Regional Trends

No. 38

2004 edition

Editors: Peggy Causer

Dev Virdee

London: TSO

A National Statistics publication
National Statistics are produced to high professional standards set out in the National Statistics Code of Practice. They undergo regular quality assurance reviews to ensure they meet customer needs. They are produced free from any political interference.

Contact points
For enquiries about this publication, contact the Editor, Peggy Causer:
Tel: **020 7533 6128**
E-mail: **regional.trends38@ons.gov.uk**

To order this publication, call The Stationery Office on 0870 600 5522. See also back cover.

For general enquiries, contact the National Statistics Customer Enquiry Centre on **0845 601 3034** (minicom: 01633 812399)
E-mail   **info@statistics.gov.uk**
Fax: 01633 652747
Letters: Room D115,
            Government Buildings
            Cardiff Road
            Newport NP10 8XG

You can find National Statistics on the Internet – go to **www.statistics.gov.uk.**

About the Office for National Statistics
The Office for National Statistics (ONS) is the government agency responsible for compiling, analysing and disseminating many of the United Kingdom's economic, social and demographic statistics, including the retail prices index, trade figures and labour market data, as well as the periodic census of the population and health statistics. The Director of ONS is also the National Statistician and the Registrar General for England and Wales, and the agency that administers the registration of births, marriages and deaths there.

Contents

Introduction

Regional Trends No.38, published by the Office for National Statistics, seeks to contribute to decision making at national, local and European level, and to inform debate about the current state of the nation. It brings together data from a wide range of sources, both from within government and outside, to paint a comprehensive picture of the countries and regions of the United Kingdom.

In recent years there has been increased interest in local information and regional diversity across the United Kingdom. Programmes of work have been put in place to improve the scope and quality of local information. As part of our continued development of Regional Trends we anticipate that spin-offs from these initiatives will be available to enrich the content of future volumes.

Whilst it is true that regional diversity exists, there is often evidence of greater variations within the regions. For example, although average weekly earnings for full-time employees in London in 2002 were the highest in the UK at £624 compared with the UK average of £463, average weekly earnings varied considerably within the region. Some 10 per cent of men in London earned more than £1,248 but 10 per cent earned less than £278, well below the average for other areas. These variations within regions also exist in less metropolitan areas and should be born in mind when making comparisons. In the South West, for example, average weekly earnings were £422 in April 2002 which ranged from Torbay where earnings averaged £340 per week to £473 in South Gloucestershire; this compared to Northern Ireland where the average weekly earnings were £390 [table 14.5 and table 5.16].

Although London continued to have the highest gross value added (GVA) per head of over £19,000 in 2001, there was a slight reduction from 1999. During the same period the East of England and South East, whose GVA was also above the national average, continued to show a rise [table 12.1].

Living costs in London are considerably higher than elsewhere, the average cost of a dwelling in 2002 being over £240 thousand in London compared to just over £80 thousand in the North East [table 6.9]. Average household expenditure on housing amounted to £90.30 per week in London, almost twice the weekly amount in Wales (£45.90) and in the North East of England (£47.70) [table 8.11].

Differences between the north and south are often commented on, however for some statistics the distinctions are more marked between built-up and more rural areas. London had the highest number of recorded offences (4,050 in 2000/01) where firearms were reported to have been used; other areas where these type of offences were also high were the North West (3,012) and Yorkshire and the Humber (2,541). On the other hand, in Wales there were 614 similar offences reported and the North East, South West, Scotland and Northern Ireland each had less that 1,000 cases reported in 2000/01[table 9.5].

Although the standards achieved in GCSE examinations have increased in all regions over the last few years, Scotland continues to have the highest success rate in English with more than seven out of ten pupils achieved the equivalent of GCSE grades A*-C in 2001/02, compared to about five out of ten for the regions of England [table 4.8].

There has been a continued increase in the participation of three- and four-year olds in early years education and this has now reached virtually 100 per cent in all regions of England except London. Over half of the provision of early years education was in the private and voluntary sector in the South East and South West, compared to 15 per cent or less in the North East and Northern Ireland [table 4.2].

Diseases such as tuberculosis (TB) are more prevalent in cities. The rate of notification of TB in London was 40 people per thousand population, more than twice that of the next highest region the West Midlands and five times the rates in the East, North East, South East and South West. [table 7.6].

There is also a contrast in age-standardised death rates; the eastern and southern regions have standardised death rates from ischaemic heart disease of below 200 per 100,000 population for males in 2001. Regions to the north and west of the Severn/Humber estuaries are above this rate [table 7.4]. Age-standardised death rates from breast cancer were lowest in the Northern and Yorkshire Health Region and the West Midlands Health Region at 51.5 and 51.9 per 100,000 women in 2001 [table 7.6].

The content of Regional Trends has been developed to reflect changing policies and data improvements included. For example, new tables have been introduced based on results from the Census held in 2001, also developments in health data and geography are reflected.

Comprehensive and up-to-date statistics about regions and subregional areas are increasingly in demand. The Region in Figures series, issued twice a year, has been produced to complement Regional Trends. The set of nine publications presents a wide range of subregional data at lower administrative levels for each Government Office Region in England giving comparative information relating to UK or GB where possible. Regional Trends and Region in Figures provide authoritative and consistent information across a spectrum of topics, which will be valuable in facilitating regional decision making.

Further development of subregional data, which will also affect regional data, will be influenced by the Neighbourhood Statistics programme being led by the Office for National Statistics. The aim of this programme is to develop and make available new statistics for small areas to meet the needs of the National Strategy Action Plan *'A New Commitment to Neighbourhood Renewal'*. As these statistics become available over a number of years they will grow to cover an increasing range of subjects, such as crime, education and health. More information about the service can be found on the Neighbourhood Statistics web pages at www.statistics.gov.uk/neighbourhood.

Overview

Regional Trends provides a unique description of the regions and countries of the United Kingdom. In 17 chapters it covers a wide range of demographic, social, industrial and economic statistics, taking a look at most aspects of life. The chapters fall broadly into four sections: regional profiles (Chapter 1), the European Union (Chapter 2), the main topic areas (Chapters 3 to 13) and subregional statistics (Chapters 14 to 17). To make comparison between regions easy, information is given in clear tables, footnotes highlighting differences in coverage where appropriate.

Regional statistics are essential for a wide range of people including policy-makers and planners in both the public and private sectors; marketing professionals; researchers; students and teachers; journalists; and anyone with a general interest in regional information. *Regional Trends 38* brings together data from diverse sources and, for some topics, is the only publication where data for the whole of the United Kingdom are available in one place. Wherever data for the component parts of the United Kingdom are sufficiently comparable, figures have been aggregated to give a national average or total.

Coverage and definitions

A section of Notes and Definitions provides details of coverage to assist in analysing and interpreting the information; additional data are also included in some instances. Maps showing the geographic boundaries applicable to various data can also be found in this section of the publication. Due to variations in coverage and definitions, some care may be needed when comparing data from more than one source. Readers are encouraged to consult the Notes and Definitions, footnotes to the tables and other references provided.

Availability of electronic data

The contents of *Regional Trends 38* will be available free of charge via the national Statistics web site, both in PDF format and as downloadable Excel files from StatBase. Previous editions of Regional Trends are also available from this site (www.statistics.gov.uk).

Further information

Regional and subregional statistics can be found in a range of other GSS publications, statistical bulletins and regular press releases. Much of the information relating to population, households and the labour market presented in *Regional Trends* can be found on Nomis®, the on-line database run by Durham University under contract to the Office for National Statistics (ONS). It contains government statistics down to the smallest available geographic area, which may be unpublished elsewhere. Additional subregional data can be accessed from the Neighbourhood Statistics web pages (http://www.statistics.gov.uk/neighbourhood). In addition, subregional data for the Government Office Regions in England can be found in the series Region in Figures; data for Wales are published on the National Assembly for Wales website, (www.wales.gov.uk); data for Scotland are published on the Scottish Executive website, (www.scotland.gov.uk); data for Northern Ireland are published on the Northern Ireland Office website, (www.northernireland.gov.uk). Details of these sources, and others, are available on the National Statistics website (www.statistics.gov.uk).

Acknowledgements

The editors would like to thank the following people for their help in producing this book:

Assistant Editor:	Eve MacSearraigh
Production Manager:	Nicola Longmuir
Authors and Production Team:	Linda Alderslade
	Francesca Ambrose
	Peter Culver
	Peter Gibb
	Martin Higgitt
	Rukshinda Jahangir
	Richard Seymour
	Katie Shaw
	Sharan Virdee
	Iain Wilson
Maps:	Alistair Dent
	Jeremy Brocklehurst
Data collection:	Data Collection Team

Contributors

The editors, authors and production team wish to thank all their colleagues in the ONS, contributing government departments and other organisations for their generous support and helpful comments, without whose help this publication would not be possible.

Data providers:

Broadcasters' Audience Research Board
Central Services Agency, Northern Ireland
Centre for Ecology and Hydrology
Civil Aviation Authority
Communicable Disease Surveillance Centre
Countryside Commission
Countryside Council for Wales
Court Service
Department for Culture, Media and Sport
Department for Education and Skills
Department for Employment & Learning, Northern Ireland
Department for Environment, Food and Rural Affairs
Department for Social Development in Northern Ireland
Department for Transport
Department for Work and Pensions
Department of Agriculture and Rural Development for Northern Ireland
Department of Economic Development, Northern Ireland
Department of Education, Northern Ireland
Department of Enterprise, Trade and Investment, Northern Ireland
Department of Health
Department of Health, Social Services and Public Safety, Northern Ireland
Department of the Environment in Northern Ireland
Department of Trade and Industry
English Nature
Environment Agency
Environment and Heritage Service, Northern Ireland
Eurostat
General Register Office for Scotland
Higher Education Statistics Agency
HM Customs and Excise
Home Office
Inland Revenue
Institute of Child Health
Land Registry
Loughborough University
Medicines and Healthcare Products Regulatory Agency
National Assembly for Wales
National Tourist Boards
Northern Ireland Cancer Registry
Northern Ireland Court Service
Northern Ireland Office
Northern Ireland Statistics and Research Agency
Office of the Deputy Prime Minister
OFWAT
Police Service of Northern Ireland
RSMB Television Research Limited
Scottish Centre for Infection and Environmental Health
Scottish Environment Protection Agency
Scottish Executive
Scottish Executive Environment and Rural Affairs Department
Scottish Health Service
Scottish National Heritage
Small Business Service

Information

Regional boundaries

The United Kingdom comprises Great Britain and Northern Ireland; Great Britain consists of England, Wales and Scotland. The Isle of Man and the Channel Isles are not part of the United Kingdom. The Scilly Isles are included as part of Cornwall throughout.

The Statistical Regions of the United Kingdom comprise the Government Office Regions for England, plus Wales, Scotland and Northern Ireland. The local government administrative structure provides the framework for breaking down the regions into smaller areas. A map of the statistical regions of the United Kingdom, along with other key boundaries used in the tables, are given in the Notes and Definitions section.

Nomenclature for Territorial Units (NUTS)

Some data are presented using the European Nomenclature for Territorial Units (NUTS) area classification, primarily economic data in chapters 12 and 13 and also in Chapter 2. The highest level of this classification – NUTS1 – corresponds to the 9 regions of England plus Wales, Scotland and Northern Ireland used as the standard breakdown throughout this publication. Further information on the NUTS classification is contained in the Notes and Definitions.

Subregional geography

The subregional information presented in Chapters 14 to 17 reflect the complete implementation of the local government reorganisation that happened between 1 April 1995 and 1 April 1998. Data for England in Chapter 14 are presented firstly by region. Within each region Unitary Authorities (UAs) are listed first in alphabetical order. Counties are listed next in alphabetical order. Within each County the Local Authority Districts (LAD) are listed alphabetically. Where still available, figures for former counties are shown at the end of the region. Chapter 15 on Wales and Chapter 16 on Scotland present data for the UAs and the New Councils respectively which replaced the former two-tier systems on 1 April 1996. Chapter 17 on Northern Ireland continues to give figures at Board or district level as available.

Full details of the local government reorganisation and the NUTS area classification are given in the *Gazetteer of old and new geographies of the United Kingdom* available from the National Statistics website.
(www.statistics.gov.uk/geography/gazetteer)

Chapter 1 **Regional Profiles**

Statistical Regions of the United Kingdom

SCOTLAND

NORTHERN
IRELAND

NORTH
EAST

NORTH
WEST

YORKSHIRE
AND THE
HUMBER

EAST
MIDLANDS

WEST
MIDLANDS

WALES

EAST

LONDON

SOUTH EAST

SOUTH WEST

ENGLAND

——————— Government
Office Region
boundary

1 *For the purposes of statistical analyses, the United Kingdom has been divided into 12 'statistical regions'.*

Table **1.1**   Key statistics for the North East

	North East	United Kingdom		North East	United Kingdom
Population, 2002[1] (thousands)	2,513	59,229	Gross value added, 2001 (£ million)	27,729	874,227
Percentage aged under 16[1]	19.4	19.9	Gross value added per head index, 2001 (UK=100)	76.1	100.0
Percentage pension age and over[1]	19.3	18.4	Total business sites, 2002 (thousands)	74.6	2,538.1
Standardised mortality ratio (UK=100), 2002	111	100	Average dwelling price, 2002 (£)[3]	81,387	145,320
Infant mortality rate,[2] 2002	5.0	5.3			
Percentage of pupils achieving 5 or more grades A*-C			Motor cars currently licensed,[4] 2002 (thousands)	922	25,782
at GCSE level or equivalent, 2001/02	45.6	52.5	Fatal and serious accidents on roads,[5] 2002		
			(rates per 100,000 population)	42	59
Economic activity rate,[6]			Recorded crime rate, 2002/03		
spring 2003 (percentages)	73.0	78.8	(notifiable offences per 100,000 population)[3]	11,543	11,327
Employment rate,[6] spring 2003 (percentages)	68.2	74.7			
Unemployment rate,6 spring 2003 (percentages)	6.6	5.1	Average gross weekly household income, 1999-2002[7] (£)	406	510
Average gross weekly earnings: males in full-time					
employment, April 2002 (£)	439.1	511.3	Average weekly household expenditure, 1999-2002[7] (£)	308.8	379.7
Average gross weekly earnings: females in full-time			Households in receipt of Income Support/Working		
employment, April 2002 (£)	332.1	382.1	Families Tax Credit,[5] 2001/02 (percentages)	22	17

1 Population figures for 2002 are mid- year population estimates and include provisional results from the Manchester matching exercise. Pension age is men aged 65 and over and women aged 60 and over.
2 Deaths of infants under one year of age per 1,000 live births.
3 Figure labelled as the United Kingdom relate to Great Britain.
4 Totals for the United Kingdom include vehicles where the country of the registered vehicle is unknown, that are under disposal or from counties unknown within Great Britain.
5 Figure labelled as the United Kingdom relates to Great Britain.
6 For people of working age, men aged 16 to 64 and women aged 16 to 59. Data are seasonally adjusted.
7 Data combined for years1999/2000, 2000/01 and 2001/02.

Map **1.2**   Population density: by local or unitary authority, 2002

Population density, 2002 (people per sq km)

- 2,500 or over
- 1,000 - 2,499
- 500 - 999
- 250 - 499
- 100 - 249
- 99 or under

1 Wansbeck
2 Newcastle upon Tyne
3 Chester-le-Street
4 Hartlepool UA
5 Stockton-on-Tees UA
6 Middlesbrough UA

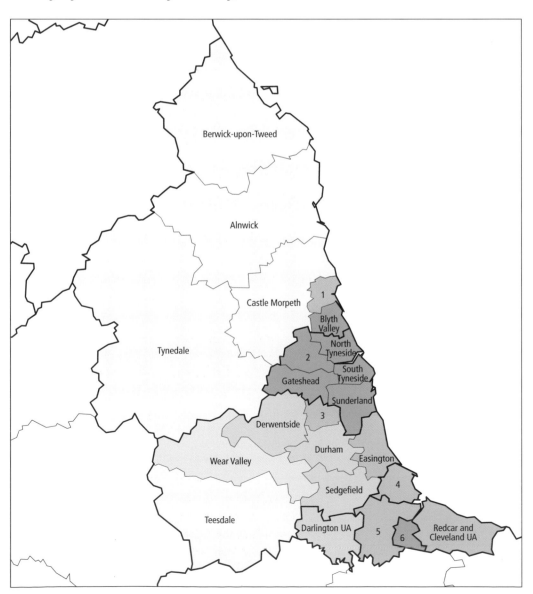

North East

In 2002, the North East had a population of 2.5 million people. Within the North East, population density was highest in Middlesbrough UA (2,485 people per sq km) and lowest in the local authority districts of Berwick-upon-Tweed and Tynedale (27 people per sq km each). (Table 3.1 and Map 3.3)

The population of the North East decreased by 4.2 per cent between 1982 and 2002, according to the mid-year population estimates. The largest percentage movement was in Middlesbrough UA with a 10.6 per cent decrease in population. (Map 3.8)

In the North East, the Standardised Mortality Ratio (SMR) in 2001 was 11 per cent higher than in the UK as a whole. Infant Mortality was similar to the UK rate; (5.6 and 5.5 deaths of infants under one year per 1,000 live births respectively). (Table 3.14)

The North East had the highest proportion of conceptions leading to maternities (for women aged under 18) in the UK in 2001, although the region's Total Fertility Rate was one of the lowest. (Tables 3.12 and 3.13)

The North East had the largest decline in the number of marriages: a decrease of 47 per cent between 1976 and 2001, compared with the UK average decrease of less than 30 per cent. (Table 3.17)

The proportion of people of working age qualified to GCE A level/equivalent or higher in the North East was around 45 per cent in spring 2003. In 2002 the proportion of full-time first degree graduates studying in the North East who subsequently gained permanent UK employment was higher than the UK average. (Tables 4.13 and 4.14)

The North East had the lowest employment rate (for people of working age) in the UK, at 68.2 per cent in spring 2003. (Table 5.1)

In December 2001 the North East had a higher proportion of employee jobs in the construction, public adminstration and defence sectors than elsewhere in the UK. (Table 5.4)

Almost one-third of males in the North East did not drink any alcohol in the week prior to being surveyed in 2001. However a slightly lower proportion consumed more than eight units of alcohol in the same period. (Table 7.12)

In April 2002, average gross weekly earnings for full-time employees on adult rates in the North East were £399.30. (Table 5.16)

Each household in the region produced on average 23.4 kilos of household waste per week in 2001/02, and recycled only 62 kilos in the year, the lowest amount in England. (Tables 11.15 and 11.16)

In the North East, manufacturing industry accounted for 24 per cent of gross value added (GVA) in 2000, compared with 19 per cent for the UK. Agriculture, hunting, forestry and fishing accounted for 0.7 per cent of GVA, compared with 1.1 per cent for the UK. (Table 12.5)

In 1999 gross disposable household income for the North East was £9,018 per head. (Table 12.9)

In March 2002, around a third of business sites in the North East were in distribution, hotels and catering and repairs, the highest rate in the UK; the UK average was 28.2 per cent. (Table 13.3)

Nearly three-quarters of the North East's exports in 2002 were to the European Union (EU), the highest rate of any area of the UK. Imports from the EU, at 52 per cent, were slightly below the average for the UK . (Table 13.7)

Table **1.3**   **Key statistics for the North West**

	North West	United Kingdom		North West	United Kingdom
Population, 2002[1] (thousands)	6,771	59,229	Gross value added, 2001 (£ million)	87,584	874,227
Percentage aged under 16[1]	20.3	19.9	Gross value added per head index, 2001 (UK=100)	89.8	100.0
Percentage pension age and over[1]	18.6	18.4	Total business sites, 2002 (thousands)	253.9	2,538.1
Standardised mortality ratio (UK=100), 2002	109	100	Average dwelling price, 2002 (£)[3]	92,433	145,320
Infant mortality rate,[2] 2002	5.4	5.3			
Percentage of pupils achieving 5 or more grades A*-C			Motor cars currently licensed,[4] 2002 (thousands)	2,876	25,782
at GCSE level or equivalent, 2001/02	49.7	52.5	Fatal and serious accidents on roads,[5] 2002		
			(rates per 100,000 population)	54	59
Economic activity rate,[6]			Recorded crime rate, 2002/03		
spring 2003 (percentages)	77.2	78.8	(notifiable offences per 100,000 population)[3]	11,810	11,327
Employment rate,[6] spring 2003 (percentages)	73.3	74.7			
Unemployment rate,[6] spring 2003 (percentages)	5.1	5.1	Average gross weekly household income, 1999-2002[7] (£)	444	510
Average gross weekly earnings: males in full-time					
employment, April 2002 (£)	471.1	511.3	Average weekly household expenditure, 1999-2002[7] (£)	351.0	379.7
Average gross weekly earnings: females in full-time			Households in receipt of Income Support/Working		
employment, April 2002 (£)	354.3	382.1	Families Tax Credit,[5] 2001/02 (percentages)	22	17

1 Population figures for 2002 are mid- year population estimates and include provisional results from the Manchester matching exercise. Pension age is men aged 65 and over and women aged 60 and over.
2 Deaths of infants under one year of age per 1,000 live births.
3 Figure labelled as the United Kingdom relate to Great Britain.
4 Totals for the United Kingdom include vehicles where the country of the registered vehicle is unknown, that are under disposal or from counties unknown within Great Britain.
5 Figure labelled as the United Kingdom relates to Great Britain.
6 For people of working age, men aged 16 to 64 and women aged 16 to 59. Data are seasonally adjusted.
7 Data combined for years, 1999/2000, 2000/01 and 2001/02.

Map **1.4**   **Population density: by local or unitary authority, 2002**

**Population density, 2002
(people per sq km)**

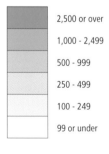

- 2,500 or over
- 1,000 - 2,499
- 500 - 999
- 250 - 499
- 100 - 249
- 99 or under

1 Barrow-in-Furness
2 Blackpool UA
3 Preston
4 Hyndburn
5 South Ribble
6 Blackburn with Darwen UA
7 Rossendale
8 Sefton
9 Bury
10 Rochdale
11 Salford
12 Manchester
13 Tameside
14 Trafford
15 Liverpool
16 Knowsley
17 St. Helens
18 Warrington UA
19 Halton UA
20 Stockport
21 Ellesmere Port & Neston
22 Congleton

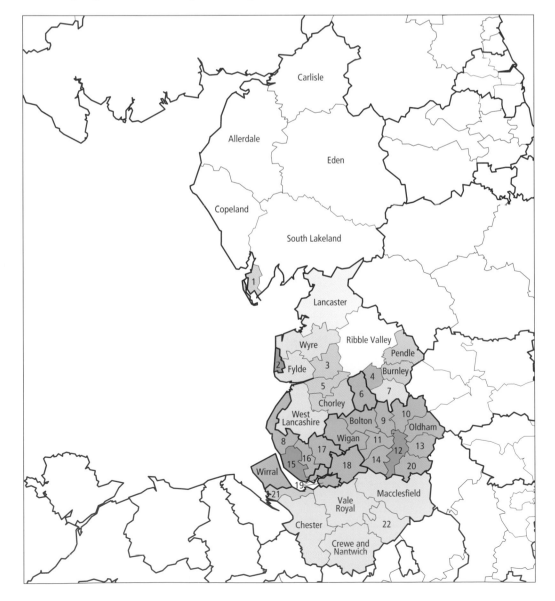

North West

In 2002, the North West had a population of 6.8 million people. Within the North West the population density was highest in Blackpool UA at 4,065 people per sq km and lowest in the local authority district of Eden (23 people per sq km). (Table 3.1 and Map 3.3)

The population of the North West fell by 2 per cent between 1982 and 2002 (based on the mid-year population estimates). The largest decrease (9.9 per cent) was in Merseyside, but the greatest percentage movement overall was in Warrington Unitary Authority where there was a population increase of 11.8 per cent. (Map 3.8)

In the North West, the Standardised Mortality Ratio (SMR) was 9 per cent higher than the UK as a whole in 2001. Infant Mortality rate in the North West was higher than the UK rate; (5.9 and 5.5 deaths of infants under one year of age per 1,000 live births respectively). During the same period the Total Fertility Rate (TFR) was also above the UK average. (Tables 3.13 and 3.14)

The North West had a large reduction in the number of marriages between 1976 and 2001, a decrease of 42 per cent. (Table 3.17)

In 2002, the North West had the highest percentage of households which consist of a lone parent with dependent children. (Table 3.20)

In 2001/02, the proportion of pupils in their last year of compulsory education in the North West achieving 5 or more GCSE grades A*- C (or equivalent) was lower than the UK average. (Table 4.6)

In 2002 the proportion of full-time first degree graduates studying in the North West who subsequently gained permanent UK employment was higher than the UK national average. (Table 4.13)

The North West employment rate (for people of working age) was 73.3 per cent in spring 2003, among the lowest proportions in the UK. (Table 5.1)

In April 2002, average gross weekly earnings for full-time employees on adult rates in the North West were £426.80. (Table 5.16)

Almost one-third of 16- to 29-year-olds in the North West had used illegal drugs in 2001-02; the percentage of youngsters using hallucinants and cannabis was highest in this region. (Figure 7.13)

The North West produced the highest average amount of household waste in 2001/02 of all the English regions (26.4 kilos per household per week). The region recycled 121 kilos of waste per year, among the lowest amounts in England. (Tables 11.15 and 11.16)

In the North West, manufacturing industry accounted for 23 per cent of GVA in 2000, compared with 19 per cent for the UK as a whole. Agriculture, hunting, forestry and fishing accounted for 0.8 per cent of GVA compared with 1.1 per cent for the UK. (Table 12.5)

Table **1.5**   Key statistics for Yorkshire and the Humber

	Yorkshire and the Humber	United Kingdom		Yorkshire and the Humber	United Kingdom
Population, 2002[1] (thousands)	4,983	59,229	Gross value added, 2001 (£ million)	61,929	874,227
Percentage aged under 16[1]	20.2	19.9	Gross value added per head index, 2001 (UK=100)	86.4	100.0
Percentage pension age and over[1]	18.7	18.4	Total business sites, 2002 (thousands)	187.0	2,538.1
Standardised mortality ratio (UK=100), 2002	101	100	Average dwelling price, 2002 (£)[3]	92,157	145,320
Infant mortality rate,[2] 2002	6.2	5.3			
Percentage of pupils achieving 5 or more grades A*-C			Motor cars currently licensed,[4] 2002 (thousands)	2,000	25,782
at GCSE level or equivalent, 2001/02	45.6	52.5	Fatal and serious accidents on roads,[5] 2002		
			(rates per 100,000 population)	64	59
Economic activity rate,[6]			Recorded crime rate, 2002/03		
spring 2003 (percentages)	78.4	78.8	(notifiable offences per 100,000 population)[3]	13,597	11,327
Employment rate,[6] spring 2003 (percentages)	74.1	74.7			
Unemployment rate,[6] spring 2003 (percentages)	5.5	5.1	Average gross weekly household income, 1999-2002[7] (£)	444	510
Average gross weekly earnings: males in full-time					
employment, April 2002 (£)	447.1	511.3	Average weekly household expenditure, 1999-2002[7] (£)	340.5	379.7
Average gross weekly earnings: females in full-time			Households in receipt of Income Support/Working		
employment, April 2002 (£)	345.0	382.1	Families Tax Credit,[5] 2001/02(percentages)	19	17

1 Population figures for 2002 are mid-year population estimates and include provisional results from the Manchester matching exercise. Pension age is men aged 65 and over and women aged 60 and over.
2 Deaths of infants under one year of age per 1,000 live births.
3 Figure labelled as the United Kingdom relate to Great Britain.
4 Totals for the United Kingdom include vehicles where the country of the registered vehicle is unknown, that are under disposal or from counties unknown within Great Britain.
5 Figure labelled as the United Kingdom relates to Great Britain.
6 For people of working age, men aged 16 to 64 and women aged 16 to 59. Data are seasonally adjusted.
7 Data combined for years, 1999/2000, 2000/01 and 2001/02.

Map **1.6**   Population density: by local or unitary authority, 2002

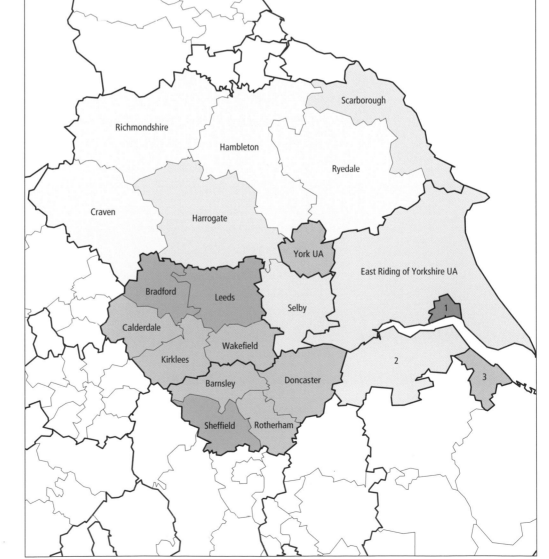

Population density, 2002 (people per sq km)

- 2,500 or over
- 1,000 - 2,499
- 500 - 999
- 250 - 499
- 100 - 249
- 99 or under

1 City of Kingston upon Hull UA
2 North Lincolnshire UA
3 North East Lincolnshire UA

Yorkshire and the Humber

In 2002, Yorkshire and the Humber had a population of 5 million people. Within Yorkshire and the Humber the population density was highest in the City of Kingston upon Hull UA (3,379 people per sq km) and lowest in the local authority district of Ryedale in North Yorkshire (34 people per sq km). (Table 3.1 and Map 3.3)

The population of Yorkshire and the Humber increased by 1.5 per cent between 1982 and 2002 (based on the mid-year population estimates). The largest percentage change in population was in the East Riding of Yorkshire UA, where there was an increase of 16.6 per cent. (Map 3.8)

Yorkshire and the Humber followed the UK trend with a decline in the number of marriages, with a decrease of 38 per cent in the region between 1976 and 2001. (Table 3.17)

In 2001/02, the proportion of pupils in their last year of compulsory education in Yorkshire and the Humber achieving 5 or more GCSE grades A*-C (or equivalent) was one of the lowest in the UK. (Table 4.6)

In April 2002, average gross weekly earnings for full-time employees on adult rates in Yorkshire and the Humber were £409.90. (Table 5.16)

Sixteen per cent of all dwellings in Yorkshire and the Humber were rented from local authorities in 2003 compared with an average of 11 per cent in England as a whole. (Table 6.4)

Forty per cent of the females in Yorkshire and the Humber did not have anything alcoholic to drink in the week prior to being surveyed in 2001/02. (Table 7.12)

Yorkshire and the Humber had a high incidence of recorded burglaries in 2002/03. There were 2,879 burglaries per 100,000 population, almost 70 per cent higher than the England and Wales rate. (Table 9.1)

In 1998, nearly 40 per cent of the land in Yorkshire and the Humber was grassland and nearly 30 per cent was put to arable and horticultural uses. (Table 11.11)

Manufacturing industry in Yorkshire and the Humber accounted for 22 per cent of GVA in 2000, compared with 19 per cent for the UK as a whole. Agriculture, hunting, forestry and fishing accounted for 1.3 per cent of GVA, compared with 1.1 per cent for the UK. (Table 12.5)

In 1999, gross disposable household income for Yorkshire and the Humber was £9,325 per head. (Table 12.9)

Between 1998/99 and 2002/03, Yorkshire and the Humber had a decrease, of more than two-thirds, in the number of project sucesses from inward investment in manufacturing. The UK figure decreased by less than one third over the same period. (Table 13.8)

Table **1.7**   Key statistics for the East Midlands

	East Midlands	United Kingdom		East Midlands	United Kingdom
Population, 2002[1] (thousands)	4,216	59,229	Gross value added, 2001 (£ million)	55,394	874,227
Percentage aged under 16[1]	19.8	19.9	Gross value added per head index, 2001 (UK=100)	91.9	100.0
Percentage pension age and over[1]	18.6	18.4	Total business sites, 2002 (thousands)	171.4	2,538.0
Standardised mortality ratio (UK=100), 2002	99	100	Average dwelling price, 2002 (£)[3]	111,717	145,320
Infant mortality rate,[2] 2002	5.6	5.3			
Percentage of pupils achieving 5 or more grades A*-C			Motor cars currently licensed,[4] 2002 (thousands)	1,927	25,782
at GCSE level or equivalent, 2001/02	50.8	52.5	Fatal and serious accidents on roads,[5] 2002		
			(rates per 100,000 population)	66	59
Economic activity rate,[6]			Recorded crime rate, 2002/03		
spring 2003 (percentages)	79.5	78.8	(notifiable offences per 100,000 population)[3]	11,884	11,327
Employment rate,[6] spring 2003 (percentages)	76.1	74.7			
Unemployment rate,[6] spring 2003 (percentages)	4.3	5.1	Average gross weekly household income, 1999-2002[7] (£)	480	510
Average gross weekly earnings: males in full-time					
employment, April 2002 (£)	454.2	511.3	Average weekly household expenditure, 1999-2002[7] (£)	363.1	379.7
Average gross weekly earnings: females in full-time			Households in receipt of Income Support/Working		
employment, April 2002 (£)	334.8	382.1	Families Tax Credit,[5] 2001/02 (percentages)	17	17

1 Population figures for 2002 are mid- year population estimates and include provisional results from the Manchester matching exercise. Pension age is men aged 65 and over and women aged 60 and over.
2 Deaths of infants under one year of age per 1,000 live births.
3 Figure labelled as the United Kingdom relate to Great Britain.
4 Totals for the United Kingdom include vehicles where the country of the registered vehicle is unknown, that are under disposal or from counties unknown within Great Britain.
5 Figure labelled as the United Kingdom relates to Great Britain.
6 For people of working age, men aged 16 to 64 and women aged 16 to 59. Data are seasonally adjusted.
7 Data combined for years, 1999/2000, 2000/01 and 2001/02.

Map **1.8**   Population density: by local or unitary authority, 2002

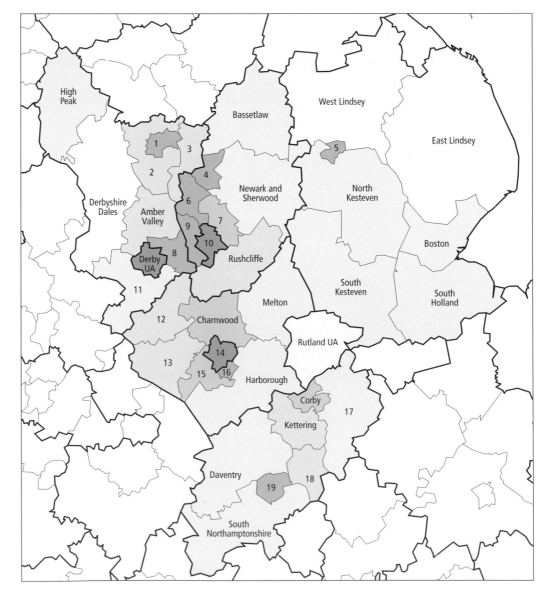

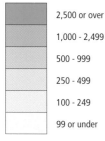

Population density, 2002
(people per sq km)

- 2,500 or over
- 1,000 - 2,499
- 500 - 999
- 250 - 499
- 100 - 249
- 99 or under

1 Chesterfield
2 North East Derbyshire
3 Bolsover
4 Mansfield
5 Lincoln
6 Ashfield
7 Gedling
8 Erewash
9 Broxtowe
10 Nottingham UA
11 South Derbyshire
12 North West Leicestershire
13 Hinckley and Bosworth
14 Leicester UA
15 Blaby
16 Oadby and Wigston
17 East Northamptonshire
18 Wellingborough
19 Northampton

East Midlands

In 2002, the East Midlands had a population of 4.2 million. The resident population of the East Midlands increased by the highest percentage in England (0.8 per cent) between mid-2001 and mid-2002. (Tables 3.1 and 3.11)

The population of the East Midlands increased by 9.5 per cent in the 20 years between 1982 and 2002, according to the mid-year population estimates. The largest percentage increase was in Lincolnshire, at 19.2 per cent. (Map 3.8)

In 2001, the Infant Mortality rate in the East Midlands was lower than the UK rate; (5.0 and 5.5 deaths of infants under one year of age per 1,000 live births respectively). (Table 3.14)

The East Midlands had the highest proportion (nearly 17 per cent) of maintained primary school classes with more than 30 pupils compared with 13 per cent in Great Britain as a whole in 2002/03. (Table 4.3)

In 2000/01, 77 per cent of 16-year-olds in the East Midlands were in some form of post-compulsory education or government-supported training. This compared with a UK rate of 79 per cent. (Table 4.10)

The proportion of people of working age qualified to GCE A level/equivalent or higher in the East Midlands was around 46 per cent in spring 2003. In 2002 the proportion of full-time first degree graduates studying in the East Midlands who subsequently gained permanent UK employment was higher than the UK national average. (Tables 4.13 and 4.14)

In spring 2003 the East Midlands employment rate (for people of working age), at 76.1 per cent, was among the highest of the countries and regions of the UK. (Table 5.1)

Around a fifth of employee jobs in the East Midlands in 2001 were in the manufacturing sector. (Table 5.4)

In April 2002, average gross weekly earnings for full-time employees on adult rates in the East Midlands were £413.00. (Table 5.16)

The number of cars currently licensed in the East Midlands increased by 13 per cent between 1998 and 2002. (Table 10.1)

In the East Midlands, manufacturing accounted for 26 per cent of GVA in 2000, compared with 19 per cent for the UK as a whole. Agriculture, hunting, forestry and fishing accounted for 1.6 per cent of GVA compared with 1.1 per cent for the UK. (Table 12.5)

In 1999, gross disposable household income for the East Midlands was £9,409 per head. (Table 12.9)

In March 2002, 29 per cent of businesses in the East Midlands were in the areas of distribution, hotels and catering or repairs; this was slightly higher than the UK average. (Table 13.3)

Over 57 per cent of the exports of the East Midlands in 2002 were destined for the European Union, slightly below the UK average of 58.3 per cent. The proportion of trade from the European Union, at 50.8 per cent, was also slightly less than the UK average of 52.8 per cent. (Table 13.7)

Table **1.9**   **Key statistics for the West Midlands**

	West Midlands	United Kingdom		West Midlands	United Kingdom
Population, 2002[1] (thousands)	5,304	59,229	Gross value added, 2001 (£ million)	68,839	874,227
Percentage aged under 16[1]	20.5	19.9	Gross value added per head index, 2001UK=100)	90.4	100.0
Percentage pension age and over[1]	18.6	18.4	Total business sites, 2002 (thousands)	209.4	2,538.1
Standardised mortality ratio (UK=100), 2002	101	100	Average dwelling price, 2002 (£)[3]	118,845	145,320
Infant mortality rate,[2] 2002	6.5	5.3			
Percentage of pupils achieving 5 or more grades A*-C			Motor cars currently licensed,[4] 2002 (thousands)	2,562	25,782
at GCSE level or equivalent, 2001/02	49.7	52.5	Fatal and serious accidents on roads,[5] 2002		
			(rates per 100,000 population)	51	59
Economic activity rate,[6]			Recorded crime rate, 2002/03		
spring 2003 (percentages)	78.6	78.8	(notifiable offences per 100,000 population)[3]	11,546	11,327
Employment rate,[6] spring 2003 (percentages)	74.0	74.7			
Unemployment rate,[6] spring 2003 (percentages)	5.9	5.1	Average gross weekly household income, 1999-2002[7] (£)	476	510
Average gross weekly earnings: males in full-time					
employment, April 2002 (£)	469.6	511.3	Average weekly household expenditure, 1999-2002[7] (£)	360.3	379.7
Average gross weekly earnings: females in full-time			Households in receipt of Income Support/Working		
employment, April 2002 (£)	353.0	382.1	Families Tax Credit,[5] 2001/02 (percentages)	17	17

1 Population figures for 2002 are mid- year population estimates and include provisional results from the Manchester matching exercise. Pension age is men aged 65 and over and women aged 60 and over.
2 Deaths of infants under one year of age per 1,000 live births.
3 Figure labelled as the United Kingdom relate to Great Britain.
4 Totals for the United Kingdom include vehicles where the country of the registered vehicle is unknown, that are under disposal or from counties unknown within Great Britain.
5 Figure labelled as the United Kingdom relates to Great Britain.
6 For people of working age, men aged 16 to 64 and women aged 16 to 59. Data are seasonally adjusted.
7 Data combined for years, 1999/2000, 2000/01 and 2001/02.

Map **1.10**   **Population density: by local or unitary authority, 2002**

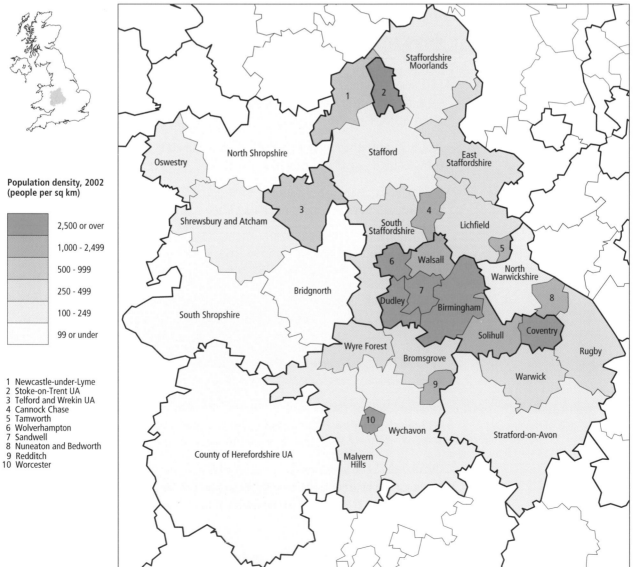

Population density, 2002 (people per sq km)

- 2,500 or over
- 1,000 - 2,499
- 500 - 999
- 250 - 499
- 100 - 249
- 99 or under

1 Newcastle-under-Lyme
2 Stoke-on-Trent UA
3 Telford and Wrekin UA
4 Cannock Chase
5 Tamworth
6 Wolverhampton
7 Sandwell
8 Nuneaton and Bedworth
9 Redditch
10 Worcester

West Midlands

In 2002, West Midlands had a population of 5.3 million. Birmingham was the area with the highest population density (3,697 people per sq km). In marked contrast, the predominantly rural district of South Shropshire had the lowest population density at 40 people per sq km. (Table 3.1 and Map 3.3)

The population of the West Midlands increased by 2.4 per cent between mid-year 1982 and 2002. (Map 3.8)

In 2001, West Midlands had the highest Infant Mortality rate in the UK, at 6.4 deaths of infants under one year of age per 1,000 live births. The region also had one of the highest Total Fertility Rates, at 1.74, second only to the Northern Ireland figure of 1.81. (Table 3.14)

The West Midlands had a 36 per cent reduction in the number of marriages between 1976 and 2001. This compared with a 30 per cent decrease in the UK as a whole. (Table 3.17)

The proportion of people of working age qualified to GCE A level/equivalent or higher in the West Midlands was around 45 per cent in spring 2003. In 2002 the proportion of full-time first degree graduates studying in the West Midlands who subsequently gained permanent UK employment was lower than the UK national average. (Tables 4.13 and 4.14)

The employment rate for people of working age in spring 2003, at 74 per cent was among the lowest in the UK. Around a fifth of employee jobs in the West Midlands in 2001 were in the manufacturing sector. (Tables 5.1 and 5.4)

In April 2002, average gross weekly earnings for full-time employees on adult rates in the West Midlands were £427.30. (Table 5.16)

The number of houses built by private enterprise in the West Midlands was lower in 2002/03 than in 1992/93. The East was the only other region to show a decline. (Table 6.2)

West Midlands had the second highest rate of tuberculosis in 2002 (14.9 cases per 100,000 population), although this rate showed a slight reduction compared to ten years earlier. (Table 7.8)

Households in the West Midlands spent on average £4.50 per week participating in the National Lottery between 1999 and 2002; this was one of the highest amounts in the UK. (Table 8.20)

The West Midlands had the highest proportion of women police officers of all regions in 2002, at 20.9 per cent. (Table 9.7)

In the West Midlands, manufacturing industry accounted for 25 per cent of GVA in 2000, compared with 19 per cent for the UK as a whole. (Table 12.5)

In March 2002, almost 30 per cent of business sites in the West Midlands were in distribution, hotels and catering or repairs, slightly above the UK average of 28.2. (Table 13.3)

The West Midlands received the highest amount of EU objective 2 funding coming to the UK in 2003 (18 per cent of the overall total). (Table 13.11)

Table **1.11** Key statistics for the East of England

	East	United Kingdom		East	United Kingdom
Population, 2002[1] (thousands)	5,420	59,229	Gross value added, 2001 (£ million)	85,775	874,227
Percentage aged under 16[1]	19.9	19.9	Gross value added per head index, 2002 (UK=100)	110.1	100.0
Percentage pension age and over[1]	19.1	18.4	Total business sites, 2002 (thousands)	248.0	2,538.1
Standardised mortality ratio (UK=100), 2002	92	100	Average dwelling price, 2001 (£)[3]	160,495	145,320
Infant mortality rate,[2] 2002	4.4	5.3			
Percentage of pupils achieving 5 or more grades A*-C			Motor cars currently licensed,[4] 2002 (thousands)	2,694	25,782
at GCSE level or equivalent, 2001/02	55.3	52.5	Fatal and serious accidents on roads,[5] 2002		
			(rates per 100,000 population)	63	59
Economic activity rate,[6]			Recorded crime rate, 2002/03		
spring 2003 (percentages)	81.9	78.8	(notifiable offences per 100,000 population)[3]	9,084	11,327
Employment rate,[6] spring 2003 (percentages)	78.5	74.7			
Unemployment rate,[6] spring 2003 (percentages)	4.2	5.1	Average gross weekly household income, 1999-2002[7] (£)	538	510
Average gross weekly earnings: males in full-time					
employment, April 2002 (£)	506.3	511.3	Average weekly household expenditure, 1999-2002[7] (£)	400.5	379.7
Average gross weekly earnings: females in full-time			Households in receipt of Income Support/Working		
employment, April 2002 (£)	375.1	382.1	Families Tax Credit,[5] 2001/02 (percentages)	12	17

1 Population figures for 2002 are mid- year population estimates and include provisional results from the Manchester matching exercise. Pension age is men aged 65 and over and women aged 60 and over.
2 Deaths of infants under one year of age per 1,000 live births.
3 Figure labelled as the United Kingdom relate to Great Britain.
4 Totals for the United Kingdom include vehicles where the country of the registered vehicle is unknown, that are under disposal or from counties unknown within Great Britain.
5 Figure labelled as the United Kingdom relates to Great Britain.
6 For people of working age, men aged 16 to 64 and women aged 16 to 59. Data are seasonally adjusted.
7 Data combined for years, 1999/2000, 2000/01 and 2001/02.

Map **1.12** Population density: by local or unitary authority, 2002

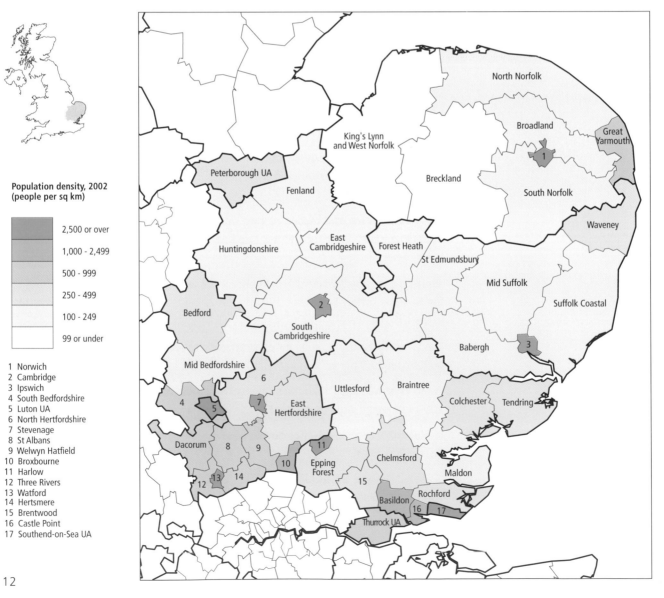

Population density, 2002 (people per sq km)

- 2,500 or over
- 1,000 - 2,499
- 500 - 999
- 250 - 499
- 100 - 249
- 99 or under

1 Norwich
2 Cambridge
3 Ipswich
4 South Bedfordshire
5 Luton UA
6 North Hertfordshire
7 Stevenage
8 St Albans
9 Welwyn Hatfield
10 Broxbourne
11 Harlow
12 Three Rivers
13 Watford
14 Hertsmere
15 Brentwood
16 Castle Point
17 Southend-on-Sea UA

East of England

In 2002, the East of England had a population of 5.4 million people. Population density was highest in Luton Unitary Authority (4,295 people per sq km), one of the highest densities outside London and lowest in the local authority district of Breckland in Norfolk (94 people per sq km). (Table 3.1 and Map 3.3)

The East of England population increased by 11.2 per cent between 1982 and 2002 based on the mid-year population estimates. The largest percentage population change was in Cambridgeshire where there was an increase of 21.5 per cent. (Map 3.8)

In the East of England the Standardised Mortality Ratio (SMR) was 8 per cent lower than the UK as a whole in 2001, at 92 (UK=100). (Table 3.14)

There was a 17 per cent decline in the number of marriages in the East of England between 1976 and 2001, lower than the decline in the United Kingdom overall. (Table 3.17)

In the East of England in 2000/01, 81 per cent of 16-year-olds were in full-time education or on a Government Supported Training scheme, one of the highest proportions in the country. (Table 4.10)

The proportion of people of working age qualified to GCE A level/equivalent or higher in the East of England was 46.6 per cent (spring 2003). In 2002 the proportion of full-time first degree graduates studying in the East of England and who gained permanent UK employment was lower than the UK national average. (Tables 4.13 and 4.14)

The employment rate for people of working age in spring 2003 was 78.5 per cent, amongst the highest rates in the UK. (Table 5.1)

In 2002, average gross weekly earnings for full-time employees on adult rates in the East of England were £459.60 per person. (Table 5.16)

Seventy per cent of residents supported by the local council were cared for in independent residential homes in March 2003, eight percentage points higher than any other region. (Table 7.19)

The East of England had the lowest expenditure per week on alcoholic beverages and tobacco, spending £17 per household, over £3 per week below the average for the UK. (Table 8.11)

Households in the East of England produced on average of 23.9 kilos of household waste per week in 2001/02, and recycled 213.3 kilos per year, amongst the highest in the country. (Table 11.15 and 11.16)

Gross value added (GVA) per head in the East of England was ten percentage points above the UK average in 2001, at £15,881. (Table 12.1)

In 1999 the gross disposable household income for the East of England was £10,638 per head. (Table 12.9)

Almost three-quarters of land in the East of England in 2002 was arable, with the highest proportion of agricultural holdings (24.8 per cent) devoted to cereal production. (Tables 13.18 and 13.19)

Table **1.13** Key statistics for London

	London	United Kingdom		London	United Kingdom
Population, 2002[1] (thousands)	7,355	59,229	Gross value added, 2001 (£ million)	140,354	874,227
Percentage aged under 16[1]	19.6	19.9	Gross value added per head index, 2001 (UK=100)	133.2	100.0
Percentage pension age and over[1]	14.0	18.4	Total business sites, 2002 (thousands)	384.9	2,538.1
Standardised mortality ratio (UK=100), 2002	98	100	Average dwelling price, 2002 (£)[3]	241,080	145,320
Infant mortality rate,[2] 2002	5.6	5.3			
Percentage of pupils achieving 5 or more grades A*-C			Motor cars currently licensed,[4] 2002 (thousands)	2,473	25,782
at GCSE level or equivalent, 2001/02	50.6	52.5	Fatal and serious accidents on roads,[5] 2002		
			(rates per 100,000 population)	71	59
Economic activity rate,[6]			Recorded crime rate, 2002/03		
spring 2003 (percentages)	75.6	78.8	(notifiable offences per 100,000 population)[3]	15,175	11,327
Employment rate,[6] spring 2003 (percentages)	70.3	74.7			
Unemployment rate,[6] spring 2003 (percentages)	7.1	5.1	Average gross weekly household income, 1999-2002[7] (£)	676	510
Average gross weekly earnings: males in full-time					
employment, April 2002 (£)	704.8	511.3	Average weekly household expenditure, 1999-2002[7] (£)	463.0	379.7
Average gross weekly earnings: females in full-time			Households in receipt of Income Support/Working		
employment, April 2002 (£)	503.6	382.1	Families Tax Credit,[5] 2001/02 (percentages)	17	17

1 Population figures for 2002 are mid- year population estimates and include provisional results from the Manchester matching exercise. Pension age is men aged 65 and over and women aged 60 and over.
2 Deaths of infants under one year of age per 1,000 live births.
3 Figure labelled as the United Kingdom relate to Great Britain.
4 Totals for the United Kingdom include vehicles where the country of the registered vehicle is unknown, that are under disposal or from counties unknown within Great Britain.
5 Figure labelled as the United Kingdom relates to Great Britain.
6 For people of working age, men aged 16 to 64 and women aged 16 to 59. Data are seasonally adjusted.
7 Data combined for years, 1999/2000, 2000/01 and 2001/02.

Map **1.14** Population density: by local or unitary authority, 2002

Population density, 2002 (people per sq km)

- 10,000 or over
- 7,500 - 9,999
- 5,000 - 7,499
- 2,500 - 4,999
- 2,499 or under

1 Waltham Forest
2 Camden
3 Islington
4 Hackney
5 Tower Hamlets
6 Newham
7 Barking and Dagenham
8 Hammersmith and Fulham
9 Kensington and Chelsea
10 Westminster
11 City of London
12 Richmond upon Thames
13 Wandsworth
14 Lambeth
15 Southwark
16 Lewisham
17 Kingston upon Thames

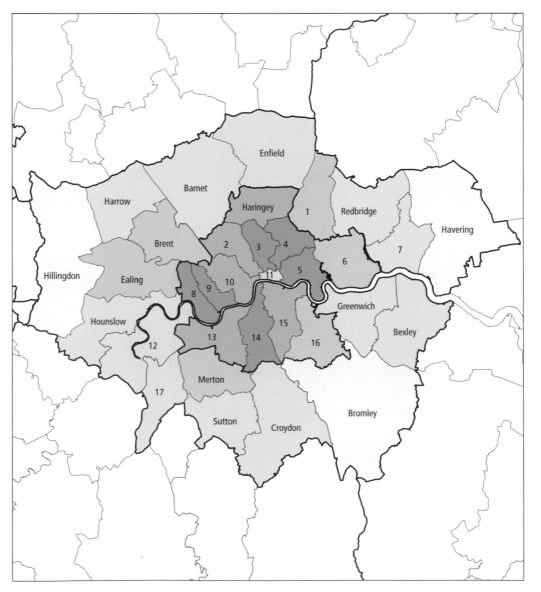

London

In 2002, London's population was 7.4 million, which equated to a population density of 4,679 people per sq km, appreciably higher than in any other region; there were 8,980 people per sq km in Inner London. Resident population grew by 8.7 per cent between 1982 and 2002. (Table 3.1, Maps 3.3 and 3.8)

London had the largest proportion of its population aged between 25 and 44 in 2002 (37 per cent). The UK proportion for that age group was 29 per cent in 2002. (Table 3.2)

The proportion of London's population who are of retirement age is the lowest of all the regions. Only 11.5 per cent of the population of Inner London were of retirement age compared to the UK average of 18.4 in 2002. (Map 3.5)

London had the highest crude live birth rate in 2001, and was the only region which had a higher rate in 2001 than in 1981. London had the lowest death rate in 2001. Between 2001 and 2002 the number of births in London was almost double the number of deaths. (Tables 3.10 and 3.11)

In 2001, birth rates in London were highest for women aged 30 to 34, whereas in many other areas the highest birth rates were to women between the ages of 25 and 29. (Table 3.13)

London had the highest proportion of households comprising two or more unrelated adults sharing in spring 2002. (Table 3.20)

In 2001/02, the proportion of pupils in their last year of compulsory education achieving 5 or more GCSE grades A*-C (or equivalent) was lower in London than the UK average. A slightly higher proportion of pupils than the UK average achieved no graded GCSE results. (Table 4.6)

Around 25 per cent of people of working age in London were qualified to degree level or equivalent in 2003. (Table 4.14)

In 2002, the highest average gross weekly earnings (by full-time employees on adult rates) in the UK were in London (£624.10). (Table 5.16)

Average gross weekly earnings for full-time male employees in London were 40 per cent higher than for females in April 2002. Average weekly earnings for males working in the financial and business services sector in April 2002 were almost 45 per cent higher than the UK rate. (Tables 5.16 and 5.17)

London had by far the highest rate of notification of tuberculosis in 2002 at 38.6 cases per 100,000 population, more than double the next highest rate. (Table 7.6)

The average number of patients for each General Practitioner (GP) in September 2002 was highest in London, with GPs having on average over 2,000 patients on their lists. Over two-fifths of the GPs in London were female, which was the highest proportion in the UK. (Table 7.18)

There were 592 robberies recorded per 100,000 population in London in 2002/03, which was the highest rate for any region. (Table 9.01)

In 1999, gross disposable household income for London was £12,207 per head, the highest in the country. (Table 12.9)

Table **1.15** Key statistics for the South East

	South East	United Kingdom		South East	United Kingdom
Population, 2002[1] (thousands)	8,037	59,229	Gross value added, 2001 (£ million)	138,877	874,227
Percentage aged under 16[1]	*19.7*	*19.9*	Gross value added per head index, 2001 (UK=100)	120.1	100.0
Percentage pension age and over[1]	*18.9*	*18.4*	Total business sites, 2002 (thousands)	384.6	2,538.1
Standardised mortality ratio (UK=100), 2002	91	100	Average dwelling price, 2002 (£)[3]	193,339	145,320
Infant mortality rate,[2] 2002	4.5	5.3			
Percentage of pupils achieving 5 or more grades A*-C			Motor cars currently licensed,[4] 2002 (thousands)	4,103	25,782
at GCSE level or equivalent, 2001/02	*56*	*52.5*	Fatal and serious accidents on roads,[5] 2002		
			(rates per 100,000 population)	59	59
Economic activity rate,[6]			Recorded crime rate, 2002/03		
spring 2003 (percentages)	*82.5*	*78.8*	(notifiable offences per 100,000 population)[3]	8,631	11,327
Employment rate,[6] spring 2003 (percentages)	*79.3*	*74.7*			
Unemployment rate,[6] spring 2003 (percentages)	*3.9*	*5.1*	Average gross weekly household income, 1999-2002[7] (£)	630	510
Average gross weekly earnings: males in full-time					
employment, April 2002 (£)	555.3	511.3	Average weekly household expenditure, 1999-2002[7] (£)	443.0	379.7
Average gross weekly earnings: females in full-time			Households in receipt of Income Support/Working		
employment, April 2002 (£)	398.6	382.1	Families Tax Credit,[5] 2001/02 (percentages)	*10*	*17*

1 Population figures for 2002 are mid- year population estimates and include provisional results from the Manchester matching exercise. Pension age is men aged 65 and over and women aged 60 and over.
2 Deaths of infants under one year of age per 1,000 live births.
3 Figure labelled as the United Kingdom relate to Great Britain.
4 Totals for the United Kingdom include vehicles where the country of the registered vehicle is unknown, that are under disposal or from counties unknown within Great Britain.
5 Figure labelled as the United Kingdom relates to Great Britain.
6 For people of working age, men aged 16 to 64 and women aged 16 to 59. Data are seasonally adjusted.
7 Data combined for years, 1999/2000, 2000/01 and 2001/02.

Map **1.16** Population density: by local or unitary authority, 2002

Population density, 2002 (people per sq km)

- 2,500 or over
- 1,000 - 2,499
- 500 - 999
- 250 - 499
- 100 - 249
- 99 or under

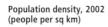

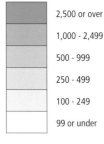

1 Milton Keynes UA	20 Sevenoaks
2 Cherwell	21 Dartford
3 Oxford	22 Gravesham
4 Wycombe	23 Medway UA
5 Chiltern	24 Tonbridge and Malling
6 South Bucks	25 Canterbury
7 Windsor and Maidenhead UA	26 Tunbridge Wells
8 Slough UA	27 Shepway
9 Reading UA	28 Rushmoor
10 Wokingham UA	29 Southampton UA
11 Bracknell Forest UA	30 Eastleigh
12 Runnymede	31 Fareham
13 Spelthorne	32 Gosport
14 Surrey Heath	33 Portsmouth UA
15 Woking	34 Havant
16 Elmbridge	35 Isle of Wight UA
17 Epsom and Ewell	36 Crawley
18 Reigate and Banstead	37 Worthing
19 Tandridge	38 Brighton and Hove UA
	39 Eastbourne
	40 Hastings

South East

In 2002, the South East's population was 8.0 million people. Within the South East the population was most concentrated in Portsmouth Unitary Authority (4,671 people per sq km) and least concentrated in the local authority district of West Oxfordshire (135 people per sq km). Since 1971 the population in the South East has been steadily increasing (including an increase of 10.5 per cent between 1982 and 2002), and it is now the largest region in terms of population. (Table 3.1, Maps 3.3 and 3.8)

Overall in the South East the Standardised Mortality Ratio (SMR) was one of the lowest, 9 per cent lower than the UK as a whole in 2001. (Table 3.14)

In January 2003, over 50 per cent of early years education (education for three- and four-year-olds) in the South East was provided by the private and voluntary sectors. This compared with around one third for the UK as a whole. (Table 4.2)

In 2001/02, the proportion of pupils in their last year of compulsory education achieving 5 or more GCSE grades A*-C results (or equivalent) was higher in the South East, at 56 per cent, than in other regions of England. (Table 4.6)

The employment rate for people of working age in spring 2003, at 79.3 per cent, was the highest in the UK. In 2002, the proportion of the working age population who were self-employed in the South East was among the highest in the UK, at 10.5 per cent. (Tables 5.1 and 5.3)

In 2003, employee absence from work due to sickness was highest in the South East at 3.3 per cent, compared with the UK average of 3 per cent. (Figure 5.14)

The South East had the largest number of dwellings in the UK in 2003 (over 3.4 million). The region also had the highest proportion of owner-occupied dwellings, at 76 per cent, in 2002. (Tables 6.1 and 6.4)

Between 1991 and 2002, actions for County Court mortgage possession orders in the South East decreased by around three-quarters. (Table 6.13)

The perinatal mortality rate was lowest in the South East (6.8 per 1,000 live and still births), compared with an average for the United Kingdom of 8.2 per 1,000 live and still births in 2002. (Table 7.3)

The South East had the lowest proportion of children looked after by Local Authorities in March 2002: 41 children per 10,000 population under 18. (Table 7.21)

In 2002/03, 8.9 per cent of households in the South East were victims of vandalism at least once, the highest rate in the UK. (Table 9.3)

Average weekly household motoring expenditure per car or van in the South East was £74.27, higher than any other of the countries and regions of the UK in 2002. (Table 10.11)

Each household in the South East produced on average 24.3 kilos of household waste per week in 2001/02 and recycled 222 kilos in the year, the latter figure being the highest in England. (Tables 11.15 and 11.16)

In the South East, manufacturing industries accounted for 15 per cent of gross value added in 2000, four percentage points lower than the UK average. (Table 12.5)

In 1999 gross disposable household income for the South East was £11,055 per head. (Table 12.9)

Table **1.17** Key statistics for the South West

	South West	United Kingdom		South West	United Kingdom
Population, 2002[1] (thousands)	4,960	59,229	Gross value added, 2001 (£ million)	63,554	874,227
Percentage aged under 16[1]	18.8	19.9	Gross value added per head index, 2001 (UK=100)	89.3	100.0
Percentage pension age and over[1]	21.5	18.4	Total business sites, 2002 (thousands)	235.1	2,538.1
Standardised mortality ratio (UK=100), 2002	90	100	Average dwelling price, 2002 (£)[3]	157,068	145,320
Infant mortality rate,[2] 2002	4.4	5.3			
Percentage of pupils achieving 5 or more grades A*-C			Motor cars currently licensed,[4] 2002 (thousands)	2,495	25,782
at GCSE level or equivalent, 2001/02	56.0	52.5	Fatal and serious accidents on roads,[5] 2002		
			(rates per 100,000 population)	53	59
Economic activity rate,[6]			Recorded crime rate, 2002/03		
spring 2003 (percentages)	81.8	78.8	(notifiable offences per 100,000 population)[3]	9,473	11,327
Employment rate,[6] spring 2003 (percentages)	78.6	74.7			
Unemployment rate,[6] spring 2003 (percentages)	3.9	5.1	Average gross weekly household income, 1999-2002[7] (£)	483	510
Average gross weekly earnings: males in full-time					
employment, April 2002 (£)	463.3	511.3	Average weekly household expenditure, 1999-2002[7] (£)	366.4	379.7
Average gross weekly earnings: females in full time			Households in receipt of Income Support/Working		
employment, April 2002 (£)	350.0	382.1	Families Tax Credit,[5] 2001/02 (percentages)	13	17

1 Population figures for 2002 are mid- year population estimates and include provisional results from the Manchester matching exercise. Pension age is men aged 65 and over and women aged 60 and over.
2 Deaths of infants under one year of age per 1,000 live births.
3 Figure labelled as the United Kingdom relate to Great Britain.
4 Totals for the United Kingdom include vehicles where the country of the registered vehicle is unknown, that are under disposal or from counties unknown within Great Britain.
5 Figure labelled as the United Kingdom relates to Great Britain.
6 For people of working age, men aged 16 to 64 and women aged 16 to 59. Data are seasonally adjusted.
7 Data combined for years, 1999/2000, 2000/01 and 2001/02.

Map **1.18** Population density: by local or unitary authority, 2002

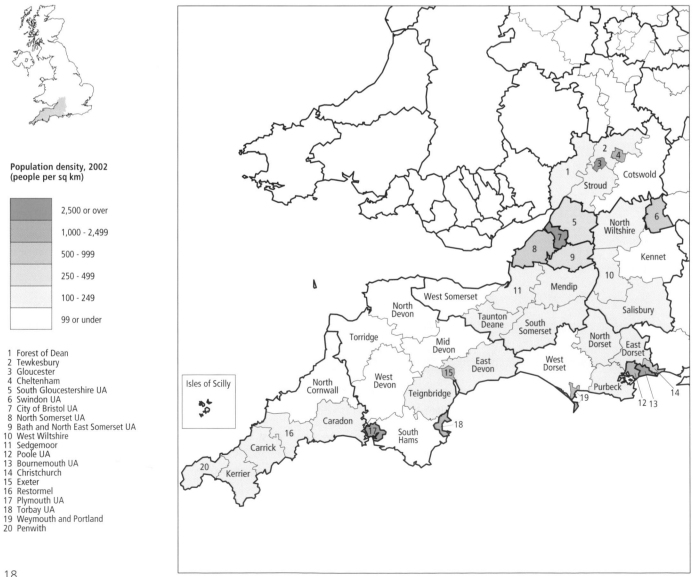

Population density, 2002 (people per sq km)

- 2,500 or over
- 1,000 - 2,499
- 500 - 999
- 250 - 499
- 100 - 249
- 99 or under

1 Forest of Dean
2 Tewkesbury
3 Gloucester
4 Cheltenham
5 South Gloucestershire UA
6 Swindon UA
7 City of Bristol UA
8 North Somerset UA
9 Bath and North East Somerset UA
10 West Wiltshire
11 Sedgemoor
12 Poole UA
13 Bournemouth UA
14 Christchurch
15 Exeter
16 Restormel
17 Plymouth UA
18 Torbay UA
19 Weymouth and Portland
20 Penwith

South West

In 2002, the South West had a population of 5.0 million. Within the South West, population density was highest in Bournemouth UA, at 3,547 people per sq km. In marked contrast, the predominantly rural local authority district of West Devon had only 44 people per sq km. (Table 3.1 and Map 3.3)

The proportion of the population over retirement age was highest in the South West in 2002. More than a quarter of the population of Torbay and of Dorset were over retirement age. (Map 3.5)

Population growth in the United Kingdom between 1982 and 2002 was highest in the South West (a 12.7 per cent increase). Only the cities of Bristol and Plymouth showed declines of 4.8 and 6.2 per cent respectively. (Map 3.8)

In 2001, the Infant Mortality rate (deaths of infants under one year of age per 1,000 live births) for the South West was virtually the same as the overall UK rate: 5.4 and 5.5 respectively. The region had the lowest Age-Standardised Mortality Rate, at 849 per 100,000 population, compared with the United Kingdom average of 954. (Tables 3.14, 7.4 and 7.5)

The number of marriages in the South West decreased by 14 per cent between 1976 and 2001. Between 2000 and 2002 the region had the highest proportion (31 per cent) of non-married people aged 16 to 59 who were cohabiting. (Tables 3.17 and 3.18)

At nearly one in three in spring 2002, the proportion of households consisting of a married couple with no children was highest in the South West. (Table 3.20)

In 2002/03, almost 16 per cent of classes in maintained primary schools in the South West had over 30 pupils, one of the highest proportions in the UK. (Table 4.3)

The proportion of pupils in their last year of compulsory education achieving 5 or more GCSE grades A*-C (or equivalent) was 56 per cent in the South West, one of the highest proportions of all English regions in 2001/02. (Table 4.6)

The employment rate for people of working age in spring 2003, at 78.6 per cent, was among the highest in the UK. (Table 5.1)

One-quarter of females in the South West were ex-regular smokers in 2001/02, the highest proportion in any area. (Table 7.12)

In 1998 over 43 per cent of the land area in the South West was categorised as grassland. (Table 11.11)

On average, each household in the South West produced 23.7 kilos of waste per week in 2001/02 and recycled 195 kilos per year. (Tables 11.15 and 11.16)

In 1999, gross disposable household income for the South West was £10,073 per head. (Table 12.9)

Over 68 per cent of the South West's export trade in 2002 was to the European Union, higher than the average proportion for the United Kingdom overall. However, the proportion of trade from the European Union was lower than the UK average; 41.3 per cent compared with 52.8. (Table 13.7)

Table **1.19** Key statistics for Wales

	Wales	United Kingdom		Wales	United Kingdom
Population, 2002[1] (thousands)	2,919	59,229	Gross value added, 2001 (£ million)	33,086	874,227
Percentage aged under 16[1]	19.9	19.9	Gross value added per head index, 2001 (UK=100)	78.9	100.0
Percentage pension age and over[1]	20.2	18.4	Total business sites, 2002 (thousands)	114.4	2,538.1
Standardised mortality ratio (UK=100), 2002	103	100	Average dwelling price, 2002 (£)[3]	90,163	145,320
Infant mortality rate,[2] 2002	4.7	5.3			
Percentage of pupils achieving 5 or more grades A*-C			Motor cars currently licensed,[4] 2002 (thousands)	1,269	25,782
at GCSE level or equivalent, 2001/02	50.5	52.5	Fatal and serious accidents on roads,[5] 2002		
			(rates per 100,000 population)	45	59
Economic activity rate,[6]			Recorded crime rate, 2002/03		
spring 2003 (percentages)	76.5	78.8	(notifiable offences per 100,000 population)[3]	10,156	11,327
Employment rate,[6] spring 2003 (percentages)	73.0	74.7			
Unemployment rate,[6] spring 2003 (percentages)	4.6	5.1	Average gross weekly household income, 1999-2002[7] (£)	407	510
Average gross weekly earnings: males in full-time					
employment, April 2002 (£)	432.9	511.3	Average weekly household expenditure, 1999-2002[7] (£)	322.5	379.7
Average gross weekly earnings: females in full-time			Households in receipt of Income Support/Working		
employment, April 2002 (£)	345.1	382.1	Families Tax Credit,[5] 2001/02 (percentages)	20	17

1 Population figures for 2002 are mid- year population estimates and include provisional results from the Manchester matching exercise. Pension age is men aged 65 and over and women aged 60 and over.
2 Deaths of infants under one year of age per 1,000 live births.
3 Figure labelled as the United Kingdom relate to Great Britain.
4 Totals for the United Kingdom include vehicles where the country of the registered vehicle is unknown, that are under disposal or from counties unknown within Great Britain.
5 Figure labelled as the United Kingdom relates to Great Britain.
6 For people of working age, men aged 16 to 64 and women aged 16 to 59. Data are seasonally adjusted.
7 Data combined for years, 1999/2000, 2000/01 and 2001/02.

Map **1.20** Population density: by local or unitary authority, 2002

Population density, 2002 (people per sq km)

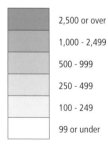

2,500 or over

1,000 - 2,499

500 - 999

250 - 499

100 - 249

99 or under

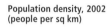

1 Swansea UA
2 Neath Port Talbot UA
3 Bridgend UA
4 Rhondda, Cynon, Taff UA
5 Merthyr Tydfil UA
6 Caerphilly UA
7 Blaenau Gwent UA
8 Torfaen UA
9 The Vale of Glamorgan UA
10 Newport UA

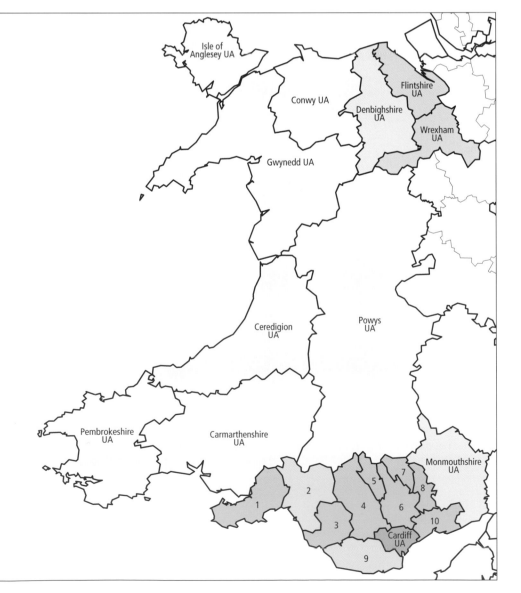

Wales

In 2002, Wales had a population of just over 2.9 million. Within Wales the population density was most concentrated in Cardiff (2,222 people per sq km) and least concentrated in Powys (25 people per sq km). (Table 3.1 and Map 3.3)

The population of Wales increased by 4.1 per cent between 1982 and 2002 (based on the mid-year population estimates). The largest increase was in Ceredigion where the population increased by more than a quarter during the twenty years. (Map 3.8)

The highest death rate throughout the United Kingdom was in Wales (11.4 per 1,000 population in 2001). (Table 3.10)

The proportion of pupils in education achieving 2 or more A levels (or equivalent) in 2001/02 was lowest in Wales, at 30.6 per cent, compared with a UK average of 37.6 per cent. (Table 4.6)

The employment rate for people of working age in spring 2003, at 73.0 per cent, was among the lowest in the UK. However, the employment rate increased in Wales by more than 4 percentage points between 1999 and 2003. (Table 5.1)

The highest proportion of males with second jobs in spring 2003 was in Wales (4.3 percent of those in employment). (Table 5.11)

In April 2002, average gross weekly earnings for full-time employees on adult rates in Wales were £399.70. (Table 5.16)

Almost a third of households in Wales in 2001/02 had lived at their current address for 20 years or more. (Table 6.6)

In 2001/02 Wales had the lowest percentage of 16 to 29 year olds using illegal drugs. Use of hallucinants and opiate substances was also much lower than in other areas. (Figure 7.13)

Wales had the highest number of prescription items (16.8) dispensed per head of population in 2002; this was around 4 more than the average for England. (Table 7.14)

Over the period 1999 to 2002, Wales has the lowest proportion of households in the UK with a weekly income of £750 or over. (Table 8.2)

The detection rate by police for recorded crimes in England and Wales was highest in Wales (36 per cent in 2002/03). (Table 9.4)

In Wales, manufacturing industry accounted for 25 per cent of GVA in 2000, compared with 19 per cent for the UK as a whole. Agriculture, hunting, forestry and fishing accounted for 1.5 per cent of GVA compared with 1.1 per cent for the UK. (Table 12.5)

In Wales over a fifth of total businesses were agricultural enterprises, the highest proportion of all regions in Great Britain in 2002. (Table 13.17)

Table **1.21** Key statistics for Scotland

	Scotland	United Kingdom		Scotland	United Kingdom
Population, 2002[1] (thousands)	5,055	59,229	Gross value added, 2001 (£ million)	69,179	874,227
Percentage aged under 16[1]	18.9	19.9	Gross value added per head index, 2001 (UK=100)	94.7	100.0
Percentage pension age and over[1]	18.8	18.4	Total business sites, 2002 (thousands)	195.9	2,358.1
Standardised mortality ratio (UK=100), 2002	114	100			
Infant mortality rate,[2] 2002	5.2	5.3	Motor cars currently licensed,[3] 2002 (thousands)	1,993	25,782
Percentage of pupils achieving 5 or more grades A*-C			Fatal and serious accidents on roads,[4] 2002		
at GCSE level or equivalent, 2001/02	60.4	52.5	(rates per 100,000 population)	58	59
Economic activity rate,[6]			Recorded crime rate, 2002		
spring 2003 (percentages)	79.1	78.8	(notifiable offences per 100,000 population)[6]	8,448	11,327
Employment rate,[6] spring 2003 (percentages)	74.6	74.7			
Unemployment rate,[6] spring 2003 (percentages)	5.7	5.1	Average gross weekly household income, 1999-2002[7] (£)	446	510
Average gross weekly earnings: males in full-time					
employment, April 2002 (£)	473.7	511.3	Average weekly household expenditure, 1999-2002[7] (£)	344.7	379.7
Average gross weekly earnings: females in full-time			Households in receipt of Income Support/Working		
employment, April 2002 (£)	360.1	382.1	Families Tax Credit,[5] 2001/02 (percentages)	19	17

1 Population figures for 2002 are mid- year population estimates and include provisional results from the Manchester matching exercise. Pension age is men aged 65 and over and women aged 60 and over.
2 Deaths of infants under one year of age per 1,000 live births.
3 Figure labelled as the United Kingdom relate to Great Britain.
4 Totals for the United Kingdom include vehicles where the country of the registered vehicle is unknown, that are under disposal or from counties unknown within Great Britain.
5 Figure labelled as the United Kingdom relates to Great Britain.
6 For people of working age, men aged 16 to 64 and women aged 16 to 59. Data are seasonally adjusted.
7 Data combined for years, 1999/2000, 2000/01 and 2001/02.

Map **1.22** Population density: by local or unitary authority, 2002

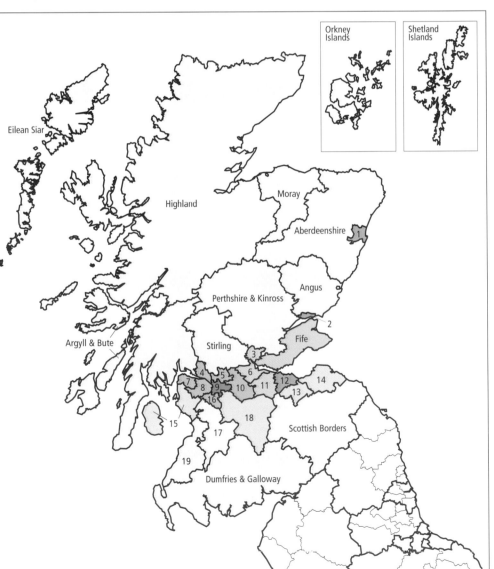

Population density, 2002 (people per sq km)

- 2,500 or over
- 1,000 - 2,499
- 500 - 999
- 250 - 499
- 100 - 249
- 99 or under

1 Aberdeen City
2 Dundee City
3 Clackmannanshire
4 West Dunbartonshire
5 East Dunbartonshire
6 Falkirk
7 Inverclyde
8 Renfrewshire
9 Glasgow City
10 North Lanarkshire
11 West Lothian
12 City of Edinburgh
13 Midlothian
14 East Lothian
15 North Ayrshire
16 East Renfrewshire
17 East Ayrshire
18 South Lanarkshire
19 South Ayrshire

Scotland

In 2002, Scotland had a population of 5.1 million. Within Scotland, population density was highest in Glasgow (3,290 people per sq km) and lowest in the Highland council area (8 people per sq km), the lowest for any local authority in the UK. (Table 3.1 and Map 3.3)

Edinburgh had one of the lowest proportions of young people (aged under 16) in the UK, 16.1 per cent of its population in 2002. This compared with a UK average of 19.9 per cent. (Map 3.4)

Scotland's population decreased by 2.1 per cent between 1982 and 2002, based on the mid-year population estimates. The largest percentage change in population was in Aberdeenshire, where there was an increase of 18.0 per cent, although there were several districts which had large declines. (Map 3.8)

Scotland's Standardised Mortality Ratio (SMR) was 14 per cent higher than the UK average in 2001, at 114 (UK=100). The Infant Mortality rate in Scotland was the same as the UK rate (5.5 deaths of infants under one year of age per 1,000 live births). (Table 3.14)

Between 1976 and 2001 the number of marriages in Scotland decreased by 21 per cent, less than the UK average. Within Great Britain, Scotland had the lowest proportion (one-fifth) of non-married people aged between 16 and 59 who were cohabiting. (Tables 3.17 and 3.18)

In 2001/02, the highest proportion, three-fifths, of pupils achieving the equivalent of 5 or more GCSE grades A*-C was in Scotland. A lower proportion of pupils than the UK average achieved no graded results. (Table 4.6)

The employment rate for people of working age in spring 2003 in Scotland was 74.6 per cent, very similar to the UK average. However, the employment rate for males rose by over 3 percentage points between 1999 and 2003. (Table 5.1)

In April 2002, average gross weekly earnings for full-time employees on adult rates in Scotland were £427.00. (Table 5.16)

Almost two-fifths of dwellings in Scotland in 2001/02 were purpose-built flats or maisonettes, the highest proportion in the United Kingdom. (Table 6.5)

Around one in eight males aged 16 and over in Scotland smoked 20 or more cigarettes a day in 2001/02, the highest proportion in the United Kingdom. (Table 7.11)

In Scotland, 102 per 10,000 young people under 18 years old were in the care of local authorities in March 2002. Of these, 14 per cent were looked after in children's homes and hostels. (Table 7.20)

Children's spending was highest in Scotland in 1999-2002. On average children spent almost £14 per week, £3 more than the average for Great Britain. (Table 8.10)

In 1999, gross disposable household income for Scotland was £9,870 per head. (Table 12.9)

Between 1992/93 and 2001/02, an average of nearly £130 million per year was spent by government on preferential assistance to industry in Scotland. The highest amount in a single year was £158.7 million in 2000/01. (Table 13.10)

Table **1.23** **Key statistics for Northern Ireland**

	Northern Ireland	United Kingdom		Northern Ireland	United Kingdom
Population, 2002[1] (thousands)	1,697	59,229	Gross value added, 2001 (£ million)	19,108	874,227
Percentage aged under 16[1]	23.2	19.9	Gross value added per head index, 2001 (UK=100)	78.4	100.0
Percentage pension age and over[1]	15.7	18.4	Total business sites, 2002 (thousands)	79.0	2,358.1
Standardised mortality ratio (UK=100), 2002	99	100			
Infant mortality rate,[2] 2002	4.7	5.3	Motor cars currently licensed,[3] 2002 (thousands)	671	25,782
Percentage of pupils achieving 5 or more grades A*-C			Fatal and serious accidents on roads,[4] 2002		
at GCSE level or equivalent, 2001/02	58.7	52.5	(rates per 100,000 population)	73	59
			Recorded crime rate, 2002/03		
Economic activity rate,[6]			(notifiable offences per 100,000 population)[6]	8,435	11,327
spring 2003 (percentages)	73.7	78.8			
Employment rate,[6] spring 2003 (percentages)	69.7	74.7	Average gross weekly household income, 1999-2002[7] (£)	399	510
Unemployment rate,[6] spring 2003 (percentages)	5.4	5.1			
Average gross weekly earnings: males in full-time			Average weekly household expenditure, 1999-2002[7] (£)	347.3	379.7
employment, April 2002 (£)	422.5	511.3			
Average gross weekly earnings: females in full-time					
employment, April 2002 (£)	340.9	382.1			

1 Population figures for 2002 are mid- year population estimates and include provisional results from the Manchester matching exercise. Pension age is men aged 65 and over and women aged 60 and over.
2 Deaths of infants under one year of age per 1,000 live births.
3 Figure labelled as the United Kingdom relate to Great Britain.
4 Totals for the United Kingdom include vehicles where the country of the registered vehicle is unknown, that are under disposal or from counties unknown within Great Britain.
5 Figure labelled as the United Kingdom relates to Great Britain.
6 For people of working age, men aged 16 to 64 and women aged 16 to 59. Data are seasonally adjusted.
7 Data combined for years, 1999/2000, 2000/01 and 2001/02.

Map **1.24** **Population density: by local or unitary authority, 2002**

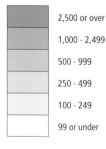

Population density, 2002 (people per sq km)

- 2,500 or over
- 1,000 - 2,499
- 500 - 999
- 250 - 499
- 100 - 249
- 99 or under

1 Newtownabbey
2 Carrickfergus
3 Belfast
4 North Down
5 Castlereagh

Northern Ireland

In 2002, Northern Ireland had a population of 1.7 million. Within Northern Ireland, population density was highest in Belfast (2,501 people per sq km) and lowest in Moyle (33 people per sq km). (Table 3.1 and Map 3.3)

Derry, in the Western district council area of Northern Ireland, had the highest percentage of its population aged under 16 in 2002 (26.3 per cent compared with the UK average of 19.9). (Map 3.4)

The population of Northern Ireland increased by 9.8 per cent between 1982 and 2002, based on the mid-year population estimates. The largest percentage change in population was in Banbridge in the Southern district where there was an increase of 40 per cent. (Map 3.8)

Northern Ireland had the highest birth rates for women aged 30 to 34 and 25 to 29 in 2001. (Table 3.13)

Between 1976 and 2001 the number of marriages in Northern Ireland decreased by 26 per cent, less than the rate of decline for the UK as a whole. (Table 3.17)

In 2001/02, the proportion of pupils in their last year of compulsory education achieving 5 or more GCSE grades A*-C (or equivalent) was higher in Northern Ireland than the UK average. (Table 4.6)

The proportion of people of working age qualified to GCE A level/equivalent or higher in Northern Ireland was around 48 per cent in spring 2003. (Table 4.14)

The employment rate for people of working age in spring 2003, at 69.7 per cent, was among the lowest in the UK. (Table 5.1)

In April 2002, average gross weekly earnings for full-time employees on adult rates in Northern Ireland were £390.10. (Table 5.16)

Less than three-quarters of females aged 25 to 64 in the target population for screening in Northern Ireland participated in cervical cancer screening programmes in 2002. (Table 7.7)

In Northern Ireland, manufacturing industry accounted for 20 per cent of GVA in 2000, compared with 19 per cent for the UK as a whole. Agriculture, hunting, forestry and fishing accounted for 2.4 per cent of GVA compared with 1.1 per cent for the UK. (Table 12.5)

In 1999, gross disposable household income for Northern Ireland was £8,998 per head. (Table 12.9)

In March 2002, just over a quarter of business sites in Northern Ireland were in distribution, hotels and catering or repairs, compared with the UK average of 28.2 per cent. (Table 13.3)

Over 64 per cent of Northern Ireland's export trade in 2002 was to the European Union, higher than the UK proportion overall. Trade from the European Union was higher than the UK average, at 56 per cent of Northern Ireland's imports. (Table 13.7)

Chapter 2 **European Union**

Population and population density

Total population in Germany, in 2001 was over 82 million, accounting for over one-fifth of total European Union population (over 376 million in 2001). (Table 2.1)

Brussels in Belgium was the most densely populated region of the European Union with over 5,900 people per sq. km in 2001, followed by London in the United Kingdom (UK) at over 4,600 people per sq. km and Berlin in Germany with 3,800 people per sq. km. (Table 2.1)

Age structure of population in the European Union varied between countries and regions. Northern Ireland in the UK had the highest proportion of the population aged under 15 years (23.2 per cent in 2002). Emilia-Romagna in Italy was the region with the largest proportion (22 per cent) of its population over the age of 65 in 2001. (Table 2.1)

Vital statistics

In 2000, the region with the highest birth rate was Île de France in France with 15.8 births per 1,000 population. Canarias in Spain had the lowest death rate of 7.3 per 1,000 population. (Table 2.1)

An important social indicator is infant mortality. The highest number of deaths of infants under 1 year of age was in Portugal, in the regions of Acores and Maderia. Both regions had an infant mortality rate of 8.1 per 1,000 births in 2001. Although the Nord Est in Italy, had the lowest infant mortality rate of 3.2, the country with the lowest rate overall was Sweden; 3.4 per 1,000 births. (Table 2.1)

Education and training

The country with the highest proportion of 16 to18 year olds in education or training was Sweden (97 per cent), the lowest percentage of all European Union countries in 2000 was in the United Kingdom with only 71 per cent of 16 to18 year olds participating in education or training. Within the UK this varied from 60 per cent in the East to 80 per cent in Northern Ireland. (Table 2.2)

Number of doctors

In 2000, Lazio in Italy had 7.7 doctors (or physicians) per 1,000 population, the highest proportion of all EU regions. Wales had the lowest number of doctors; 1.3 per 1,000 population. (Table 2.2)

Transport

The European transport network is key to the increasing demand for passenger and goods transport services. In 2002, motorway density (length of motorways (km) per 1,000 sq. km of area) was highest in the German region of Bremen; 146 km per 1,000 sq. km. Hamburg was the only other region with motorway density in excess of 100 km per sq. km. (Table 2.2)

Car ownership

Luxembourg, Italy, Sweden and Germany had the highest numbers of privately owned cars in the European Union in 2002 (over 500 privately owned cars per 1,000 population). Kentriki Ellada (Greece) had the lowest number of privately owned cars where there were 128 cars per 1,000 population, compared to Lazio in Italy where the rate was almost fives higher at 593 cars per 1,000 population. (Table 2.2)

Unemployment

Luxembourg and the Netherlands had the lowest unemployment rates in the European Union in 2002 (2.6 and 2.8 per cent respectively). The country with the highest rate was Spain where 11.4 per cent of the population were unemployed. In Spain the rate reached 18.3 per cent in the Sur region, however the regions with the highest unemployment rate were in Germany, Mecklenburg-Vorpommern and Sacheen-Anhalt at 23.6 and 23.5 per cent respectively. (Table 2.3)

The highest rate of long-term unemployment expressed as a percentage of all unemployed in 2002 was in Italy, where almost 60 per cent of the unemployed were classified as long-term unemployed, (those unemployed for 12 months or more). Long-term unemployment in the Campania region of Italy was over 70 per cent. Conversely, the South East and South West regions of the UK were the only two EU regions with rates below 15 per cent. (Table 2.3)

Employment

In each region of Europe, the services sector in 2002 employed the highest proportion of people. Over 85 per cent of London's workforce were in the service sector as was the case in Brussels. Greece had the highest proportion of people working in agriculture. In the regions of Kentriki Ellada and Nisia Algaiou, Kriti over a quarter of all people worked in agriculture. (Table 2.3)

GDP

Estimates of the percentage of GDP in 2000 derived from agriculture, showed that Luxembourg and the UK had the lowest rates (0.7 and 1.0 respectively). Ireland had the highest percentage (42.6) of GDP derived from industry. (Table 2.3)

Land use and agricultural statistics

Over 40 per cent of land in the European Union in 2001 was agricultural. Over two-thirds of land in the UK was agricultural land, the highest proportion of all countries in the EU. In Sweden and Finland only 7 per cent of the land was agricultural, of which over 90 per cent was arable. (Table 2.4)

Ireland produced the highest yield of wheat of all EU countries in 2002, (relative to arable land available); 84 kg per hectare. However, the German region of Schleswig-Holstein yielded 98 kg per hectare. Portugal produced 8 kg of wheat and 11 kg of barley per hectare, the lowest of all European Union countries. Barley production was highest in Belgium at 72 kg per hectare, although some regions of Germany and France had higher yields. (Table 2.4)

Belgium had the greatest livestock density of cattle per 1,000 hectare of utilised agricultural land in 2001 whilst the Netherlands had the highest density of pigs. Greece had the fewest cattle relative to agricultural area. (Table 2.4)

NUTS level 1 areas in the European Union[1]

NETHERLANDS
1 Noord-Nederland
2 Oost-Nederland
3 Zuid-Nederland
4 West-Nederland

BELGIUM
5 Vlaams Gewest
6 Région Wallonne
7 Bruxelles-Brussels

8 **LUXEMBOURG**

GERMANY
9 Saarland
10 Rheinland-Pfalz
11 Baden-Württemberg
12 Mecklenburg-Vorpommern
13 Hamburg
14 Schleswig-Holstein

non-EU countries

Açores (Portugal)

Madeira (Portugal)

Ceuta y Melilla (Spain-Sur)

Canarias (Spain)

1 NUTS (Nomenclature of Units for Territorial Statistics) is a hierachical classfication of areas that provides a breakdown of the EU's economic territory. See Notes and Definitions.

Table **2.1**   Population and vital statistics, 2001

| | | | | Percentage of population | | | | Infant |
	Area (sq km)[1]	Popu-lation[1,2,3] (thousands)	People per sq. km	Aged under 15[3]	Aged 65 and over[3,4]	Births[5] (per 1,000 population)	Deaths[5,6] (per 1,000 population)	mortality[5,6,7] (per 1,000 births)
EUR 15	**3,191,120**	**376,541**	**118**	..	..	**10.7**	**9.9**	..
Austria	**83,859**	**8,103**	**97**	*16.8*	*15.5*	**9.7**	**9.5**	**4.8**
Ostösterreich	23,554	3,424	145	*15.8*	*16.3*	9.3	10.6	5.2
Südösterreich	25,921	1,767	68	*16.5*	*16.4*	9.0	9.6	3.9
Westösterreich	34,384	2,912	85	*18.2*	*14.0*	10.5	8.1	4.9
Belgium	**30,518**	**10,239**	**336**	*17.6*	*16.8*	**11.2**	**10.2**	**4.8**
Bruxelles-Brussels	161	959	5,942	*17.8*	*16.8*	14.2	10.6	5.4
Vlaams Gewest	13,512	5,940	440	*17.0*	*16.7*	10.4	9.7	4.8
Région Wallonne	16,844	3,340	198	*18.6*	*16.8*	11.8	11.1	4.7
Denmark	**43,094**	**5,330**	**124**	*18.4*	*14.8*	**12.6**	**10.9**	**5.3**
Finland	**304,529**	**5,171**	**17**	*18.2*	*14.8*	**11.0**	**9.5**	**3.8**
Manner-Suomi	303,003	5,146	17	*18.2*	*14.8*	11.0	9.5	3.8
Åland	1,527	26	17	*18.7*	*16.0*	10.0	9.6	3.9
France	**543,965**	**58,749**	**108**	*18.9*	*16.0*	**13.1**	**9.0**	**4.2**
Île de France	12,012	10,979	914	*19.8*	*12.1*	15.8	6.8	4.7
Bassin Parisien	145,645	10,480	72	*19.2*	*16.4*	12.7	9.6	4.3
Nord - Pas-de-Calais	12,414	4,005	323	*21.3*	*13.9*	14.4	9.2	5.8
Est	48,030	5,179	108	*19.1*	*15.0*	12.6	8.7	5.4
Ouest	85,099	7,809	92	*18.4*	*17.7*	12.6	9.8	3.9
Sud-Ouest	103,599	6,202	60	*16.6*	*19.6*	11.2	10.6	4.2
Centre-Est	69,711	6,987	100	*18.9*	*15.8*	12.9	8.7	3.9
Méditerranée	67,455	7,109	105	*17.8*	*18.7*	11.7	10.1	4.6
Germany	**357,020**	**82,164**	**230**	*15.7*	*16.2*	**9.4**	**10.3**	**4.5**
Baden-Württemberg	35,751	10,476	293	*16.8*	*15.5*	10.3	9.3	4.3
Bayern	70,548	12,155	172	*16.4*	*16.0*	10.2	9.9	4.2
Berlin	891	3,387	3,800	*13.8*	*14.2*	8.8	10.3	4.4
Brandenburg	29,477	2,601	88	*14.1*	*14.9*	6.9	10.0	3.4
Bremen	404	663	1,640	*14.0*	*18.1*	9.2	11.5	3.1
Hamburg	755	1,705	2,257	*13.5*	*16.7*	9.4	10.9	4.5
Hessen	21,114	6,052	287	*15.5*	*16.2*	9.8	10.1	4.5
Mecklenburg-Vorpommern	23,172	1,789	77	*14.5*	*14.5*	7.0	9.7	4.9
Niedersachsen	47,614	7,899	166	*16.6*	*16.5*	10.2	10.5	5.3
Nordrhein-Westfalen	34,080	18,000	528	*16.3*	*16.6*	9.8	10.5	4.8
Rheinland-Pfalz	19,847	4,031	203	*16.4*	*17.0*	9.5	10.6	4.6
Saarland	2,570	1,072	417	*15.0*	*17.8*	8.3	11.9	5.6
Sachsen	18,413	4,460	242	*13.0*	*18.0*	7.0	11.3	4.2
Sachsen-Anhalt	20,447	2,649	130	*13.4*	*16.9*	6.8	11.3	3.9
Schleswig-Holstein	15,765	2,777	176	*16.1*	*16.4*	9.9	10.9	3.5
Thüringen	16,172	2,449	151	*13.5*	*16.3*	6.9	10.8	5.2
Greece	**131,626**	**10,554**	**80**	*15.2*	*17.3*	**9.5**	**9.6**	**5.9**
Voreia Ellada	56,457	3,423	61	*15.4*	*17.0*	9.7	9.5	6.3
Kentriki Ellada	53,902	2,657	49	*14.0*	*19.4*	8.5	11.0	6.6
Attiki	3,808	3,451	906	*15.3*	*15.9*	9.6	8.9	5.3
Nisia Aigaiou, Kriti	17,458	1,023	59	*16.8*	*17.6*	10.3	9.7	5.5
Ireland	**70,273**	**3,777**	**54**	*21.9*	*11.2*	**14.3**	**8.2**	**5.9**

Table **2.1**   (continued)

	Area (sq km)[1]	Population[1,2,3] (thousands)	People per sq. km	Percentage of population Aged under 15[3]	Aged 65 and over[3,4]	Births[5] (per 1,000 population)	Deaths[5,6] (per 1,000 population)	Infant mortality[5,6,7] (per 1,000 births)
Italy	301,333	57,680	191	*14.4*	*18.0*	9.4	9.7	4.5
Nord Ovest	34,082	6,034	177	*11.5*	*21.5*	8.0	11.9	3.5
Lombardia	23,863	9,065	380	*13.0*	*17.5*	9.4	9.4	3.4
Nord Est	39,853	6,633	166	*13.3*	*18.2*	9.5	9.7	3.2
Emilia-Romagna	22,123	3,981	180	*11.2*	*22.0*	8.5	11.4	3.6
Centro	41,138	5,833	142	*12.0*	*21.8*	8.1	11.2	4.1
Lazio	17,208	5,264	306	*14.2*	*17.0*	9.3	9.0	4.7
Abruzzo-Molise	15,235	1,607	105	*14.4*	*19.9*	8.4	10.3	4.4
Campania	13,593	5,781	425	*19.3*	*13.6*	11.6	8.2	4.9
Sud	44,447	6,742	152	*17.2*	*15.7*	10.1	8.3	5.4
Sicilia	25,703	5,088	198	*18.0*	*16.1*	10.5	9.2	6.1
Sardegna	24,090	1,652	69	*14.5*	*15.3*	8.4	8.3	4.1
Luxembourg	2,586	440	170	*18.9*	*14.3*	13.0	8.7	5.0
Netherlands	33,873	15,864	468	*18.6*	*13.6*	13.0	8.8	5.1
Noord-Nederland	8,346	1,657	199	*18.1*	*14.7*	12.2	9.5	5.7
Oost-Nederland	9,741	3,314	340	*19.6*	*13.2*	13.6	8.6	5.2
West-Nederland	8,693	7,396	851	*18.4*	*13.6*	13.2	8.9	4.9
Zuid-Nederland	7,093	3,497	493	*18.2*	*13.4*	12.2	8.5	5.4
Portugal	91,906	10,198	111	*16.1*	*16.1*	11.8	10.4	5.5
Continent	88,797	9,715	109	*15.8*	*16.3*	11.6	10.3	5.3
Açores	2,330	238	102	*22.4*	*12.2*	14.5	10.9	8.1
Madeira	779	245	315	*19.9*	*13.1*	13.2	10.9	8.1
Spain	504,790	39,733	79	*14.9*	*16.8*	9.9	9.0	4.3
Noroeste	45,297	4,287	95	*12.0*	*19.8*	7.1	10.8	3.7
Noreste	70,366	4,030	57	*12.6*	*18.6*	8.7	9.5	4.1
Comunidad de Madrid	7,995	5,112	639	*14.6*	*15.4*	11.0	7.5	4.1
Centro	215,025	5,251	24	*14.4*	*20.1*	8.4	9.7	4.2
Este	60,249	10,927	181	*14.5*	*16.8*	10.3	9.3	3.6
Sur	98,616	8,464	86	*17.8*	*14.1*	11.4	8.3	5.3
Canarias	7,242	1,662	229	*17.1*	*11.9*	11.1	7.3	6.4
Sweden	410,934	8,861	22	*18.5*	*17.3*	10.2	10.5	3.4
United Kingdom[8]	242,514	59,229	244	*19.9*	*18.4*	11.4	10.3	5.5
North East	8,573	2,513	293	*19.4*	*19.3*	10.3	11.3	5.6
North West	14,106	6,771	480	*20.3*	*18.6*	11.2	11.1	5.9
Yorkshire and the Humber	15,408	4,983	323	*20.2*	*18.7*	11.2	10.5	5.8
East Midlands	15,607	4,216	270	*19.8*	*18.6*	10.7	10.2	5.0
West Midlands	12,998	5,304	408	*20.5*	*18.6*	11.5	10.3	6.4
East	19,110	5,420	284	*19.9*	*19.1*	11.1	9.9	4.5
London	1,572	7,355	4,679	*19.6*	*14.0*	14.5	8.2	6.1
South East	19,069	8,037	421	*19.7*	*18.9*	11.1	9.9	4.2
South West	23,837	4,960	208	*18.8*	*21.5*	9.9	11.0	5.4
Wales	20,732	2,919	141	*19.9*	*20.2*	10.5	11.3	5.4
Scotland	77,925	5,055	65	*19.9*	*18.8*	10.4	11.4	5.5
Northern Ireland	13,576	1,697	125	*23.2*	*15.7*	13.0	8.6	6.0

1 Sum of all countries does not add to the total for area and population of EUR 15.
2 Estimates for EUR 15 relate to 2000. Data for France are provisional. Data for Luxembourg are estimated values.
3 Population estimates for UK relate to 2002 and include provisional results from the 'Manchester matching exercise', published November 2003.
4 Data for the UK are for pension age and over.
5 Data are for 2000. 2001 for UK. 1999 for EUR 15 and Germany.
6 Deaths are by date of occurrence and not date of registration.
7 Death of infants under 1 year of age per 1,000 live births. Data for Germany are for 1999.
8 Government Office Regions for the United Kingdom equal NUTS 1 regions for the European Union. See Notes and Definitions.

Source: Eurostat

Table **2.2**   **Social statistics**

	Dependency rate[1] 2000	Proportion of 16 to 18 year olds in education or training (percentages) 2000[2,3]	Number of physicians or doctors per 1,000 population, 2000[4]	Deaths and people injured in road traffic accidents per 1,000 population 2001[5]	Transport 2002 Length of motorways (km) per 1,000 sq km[6]	Private cars per 1,000 population
EUR 15	115	..	..	..	16	..
Austria	**106**	**82**	**3.1**	..	**19**	**496**
Ostösterreich	102	82	3.6	18	18	475
Südösterreich	118	82	3.0	14	21	534
Westösterreich	103	82	2.7	25	19	496
Belgium	**132**	**95**	**4.1**	..	**57**	**449**
Bruxelles-Brussels	136	126	7.0	..	70	502
Vlaams Gewest	125	91	3.6	..	63	457
Région Wallonne	144	94	4.1	..	51	420
Denmark	**86**	**83**	**2.8**	..	**22**	**347**
Finland	**93**	**92**	**3.1**	**9**	**2**	**403**
Manner-Suomi	94	92	3.1	9	2	403
Åland	85	91	2.4	-	-	527
France	**122**	**90**	**3.4**	..	**18**	**490**
Île de France	104	90	4.2	35	50	452
Bassin Parisien	124	88	2.6	27	19	501
Nord - Pas-de-Calais	144	88	2.8	7	48	426
Est	113	89	3.1	13	20	504
Ouest	125	92	2.8	17	10	492
Sud-Ouest	125	90	3.5	19	11	517
Centre-Est	118	90	3.1	18	22	505
Méditerranée	142	89	3.9	28	18	521
Germany	**106**	**92**	**3.3**	..	**33**	**516**
Baden-Württemberg	103	90	3.4	59	29	540
Bayern	98	92	3.5	90	32	553
Berlin	95	93	4.6	18	70	352
Brandenburg	89	87	2.6	17	26	507
Bremen	113	108	4.4	4	146	429
Hamburg	96	97	4.6	12	107	440
Hessen	107	93	3.4	37	45	556
Mecklenburg-Vorpommern	92	89	3.0	12	15	477
Niedersachsen	114	90	2.9	53	28	532
Nordrhein-Westfalen	120	98	3.3	94	64	504
Rheinland-Pfalz	109	87	3.0	25	42	549
Saarland	120	93	3.6	7	92	558
Sachsen	95	91	2.8	25	25	492
Sachsen-Anhalt	97	87	2.8	15	16	479
Schleswig-Holstein	108	88	3.3	19	30	526
Thüringen	91	88	2.9	15	18	499
Greece	**133**	**84**	**4.5**	..	**2**	**252**
Voreia Ellada	133	..	3.9	7	1	195
Kentriki Ellada	138	..	3.0	6	3	128
Attiki	130	..	6.0	14	18	416
Nisia Aigaiou, Kriti	129	..	4.0	2	-	208
Ireland	**117**	**82**	**2.5**	**11**	**1**	**339**

Table **2.2** (continued)

	Dependency rate[1] 2000	Proportion of 16 to 18 year olds in education or training (percentages) 2000[2,3]	Number of physicians or doctors per 1,000 population, 2000[4]	Deaths and people injured in road traffic accidents per 1,000 population 2001[5]	Transport 2002	
					Length of motorways (km) per 1,000 sq km[6]	Private cars per 1,000 population
Italy	**143**	*75*	**6.0**	..	**21**	**535**
Nord Ovest	130	*75*	..	..	36	554
Lombardia	123	*72*	5.5	..	23	557
Nord Est	123	*74*	..	..	22	545
Emilia-Romagna	116	*83*	6.5	..	28	585
Centro	133	*84*	..	..	16	561
Lazio	142	*84*	7.7	..	28	593
Abruzzo-Molise	161	*85*	..	..	24	499
Campania	181	*70*	..	..	33	521
Sud	176	*73*	..	..	14	442
Sicilia	185	*68*	6.3	..	22	498
Sardegna	153	*76*	6.5	..	-	477
Luxembourg	**132**	*79*	**3.2**	**1**	**44**	**586**
Netherlands	**94**	*93*	**3.0**	**1**	**68**	**401**
Noord-Nederland	101	..	3.0	-	39	388
Oost-Nederland	94	..	2.6	-	63	403
West-Nederland	92	..	3.5	-	87	389
Zuid-Nederland	95	..	2.4	-	84	433
Portugal	**96**	..	**2.6**	..	**16**	**430**
Continent	94	..	2.7	..	17	510
Açores	144	..	..	..	-	..
Madeira	120	..	..	..	-	..
Spain	**133**	*81*	**3.5**	..	**18**	**425**
Noroeste	141	*85*	3.0	16	20	397
Noreste	126	*90*	3.3	16	16	392
Comunidad de Madrid	121	*93*	4.8	19	62	527
Centro	148	*83*	3.1	21	10	364
Este	122	*75*	3.6	52	37	469
Sur	147	*77*	3.3	27	19	365
Canarias	126	*80*	2.8	4	26	477
Sweden	**103**	*97*	**2.7**	**23**	**4**	**527**
United Kingdom[7]	**99**	*71*	..	..	**14**	**403**
North East	114	*67*	..	12	8	327
North West	106	*67*	1.9	43	41	391
Yorkshire and the Humber	102	*72*	4.3	30	21	368
East Midlands	93	*68*	..	23	12	415
West Midlands	103	*75*	1.8	29	28	435
East	92	*60*	..	31	14	460
London	96	*68*	2.6	45	44	330
South East	87	*71*	1.8	45	34	472
South West	95	*70*	1.9	26	13	468
Wales	118	*71*	1.3	14	6	397
Scotland	99	*79*	2.3	20	5	356
Northern Ireland	128	*80*	1.6	13	..	..

1 *Dependency rates are calculated as the number of non-active persons (total population less labour force) expressed as a percentage of those economically active.*

2 *Participation rates are calculated by dividing the number of pupils aged 16 to 18 years enrolled in a region by the resident population aged 16 to 18 years in that region. As some young people may be resident in one region and in education in another, this interregional movement may influence the results. The UK data exclude Open University, independent and special schools in Wales, and Youth Training with employers, all of which are not available by region and age. For all countries, age is taken at 1 January except for the UK where it is taken at 31 August (the start of the academic year). Eurostat estimates.*

3 *Data for Austria and all its regions was for 1999. 2001 data for Belgium, France, Italy and Spain.*

4 *Data for Germany, Greece, Portugal and Finland are for 2001. Data for Denmark are for 1999.*

5 *Data for Greece and France are provisional. Data for the Netherlands are for deaths only. Data for Belgium, Italy and Portugal are not available.*

6 *1994 for Italian regions.*

7 *Government Office Regions for the United Kingdom equals NUTS 1 regions for the European Union. See Notes and Definitions.*

Source: Eurostat

Table **2.3**   Economic statistics

	People in employment[1], 2002 (thousands)	Employment[1,2], 2002 percentage in			Unemployment rate[1] (percentages) 2002	Long-term unemployed[1] as a percentage of all unemployed, 2002[3]	Gross domestic product per head (PPS)[4] EUR 15=100 2000	Estimates[5] of the percentage of GDP in 2000 derived from		
		Agriculture	Industry	Services				Agriculture	Industry	Services
EUR 15	**163,101**	*4.0*	*28.2*	*67.7*	*7.8*	*39.7*	**100**	..	..	..
Austria	**3,776**	*5.7*	*29.4*	*65.0*	*4.0*	*28.1*	**114**	*2.3*	*31.2*	*66.5*
Ostösterreich	1,591	4.8	25.2	70.0	5.4	33.3	123	2.2	25.1	72.7
Südösterreich	798	8.0	32.6	59.4	3.4	26.9	97	3.4	36.2	60.4
Westösterreich	1,388	5.3	32.3	62.4	2.7	17.0	115	2.0	36.2	61.8
Belgium	**4,071**	*1.7*	*25.4*	*72.9*	*7.5*	*48.6*	**106**	*1.4*	*26.8*	*71.8*
Bruxelles-Brussels	354	0.1	13.1	86.8	14.5	54.7	214	0.0	12.1	87.8
Vlaams Gewest	2,516	1.8	28.1	70.2	4.9	35.1	104	1.6	31.9	66.5
Région Wallonne	1,201	2.0	23.5	74.4	10.5	58.5	77	1.8	26.5	71.7
Denmark	**2,724**	*3.3*	*24.2*	*72.3*	*4.6*	*19.0*	**115**	*2.7*	*25.9*	*71.4*
Finland	**2,372**	*5.3*	*26.9*	*67.4*	*9.1*	*24.7*	**104**	*3.8*	*33.4*	*62.8*
Manner-Suomi	2,359	5.3	27.0	67.3	9.1	24.8	104	3.8	33.6	62.6
Åland	13	5.3	17.7	77.0	2.9	..	139	4.4	12.1	83.5
France	**23,885**	*4.1*	*25.4*	*70.5*	*8.7*	*32.8*	**104**	*2.7*	*24.8*	*72.5*
Île de France	5,029	0.3	17.3	82.4	8.1	33.5	159	0.2	17.7	82.1
Bassin Parisien	4,058	5.6	30.3	64.0	8.6	32.7	89	5.3	31.1	63.6
Nord - Pas-de-Calais	1,449	2.4	29.7	67.9	13.4	39.7	79	2.0	30.6	67.3
Est	2,300	3.1	33.4	63.5	7.5	24.0	91	2.5	32.5	65.0
Ouest	3,144	6.5	29.0	64.5	7.4	27.6	87	5.1	27.3	67.6
Sud-Ouest	2,573	6.4	23.8	69.8	8.5	31.6	88	4.8	23.5	71.8
Centre-Est	2,864	4.7	28.6	66.7	6.9	25.5	100	1.8	31.3	66.9
Méditerranée	2,469	5.2	17.4	77.3	12.0	41.2	87	3.0	18.7	78.3
Germany	**36,275**	*2.5*	*32.4*	*65.1*	*9.4*	*47.0*	**102**	*1.2*	*29.4*	*69.5*
Baden-Württemberg	4,990	2.1	39.9	58.0	4.7	36.9	116	1.0	38.5	60.5
Bayern	5,887	3.3	35.3	61.3	5.0	36.5	120	1.2	30.7	68.1
Berlin	1,448	0.6	19.3	80.0	18.7	50.8	93	0.2	19.5	80.4
Brandenburg	1,115	4.2	28.4	67.4	20.4	53.5	68	2.3	27.2	70.5
Bremen	266	1.1	25.2	73.7	11.2	44.8	137	0.2	28.7	71.1
Hamburg	792	0.9	20.5	78.5	9.0	43.8	174	0.2	18.1	81.7
Hessen	2,764	1.6	30.3	68.1	6.3	44.3	125	0.6	24.7	74.7
Mecklenburg-Vorpommern	726	7.4	25.8	66.8	23.6	51.6	67	4.0	20.8	75.2
Niedersachsen	3,390	3.4	30.9	65.7	7.9	49.9	92	2.3	30.8	66.9
Nordrhein-Westfalen	7,562	1.4	32.8	65.8	7.9	44.0	103	0.7	28.5	70.7
Rheinland-Pfalz	1,779	2.5	32.5	65.0	5.9	37.0	92	1.4	32.0	66.6
Saarland	437	1.4	33.0	65.6	8.3	43.5	94	0.3	30.3	69.4
Sachsen	1,807	2.4	32.8	64.9	21.3	53.0	67	1.4	29.2	69.4
Sachsen-Anhalt	1,045	4.0	31.0	65.0	23.5	59.0	66	2.6	26.9	70.5
Schleswig-Holstein	1,219	4.0	23.5	72.5	8.5	42.9	94	2.2	23.4	74.3
Thüringen	1,050	3.1	35.0	61.8	17.6	47.6	67	2.0	28.7	69.3
Greece	**3,940**	*16.1*	*22.5*	*61.5*	*10.0*	*51.2*	**66**	*7.3*	*21.0*	*71.7*
Voreia Ellada	1,199	22.8	23.4	53.8	11.3	53.0	64	11.8	22.9	65.3
Kentriki Ellada	798	30.3	19.7	50.0	9.3	57.2	66	11.6	26.9	61.5
Attiki	1,556	1.2	24.5	74.3	9.2	51.9	69	0.4	18.7	80.9
Nisia Aigaiou, Kriti	387	25.5	17.1	57.4	9.7	31.3	66	9.7	10.9	79.5
Ireland	**1,750**	*6.9*	*27.7*	*64.9*	*4.3*	*29.2*	**114**	*3.8*	*42.6*	*53.7*

Table **2.3** (continued)

	People in employment[1], 2002 (thousands)	Employment[1,2], 2002 percentage in			Unem- ployment rate[1] (percentages) 2002	Long-term unemployed[1] as a percentage of all unem- ployed, 2002[3]	Gross domestic product per head (PPS)[4] EUR 15=100 2000	Estimates[5] of the percentage of GDP in 2000 derived from		
		Agriculture	Industry	Services				Agriculture	Industry	Services
Italy	**21,829**	**5.0**	**31.8**	**63.2**	**9.0**	**59.1**	**103**	**2.8**	**27.9**	**69.4**
Nord Ovest	2,458	3.5	34.0	62.5	5.4	49.4	117	2.0	30.1	67.9
Lombardia	4,023	1.9	40.1	58.0	3.8	36.0	135	1.6	34.7	63.7
Nord Est	2,911	4.4	37.2	58.4	3.3	25.9	122	2.8	31.8	65.4
Emilia-Romagna	1,822	5.4	35.5	59.0	3.3	25.0	130	3.5	33.0	63.4
Centro	2,400	4.0	35.0	61.0	4.8	38.5	109	2.2	29.4	68.4
Lazio	2,024	3.3	19.9	76.7	8.6	68.5	114	1.6	17.2	81.2
Abruzzo-Molise	582	6.6	31.1	62.3	7.5	55.6	84	4.0	29.4	66.6
Campania	1,644	6.4	24.4	69.3	21.1	73.3	66	3.2	20.7	76.1
Sud	2,015	10.9	25.5	63.6	17.4	63.4	66	5.8	20.5	73.7
Sicilia	1,407	9.3	20.4	70.3	20.1	69.0	66	4.7	16.7	78.6
Sardegna	543	8.7	23.5	67.8	18.5	57.9	76	4.2	19.9	76.0
Luxembourg	**188**	**2.0**	**20.1**	**77.8**	**2.6**	**27.4**	**198**	**0.7**	**17.5**	**81.9**
Netherlands	**8,168**	**3.0**	**20.8**	**76.2**	**2.8**	**19.2**	**109**	**2.8**	**25.9**	**71.4**
Noord-Nederland	817	4.1	23.8	72.1	3.5	18.8	100	4.3	36.4	59.2
Oost-Nederland	1,706	3.6	22.7	73.7	2.7	18.6	92	3.4	27.2	69.3
West-Nederland	3,849	2.5	16.2	81.3	2.6	19.9	121	2.4	19.2	78.4
Zuid-Nederland	1,797	3.3	27.4	69.2	2.7	18.9	104	2.7	32.9	64.4
Portugal	**5,107**	**12.4**	**33.8**	**53.8**	**5.1**	**34.4**	**71**	**3.4**	**28.5**	**68.0**
Continent	4,892	12.3	34.1	53.6	5.2	34.4	71	3.3	29.1	67.5
Açores	100	13.7	29.0	57.2	2.5	37.8	55	10.2	17.0	72.9
Madeira	114	12.8	27.4	59.8	2.5	33.4	83	2.5	18.9	78.5
Spain	**16,258**	**5.9**	**31.2**	**62.9**	**11.4**	**34.2**	**83**	**3.5**	**29.2**	**67.2**
Noroeste	1,652	10.8	32.6	56.6	11.4	42.7	68	4.8	32.0	63.2
Noreste	1,709	4.5	37.3	58.2	7.7	36.4	98	3.3	36.8	59.9
Comunidad de Madrid	2,318	0.8	24.5	74.7	7.1	39.7	110	0.2	23.7	76.2
Centro	1,942	10.0	30.9	59.1	11.9	33.3	68	8.8	29.4	61.8
Este	4,898	3.0	36.8	60.2	9.7	31.3	92	2.0	33.0	65.1
Sur	3,000	10.3	25.6	64.1	18.3	32.6	63	6.4	23.2	70.4
Canarias	738	4.6	21.3	74.1	11.1	32.1	78	2.4	18.9	78.6
Sweden	**4,324**	**2.5**	**23.0**	**74.4**	**5.1**	**19.9**	**110**	**1.9**	**28.8**	**69.3**
United Kingdom[6]	**28,435**	**1.3**	**24.3**	**74.2**	**5.1**	**21.9**	**104**	**1.0**	**27.3**	**71.7**
North East	1,098	0.9	27.2	71.8	6.8	26.9	77	0.6	32.5	66.8
North West	3,136	0.8	26.0	73.1	5.3	26.6	92	0.8	29.7	69.5
Yorkshire and the Humber	2,350	1.2	27.1	71.6	5.2	21.5	89	1.2	29.9	68.8
East Midlands	2,047	1.4	30.2	68.2	4.5	23.0	94	1.6	34.0	64.4
West Midlands	2,489	1.0	30.5	68.3	5.6	20.7	93	1.2	32.2	66.6
East	2,760	1.5	25.0	73.3	3.7	18.2	98	1.5	26.4	72.0
London	3,551	0.3	13.9	85.6	6.7	23.6	172	0.0	13.7	86.2
South East	4,162	1.4	22.3	76.0	3.7	14.8	112	0.7	22.4	76.9
South West	2,468	2.0	23.7	74.3	3.7	14.1	92	2.0	27.0	71.0
Wales	1,268	2.6	26.1	71.0	5.6	20.1	80	1.5	32.1	66.4
Scotland	2,385	1.9	23.5	74.5	6.5	23.5	98	1.8	28.4	69.9
Northern Ireland	722	4.5	25.9	69.3	5.8	37.3	80	2.3	29.2	68.5

1 See Notes and Definitions.
2 Data for EUR 15 does not total 100 per cent due to rounding.
3 Data for Aland in Finland relate to 2000
4 Purchasing Power Standard. See Notes and Definitions
5 Estimates for GDP by sector are based on the gross value added (GVA) figures for each area.
6 Government Office Regions for the United Kingdom equals NUTS 1 regions for the European Union. See Notes and Definitions.

Source: Eurostat; Office for National Statistics

Table **2.4**   Agricultural statistics, 2001

| | Agricultural land as a percentage of total land area[1] | Arable land as a percentage of agricultural land[1] | Average yield[2] | | Livestock per 1,000 ha of utilised agricultural land[3] | | |
			Wheat 100kg/ha	Barley 100kg/ha	All cattle	All sheep and lambs	All pigs
EUR 15	*40.4*	*56.4*	60	49	613	678	924
Austria	*40.2*	*40.9*	52	47	628	95	1,019
Ostosterreich	*48.5*	*75.0*	50	46	448	55	914
Suedosterreich	*31.5*	*25.7*	60	50	675	124	1,356
Westosterriech	*41.2*	*22.1*	60	47	745	110	911
Belgium	*45.5*	*60.8*	81	72	2,185	112	4,916
Bruxelles-Brussels	*2.5*	*75.0*	50	40	1,000	0	0
Vlamms Gewest	*47.0*	*68.2*	78	66	2,404	156	10,246
Region Wallone	*44.8*	*54.6*	82	74	2,001	75	431
Denmark	*62.5*	*92.7*	74	54	683	41	4,816
Finland	*6.6*	*98.6*	34	33	459	30	654
Manner-Suomi	-	-	-	-	-	-	-
Aland	-	-	-	-	-	-	-
France	*53.9*	*61.8*	74	67	684	312	515
Ile de France	*48.8*	*95.6*	83	71	56	..	19
Bassin Parisien	*64.2*	*71.4*	80	71	591	..	180
Nord-Pas-de-Calais	*69.0*	*77.2*	85	79	829	..	632
Est	*46.5*	*54.0*	70	63	802	..	143
Ouest	*68.7*	*78.0*	73	64	992	..	1,787
Sud-Ouest	*48.5*	*56.4*	57	50	654	766	252
Centre-Est	*45.5*	*35.9*	64	57	808	..	219
Mediterranee	*33.4*	*22.5*	38	36	151	..	54
Germany	*47.7*	*69.3*	79	64	857	163	1,513
Baden-Wuttemberg	*41.0*	*57.5*	70	56	827	210	1,580
Bayern	*46.2*	*64.1*	70	56	1,254	145	1,156
Berlin	*2.1*	*68.4*	..	..	263	158	53
Brandenburg	*45.6*	*77.5*	65	65	484	117	546
Bremen	*21.0*	*17.6*	..		1,400	24	94
Hamburg	*18.5*	*39.3*	..	..	586	264	179
Hessen	*36.3*	*63.4*	81	61	708	236	1,079
Mecklenburg-Vorpommern	*58.6*	*79.3*	79	77	436	82	466
Niedersachsen	*55.1*	*68.8*	89	66	1,078	104	2,861
Nordrhein-Westfalen	*44.0*	*71.1*	92	74	1,010	150	4,084
Rheinland-Pfalz	*35.7*	*55.4*	72	48	630	195	511
Saarland	*30.9*	*48.9*	61	48	784	207	284
Sachsen	*50.1*	*78.9*	72	66	597	156	666
Sachsen-Anhalt	*57.3*	*85.5*	77	73	334	117	696
Schleswig-Holstein	*64.8*	*60.4*	98	81	1,292	358	1,355
Thuringen	*49.6*	*77.6*	75	65	486	297	856
Greece	*29.2*	*57.4*	24	23	145	2,349	223
Voreia Ellada	*32.9*	*82.0*	24	25	222	1,705	178
Kentriki Ellada	*25.4*	*41.6*	27	24	74	2,817	325
Attiki	*26.1*	*13.8*	17	14	74	1,346	133
Nisia Aigiou, Kriti	*29.6*	*18.4*	13	12	66	3,634	136
Ireland	*62.2*	*17.2*	84	55	1,478	1,107	400

Table **2.4**   (continued)

	Agricultural land as a percentage of total land area[1]	Arable land as a percentage of agricultural land[1]	Average yield[2]		Livestock per 1,000 ha of utilised agricultural land[3]		
			Wheat 100kg/ha	Barley 100kg/ha	All cattle	All sheep and lambs	All pigs
Italy	*51.8*	*54.1*	**28**	**34**	**444**	**532**	**561**
Nord Ovest	*40.9*	*50.1*	49	50	667	87	684
Lombardia	*47.9*	*72.0*	53	53	1,632	75	3,128
Nord Est	*40.9*	*51.6*	53	49	800	56	577
Emilia-Romangna	*56.7*	*77.1*	50	47	562	65	1,307
Centro	*43.5*	*66.7*	34	36	157	518	365
Lazio	*51.4*	*54.1*	25	28	345	969	131
Abruzzo-Molise	*50.3*	*52.8*	33	36	199	581	236
Campania	*53.2*	*55.5*	27	32	511	370	222
Sud	*63.8*	*51.7*	17	23	142	321	92
Sicilia	*63.9*	*48.8*	21	20	208	562	27
Sardegna	*64.6*	*23.9*	15	18	176	2,316	151
Luxembourg	*49.5*	*48.0*	**55**	**46**	**1,550**	**57**	**596**
Netherlands	*45.8*	*51.9*	**78**	**55**	**1,980**	**608**	**5,977**
Noord-Nederland	*48.3*	*46.4*	73	55	1,686	650	961
Oost-Nederland	*44.9*	*43.8*	67	54	2,710	427	6,818
West-Nederland	*39.7*	*52.1*	84	59	1,295	993	1,347
Zuid-Nederland	*51.0*	*71.7*	81	55	2,198	328	18,027
Portugal	*41.0*	*42.2*	**8**	**11**	**373**	**918**	**634**
Continente	*41.0*	*43.3*	8	11	321	947	633
Acores	*52.1*	*9.8*	..	..	1,912	36	495
Maderia	*8.1*	*45.8*	13	..	705	951	3,666
Spain	*50.4*	*53.5*	**31**	**34**	**242**	**959**	**871**
Noroeste	*28.9*	*29.2*	28	25	1,367	374	799
Noreste	*50.9*	*56.7*	28	33	174	1,318	1,162
Madrid	*42.6*	*55.2*	27	30	250	560	128
Centro	*57.4*	*62.8*	36	36	181	1,044	465
Este	*37.3*	*36.5*	30	26	376	967	3,143
Sur	*56.3*	*43.7*	25	14	102	702	730
Canarias	*10.0*	*22.4*	10	10	373	768	846
Sweden	*6.6*	*90.8*	**59**	**41**	**545**	**152**	**647**
United Kingdom	*67.8*	*39.1*	**80**	**56**	**615**	**1,479**	**344**
North East	*66.4*	*35.6*	81	62	426	2,247	171
North West	*62.4*	*24.6*	68	49	873	1,599	205
Yorkshire and the Humber	*68.4*	*58.5*	85	64	494	1,364	1,461
East Midlands	*75.8*	*73.6*	83	60	460	813	417
West Midlands	*70.3*	*54.9*	75	60	860	1,842	288
Eastern	*71.4*	*86.6*	82	60	170	194	832
London	*7.9*	*54.2*	..	..	..	..	..
South East	*57.3*	*64.1*	81	59	475	921	346
South West	*72.7*	*45.3*	74	53	1,027	1,391	315
Wales	*67.0*	*13.5*	73	49	856	4,801	36
Scotland	*67.1*	*18.6*	76	52	365	1,115	110
Northern Ireland	*74.2*	*18.7*	65	39	1,563	1,344	387

1 Data for Spain are for 2000; France, Ireland, and the Netherlands are for 2002.
2 Data for Spain are for 2000; France, Ireland, and the Netherlands and UK are for 2002.
3 Data for Spain are for 2000 and Netherlands for 2002.

Source: Eurostat

Chapter 3 **Population and Migration**

Resident population

London had the highest growth rate between 1991 and 2001 of 9.1 per cent in male resident population. The greatest rate of decline in male population was in the North East (–2.6 per cent). The highest percentage growth of female resident population was in the East of England (5.5 per cent) with the largest percentage decrease in the North East (–2.7 per cent).

The highest percentage growth in the overall population was in London (7.0 per cent), and the lowest was in the North East (–2.6 per cent). Between 1991 and 2001 the number of males in the UK increased by 3 per cent compared to an increase of 2 per cent for females. (Table 3.1)

In 2002, London had the highest regional proportion of residents aged between 25 to 44 (36.7 per cent); the lowest was in Wales (26.3 per cent). The South West had the highest percentage of people in each age group from 45 and upwards. (Table 3.2)

Population density

Kensington and Chelsea in Inner London had the highest population density of any area in the UK in 2002 (13,609 people per sq km). The Highlands in Scotland had the lowest density at 8 people per sq km, followed by Eilean Siar with 9. Portsmouth Unitary Authority in the South East had the highest population density (4,671 people per sq km) outside London. (Map 3.3)

Population by age

Several areas (districts) in Northern Ireland had more than a quarter of their population aged under 16 in 2002. The proportion was highest in Derry where 26.3 per cent of the population were aged under 16 and the City of Edinburgh in Scotland had the lowest (16.1 per cent). (Map 3.4)

Conversely, over a quarter of the population (26.8 per cent) in Dorset (South West), were of retirement age compared to Inner London with only 11.5 per cent in 2002. (Map 3.5)

Socio-economic classification

In summer 2003, the largest category of workers in the UK was those employed in lower managerial and professional occupations. London and the South East shared the highest percentage (25.3 per cent) in this category with the lowest proportion in the North East (18.8 per cent) and in Northern Ireland (18.6 per cent). The North East also had the highest percentages of workers in semi-routine and routine occupations (16.2 and 12.9 per cent respectively) and London had the lowest (8.9 per cent). Northern Ireland had the highest percentage of long-term unemployed workers (23.4 per cent), whereas the South West had the lowest proportion of working-age people who were unemployed long-term (12.6 per cent). (Table 3.6)

Ethnic groups

In 2001, London was the most prominent multi-cultural region in the UK. London had the highest percentage of most ethnic groups with the exception of white and Pakistani populations. The population in Northern Ireland was 99.25 per cent white. (Map 3.7)

Population change

The South West had the highest population growth (12.7 per cent) between 1982 and 2002, in contrast population in the North East declined by –4.5 per cent. Over the same period Milton Keynes in the South East region had the greatest population growth (58.3 per cent) and Glasgow City the largest decline in population (–17.8 per cent). (Map 3.8)

Growth in Milton Keynes Unitary Authority is predicted to continue with the highest projected population change (9.8 per cent) for 2002–2011. Dundee City, Scotland has the highest projected decrease (-10.9 per cent). The South East is projected to have the highest population change at 4.4 per cent and Scotland the lowest with a decrease of –1.6 per cent. (Map 3.9)

Conceptions and birth rates

In 2001, London had the highest rate of live births (14.3 per 1,000 population), the South West had the lowest (9.9 per 1,000 population). All areas continued to show a decline in their birth rates since 1991. The highest death rates were in Wales, Scotland and the North East with 11.4, 11.3 and 11.3 per 1,000 population respectively; the lowest rate was in London at 8.0 deaths per 1,000 population. (Table 3.10)

The East Midlands had the highest proportionate change in the resident population from mid-2001 to mid-2002, with an increase of just under 1 per cent. The North East and Scotland were the only regions to have a reduction in the population during this period. (Table 3.11)

In 2001, the highest proportion of pregnancies (leading to maternities) for women under the age of 18 was in the North East (62.8 per cent). London had the highest proportion of conceptions leading to abortions (58.5 per cent for women aged under 18). Overall the percentage of pregnancies to women under the age of 18 leading to abortions has increased by five points since 1997; a similar level of increase was evident in each region. (Table 3.12)

In 2001, Northern Ireland had the highest birth rate for women of all ages and Scotland the lowest; (60 and 49 live births per 1,000 women respectively). In the UK the highest birth rates were to women aged between 25 to 29. However, in Northern Ireland the birth rate was highest in the 30 to 34 age band. The North East and Wales had the highest rate of live births to women under the age of 20, (35 live births per 1,000 women in each area). London had the highest rate of births to women aged between 35 to 39 (59 live births per 1,000 women). (Table 3.13)

Death rates

In 2001, death rates for men were generally higher than for women, across all age groups. Scotland had the highest rate of deaths for males in the 55 to 64 age group at 14.1 per 1,000 population in that age group. The lowest rates for this age group were in the South West, South East and East with 8.6, 8.7 and 8.7 per 1,000 population aged 55 to 64. Deaths for females in this age group were also highest in Scotland (8.3 per 1,000 population) and lowest in the South West (5.2 per 1,000 population). (Table 3.14)

Migration

In 2002, the South East had the highest inflow of migrants from other regions (229 thousand) and the North East had the lowest at 43 thousand. The South East also had a high outflow of interregional migrants (220 thousands people), but London had the highest outflow at 262 thousand and the North East the lowest of any English region at 41 thousand. (Table 3.15)

The highest volumes of interregional movements occurred between London and the South East and East regions. Approximately 98 thousand people moved from London to the South East. (Table 3.16)

Marriage and cohabiting

The South East had the highest number of marriages; 41.7 thousand in 2001 and Northern Ireland the lowest number of marriages in the UK, at 7.3 thousand. All areas have shown a reduction in the number of marriages in the twenty-five years to 2001. (Table 3.17)

Between 2000 and 2002, the proportion of non-married couples aged between 16 and 59 who were cohabiting was highest in the South West (31 per cent) and lowest in Scotland (20 per cent). (Table 3.18)

Households and marital status

In spring 2002, the most common type of household in the UK overall was a one-person household, although in many areas the most frequent type of household was a married couple with no children. Scotland had the greatest percentage of one-person households, 32.8 per cent. Northern Ireland was lowest at 26.6 per cent of households. The North West had the highest proportion (8.7 per cent) of lone parent households with dependent children, followed by London at 8.3 per cent. (Table 3.20)

In 2001, London had the highest proportion of the population whose marital status was single (53.1 per cent), appreciably higher than any other region. Northern Ireland had the lowest percentage of divorced people (3.1 per cent) and re-married individuals (2.0 per cent). Throughout the UK, there are more widowed females than males, 10.3 per cent of the overall female population compared to 2.9 per cent for males. However, men are more likely to have never been married at 47.9 per cent to 40.9 per cent for women. (Table 3.21)

Religion

Four in five of the people that live in the North East are Christians. This compares to just under three in five in London, where there are the highest percentages of people of all other religions except Sikh. The proportion who stated that they had no religion varied from around 11 per cent in the North East and North West to 19 per cent in Wales. (Table 3.22)

Table **3.1**   Resident population:[1] by sex

Thousands and percentages

	Population (thousands)					Total population growth (percentages)		
	1971	1981	1991	2001[2]	2002[2]	1971 to 1981	1981 to 1991	1991 to 2001[2]
Males								
United Kingdom	27,167.3	27,411.6	27,909.0	28,809.6	28,911.3	0.9	1.8	3.2
North East	1,304.0	1,283.1	1,253.7	1,221.6	1,219.2	−1.6	−2.3	−2.6
North West	3,422.4	3,357.6	3,311.4	3,284.5	3,286.8	−1.9	−1.4	−0.8
Yorkshire and the Humber	2,384.9	2,395.0	2,398.5	2,416.8	2,423.7	0.4	0.1	0.8
East Midlands	1,797.8	1,894.8	1,968.4	2,058.0	2,074.3	5.4	3.9	4.6
West Midlands	2,542.4	2,555.6	2,563.9	2,590.9	2,602.4	0.5	0.3	1.1
East	2,194.6	2,386.0	2,511.3	2,648.5	2,657.4	8.7	5.3	5.5
London	3,611.4	3,277.3	3,296.4	3,598.0	3,631.8	−9.3	0.6	9.1
South East	3,321.1	3,527.2	3,717.4	3,923.1	3,931.1	6.2	5.4	5.5
South West	1,989.9	2,118.5	2,269.6	2,402.6	2,413.3	6.5	7.1	5.9
England	22,568.5	22,795.0	23,290.6	24,143.9	24,239.9	1.0	2.2	3.7
Wales	1,328.5	1,365.1	1,390.7	1,407.6	1,410.7	2.8	1.9	1.2
Scotland	2,515.7	2,494.9	2,444.5	2,433.7	2,431.8	−0.8	−2.0	−0.4
Northern Ireland	754.6	756.6	783.2	824.4	828.9	0.3	3.5	5.3
Females								
United Kingdom	28,760.7	28,945.9	29,529.7	30,241.2	30,317.7	0.6	2.0	2.4
North East	1,374.5	1,353.1	1,333.3	1,297.2	1,294.1	−1.6	−1.5	−2.7
North West	3,685.4	3,582.7	3,531.7	3,482.7	3,484.2	−2.8	−1.4	−1.4
Yorkshire and the Humber	2,517.4	2,523.5	2,537.6	2,553.7	2,558.8	0.2	0.6	0.6
East Midlands	1,854.1	1,957.9	2,043.0	2,124.8	2,141.2	5.6	4.3	4.0
West Midlands	2,603.6	2,631.1	2,665.8	2,691.9	2,701.7	1.1	1.3	1.0
East	2,259.7	2,469.0	2,609.8	2,752.8	2,763.0	9.3	5.7	5.5
London	3,918.0	3,527.7	3,532.9	3,709.9	3,723.6	−10.0	0.1	5.0
South East	3,508.6	3,715.8	3,911.8	4,098.3	4,106.0	5.9	5.3	4.8
South West	2,121.9	2,264.9	2,418.6	2,534.4	2,546.3	6.7	6.8	4.8
England	23,843.2	24,025.8	24,584.4	25,245.8	25,318.9	0.8	2.3	2.7
Wales	1,411.8	1,448.4	1,482.3	1,500.0	1,508.0	2.6	2.3	1.2
Scotland	2,719.9	2,685.3	2,638.8	2,630.5	2,623.0	−1.3	−1.7	−0.3
Northern Ireland	785.8	786.3	824.1	864.9	867.8	0.1	4.8	4.9
All Persons								
United Kingdom	55,928.0	56,357.5	57,438.7	59,050.8	59,228.9	0.8	1.9	2.8
North East	2,678.5	2,636.2	2,587.0	2,518.8	2,513.3	−1.6	−1.9	−2.6
North West	7,107.8	6,940.3	6,843.0	6,767.2	6,771.0	−2.4	−1.4	−1.1
Yorkshire and the Humber	4,902.3	4,918.5	4,936.1	4,970.6	4,982.5	0.3	0.4	0.7
East Midlands	3,651.9	3,852.7	4,011.4	4,182.8	4,215.5	5.5	4.1	4.3
West Midlands	5,146.0	5,186.6	5,229.7	5,282.8	5,304.1	0.8	0.8	1.0
East	4,454.3	4,855.0	5,121.1	5,401.3	5,420.4	9.0	5.5	5.5
London	7,529.4	6,805.0	6,829.3	7,307.9	7,355.4	−9.6	0.4	7.0
South East	6,829.7	7,243.1	7,629.2	8,021.4	8,037.1	6.1	5.3	5.1
South West	4,111.8	4,383.4	4,688.2	4,937.0	4,959.6	6.6	7.0	5.3
England	46,411.7	46,820.8	47,875.0	49,389.7	49,558.8	0.9	2.3	3.2
Wales	2,740.3	2,813.5	2,873.0	2,907.6	2,918.7	2.7	2.1	1.2
Scotland	5,235.6	5,180.2	5,083.3	5,064.2	5,054.8	−1.1	−1.9	−0.4
Northern Ireland	1,540.4	1,543.0	1,607.3	1,689.3	1,696.6	0.2	4.2	5.1

1 Population estimates exclude HM Forces stationed outside UK, includes foreign forces stationed here. Students are considered resident at their term-time address. See Notes and Definitions.

2 Population estimates for 2001 and 2002 include provisional results from the Manchester matching exercise, published November 2003.

Source: Office for National Statistics; General Register Office for Scotland; Northern Ireland Statistics and Research Agency

Table **3.2**   Resident population:[1] by age and sex, 2002[2]

Thousands and percentages

	0 to 4	5 to 15	16 to 19	20 to 24	25 to 44	45 to 59	60 to 64	65 to 79	80 and over	All ages
Males (thousands)										
United Kingdom	1,744.5	4,280.0	1,532.8	1,806.2	8,560.7	5,597.2	1,413.1	3,140.8	835.9	28,911.3
North East	68.9	181.0	68.0	77.6	337.6	246.7	62.8	143.2	33.3	1,219.2
North West	197.2	507.8	181.4	198.6	932.4	647.7	168.1	363.8	89.7	3,286.8
Yorkshire and the Humber	145.5	367.7	134.2	157.1	684.9	476.2	120.7	267.7	69.6	2,423.7
East Midlands	120.9	308.2	110.1	128.5	591.7	416.8	104.4	232.5	61.2	2,074.3
West Midlands	159.9	396.4	141.9	159.9	742.7	507.0	132.7	288.0	73.8	2,602.4
East	161.1	390.9	132.2	152.6	768.9	531.7	132.0	304.2	83.7	2,657.4
London	241.0	493.7	178.8	251.3	1,385.6	572.6	133.2	293.9	81.6	3,631.8
South East	236.7	578.3	202.6	237.6	1,143.5	785.0	191.0	429.9	126.6	3,931.1
South West	134.5	345.1	123.6	140.3	653.1	491.9	130.4	303.6	90.7	2,413.3
England	1,465.9	3,569.1	1,272.8	1,503.4	7,240.5	4,675.6	1,175.3	2,626.9	710.3	24,239.9
Wales	83.4	215.1	76.6	85.8	373.0	285.3	76.6	170.2	44.7	1,410.7
Scotland	137.4	352.0	129.6	161.0	706.5	489.5	124.9	268.2	62.7	2,431.8
Northern Ireland	57.8	143.8	53.8	56.0	240.7	146.8	36.3	75.5	18.2	828.9
Females (thousands)										
United Kingdom	1,663.3	4,071.6	1,453.1	1,818.6	8,679.1	5,703.7	1,475.4	3,765.0	1,688.0	30,317.7
North East	65.2	172.3	66.3	77.6	354.4	248.6	66.4	174.3	68.9	1,294.1
North West	187.6	483.3	176.3	206.6	966.1	656.5	174.8	441.0	192.1	3,484.2
Yorkshire and the Humber	139.7	352.4	127.6	158.6	706.4	479.9	125.7	324.8	143.9	2,558.8
East Midlands	113.8	291.2	103.3	124.9	598.7	417.3	106.2	268.0	117.7	2,141.2
West Midlands	152.4	378.5	134.0	160.2	743.9	509.2	135.1	339.9	148.5	2,701.7
East	154.2	372.9	124.6	149.1	772.6	541.5	136.5	351.1	160.6	2,763.0
London	231.6	473.4	167.9	275.5	1,317.2	601.7	142.9	353.6	159.9	3,723.6
South East	225.2	545.8	188.5	232.6	1,156.5	795.7	197.6	511.1	253.0	4,106.0
South West	128.5	326.7	114.0	131.2	668.8	507.2	134.9	357.7	177.2	2,546.3
England	1,398.2	3,396.3	1,202.5	1,516.3	7,284.6	4,757.6	1,220.1	3,121.5	1,421.9	25,318.9
Wales	79.3	203.8	74.5	88.5	395.4	293.0	79.5	202.4	91.6	1,508.0
Scotland	131.1	334.8	124.7	159.0	750.6	503.9	136.9	344.8	137.2	2,623.0
Northern Ireland	54.7	136.7	51.4	54.8	248.5	149.2	38.8	96.4	37.3	867.8
All people (percentages)										
United Kingdom	5.8	14.1	5.0	6.1	29.1	19.1	4.9	11.7	4.3	100.0
North East	5.3	14.1	5.3	6.2	27.5	19.7	5.1	12.6	4.1	100.0
North West	5.7	14.6	5.3	6.0	28.0	19.3	5.1	11.9	4.2	100.0
Yorkshire and the Humber	5.7	14.5	5.3	6.3	27.9	19.2	4.9	11.9	4.3	100.0
East Midlands	5.6	14.2	5.1	6.0	28.2	19.8	5.0	11.9	4.2	100.0
West Midlands	5.9	14.6	5.2	6.0	28.0	19.2	5.0	11.8	4.2	100.0
East	5.8	14.1	4.7	5.6	28.4	19.8	5.0	12.1	4.5	100.0
London	6.4	13.1	4.7	7.2	36.7	16.0	3.8	8.8	3.3	100.0
South East	5.7	14.0	4.9	5.8	28.6	19.7	4.8	11.7	4.7	100.0
South West	5.3	13.5	4.8	5.5	26.7	20.1	5.3	13.3	5.4	100.0
England	5.8	14.1	5.0	6.1	29.3	19.0	4.8	11.6	4.3	100.0
Wales	5.6	14.4	5.2	6.0	26.3	19.8	5.3	12.8	4.7	100.0
Scotland	5.3	13.6	5.0	6.3	28.8	19.7	5.2	12.1	4.0	100.0
Northern Ireland	6.6	16.5	6.2	6.5	28.8	17.4	4.4	10.1	3.3	100.0

1 *Population estimates exclude HM Forces stationed outside UK, includes foreign forces stationed here. Students are considered resident at their term time address. See Notes and Definitions.*

2 *Population figures for 2002 include provisional results from the Manchester matching exercise, published in November 2003.*

Source: Office for National Statistics; General Register Office for Scotland; Northern Ireland Statistics and Research Agency

Map **3.3**

Population density,[1] 2002[2]

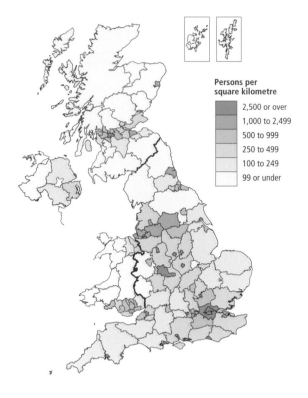

Persons per
square kilometre

2,500 or over
1,000 to 2,499
500 to 999
250 to 499
100 to 249
99 or under

1 See Notes and Definitions.
2 Mid-2002 Population Estimates for the UK, England and Manchester include provisional results from the Manchester matching exercise, published in November 2003.

Source: Office for National Statistics; General Register Office for Scotland; Northern Ireland Statistics and Research Agency

Map **3.4**

Population under 16,[1] 2002[2]

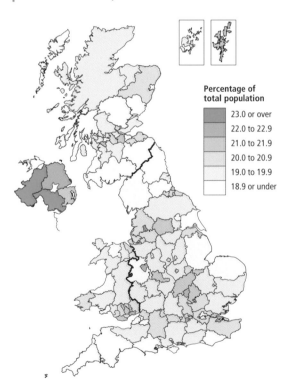

Percentage of
total population

23.0 or over
22.0 to 22.9
21.0 to 21.9
20.0 to 20.9
19.0 to 19.9
18.9 or under

1 See Notes and Definitions.
2 Mid-2002 Population Estimates for the UK, England and Manchester include provisional results from the Manchester matching exercise, published in November 2003.

Source: Office for National Statistics; General Register Office for Scotland; Northern Ireland Statistics and Research Agency

Map **3.5**

Population of retirement age,[1] 2002[2]

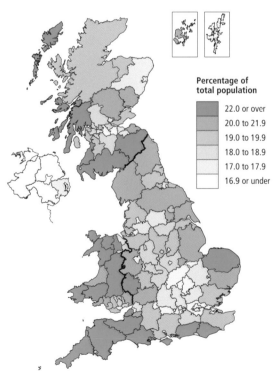

Percentage of
total population

22.0 or over
20.0 to 21.9
19.0 to 19.9
18.0 to 18.9
17.0 to 17.9
16.9 or under

1 Men aged 65 and over, women aged 60 and over as a percentage of the
total population.
2 Mid-2002 population estimates for the UK, England and Manchester include
provisional results from the Manchester matching exercise, published in
November 2003. See Notes and Definitions.

**Source: Office for National Statistics; General Register Office for
Scotland; Northern Ireland Statistics and Research Agency**

Table **3.6**   Socio-economic classification[1] of working-age[2] population, summer 2003

Percentages and thousands

	Social class (NS-SEC)								Total working-age population (=100%) (thousands)
	Higher managerial and professional occupations	Lower managerial and professional occupations	Intermediate occupations	Small employers and own account workers	Lower supervisory and technical occupations	Semi-routine occupations	Routine occupations	Never worked, long-term unemployed and n.e.c.[3]	
United Kingdom	10.8	22.2	10.3	7.7	9.4	13.3	9.8	16.5	37,248
North East	7.9	18.8	9.9	4.9	10.8	16.2	12.9	18.5	1,579
North West	8.7	20.5	11.6	6.7	9.4	14.3	11.0	17.7	4,229
Yorkshire and the Humber	8.7	20.5	10.3	6.8	10.7	14.6	12.0	16.5	3,121
East Midlands	9.8	19.9	9.7	7.4	10.6	14.6	12.0	15.9	2,623
West Midlands	8.9	20.7	9.3	7.1	10.4	15.7	11.5	16.5	3,262
East	12.0	23.6	11.1	9.1	8.8	13.1	9.3	12.8	3,396
London	14.3	25.3	9.8	7.9	5.8	8.9	6.6	21.4	4,958
South East	14.7	25.3	10.9	8.7	8.6	11.8	7.3	12.6	5,068
South West	10.5	23.3	9.4	9.5	10.3	14.2	9.1	13.8	3,014
England	11.2	22.5	10.3	7.8	9.1	13.2	9.7	16.2	31,251
Wales	8.2	20.0	9.5	8.5	11.8	14.4	10.9	16.7	1,779
Scotland	9.5	21.9	10.3	6.0	11.0	13.8	10.4	17.1	3,173
Northern Ireland	6.6	18.6	9.0	9.4	8.9	13.2	10.7	23.4	1,044

1 Based on the National Statistics Socio-economic Classification (NS-SEC). See Notes and Definitions.
2 Men aged 16 to 64 and women aged 16 to 59.
3 Includes those who have never worked, long-term unemployed and those not elsewhere classified. The latter include some full-time students, those with occupations not stated or inadequately described. See Notes and Definitions.

Source: Labour Force Survey, Office for National Statistics

Table **3.7**   Resident population by ethnic group, 2001[1]

Percentages and thousands

	White[1]	Mixed[1]	Indian	Pakistani	Bangla-deshi	Other Asian	Caribb-ean	African	Other Black	Chinese	Other Ethnic Group	All People
United Kingdom	92.12	1.15	1.79	1.27	0.48	0.42	0.96	0.83	0.17	0.42	0.39	58,789.2
North East	97.62	0.49	0.40	0.56	0.25	0.13	0.04	0.10	0.02	0.24	0.17	2,515.4
North West	94.43	0.93	1.07	1.74	0.39	0.22	0.30	0.24	0.08	0.40	0.20	6,729.8
Yorkshire and the Humber	93.48	0.91	1.04	2.95	0.25	0.25	0.43	0.19	0.07	0.25	0.19	4,964.8
East Midlands	93.48	1.03	2.93	0.67	0.17	0.28	0.64	0.22	0.09	0.31	0.18	4,172.2
West Midlands	88.74	1.39	3.39	2.93	0.60	0.40	1.56	0.23	0.19	0.31	0.27	5,267.3
East	95.12	1.08	0.95	0.72	0.34	0.25	0.49	0.31	0.10	0.38	0.27	5,388.1
London	71.15	3.15	6.09	1.99	2.15	1.86	4.79	5.28	0.84	1.12	1.58	7,172.1
South East	95.10	1.07	1.12	0.73	0.19	0.29	0.34	0.31	0.06	0.41	0.37	8,000.6
South West	97.71	0.76	0.33	0.14	0.10	0.10	0.25	0.13	0.05	0.26	0.19	4,928.4
England	90.92	1.31	2.09	1.44	0.56	0.48	1.14	0.97	0.19	0.45	0.44	49,138.8
Wales	97.88	0.61	0.28	0.29	0.19	0.12	0.09	0.13	0.03	0.22	0.18	2,903.1
Scotland	97.99	0.25	0.30	0.63	0.04	0.12	0.04	0.10	0.02	0.32	0.19	5,062.0
Northern Ireland[2]	99.25	0.20	0.09	0.04	0.01	0.01	0.02	0.03	0.02	0.25	0.08	1,685.3

1 Ethnic categories used are based on the census, April 2001, and different to those used in previous editions of Regional Trends. They are therefore not comparable to previous years. See Notes and Definitions.
2 Northern Ireland figures for White category includes White Irish traveller.

Source: Office for National Statistics; General Register Office for Scotland; Northern Ireland Statistics and Research Agency

Map **3.8**

Population change, 1982-2002[1]

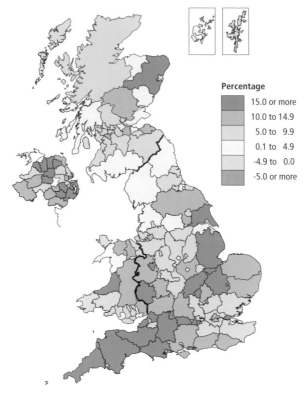

Percentage

- 15.0 or more
- 10.0 to 14.9
- 5.0 to 9.9
- 0.1 to 4.9
- -4.9 to 0.0
- -5.0 or more

1 See Notes and Definitions.

Source: Office for National Statistics; General Register Office for Scotland; Northern Ireland Statistics and Research Agency

Map **3.9**

Projected population change,[1] 2002-2011

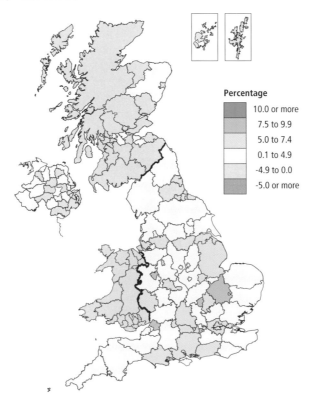

Percentage

- 10.0 or more
- 7.5 to 9.9
- 5.0 to 7.4
- 0.1 to 4.9
- -4.9 to 0.0
- -5.0 or more

1 1996-based subnational projections for England; 1998-based projections for Scotland and Wales; 1999 mid-year estimates for Northern Ireland.
See Notes and Definitions.

Source: Office for National Statistics; National Assembly for Wales; General Register Office for Scotland; Northern Ireland Statistics and Research Agency

Table **3.10**   Live births, deaths and natural change in population

Thousands and rates

	Thousands					Rates per 1,000 population				
	1981	1986	1991	1996	2001	1981	1986	1991	1996	2001
Live births[1]										
United Kingdom	730.8	755.0	792.3	733.2	669.1	13.0	13.3	13.8	12.6	11.3
North East	34.2	34.7	34.9	30.1	25.9	13.0	13.3	13.4	11.7	10.3
North West	90.4	93.4	97.5	85.0	75.2	13.0	13.6	14.2	12.5	11.1
Yorkshire and the Humber	62.6	65.3	68.6	62.0	55.6	12.7	13.3	13.8	12.5	11.2
East Midlands	49.2	50.3	54.0	49.4	44.6	12.8	12.8	13.4	12.0	10.7
West Midlands	67.5	70.4	74.2	67.5	60.8	13.0	13.5	14.1	12.8	11.5
East	62.6	64.4	68.4	64.6	60.1	12.9	12.8	13.3	12.3	11.1
London	92.4	97.7	105.8	105.4	104.2	13.6	14.4	15.5	15.3	14.3
South East	89.0	92.9	99.8	95.3	88.5	12.3	12.4	13.0	12.2	11.0
South West	50.4	54.5	57.6	54.8	48.7	11.5	12.0	12.2	11.4	9.9
England	598.2	623.6	660.8	614.2	563.7	12.8	13.2	13.7	12.7	11.4
Wales	35.8	37.0	38.1	34.9	30.6	12.7	13.1	13.2	12.1	10.5
Scotland	69.1	65.8	67.0	59.3	52.5	13.3	12.8	13.1	11.6	10.4
Northern Ireland	27.3	28.2	26.3	24.4	22.0	17.6	17.8	16.2	14.7	13.0
Deaths[2]										
United Kingdom	658.0	660.7	646.2	638.9	604.4	11.7	11.6	11.2	11.0	10.2
North East	32.1	32.0	31.8	30.2	28.4	12.2	12.3	12.2	11.8	11.3
North West	86.6	85.5	82.7	79.5	75.0	12.5	12.5	12.0	11.7	11.1
Yorkshire and the Humber	59.1	58.9	57.3	55.4	52.0	12.0	12.0	11.5	11.2	10.5
East Midlands	42.8	43.5	43.9	43.9	42.6	11.1	11.1	10.9	10.0	10.2
West Midlands	56.4	57.7	57.0	56.1	54.1	10.9	11.1	10.8	10.0	10.2
East	50.7	52.4	53.3	53.8	53.4	10.4	10.5	10.3	10.3	9.9
London	77.6	73.9	68.9	65.4	58.6	11.4	10.9	10.1	9.5	8.0
South East	81.3	84.2	83.0	83.7	79.6	11.2	11.2	10.8	10.7	9.9
South West	54.4	56.4	56.2	55.9	54.3	12.4	12.4	11.9	11.7	11.0
England	541.0	544.5	534.0	524.0	497.9	11.6	11.5	11.1	10.8	10.1
Wales	35.0	34.7	34.1	34.6	33.2	12.4	12.3	11.8	12.0	11.4
Scotland	63.8	63.5	61.0	60.7	57.4	12.3	12.4	12.0	11.9	11.3
Northern Ireland	16.3	16.1	15.1	15.2	14.5	10.5	10.2	9.4	9.2	8.6
Natural Change										
United Kingdom	72.8	94.2	146.3	94.3	64.7	1.3	1.7	2.6	1.6	1.1
North East	2.1	2.7	3.1	−0.1	−2.5	0.8	1.0	1.2	0.1	−1.0
North West	3.8	7.9	14.8	5.5	0.2	0.5	1.2	2.2	0.8	0.0
Yorkshire and the Humber	3.5	6.4	11.3	6.6	3.6	0.7	1.3	2.3	1.3	0.7
East Midlands	6.4	6.8	10.1	5.5	2.0	1.7	1.7	2.5	2.0	0.5
West Midlands	11.1	12.7	17.2	11.4	6.7	2.1	2.4	3.3	2.8	1.3
East	11.9	12.0	15.1	10.7	6.7	2.5	2.4	3.0	2.0	1.2
London	14.8	23.8	36.9	40.0	45.6	2.2	3.5	5.4	5.8	6.3
South East	7.7	8.8	16.8	11.6	8.9	1.1	1.2	2.2	1.5	1.1
South West	−4.0	−1.9	1.4	−1.0	−5.6	−0.9	−0.4	0.3	−0.3	−1.1
England	57.2	79.1	126.8	90.2	65.8	1.2	1.7	2.6	1.9	1.3
Wales	0.8	2.3	4.0	0.3	−2.6	0.3	0.8	1.4	0.1	−0.9
Scotland	5.3	2.3	6.0	−1.4	−4.9	1.0	0.5	1.1	−0.3	−0.9
Northern Ireland	10.9	11.9	10.9	9.2	7.5	7.2	7.7	6.8	5.5	4.4

1 Based on the usual area of residence of the mother. See Notes and Definitions for details of the inclusion or exclusion of births to non-resident mothers in the individual countries and regions of England. The United Kingdom figures have been calculated on all births registered in the United Kingdom, including births to mothers usually resident outside the United Kingdom. Data relate to year of occurrence in England and Wales, and year of registration in Scotland and Northern Ireland.

2 Based on the usual area of residence of the deceased. See Notes and Definitions for details of the inclusion or exclusion of deaths of non-resident people in the individual countries and regions of England. The figures for the United Kingdom have been calculated on all deaths registered in the United Kingdom in 2001, including deaths of people usually resident outside the United Kingdom.

Source: Office for National Statistics; General Register Office for Scotland; Northern Ireland Statistics and Research Agency

Table 3.11 Components of population change[1], mid-2001 to mid-2002[2]

Thousands

	Resident population mid-2001	Births	Deaths	Net natural change	Net migration and other changes	Total change	Resident population mid-2002
United Kingdom	59,050.8	663.3	601.3	61.9	116.2	178.1	59,228.9
North East	2,518.8	25.8	28.3	−2.6	−3.0	−5.5	2,513.3
North West	6,767.2	74.4	74.9	−0.5	4.2	3.8	6,771.0
Yorkshire and the Humber	4,970.6	55.4	52.4	3.1	8.9	12.0	4,982.5
East Midlands	4,182.8	44.6	42.3	2.2	30.5	32.7	4,215.5
West Midlands	5,282.8	60.7	53.8	6.9	14.4	21.3	5,304.1
East	5,401.3	59.6	53.7	5.9	13.2	19.1	5,420.4
London	7,307.9	104.3	57.4	47.0	0.5	47.4	7,355.4
South East	8,021.4	87.2	79.6	7.6	8.1	15.8	8,037.1
South West	4,937.0	48.5	54.6	−6.1	28.7	22.6	4,959.6
England	49,389.7	560.5	497.0	63.5	105.6	169.1	49,558.8
Wales	2,907.6	30.1	32.8	−2.7	13.8	11.1	2,918.7
Scotland	5,064.2	51.2	57.3	−6.1	−3.3	−9.4	5,054.8
Northern Ireland	1,689.3	21.5	14.2	7.2	0.1	28.7	1,696.6

1 See Notes and Definitions.
2 Mid-2001 and mid-2002 population estimates for the UK, England and North West include provisional results from the Manchester Matching Exercise, published in November 2003.

Source: Office for National Statistics; General Register Office for Scotland; Northern Ireland Statistics and Research Agency

Table 3.12 Conceptions[1,2] to women aged under 18: by outcome

	1997[3]				2001[5] (Provisional)			
	Percentage of conceptions				Percentage of conceptions			
	Leading to maternities	Leading to abortions	Total number	Rate per 1,000 population[4]	Leading to maternities	Leading to abortions	Total number	Rate per 1,000 population[4]
England and Wales	59.4	40.6	43,358	46.4	54.3	45.7	40,966	42.7
North East	66.3	33.7	2,921	61.3	62.8	37.2	2,389	48.7
North West	62.4	37.6	6,307	50.1	57.0	43.0	6,020	45.2
Yorkshire and the Humber	64.9	35.1	4,723	52.7	61.4	38.6	4,434	47.2
East Midlands	64.1	35.9	3,359	45.2	59.4	40.6	3,076	40.3
West Midlands	59.3	40.7	5,221	52.9	55.5	44.5	4,759	47.2
East	57.1	42.9	3,487	36.2	52.6	47.4	3,308	34.1
London	48.1	51.9	5,975	49.8	41.5	58.5	6,201	50.4
South East	56.6	43.4	5,268	36.3	51.0	49.0	5,022	35.0
South West	57.6	42.4	3,202	37.5	54.0	46.0	3,230	37.1
England	59.0	41.0	40,463	46.0	54.0	46.0	38,439	42.5
Wales	65.5	34.5	2,895	53.8	59.9	40.1	2,527	45.5

1 Conception statistics are derived from numbers of registered births and abortions. They do not include spontaneous miscarriages and illegal abortions. See Notes and Definitions.
2 Based on place of usual residence. Information about usual residence of women undergoing abortions is known to be not wholly accurate. Some women living outside London or other large cities may have given a temporary address in the city as their usual place of residence.
3 Overall rates for England and Wales for 1997 have been calculated using the population estimates released in October 2003. Rates for individual regions of England have been calculated using the population estimates released in Autumn 2002.
4 The rates for girls aged under 18 are based on the population of girls aged 15 to 17.
5 Rates for 2001 have been calculated using the population estimates released in October 2003.

Source: Office for National Statistics

Table **3.13** Age specific birth rates[1]

Rates

	Under 20	20 to 24	25 to 29	30 to 34	35 to 39	40 and over	All ages[3]	TFR[4]
	Live births per 1,000 women in age groups[2]							
1981								
United Kingdom	28	107	130	70	22	5	62	1.82
North East	34	114	128	60	18	4	62	1.79
North West	35	114	130	65	21	5	63	1.85
Yorkshire and the Humber	31	117	128	59	18	6	62	1.80
East Midlands	30	113	127	63	19	4	61	1.79
West Midlands	32	108	133	69	20	7	62	1.84
East	22	110	138	70	20	4	61	1.82
London	29	83	114	80	31	6	62	1.71
South East	20	97	138	73	23	4	59	1.77
South West	24	103	131	63	18	3	57	1.71
England	28	104	129	69	22	5	61	1.78
Wales	30	121	127	67	21	6	63	1.86
Scotland	31	112	131	66	21	4	63	1.84
Northern Ireland	27	135	172	117	52	13	86	2.60
1991								
United Kingdom	33	89	120	87	32	5	64	1.82
North East	44	102	120	72	23	4	63	1.82
North West	42	101	124	84	29	5	67	1.93
Yorkshire and the Humber	41	99	122	78	26	4	64	1.85
East Midlands	34	95	126	81	26	4	63	1.83
West Midlands	39	102	126	84	31	5	67	1.93
East	24	86	129	91	31	4	62	1.83
London	29	69	97	96	47	10	64	1.74
South East	23	78	122	95	35	5	61	1.80
South West	25	84	125	87	30	5	60	1.77
England	33	89	119	88	32	5	64	1.81
Wales	39	103	127	77	27	5	64	1.88
Scotland	33	82	117	78	27	4	60	1.69
Northern Ireland	29	97	146	105	46	10	75	2.16
2001								
United Kingdom	28	68	92	88	41	9	55	1.63
North East	35	77	93	75	29	5	50	1.58
North West	32	78	97	83	36	7	54	1.67
Yorkshire and the Humber	33	80	99	81	33	6	54	1.67
East Midlands	29	70	99	83	36	7	53	1.61
West Midlands	32	83	103	86	36	8	57	1.74
East	22	67	98	95	43	9	56	1.67
London	26	59	73	94	59	15	59	1.62
South East	22	58	91	98	47	10	54	1.62
South West	23	63	95	87	40	8	52	1.58
England	28	69	92	89	42	9	55	1.64
Wales	35	76	100	80	34	7	54	1.66
Scotland	28	58	85	82	37	7	49	1.49
Northern Ireland	24	68	105	106	48	10	60	1.81

1 Based on the usual area of residence of the mother. See Notes and Definitions for details of the inclusion or exclusion of births to non-resident mothers in the individual countries and regions of England. The United Kingdom figures have been calculated on all births registered in the United Kingdom, i.e. including births to mothers usually resident outside the United Kingdom apart from the non-residents of Northern Ireland which are excluded. The England and Wales figures have been calculated on all births registered in England and Wales apart from the non-residents. Data relate to year of occurrence in England and Wales, and year of registration in Scotland and Northern Ireland.

2 The rates for women aged under 20, 40 and over and all ages are based upon the population of women aged 15 to 19, 40 to 44 and 15 to 44 respectively. See Notes and Definitions.

3 The 'All ages' figure for Scotland for year 2001 includes births to mothers whose age was not known.

4 The Total Fertility Rate (TFR) is the average number of children which would be born to a woman if the current pattern of fertility persisted throughout her child-bearing years. Previously known as Total Period Fertility. See Notes and Definitions.

Source: Office for National Statistics; General Register Office for Scotland; Northern Ireland Statistics and Research Agency

Table **3.14** Age specific death rates: by sex, 2001[1]

Rates and Standardised Mortality Ratios

	Deaths per 1,000 population for specific age groups											SMR[3] (UK = 100)
	Under 1[2]	1 to 4	5 to 15	16 to 24	25 to 34	35 to 44	45 to 54	55 to 64	65 to 74	75 to 84	85 and over	
Males												
United Kingdom	6.0	0.2	0.2	0.8	1.1	1.7	4.1	10.4	28.8	75.0	187.4	100
North East	6.1	0.4	0.2	0.7	1.1	1.7	4.8	11.9	33.8	84.7	192.0	112
North West	6.1	0.3	0.2	0.7	1.3	1.9	4.7	11.7	32.2	81.3	198.9	110
Yorkshire and the Humber	6.1	0.3	0.2	0.8	1.1	1.6	4.0	10.3	29.4	78.5	189.0	102
East Midlands	4.9	0.2	0.1	0.7	1.1	1.6	3.6	9.3	27.3	75.0	191.4	97
West Midlands	6.8	0.2	0.1	0.8	1.0	1.6	4.2	10.6	29.5	75.7	190.1	101
East	5.2	0.2	0.1	0.7	0.8	1.4	3.3	8.7	24.6	69.5	184.6	90
London	7.1	0.3	0.2	0.6	0.8	1.6	4.3	11.2	28.8	74.0	179.4	99
South East	4.8	0.2	0.1	0.7	0.9	1.3	3.3	8.7	24.7	69.2	178.8	89
South West	5.6	0.2	0.1	0.7	1.0	1.4	3.4	8.6	24.2	66.7	186.3	89
England	5.9	0.3	0.2	0.7	1.0	1.6	3.9	10.0	27.9	74.0	186.7	98
Wales	6.2	0.3	0.1	0.8	1.3	1.9	3.9	10.8	30.2	77.3	187.5	103
Scotland	5.7	0.2	0.2	1.0	1.5	2.4	5.3	14.1	34.7	81.7	191.3	117
Northern Ireland	7.0	0.1	0.2	1.0	1.0	1.6	4.2	9.9	30.0	79.4	193.6	104
Females												
United Kingdom	5.0	0.2	0.1	0.3	0.4	1.0	2.6	6.4	17.9	51.0	156.3	100
North East	5.0	0.3	0.1	0.3	0.5	0.9	3.1	7.1	21.2	57.1	161.1	110
North West	5.7	0.2	0.1	0.3	0.5	1.1	3.1	7.4	20.1	56.0	164.5	109
Yorkshire and the Humber	5.5	0.4	0.1	0.2	0.4	1.0	2.7	6.3	18.6	52.1	153.4	100
East Midlands	5.0	0.1	0.1	0.3	0.5	1.0	2.5	6.1	17.3	51.8	158.9	100
West Midlands	6.0	0.2	0.1	0.2	0.5	1.0	2.6	6.4	17.6	51.7	156.9	100
East	3.9	0.2	0.1	0.3	0.4	0.9	2.3	5.5	15.7	48.2	154.9	94
London	5.1	0.3	0.1	0.2	0.4	1.0	2.5	6.6	17.7	47.9	149.9	96
South East	3.6	0.2	0.1	0.3	0.4	0.9	2.3	5.6	15.3	46.5	153.0	93
South West	5.2	0.2	0.1	0.3	0.3	0.9	2.3	5.2	14.8	44.9	150.0	90
England	4.9	0.2	0.1	0.3	0.4	1.0	2.6	6.2	17.3	50.1	155.3	98
Wales	4.8	0.2	0.1	0.3	0.5	1.1	2.6	6.8	19.2	53.2	159.8	104
Scotland	5.2	0.2	0.1	0.4	0.5	1.2	3.2	8.3	21.3	57.5	162.4	112
Northern Ireland	5.2	0.2	0.1	0.2	0.3	1.1	2.6	6.1	18.6	50.8	163.3	102
All people												
United Kingdom	5.5	0.2	0.1	0.5	0.7	1.3	3.4	8.4	23.0	60.5	164.9	100
North East	5.6	0.3	0.1	0.5	0.8	1.3	4.0	9.5	27.0	67.9	169.3	111
North West	5.9	0.3	0.2	0.5	0.9	1.5	3.9	9.5	25.7	65.9	173.4	109
Yorkshire and the Humber	5.8	0.3	0.1	0.5	0.8	1.3	3.3	8.3	23.6	62.6	163.0	101
East Midlands	5.0	0.2	0.1	0.5	0.8	1.3	3.1	7.7	22.1	61.4	168.1	99
West Midlands	6.4	0.2	0.1	0.5	0.8	1.3	3.4	8.5	23.2	61.2	166.1	101
East	4.5	0.2	0.1	0.5	0.6	1.2	2.8	7.1	19.9	56.9	163.5	92
London	6.1	0.3	0.2	0.4	0.6	1.3	3.4	8.8	22.9	58.3	158.2	98
South East	4.2	0.2	0.1	0.5	0.7	1.1	2.8	7.1	19.7	55.5	160.3	91
South West	5.4	0.2	0.1	0.5	0.7	1.2	2.8	6.9	19.2	53.7	160.5	90
England	5.4	0.2	0.1	0.5	0.7	1.3	3.2	8.1	22.3	59.7	164.0	98
Wales	5.5	0.2	0.1	0.6	0.9	1.5	3.3	8.7	24.4	62.7	167.4	103
Scotland	5.5	0.2	0.2	0.7	1.0	1.8	4.3	11.1	27.3	66.7	169.9	114
Northern Ireland	6.1	0.2	0.2	0.6	0.7	1.3	3.4	7.9	23.8	61.8	171.5	99

1 Based on the usual area of residence of the deceased. See Notes and Definitions for details of the inclusion or exclusion of deaths of non-resident persons in the individual countries and regions of England. The UK figures have been calculated on all deaths registered in the UK in 2001, i.e. including deaths of persons usually resident outside the UK.
2 Deaths of infants under 1 year of age per 1,000 live births.
3 Standardised Mortality Ratio (SMR) is the ratio of observed deaths to those expected by applying a standard death rate to the regional population. See Notes and Definitions.

Source: Office for National Statistics; General Register Office for Scotland; Northern Ireland Statistics and Research Agency

Table 3.15   Migration

Thousands

	Inflow					Outflow				
	1991	1996	2000	2001	2002	1991	1996	2000	2001	2002
Interregional migration[1,2]										
North East	40	39	39	40	43	41	45	43	43	41
North West	96	105	106	106	109	105	114	111	110	108
Yorkshire and the Humber	85	91	97	96	100	85	98	96	96	95
East Midlands	90	102	112	115	120	81	94	95	96	97
West Midlands	83	91	94	95	99	88	101	101	102	103
East	122	139	146	147	150	113	121	125	127	130
London	149	168	163	160	155	202	213	232	244	262
South East	198	228	224	224	229	185	199	210	216	220
South West	121	139	140	143	146	99	110	111	111	111
England	96	111	109	104	101	112	105	111	120	119
Wales	51	55	59	60	64	47	53	52	51	50
Scotland	56	47	49	56	53	47	54	53	50	48
Northern Ireland	12	11	11	13	11	9	12	12	11	11
International migration[3,4,5]										
United Kingdom	328	318	483	480	..	285	264	321	308	..
North East	7	3	9	11	..	4	5	7	6	..
North West	18	18	27	34	..	22	21	20	23	..
Yorkshire and the Humber	22	14	30	27	..	17	12	13	19	..
East Midlands	14	14	15	15	..	9	11	17	13	..
West Midlands	16	25	23	39	..	21	20	17	17	..
East	28	25	33	27	..	25	16	20	30	..
London	116	127	223	199	..	84	72	103	95	..
South East	53	46	64	65	..	43	56	64	50	..
South West	21	18	30	25	..	22	16	23	20	..
England	294	291	453	443	..	245	230	284	271	..
Wales	10	8	6	14	..	8	8	7	9	..
Scotland	21	16	20	20	..	27	22	23	24	..
Northern Ireland	4	3	5	3	..	5	4	6	4	..

1 Based on patients re-registering with NHS doctors in other parts of the United Kingdom. See Notes and Definitions.

2 At the time this table was being prepared for publication, research was ongoing into whether there was a need to revise internal migration estimates in light of the results of the 2001 Census. By the time of publication, ONS will have reported on the necessity and feasibility of producing revised internal migration estimates. Future editions of this publication will reflect any revisions that are made.

3 Subject to relatively large sampling errors where estimates are based on small numbers of contacts. See Notes and Definitions.

4 The figures in this table combine migration data from three sources to provide total international migration. See Notes and Definitions.

5 These estimates of total international migration have been derived using a consistent methodology based primarily on the International Passenger Survey (IPS) to allocate migration to the constituent countries of the UK, and to Government Office Regions within England. This methodology is currently under review as part of the National Statistics Quality Review of International Migration. Given the small sample size of the IPS for Scotland and Northern Ireland residents, adjustment of these estimates using data from administrative records is currently made for the purposes of population estimation in Scotland and Northern Ireland.

Source: National Health Service Central Register and International Passenger Survey, Office for National Statistics; General Register Office for Scotland; Northern Ireland Statistics and Research Agency; Home Office; Irish Central Statistical Office.

Table **3.16** Interregional movements,[1,2] 2002

Thousands

	United Kingdom	England	North East	North West	York-shire and the Humber	East Mid-lands	West Mid-lands	East	London	South East	West	Wales	Scot-land	Nor-thern Ireland
														Area of origin (header spans)
United Kingdom[3]	.	119	41	108	95	97	103	130	262	220	111	50	48	11
Area of destination														
England	101	.	36	87	86	90	89	120	247	199	94	48	45	9
North East	43	37	.	6	9	3	3	3	5	5	2	1	4	1
North West	109	91	6	.	18	10	13	8	14	14	8	9	7	2
Yorkshire and the Humber	100	92	9	18	.	17	8	9	11	13	6	3	5	1
East Midlands	120	113	3	10	18	.	17	20	15	22	8	3	3	1
West Midlands	99	87	3	12	8	14	.	8	13	16	13	8	3	1
East	150	142	3	7	7	13	7	.	66	28	9	3	4	1
London	155	142	5	12	10	10	11	28	.	51	15	5	7	1
South East	229	213	4	12	9	14	14	29	98	.	33	8	7	1
South West	146	132	2	9	6	9	16	14	25	50	.	9	4	1
Wales	64	62	1	11	3	3	10	4	6	11	12	.	2	-
Scotland	53	49	4	8	5	3	3	5	7	9	4	2	.	2
Northern Ireland	11	8	-	1	1	1	1	1	2	1	1	-	2	.

1 Based on patients re-registering with NHS doctors in other parts of the United Kingdom. See Notes and Definitions. Figures have been adjusted for minor changes caused by database realignment during Health Authority organisation.

2 At the time this table was being prepared for publication, research was ongoing into whether there was a need to revise internal migration estimates in light of the results of the 2001 Census. By the time of publication, ONS will have reported on the necessity and feasibility of producing revised internal migration estimates. Future editions of this publication will reflect any revisions that are made.

3 Total number of people moving from other parts of the United Kingdom.

Source: National Health Service Central Register; General Register Office for Scotland; Northern Ireland Statistics and Research Agency.

Table **3.17** Marriages[1,2]

Thousands

	1976	1986	2001
United Kingdom	406.0	393.9	286.1
North East	20.1	17.6	10.7
North West	50.3	46.3	29.2
Yorkshire and the Humber	36.3	35.2	22.5
East Midlands	26.7	27.4	19.8
West Midlands	36.6	35.2	23.5
East	32.2	34.7	26.6
London	58.4	47.5	36.4
South East	48.5	52.0	41.7
South West	30.1	32.5	25.9
England	339.0	328.4	236.2
Wales	19.5	19.5	13.0
Scotland	37.5	35.8	29.6
Northern Ireland	9.9	10.2	7.3

1 Marriages solemnised outside the United Kingdom are not included.

2 Region of occurrence of marriage.

Source: Office for National Statistics; General Register Office for Scotland; Northern Ireland Statistics and Research Agency

Figure **3.18** Cohabitation among non-married people aged 16 to 59, 2000-02[1]

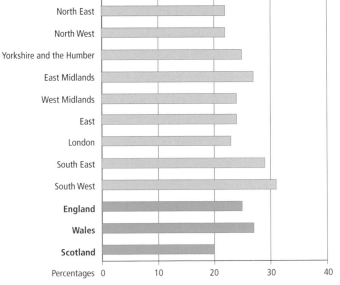

1 Combined data from the 2000/01 and 2001/02 surveys.

Source: General Household Survey, Office for National Statistics; Continuous Household Survey, Northern Ireland Statistics and Research Agency

Table **3.19** Household numbers and projections

Millions

	Household numbers[1]			Household projections[2]			
	1981	1991	2001	2006	2011	2016	2021
Great Britain	20.18	22.39	24.14	25.29	26.20	..	..
North East	0.98	1.05	1.07	1.12	1.14	1.15	1.17
North West	2.55	2.72	2.82	2.93	3.00	3.06	3.11
Yorkshire and the Humber	1.83	1.99	2.09	2.20	2.26	2.32	2.37
East Midlands	1.41	1.60	1.74	1.83	1.90	1.97	2.03
West Midlands	1.86	2.04	2.16	2.24	2.30	2.35	2.40
East	1.76	2.04	2.26	2.39	2.49	2.60	2.70
London	2.64	2.84	3.17	3.25	3.38	3.52	3.65
South East	2.64	3.03	3.35	3.57	3.74	3.91	4.06
South West	1.64	1.90	2.10	2.21	2.32	2.42	2.52
England	17.31	19.21	20.75	21.73	22.52	23.31	24.00
Wales	1.02	1.13	1.19	1.24	1.28	1.31	1.34
Scotland	1.85	2.05	2.19	2.31	2.41	..	..

1 Estimates for 2001 are based on mid-year population estimates which take into account 2001 census results. Estimates for 1981 onwards are subject to revision following revisions to population estimates.
2 For England and Wales figures for 2006 onwards are 1996-based projections. For Scotland figures for 2006 onwards are 2000-based projections. All projections do not take account of the 2001 census results.

Source: Office of the Deputy Prime Minister; National Assembly for Wales; Scottish Executive

Table **3.20** Households: by type, spring 2002

Percentages and thousands

	Types of households (percentages)								
			Married couple			Lone parent			Total house-holds (=100%) (thou-sands)
	One person	Two or more un-related adults	With dependent children	With non-dependent children only	With no children	With dependent children	With non-dependent children only	Two or more families[1]	
United Kingdom	29.1	3.1	22.6	6.4	28.4	6.5	3.0	0.9	25,026
North East	31.2	2.1	21.4	6.6	27.8	7.1	3.3	..	1,105
North West	29.1	2.0	22.2	7.4	26.6	8.7	3.3	0.7	2,872
Yorkshire and the Humber	29.7	2.8	21.2	6.0	30.4	6.3	2.8	0.9	2,158
East Midlands	26.7	2.7	23.4	7.0	31.1	6.0	2.4	0.8	1,748
West Midlands	28.4	2.4	23.5	6.6	28.5	6.4	3.1	1.1	2,187
East	27.2	2.4	24.4	6.3	31.0	5.2	2.6	0.8	2,285
London	30.7	6.1	22.1	5.5	22.2	8.3	3.3	1.8	3,018
South East	28.1	2.9	23.6	6.4	30.8	5.1	2.3	0.9	3,396
South West	28.7	3.1	22.3	5.4	32.6	4.9	2.4	0.7	2,135
England	28.8	3.1	22.8	6.3	28.8	6.5	2.8	1.0	20,904
Wales	28.8	2.9	23.1	6.7	27.6	6.8	3.1	0.9	1,218
Scotland	32.8	3.2	19.8	7.0	26.9	6.0	3.7	0.6	2,256
Northern Ireland	26.6	3.2	27.9	7.9	22.6	6.9	4.0	..	648

1 For some regions, sample sizes are too small to provide a reliable estimate.

Source: Labour Force Survey Household Datasets, Office for National Statistics; Department of Economic Development, Northern Ireland

Table **3.21**   Marital Status: by sex, 2001[1]

Thousands and percentages

	Total (=100%)	Single (never married)	Married (first marriage)	Re-married	Separated (still legally married)	Divorced	Widowed
Males							
United Kingdom	28,579.9	13,699.7	10,255.2	1,697.4	493.2	1,601.0	833.3
North East	1,218.6	569.0	444.8	69.4	20.3	73.6	41.6
North West	3,259.0	1,571.8	1,142.2	189.8	53.6	196.5	105.1
Yorkshire and the Humber	2,411.9	1,128.7	870.5	157.2	37.2	145.8	72.6
East Midlands	2,048.9	940.7	753.5	139.6	33.9	120.1	61.1
West Midlands	2,575.1	1,219.3	946.6	149.2	40.0	143.0	77.0
East	2,638.3	1,198.4	993.4	179.1	42.8	151.1	73.4
London	3,468.8	1,959.0	1,062.6	134.0	65.0	170.4	77.8
South East	3,905.2	1,811.1	1,429.9	273.5	63.7	221.9	105.0
South West	2,396.4	1,069.4	881.0	184.1	38.1	151.5	72.2
England	23,922.1	11,467.5	8,524.4	1,475.8	394.6	1,373.9	685.9
Wales	1,403.8	651.7	515.5	87.4	17.7	85.4	46.1
Scotland	2,432.5	1,150.1	904.4	116.2	61.6	119.8	80.5
Northern Ireland	821.4	430.4	311.0	17.9	19.4	21.9	20.9
Females							
United Kingdom	30,209.3	12,345.8	10,280.2	1,620.5	688.1	2,160.2	3,114.5
North East	1,296.9	513.0	442.5	68.5	28.7	97.8	146.3
North West	3,470.8	1,429.3	1,144.4	182.9	77.5	261.7	375.0
Yorkshire and the Humber	2,552.9	1,015.7	867.6	154.0	52.5	191.5	271.6
East Midlands	2,123.3	820.3	752.9	136.5	43.7	152.0	218.0
West Midlands	2,692.2	1,077.1	947.0	144.6	55.4	183.9	284.2
East	2,749.8	1,051.9	993.9	172.7	55.4	201.1	274.8
London	3,703.3	1,849.1	1,076.2	113.5	102.8	253.3	308.5
South East	4,095.5	1,601.5	1,435.2	259.1	83.1	303.5	413.0
South West	2,532.0	937.6	885.3	177.6	48.4	201.3	281.8
England	25,216.7	10,295.6	8,545.1	1,409.4	547.4	1,846.0	2,573.3
Wales	1,499.3	584.9	516.0	85.0	26.1	115.6	171.6
Scotland	2,629.5	1,071.4	906.4	109.7	84.6	167.4	290.0
Northern Ireland	863.8	393.9	312.7	16.5	30.0	31.1	79.6
All Persons							
United Kingdom	58,789.2	*44.3*	*34.9*	*5.6*	*2.0*	*6.4*	*6.7*
North East	2,515.4	*43.0*	*35.3*	*5.5*	*1.9*	*6.8*	*7.5*
North West	6,729.8	*44.6*	*34.0*	*5.5*	*1.9*	*6.8*	*7.1*
Yorkshire and the Humber	4,964.8	*43.2*	*35.0*	*6.3*	*1.8*	*6.8*	*6.9*
East Midlands	4,172.2	*42.2*	*36.1*	*6.6*	*1.9*	*6.5*	*6.7*
West Midlands	5,267.3	*43.6*	*35.9*	*5.6*	*1.8*	*6.2*	*6.9*
East	5,388.1	*41.8*	*36.9*	*6.5*	*1.8*	*6.5*	*6.5*
London	7,172.1	*53.1*	*29.8*	*3.5*	*2.3*	*5.9*	*5.4*
South East	8,000.6	*42.7*	*35.8*	*6.7*	*1.8*	*6.6*	*6.5*
South West	4,928.4	*40.7*	*35.8*	*7.3*	*1.8*	*7.2*	*7.2*
England	49,138.8	*44.3*	*34.7*	*5.9*	*1.9*	*6.6*	*6.6*
Wales	2,903.1	*42.6*	*35.5*	*5.9*	*1.5*	*6.9*	*7.5*
Scotland	5,062.0	*43.9*	*35.8*	*4.5*	*2.9*	*5.7*	*7.3*
Northern Ireland	1,685.3	*48.9*	*37.0*	*2.0*	*2.9*	*3.1*	*6.0*

1 Cells in this table have been randomly adjusted to avoid the release of confidential data.

Source: Office for National Statistics; General Register Office for Scotland; Northern Ireland Statistics and Research Agency

Table **3.22**   Religion[1], 2001

Millions and percentages

	Total (millions = 100%)	Percentage of people stating religion as:								
		Christian	Buddhist	Hindu	Jewish	Muslim	Sikh	Other religions	No religion	Religion not stated
North East	2.5	80.1	0.1	0.2	0.1	1.1	0.2	0.2	11.0	7.1
North West	6.7	78.0	0.2	0.4	0.4	3.0	0.1	0.2	10.5	7.2
Yorkshire and the Humber	5.0	73.1	0.1	0.3	0.2	3.8	0.4	0.2	14.1	7.8
East Midlands	4.2	72.0	0.2	1.6	0.1	1.7	0.8	0.2	15.9	7.5
West Midlands	5.3	72.6	0.2	1.1	0.1	4.1	2.0	0.2	12.3	7.5
East	5.4	72.1	0.2	0.6	0.6	1.5	0.3	0.3	16.7	7.8
London	7.2	58.2	0.8	4.1	2.1	8.5	1.5	0.5	15.8	8.7
South East	8.0	72.8	0.3	0.6	0.2	1.4	0.5	0.4	16.5	7.5
South West	4.9	74.0	0.2	0.2	0.1	0.5	0.1	0.4	16.8	7.8
England	49.1	71.7	0.3	1.1	0.5	3.1	0.7	0.3	14.6	7.7
Wales	2.9	71.9	0.2	0.2	0.1	0.8	0.1	0.2	18.5	8.1

1 Figures in this table have been adjusted to avoid the release of confidential data.

Source: Census 2001, Office for National Statistics

Chapter 4 **Education and Training**

Pupils and teachers

Within England, pupil/teacher ratios in 2002/03 in public sector primary schools varied from 21.9 in the North East to 23.3 in London. This compared with a ratio of 18.0 in Scotland. For public sector secondary schools, numbers in all English regions (ranging from 16.4 in the North West to 17.5 in the East of England) were also higher than in Scotland, which had a ratio of 12.7. (Table 4.1)

More than half of all pupils in UK public sector nursery schools in 2002/03 were in Scotland. The Scottish nursery school pupil/teacher ratio, at 29.8, was much higher than in all English regions (where ratios ranged from 14.6 to 18.8). (Table 4.1)

Early years education

Participation rates in early years education by three- and four-year-olds rose in all English regions between January 2002 and January 2003, reaching around 100 per cent in all regions. (Table 4.2)

The highest participation rates in the private and voluntary sector of early years education in January 2003 were in the South East and South West regions, at over 50 per cent. This compared with 15 per cent or less in the North East and Northern Ireland. (Table 4.2)

Class sizes

The proportion of classes with more than 30 pupils in maintained primary schools in 2002/03 was highest in the East Midlands and the North West, at over 16 per cent. The lowest proportions were in London, at 8 per cent, and Northern Ireland, at 4 per cent. (Table 4.3)

School meals

The percentage of pupils taking free school meals in maintained nursery, primary and secondary schools in London in 2002/03 was around three times that in the South East. (Table 4.4)

Unauthorised absence

Rates of unauthorised absence from maintained primary and secondary schools in England fell slightly between 2001/02 and 2002/03. For primary schools in 2002/03, the highest rate was in London, at 0.79 per cent, which compared with a rate of 0.24 per cent in the North East. Unauthorised rates in secondary schools were higher, ranging from 1.47 per cent in Yorkshire and the Humber and 1.34 per cent in London to 0.84 per cent in the North East and 0.81 per cent in the South West. (Table 4.5)

Examination achievements

In England, the proportions of pupils in their last year of compulsory education achieving 5 or more GCSEs at grades A*-C (or equivalent) in 2001/02 were highest in the South East and South West regions at 56 per cent and lowest in the North East and Yorkshire and the Humber at 46 per cent. This compared with 59 per cent in

Northern Ireland and 60 per cent in the equivalent at Standard Grade in Scotland. (Table 4.6)

The proportion of pupils who achieved no graded GCSEs or SCE Standard Grades (or equivalent) in 2001/02 was lowest in Northern Ireland at 4.4 per cent and highest in Wales at 7.6 per cent. (Table 4.6)

The proportion of pupils who achieved 2 or more A levels or 3 or more SCE/NQ Highers (or equivalent) in 2001/02 was lowest in Wales at 31 per cent and the North East at 32 per cent. This compared with 43 per cent in Northern Ireland and 44 per cent in the South East. (Table 4.6)

In their last year of compulsory education in 2001/02, 71 per cent of pupils in Scotland achieved the equivalent of GCSE grades A*-C in English and 61 per cent in a science subject. The North East was the region with the lowest figures in these subjects: 49 per cent in English and 41 per cent in science. For mathematics, the highest proportion of pupils achieving GCSE grades A*-C was in the South East, at 54 per cent. The lowest proportion was in Yorkshire and the Humber, at 43 per cent. (Table 4.8)

Key stage assessments

In summer 2003 in England and Wales, the region with the lowest proportion of pupils reaching or exceeding the expected standards in Key Stage 3 Teacher Assessments was London, with figures of 63 per cent in English, 68 per cent in mathematics and 62 per cent in science. This compared with proportions of 71, 76 and 74 per cent respectively in the South East. At Key Stage 2, pupils in Wales performed the best, with 76 per cent meeting or exceeding the expected standards in English, 76 per cent in mathematics and 84 per cent in science. (Table 4.9)

Post-compulsory education

Wales, London and the East of England had the highest proportion of 16-year-olds in England and Wales in full-time education or on a government-supported training scheme in 2000/01, at 81 per cent. Regions with the lowest proportion were the East Midlands and Yorkshire and the Humber, at 77 per cent. (Table 4.10)

Further education

For home students in further education in England in 2001/02, London was the region with the lowest proportion of students undertaking a course leading to NVQ/GNVQ or equivalent academic qualifications, at less than 65 per cent. Proportions in other regions were much higher, ranging from 83 per cent in the East of England to 88 per cent in the North East. (Table 4.11)

Higher education

Higher education students whose home was in the East of England were the least likely to be studying within their own region in 2001/02, with only 41 per cent of students doing so. In contrast, 95 per cent of higher education students domiciled in Scotland also studied in Scotland. (Table 4.12)

Graduate destinations

Of those graduating in the UK with a first degree in 2002, people who had studied in the East of England were the most likely still to be in education or training 6 months after graduating, with 26.5 per cent doing so. They were also the least likely to be thought unemployed, at 5.6 per cent. Graduates who had studied in the South West were the least likely still to be in education or training, at 16.0 per cent, while those who had studied in London were the most likely to be believed unemployed, at 9.1 per cent. (Table 4.13)

Qualifications

Around a quarter of people of working age in London were qualified to degree level or equivalent in spring 2003, compared with around one in six in the UK as a whole. (Table 4.14)

The proportion of working age people without qualifications in Northern Ireland in spring 2003 was the highest in the UK, at 24 per cent. This compared with fewer than 11 per cent in the South East and South West. (Table 4.14)

The proportion of 19-year-olds qualified to at least level 3 in spring 2003 was highest in the South East, at 57 per cent, and lowest in the North West, at 46 per cent. The National Target for 2004 is 55 per cent. (Table 4.15)

Training

For both males (at 16 per cent) and females (at 21 per cent), Wales had the highest proportion in the UK of employees of working age receiving job-related training in spring 2003. The lowest proportion for males was in the East Midlands, at 11 per cent, and for females was in Northern Ireland, at 15 per cent. (Table 4.16)

Of those who left the Work-based Learning for Young People programme in England, Wales and Northern Ireland in 2000/01, the regions with the highest proportions in employment and the lowest proportions unemployed six months later were the South East and South West. In contrast, Northern Ireland (which had different schemes from those in England and Wales) had the lowest proportion in employment and the highest proportion unemployed. (Table 4.17)

Examination achievements (subregional)

Percentages of pupils in their final year of compulsory schooling in England gaining 5 or more GCSE passes at grades A*-C (or equivalent) in 2001/02 ranged from 28.9 in Kingston upon Hull to 64.8 in Sutton. Percentages gaining no graded results varied from 0.6 in Newham to 12.6 in Manchester. (Table 14.4)

Average A/AS level points scores in Wales in 2001/02 ranged from 14.9 in Blaenau Gwent to 22.5 in Ceredigion. (Table 15.4)

Percentages of pupils in their final year of compulsory schooling in Scotland gaining 5 or more grades 1-3 at SCE Standard Grade (or equivalent) in 2001/02 ranged from 48.0 in Dundee City to 83.3 in East Renfrewshire. Percentages gaining no graded results varied from 0.7 in Renfrewshire and 1.0 in East Renfrewshire to 9.1 in Clackmannanshire and 9.3 in Moray. (Table 16.3)

Percentages of pupils in their final year of compulsory schooling in Northern Ireland gaining 5 or more GCSE passes at grades A*-C (or equivalent) in 2001/02 ranged from 56.3 in the South Eastern Board area to 60.1 in Belfast. (Table 17.3)

Table **4.1**   Pupils and teachers[1]: by type of school, 2002/03[2]

Thousands and numbers

	Public sector schools				Non-maintained schools[4,5]	All special schools	All schools
	Nursery schools	Primary schools[3]	Secondary schools	Pupil Referral Units			
Pupils[6] (thousands)							
United Kingdom	84.6	5,023.3	3,995.2	..	623.6	110.6	9,849.1
North East	2.2	214.4	180.4	0.7	17.1	6.0	420.8
North West	3.8	611.0	470.9	2.0	56.1	15.0	1,158.9
Yorkshire and the Humber	2.2	445.5	347.5	1.3	33.4	7.9	837.8
East Midlands	1.5	359.4	297.4	0.7	36.9	5.9	701.8
West Midlands	3.5	471.2	378.7	1.2	44.4	12.4	911.3
East	2.1	440.7	383.8	0.9	63.1	9.0	899.7
London	5.5	607.4	418.1	2.6	127.3	12.0	1,172.8
South East	2.3	630.3	507.2	1.3	144.1	17.3	1,302.5
South West	1.2	387.2	324.3	1.0	61.1	7.5	782.4
England	24.3	4,167.3	3,308.3	11.7	583.5	93.0	8,188.0
Wales	1.4	267.7	214.3	..	9.7	3.8	496.9
Scotland	54.0	413.7	316.9	.	29.4	9.0	823.0
Northern Ireland	5.0	174.7	155.7	.	0.9	4.9	341.3
Teachers[1,6] (thousands)							
United Kingdom	3.6	228.8	243.3	..	64.0	18.3	560.7
North East	0.1	9.8	10.8	0.1	1.5	0.9	23.2
North West	0.2	27.4	28.8	0.3	5.2	2.4	64.3
Yorkshire and the Humber	0.1	19.6	20.5	0.3	3.1	1.3	44.9
East Midlands	0.1	15.6	17.3	0.1	3.6	0.9	37.6
West Midlands	0.2	20.9	22.3	0.4	4.5	1.9	50.2
East	0.1	19.4	21.9	0.4	6.6	1.3	49.8
London	0.3	26.1	24.7	0.6	12.4	2.0	66.1
South East	0.2	28.1	29.2	0.4	16.2	2.7	76.7
South West	0.1	17.3	18.8	0.2	6.7	1.2	44.3
England	1.5	184.0	194.4	2.7	59.9	14.6	457.2
Wales	0.1	12.9	13.0	..	1.0	0.6	27.6
Scotland	1.8	23.0	25.0	.	2.9	2.3	55.1
Northern Ireland	0.2	9.0	10.8	.	0.1	0.8	20.9
Pupils per teacher[6] (numbers)							
United Kingdom	23.7	22.0	16.4	..	9.7	6.0	17.6
North East	18.3	21.9	16.7	5.5	11.5	6.7	18.1
North West	16.2	22.3	16.4	6.7	10.8	6.2	18.0
Yorkshire and the Humber	16.7	22.7	16.9	4.9	10.7	6.3	18.7
East Midlands	16.2	23.1	17.2	5.8	10.2	6.6	18.7
West Midlands	18.8	22.5	17.0	3.4	9.8	6.5	18.2
East	15.6	22.8	17.5	2.3	9.5	6.8	18.1
London	16.1	23.3	16.9	4.6	10.3	6.0	17.7
South East	14.6	22.5	17.3	3.5	8.9	6.5	17.0
South West	15.5	22.4	17.2	4.8	9.1	6.2	17.7
England	16.4	22.6	17.0	4.3	9.7	6.4	17.9
Wales[7]	16.7	20.7	16.5	..	9.7	6.6	18.0
Scotland	29.8	18.0	12.7	.	10.0	3.9	14.9
Northern Ireland[8]	24.1	19.6	14.4	.	8.5	6.0	16.3

1 Qualified teachers only. See Notes and Definitions.
2 Provisional.
3 For Northern Ireland, figures include the preparatory departments of grammar schools.
4 Excluding special schools.
5 Includes Direct Grant Nursery Schools, City Technology Colleges and City Academies in England.
6 Based on full-time equivalent pupils and teachers.
7 Pupils per teacher data for all schools exclude Pupil Referral Units as information on teachers is not collected for Wales.
8 The 'All schools' pupil/teacher ratio in this table includes data for Independent schools, but is more usually reported for Grant-aided schools only in figures published by the Northern Ireland Department of Education.

Source: Department for Education and Skills; National Assembly for Wales; Scottish Executive; Northern Ireland Department of Education

Table **4.2**   Three- and four-year-olds[1,2,3] by type of early years education provider[4]

Thousands and percentages

	January 2002						January 2003[5]					
		Participation rates[6] (percentages)						Participation rates[6] (percentages)				
	Three- and four-year -olds in early years education (thousands)	Maintained nursery and primary schools	Independent and special schools	All schools	Private and voluntary providers[7]	All providers	Three- and four-year -olds in early years education (thousands)	Maintained nursery and primary schools	Independent and special schools	All schools	Private and voluntary providers[7]	All providers
United Kingdom	1,325.7	..	..	64	29	93	1,379.9	..	..	65	34	99
North East	56.5	85	2	87	12	99	56.5	85	2	87	15	102
North West	157.2	67	3	70	27	97	160.7	67	3	70	32	102
Yorkshire and the Humber	116.5	70	3	73	24	97	119.6	70	3	73	29	102
East Midlands	96.5	60	4	64	34	98	101.2	60	4	64	41	104
West Midlands	124.0	65	4	69	25	95	128.1	66	4	70	30	100
East	125.6	51	5	56	40	95	133.9	51	5	56	47	103
London	174.9	65	7	72	20	92	181.5	66	8	73	24	98
South East	180.6	40	8	48	45	93	192.9	41	8	48	53	101
South West	110.9	44	5	49	51	100	116.3	43	6	49	58	106
England	1,142.7	59	5	64	32	96	1,190.6	59	5	64	38	102
Wales	55.6	78	1	79	0	79	55.6	78	1	79	0	79
Scotland	95.3	..	..	60	22	82	100.7	..	..	65	26	91
Northern Ireland	32.2	55	1	56	11	67	32.9	58	1	59	13	71

1 Headcounts of children aged three and four at 31 December in the previous calendar year.
2 Numbers of three- and four-year-olds in schools may include some two-year-olds.
3 Any child attending more than one provider in England, and in Scotland may have been counted twice.
4 These figures must be interpreted carefully in the light of differing types of education providers between the countries. See Notes and Definitions.
5 Provisional. Data for Wales refer to 2002.
6 Number of three- and four-year-olds attending provider expressed as a percentage of the three- and four-year-old population.
7 Includes some Local Authority providers (other than schools) registered to receive nursery education grants.

Source: Department for Education and Skills; National Assembly for Wales; Scottish Executive; Northern Ireland Department of Education

Table **4.3**   Class sizes for all classes[1], 2002/03[2]

Numbers and percentages

	Primary schools						Secondary schools	
	Key Stage 1[3]		Key Stage 2[3]		All primary schools[4]			
	Average number in class	Percentage of classes with 31 or more pupils	Average number in class	Percentage of classes with 31 or more pupils	Average number in class	Percentage of classes with 31 or more pupils	Average number in class	Percentage of classes with 31 or more pupils
Great Britain	25.3	1.7	27.1	22.4	26.0	13.1	21.9	..
North East	24.6	1.2	26.5	19.7	25.4	11.6	21.8	7.8
North West	25.0	1.3	27.5	28.8	26.2	16.2	21.8	8.9
Yorkshire and the Humber	25.5	2.4	27.4	24.6	26.5	15.6	22.1	8.4
East Midlands	24.9	1.9	27.7	28.2	26.3	16.8	22.0	8.0
West Midlands	25.7	1.8	27.3	22.9	26.2	13.3	21.9	8.7
East	25.4	2.2	27.4	21.9	26.2	12.7	21.6	7.7
London	27.0	1.5	27.4	12.7	27.0	8.1	22.1	6.6
South East	25.6	1.4	27.5	25.3	26.4	14.5	21.8	7.3
South West	25.5	1.3	27.3	27.9	26.2	15.6	22.3	10.5
England	25.6	1.7	27.4	23.5	26.3	13.8	21.9	8.2
Wales[2]	24.2	2.6	25.9	17.5	24.4	9.5	21.2	..
Scotland[2,3]	23.6	1.5	25.3	16.1	24.3	9.4	..	..
Northern Ireland	22.9	1.7	24.1	8.0	23.0	4.1	..	..

1 Maintained schools only. Figures relate to all classes - not just those taught by one teacher. In Northern Ireland a class is defined as a group of pupils normally under the control of one teacher.
2 Provisional. Data for Wales and Scotland refer to 2001/02.
3 In Scotland primary P1-P3 is interpreted to be Key Stage 1 and P4-P7, Key Stage 2. See Notes and Definitions.
4 For all countries, pupils in composite classes which overlap Key Stage 1 and Key Stage 2 are included in the 'All primary schools' total, but are excluded from all other categories.

Source: Department for Education and Skills; National Assembly for Wales; Scottish Executive; Northern Ireland Department of Education

Table **4.4**   School meal arrangements, 2002/03[1]

Thousands and percentages

	Maintained nursery and primary schools[2,3]			Maintained secondary schools[2]			All special schools[5]		
	Number on roll (thousands)	Percentage known to be eligible for free meals	Percentage taking free school meals[4]	Number on roll (thousands)	Percentage known to be eligible for free meals	Percentage taking free school meals[4]	Number on roll (thousands)	Percentage known to be eligible for free meals	Percentage taking free school meals[4]
United Kingdom	5,232.8	17.4	14.3	3,984.3	14.9	10.8	106.0	37.4	31.4
North East	230.1	22.1	19.1	180.4	18.1	12.6	6.0	49.8	42.6
North West	636.4	20.6	17.2	470.9	18.8	13.9	15.0	43.5	36.1
Yorkshire and the Humber	470.5	17.4	14.3	347.6	16.0	10.9	8.1	36.8	30.6
East Midlands	375.9	12.7	10.5	297.5	11.2	8.3	6.1	32.9	27.6
West Midlands	493.0	18.5	15.5	378.6	15.9	11.4	12.9	36.8	31.8
East	459.0	11.7	9.5	383.9	9.6	7.0	9.2	26.3	21.6
London	640.7	25.7	21.3	417.9	24.0	18.5	12.0	43.9	36.0
South East	649.7	10.1	7.9	507.3	8.4	6.0	17.7	24.4	19.2
South West	395.0	11.3	9.2	324.3	8.9	6.6	7.6	28.4	24.5
England	4,350.3	16.8	13.9	3,308.5	14.5	10.6	94.7	35.3	29.4
Wales	284.8	19.4	17.7	212.0	16.8	13.4	3.7	47.3	44.8
Scotland	414.7	20.2	16.8	308.1	16.0	10.5	7.6	58.1	59.9
Northern Ireland	183.1	21.0	17.3	155.7	20.4	16.5	..	..	..

1 Provisional, based on full-time and part-time headcounts. Figures throughout England now include boarding pupils as well as solely and dually registered pupils. Figures for Wales refer to 2001/02.

2 Includes middle schools as deemed.

3 Figures for Northern Ireland include reception pupils and pupils in preparatory departments of grammar schools. Figures for Scotland are mainly for primary schools but include some nursery pupils based in primary schools.

4 Figures shown for Wales and Scotland are calculated as the percentage of the day pupils present on the census day, therefore the percentage taking free school meals may exceed the percentage known to be eligible. Figures for England, Northern Ireland and the UK, however, are percentages of the numbers of pupils on the school roll.

5 Figures in UK row for "all special schools" refer to Great Britain.

Source: Department for Education and Skills; National Assembly for Wales; Scottish Executive; Northern Ireland Department of Education

Table **4.5**   Pupil absence from maintained primary and secondary schools

Percentages[1]

	2001/02				2002/03			
	Primary schools		Secondary schools		Primary schools		Secondary schools	
	Authorised	Unauthorised	Authorised	Unauthorised	Authorised	Unauthorised	Authorised	Unauthorised
England	5.40	0.45	7.63	1.09	5.38	0.43	7.21	1.07
North East	5.62	0.24	8.06	0.86	5.68	0.24	7.72	0.84
North West	5.43	0.41	7.97	1.09	5.20	0.39	7.39	1.07
Yorkshire and the Humber	5.40	0.49	7.85	1.49	5.34	0.45	7.35	1.47
East Midlands	5.24	0.43	7.47	1.26	5.35	0.40	7.07	1.27
West Midlands	5.65	0.37	7.69	0.96	5.71	0.38	7.24	0.98
East	5.16	0.38	7.24	0.88	5.37	0.38	7.10	0.87
London	5.70	0.85	7.46	1.45	5.58	0.79	6.92	1.34
South East	5.20	0.36	7.39	0.96	5.17	0.34	7.01	0.93
South West	5.29	0.34	7.72	0.81	5.27	0.32	7.38	0.81

1 Number of half-day sessions missed as a percentage of total possible pupil sessions. See Notes and Definitions.

Source: Department for Education and Skills

Table 4.6   Examination achievements[1]: by sex, 2001/02

	Pupils in their last year of compulsory education[1]					Pupils/students in education[2,3,4] achieving 2 or more A levels[7]/ 3 or more SCE/NQ[6] Highers (percentages)	Average A/AS level and Advanced GNVQ point scores[2,3,4,9]
	Percentage achieving GCSE[5] or SCE Standard Grade/National Qualifications(NQ)[6]				Total (=100%) (thousands)		
	5 or more grades A*-C	1-4 grades A*-C	Grades D-G only[8]	No graded GCSEs/SCEs			
Males							
United Kingdom	47.2	24.4	22.0	6.4	374.0	33.2	..
North East	40.5	24.2	27.3	8.0	16.9	28.6	227.7
North West	44.7	25.2	23.3	6.8	45.6	31.3	248.1
Yorkshire and the Humber	40.2	23.7	28.4	7.7	32.6	29.2	242.8
East Midlands	45.8	23.1	24.8	6.3	26.8	31.5	245.8
West Midlands	44.3	25.0	24.1	6.6	34.7	31.1	239.4
East	50.1	23.5	20.9	5.5	33.9	37.5	241.0
London	45.4	25.6	22.4	6.6	39.5	32.8	232.4
South East	51.5	22.7	20.2	5.6	49.3	39.7	256.1
South West	50.3	23.1	21.1	5.5	30.4	35.5	248.6
England	46.4	24.0	23.2	6.4	309.7	33.6	244.1
Wales	44.8	23.9	22.0	9.2	19.0	26.0	18.5
Scotland	55.2	28.0	11.6	5.2	32.2	33.7	.
Northern Ireland	51.9	23.6	18.3	6.1	13.1	34.5	..
Females							
United Kingdom	58.0	23.1	14.6	4.3	358.5	42.1	..
North East	50.9	24.3	19.3	5.4	16.3	34.9	239.6
North West	55.0	24.1	16.5	4.5	44.1	39.3	268.3
Yorkshire and the Humber	51.3	24.1	19.5	5.1	31.0	36.6	264.6
East Midlands	56.0	23.4	16.5	4.1	25.3	38.3	267.3
West Midlands	55.4	24.4	16.2	4.1	33.1	39.2	260.8
East	60.8	21.6	13.8	3.8	32.2	44.5	266.3
London	55.9	25.1	14.7	4.3	38.8	42.8	243.3
South East	61.4	21.3	13.0	4.3	46.8	48.5	276.6
South West	61.9	21.4	12.9	3.9	29.2	45.4	268.7
England	57.0	23.2	15.5	4.3	296.8	41.8	263.5
Wales	56.4	22.8	14.9	5.9	18.1	35.3	20.2
Scotland	65.7	22.5	7.7	4.0	30.9	45.2	.
Northern Ireland	65.7	20.8	11.0	2.6	12.7	52.4	..
All pupils/students							
United Kingdom	52.5	23.7	18.4	5.4	732.5	37.6	..
North East	45.6	24.3	23.4	6.7	33.1	31.8	234.2
North West	49.7	24.7	20.0	5.6	89.7	35.2	259.0
Yorkshire and the Humber	45.6	23.9	24.1	6.4	63.6	32.8	254.4
East Midlands	50.8	23.2	20.8	5.2	52.1	34.8	257.1
West Midlands	49.7	24.7	20.2	5.4	67.8	35.0	250.8
East	55.3	22.6	17.4	4.7	66.1	40.9	254.1
London	50.6	25.4	18.6	5.5	78.3	37.6	238.3
South East	56.4	22.0	16.7	4.9	96.1	43.9	266.9
South West	56.0	22.2	17.1	4.7	59.6	40.3	259.4
England	51.6	23.6	19.4	5.4	606.6	37.6	254.4
Wales	50.5	23.4	18.5	7.6	37.1	30.6	19.5
Scotland	60.4	25.3	9.7	4.6	63.0	39.4	.
Northern Ireland	58.7	22.2	14.7	4.4	25.8	43.4	..

1 See Notes and Definitions.

2 Pupils in schools and students in further education institutions aged 18 to 19 at the end of the academic year in England, aged 18 in Wales, and aged 17 to 19 in Northern Ireland, as a percentage of the 18-year-old population. Pupils in Scotland generally sit Highers one year earlier and the figures relate to the results of pupils in Year S5/S6 as a percentage of the 17-year-old population.

3 Figures for England are cumulative GCE A/AS/VCE/AGNVQ results obtained in the academic years 2000/01 and 2001/02 and are not therefore directly comparable with pre-2002 editions of Regional Trends.

4 Including students in England who were entered for a pre-September 2001 or post-September 2001 A level, are at the end of their second year of an Advanced GNVQ or have entered for a double award VCE A level in Summer 2002.

5 Figures for England and Wales include GNVQ equivalents.

6 From 1999/2000 National Qualifications (NQ) were introduced in Scotland. NQs include Standard Grades, Intermediate 1 & 2 and Higher Grades. The figures for Higher Grades combine the new NQ Higher and the old SCE Higher. Figures for Scotland include those with two or more Advanced Higher or combination of two or more Highers plus an Advanced Higher.

7 Including Vocational Certificates of Education (VCE) and equivalent in England, Wales and Northern Ireland.

8 No grades above D and at least one in the D-G range. Figures for Wales, England and the English regions include pupils with one GCSE short course only.

9 The point scores for 2001/02 throughout England reflect the Universities and Colleges Admissions Service (UCAS) Tariff, and data are not directly comparable with earlier years, or with Wales. See Notes and Definitions for derivation of points scores.

Source: Department for Education and Skills; National Assembly for Wales; Scottish Executive; Northern Ireland Department of Education

Map **4.7**

Pupils[1,2] achieving 5 or more GCSE Grades A*-C/ Standard Grades 1-3 (or equivalent),[3] 2001/02

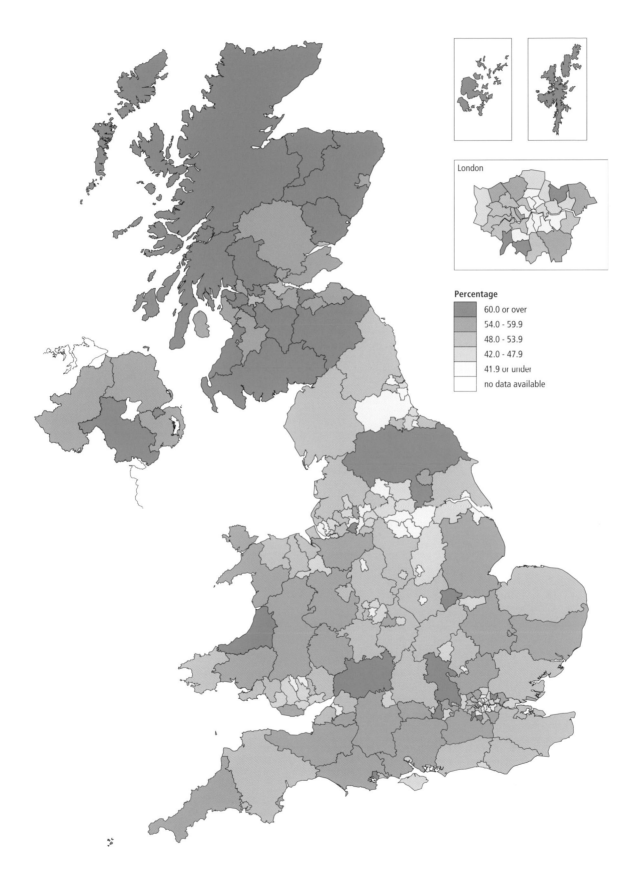

London

Percentage

60.0 or over
54.0 - 59.9
48.0 - 53.9
42.0 - 47.9
41.9 or under
no data available

1 Pupils in their last year of compulsory schooling as a percentage of the school population of the same age.
2 Figures for England and Wales relate to maintained schools only, while figures for Scotland and Northern Ireland are for all schools.
3 Figures are presented by Local Education Authority in England, by unitary authority in Wales and Scotland and by Education and Library Board in Northern Ireland.

Source: Department for Education and Skills; Scottish Executive; National Assembly for Wales; Northern Ireland Department of Education

Table **4.8** Pupils[1] achieving GCSE grades A*-C[2]: by selected subjects and sex, 2001/02[3]

Percentages

	English	Mathe-matics	Any science[4]	Single award[5]	Double award	Any modern langu-age[6]	French	Geo-graphy	History	Craft Design Techno-logy	All core sub-jects[7]
			Science								
Males											
United Kingdom	49.0	48.1	47.6	2.0	34.3	32.4	21.9	22.1	18.9	30.1	26.6
North East	40.8	42.6	39.9	1.1	32.0	23.8	16.3	16.8	15.3	28.7	19.2
North West	46.1	46.7	45.0	1.3	36.6	29.3	19.4	19.7	17.7	30.8	23.6
Yorkshire and the Humber	41.9	42.0	40.8	0.8	34.7	26.2	16.8	18.8	16.1	30.5	20.4
East Midlands	46.5	47.4	46.8	1.1	40.5	31.5	22.0	21.2	17.5	31.8	24.8
West Midlands	45.5	46.2	44.1	1.1	36.6	29.4	19.5	20.7	17.4	30.0	23.0
East	50.6	51.7	50.5	1.2	43.1	34.5	23.1	24.0	20.7	33.5	27.9
London	47.1	47.5	43.6	1.5	34.3	33.5	21.1	18.4	18.3	24.5	24.9
South East	52.8	53.4	51.0	1.8	38.5	37.0	25.7	24.8	22.2	30.3	30.5
South West	50.8	51.7	51.4	1.2	42.1	34.1	23.5	26.1	19.9	35.6	28.2
England	47.5	48.2	46.3	1.3	37.7	31.7	21.2	21.4	18.7	30.5	25.3
Wales	46.3	43.0	45.9	1.7	35.1	17.7	13.2	24.3	19.6	23.5	33.6
Scotland	64.4	49.9	58.3	6.9	.	45.7	31.4	26.7	19.5	32.9	35.0
Northern Ireland	50.9	49.8	52.3	8.5	35.8	38.8	26.4	23.8	21.3	22.7	28.8
Females											
United Kingdom	65.0	50.3	51.0	2.4	38.6	48.4	33.3	20.0	21.9	36.1	36.8
North East	56.6	44.3	42.7	1.6	35.2	38.9	27.8	16.5	17.3	42.1	28.9
North West	61.3	48.7	47.9	1.8	40.7	44.6	30.3	16.1	19.5	40.2	33.8
Yorkshire and the Humber	58.7	44.3	44.2	1.5	38.2	42.4	27.4	16.9	18.6	43.1	30.8
East Midlands	62.7	48.3	48.8	1.5	43.9	47.4	33.7	18.0	20.6	44.2	34.6
West Midlands	61.9	47.3	46.9	1.2	40.8	45.0	30.4	19.5	20.6	39.7	32.9
East	66.4	53.0	52.9	2.0	46.0	50.2	34.7	21.6	23.5	44.1	38.0
London	62.6	50.0	48.5	2.3	42.0	48.3	30.5	18.8	21.6	33.0	34.7
South East	67.9	55.2	53.8	2.0	44.5	51.8	35.5	22.8	23.5	39.0	40.5
South West	68.6	54.5	55.0	1.8	46.0	52.0	36.6	24.8	23.0	46.7	40.8
England	63.4	50.0	49.4	1.8	42.3	47.3	32.1	19.6	21.2	40.8	35.5
Wales	64.6	46.6	49.2	2.6	39.5	32.7	25.6	19.3	24.8	17.3	40.4
Scotland	78.2	52.1	63.0	4.9	.	64.4	46.5	21.4	25.5	13.9	45.0
Northern Ireland	69.5	56.5	61.4	10.9	43.6	56.6	40.4	25.5	25.0	7.2	42.5
All pupils											
United Kingdom	56.8	49.2	49.3	2.2	36.4	40.2	27.5	21.1	20.4	33.0	31.6
North East	48.6	43.5	41.3	1.3	33.5	31.2	21.9	16.7	16.2	35.2	24.0
North West	53.5	47.7	46.4	1.5	38.6	36.8	24.8	17.9	18.6	35.4	28.6
Yorkshire and the Humber	50.1	43.1	42.4	1.1	36.4	34.1	22.0	17.9	17.3	36.7	25.5
East Midlands	54.4	47.8	47.8	1.3	42.1	39.2	27.7	19.6	19.0	37.8	29.6
West Midlands	53.5	46.7	45.5	1.2	38.6	37.0	24.8	20.1	19.0	34.8	27.8
East	58.3	52.4	51.7	1.6	44.5	42.1	28.8	22.8	22.1	38.7	32.8
London	54.8	48.7	46.0	1.9	38.1	40.8	25.7	18.6	19.9	28.7	29.8
South East	60.1	54.3	52.4	1.9	41.4	44.2	30.5	23.8	22.8	34.5	35.4
South West	59.5	53.1	53.2	1.5	44.0	42.8	29.9	25.5	21.4	41.0	34.4
England	55.3	49.1	47.9	1.5	40.0	39.3	26.6	20.5	19.9	35.6	30.3
Wales	55.2	44.8	47.5	2.1	37.2	25.0	19.3	21.9	22.1	20.5	36.9
Scotland	71.1	51.0	60.6	5.9	.	54.9	38.8	24.1	22.4	23.6	39.9
Northern Ireland	60.0	53.1	56.7	9.7	39.6	47.5	33.3	24.6	23.1	15.1	35.5

1 Pupils in their last year of compulsory education.
2 SCE Standard Grade awards at levels 1-3/Intermediate 2 at A-C/Intermediate 1 at A-B (temporary benchmark) in Scotland.
3 See Notes and Definitions for information on comparisons for England, Wales and Northern Ireland with Scotland.
4 Includes double award, single award and individual science subjects. In Scotland, 'Any science' includes Biology, Chemistry, Physics or General Science Standard Grade. See Notes and Definitions.
5 General Science in Scotland.
6 Including French.
7 The core subjects of the National Curriculum applicable in England and Northern Ireland are English, mathematics and a science. Figures in this column for England and Northern Ireland also include a modern language. The core subjects applicable in Wales are mathematics, a science, and either English or Welsh (as a first language). In 2001/02, 9.0 per cent of pupils achieved GCSE grade A*-C in Welsh as a first language. The National Curriculum does not apply in Scotland. However, figures in this column include those who obtained English, mathematics, a science and a modern language.

Source: Department for Education and Skills; National Assembly for Wales; Scottish Executive; Northern Ireland Department of Education

Table **4.9**   **Pupils reaching or exceeding expected standards:[1] by Key Stage Teacher Assessment, summer 2003[2]**

Percentages

	Key Stage 1[3]			Key Stage 2[4]			Key Stage 3[5]		
	English	Mathematics	Science	English	Mathematics	Science	English	Mathematics	Science
England[6]	85	89	89	72	74	82	68	72	69
North East	85	89	89	71	74	81	65	70	65
North West	85	88	89	73	75	83	69	72	68
Yorkshire and the Humber	85	88	89	69	72	79	65	69	66
East Midlands	86	89	90	72	74	81	66	73	70
West Midlands	83	87	87	70	71	80	67	70	68
East	86	90	91	73	74	82	70	75	72
London	82	86	87	69	72	78	63	68	62
South East	86	90	91	74	75	83	71	76	74
South West	85	89	91	73	75	83	71	75	73
Wales	82	87	88	76	76	84	65	69	69
Northern Ireland[7,8]	95	95	.	74	77	.	74	72	72

1 For information about the National Curriculum in England and Wales and the common curriculum in Northern Ireland, see Notes and Definitions.
2 Provisional. Data for Northern Ireland refer to 2002.
3 Percentage of pupils achieving level 2 or above at Key Stage 1.
4 Percentage of pupils achieving level 4 or above at Key Stage 2.
5 Percentage of pupils achieving level 5 or above at Key Stage 3.
6 Includes non-LEA maintained schools. These are not included in the regional figures.
7 In Northern Ireland Key Stage 1, pupils are assessed at the age of 8. Pupils are not assessed in science at Key Stages 1 and 2.
8 As a result of industrial action, approximately 10% of schools did not submit Key Stage 1 results and 9% of schools did not submit Key Stage 2 results.

Source: Department for Education and Skills; National Assembly for Wales; Northern Ireland Department of Education

Table **4.10**   **16- and 17-year-olds participating in post-compulsory education[1] and government-supported training: by region, 2000/01**

Percentages[2]

	16-year-olds					17-year-olds				
	At school[1]	In further education[1,3]		Government-supported training (GST)[4]	All in full-time education and GST[4,5]	At school[1]	In further education[1,3]		Government-supported training (GST)[4]	All in full-time education and GST[4,5]
		Full-time	Part-time				Full-time	Part-time		
United Kingdom	39	34	6	8	79	30	28	8	10	68
North East	27	38	9	15	79	20	31	9	16	67
North West	25	43	6	11	78	20	34	8	14	68
Yorkshire and the Humber	31	36	9	11	77	24	29	10	13	66
East Midlands	38	31	7	9	77	31	26	9	11	68
West Midlands	32	37	7	10	78	26	31	9	11	67
East	42	33	5	7	81	33	27	7	8	68
London	41	36	4	4	81	32	32	6	6	69
South East	39	35	4	6	79	33	29	6	8	69
South West	39	34	5	7	80	32	29	7	11	71
England	35	36	6	8	79	28	30	8	10	68
Wales	39	34	6	8	81	29	28	8	11	68
Scotland[6]	71	14	8	..	..	41	12	11	..	..
Northern Ireland[7]	47	29	10	..	..	40	28	7	..	..

1 See Notes and Definitions.
2 As a percentage of the estimated 16- and 17-year-old population respectively. Population data do not include post-Census revisions.
3 Including sixth form colleges in England and a small element of further education in higher education institutions in England, Wales and Scotland.
4 Figures in the United Kingdom row relate to England and Wales.
5 Figures for England exclude overlap between full-time education and government-supported training.
6 The estimates of 16-year-olds at school exclude those pupils who leave school in the winter term at the minimum statutory school-leaving age.
7 Participation in part-time FE should not be aggregated with full-time FE or schools activity due to the unquantifiable overlap of these activities.

Source: Department for Education and Skills; National Assembly for Wales; Scottish Executive; Northern Ireland Department of Education

Table **4.11** Home students in further education[1] in England: by level of course of study[2], 2001/02

Percentages and thousands

	Courses leading to NVQ/GNVQ or equivalent academic qualifications (percentages)					Total FE students[1] studying in England (=100%) (thousands)
	Level 1 and entry	Level 2	Level 3	Level 4, 5 and higher education	Other courses	
Region of study[3]						
North East	25.4	29.7	27.4	5.7	11.8	184.2
North West	21.3	27.7	30.1	4.9	15.9	430.3
Yorkshire and the Humber	25.6	26.8	28.7	4.3	14.5	283.5
East Midlands	24.7	28.8	28.9	3.0	14.6	194.2
West Midlands	25.3	25.8	28.4	4.8	15.7	350.0
East	21.2	24.5	31.7	5.3	17.3	198.3
London	18.9	20.2	22.5	3.0	35.5	396.9
South East	22.5	23.3	32.8	5.2	16.2	348.2
South West	22.9	26.0	30.5	4.6	15.9	216.9
England	22.8	25.5	28.8	4.5	18.5	2,602.6
Other[4]	12.2	23.4	30.8	14.8	18.7	9.4

1 Further education (FE) institutions only. See Notes and Definitions. Due to a change in methodology, figures are not directly comparable with those published previously in Regional Trends before 2001.
2 Highest level of qualification aimed for by students.
3 English domiciled students only.
4 Those studying within England domiciled in Wales, Scotland, Northern Ireland, Channel Islands and the Isle of Man.

Source: Department for Education and Skills

Table **4.12** Home domiciled higher education students[1]: by area of study and domicile, 2001/02

Percentages and thousands

	Area of study												All students (=100%) (thousands)
	North East	North West	York-shire and the Humber	East Mid-lands	West Mid-lands	East	London	South East	South West	Wales	Scot-land	Nor-thern Ireland	
Area of domicile													
United Kingdom[2]	4.6	11.3	9.8	6.7	8.3	5.4	15.0	10.3	6.7	5.5	13.5	2.9	1,688.2
North East	**72.7**	5.5	9.4	2.7	1.5	1.0	1.7	1.4	0.7	0.5	2.9	0.1	66.5
North West	3.3	**68.3**	10.7	3.4	3.9	1.2	2.3	1.9	1.3	1.9	1.9	-	178.1
Yorkshire and the Humber	6.0	8.1	**67.5**	5.8	2.6	1.5	2.4	1.9	1.3	1.0	1.7	0.1	120.4
East Midlands	2.5	6.3	17.2	**48.0**	8.3	3.9	4.3	4.0	2.7	1.6	1.1	-	99.3
West Midlands	1.2	7.1	6.1	8.4	**58.0**	1.7	3.7	3.9	4.5	4.2	1.0	-	130.0
East	1.8	3.6	6.3	9.4	4.5	**41.3**	15.7	9.8	4.5	1.8	1.3	-	125.6
London	0.9	2.3	2.5	2.8	2.4	5.1	**69.7**	9.3	2.8	1.0	1.1	-	231.8
South East	1.5	3.0	3.9	5.4	3.9	4.2	16.6	**48.2**	9.0	2.9	1.4	-	209.4
South West	1.1	3.0	3.2	3.7	4.6	2.3	6.9	13.1	**53.6**	7.2	1.2	-	115.0
England[2]	5.7	13.6	12.1	8.3	10.2	6.7	18.7	12.8	8.1	2.4	1.5	-	1,329.0
Wales	0.6	6.2	2.6	2.3	3.5	1.1	2.8	3.3	5.6	**71.3**	0.7	-	84.1
Scotland	0.7	0.9	0.6	0.3	0.4	0.3	0.7	0.6	0.3	0.3	**94.8**	-	212.6
Northern Ireland	1.4	4.0	1.2	1.0	0.8	0.8	1.6	1.1	0.4	0.7	8.7	**78.4**	62.5

1 Including higher education students in further education institutions for England, Wales, Scotland and Northern Ireland. Excluding Open University students. These data are not comparable with figures prior to those shown in Regional Trends 35. See Notes and Definitions.
2 Including students from the Channel Islands and Isle of Man and students whose area of domicile was unknown or unclassified.

Source: Department for Education and Skills; Higher Education Statistics Agency; National Assembly for Wales; Scottish Executive; Northern Ireland Department for Employment and Learning

Table **4.13**   Destination of full-time first degree graduates, 2002[1]

Percentages and thousands

	UK employment		Overseas employment[2]	Total employment	Continuing education or training	Believed unemployed	Other destinations[3]	All first degree graduates[4] (thousands)
	Permanent	Temporary						
Area of study								
United Kingdom	42.8	20.1	2.1	65.0	19.8	6.8	8.4	223.9
North East	44.9	17.2	2.4	64.5	21.6	6.0	7.9	11.7
North West	44.5	21.3	1.7	67.6	18.9	6.5	7.1	25.6
Yorkshire and the Humber	47.5	18.5	2.6	68.6	17.7	6.1	7.6	24.5
East Midlands	47.1	18.9	1.9	67.9	17.7	6.1	8.2	17.1
West Midlands	42.0	21.1	2.1	65.2	20.6	7.1	7.1	17.9
East	38.9	19.1	1.9	59.9	26.5	5.6	8.0	12.0
London	40.2	19.5	1.2	61.0	19.6	9.1	10.4	30.2
South East	42.0	21.0	2.1	65.1	19.6	6.5	8.8	26.7
South West	45.7	19.0	2.4	67.0	16.0	6.9	10.1	16.8
England	43.7	19.7	2.0	65.3	19.3	6.8	8.5	182.4
Wales	40.8	19.6	2.1	62.6	23.6	6.5	7.3	13.4
Scotland	38.3	24.3	2.7	65.3	19.7	6.3	8.7	22.3
Northern Ireland	36.9	18.7	3.5	59.1	25.1	7.3	8.5	5.7

1 Home and EU students graduating from higher education institutions in 2002. As a percentage of known destinations. As from 1999/2000 the target population excludes non-EU overseas domiciled students.
2 Home students only.
3 Includes overseas graduates leaving the United Kingdom and graduates not available for employment.
4 Includes known and unknown destinations.

Source: Department for Education and Skills; Higher Education Statistics Agency

Table **4.14**   Population of working age[1]: by highest qualification[2], spring 2003

Percentages

	Degree or equivalent	Higher education qualifications[3]	GCE A level or equivalent[4]	GCSE grades A*-C or equivalent	Other qualifications	No qualifications
United Kingdom	16.3	8.5	24.1	21.7	13.7	15.0
North East	11.3	9.1	25.1	22.7	12.6	18.8
North West	13.3	8.3	24.6	24.1	11.4	17.5
Yorkshire and the Humber	13.4	7.7	25.6	22.1	14.4	16.2
East Midlands	13.0	7.6	25.1	22.6	13.4	17.1
West Midlands	12.7	8.3	23.6	22.7	14.1	17.6
East	16.2	7.7	22.7	25.0	14.0	14.0
London	24.7	6.0	18.5	16.7	20.2	13.4
South East	19.9	8.6	24.2	22.4	13.7	10.6
South West	16.2	9.8	24.9	24.1	13.4	10.7
England	16.6	8.0	23.5	22.2	14.5	14.6
Wales	14.6	8.8	23.2	23.4	11.6	17.1
Scotland	15.4	13.3	29.9	16.4	9.7	14.7
Northern Ireland	13.1	7.7	26.9	21.0	6.7	23.7

1 Males aged 16 to 64 and females aged 16 to 59.
2 For information on equivalent level qualifications, see Notes and Definitions.
3 Below degree level.
4 Includes recognised trade apprenticeship.

Source: Department for Education and Skills; from the Labour Force Survey, Office for National Statistics

Table **4.15** **Progress towards achieving National Targets[1] for England for young people and adults[2], spring 2003**

Percentages and thousands

	Young people							Adults[2]						
	19-year-olds qualified to at least level 2[3,4]				19-year-olds qualified to at least level 3[4,5]			Economically Active adults qualified to at least level 2[6]			Number of adults achieving NVQ level 2[6] (thousands)	Economically Active adults qualified to at least level 3[7]		
	spring 2002 (baseline)	spring 2003			spring 2003			spring 2003			spring 2003	spring 2003		
	All	All	Males	Females	All	Males	Females	All	Males	Females	All	All	Males	Females
Region of residence														
North East	73	72	62	82	49	40	57	69	71	67	780	47	50	45
North West	72	73	69	78	46	44	48	70	71	68	2,211	48	51	43
Yorkshire and the Humber	71	77	78	77	53	53	54	68	71	65	1,622	46	49	42
East Midlands	78	78	76	79	55	56	54	68	72	64	1,371	46	50	41
West Midlands	70	75	69	82	49	45	52	68	70	65	1,693	46	48	42
East	72	74	73	75	50	49	51	69	71	66	1,871	46	50	42
London	76	73	72	74	50	48	51	73	74	72	2,678	54	55	52
South East	80	79	76	83	57	57	57	73	75	70	2,959	52	56	48
South West	79	78	78	77	54	51	57	72	74	69	1,704	51	54	47
England	75	76	73	78	52	50	53	70	72	68	16,889	49	52	45

1 These targets have superseded the former 2002 National Learning Targets. See Notes and Definitions for details of the targets.
2 Males aged 18 to 64 and females aged 18 to 59 in employment or actively seeking employment.
3 DfES Public Service Agreement (PSA) Target: By 2004, increase by 3 percentage points the number of 19-year-olds achieving a qualification equivalent to level 2, compared to 2002, with a further increase of 3 percentage points by 2006. Learning and Skills Council (LSC) Target: By 2004, 85 per cent to achieve level 2 by age 19.
4 The achievement of 19- to 21-year-olds is used as a proxy for attainment at age 19.
5 DfES Delivering Results Target: Increase the proportion of 19-year-olds achieving a level 3 qualification from 51 per cent in 2000 to 55 per cent in 2004. LSC Target: By 2004, 55 per cent to achieve level 3 by age 19.
6 DfES PSA Target: Reduce by at least 40 per cent the number of adults who lack level 2 by 2010. Working towards this, 1 million adults already in the workforce to achieve level 2 between 2003 and 2006.
7 DfES Delivering Results Target: Increase the percentage of adults attaining a level 3 qualification from 47 per cent to 52 per cent in 2004. LSC Target: By 2004, 52 per cent of adults to achieve level 3.

Source: Department for Education and Skills

Table **4.16** **Employees of working age[1] receiving job-related training:[2] by sex, spring 2003**

Percentages[3]

| | Males | | | | Females | | | |
	On-the-job training only	Off-the-job training only	Both on- and off-the-job training	Any job-related training	On-the-job training only	Off-the-job training only	Both on- and off-the-job training	Any job-related training
United Kingdom	4.6	6.6	2.7	13.9	5.3	8.7	3.5	17.5
North East	5.2	6.1	3.4	14.8	6.2	6.7	4.4	17.3
North West	4.9	6.1	3.0	14.0	5.5	8.6	3.6	17.7
Yorkshire and the Humber	5.4	6.1	2.6	14.2	6.3	9.1	3.6	19.1
East Midlands	3.8	5.0	2.3	11.1	6.0	7.5	3.8	17.3
West Midlands	4.2	5.7	2.7	12.5	6.2	8.5	3.4	18.2
East	3.4	7.0	2.7	13.1	4.7	8.3	3.5	16.5
London	5.0	7.4	3.0	15.4	4.7	9.3	3.4	17.4
South East	4.3	7.1	2.5	14.0	4.8	9.3	3.2	17.4
South West	4.6	7.7	2.2	14.5	5.0	9.6	3.2	17.8
England	4.5	6.6	2.7	13.8	5.4	8.7	3.5	17.6
Wales	5.5	7.3	3.3	16.0	6.4	10.1	4.2	20.7
Scotland	4.8	6.5	3.2	14.5	4.7	7.3	3.8	15.9
Northern Ireland	5.1	5.4	1.7	12.2	4.5	8.6	2.0	15.2

1 Males aged 16 to 64 and females aged 16 to 59.
2 Job-related education or training received in the four weeks before interview.
3 As a percentage of all employees of working age.

Source: Department for Education and Skills; Labour Force Survey, Office for National Statistics

Table **4.17** Work-based learning,[1] 2000/01

Percentages and thousands

	Work-based Learning for Adults						Work-based Learning for Young People[2]					
	Status six months after leaving (percentages)						Status six months after leaving (percentages)					
	In employ-ment	In further educ-ation or training	Unemp-loyed	Other	Gained full qualifi-cation (percent-ages)	All leavers[3] (thou-sands)	In employ-ment	In further educ-ation or training	Unemp-loyed	Other	Gained full qualifi-cation (percent-ages)	All leavers[3] (thou-sands)
England and Wales	42	4	47	7	41	117.9	71	11	11	7	52	282.7
North East	37	4	52	7	40	8.1	64	14	16	6	52	21.2
North West	40	4	50	6	41	18.3	73	10	11	6	54	49.0
Yorkshire and the Humber	36	4	53	7	38	11.4	69	11	13	7	47	31.8
East Midlands	40	4	48	7	42	7.7	73	10	10	8	53	24.2
West Midlands	43	4	46	7	45	14.1	69	13	10	7	51	31.5
East	46	3	43	8	48	8.4	73	10	10	8	56	23.2
London	40	5	48	7	34	25.6	67	12	12	9	50	25.8
South East	49	4	40	7	45	9.7	79	7	6	8	55	29.4
South West	47	3	42	7	43	8.1	79	9	6	6	57	22.2
England	42	4	47	7	41	111.5	72	10	10	7	53	258.3
Wales	48	4	43	5	41	6.4	60	16	17	7	46	24.4
Scotland	..	..	..	..	..	..	..	..	..	..	..	..
Northern Ireland[1]	62	5	27	6	91	0.3	53	6	21	20	47	11.2

1 Schemes in Northern Ireland differ from those in England and Wales. See Notes and Definitions.
2 Work Based Learning for Young People data in England and Wales consist of Advanced Modern Apprenticeships (known as Modern Apprenticeships in Wales), Foundation Modern Apprenticeships (known as National Traineeships in Wales), Life Skills (Skill Build in Wales) and Other Training for Young People.
3 All those who left the programme during 2000/01.

Source: Department for Education and Skills; National Assembly for Wales; Northern Ireland Department for Employment and Learning

Chapter 5 **Labour Market**

Employment

Employment rates in the United Kingdom as a whole increased between spring 1999 and spring 2003, from 73.8 to 74.7 per cent. There were rises of around three or four percentage points in Wales, Scotland, Northern Ireland and the North East, while in London and the South East there were falls. The overall effect was to reduce disparities between the countries and regions of the UK. (Table 5.1)

The employment rate for males rose more than three percentage points between 1999 and 2003 in the North East, Scotland and Northern Ireland but fell by more than one percentage point in London and the South East. For females, there were rises of more than six percentage points in Wales and three in Scotland, but there was a fall of more than two percentage points in London. (Table 5.1)

The labour force

London and Northern Ireland both had relatively young labour forces in spring 2003, with around 42 per cent being less than 35 years old. Elsewhere in the UK, the under-35 section of the labour force made up around 36 to 38 per cent of the total. (Table 5.2)

In spring 2003, London was the region with the highest proportion of the working-age population in self-employment (10.6 per cent) and the lowest proportion working as part-time employees (11.6 per cent). In the South West, the proportion in self-employment was similar, at 10.5 per cent, but the proportion working as part-time employees was much higher, at 19.3 per cent. (Table 5.3)

Employee jobs

One in three employee jobs in London in December 2001 were in financial and business services compared with around one in nine in Wales. The proportion of employee jobs in manufacturing was highest in the East Midlands and West Midlands at around 20 per cent, while the lowest was in London at 6.5 per cent. (Table 5.4)

The highest numbers of self-employment and of employee jobs for both males and females in 2002 were in London and the South East. (Table 5.5)

Self-employed

In Northern Ireland in spring 2003, more than 20 per cent of self-employed people worked in agriculture and fishing, compared with fewer than 6 per cent in all English regions for which a reliable estimate could be made. (Table 5.6)

In London in spring 2003, around three-quarters of self-employed people worked in the services sector, while in Northern Ireland the figure was one in two. (Table 5.6)

Economic activity

Between spring 2000 and spring 2003, economic activity rates changed little in the United Kingdom, falling 0.5 per cent among males and remaining almost unchanged among females. However, disparities in rates between different areas of the UK were reduced over this period. (Table 5.7)

The regions with the highest rates of economic activity in spring 2000 (the South East and the South West) both showed lower rates in 2003. In contrast, there were relatively large increases in economic activity rates in Wales and Northern Ireland, which had the lowest rates in 2000. (Table 5.7)

Part-time working

The South West was the region with the highest proportions of part-time workers in spring 2003: among employees and the self-employed in this region, more than a half of females and more than one in eight males worked part-time. (Figure 5.8)

The proportion of men who said that the reason they were working part-time was because they could not find a full-time job was highest in the North East in spring 2003, at 27.4 per cent, more than two and a half times the proportion in the South East and East of England. Proportions for women were generally about one third of those for men, with the North East and Northern Ireland showing the highest rates, at 9.1 per cent, again around two and a half times the proportion in the South East and East of England. (Table 5.9)

Flexible working

In spring 2003, female employees in all areas of the UK were more likely to have flexible working patterns than male employees. Flexible working patterns among male employees were most common in Wales and Scotland, at 21 per cent, while for females the highest prevalence of employees with flexible working patterns was in the North East, at 30 per cent. (Figure 5.10)

Second jobs

Among people in employment in spring 2003, women in all areas of the UK were more likely than men to have a second job. The highest proportion of females with second jobs was in the South West, at 6.9 per cent, while for males the highest proportion was in Wales, at 4.3 per cent. (Table 5.11)

Hours of work

The highest average hours worked by full-time employees in spring 2003 were those in the East Midlands and the East of England at 43.7, while the lowest hours worked were in Northern Ireland, at 42.0. These figures are from the Labour Force Survey and include both paid and unpaid overtime. All parts of the UK tended to reflect the national pattern: with a few exceptions, the longest hours worked in each country and region were by people in three groups: managers and senior officials; professional occupations; and process, plant and machine operatives. (Table 5.12)

Figures from the New Earnings Survey 2002, which excludes unpaid overtime, show that for males the longest hours worked by full-time employees were in the East Midlands at 41.7 hours per week, and that for females the longest hours worked were in the South East at 37.9 hours per week. Shortest average hours for males were in London at 39.7 hours per week and for females in London and Northern Ireland, each at 37.2 hours per week. People in London also worked the least amount of paid overtime. (Table 5.17)

Labour disputes

Apart from in Scotland, the number of working days per 1,000 employees lost due to labour disputes was higher in 2002 in all countries and regions of the UK than in any of the four preceding years. The North East had the highest number of days lost per 1,000 employees in 2002, at 119, while the lowest rates were in the East, the South

West, Northern Ireland and the South East, at between 26 and 36 days per 1,000 employees. (Table 5.13)

Sickness absence

Sickness absence from work in spring 2003 was highest among employees in the South East and in Scotland and lowest in Northern Ireland. (Figure 5.14)

Trade unions

Trade union membership rates among employees in autumn 2002 were highest in Northern Ireland, Wales and the North East, each at more than 38 per cent. Lowest rates of membership were in the South East, the East of England and London, at below 25 per cent. (Table 5.15)

Earnings

In industrial sectors where average weekly earnings for full-time employees could be reliably estimated, rates for males in April 2002 varied from £965 in financial and business services in London to £251 in agriculture, forestry, fishing and hunting in Northern Ireland. For females, earnings varied from £602 in financial and business services in London to £235 in distribution, hotels, catering and repairs in Wales. (Table 5.16)

Average weekly earnings for full-time employees in the UK in April 2002 stood at £463 (£511 for males and £382 for females). Only two regions were above the UK average: London at £624 and the South East at £497. The lowest rates for males were in Northern Ireland at £423 and Wales at £433, while for females the lowest rates were in the North East at £332 and the East Midlands at £335. (Tables 5.16 and 5.17)

Unemployment

Between spring 1999 and spring 2003, unemployment rates fell in all countries and regions of the UK, except in the South East (where there was a fall to 3.2 in 2001, but a rise to 3.9 by 2003). The largest falls were in the North East (down 3.5 percentage points to 6.6 per cent) and in Wales (down 2.8 percentage points to 4.6 per cent). (Table 5.18)

The highest unemployment rates in the UK in spring 2003 were in London at 7.1 per cent and the North East at 6.6 per cent. The lowest rates were in the South East and South West, each at 3.9 per cent. (Table 5.18)

Average unemployment rates for 16- to 24-year-olds in 2002/03 ranged from less than 10 per cent in the South East and South West to more than 15 per cent in London and the North East. (Table 5.20)

In areas where a reliable estimate could be made, the proportion of unemployed people in spring 2003 who had been unemployed for six months or more was lowest in the South East, South West and East of England. For males, the proportion was less than 34 per cent in each region, while for females it was less than 26 per cent. The highest proportion for males was in the North West at more than 46 per cent and for females was in the North West and the East Midlands, each at more than 36 per cent. (Table 5.23)

For working-age people with no qualifications, unemployment rates in spring 2003 varied from 5.5 per cent in the East of England to around 12 per cent in London and the North East. (Table 5.24)

Claimant count

Workplace-based claimant count rates fell in all parts of the United Kingdom between 1998 and 2002, from a fall of 2.8 percentage points in Northern Ireland to a fall of 0.9 in the South East. Claimant count rates in 2002 ranged from 1.7 per cent in the South East to 5.2 per cent in the North East. (Table 5.19)

Of those claiming unemployment-related benefits in the UK in March 2003, London had the lowest proportion aged 50 or over, at around 13 per cent. Regions with the highest proportions aged 50 or over were the South West, East and South East of England, each at over 19 per cent. (Table 5.21)

Claimant count rates (residence-based) in March 2003 varied from 0.7 per cent in the Ribble Valley (Lancashire), Rutland and North Dorset to 6.2 per cent in the Inner London boroughs of Hackney and Tower Hamlets. The long-term claimant count proportion, i.e. those claiming for more than 12 months, varied from 1.5 per cent in Rutland to more than 30 per cent in the Isle of Anglesey, Fermanagh and Strabane. (Map 5.22)

Redundancies

Redundancy rates in spring 2003 in London were just over half of the rates in the South East, North West and West Midlands. (Figure 5.25)

New Deal

Between 2000 and 2002, the number of starts on the New Deal for young unemployed people aged 18 to 24 fell in all countries and regions of Great Britain except in London and the West Midlands. Of young people starting on the New Deal, the highest female proportion was in London, at around one in three of the total. (Table 5.27)

Economic inactivity

More than four fifths of economically inactive people of working age in Northern Ireland in spring 2003 said that the reason they were inactive was because they did not want a job. In Scotland, the corresponding figure was much lower, at 65 per cent. (Table 5.28)

Jobs density

Jobs density is defined as the number of filled jobs in an area divided by the number of working-age people resident in that area. Across the UK as a whole, there were just over 0.8 jobs per person of working age in 2001. Around 50 local authorities had at least one job per person of working age. But only three had more than one and a half jobs per person: City of London (60.1), Westminster (4.56) and Camden (2.05). (Map 5.29)

Table **5.1**   Labour force and employment rates[1]

Thousands and percentages

	Labour force (thousands)					Employment rates[2] (percentages)				
	1999	2000	2001	2002	2003	1999	2000	2001	2002	2003
Males										
United Kingdom	15,485	15,590	15,594	15,652	15,774	78.7	79.4	79.5	79.0	79.4
North East	611	630	625	603	615	68.7	71.8	72.9	70.4	72.3
North West	1,711	1,738	1,706	1,685	1,729	75.4	78.1	76.2	75.0	77.6
Yorkshire and the Humber	1,284	1,291	1,270	1,288	1,308	77.0	78.0	77.5	77.9	78.5
East Midlands	1,120	1,134	1,125	1,133	1,141	80.6	81.4	80.9	81.1	81.2
West Midlands	1,408	1,384	1,398	1,412	1,410	78.8	78.1	79.5	79.6	78.6
East	1,471	1,471	1,490	1,491	1,486	84.1	84.0	85.0	84.7	83.7
London	1,968	1,995	2,044	2,089	2,095	77.7	77.5	78.2	77.8	76.6
South East	2,214	2,224	2,217	2,234	2,217	86.0	85.9	85.6	85.1	83.9
South West	1,291	1,299	1,295	1,300	1,304	82.7	83.2	83.1	82.4	82.4
England	13,078	13,165	13,172	13,233	13,303	79.7	80.3	80.4	79.9	79.8
Wales	705	708	690	703	710	72.4	73.9	72.5	73.7	74.8
Scotland	1,297	1,320	1,317	1,308	1,325	74.3	75.7	77.1	75.8	78.1
Northern Ireland	405	403	417	410	431	72.3	71.9	74.4	73.3	76.9
Females										
United Kingdom	12,477	12,616	12,679	12,800	12,864	68.6	69.1	69.5	69.6	69.8
North East	504	510	510	525	501	62.1	63.7	64.7	66.9	63.9
North West	1,371	1,390	1,425	1,428	1,433	66.4	66.9	69.0	68.5	68.7
Yorkshire and the Humber	1,032	1,053	1,056	1,043	1,065	68.0	69.2	69.3	67.8	69.4
East Midlands	901	918	901	918	914	71.1	72.0	70.1	71.4	70.6
West Midlands	1,113	1,103	1,098	1,110	1,117	68.6	68.1	68.6	68.4	69.1
East	1,157	1,165	1,204	1,197	1,206	71.5	72.1	73.8	73.3	72.8
London	1,579	1,595	1,578	1,609	1,606	65.6	65.4	64.2	64.3	63.5
South East	1,769	1,809	1,803	1,826	1,824	73.0	74.7	74.4	74.5	74.4
South West	1,059	1,070	1,082	1,094	1,094	73.4	73.9	74.6	75.4	74.6
England	10,486	10,611	10,657	10,750	10,760	69.1	69.8	70.0	70.1	69.8
Wales	566	575	567	570	624	64.7	65.1	63.9	63.6	71.0
Scotland	1,104	1,121	1,132	1,155	1,149	67.8	68.7	70.3	70.7	70.9
Northern Ireland	322	308	318	328	330	61.6	58.6	60.6	62.2	62.1
All people										
United Kingdom	27,961	28,206	28,272	28,451	28,638	73.8	74.4	74.7	74.5	74.7
North East	1,115	1,139	1,135	1,127	1,116	65.5	67.9	68.9	68.7	68.2
North West	3,082	3,127	3,131	3,113	3,162	71.0	72.6	72.7	71.8	73.3
Yorkshire and the Humber	2,316	2,344	2,326	2,331	2,373	72.6	73.8	73.5	73.0	74.1
East Midlands	2,021	2,052	2,026	2,051	2,054	76.0	76.9	75.7	76.5	76.1
West Midlands	2,522	2,487	2,496	2,522	2,527	73.9	73.3	74.3	74.3	74.0
East	2,627	2,635	2,694	2,688	2,692	78.0	78.3	79.6	79.2	78.5
London	3,547	3,590	3,623	3,698	3,701	71.7	71.6	71.4	71.2	70.3
South East	3,983	4,033	4,021	4,060	4,041	79.7	80.5	80.2	80.0	79.3
South West	2,350	2,369	2,378	2,394	2,397	78.2	78.7	79.0	79.0	78.6
England	23,564	23,777	23,829	23,984	24,063	74.6	75.2	75.4	75.1	75.0
Wales	1,272	1,282	1,258	1,273	1,334	68.7	69.6	68.3	68.8	73.0
Scotland	2,401	2,441	2,449	2,463	2,475	71.1	72.2	73.8	73.3	74.6
Northern Ireland	727	712	735	738	761	67.0	65.4	67.7	67.9	69.7

1 At spring of each year, seasonally adjusted. Based on the population of working age in private households, student halls of residence and NHS accommodation. These data
have been adjusted to reflect the 2001 Census population estimates. See Notes and Definitions.
2 Total in employment as a percentage of all people of working age in each area.

Source: Labour Force Survey, Office for National Statistics

Table 5.2 Labour force:[1] by age, spring 2003[2]

Percentages and thousands

	Percentage aged:					All ages (=100%) (thousands)
	16 to 24	25 to 34	35 to 49	Males 50 to 64/ females 50 to 59	Males 65 or over/ females 60 or over	
United Kingdom	15.0	22.8	37.5	21.5	3.1	29,455
North East	16.2	21.1	39.9	21.0	1.8	1,131
North West	15.6	22.6	37.4	21.9	2.6	3,240
Yorkshire and the Humber	16.2	21.4	38.1	21.7	2.5	2,420
East Midlands	14.6	21.3	37.9	23.0	3.2	2,112
West Midlands	15.4	21.4	37.7	22.6	2.9	2,587
East	14.1	23.0	36.4	23.0	3.5	2,789
London	13.6	28.3	38.0	17.2	2.9	3,796
South East	14.1	22.3	37.2	22.5	3.9	4,206
South West	15.0	21.1	36.6	23.3	4.1	2,487
England	14.8	22.9	37.5	21.6	3.2	24,770
Wales	16.4	21.1	37.3	22.0	3.3	1,370
Scotland	15.9	21.9	38.7	20.7	2.8	2,528
Northern Ireland	17.4	25.0	35.7	18.8	3.2	782

1 The labour force includes those in employment and unemployment. See Notes and Definitions.
2 Not seasonally adjusted. The percentage figures in this table are based on data that have not been adjusted to take account of the Census 2001 population estimates. However, the totals figures in the final column have been adjusted in line with the Census population estimates.

Source: Labour Force Survey, Office for National Statistics

Table 5.3 Employment status and rates, spring 2003[1]

Percentages and thousands

	In employment				Econom- ically active[3]	Econom- ically inactive	All of working age[4] (=100%) (thousands)	Unemploy- ment rate[5]
	Employees							
	Full- time	Part- time	Self- employed	Total[2]				
United Kingdom	49.7	15.9	8.6	74.7	78.6	21.4	36,366	4.9
North East	46.4	15.9	5.2	68.1	73.0	27.0	1,529	6.7
North West	50.2	15.3	7.4	73.4	77.2	22.8	4,096	4.9
Yorkshire and the Humber	49.2	17.2	7.2	74.1	78.3	21.7	3,028	5.4
East Midlands	50.8	16.6	8.0	75.9	79.1	20.9	2,584	4.1
West Midlands	50.7	15.8	6.9	74.0	78.4	21.6	3,214	5.6
East	52.3	16.4	9.7	78.7	82.0	18.0	3,286	4.0
London	47.7	11.6	10.6	70.3	75.3	24.7	4,894	6.7
South East	51.3	17.4	10.5	79.5	82.6	17.4	4,898	3.8
South West	48.4	19.3	10.5	78.4	81.4	18.6	2,931	3.7
England	49.8	16.0	8.8	75.0	78.9	21.1	30,461	4.9
Wales	47.5	15.6	8.9	72.6	76.1	23.9	1,745	4.6
Scotland	50.4	16.6	7.0	74.3	78.6	21.4	3,129	5.5
Northern Ireland	46.6	13.6	8.0	69.5	73.4	26.6	1,033	5.3

1 For people of working age only. Not seasonally adjusted. The percentage figures in this table are based on data that have not been adjusted to take account of the Census 2001 population estimates. However, the totals figures in the penultimate column have been adjusted in line with the Census population estimates.
2 Total in employment also includes those on government-supported employment and training schemes and unpaid family workers.
3 The economically active population consists of people in employment and people who are unemployed according to the ILO definition. See Notes and Definitions.
4 Based on the population of men aged 16 to 64 and women aged 16 to 59 in private households, student halls of residence and NHS accommodation. See Notes and Definitions.
5 The unemployment rate shown here is the number of unemployed people of working age as a percentage of the economically active population in the area. Other percentage figures in this table are percentages of the working-age population.

Source: Labour Force Survey, Office for National Statistics

Table **5.4**   Employee jobs: by industry[1] and sex, December 2001

Percentages and thousands

	Agriculture, hunting, forestry and fishing	Mining, quarrying (inc oil and gas extraction)	Manu-facturing	Electricity, gas, water	Construction	Distribution, hotels and catering, repairs	Transport, storage and commun-ication	Financial and business services	Public adminis-tration and defence	Education, social work and health services	Other	Whole economy (=100%) (thousands)
Males												
Great Britain	1.3	0.5	20.2	0.8	7.6	22.1	8.8	20.2	5.2	8.4	5.0	12,996
North East	0.8	0.6	24.6	0.9	10.3	17.9	7.8	14.8	6.7	10.0	5.4	492
North West	0.8	0.2	23.6	0.8	7.9	22.7	8.5	16.7	5.3	9.2	4.2	1,479
Yorkshire and the Humber	1.2	0.6	26.2	0.9	8.7	21.2	8.9	13.7	4.9	9.2	4.5	1,070
East Midlands	1.8	0.7	28.5	0.8	8.4	21.0	8.3	14.4	4.4	8.0	3.6	901
West Midlands	1.2	0.2	28.8	0.9	7.0	21.6	8.1	15.7	4.5	7.7	4.4	1,203
East	2.0	0.2	20.6	0.8	8.1	23.1	9.3	19.5	4.0	7.6	4.6	1,154
London	0.1	0.1	8.0	0.3	5.4	22.0	10.9	34.3	5.0	7.0	6.9	2,117
South East	1.4	0.2	16.1	0.7	7.0	24.3	8.5	24.5	4.6	7.8	4.9	1,837
South West	2.0	0.6	21.0	1.0	7.6	23.6	7.5	17.1	6.1	9.2	4.3	1,055
England	1.2	0.3	20.2	0.7	7.4	22.3	8.9	20.9	5.0	8.2	4.9	11,308
Wales	2.0	0.5	25.8	1.0	8.1	20.3	6.9	11.7	7.1	11.9	4.8	542
Scotland	2.5	1.8	18.2	1.2	9.0	20.6	8.3	17.1	6.2	9.4	5.6	1,146
Females												
Great Britain	0.6	0.1	7.8	0.3	1.3	26.5	3.4	19.0	5.2	30.3	5.5	12,460
North East	0.3	0.1	8.0	0.2	1.7	25.7	3.1	12.0	7.2	36.1	5.6	482
North West	0.4	0.1	8.8	0.4	1.2	27.3	3.1	15.7	5.8	32.4	4.9	1,408
Yorkshire and the Humber	0.5	0.1	9.2	0.2	1.3	27.3	2.8	14.7	4.9	33.8	5.2	1,015
East Midlands	0.9	0.1	11.8	0.3	1.5	27.1	2.6	14.0	5.0	31.4	5.2	854
West Midlands	0.6	-	10.2	0.3	1.4	26.4	2.9	16.4	5.0	31.9	4.8	1,111
East	1.0	0.1	8.0	0.3	1.7	28.1	3.8	18.7	4.1	29.2	5.0	1,117
London	0.1	-	4.8	0.1	1.1	22.5	4.8	31.6	5.1	22.5	7.3	1,897
South East	0.9	0.1	6.1	0.3	1.4	27.2	3.7	21.9	4.2	28.6	5.6	1,819
South West	0.8	0.1	7.5	0.3	1.3	28.9	2.8	16.7	5.0	31.9	4.8	1,045
England	0.6	0.1	7.8	0.3	1.4	26.5	3.5	19.6	5.0	29.8	5.5	10,749
Wales	0.6	0.1	9.0	0.3	1.2	27.2	2.2	11.0	6.6	36.9	4.9	548
Scotland	0.9	0.4	7.4	0.5	1.1	26.3	3.0	17.1	6.5	31.3	5.6	1,163
All persons												
Great Britain	1.0	0.3	14.2	0.5	4.5	24.3	6.1	19.6	5.2	19.1	5.2	25,456
North East	0.6	0.4	16.4	0.6	6.0	21.8	5.5	13.4	7.0	23.0	5.5	974
North West	0.6	0.1	16.4	0.6	4.6	24.9	5.9	16.2	5.6	20.5	4.6	2,887
Yorkshire and the Humber	0.9	0.4	17.9	0.6	5.1	24.2	5.9	14.2	4.9	21.2	4.8	2,085
East Midlands	1.4	0.4	20.4	0.6	5.1	24.0	5.6	14.2	4.7	19.4	4.4	1,756
West Midlands	0.9	0.1	19.9	0.6	4.3	23.9	5.6	16.0	4.8	19.3	4.6	2,314
East	1.5	0.2	14.4	0.6	4.9	25.6	6.6	19.1	4.1	18.2	4.8	2,271
London	0.1	0.1	6.5	0.2	3.3	22.2	8.0	33.0	5.1	14.4	7.1	4,015
South East	1.1	0.1	11.1	0.5	4.2	25.8	6.1	23.2	4.4	18.1	5.2	3,656
South West	1.4	0.3	14.3	0.7	4.5	26.2	5.1	16.9	5.6	20.5	4.5	2,099
England	0.9	0.2	14.1	0.5	4.5	24.4	6.3	20.3	5.0	18.7	5.2	22,057
Wales	1.3	0.3	17.3	0.6	4.6	23.8	4.5	11.3	6.9	24.5	4.9	1,091
Scotland	1.7	1.1	12.7	0.8	5.0	23.4	5.6	17.1	6.4	20.4	5.6	2,309

1 Based on Standard Industrial Classification 1992. See Notes and Definitions for the Industry and Agriculture chapter.

Source: Annual Business Inquiry, Office for National Statistics

Table **5.5**   Employee jobs and self-employment jobs[1]: by sex

Thousands

| | Employee jobs | | | | | | Self-employment jobs[2] | | | | | |
| | Males | | | Females | | | Males | | | Females | | |
	2000	2001	2002	2000	2001	2002	2000	2001	2002	2000	2001	2002
United Kingdom	12,973	13,087	12,987	12,769	12,817	12,853	2,346	2,392	2,452	953	914	961
North East	480	471	488	494	475	478	63	58	66	28	23	21
North West	1,420	1,467	1,457	1,417	1,413	1,416	220	236	241	84	69	82
Yorkshire and the Humber	1,052	1,034	1,031	1,040	1,038	1,043	178	175	181	63	57	68
East Midlands	874	869	854	883	885	882	157	165	168	61	58	57
West Midlands	1,190	1,165	1,166	1,095	1,121	1,136	182	193	183	70	68	71
East	1,136	1,164	1,131	1,085	1,107	1,113	248	247	260	103	93	104
London	2,076	2,123	2,078	1,954	1,909	1,892	328	331	344	153	154	151
South East	1,821	1,817	1,784	1,789	1,771	1,798	372	377	397	166	167	169
South West	967	1,013	1,041	1,039	1,067	1,055	242	250	246	109	106	108
England	11,016	11,123	11,030	10,796	10,786	10,813	1,989	2,033	2,088	835	795	830
Wales	513	536	524	569	541	551	113	106	114	44	36	48
Scotland	1,125	1,107	1,110	1,080	1,159	1,150	166	173	176	59	66	68
Northern Ireland	319	320	324	324	331	339	78	79	74	15	16	15

1 At September each year. See Notes and Definitions.
2 With or without employees.

Source: Short-term Employment and Labour Force Surveys, Office for National Statistics; Quarterly Employment and Labour Force Surveys, Department of Economic Development, Northern Ireland

Table **5.6**   Self-employment:[1] by broad industry group[2], spring 2003[3]

Percentages and thousands

| | Agriculture and fishing | Industry | | | | Services | Total self-employed[5] (=100%) (thousands) |
		Manufacturing	Construction	All industry[4]			
United Kingdom	5.3	6.3	22.7	29.2	65.5	3,337
North East	..	..	22.4	30.4	63.8	82
North West	..	4.8	25.0	30.1	67.6	321
Yorkshire and the Humber	5.7	5.3	24.2	29.5	64.8	223
East Midlands	5.9	8.9	23.3	32.4	61.7	222
West Midlands	5.3	6.2	26.2	32.5	62.2	236
East	5.6	6.4	26.2	32.6	61.8	339
London	..	6.5	17.4	23.9	75.6	547
South East	2.9	6.9	24.9	32.2	64.9	548
South West	5.9	6.5	23.6	30.4	63.7	331
England	3.8	6.5	23.3	30.0	66.2	2,849
Wales	16.9	..	20.7	26.0	57.0	166
Scotland	9.2	6.1	15.4	22.2	68.6	231
Northern Ireland	21.0	..	25.6	28.8	50.2	91

1 Main job only.
2 Based on Standard Industrial Classification 1992. In some cases, sample sizes are too small to provide a reliable estimate.
3 Not seasonally adjusted. The percentage figures in this table are based on data that have not been adjusted to take account of the Census 2001 population estimates. However, the totals figures in the final column have been adjusted in line with the Census population estimates.
4 Includes Standard Industrial Classification groups C and E: Quarrying, Energy and Water.
5 Total includes those who did not state their industry and those whose workplace is outside the United Kingdom, but percentages are based on figures which exclude them.

Source: Labour Force Survey, Office for National Statistics

Table **5.7** Economic activity rates:[1] by sex

Percentages

	Males				Females				All people			
	2000	2001	2002	2003	2000	2001	2002	2003	2000	2001	2002	2003
United Kingdom	84.6	84.1	83.9	84.1	72.9	72.8	73.0	73.0	79.0	78.6	78.6	78.8
North East	80.1	79.6	76.8	78.4	68.8	68.8	70.6	67.3	74.6	74.4	73.8	73.0
North West	83.0	81.4	80.2	82.2	70.5	72.1	71.9	71.9	77.0	76.9	76.2	77.2
Yorkshire and the Humber	84.0	82.2	82.9	84.0	73.0	72.6	71.2	72.4	78.6	77.6	77.3	78.4
East Midlands	86.3	85.1	85.0	85.1	75.6	73.7	74.4	73.5	81.1	79.6	79.9	79.5
West Midlands	83.7	84.4	84.7	84.3	72.4	71.8	72.2	72.4	78.3	78.3	78.7	78.6
East	87.5	88.2	88.0	87.3	74.6	76.7	76.0	76.1	81.3	82.7	82.2	81.9
London	84.0	83.7	83.9	82.9	70.1	68.2	68.7	67.9	77.2	76.2	76.5	75.6
South East	89.0	88.3	88.8	87.6	77.5	76.9	77.6	77.0	83.5	82.8	83.4	82.5
South West	87.1	86.3	86.2	86.0	77.1	77.4	77.7	77.3	82.3	82.0	82.1	81.8
England	85.3	84.7	84.6	84.5	73.5	73.3	73.4	73.1	79.6	79.2	79.2	79.0
Wales	79.7	77.7	78.9	79.5	68.9	67.6	67.4	73.3	74.5	72.8	73.3	76.5
Scotland	83.0	82.8	82.1	83.1	73.3	73.8	75.2	74.9	78.3	78.4	78.7	79.1
Northern Ireland	78.3	80.2	78.1	81.6	62.4	63.9	65.4	65.4	70.5	72.2	71.9	73.7

1 At spring of each year, seasonally adjusted. Based on the population of working age in private households, student halls of residence and NHS accommodation. These data have been adjusted to reflect the 2001 Census population estimates. See Notes and Definitions.

Source: Labour Force Survey, Office for National Statistics

Figure **5.8** Part-time[1] working: by sex, spring 2003[2]

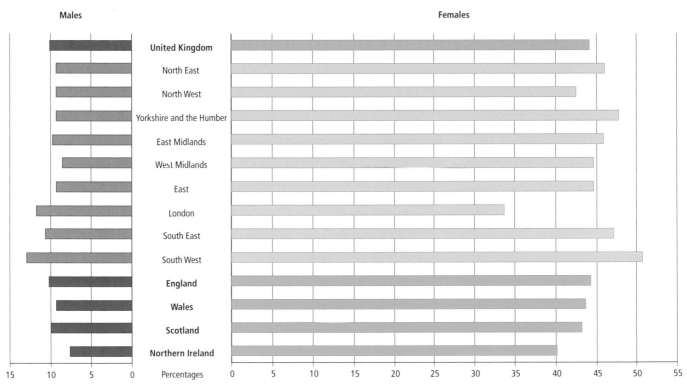

1 Part-time workers as a percentage of all in employment (employees and the self-employed only). Based on respondents' own definition of part-time.
2 These data are not seasonally adjusted and have not been adjusted in line with the Census 2001 population estimates.

Source: Labour Force Survey, Office for National Statistics

Table **5.9**   **Reasons given for working part-time,[1] spring 2003[2]**

Percentages and thousands

	Males				Females			
	Did not want a full-time job	Could not find a full-time job	Student or at school	All part-time workers[3,4] (=100%) (thousands)	Did not want a full-time job	Could not find a full-time job	Student or at school	All part-time workers[3,4] (=100%) (thousands)
United Kingdom	46.3	16.1	33.3	1,591	80.8	5.8	11.9	5,647
North East	34.3	27.4	30.3	56	79.2	9.1	10.9	225
North West	43.0	20.1	33.4	162	82.0	6.5	10.4	608
Yorkshire and the Humber	44.8	18.0	31.9	123	81.6	6.7	10.5	502
East Midlands	51.9	13.4	31.8	112	84.1	4.5	10.3	416
West Midlands	46.6	17.8	30.6	118	79.8	6.6	11.3	490
East	52.8	10.5	31.5	142	85.4	3.7	9.7	551
London	43.8	18.6	35.0	237	74.5	7.2	17.1	517
South East	52.1	10.0	34.0	240	83.1	3.2	12.0	893
South West	51.2	13.9	31.4	173	82.0	4.4	11.8	565
England	47.6	15.7	32.7	1,363	81.6	5.4	11.6	4,767
Wales[5]	50.6	..	30.4	67	77.9	6.9	13.1	268
Scotland	33.1	20.9	41.9	130	75.8	8.7	13.9	483
Northern Ireland[5]	34.4	..	32.4	31	76.8	9.1	13.3	129

1 Based on respondents' own definition of part-time.
2 Not seasonally adjusted. The data in this table have not been adjusted to take account of the Census 2001 population estimates.
3 Employees and the self-employed only.
4 Includes people who said they worked part-time because they were ill or disabled. Hence percentages shown do not add to 100 per cent. In addition, the totals (thousands) figures include those who did not state a reason for working part-time, while percentages are based on figures which exclude them.
5 Some sample sizes are too small to provide reliable estimates.

Source: Labour Force Survey, Office for National Statistics

Figure **5.10** **Employees with flexible working patterns:[1] by sex, spring 2003[2]**

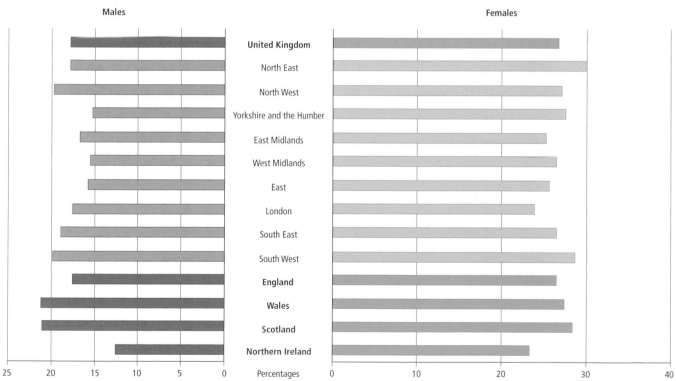

1 Includes those on flexi-time, annualised hours, term-time working, job sharing, nine day fortnight, four and a half day week and zero hours contract (not contracted to work a set number of hours but paid for the actual number of hours worked).
2 These data are not seasonally adjusted and have not been adjusted in line with the Census 2001 population estimates.

Source: Labour Force Survey, Office for National Statistics; Department of Economic Development, Northern Ireland

Table **5.11** People in employment with a second job: by sex, spring 2003[1]

Thousands and percentages

	People with a second job (thousands)			As a percentage of all in employment		
	Males	Females	All people	Males	Females	All people
United Kingdom	463	687	1,150	3.1	5.3	4.1
North East	10	20	30	1.8	4.1	2.8
North West	48	55	103	2.9	3.8	3.3
Yorkshire and the Humber	35	67	101	2.8	6.3	4.4
East Midlands	30	56	87	2.7	6.1	4.2
West Midlands	38	57	94	2.8	5.1	3.8
East	40	64	105	2.8	5.3	3.9
London	55	71	126	2.8	4.5	3.5
South East	72	110	182	3.3	5.9	4.5
South West	50	77	127	3.9	6.9	5.3
England	378	577	955	2.9	5.4	4.0
Wales	29	31	61	4.3	4.9	4.6
Scotland	43	62	105	3.4	5.5	4.4
Northern Ireland	13	16	29	3.1	5.0	3.9

1 Not seasonally adjusted. The percentage figures in this table are based on data that have not been adjusted to take account of the Census 2001 population estimates. However, the totals figures in the first three columns have been adjusted in line with the Census population estimates.

Source: Labour Force Survey, Office for National Statistics

Table **5.12** Average usual weekly hours[1] of work of full-time employees: by occupational group, spring 2003[2]

Hours

	Managers & senior officials	Professional occupations	Associate professional & technical	Administrative & secretarial	Skilled trades occupations	Personal service occupations	Sales & customer service occupations	Process, plant & machine operatives	Elementary occupations	All occu-pations[3]
United Kingdom	46.3	45.0	42.2	38.8	44.0	39.5	40.0	45.3	42.6	43.2
North East	44.6	44.6	42.1	39.1	43.8	39.6	39.8	45.0	42.1	42.7
North West	45.6	44.7	41.0	38.1	42.7	39.3	39.2	44.9	41.5	42.3
Yorkshire and the Humber	46.6	45.6	42.3	39.0	44.3	39.9	40.5	45.9	42.7	43.5
East Midlands	47.1	45.6	42.4	39.0	45.0	38.6	41.1	45.1	43.1	43.7
West Midlands	45.8	45.6	41.8	38.8	43.4	39.3	40.2	44.1	41.8	42.9
East	46.6	45.0	42.5	39.0	45.1	39.3	40.2	46.5	43.3	43.7
London	46.3	45.0	42.7	39.1	44.4	40.9	40.5	45.6	43.0	43.4
South East	46.7	45.1	42.4	39.1	44.6	39.8	40.1	45.9	42.8	43.6
South West	47.0	45.3	42.6	38.3	43.7	39.1	40.1	45.4	43.1	43.4
England	46.4	45.1	42.2	38.8	44.1	39.6	40.1	45.3	42.6	43.3
Wales	45.1	44.0	41.6	37.8	43.1	39.3	39.2	44.4	43.2	42.4
Scotland	46.1	44.4	42.2	38.9	43.9	38.2	39.6	46.4	42.8	43.0
Northern Ireland	44.2	42.7	41.0	39.3	43.7	39.9	38.9	44.0	41.9	42.0

1 Includes paid and unpaid overtime and excludes meal breaks. The table excludes those who did not state the number of hours they worked.
2 These data are not seasonally adjusted and have not been adjusted in line with the Census 2001 population estimates.
3 Includes those whose workplace is outside the United Kingdom, and those who did not specify their occupation.

Source: Labour Force Survey, Office for National Statistics

Table **5.13**   **Working days lost due to labour disputes**[1]

Days lost per 1,000 employees

	1998	1999	2000	2001	2002
United Kingdom	11	10	20	20	51
North East	9	3	6	12	119
North West	9	4	20	32	76
Yorkshire and the Humber	1	11	4	24	44
East Midlands	1	1	5	8	50
West Midlands	7	1	20	33	41
East	11	2	6	11	26
London	12	15	7	24	60
South East	1	4	4	4	36
South West	1	2	1	8	32
England	6	5	8	17	54
Wales	2	4	6	17	74
Scotland	23	21	136	29	54
Northern Ireland	6	10	33	1	34

1 Regional rates are based on data for stoppages that exclude widespread disputes that cannot be allocated to a specific region. These are included in the United Kingdom strike rate only. See Notes and Definitions.

Source: Office for National Statistics

Figure **5.14**   **Employees absent due to sickness,**[1] **spring 2003**[2]

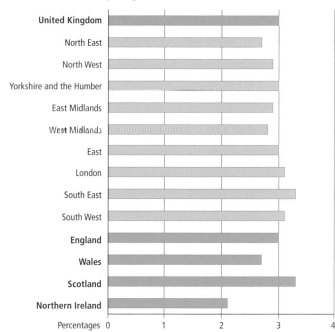

1 Percentages of employees absent from work due to illness or injury for at least one day in the week before interview.
2 These data are not seasonally adjusted and have not been adjusted in line with the Census 2001 population estimates.

Source: Labour Force Survey, Office for National Statistics

Table **5.15** Trade union membership, autumn 2002[1]

Percentages[2]

	Public Sector			Private sector			
	Males	Females	All public sector employees	Males	Females	All private sector employees	All employees[3]
United Kingdom	64.0	57.2	59.6	21.5	13.6	18.2	28.9
North East	71.1	67.2	68.5	31.8	16.1	25.3	38.2
North West	69.9	59.3	63.2	28.0	16.6	23.3	34.2
Yorkshire and the Humber	68.3	58.9	62.0	24.6	17.3	21.7	32.3
East Midlands	66.2	59.8	62.0	21.3	13.7	18.1	28.3
West Midlands	60.2	57.1	58.2	24.3	14.7	20.5	29.8
East	51.8	49.0	50.0	17.2	10.3	14.3	22.5
London	65.0	55.1	59.0	14.9	11.1	13.4	24.9
South East	55.2	47.3	50.2	15.2	10.6	13.2	21.4
South West	57.6	51.2	53.4	20.2	11.5	16.4	25.5
England	62.5	55.2	57.8	20.8	13.1	17.6	27.5
Wales	68.9	68.9	68.9	28.6	17.7	24.2	38.9
Scotland	69.3	63.1	65.3	22.8	16.6	20.2	33.8
Northern Ireland	73.5	68.8	70.7	28.1	17.9	23.9	40.8

1 These data are not seasonally adjusted and have not been adjusted in line with the Census 2001 population estimates.

2 As a percentage of all employees in each region, excluding the armed forces and those who did not say whether they belonged to a trade union.

3 Includes some people who did not state whether they were in the public or private sector.

Source: Labour Force Survey, Office for National Statistics

Table 5.16 Average weekly earnings:[1] by industry[2] and sex, April 2002

£ per week

	Whole economy			Agriculture, forestry, fishing & hunting		Manufacturing	
	Males	Females	All people	Males	Females	Males	Females
United Kingdom	511.3	382.1	462.6	338.5	278.7	480.9	349.7
North East	439.1	332.1	399.3	..	..	431.0	304.6
North West	471.1	354.3	426.8	..	..	482.3	339.0
Yorkshire and the Humber	447.1	345.0	409.9	..	..	443.4	308.3
East Midlands	454.2	334.8	413.0	..	..	449.4	299.4
West Midlands	469.6	353.0	427.3	..	..	452.6	311.4
East	506.3	375.1	459.6	328.6	..	505.0	..
London	704.8	503.6	624.1	..	..	627.5	516.3
South East	555.3	398.6	496.7	369.5	..	565.0	399.2
South West	463.3	350.0	421.7	315.1	..	475.5	354.6
England	521.3	388.0	471.7	345.8	277.0	487.8	358.5
Wales	432.9	345.1	399.7	..	..	432.9	292.9
Scotland	473.7	360.1	427.0	334.9	..	474.6	314.6
Northern Ireland	422.5	340.9	390.1	251.3	..	378.8	284.3

	Mining, quarrying & electricity, gas, water		Construction		Distribution, hotels & catering, repairs		Transport, storage & communication	
	Males	Females	Males	Females	Males	Females	Males	Females
United Kingdom	588.1	408.6	477.5	355.9	432.7	300.7	458.6	390.4
North East	550.0	..	439.1	..	376.7	248.2	388.2	..
North West	..	..	451.8	296.3	399.1	287.3	425.3	342.0
Yorkshire and the Humber	512.8	..	445.5	..	397.8	276.2	418.8	335.8
East Midlands	523.7	..	459.4	..	425.3	279.6	404.6	318.1
West Midlands	..	..	451.5	..	425.5	280.4	401.7	..
East	..	..	511.2	..	445.7	302.4	473.5	378.8
London	..	..	610.1	..	493.7	375.4	560.3	497.0
South East	..	..	531.2	..	502.4	354.8	480.0	386.5
South West	..	..	439.3	..	394.2	259.2	430.6	..
England	581.5	416.5	488.2	360.6	441.2	309.3	465.7	394.6
Wales	..	..	396.1	..	349.4	234.8	394.6	337.1
Scotland	..	..	456.6	..	391.3	261.5	416.6	376.2
Northern Ireland	479.5	..	366.5	277.4	350.6	237.2	399.9	314.7

	Financial & business services		Public administration & defence		Education, social work & health services		Other	
	Males	Females	Males	Females	Males	Females	Males	Females
United Kingdom	668.7	430.3	490.4	369.1	509.1	402.9	514.6	369.7
North East	..	339.1	396.7	325.0	477.5	367.7	..	..
North West	535.7	367.9	467.1	343.7	489.9	390.6	..	283.0
Yorkshire and the Humber	497.5	350.4	466.8	364.1	482.8	385.6	394.5	285.4
East Midlands	496.2	348.3	463.3	372.5	499.3	381.1	363.8	262.5
West Midlands	544.0	372.9	465.4	355.2	519.7	390.3	..	..
East	593.5	376.9	495.9	364.5	511.6	408.3	444.3	312.0
London	964.5	601.6	606.9	464.0	595.4	470.9	648.6	503.3
South East	675.4	433.2	487.1	373.8	530.5	405.0	..	350.9
South West	527.6	364.8	467.2	348.3	488.3	379.9	407.6	..
England	684.9	441.4	495.7	374.1	517.0	403.6	523.5	377.7
Wales	..	335.4	445.0	364.4	481.4	387.9	356.2	..
Scotland	563.2	357.4	468.9	365.1	471.8	399.9	..	319.4
Northern Ireland	505.2	321.3	500.6	320.1	518.6	420.5	379.5	298.6

1 Average gross weekly earnings. Data relate to full-time employees on adult rates whose pay for the survey pay-period was not affected by absence. See Notes and Definitions.
2 Classification is based on Standard Industrial Classification 1992.

Source: New Earnings Survey, Office for National Statistics; Department of Enterprise, Trade and Investment, Northern Ireland

Table 5.17 Average weekly earnings and hours: by sex, April 2002[1]

| | Average gross weekly earnings | | | | | | | | Percentage of employees who received overtime pay | Average weekly hours | |
| | Total (£) | Overtime pay (£) | PBR pay[2] (£) | Shift premium pay (£) | Percentage earning under | | | | | Total including overtime (hours) | Overtime (hours) |
					£200	£300	£400	£500			
All full-time male employees											
United Kingdom	511.3	25.9	21.5	6.8	4.2	24.0	46.4	64.3	30.1	40.9	2.4
North East	439.1	28.6	14.2	10.3	6.2	30.5	54.0	72.8	34.5	40.9	2.6
North West	471.1	25.5	16.1	8.0	4.9	27.3	50.5	69.4	31.2	40.9	2.4
Yorkshire and the Humber	447.1	30.0	17.2	7.0	5.0	28.0	53.3	71.8	33.9	41.6	2.9
East Midlands	454.2	28.9	17.0	6.7	4.4	26.0	52.6	70.8	33.3	41.7	2.9
West Midlands	469.6	26.3	22.1	6.6	4.2	25.6	50.6	69.2	31.4	41.1	2.5
East	506.3	27.7	19.4	6.1	3.4	22.3	44.2	62.7	31.4	41.4	2.6
London	704.8	20.5	37.2	5.2	2.3	13.1	29.6	45.2	21.9	39.7	1.7
South East	555.3	24.1	26.7	5.8	2.7	18.2	39.3	57.5	27.3	41.0	2.2
South West	463.3	25.2	14.9	5.6	4.4	27.0	50.3	68.1	31.0	41.0	2.3
England	521.3	25.6	22.3	6.5	3.9	22.8	45.2	63.1	29.7	40.9	2.4
Wales	432.9	24.2	15.7	10.2	6.4	32.1	55.3	74.0	31.2	40.7	2.3
Scotland	473.7	27.7	18.7	7.7	5.0	27.6	49.8	67.8	32.4	41.0	2.6
Northern Ireland	422.5	32.4	10.2	7.8	7.3	35.6	57.9	73.0	33.6	41.2	2.9
Full-time manual male employees											
United Kingdom	366.6	43.3	12.0	11.0	6.2	35.6	66.9	85.5	48.3	43.9	4.3
North East	357.8	44.0	13.4	15.8	7.3	38.6	67.6	85.5	50.2	43.2	4.2
North West	357.8	41.0	10.6	12.2	6.6	37.6	68.1	87.3	47.2	43.4	4.1
Yorkshire and the Humber	360.9	48.6	14.3	10.9	6.5	36.5	69.0	87.2	52.0	44.4	5.0
East Midlands	363.8	46.4	14.4	10.7	5.7	35.4	69.0	86.9	50.2	44.5	4.9
West Midlands	361.3	40.9	13.2	10.8	5.8	35.0	68.8	86.6	47.7	43.6	4.1
East	374.6	44.9	12.0	9.1	4.9	32.9	64.1	84.4	50.6	44.3	4.5
London	409.1	41.1	9.8	10.3	4.7	25.5	55.5	76.6	42.5	43.9	3.9
South East	395.1	47.2	10.2	9.6	4.1	28.3	59.8	81.1	48.9	44.6	4.6
South West	350.6	40.3	8.5	8.9	7.0	39.4	71.7	88.6	48.8	43.9	4.1
England	371.0	43.8	11.7	10.7	5.8	34.1	65.8	84.9	48.6	44.0	4.4
Wales	345.2	33.4	11.1	15.6	8.5	43.3	70.5	87.9	44.2	42.8	3.5
Scotland	356.1	44.3	14.9	10.7	7.2	39.8	70.3	87.8	49.0	43.7	4.4
Northern Ireland	324.2	41.8	11.6	10.5	10.6	50.6	79.1	91.6	45.4	43.2	4.3
Full-time non-manual male employees											
United Kingdom	608.7	14.2	27.9	4.0	2.8	16.1	32.5	49.9	17.8	38.9	1.1
North East	516.0	13.9	15.0	5.0	5.2	22.8	41.1	60.7	19.5	38.8	1.1
North West	555.7	13.9	20.3	4.9	3.6	19.5	37.3	55.9	19.1	39.0	1.1
Yorkshire and the Humber	522.2	13.7	19.8	3.5	3.7	20.6	39.6	58.4	18.1	39.1	1.1
East Midlands	531.0	14.0	19.2	3.2	3.4	17.9	38.7	57.1	19.0	39.3	1.2
West Midlands	558.5	14.2	29.4	3.1	2.9	17.8	35.7	54.9	18.1	39.0	1.1
East	597.1	15.9	24.5	4.1	2.3	15.0	30.5	47.7	18.2	39.4	1.2
London	806.7	13.4	46.7	3.4	1.5	8.9	20.7	34.4	14.9	38.3	0.9
South East	636.2	12.4	35.0	3.9	2.0	13.0	29.0	45.6	16.4	39.2	0.9
South West	543.9	14.4	19.5	3.3	2.6	18.1	35.1	53.5	18.4	38.9	1.1
England	618.7	13.8	29.2	3.8	2.7	15.5	31.8	49.0	17.4	38.9	1.0
Wales	510.6	16.1	19.9	5.5	4.6	22.2	41.9	61.7	19.7	38.9	1.3
Scotland	560.0	15.6	21.4	5.5	3.4	18.6	34.8	53.2	20.3	38.9	1.2
Northern Ireland	532.0	21.9	8.7	4.8	3.6	18.8	34.2	52.3	20.4	38.9	1.4

Table **5.17** (continued)

| | Average gross weekly earnings | | | | | | | | Percentage of employees who received overtime pay | Average weekly hours | |
| | Total (£) | of which | | | Percentage earning under | | | | | Total including overtime (hours) | Overtime (hours) |
		Overtime pay (£)	PBR pay[2] (£)	Shift premium pay (£)	£200	£300	£400	£500			
All full-time female employees											
United Kingdom	382.1	7.3	9.1	3.9	11.5	43.4	65.7	79.4	16.2	37.4	0.7
North East	332.1	7.0	4.8	3.3	15.7	55.2	74.8	86.5	17.1	37.3	0.7
North West	354.3	7.6	8.6	3.9	13.3	47.6	70.6	83.4	16.6	37.3	0.8
Yorkshire and the Humber	345.0	6.9	6.1	3.8	14.8	50.6	72.4	83.8	17.4	37.4	0.7
East Midlands	334.8	7.7	6.9	3.7	16.4	53.4	73.9	86.2	18.3	37.7	0.9
West Midlands	353.0	7.2	9.8	3.5	13.6	49.1	71.7	83.5	16.7	37.5	0.8
East	375.1	7.9	12.4	3.5	10.5	43.7	68.6	81.3	17.5	37.7	0.8
London	503.6	6.7	14.4	3.2	4.4	21.0	43.3	62.7	11.7	37.2	0.5
South East	398.6	7.6	12.0	3.7	8.1	37.9	63.0	78.2	16.6	37.9	0.8
South West	350.0	7.1	7.0	3.7	13.0	50.2	72.8	84.5	18.0	37.4	0.7
England	388.0	7.3	10.0	3.6	11.0	42.1	64.9	78.9	16.1	37.5	0.7
Wales	345.1	7.6	5.4	4.7	15.2	53.0	71.4	82.7	16.5	37.4	0.8
Scotland	360.1	7.0	4.4	5.5	12.1	47.6	68.4	80.7	16.7	37.3	0.7
Northern Ireland	340.9	6.8	3.5	6.6	17.6	51.0	69.7	82.8	14.7	37.2	0.6
Full-time manual female employees											
United Kingdom	250.3	13.8	6.1	6.9	33.3	78.0	93.5	97.9	28.9	39.7	1.7
North East	232.2	13.3	2.8	6.4	41.6	84.3	96.5	99.6	30.2	39.8	1.8
North West	241.4	12.3	7.2	5.4	39.3	78.7	94.7	99.1	23.7	39.3	1.6
Yorkshire and the Humber	234.1	13.3	4.8	6.5	36.8	85.3	96.8	98.8	31.2	39.6	1.8
East Midlands	238.5	14.0	9.6	6.7	39.4	82.7	94.5	97.6	29.4	39.6	1.8
West Midlands	247.8	14.6	8.6	6.6	36.4	78.3	92.9	97.5	31.2	39.8	1.9
East	259.7	16.5	6.2	7.3	28.4	75.6	92.0	96.4	29.8	39.9	2.0
London	292.8	15.2	4.5	6.9	18.1	62.3	85.5	94.7	28.4	40 1	1.8
South East	274.7	15.7	3.7	8.5	22.6	70.6	90.0	96.8	31.3	40.2	1.9
South West	245.4	11.6	6.2	6.6	33.2	79.7	95.9	99.2	31.1	39.2	1.4
England	253.8	14.1	6.1	6.8	32.1	76.8	92.9	97.6	29.5	39.7	1.8
Wales	233.0	13.4	2.4	6.6	39.1	84.4	95.9	99.7	27.6	39.7	1.7
Scotland	237.5	11.4	6.4	7.0	38.2	81.3	96.7	99.0	27.2	39.3	1.4
Northern Ireland	230.1	12.9	9.8	8.3	40.3	87.2	96.5	99.1	23.5	39.1	1.6
Full-time non-manual female employees											
United Kingdom	404.0	6.2	9.7	3.4	7.9	37.6	61.1	76.3	14.0	37.1	0.5
North East	349.8	5.9	5.2	2.8	11.1	50.0	71.0	84.2	14.8	36.9	0.6
North West	372.7	6.8	8.8	3.7	9.0	42.5	66.7	80.8	15.4	37.0	0.6
Yorkshire and the Humber	367.0	5.7	6.4	3.3	10.4	43.7	67.6	80.9	14.6	36.9	0.5
East Midlands	357.9	6.2	6.2	3.0	10.8	46.3	69.0	83.5	15.7	37.2	0.6
West Midlands	374.9	5.7	10.1	2.8	8.9	43.0	67.2	80.6	13.7	37.0	0.6
East	394.3	6.5	13.5	2.9	7.5	38.4	64.7	78.8	15.5	37.3	0.6
London	523.5	5.9	15.4	2.9	3.1	17.1	39.3	59.7	10.2	36.9	0.4
South East	417.4	6.4	13.3	3.0	5.9	32.9	58.9	75.4	14.3	37.5	0.6
South West	368.3	6.3	7.1	3.2	9.5	45.0	68.8	81.9	15.8	37.1	0.6
England	409.8	6.2	10.7	3.1	7.6	36.4	60.4	75.9	14.0	37.1	0.6
Wales	365.9	6.5	6.0	4.3	10.8	47.2	66.8	79.6	14.4	37.0	0.6
Scotland	381.1	6.3	4.0	5.3	7.7	41.9	63.5	77.5	14.9	36.9	0.6
Northern Ireland	364.9	5.5	2.1	6.2	12.7	43.2	63.9	79.2	12.8	36.8	0.4

1 Data relate to full-time employees on adult rates whose pay for the survey pay-period was not affected by absence. See Notes and Definitions.
2 PBR pay is payments-by-results, bonuses, commission and all other incentive payments plus profit-related payments.

Source: New Earnings Survey, Office for National Statistics; Department of Enterprise, Trade and Investment, Northern Ireland

Table **5.18** Unemployment rates[1]

Percentages

	Spring quarter of each year				
	1999	2000	2001	2002	2003
United Kingdom	6.2	5.8	5.0	5.3	5.1
North East	10.1	9.1	7.4	6.9	6.6
North West	6.5	5.7	5.4	5.7	5.1
Yorkshire and the Humber	6.7	6.2	5.2	5.5	5.5
East Midlands	5.3	5.3	5.0	4.3	4.3
West Midlands	6.9	6.4	5.2	5.7	5.9
East	4.4	3.8	3.8	3.7	4.2
London	7.8	7.3	6.3	6.9	7.1
South East	3.8	3.5	3.2	4.0	3.9
South West	5.0	4.3	3.7	3.7	3.9
England	6.0	5.5	4.8	5.1	5.1
Wales	7.4	6.5	6.2	6.2	4.6
Scotland	7.5	7.7	5.9	6.9	5.7
Northern Ireland	7.6	7.2	6.3	5.6	5.4

1 For those of working age. Seasonally adjusted. These data have been adjusted in line with the Census 2001 population estimates. See Notes and Definitions.

Source: Labour Force Survey, Office for National Statistics

Table **5.19** Claimant count rates[1]

Percentages

	Seasonally adjusted annual averages				
	1998	1999	2000	2001	2002
United Kingdom	4.6	4.2	3.6	3.2	3.1
North East	7.1	7.1	6.3	5.7	5.2
North West	5.1	4.6	4.1	3.7	3.6
Yorkshire and the Humber	5.4	5.0	4.4	4.0	3.7
East Midlands	4.0	3.7	3.4	3.1	2.9
West Midlands	4.5	4.5	4.0	3.7	3.5
East	3.3	2.9	2.4	2.1	2.1
London	5.2	4.5	3.7	3.3	3.6
South East	2.6	2.3	1.9	1.6	1.7
South West	3.4	3.1	2.5	2.1	2.0
England	4.3	3.9	3.4	3.0	3.0
Wales	5.5	5.0	4.4	4.0	3.6
Scotland	5.4	5.1	4.6	4.0	3.9
Northern Ireland	7.3	6.4	5.3	4.9	4.5

1 Claimant count rates are calculated by expressing the number of claimants as a percentage of the estimated total workforce. Claimants are people receiving unemployment related benefits such as Jobseeker's Allowance (JSA) and National Insurance credits. See Notes and Definitions.

Source: Office for National Statistics

Table **5.20** Unemployment rates: by age, 2002/03[1]

Percentages and thousands

	Percentage of the economically active[2] who were unemployed and aged:				All unemployed of working age (thousands)
	16 to 24	25 to 34	35 to 49	Males 50 to 64, females 50 to 59	
United Kingdom	12.4	4.7	3.5	3.5	1,527
North East	15.6	5.8	4.1	5.2	77
North West	12.3	5.2	3.5	3.0	171
Yorkshire and the Humber	12.6	5.5	3.3	3.0	129
East Midlands	10.9	4.2	3.0	3.3	96
West Midlands	14.6	5.3	3.9	3.8	152
East	10.8	3.8	2.7	2.6	116
London	15.5	5.7	5.4	5.1	258
South East	9.5	3.4	2.7	2.8	164
South West	9.7	3.6	2.3	3.0	98
England	12.2	4.7	3.5	3.4	1,260
Wales	12.9	4.4	3.2	3.4	69
Scotland	14.3	5.1	4.1	4.6	155
Northern Ireland	11.4	5.0	4.5	4.1	44

1 Average of four quarters ending spring 2003. The figures in this table have not been adjusted to take account of the Census 2001 population estimates. See Notes and Definitions.
2 Those economically active in the relevant age group.

Source: Labour Force Survey, Office for National Statistics

Table **5.21**   Claimant count:[1] by age and sex – computerised claims only[2], March 2003

Percentages and thousands

	Under 20	20 to 29	30 to 39	40 to 49	50 to 59	60 or over	Total (=100%) (thousands)
Males							
United Kingdom	9.2	30.7	25.9	17.8	15.0	1.5	739.0
North East	11.3	31.4	23.2	17.0	15.9	1.2	45.1
North West	10.8	33.0	25.0	16.5	13.5	1.1	93.3
Yorkshire and the Humber	10.0	32.2	25.0	16.6	15.0	1.2	68.0
East Midlands	9.3	31.0	24.5	17.4	15.9	1.8	45.5
West Midlands	9.4	31.6	25.1	17.3	14.8	1.8	74.4
East	8.6	28.7	25.1	18.6	16.9	2.0	45.0
London	6.6	29.7	31.4	19.2	11.9	1.1	123.8
South East	7.5	27.5	25.9	19.9	17.1	2.1	59.0
South West	8.6	29.3	24.6	18.2	17.4	1.9	38.7
England	8.9	30.7	26.2	17.9	14.7	1.5	593.0
Wales	10.8	32.8	23.4	16.6	15.2	1.1	37.4
Scotland	9.7	30.1	24.7	18.1	15.9	1.4	82.0
Northern Ireland	9.8	31.7	24.0	17.2	16.4	1.0	26.7
Females							
United Kingdom	16.9	29.3	18.7	17.9	17.2	-	241.6
North East	23.8	27.4	15.5	17.5	15.7	-	12.4
North West	21.2	30.5	16.7	16.3	15.2	-	26.7
Yorkshire and the Humber	20.1	29.4	17.2	16.6	16.6	-	21.0
East Midlands	16.3	27.9	17.4	18.6	19.7	-	16.0
West Midlands	17.4	30.0	17.2	17.4	17.9	-	23.2
East	15.6	27.1	18.2	18.3	20.8	-	16.8
London	11.3	32.2	23.5	18.6	14.4	-	47.8
South East	13.9	25.6	20.7	20.1	19.7	-	20.2
South West	15.8	27.6	17.8	18.3	20.4	-	14.0
England	16.4	29.3	19.0	18.0	17.2	-	198.3
Wales	19.8	29.8	16.2	17.0	17.2	-	11.3
Scotland	19.2	27.3	17.7	18.6	17.2	-	24.4
Northern Ireland	17.0	32.4	15.8	16.1	18.6	-	7.6
All people							
United Kingdom	11.1	30.4	24.1	17.9	15.5	1.1	980.7
North East	14.0	30.6	21.5	17.1	15.9	0.9	57.5
North West	13.1	32.4	23.2	16.5	13.9	0.9	120.0
Yorkshire and the Humber	12.4	31.6	23.2	16.6	15.4	0.9	89.1
East Midlands	11.2	30.2	22.7	17.8	16.9	1.4	61.5
West Midlands	11.3	31.2	23.2	17.3	15.5	1.3	97.6
East	10.5	28.3	23.2	18.5	18.0	1.5	61.8
London	7.9	30.4	29.2	19.1	12.6	0.8	171.6
South East	9.1	27.0	24.6	20.0	17.8	1.6	79.3
South West	10.5	28.8	22.8	18.2	18.2	1.4	52.8
England	10.8	30.3	24.4	17.9	15.4	1.1	791.3
Wales	12.9	32.1	21.7	16.7	15.7	0.9	48.7
Scotland	11.9	29.4	23.1	18.2	16.2	1.1	106.4
Northern Ireland	11.4	31.9	22.1	17.0	16.9	0.8	34.3

1 Not seasonally adjusted. See Notes and Definitions.
2 Only computerised claims are analysed by age and duration on a monthly basis.

Source: Office for National Statistics

Map 5.22a

Claimant count rate: by county or unitary authority,[1] March 2003

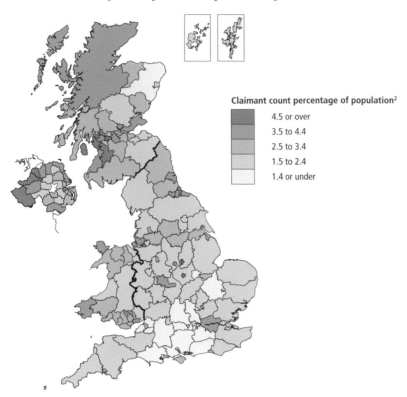

Claimant count percentage of population[2]

- 4.5 or over
- 3.5 to 4.4
- 2.5 to 3.4
- 1.5 to 2.4
- 1.4 or under

1 County or unitary authorities in England, unitary authorities in Wales, council areas in Scotland and district council areas in Northern Ireland.
2 Percentages of resident working-age population claiming Jobseeker's Allowance. Not seasonally adjusted.

Source: Office for National Statistics

Map 5.22b

Percentage claiming for more than 12 months:[1] by county or unitary authority,[2] March 2003

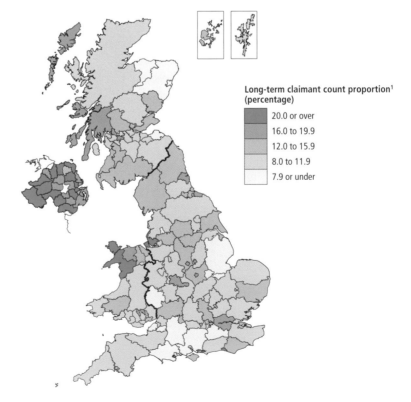

Long-term claimant count proportion[1]
(percentage)

- 20.0 or over
- 16.0 to 19.9
- 12.0 to 15.9
- 8.0 to 11.9
- 7.9 or under

1 People who have been claiming for more than 12 months (computerised claims only), as a percentage of total computerised claimants in each area.
2 County or unitary authorities in England, unitary authorities in Wales, council areas in Scotland and district council areas in Northern Ireland.

Source: Office for National Statistics

Table 5.23 Contributions to unemployment rates:[1,2] by duration and sex, spring 2003

Percentages and thousands

	Males						Females					
	under 6 months	6 months but under 12 months	1 year but under 2 years	2 years and over	Total unem-ployment rate	Total unem-ployed (thousands)	under 6 months	6 months but under 12 months	1 year but under 2 years	2 years and over	Total unem-ployment rate	Total unem-ployed (thousands)
United Kingdom	3.2	0.8	0.7	0.8	5.4	877	2.8	0.6	0.4	0.3	4.1	548
North East	4.5	..	..	1.6	7.7	48	3.5	..	..	..	5.1	26
North West	2.9	0.8	0.9	0.8	5.5	95	2.5	0.8	..	..	4.0	60
Yorkshire and the Humber	3.5	0.8	1.0	0.9	6.3	85	2.6	..	..	..	4.0	44
East Midlands	2.5	..	..	..	4.4	52	2.2	..	..	..	3.5	33
West Midlands	3.8	1.1	..	0.8	6.3	91	2.9	..	..	..	4.5	52
East	2.6	..	..	..	3.9	59	2.9	..	..	..	3.9	50
London	4.0	0.9	0.9	1.2	7.0	149	4.1	0.8	0.7	..	5.9	101
South East	2.8	0.7	0.4	..	4.2	96	2.3	..	..	..	3.1	60
South West	2.9	..	..	..	4.1	54	2.3	..	..	..	3.1	35
England	3.2	0.8	0.6	0.7	5.4	729	2.8	0.6	0.4	0.3	4.1	461
Wales	3.6	..	..	..	5.8	42	1.8	..	..	..	2.7	17
Scotland	3.4	0.8	0.9	1.0	6.1	81	3.2	..	..	..	4.6	55
Northern Ireland	..	..	..	..	5.5	25	..	..	..	..	4.6	16

1 For those aged 16 and over. Not seasonally adjusted. The percentage figures in this table are based on data that have not been adjusted to take account of the Census 2001 population estimates. However, the totals (thousands) figures have been adjusted in line with the Census population estimates. See Notes and Definitions.
2 The sample size for some categories for some countries and regions is too small to provide reliable estimates (i.e. the cells containing '..').

Source: Labour Force Survey, Office for National Statistics

Table 5.24 Unemployment[1]: by highest qualification, spring 2003

Percentages and thousands

	Unemployment rates						Total[4] (=100%) (thousands)
	Degree or equivalent	Higher education qualification[2]	GCE A level or equivalent[3]	GCSE grades A*-C or equivalent	Other qualifications	No qualifications	
United Kingdom	2.7	2.2	3.8	5.5	6.9	8.9	1,407
North East	..	..	4.1	9.3	8.7	11.9	74
North West	2.9	..	3.0	5.5	8.3	8.7	153
Yorkshire and the Humber	..	..	4.2	5.5	8.3	9.0	128
East Midlands	..	..	3.1	4.4	4.4	8.0	83
West Midlands	3.5	..	3.8	5.5	7.4	10.2	141
East	2.0	..	3.0	4.4	6.2	5.5	107
London	3.9	..	6.1	8.1	8.9	12.0	248
South East	2.7	..	3.0	3.8	4.8	7.1	153
South West	2.5	..	3.1	4.3	4.1	7.2	87
England	2.8	2.0	3.6	5.3	6.8	8.7	1,174
Wales	..	..	3.5	4.6	..	10.9	59
Scotland	..	2.6	4.7	8.2	7.7	9.4	134
Northern Ireland	..	..	4.2	..	..	8.0	41

1 For people of working age (males aged 16 to 64 and females aged 16 to 59). Not seasonally adjusted. The percentage figures in this table are based on data that have not been adjusted to take account of the Census 2001 population estimates. However, the totals figures in the final column have been adjusted in line with the Census population estimates. The sample size for some categories for some countries and regions is too small to provide reliable estimates (i.e. the cells containing '..').
2 Below degree level.
3 Includes recognised trade apprenticeships.
4 Includes those who did not state their qualifications.

Source: Labour Force Survey, Office for National Statistics

Figure **5.25** Redundancies,[1] spring 2003[2]

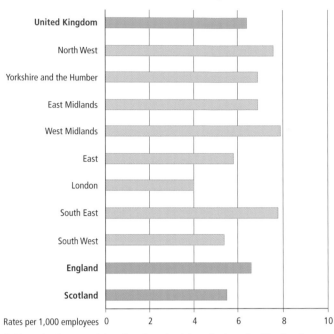

Rates per 1,000 employees

1 The redundancy rate is based on the ratio of the redundancy level for the given quarter to the number of employees in the previous quarter, multiplied by 1,000. For some areas, the sample sizes are too small to provide reliable estimates but are included in the UK total.
2 These data are not seasonally adjusted and have not been adjusted in line with the Census 2001 population estimates.

Source: Labour Force Survey, Office for National Statistics

Table **5.26** Vacancies at jobcentres[1,2]

Thousands

	1998	1999[3]	2000[3]
United Kingdom	295.9	314.3	358.3
North East	11.0	16.0	19.7
North West	40.9	37.1	41.1
Yorkshire and the Humber	22.6	24.1	32.6
East Midlands	20.6	21.2	22.4
West Midlands	30.1	35.7	35.8
East	24.0	24.0	24.5
London	28.2	32.0	36.4
South East	34.8	37.5	43.5
South West	26.1	27.8	34.5
England	238.1	255.4	290.4
Wales	17.9	17.0	19.0
Scotland	31.0	32.9	39.9
Northern Ireland	8.9	..	..

1 Vacancies remaining unfilled, seasonally adjusted annual averages.
2 Publication of the Jobcentre vacancy series has been deferred since April 2001 due to distortions to the data as a result of the introduction of Employer Direct by Jobcentre Plus.
3 The publication of the vacancy figures for Northern Ireland has been suspended since March 1999 as a result of a discontinuity identified during the introduction of a new computer system for processing vacancies to local offices of the Department for Employment and Learning. For the purposes of the seasonally adjusted United Kingdom figures it has been assumed provisionally that the Northern Ireland figures have remained constant since February 1999.

Source: Jobcentre Plus

Table **5.27** Number of starts on the New Deal 18 to 24:[1] by sex

Thousands

	Males			Females			All people		
	2000	2001	2002	2000	2001	2002	2000	2001	2002
Great Britain[2]	123.8	116.1	117.3	50.9	46.8	47.5	174.8	162.9	164.8
North East	10.0	9.5	9.0	3.7	3.4	3.3	13.7	13.0	12.3
North West	18.2	17.0	16.8	6.8	6.2	6.1	25.0	23.2	22.9
Yorkshire and the Humber	13.8	12.9	12.4	5.8	5.2	5.1	19.6	18.1	17.4
East Midlands	7.9	7.6	7.1	3.3	3.1	2.9	11.2	10.7	9.9
West Midlands	13.0	13.2	13.5	5.8	5.7	5.6	18.8	18.9	19.0
East	6.1	5.3	5.7	2.7	2.3	2.4	8.9	7.6	8.1
London	17.7	15.8	18.6	8.8	8.1	9.5	26.5	23.9	28.0
South East	7.5	6.2	6.5	2.9	2.5	2.4	10.4	8.7	8.9
South West	7.0	6.3	6.0	2.8	2.4	2.4	9.8	8.7	8.4
England	101.1	93.7	95.5	42.6	38.9	39.6	143.8	132.6	135.1
Wales	8.1	8.0	7.4	2.9	2.8	2.6	11.0	10.8	9.9
Scotland	14.6	14.4	14.5	5.4	5.1	5.3	20.0	19.5	19.8

1 The New Deal for the young unemployed is available to young people aged 18 to 24 who have been unemployed for more than six months.
2 Includes clients for whom the region is recorded as unknown.

Source: Department for Work and Pensions

Table **5.28** Reasons for economic inactivity, spring 2003[1]

Percentages and thousands

	Does not want a job					Wants a job but not seeking in last four weeks						Wants a job and seeking work but not able to start[3]	All inactive (=100%) (thousands)
	Looking after family or home	Long-term sick or disabled	Student	Other	All	Looking after family or home	Long-term sick or disabled	Student	Dis-couraged worker[2]	Other	All		
United Kingdom	22.5	18.1	18.3	13.8	72.8	7.1	8.9	3.5	0.5	4.4	24.3	2.9	7,867
North East	19.6	24.8	17.6	10.2	72.2	6.6	10.5	3.5	..	5.1	26.1	..	418
North West	21.8	23.5	19.0	11.4	75.6	6.0	9.4	2.9	..	3.6	22.3	2.1	944
Yorkshire and the Humber	24.6	17.9	16.8	14.3	73.6	7.0	8.9	3.6	..	3.8	23.5	2.9	671
East Midlands	24.1	16.6	19.8	13.5	74.1	7.0	9.3	3.2	..	3.0	23.1	2.8	543
West Midlands	24.1	18.6	18.1	13.2	74.0	7.1	8.3	3.3	..	4.5	23.5	2.5	704
East	26.5	13.6	15.5	17.6	73.2	6.7	8.5	3.2	..	4.5	23.3	3.6	599
London	24.0	13.7	23.5	11.7	72.9	6.5	7.0	4.3	..	5.4	23.8	3.3	1,209
South East	24.8	10.9	16.8	18.8	71.3	7.9	8.4	3.2	..	4.7	24.7	4.0	862
South West	19.8	15.0	15.7	18.7	69.3	8.2	10.6	3.0	..	5.2	27.6	3.2	551
England	23.4	16.8	18.6	14.2	73.0	6.9	8.7	3.4	0.4	4.5	24.0	3.0	6,501
Wales	18.6	27.3	16.6	13.8	76.3	5.9	8.1	3.7	..	3.5	21.5	..	421
Scotland	16.5	22.3	15.0	11.2	65.0	8.9	11.6	4.6	..	5.7	31.7	3.3	675
Northern Ireland	21.8	25.7	23.6	10.2	81.3	7.9	6.3	..	..	..	17.6	..	276

1 For people of working age (males aged 16 to 64 and females aged 16 to 59). Not seasonally adjusted. The percentage figures in this table are based on data that have not been adjusted to take account of the Census 2001 population estimates. However, the totals figures in the final column have been adjusted in line with the Census population estimates. The sample size for some categories for some countries and regions is too small to provide reliable estimates (i.e. the cells containing '..').

2 People who believed no jobs were available.

3 Not available for work in the next two weeks. Includes those who did not state whether or not they were available.

Source: Labour Force Survey, Office for National Statistics

Map **5.29**

Jobs density:[1] by unitary authority or local authority, 2001[2]

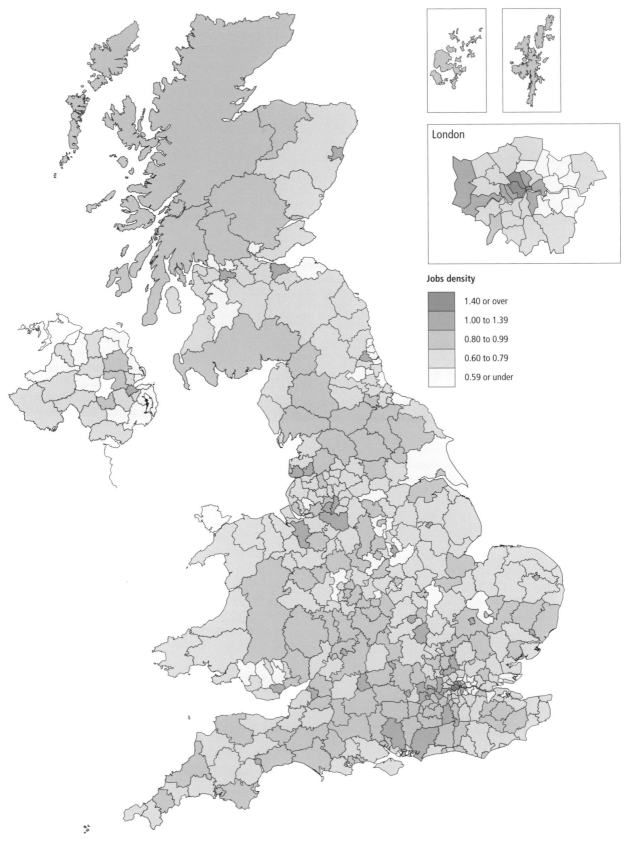

London

Jobs density

1.40 or over
1.00 to 1.39
0.80 to 0.99
0.60 to 0.79
0.59 or under

1 Jobs density is defined as the number of filled jobs in an area divided by the number of working-age people resident in that area.
2 Data are not seasonally adjusted. Includes data on self-employment jobs from the Labour Force Survey which have not been adjusted to take account
   of the Census 2001 population estimates.

Source: Office for National Statistics

Chapter 6 **Housing**

Dwelling stock

There were over 3 million dwellings in the South East in 2003 and the region has continuously had the highest number in the United Kingdom since 1992. Although Northern Ireland had the lowest number of dwellings in 2003, it had the largest percentage increase (16.8 per cent to 669 thousand dwellings) between 1992 and 2003. (Table 6.1)

New homes

Private enterprises constructed 89 per cent of new houses in the UK in 2002/03. Houses built by registered social landlords decreased in each region of England and Wales, and increased in Scotland and in Northern Ireland between 1992/93 and 2002/03. Over the same time period the number of new homes built by local authorities decreased in the UK, from 4,400 to 400 in the UK. (Table 6.2)

Council house sales and transfers

Between 1979 and 2003 local authorities in the South East sold or transferred nearly two-thirds of their housing stock, compared to over a third in Yorkshire and the Humber. In 2002/03 the North West sold and transferred 74 thousand dwellings compared to 3 thousand in Wales. (Table 6.3)

Tenure of dwelling

The percentage of owner-occupied dwellings increased throughout the UK while the proportion of dwellings rented from the local authorities decreased between 1993 and 2003. The South East had the highest proportion (76 per cent) of owner-occupied dwellings in 2003 while the North East had the highest proportion of rentals (18 per cent) through local authorities. London continued to have the highest percentage of privately rented accommodation, 16 per cent in 2003. (Table 6.4)

Type of dwelling

The detached house was the most common dwelling type in the South East and Northern Ireland during 2001/02, with 29 and 36 per cent respectively. Almost 40 per cent of dwellings in Scotland and London were purpose-built flats or maisonettes compared to only 6 per cent of the dwellings in Northern Ireland in the same year. (Table 6.5)

Owner-occupier housing costs

Average weekly mortgage payments for owner-occupiers ranged from £41 in the North East to £93 in London in 2001/02. Owner-occupiers in Wales and the North East had the lowest average weekly housing costs, around half the amount paid in London (£71). (Table 6.8)

Dwelling prices

Average house prices continued to increase throughout England and Wales between 2001 and 2002. The East Midlands and the South West had a 27 per cent increase while London, the North East and the North West each had rises under 20 per cent.

Increases in average house prices between 2001 and 2002 were considerably greater throughout England and Wales compared to the previous year. London had the greatest twelve-month increase – more than 6.5 times higher than the percentage rise between 2000 and 2001. (Table 6.9)

Mortgages

During 2002, more than one-in-three mortgage loans in the UK were to first-time buyers. London and Northern Ireland had the greatest proportion (44 per cent in each region) of loans given to first-time buyers; Yorkshire and the Humber had the lowest with 35 per cent. The average age of borrowers in the UK decreased by two years for first-time buyers and three for previous owner-occupiers from 2001. (Table 6.10)

Weekly rents

Renting from a London Local Authority cost on average 50 per cent more per week in 2001/02 than renting in Yorkshire and the Humber or from a Scottish Local Authority. (Table 6.11)

Council tax

Eight per cent of London dwellings were in the highest council tax bands G-H, with only 17 per cent in lowest band A-B. Almost three-quarters of dwellings in the North East were in council tax bands A-B. (Table 6.12)

Mortgage possession orders

The North West had 3,000 County Court mortgage possessions orders made in 2002, compared to 800 in the North East and 500 in Northern Ireland. The number of 'actions entered' for mortgage possession orders, dropped by 75 per cent in the South East between 1991 and 2002, while 'orders made' dropped by 86 per cent. (Table 6.13)

Homelessness

The West Midlands had the highest incidence of homelessness in 2001/02 outside London, with 14,670 households accepted as being homeless. Wales had the lowest number of households at 5,333. No longer being able or willing to remain with parents, relatives or friends was cited by one-in-three households in most areas in Great Britain as a reason for homelessness; in Northern Ireland the proportion was one-in-five. Breakdown of relationships with a partner was cited by one-in-three in the West Midlands and North East, while similar proportions in the South West, South East and the East cited loss of rented accommodation. (Table 6.14)

Table **6.1** Stock of dwellings[1]

	Thousands												Percentage increase 1992-2002
	1992	1993	1994	1995	1996	1997	1998	1999	2000	2001	2002	2003	
United Kingdom	23,762	23,946	24,135	24,341	24,529	24,720	24,913	25,097	25,283	25,456	25,617	..	7.8
North East[2]	1,077	1,082	1,086	1,091	1,094	1,099	1,104	1,108	1,112	1,115	1,118	1,122	3.8
North West[2]	2,807	2,822	2,838	2,855	2,874	2,890	2,905	2,920	2,935	2,945	2,954	2,966	5.2
Yorkshire and the Humber[2]	2,035	2,048	2,060	2,076	2,090	2,105	2,120	2,132	2,144	2,155	2,165	2,176	6.4
East Midlands[2]	1,651	1,666	1,682	1,700	1,717	1,732	1,748	1,764	1,782	1,797	1,812	1,828	9.8
West Midlands[2]	2,094	2,110	2,124	2,141	2,156	2,170	2,183	2,197	2,211	2,225	2,236	2,248	6.8
East[2]	2,116	2,137	2,159	2,182	2,205	2,227	2,249	2,270	2,290	2,308	2,324	2,343	9.8
London[2]	2,934	2,953	2,972	2,990	3,009	3,026	3,042	3,059	3,074	3,090	3,106	3,123	5.9
South East[2]	3,131	3,159	3,188	3,219	3,250	3,280	3,310	3,338	3,365	3,392	3,415	3,441	9.1
South West[2]	1,991	2,010	2,029	2,051	2,072	2,093	2,117	2,139	2,161	2,181	2,199	2,217	10.4
England[2]	19,836	19,987	20,139	20,305	20,468	20,622	20,778	20,927	21,075	21,207	21,330	21,464	7.5
Wales[3]	1,194	1,204	1,214	1,224	1,233	1,243	1,251	1,259	1,267	1,274	1,282	..	7.4
Scotland[4]	2,160	2,175	2,193	2,210	2,230	2,248	2,267	2,285	2,305	2,325	2,345	..	8.6
Northern Ireland[5]	573	580	590	600	597	608	618	626	636	649	660	669	15.2

1 On 1 April each year, except for Scotland (and Northern Ireland up to 2001) where the figure is the one for 31 December the previous year. The figure shown for the United Kingdom is the sum of the component countries for these periods. See Notes and Definitions.
2 Series up to 2001 for England and the regions has been adjusted so that the 2001 estimates match the census. Figure for 2003 is provisional.
3 Wales figures for 2001 and 2002 are provisional.
4 Scotland figure for 2001 is provisional.
5 Northern Ireland figures are taken on 31st December until 2001. From 2002 figures are shown on 31st March of that year and are provisional.

Source: Office of the Deputy Prime Minister; National Assembly for Wales; Scottish Executive; Department for Social Development, Northern Ireland

Table **6.2** Housebuilding: permanent dwelling completed: by tenure, country and region

Thousands

	Private enterprise[1]		Registered Social Landlords		Local authorities[2]	
	1992/93	2002/03	1992/93	2002/03	1992/93	2002/03
United Kingdom	144.4	163.8	30.1	19.9	4.4	0.4
North East	5.0	5.4	1.5	0.1	0.0	-
North West	15.1	17.4	3.9	1.0	0.1	-
Yorkshire and the Humber	10.6	12.7	2.3	0.6	0.2	-
East Midlands	12.8	14.2	1.3	0.7	0.2	-
West Midlands	13.2	12.6	2.7	1.3	0.4	-
East	17.3	16.5	2.3	1.2	0.4	0.1
London	9.8	11.4	4.4	4.3	0.2	0.1
South East	19.5	19.9	3.8	2.7	0.8	0.1
South West	12.8	14.2	1.8	1.5	0.3	-
England	115.9	124.3	24.0	13.3	2.6	0.3
Wales	7.1	7.1	2.7	0.8	0.1	-
Scotland	15.6	19.2	2.6	4.7	0.8	0.1
Northern Ireland	5.8	13.2	0.9	1.1	0.9	-

1 Includes private landlords (persons or companies) and owner-occupiers.
2 Northern Ireland Housing Executive in Northern Ireland.

Source: Office of the Deputy Prime Minister; National Assembly for Wales; Scottish Executive; Department for Social Development, Northern Ireland

Table **6.3**   Sales and transfers of local authority dwellings[1]

Thousands and percentages

	April 1979 to March 2003[2,3]				2002/03[3]				Stock at 1 April 2002	Total sales and transfers April 1979 to March 2003 as a percentage of notional stock at 1 April 1979[6]
	Right-to-buy sales[4]	Large scale voluntary transfers[5]	Other sales and transfers	Total sales and transfers	Right-to-buy sales[4]	Large scale voluntary transfers[5]	Other sales and transfers	Total sales and transfers		
North East	135	52	6	192	6	12	-	17	227	46
North West	181	146	42	369	8	67	-	74	405	48
Yorkshire and the Humber	173	46	15	234	11	26	-	37	386	38
East Midlands	147	35	17	199	6	9	-	15	242	45
West Midlands	194	129	25	348	9	31	-	40	301	54
East	174	65	43	292	5	14	-	20	250	54
London	258	56	71	385	12	4	-	16	518	43
South East	194	153	52	399	4	-	-	4	225	64
South West	133	87	19	239	3	4	-	7	153	61
England	1,589	780	288	2,657	63	166	1	230	2,706	50
Wales	115	..	6	122	3	..	-	3	183	40
Scotland	329	23	1	353	13	1	-	15	527	40
Northern Ireland[7,8,9]	..	..	..	..	..	-	-	5	111	..

1 Includes shared ownership deals and dwellings transferred to housing associations and private developers. Excludes New Towns. Figures for Scotland exclude sales by Scottish Homes.
2 Figures for Wales are from October 1980 to March 2002.
3 Figures are up to 2002 for Wales, Scotland and Northern Ireland.
4 Right-to-buy sales were introduced in Great Britain in October 1980.
5 Scotland figure includes large scale voluntary transfers and trickle transfers to housing associations. For England, includes Estate Renewal Challenge Fund transfers.
6 Calculated as sales in the period April 1979 to March 2003, expressed as a percentage of stock at 1 April 2002 plus sales in the period April 1979 to March 2003.
7 The Northern Ireland Housing Executive (NIHE) is responsible for public sector housing in Northern Ireland. Under the Housing (NI) Order 1992 NIHE operates a voluntary house sales scheme which is comparable to the Right-to-buy schemes in Great Britain.
8 Figures relate to sales only (excluding Special Purchase of Evacuated Dwellings scheme (SPED) cases) and do not include transfers.
9 NIHE housing stock is at 31 March.

Source: Office of the Deputy Prime Minister; National Assembly for Wales; Scottish Executive; Department for Social Development, Northern Ireland

Table **6.4**   Tenure of dwellings[1]

Percentages

	Owner-occupied			Rented from local authority[2]			Rented from registered social landlord			Rented from private owners or with job or business		
	1993	1998	2003	1993	1998	2003	1993	1998	2003	1993	1998	2003
North East	60	62	66	30	26	18	4	4	9	7	7	7
North West	67	68	71	20	18	11	4	5	10	8	9	8
Yorkshire and the Humber	64	66	69	23	20	16	3	3	5	11	10	10
East Midlands	70	72	74	18	17	12	2	3	5	9	9	9
West Midlands	67	69	71	22	18	11	3	5	9	8	8	8
East	72	73	74	15	13	10	3	4	6	9	10	10
London	56	57	59	22	20	16	6	7	9	16	16	16
South East	75	74	76	12	8	6	3	6	7	10	11	11
South West	72	74	75	13	10	7	2	4	7	12	12	11
England[2]	67	69	71	19	16	11	4	5	8	10	11	10
Wales	71	71	..	18	16	..	3	4	..	8	8	..
Scotland	55	61	..	34	27	..	3	5	..	7	7	..
Northern Ireland	67	71	75	27	22	16	2	3	3	4	4	5

1 On 1 April each year, except for Scotland (and Northern Ireland up to 2000) where the figure is on 31 December the previous year. From 2002 the figures for Northern Ireland are from 31 March. See Notes and Definitions.
2 Data for 1993 and 1998 have been adjusted to match Census 2001 estimates.

Source: Office of the Deputy Prime Minister; National Assembly for Wales; Scottish Executive; Department for Social Development, Northern Ireland

Table **6.5**   Households: by type of dwelling, 2001/02

Percentages

	Detached house	Semi-detached house	Terraced house	Purpose-built flat or maisonette	Other[1]
United Kingdom	21	31	28	16	4
North East	14	29	47	7	2
North West	18	38	34	8	3
Yorkshire and the Humber	18	41	32	7	3
East Midlands	30	37	21	9	3
West Midlands	23	40	23	11	3
East	29	33	24	11	3
London	4	19	28	37	11
South East	29	28	25	14	4
South West	28	33	26	10	4
England	21	32	28	14	4
Wales	29	30	32	7	2
Scotland	15	21	21	39	4
Northern Ireland	36	24	32	6	2

1 Includes converted flats which are particularly common in London.

Source: Survey of English Housing, Office of the Deputy Prime Minister; General Household Survey, Office for National Statistics; Continuous Household Survey, Northern Ireland Statistics and Research Agency

Table **6.6**   Households: by length of time at current address, 2001/02

Percentages

	Less than 12 months	12 months, less than 5 years	5 years, less than 10 years	10 years, less than 20 years	20 years or more
United Kingdom	10	26	17	22	25
North East	15	22	17	21	25
North West	11	24	17	21	27
Yorkshire and the Humber	11	26	14	22	27
East Midlands	10	26	17	22	25
West Midlands	8	25	13	24	30
East	10	30	18	21	21
London	13	28	19	19	21
South East	10	29	18	20	23
South West	10	27	18	23	22
England	11	27	17	21	24
Wales	6	24	15	23	31
Scotland	10	25	16	25	24
Northern Ireland	5	24	18	23	29

Source: General Household Survey, Office for National Statistics; Continuous Household Survey, Northern Ireland Statistics and Research Agency

Table **6.7**   Householders' satisfaction with their area, 2001/02

Percentages and numbers

| | Satisfaction with area | | | | | |
	Very satisfied	Fairly satisfied	Neither satisfied nor dissatisfied	Slightly dissatisfied	Very dissatisfied	All households[1] (=100%) (numbers)
England	48.8	37.0	4.9	5.9	3.4	19,767
North East	47.8	36.0	5.1	5.8	5.3	1,046
North West	46.1	37.5	4.3	7.4	4.7	2,770
Yorkshire and the Humber	51.0	35.5	4.0	5.8	3.7	2,000
East Midlands	50.6	36.5	4.9	4.5	3.4	1,725
West Midlands	47.7	38.3	5.9	5.1	3.0	2,104
East	52.4	36.3	4.1	5.4	1.8	2,174
London	35.7	43.7	7.2	8.6	4.7	2,736
South East	52.9	35.0	4.7	4.6	2.7	3,183
South West	57.5	32.1	3.9	4.4	2.0	2,029
Scotland[2,3]	50.5	41.3	5.1	2.8	0.3	14,042

1 Excludes households where the respondent was not the household reference person nor spouse/partner.
2 Adult population.
3 Data for Scotland are for 2002. The categories of satisfaction differ in Scotland, their ratings are 'very good, fairly good, fairly poor, very poor and no opinion'. See Notes and Definitions.

Source: Survey of English Housing, Office of the Deputy Prime Minister; Scottish Household Survey, Scottish Executive.

Table **6.8**   Selected housing costs[1] of owner-occupiers, 2001/02

£ per week

| | Type of housing costs | | | | All owner-occupier[2] costs |
	Mortgages	Endowment policies	Structural insurance	Services	
Great Britain	63	22	5	7	49
North East	41	16	4	3	35
North West	52	18	5	2	40
Yorkshire and the Humber	47	17	5	3	37
East Midlands	51	18	4	6	41
West Midlands	55	19	5	6	42
East	70	24	5	11	54
London	93	29	7	14	71
South East	84	29	6	11	64
South West	69	23	5	8	48
England	66	22	5	8	50
Wales	46	17	4	2	33
Scotland	49	18	5	5	43

1 Average expenditure per week of those who made payments within each type of housing costs, e.g. average mortgage payments by those who are making mortgage payments. See Notes and Definitions.
2 Expenditure of All owner-occupiers include both home-owners with a mortgage and those who own their house outright.

Source: Family Resources Survey, Department for Work and Pensions

Table 6.9   Average dwelling prices, 2002[1]

£ and percentages

	Average sale price (£)				All dwellings		
	Detached houses	Semi-detached houses	Terraced houses	Flats/ maisonettes	Average price (£) 2001	Average price (£) 2002	Percentage increase 2001-2002
England and Wales	222,307	127,943	107,707	142,551	119,982	145,320	21.1
North East	149,372	77,541	56,070	65,575	67,915	81,387	19.8
North West	177,883	92,328	55,151	94,367	77,738	92,433	18.9
Yorkshire and the Humber	159,769	84,594	59,877	91,993	75,711	92,157	21.7
East Midlands	167,885	91,813	72,172	83,617	87,711	111,717	27.4
West Midlands	202,252	103,074	79,950	85,592	97,542	118,845	21.8
East	235,990	149,133	124,125	108,021	129,630	160,495	23.8
London	500,454	269,401	242,690	208,771	201,913	241,080	19.4
South East	315,521	180,080	146,557	123,446	160,424	193,339	20.5
South West	233,819	141,153	119,246	114,733	123,740	157,068	26.9
England	227,842	130,577	110,485	143,615	122,005	148,184	21.5
Wales	140,609	79,002	60,268	78,774	75,159	90,163	20.0

1 Excludes those bought at non-market prices. Averages are taken from the last quarter of each year. See Notes and Definitions.
Source: Land Registry

Table 6.10   Mortgage advances, and income and age of borrowers, 2002[1]

	First-time buyers				Previous owner-occupiers			
	Number of loans (thousands)	Average percentage of price advanced	Average recorded income[2] (£ per annum)	Average age of borrowers (years)	Number of loans (thousands)	Average percentage of price advanced	Average recorded income[2] (£ per annum)	Average age of borrowers (years)
United Kingdom	524	77.4	31,988	32	882	63.8	38,134	37
North East	20	84.1	24,105	33	38	69.6	28,982	37
North West	58	82.3	27,065	32	93	68.5	33,340	37
Yorkshire and the Humber	39	81.6	26,142	33	82	69.1	30,180	36
East Midlands	39	78.8	26,251	32	71	66.6	34,156	37
West Midlands	39	77.3	27,756	33	70	65.5	35,321	37
East	55	76.6	36,143	32	87	59.8	41,590	38
London	67	76.4	46,421	32	87	63.3	57,022	36
South East	74	74.1	38,253	32	134	59.0	45,751	38
South West	38	73.2	31,491	33	75	59.9	39,726	39
England	431	76.9	33,314	32	736	62.9	39,695	37
Wales	28	80.1	25,862	33	46	67.4	30,942	37
Scotland	50	82.6	24,998	34	82	74.6	30,387	38
Northern Ireland	15	79.8	28,229	32	19	69.1	27,861	36

1 Figures in this table are taken from The Survey of Mortgage Lenders, a five per cent sample survey of mortgages at completion stage. First-time buyers include sitting tenant purchases. See Notes and Definitions.
2 The income of borrowers is the total recorded income taken into account when the mortgage is granted.
Source: Office of the Deputy Prime Minister

Table **6.11** Average weekly rents: by tenure, 2001/02

£ per week

	Average weekly rents by sector[1,2]		
	Private	Local autho-rities	Registered social landlords
Great Britain	107	47	59
North East	56	41	51
North West	78	45	54
Yorkshire and the Humber	78	40	56
East Midlands	73	42	54
West Midlands	82	45	52
East	91	50	59
London	180	63	75
South East	115	55	67
South West	83	48	60
England	107	47	59
Wales	79	44	50
Scotland	83	40	49

1 See Notes and Definitions.
2 Excludes rent-free accommodation and squats.

Source: Family Resources Survey, Department for Work and Pensions

Table **6.12** Dwellings in council tax bands, 2002/03[1]

Percentages

	Council Tax Bands[2]			
	A-B	C-D	E-F	G-H
North East	72	21	5	1
North West	63	27	8	2
Yorkshire and the Humber	65	25	8	2
East Midlands	61	28	9	2
West Midlands	57	30	10	2
East	36	44	16	4
London	17	52	23	8
South East	25	46	22	7
South West	42	39	16	3
England	45	37	14	4

1 Based on number of dwellings on the valuation list on 28 March 2003.
2 For council tax band definitions see Notes and Definitions.

Source: Office of the Deputy Prime Minister

Table **6.13** County Court mortgage possession orders[1]

Thousands

	1991			2000			2001			2002		
	Actions entered	Sus-pended orders	Orders made	Actions entered	Sus-pended orders	Orders made	Actions entered	Sus-pended orders	Orders made	Actions entered	Sus-pended orders	Orders made
England and Wales	186.6	69.1	73.9	73.0	31.7	20.4	65.0	27.9	17.8	61.7	23.5	16.2
North East	6.0	2.9	1.9	4.0	1.9	1.1	3.4	1.6	1.1	3.1	1.2	0.8
North West	22.3	8.6	7.5	12.4	5.7	3.7	11.7	5.0	3.4	10.7	4.5	3.0
Yorkshire and the Humber	14.1	5.1	5.7	7.8	3.7	2.4	6.9	3.2	2.2	6.2	2.5	1.7
East Midlands	13.5	4.5	5.2	5.7	2.4	1.6	5.4	2.4	1.4	4.7	1.8	1.4
West Midlands	17.7	6.5	6.9	9.8	3.7	2.3	7.6	3.5	2.1	6.3	2.5	1.7
East	18.6	6.0	8.4	6.2	2.5	1.6	5.5	2.2	1.4	5.4	2.0	1.3
London	35.3	13.1	14.4	8.1	3.1	2.1	7.4	2.7	1.8	8.7	2.7	2.3
South East	32.2	13.2	13.2	8.6	3.9	2.6	8.2	3.4	1.9	8.0	2.9	1.8
South West	16.7	5.8	6.5	5.2	2.3	1.3	4.4	1.8	1.1	4.1	1.7	1.0
England	176.4	65.6	69.9	67.7	29.1	18.7	60.5	25.8	16.4	57.1	21.7	15.0
Wales	10.2	3.5	4.0	5.3	2.6	1.6	4.5	2.1	1.4	4.7	1.9	1.2
Northern Ireland[2]	3.1	..	..	1.7	0.2	0.6	1.6	0.2	0.7	1.6	0.2	0.5

1 Local authority and private. See Notes and Definitions.
2 Mortgage possession actions are heard in Chancery Division of Northern Ireland High Court.

Source: The Court Service; Northern Ireland Court Service

Table **6.14** Households accepted as homeless: by reason, 2001/02[1]

Percentages and numbers

	Reasons for homelessness							
	No longer willing or able to remain with			Break-down of relation-ship with partner	Mortgage arrears	Rent arrears or other reason for loss of rented or tied accomm-odation	Other reasons[2]	Total[3] (=100%) (numbers)
	Parents	Relatives or friends	Parents, relatives or friends					
England and Wales	19	15	33	22	2	24	18	123,523
North East	21	10	30	34	4	19	13	5,590
North West	15	9	23	30	3	18	25	13,260
Yorkshire and the Humber	14	14	29	29	3	21	19	10,780
East Midlands	16	10	26	33	3	23	15	7,220
West Midlands	16	12	28	31	4	19	18	14,670
East	22	10	32	23	3	32	11	10,220
London	21	24	45	10	1	23	21	30,470
South East	23	13	36	18	2	32	13	14,380
South West	18	11	29	21	2	33	14	11,270
England	19	15	33	22	2	24	18	117,840
Wales	20	9	29	26	4	25	16	5,333
Scotland[4]	17	14	31	26	1	8	34	25,923
Northern Ireland	..	..	19	12	1	11	57	7,374

1 In England and Wales the basis for these figures is households accepted for re-housing by local authorities under the homelessness provisions of Part III of the Housing Act 1985, and Part VII of the Housing Act 1996. In Scotland the basis of these figures is households assessed by the local authorities as unintentionally homeless or potentially homeless and in priority need, as defined in Section 24 of the Housing (Scotland) Act 1987. In Northern Ireland, the Housing (Northern Ireland) Order 1988 (Part II) defines the basis under which households (including one-person households) are classified as homeless. The figures relate to priority cases only.

2 A large proportion of the Northern Ireland total is classified as 'Other reasons' due to differences in the definitions used.

3 The totals may not equal the sum of components because of rounding.

4 The figures for Scotland relate to the financial year 2002/03.

Source: Office of the Deputy Prime Minister; National Assembly for Wales; Scottish Executive; Department for Social Development, Northern Ireland

Chapter 7 **Health and Care**

Organisation

On 1 April 2002 a new organisation was introduced for the National Health Service (NHS) in England and Wales, whereby Primary Care Trusts (PCTs) and care groups were created to become the lead NHS organisations in assessing need, planning and securing all health services and improving health. They will forge new partnerships with local communities and lead the NHS contribution to joint work with local government and other partners.

In order to facilitate comparison of historic data we have retained table 7.1 showing the population and vital statistics of the pre-2002 health regions in addition to providing data relating to the Strategic Health Authorities. (Tables 7.1 and 7.2)

Infant and perinatal mortality

Over the last 20 years Infant Mortality has declined in all areas of the United Kingdom, most significantly in Northern Ireland where the rate has declined from 13.2 per 1,000 live births in 1981 to 4.7 in 2002 and in Wales from 12.6 to 4.7 per 1,000 live births.

In 2002 the South East had lowest perinatal mortality rate (6.8 per 1,000 live and still births) in the UK, although London had one of the highest rates, 9.2 per 1,000 births; this was second only to the rate in West Midlands of 10.1 per 1,000 births. There were slight increases in perinatal mortality rates in 2002 compared to 2001 for several areas; there were increases in the rate of still births in 10 out of 12 parts of the United Kingdom. (Table 7.4)

Mortality rates

The age-standardised mortality ratio (SMR) makes allowance for differences in the age structure of the population over time and sex. Scotland had the highest mortality ratio of 1,085 in 2001, whereas the lowest rate was in the South West at 849 followed by the South East (863) and the East of England (879).

Circulatory disease was the highest single cause of death during 2001, averaging 378 per 100,000 for the UK as a whole. The rate for females is higher than the rate for males throughout the UK, ranging from 456 in Scotland to 358 per 100,000 females in the East. The corresponding rates for males in the same areas were 396 and 313 respectively.

Scotland had the highest incidence of suicides and open verdicts as to cause of death for both males and females (26 and 9 per 100,000 respectively); this compared with rates in the East of 11 and 4 respectively. Overall, the rate of suicides and open verdicts is three times higher for males than females. (Table 7.5)

Cervical and breast screening

Northern Ireland and London had appreciably lower proportions of women aged 25 to 64 participating in cervical screening in 2002 (72 and 76 per cent respectively). Women aged 50 to 64 in London also had the lowest breast cancer screening rate, 57 per cent, 13 percentage points below the national rate.

Age-standardised death rates from breast cancer were the highest, 58 per 100,000 population, in the health region of Trent, despite having the second highest proportion of women participating in screening programmes, 74 per cent. The lowest death rates from breast cancer, 52 per 100,000, were in Northern and Yorkshire and West Midlands Health Regions.

Deaths from cervical cancer in Wales were almost three per 100,000 more than the English average of five per 100,000. Cervical screening of Welsh women aged 20 to 34 is lower than in most other parts of the UK (despite screening commencing five years earlier in Wales than elsewhere), 73 per cent compared to 83 per cent in Trent. (Table 7.7)

Incidence of TB

London had by far the highest notification rate of tuberculosis (TB) in 2002 with 38.6 notifications per 100,000 population; almost three times the second highest rate of 14.9 per 100,000 population in the West Midlands. The lowest incidence of reported TB was 4.0 in Northern Ireland; Wales also had a low rate of notification of 4.3 per 100,000 population.

Although the West Midlands, along with several other areas, showed a slight decline in the TB rate from 16.6 to 14.9 per 100,000 population over the ten years to 2002, London had a steady growth in reported rate of TB from 29.4 in 1992. (Table 7.6)

Incidence of HIV

The number of diagnosed HIV patients increased by nearly 60 per cent between 1999 and 2002 in the UK; there are now in excess of 31,000 infected patients. Injecting drugs accounted for a quarter of the incidence in Scotland, over six times the proportion in the UK as a whole. Sexual activity accounted for four-fifths of probable routes of infection overall in the UK, but only two-thirds of the incidence in Scotland. (Table 7.9)

Cigarette smoking

People smoke less in London than in other parts of Great Britain. Both males and females had the highest percentages smoking less than 10 cigarettes per day in 2001/02 – 11 and 10 per cent respectively for males and females. London was also one of the areas with the highest proportion of people who had never or only occasionally smoked. This was only bettered by the West Midlands where almost three-fifths of females had never or only occasionally smoked.

Throughout Great Britain the proportion of males who had given up smoking was higher than for females; the biggest difference was in the West Midlands where 29 per cent of males had given up compared with 18 per cent of females. Overall, approximately one-fifth of females claimed to be ex-regular smokers, ranging from 17 per cent in London to 25 per cent in the South West. (Table 7.11)

Alcohol consumption

Almost a third (30 per cent) of males in the North East and London did not drink alcohol in the week before they were questioned. However, the North East also had the highest percentage, equal with Scotland, (28 per cent) of those that drank more than 8 units on the heaviest drinking day in the same week.

Females in the North East demonstrated a similar pattern of alcohol consumption with the highest percentage, 15 per cent, who drank more than 6 units on one day in the previous week compared with the regional average of 9 per cent. This contrasted with 45 per cent of females in the North East who had nothing to drink in the previous week; the highest proportions of females not drinking were in Wales, the West Midlands and London where 46 per cent in each area abstained.

The East Midlands had the lowest proportion of females who drank nothing, 35 per cent, followed by the South West at 36 per cent, while males in the South West had the lowest with 21 per cent abstaining, followed closely by North West, and Yorkshire and the Humber with 22 per cent. (Table 7.12)

Illegal drugs

Use of illegal drugs in Wales was less than half of that in the North West where 30 per cent of 16 to 29 year olds reported using drugs in 2001/02.

Young people in London aged 16 to 29 years were almost seven times more likely to use opiates than those of similar age in Wales (8.2 per cent compared with 1.2 per cent). Use of hallucinants and cannabis was highest in the North West. (Figure 7.13)

Prescriptions

On average we spent almost £140 per person in England on prescription drugs in 2002. This represents an increase of approximately 70 per cent over the previous 6 years, while over the same period retail prices increased by less than 20 per cent.

Wales had the highest number of prescription items,17, dispensed per person and the highest average net ingredient cost of almost £172 per person in 2002, although there was a comparatively low average net ingredient cost of £10.20 per item prescribed. More than 10 per cent of Welsh prescriptions were issued for children compared with an average in England of 7 per cent. Less than half the prescriptions dispensed in Wales were to people aged 60 or over, which was one of the lowest percentages. (Table 7.14)

NHS hospital waiting lists

Waiting times for hospital beds have fallen considerably over the last few years and four-fifths of patients in England were admitted after waiting less than 6 months in the year ending March 2003. Apart from 0.2 per cent of patients in Bedfordshire and Hertfordshire, patients in England did not have to wait longer than 12 months for an in-patient or day case admission in NHS hospitals. In Northern Ireland, Wales and Scotland, 22, 16 and 10 per cent, respectively, of patients had to wait longer than 12 months for treatment.

Half the patients in Kent and Medway waited more than 3.4 months for an appointment, which was the highest median waiting time in the UK. The median time for Scotland was the same as that for England overall, 2.7 months, although the average length of waiting in England was 3.6 months, which was two months less than in Scotland. These differences are consistent with long waits for a relatively small number of the patients in Scotland as seen in the figures of those waiting over a year. Scotland had a tenth of the total number of patients waiting in England. (Table 7.15)

Number of GPs

Approximately one-third of all English GPs were females in September 2002; the proportion in London was the highest at 42 per cent.

The average GP list size reduced slightly over the last few years and in September 2002 averaged 1,838 patients in England, which was greater than other areas of the United Kingdom. General Practitioners in London had the largest number of patients, with the northern parts of the city averaging over 2,080 for each doctor. (Table 7.18)

Council supported residents

In the East of England 70 per cent of residents who were supported by the local council were looked after in independent residential care homes. This was 10 percentage points higher than the average for England and corresponded to a lower proportion cared for in independent nursing homes compared to other regions.

One-third (32 per cent) of the people supported in London in March 2003 were aged 18 to 64 years, whereas in the North East only 15 per cent were younger than 65 years. Seventeen per cent of London residents were aged 18 to 64 years with learning disabilities, compared to 7 per cent in the North East; the proportion being looked after because of mental health problems was also highest in London. (Table 7.19)

Children looked after by local authorities

Scotland had the highest proportion of children in Local Authority care at 102 out of 10,000 young people under 18 and the next highest was London with 70, while the average for England was 54 for the year ending March 2002. Scotland also had the highest rate of new admissions at 43 per 10,000 children. The South East had the lowest proportion or young people in care, 41 per 10,000, and also the joint lowest rate for new admissions at 16.

Except in Scotland, foster homes were the most common form of accommodation accounting for around two-thirds of children in care in England, rising to almost three-quarters in Wales and the South West.

London followed by Scotland had the highest proportion of young people being cared for in children's homes and hostels, at 14.5% and 14.0% respectively; Local Authority care provided by children's homes was lowest in Wales at 6.4%. (Table 7.20)

Children and young people on child protection registers

In the year to March 2002, Northern Ireland and the North East had the highest rates of children on the child protection register (34 and 33 people per 10,000 under 18-year olds respectively). The rate in the South East was the lowest at half this with 17 people per 10,000 under-18 year olds.

Neglect was the most common single reason for a child being on the child protection register for every region, ranging from 31 per cent in London to 46 per cent in Northern Ireland. About one-fifth of the children on registers in Northern Ireland, Wales, South West and North West were as a result of physical injury.

Sexual abuse was the least common cause of children being on registers in each region except in Yorkshire and the Humber and the East Midlands where it constituted 15 and 16 per cent of the total registered. In the North East and London the proportion was lowest at 7 per cent, although in the case of the North East far more children on registers fall under multiple or other categories (30 per cent of the total) than elsewhere in England. (Table 7.21)

Table **7.1**   Population and vital statistics: by former NHS Regional Office area, 2001

| | Population[1] aged (percentages and thousands) | | | | | | Vital statistics (rates) | | | | |
	0 to 4	5 to 15	16 to 44	45 to 74	75 and over	All ages (100%)	Live births[2,3]	Still births[3,4]	Deaths[5]	Perinatal mortality[6]	Infant mortality[7]
United Kingdom	5.9	14.2	40.1	32.2	7.5	58,836.7	54.5	5.3	10.3	8.0	5.5
Northern and Yorkshire	5.7	14.4	39.3	33.1	7.5	6,219.7	52.8	5.1	10.8	7.4	5.4
North West	5.9	14.9	39.3	32.6	7.4	6,450.5	54.5	6.2	11.1	8.8	5.9
Trent	5.7	14.3	39.2	33.2	7.7	5,089.6	52.4	5.4	10.5	8.0	5.3
West Midlands	6.0	14.8	39.0	32.7	7.4	5,267.1	57.0	5.5	10.3	9.1	6.4
Eastern	6.0	14.1	38.9	33.2	7.8	5,394.9	55.6	4.8	9.9	7.1	4.5
London	6.7	13.5	47.4	26.5	5.9	7,188.0	58.5	5.9	8.2	8.9	6.1
South East	5.9	14.1	39.4	32.6	7.9	8,637.3	54.6	4.6	9.9	6.9	4.2
South West	5.5	13.6	37.1	34.6	9.3	4,934.2	51.7	4.3	11.0	7.2	5.4
England	5.9	14.2	40.2	32.1	7.6	49,181.3	54.9	5.3	10.1	8.0	5.4
Wales	5.8	14.5	37.4	34.0	8.3	2,903.2	53.5	5.0	11.5	7.5	5.4
Scotland	5.5	13.7	40.4	33.3	7.1	5,064.2	48.8	5.7	11.3	8.5	5.5
Northern Ireland	6.8	16.7	41.7	28.9	6.0	1,689.3	59.7	5.1	8.6	8.4	6.0

1 Mid-year population estimates which have not been revised to take account of the Manchester matching exercise.
2 Per 1,000 women aged 15 to 44.
3 See Notes and Definitions for the Population chapter.
4 Per 1,000 live and still births. A still birth relates to a baby born dead after 24 completed weeks gestation or more.
5 Per 1,000 population.
6 Still births and deaths of infants under 1 week of age per 1,000 live and still births.
7 Deaths of infants under 1 year of age per 1,000 live births.

Source: Office for National Statistics; General Register Office for Scotland; Northern Ireland Statistics and Research Agency

Table **7.2**   Population: by NHS Strategic Health Authority[1], sex and age, mid-2002

Percentages and thousands

| | Male population[2] aged (percentages) | | | | | Female population[2] aged (percentages) | | | | |
	0–4	5–14	15–64	65–74	75 and over	All males ('000s = 100%)	0–4	5–14	15–64	65–74	75 and over	All females ('000s = 100%)
North East												
County Durham and Tees Valley	5.9	14.0	66.1	8.6	5.4	547	5.3	12.6	63.9	9.3	8.9	584
Northumberland, Tyne and Wear	5.7	13.4	66.3	8.8	5.8	669	5.1	11.9	63.9	9.7	9.4	713
North West												
Cheshire and Merseyside	6.0	14.3	65.5	8.7	5.5	1,124	5.3	12.6	63.7	9.3	9.1	1,219
Cumbria and Lancashire	6.1	13.9	65.3	8.7	6.0	922	5.4	12.5	62.7	9.4	10.0	978
Greater Manchester	6.4	14.4	66.5	7.5	5.1	1,208	5.8	13.0	64.1	8.3	8.8	1,274
Yorkshire and the Humber												
North and East Yorkshire and												
Northern Lincolnshire	5.8	13.8	65.1	9.0	6.3	775	5.2	12.3	62.9	9.6	10.1	830
South Yorkshire	6.1	13.7	66.4	8.2	5.7	616	5.5	12.4	63.7	9.0	9.4	649
West Yorkshire	6.6	14.4	66.2	7.5	5.3	1,005	5.9	13.0	63.9	8.4	8.8	1,073
East Midlands												
Leicestershire, Northamptonshire												
and Rutland	6.3	14.0	66.8	7.5	5.4	761	5.8	12.8	64.9	8.1	8.5	789
Trent	5.8	13.6	65.7	8.7	6.2	1,277	5.3	12.3	63.5	9.3	9.7	1,334
West Midlands												
Birmingham and The Black Country	6.9	14.8	64.7	8.1	5.5	1,094	6.2	13.5	62.6	8.8	9.0	1,159
Coventry, Warwickshire, Herefordshire												
and Worcestershire	6.0	13.5	66.2	8.4	6.0	747	5.4	12.2	63.8	8.9	9.7	775
Shropshire and Staffordshire	5.9	13.5	66.7	8.4	5.5	725	5.5	12.4	64.1	8.9	9.0	757
East												
Bedfordshire and Hertfordshire	6.7	14.1	66.5	7.6	5.2	784	6.2	13.0	64.5	8.1	8.2	814
Essex	6.4	13.6	65.6	8.4	6.1	784	5.6	12.3	63.3	8.9	9.8	828
Norfolk, Suffolk and Cambridgeshire	5.9	13.1	65.0	9.2	6.9	1,041	5.3	11.8	62.9	9.6	10.4	1,097
London												
North Central London	6.8	12.8	69.7	6.3	4.4	564	6.1	11.4	69.0	6.5	7.0	615
North East London	7.6	14.6	67.1	6.3	4.3	729	6.9	13.2	66.1	6.7	7.1	769
North West London	6.6	12.0	70.6	6.4	4.4	839	5.9	10.9	69.5	6.7	6.9	890
South East London	7.1	13.2	68.9	6.3	4.6	722	6.4	11.9	67.2	6.9	7.5	769
South West London	7.0	12.6	69.5	6.2	4.7	617	6.2	11.1	68.1	6.7	7.8	663
South East												
Hampshire and Isle of Wight	6.1	13.7	65.7	8.3	6.2	847	5.5	12.2	63.6	8.8	9.9	902
Kent and Medway	6.4	14.3	65.1	8.3	6.0	762	5.6	12.8	63.0	8.8	9.8	813
Surrey and Sussex	6.0	13.0	64.9	8.8	7.2	1,226	5.3	11.4	62.0	9.5	11.8	1,322
Thames Valley	6.6	13.8	67.8	7.1	4.8	1,022	6.1	12.5	66.2	7.4	7.8	1,054
South West												
Avon, Gloucestershire and Wiltshire	6.3	13.4	66.0	8.2	6.1	1,044	5.7	12.1	63.7	8.7	9.8	1,101
Dorset and Somerset	5.4	13.0	62.9	10.2	8.4	568	4.9	11.4	60.2	10.7	12.9	616
South West Peninsula	5.5	13.1	63.6	10.1	7.7	748	4.8	11.4	61.3	10.3	12.2	814
England	6.3	13.7	66.2	8.1	5.8	23,767	5.6	12.3	64.1	8.7	9.3	25,201
Wales	6.1	14.0	64.8	8.8	6.3	1,400	5.4	12.4	62.6	9.4	10.2	1,499
Scotland	5.7	13.1	67.6	8.3	5.3	2,432	5.0	11.6	65.1	9.4	9.0	2,623
Northern Ireland	7.0	15.7	66.1	6.8	4.5	829	6.3	14.2	64.1	7.9	7.5	868

1 Strategic Health Authorities were introduced by NHS in England on 1 April 2002.
2 Mid-year estimates which have not been revised to take account of the Manchester matching exercise.

Source: Office for National Statistics; General Register Office for Scotland; Northern Ireland Statistics and Research Agency.

Table **7.3**   Proportion of population reporting 'good' state of general health: by sex and age, 2001/02

Percentages

	Males				Females			
	16 to 44	45 to 64	65 or over	All aged 16 and over	16 to 44	45 to 64	65 or over	All aged 16 and over
North East	64	44	33	53	67	49	20	51
North West	74	46	33	58	69	48	35	56
Yorkshire and the Humber	73	54	37	61	67	52	33	55
East Midlands	70	51	39	58	63	53	39	54
West Midlands	73	52	37	59	73	53	40	60
East	75	60	43	65	66	58	37	58
London	75	62	39	67	70	55	38	61
South East	77	63	41	66	68	57	42	59
South West	69	60	38	60	72	59	34	59
England	73	56	38	62	69	54	37	58
Wales	66	53	32	55	72	53	25	55
Scotland	68	53	36	58	66	59	39	57
Northern Ireland	72	48	31	57	66	47	26	52

Source: General Household Survey, Office for National Statistics; Continuous Household Survey, Northern Ireland Statistics and Research Agency.

Table **7.4**   Still births, perinatal mortality and infant mortality[1]

Rates

	Still births[2,3]		Still births[2,3]			Perinatal mortality[3,4]		Perinatal mortality[3,4]			Infant mortality[5]			
	1981	1993	1993	2001	2002	1981	1993	1993	2001	2002	1981	1993	2001	2002
United Kingdom	6.6	4.4	5.7	5.3	5.6	12.0	7.6	9.0	8.0	8.2	11.2	6.3	5.5	5.3
North East	7.5	4.6	5.9	5.2	5.8	12.6	7.9	9.2	7.9	7.7	10.4	6.7	5.6	5.0
North West	7.0	4.5	5.8	6.1	5.6	12.7	7.7	9.0	8.8	8.4	11.3	6.5	5.9	5.4
Yorkshire and the Humber	7.8	4.6	5.9	5.1	6.0	13.5	8.0	9.4	7.6	9.1	12.1	7.3	5.8	6.2
East Midlands	6.2	3.9	5.4	5.4	5.6	11.4	7.2	8.7	7.9	8.4	11.0	6.6	5.0	5.6
West Midlands	7.0	4.4	6.0	5.5	6.2	12.9	8.4	9.9	9.0	10.1	11.7	7.1	6.4	6.5
East	5.5	3.9	5.2	4.8	5.3	10.0	6.8	8.1	7.0	7.5	9.7	5.4	4.5	4.4
London	6.3	4.9	6.1	5.9	6.5	10.3	8.2	9.5	8.9	9.2	10.7	6.5	6.1	5.6
South East	5.8	4.0	5.4	4.6	4.8	10.5	7.0	8.3	6.8	6.8	10.3	5.3	4.2	4.5
South West	6.3	4.0	5.0	4.3	4.5	10.8	6.9	7.9	7.1	6.9	10.4	5.8	5.4	4.4
England	6.5	4.3	5.7	5.3	5.6	11.7	7.6	8.9	8.0	8.3	10.9	6.3	5.4	5.3
Wales	7.3	4.5	5.8	5.0	5.4	14.1	7.0	8.3	7.5	7.7	12.6	5.5	5.4	4.7
Scotland	6.3	4.8	6.4	5.7	5.4	11.6	8.0	9.6	8.5	7.5	11.3	6.5	5.5	5.2
Northern Ireland	8.8	4.1	5.2	5.1	5.7	15.3	7.7	8.8	8.4	8.8	13.2	7.1	6.0	4.7

1 See Notes and Definitions for the Population chapter.
2 Rate per 1,000 live and still births.
3 On 1 October 1992 the legal definition of a still birth was altered from a baby born dead after 28 completed weeks gestation or more to one born dead after 24 weeks gestation or more. Figures are given on both the old and new definitions for continuity.
4 Still births and deaths of infants under 1 week of age per 1,000 live and still births.
5 Deaths of infants under 1 year of age per 1,000 live births.

Source: Office for National Statistics; General Register Office for Scotland; Northern Ireland Statistics and Research Agency

Table **7.5**   Age-standardised mortality rates[1]: by cause[2] and sex, 2001

Rates per 100,000 population

	All circulatory diseases			All respiratory diseases			All injuries and poisonings			All other causes	All causes[4]
	Total	Ischaemic heart disease	Cerebro-vascular disease	Total	Bronchitis and allied conditions	Cancer[3]	Total	Road traffic accidents	Suicides and open verdicts		
Males											
United Kingdom	351	207	75	104	45	254	43	10	16	140	892
North East	395	240	88	121	56	300	44	6	16	143	1,002
North West	393	235	84	120	54	279	49	9	17	142	982
Yorkshire and the Humber	367	225	80	109	51	258	39	9	14	139	912
East Midlands	341	199	73	107	47	236	43	11	15	135	862
West Midlands	361	211	79	104	44	249	43	10	16	148	904
East	313	181	62	91	39	230	38	10	11	125	797
London	339	193	71	117	48	252	37	7	13	146	890
South East	307	172	66	90	37	231	38	10	13	124	791
South West	312	182	67	82	36	225	39	10	15	125	784
England	343	201	73	103	45	248	41	9	14	136	870
Wales	377	226	77	102	46	260	49	9	19	134	921
Scotland	396	238	92	109	54	298	61	11	26	180	1,044
Northern Ireland	366	226	76	116	43	259	47	15	17	135	924
Females											
United Kingdom	396	173	129	128	40	243	24	3	5	208	999
North East	427	200	137	147	55	275	23	2	4	223	1,095
North West	439	200	138	150	53	260	28	3	5	214	1,090
Yorkshire and the Humber	395	183	129	131	47	248	18	3	4	213	1,005
East Midlands	396	171	133	129	36	237	26	4	4	211	1,000
West Midlands	404	175	134	126	38	234	25	3	4	213	1,002
East	358	149	118	119	31	230	22	3	4	209	939
London	364	152	111	142	39	235	21	3	5	202	963
South East	359	144	119	111	30	228	22	2	4	197	917
South West	359	153	122	97	26	218	21	3	4	197	893
England	386	167	126	126	38	238	23	3	4	207	981
Wales	430	191	136	133	45	251	27	2	4	197	1,039
Scotland	456	212	155	132	54	277	34	4	9	223	1,121
Northern Ireland	421	201	130	148	36	235	23	4	3	191	1,019
All people											
United Kingdom	378	192	103	117	44	251	33	6	10	175	954
North East	415	222	113	135	56	289	33	4	10	184	1,056
North West	419	220	112	136	54	271	38	6	11	179	1,043
Yorkshire and the Humber	385	207	106	122	50	256	29	6	9	177	967
East Midlands	374	189	104	121	43	240	34	7	10	174	943
West Midlands	387	196	108	116	42	245	34	6	10	182	963
East	340	168	91	107	36	234	30	7	8	168	879
London	355	175	92	131	44	246	28	5	9	174	935
South East	337	160	93	102	35	233	30	6	9	161	863
South West	341	171	96	92	32	225	30	6	9	162	849
England	369	187	100	116	42	246	31	6	9	172	935
Wales	407	211	108	119	46	259	37	6	11	166	988
Scotland	427	225	124	121	54	288	47	7	17	202	1,085
Northern Ireland	396	214	104	134	40	249	34	9	10	164	977

1 Based on deaths registered in 2001. Rates standardised to the mid-1991 United Kingdom population for males and females separately. See Notes and Definitions.
2 Deaths at ages under 28 days occurring in England and Wales are not assigned an underlying cause.
3 Malignant neoplasms only.
4 Including deaths at ages under 28 days.

Source: Office for National Statistics; General Register Office for Scotland; Northern Ireland Statistics and Research Agency

Table **7.6**   Notification rates of tuberculosis

Rates per 100,000 population

	1992	1993	1994	1995	1996	1997	1998	1999	2000	2001	2002
United Kingdom	11.2	11.4	10.8	10.7	10.7	10.9	11.3	11.5	12.1	12.2	12.2
North East	9.4	8.7	6.5	6.9	6.6	7.0	6.6	5.9	5.7	7.7	6.4
North West	11.5	11.9	9.8	9.5	8.8	9.3	10.2	10.7	10.0	10.0	9.4
Yorkshire and the Humber	10.1	11.5	10.1	12.0	11.6	11.7	12.0	11.5	12.1	12.3	10.8
East Midlands	8.8	11.5	9.9	10.1	10.6	9.3	10.4	10.7	10.6	11.1	11.9
West Midlands	16.6	15.0	13.9	12.4	12.5	11.6	12.8	13.5	13.7	13.1	14.9
East	5.6	5.2	4.7	5.1	5.0	4.4	5.1	4.3	4.7	6.0	6.1
London	29.4	28.7	30.3	29.8	31.7	34.8	35.1	35.4	39.9	40.2	38.6
South East	4.6	5.4	5.3	5.5	5.3	5.4	5.5	5.3	6.1	6.6	7.3
South West	4.2	4.5	4.3	4.2	4.2	4.4	4.4	4.3	4.6	4.0	4.8
England	11.7	11.9	11.2	11.2	11.3	11.7	12.2	12.2	13.0	13.4	13.4
Wales	7.0	6.9	6.3	6.2	5.6	6.7	5.9	7.1	6.7	4.9	4.3
Scotland	11.0	10.9	10.7	9.4	10.0	8.5	9.0	9.8	9.3	8.7	8.3
Northern Ireland	5.2	5.5	5.7	5.5	4.5	4.5	3.6	3.6	3.5	2.8	4.0

Source: Health Protection Agency Communicable Disease Surveillance Centre; Scottish Centre for Infection and Environmental Health; Department of Health, Social Services and Public Safety, Northern Ireland

Table **7.7**   Cervical and breast cancer: screening and age-standardised death rates: by NHS Regional Office area

	Cervical screening programme at 31 March 2002						Breast screening programme at 31 March 2002				Age-standardised death rates[6], 2001	
	Percentage of target population[1] screened: women aged					Per-centage recalled early[4] 2001/02	Percentage of target population[5] screened: women aged				Cervical cancer	Breast cancer
	25 to 34[2,3]	35 to 44	45 to 54	55 to 64[3]	All aged 25 to 64[2,3]		50 to 54	55 to 59	60 to 64	All aged 50 to 64		
United Kingdom	78.1	84.5	84.1	79.4	81.6	..	61.2	76.1	74.7	70.1	5.0	54.9
Northern and Yorkshire	81.5	85.9	84.6	79.9	83.3	5.2	61.6	79.3	77.7	72.1	5.6	51.5
North West	80.2	84.0	82.6	77.5	81.4	7.2	61.1	77.2	75.4	70.7	6.1	56.4
Trent	82.9	86.8	85.2	80.8	84.2	5.6	63.7	81.1	79.8	74.3	5.0	57.9
West Midlands	79.3	84.7	83.7	79.6	82.0	6.4	62.5	79.1	77.3	72.5	5.2	51.9
Eastern	79.7	84.8	84.2	80.2	82.4	6.0	60.1	77.1	76.3	70.5	3.5	55.3
London	71.7	78.8	79.7	76.0	75.9	7.2	47.9	63.8	62.4	57.2	5.2	56.5
South East	79.8	85.7	85.1	81.3	83.1	5.7	60.4	76.8	76.0	70.4	3.9	55.2
South West	80.5	85.2	84.5	80.1	82.8	6.3	60.9	78.3	77.7	71.7	4.5	53.9
England	78.6	84.2	83.6	79.4	81.6	6.2	59.6	76.5	75.2	69.8	4.8	54.8
Wales	73.1	85.5	85.5	79.3	80.0	7.0	57.5	72.5	71.2	66.6	7.6	56.0
Scotland	79.7	91.2	91.7	87.6	86.5	..	75.0	76.0	74.0	75.0	5.3	55.0
Northern Ireland	70.0	75.5	74.3	66.8	72.2	..	73.7	72.7	71.2	72.6	4.0	53.1

1 For England and Northern Ireland the target population relates to women aged 25 to 64, for Wales to women aged 20 to 64 and for Scotland to women 20 to 60 years screened in the previous 5 years (5 and a half years in Scotland). Medically ineligible women (women who for example, as a result of surgery, do not require screening) in the target population are excluded from the figures, except in Northern Ireland. See Notes and Definitions.

2 For Wales the age groups are 20 to 34 and 20 to 64 for 'All ages' total.

3 For Scotland the age groups are 20 to 34 and 55 to 60. 'All ages' total is therefore 20 to 60.

4 Women whose screening test results are borderline or show mild dyskaryosis are recalled for a repeat smear in approximately 6 months instead of the routine 5 years; if the condition persists they are referred to a gynaecologist.

5 Percentage of the target population (women aged 50 to 64 years) screened in the previous 3 years. Medically ineligible women (women who for example, as a result of surgery, do not require screening) in the target population are excluded from the figures, except in Scotland. See Notes and Definitions.

6 Deaths registered in 2001 per 100,000 women aged 20 or over. Standardised to mid-1991 UK population. See Notes and Definitions.

Source: Office for National Statistics; Department of Health; National Assembly for Wales; General Register Office for Scotland; Information and Statistics Division, NHS Scotland; Northern Ireland Statistics and Research Agency; Department of Health, Social Services and Public Safety, Northern Ireland.

Figure **7.8** Standardised cancer registrations, 2000[1]

Standardised rate England = 100

Stomach

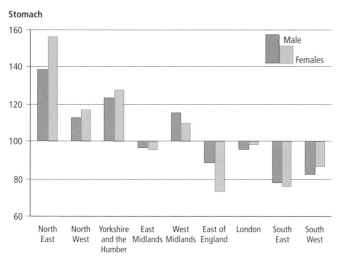

Lung

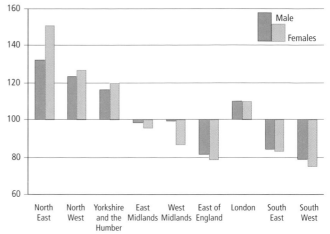

Breast

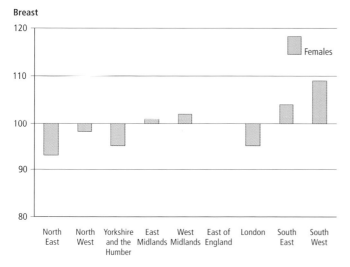

Prostate

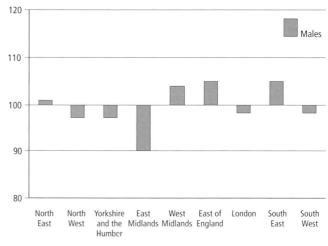

Skin[2]

Leukaemia

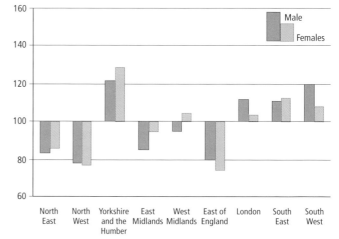

1 Standardised registration ratios by region of residence, as registered by July 2003.
2 Malignant melanoma of skin. See Notes and Definitions for detail of categories and rates for England and the UK

Source: Office for National Statistics

Table **7.9** **Diagnosed HIV-infected patients: by probable route of HIV infection and region of residence when last seen for care in 2002[1]**

Numbers

	Sex between men	Injecting drug use	Sex between men and women	Blood/ blood products	Mother to infant[2]	Other/ not known	Total
United Kingdom[3]	14,522	1,285	13,005	495	1,038	1,516	31,861
North East	184	12	185	10	7	11	409
North West	1,390	75	628	58	55	122	2,328
Yorkshire and the Humber	382	43	463	46	29	34	997
East Midlands	344	42	565	34	44	37	1,066
West Midlands	499	23	523	20	56	36	1,157
East	427	51	943	36	47	45	1,549
London	8,115	455	7,019	121	586	906	17,202
South East	1,473	115	1,340	66	98	138	3,230
South West	569	43	365	18	26	50	1,071
England[4]	13,398	860	12,047	409	950	1,380	29,044
Wales	253	16	153	30	8	8	468
Scotland	546	391	504	40	51	40	1,572
Northern Ireland	82	5	52	1	1	2	143

1 Patients reported as seen for HIV-related care at NHS medical services in the United Kingdom in 2002.

2 Includes 293 children born to HIV infected mothers in 2002 whose HIV infected status had not been confirmed: four residents in North East, 14 in North West, 13 in Yorkshire and the Humber, 16 in East Midlands, 26 in West Midlands, 18 in East of England, 133 in London, 33 in South East, three in South West, none in Wales, 17 in Scotland, none in Northern Ireland and 16 where the region was not reported.

3 United Kingdom total includes those reported to be resident abroad or whose country of residence was not reported.

4 Includes patients whose region of residence within England was not known.

Source: Health Protection Agency Communicable Disease Surveillance Centre; Institute of Child Health (London); Scottish Centre for Infection and Environmental Health.

Table **7.10** **Contributions of selected foods to nutritional intakes (household food), 1999/2000[1]**

	Percentage of fat and energy derived from										Total intake[2] per person per day		Per- centage of food energy derived from fat[2]
	Liquid and processed milk and cream		Meat and meat products		All fats		Fresh and processed fruit and vegetables		Cereals including bread				
	Fat	Energy	Fat	Energy	Fat	Energy	Fat	Energy	Fat	Energy	Fat (grams)	Energy (Kcal)	
United Kingdom	11.2	10.4	22.6	14.7	27.6	10.7	8.3	15.3	17.1	35.7	73	1,722	38
North East	11.1	10.4	23.6	15.4	26.3	10.2	8.4	15.3	18.2	36.2	72	1,694	38
North West	11.8	10.9	24.3	15.7	26.7	10.3	7.5	14.4	16.9	35.8	70	1,656	38
Yorkshire and the Humber	11.5	10.8	23.6	15.3	27.8	10.8	7.4	14.6	17.3	35.9	73	1,715	38
East Midlands	11.1	10.4	22.0	14.0	28.0	10.6	8.0	15.0	17.6	36.7	73	1,760	38
West Midlands	10.9	10.0	21.3	13.8	29.9	11.5	8.5	15.5	16.5	35.7	74	1,757	38
East	10.5	9.8	22.7	14.6	26.0	10.0	8.9	16.1	17.9	36.0	73	1,736	38
London	10.6	9.7	21.3	13.6	30.6	11.6	8.2	15.6	15.6	36.7	71	1,690	38
South East	11.0	10.3	21.8	14.3	27.0	10.6	8.9	15.7	17.0	34.9	77	1,788	39
South West	11.1	10.5	22.4	14.7	26.6	10.3	9.0	16.3	17.3	34.7	74	1,736	38
England	11.1	10.3	22.5	14.6	27.7	10.7	8.3	15.4	17.1	35.8	73	1,727	38
Wales	11.4	10.5	23.3	15.2	28.6	11.1	8.0	15.1	16.5	34.8	73	1,713	38
Scotland	12.4	11.1	23.7	15.6	24.4	9.5	8.3	14.4	17.5	35.6	71	1,660	38
Northern Ireland	12.9	11.5	22.9	14.9	31.4	12.3	7.0	15.8	16.5	35.0	76	1,775	39

1 Data collected through the National Food Survey in which 6000 households in Great Britain keep a record of the type, quantity and costs of foods entering the home during a one week period. Nutritional intakes are just estimates taken from the survey data. See Notes and Definitions.

2 Total intake from all household food, excluding household consumption of soft and alcoholic drinks and confectionery.

Source: National Food Survey, Department for Environment, Food and Rural Affairs

Table 7.11   Cigarette smoking among people aged 16 or over: by sex, 2001/02

Percentages

	Males					Females				
	Smoked per day				Never or only	Smoked per day				Never or only
	less than 10	10, less than 20	20 or more	Ex-regular smoker	occasionally smoked	less than 10	10, less than 20	20 or more	Ex-regular smoker	occasionally smoked
Great Britain	8	11	10	27	45	8	11	7	21	54
North East	6	16	11	23	44	6	12	8	20	55
North West	7	11	10	27	45	8	12	10	21	50
Yorkshire and the Humber	7	12	11	26	44	9	11	8	21	51
East Midlands	8	11	10	25	47	8	11	7	22	51
West Midlands	6	11	9	29	44	6	9	7	18	59
East	7	13	7	30	43	8	10	6	21	54
London	11	10	8	22	48	10	10	5	17	57
South East	7	10	10	29	45	8	9	6	23	54
South West	9	9	9	30	43	8	8	5	25	53
England	8	11	9	27	45	8	10	7	21	54
Wales	9	9	9	26	47	9	12	6	22	51
Scotland	6	12	13	23	45	6	15	9	18	52

Source: General Household Survey, Office for National Statistics; Continuous Household Survey, Northern Ireland Statistics and Research Agency.

Table 7.12   Alcohol consumption among people aged 16 and over: by sex, 2001/02[1]

Percentages

	Males				Females			
	Drank nothing last week	Drank up to 4 units last week[2]	Drank more than 4 and up to 8 units[2]	Drank more than 8 units last week[2]	Drank nothing last week	Drank up to 3 units last week[2]	Drank more than 3 and up to 6 units[2]	Drank more than 6 units last week[2]
North East	30	23	19	28	45	27	13	15
North West	22	31	20	27	37	35	15	13
Yorkshire and the Humber	22	35	17	26	40	35	13	12
East Midlands	25	32	21	21	35	39	14	12
West Midlands	28	39	16	17	46	38	10	7
East	28	38	14	19	41	39	12	8
London	30	35	16	19	46	36	10	8
South East	25	42	16	17	39	41	13	7
South West	21	42	17	19	36	41	14	8
England	26	36	17	21	40	38	13	9
Wales	28	36	16	20	46	33	10	11
Scotland	23	32	17	28	43	31	14	13

1   Comparative consumption levels are different for males and females. See Notes and Definitions.
2   On the heaviest drinking day last week.

Source: General Household Survey, Office for National Statistics

Figure **7.13** Drug use among 16 to 29 year olds[1], 2001/02[2]

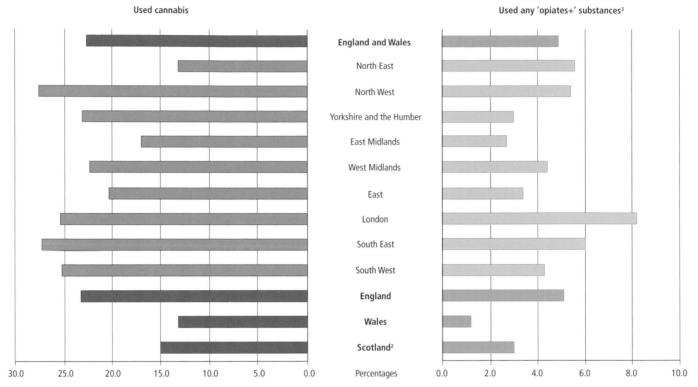

Used cannabis

Used any 'opiates+' substances[3]

England and Wales
North East
North West
Yorkshire and the Humber
East Midlands
West Midlands
East
London
South East
South West
England
Wales
Scotland[2]

1 See Notes and Definitions for where to find results.
2 Interviews were conducted between April 2001 and March 2002, asking about drug use in the previous 12 months before the date of interview. Data for Scotland relate to 2000.
3 Heroin, methadone, cocaine or crack.

Source: British Crime Survey, Home Office; Scottish Crime Survey, Scottish Executive

Table **7.14** Prescriptions dispensed, 2002

	Prescription items dispensed (millions)[1]	Percentage of prescription items exempt from charge[2,3]	Percentage of prescription items[2,4] that were for		Number of prescription items per head	Average net ingredient cost[5]	
			Children	People aged 60 or over		£ per person	£ per prescription item
North East	36.7	87.5	6.5	56.4	14.6	152.3	10.4
North West	101.5	86.9	6.8	55.8	15.1	163.1	10.8
Yorkshire and the Humber	70.9	86.2	6.8	56.8	14.3	145.3	10.1
East Midlands	52.7	84.2	6.4	57.8	12.7	133.5	10.5
West Midlands	67.8	86.2	8.1	55.6	12.9	142.7	11.1
East	64.8	83.0	6.7	57.9	12.1	139.0	11.5
London	71.4	86.1	10.0	49.2	10.0	118.8	11.9
South East	88.8	82.8	6.7	58.2	11.2	135.1	12.1
South West	62.4	85.2	5.6	61.1	12.8	137.4	10.8
England	617.0	85.3	7.1	56.5	12.6	139.8	11.1
Wales	48.8	88.2	10.7	49.6	16.8	171.6	10.2
Scotland	69.1	90.7	..	..	13.7	163.8	12.0
Northern Ireland	25.4	93.8	..	..	14.3	168.3	11.8

1 Figures relate to NHS prescription items dispensed by community pharmacies, appliance contractors (appliance suppliers in Scotland and in Northern Ireland), and dispensing doctors, and prescriptions submitted by prescribing doctors for items personally administered, known as stock orders in Scotland and Northern Ireland.
2 For England, items for personal administration are not analysed into exempt, non-exempt or other categories and are therefore excluded. Personally administered items are free of charge. For Scotland, figures relate to items dispensed by community pharmacists, appliance contractors and dispensing doctors.
3 Figures for the English regions, England and Wales exclude prescriptions for which prepayment certificates have been purchased. For Scotland and Northern Ireland they are included. Due to this, and the issues mentioned in footnote 2, comparisons across the four areas should not be made.
4 The data for England for 'people aged 60 and over' and 'children' (children aged 15 and under and young adults aged 16 to 18 who are in full-time education) are estimates based in a 1 in 20 sample of prescription items dispensed by community pharmacists, appliance contractors and dispensing doctors. Data for Wales are calculated from a 100 per cent sample of prescriptions but based on 3 months data only. Age specific data are not available in Scotland and Northern Ireland.
5 Net ingredient cost is the cost of medicines before any discounts and does not include any dispensing costs or fees. This is known as Gross Ingredient Cost in Scotland and Ingredient Cost in Northern Ireland.

Source: Department of Health; National Assembly for Wales, Information and Statistics Division, NHS in Scotland; Central Services Agency, Northern Ireland.

Table 7.15 NHS hospital waiting lists: by patients' region of residence[1,2] at 31 March 2003

	NHS hospital waiting lists[2]						
	Percentage waiting:				Total waiting (=100%) (thousands)	Mean waiting time (months)[3]	Median waiting time (months)[3]
	Less than 6 months	6 months but less than 12	Less than 12 months	12 months or longer			
Patients' region of residence[4]							
North East							
County Durham and Tees Valley	81.1	18.9	100	0	21.0	3.6	2.8
Northumberland, Tyne and Wear	84.8	15.2	100	0	25.3	3.3	2.5
North West							
Cheshire and Merseyside	79.8	20.2	100	0	53.1	3.6	2.7
Cumbria and Lancashire	81.3	18.7	100	0	43.0	3.5	2.7
Greater Manchester	82.4	17.6	100	0	61.9	3.4	2.6
Yorkshire and Humberside							
North and East Yorkshire and Northern Lincolnshire	79.3	20.7	100	0	32.7	3.7	2.8
South Yorkshire	85.7	14.3	100	0	20.6	3.2	2.4
West Yorkshire	81.3	18.7	100	0	38.4	3.5	2.7
East Midlands							
Leicestershire, Northamptonshire and Rutland	83.2	16.8	100	0	28.1	3.4	2.6
Trent	82.6	17.4	100	0	51.9	3.4	2.6
West Midlands							
Birmingham and the Black Country	93.8	6.2	100	0	29.3	2.5	2.1
Coventry, Warwickshire, Herefordshire and Worcestershire	82.2	17.8	100	0	24.5	3.5	2.6
Shropshire and Staffordshire	78.0	22.0	100	0	25.9	3.8	3.0
East							
Bedfordshire and Hertfordshire	76.7	23.2	99.8	0.2	34.3	3.9	3.0
Essex	78.9	21.1	100	0	35.4	3.8	2.9
Norfolk, Suffolk and Cambridgeshire	79.5	20.5	100	0	49.7	3.7	2.8
London							
North Central London	82.2	17.8	100	0	20.1	3.5	2.7
North East London	78.8	21.2	100	0	31.0	3.8	2.9
North West London	81.7	18.3	100	0	29.0	3.5	2.7
South East London	78.4	21.6	100	0	27.5	3.8	2.9
South West London	82.7	17.3	100	0	23.1	3.5	2.7
South East							
Hampshire and Isle of Wight	78.0	22.0	100	0	41.0	3.8	3.0
Kent and Medway	73.8	26.2	100	0	36.9	4.1	3.4
Surrey and Sussex	78.2	21.8	100	0	54.7	3.8	3.0
Thames Valley	81.6	18.4	100	0	34.7	3.5	2.7
South West							
Avon, Gloucestershire and Wiltshire	78.8	21.2	100	0	46.2	3.8	2.9
Dorset and Somerset	91.4	8.5	100	0	18.0	2.9	2.3
South West Peninsula	74.5	25.5	100	0	37.9	4.1	3.3
England	80.6	19.4	100	0	975.3	3.6	2.7
Wales	63.0	21.0	84.2	15.9	74.6	..	..
Scotland	74.9	14.8	89.7	10.3	102.5	5.6	2.7
Northern Ireland	60.0	18.0	78.0	22.0	56.0	..	..

1   In Scotland, waiting lists are based on NHS lists for each trust irrespective of the patient's residence.
2   The figures relate to people on the waiting lists on 31 March 2003 who were waiting for admission as either an in-patient or a day case and the length of time they had waited to date. Figures for Northern Ireland included all patients waiting for treatment at Northern Ireland Trusts including private patients and patients from outside Northern Ireland. Patients undergoing a series of repeat admissions and those who were temporarily suspended from the waiting list for medical or social reasons are excluded. There are differences between countries in the ways that waiting times are calculated; comparisons between countries should be made with caution.
3   Average time patients had been waiting at 31 March 2003. The mean and median are different types of 'average'.   See Notes and Definitions.
4   Data for England relate to Strategic Health Authorities.

Source: Department of Health; National Assembly for Wales; Information and Statistics Division, NHS in Scotland; Department of Health, Social Services, Northern Ireland.

Table **7.16**   NHS hospital activity:[1] by Strategic Health Authority and region, 2002/03[2]

	In-patients (all specialities)						Consultant out-patient attendances	
	Average daily available beds[3] per 1,000 population	Admissions[4] per available bed	Admissions[4] per 1,000 population	Finished consultants episodes[5] (thousands)	Average length of stay[4] (days)	Day cases (thousands)	Total accident & emergency attendances (thousands)	Total (thousands)	Of which: new[6] outpatients (percentages)
North East	4.7	40	190	799		251	771	2,648	
County Durham and Tees Valley	4.3	43	184	335	6.0	93	333	1,009	30.1
Northumberland, Tyne and Wear	5.1	38	195	464	8.3	158	438	1,639	32.7
North West	4.2	44	183	2,016		541	2,181	7,037	
Cheshire and Merseyside	4.1	44	182	695	7.3	166	785	2,622	27.6
Cumbria and Lancashire	4.0	44	175	540	7.7	156	542	1,450	30.3
Greater Manchester	4.3	44	190	780	6.9	219	855	2,965	27.4
Yorkshire and the Humber	4.0	44	175	1,436		438	1,620	4,735	
North and East Yorkshire and Northern Lincolnshire	3.3	45	147	395	6.9	124	488	1,190	28.7
South Yorkshire	4.7	43	204	437	7.7	139	418	1,591	29.2
West Yorkshire	4.1	44	179	603	9.5	175	714	1,953	26.0
East Midlands	3.4	42	142	1,011		301	916	3,126	
Leicestershire, Northamptonshire and Rutland	3.5	42	146	370	7.3	112	293	1,167	27.9
Trent	3.4	41	140	641	7.8	189	623	1,959	27.6
West Midlands	3.6	45	161	1,401		415	1,598	4,833	
Birmingham and the Black Country	4.1	46	186	687	7.6	190	757	2,564	27.0
Coventry, Warwickshire, Herefordshire and Worcestershire	3.2	44	141	338	6.9	91	454	1,128	29.9
Shropshire and Staffordshire	3.3	44	144	376	7.2	134	387	1,141	31.6
East	3.4	40	135	1,252		372	1,197	4,115	
Bedfordshire and Hertfordshire	2.8	40	111	284	6.9	82	381	1,110	30.3
Essex	3.1	39	121	332	11.1	103	355	1,196	30.0
Norfolk, Suffolk and Cambridgeshire	3.9	42	164	636	7.7	187	462	1,809	30.7
London	4.0	39	156	1,794		522	2,482	8,139	
North Central London	4.9	39	189	353	8.1	104	408	1,924	27.9
North East London	4.1	36	148	362	9.0	105	481	1,516	30.0
North West London	4.0	37	149	415	7.9	114	615	1,814	26.6
South East London	3.8	41	157	374	8.2	110	563	1,593	28.8
South West London	3.5	41	142	292	8.7	87	416	1,292	29.0
South East	3.2	42	135	1,677		454	1,892	6,097	
Hampshire and Isle of Wight	3.3	43	142	403	8.0	97	303	1,290	30.6
Kent and Medway	3.0	46	138	333	7.8	87	482	1,260	28.5
Surrey and Sussex	3.5	37	127	519	10.1	164	651	1,971	30.0
Thames Valley	2.9	47	137	421	7.2	105	457	1,576	32.5
South West	3.9	48	158	1,369		422	1,387	3,869	
Avon, Gloucestershire and Wiltshire	3.9	39	153	580	8.4	183	629	1,742	30.6
Dorset and Somerset	4.1	37	151	327	8.7	110	294	908	35.5
South West Peninsula	3.6	47	171	461	7.0	129	464	1,219	31.2
England	3.8	42	157	12,755		3,714	14,046	44,598	29.2
Wales[2]	5.0	35	174	509	6.8	133	1,010	2,762	25.2
Scotland[2]	6.0	30	188	954	7.0	420	1,563	4,707	28.0
Northern Ireland[2]	4.9	39	194	328	6.4	130	673	1,458	28.3

1   See Notes and definitions.
2   Data for Wales, Scotland and Northern Ireland relate to 2001/02.
3   Excluding cots for healthy new-born babies except in Northern Ireland.
4   Admissions and length of stay exclude day cases.
5   Finished consultant episodes in England and discharges and deaths in Wales. Data for Scotland relate to discharges and deaths and transfers to other specialities and hospitals. Data for Northern Ireland relate to discharges and deaths and transfers to another hospital. Healthy new-born babies are included for Northern Ireland but excluded for the other countries.
6   In Northern Ireland data refer to GP referrals, not first attendances.

Source: Department of Health; National Assembly for Wales; Information and Statistics Division, NHS in Scotland; Department of Health, Social Services, Northern Ireland.

Table **7.17**   NHS Hospital and Community Health Service staff: by type of staff[1], 30 September 2002

Percentages and thousands

	Medical and dental	Qualified nursing, midwifery and health visiting[2]	Qualified scientific, therapeutic and technical	Support to clinical and other direct care staff[3]	All medical and clinical staff	NHS infrastructure support staff[4]	Total staff[1] (=100%) (thousands)
North East	7.5	32.2	10.0	31.4	81.0	19.0	53.3
County Durham and Tees Valley	7.1	33.0	9.2	30.2	79.5	20.5	21.0
Northumberland, Tyne and Wear	7.7	31.6	10.4	32.2	82.0	18.0	32.4
North West	7.3	32.5	10.7	32.9	83.4	16.6	134.7
Cheshire and Merseyside	7.1	32.6	11.1	32.2	82.9	17.1	47.9
Cumbria and Lancashire	6.3	33.1	9.3	34.4	83.1	16.9	34.2
Greater Manchester	8.0	31.9	11.4	32.6	83.9	16.1	52.6
Yorkshire and the Humber	7.4	30.9	11.3	31.3	80.9	19.1	95.6
North and East Yorkshire and Northern Lincolnshire	7.0	33.2	10.8	32.8	83.8	16.2	23.2
South Yorkshire	7.3	30.1	11.5	30.2	79.2	20.8	29.4
West Yorkshire	7.6	30.3	11.3	31.3	80.6	19.4	43.0
East Midlands	7.0	31.3	11.0	31.3	80.7	19.3	66.6
Leicestershire, Northamptonshire and Rutland	8.3	32.2	11.2	29.4	81.1	18.9	22.2
Trent	6.4	30.9	11.0	32.3	80.5	19.5	44.5
West Midlands	7.3	31.6	10.4	32.8	82.1	17.9	94.3
Birmingham and The Black Country	7.7	31.6	10.4	33.1	82.9	17.1	47.0
Coventry, Warwickshire, Herefordshire and Worcestershire	7.4	31.1	10.2	34.8	83.5	16.5	23.2
Shropshire and Staffordshire	6.4	32.2	10.5	30.4	79.4	20.6	24.0
East	7.8	32.1	10.7	34.1	84.7	15.3	78.4
Bedfordshire and Hertfordshire	8.0	33.5	10.4	31.3	83.2	16.8	19.8
Essex	7.0	31.3	10.3	36.2	84.8	15.2	21.7
Norfolk, Suffolk and Cambridgeshire	8.2	31.8	11.1	34.3	85.4	14.6	36.9
London[5]	10.4	35.2	12.6	25.1	83.2	16.8	135.5
North Central London	11.1	35.9	14.1	22.8	83.8	16.2	27.3
North East London	9.7	32.9	11.3	27.6	81.5	18.5	24.6
North West London	10.6	37.4	11.4	23.9	83.2	16.8	33.3
South East London	10.5	35.0	12.5	25.7	83.6	16.4	29.2
South West London	10.0	33.7	13.9	26.4	84.0	16.0	21.1
South East	7.7	31.5	10.6	33.1	82.9	17.1	121.5
Hampshire and Isle of Wight	7.8	31.3	10.6	31.2	81.0	19.0	27.6
Kent and Medway	7.6	30.7	10.4	34.8	83.4	16.6	22.7
Surrey and Sussex	7.3	31.5	10.5	33.9	83.1	16.9	40.3
Thames Valley	8.1	32.4	10.9	32.7	84.1	15.9	31.0
South West	7.3	31.5	11.5	32.3	82.7	17.3	84.7
Avon, Gloucestershire and Wiltshire	7.8	31.5	12.2	30.9	82.5	17.5	38.2
Dorset and Somerset	7.1	31.8	10.5	35.3	84.7	15.3	18.5
South West Peninsula	6.8	31.3	11.2	32.4	81.7	18.3	27.9
England[6]	7.7	31.7	11.2	31.5	82.1	17.9	882.1
Wales	6.9	31.2	13.5	26.3	77.9	22.1	60.1
Scotland	8.0	32.8	11.9	18.3	71.0	29.0	113.6
Northern Ireland	6.8	29.8	10.1	13.6	60.3	39.7	40.0

1 Directly employed whole-time equivalents. See Notes and Definitions. The Northern Ireland figures exclude bank staff.
2 Figures for nursing, midwifery and health visiting excludes student nurses. Northern Ireland does not have any healthcare assistants.
3 Includes qualified ambulance staff.
4 The Northern Ireland figure includes administration and clercial staff working within Personal Social Services.
5 Includes data for London Ambulance Service personnel and other staff not allocated to individual health authorities.
6 Data include staff not allocated to individual region.

Source: Department of Health; National Assembly for Wales; Information and Statistics Division, NHS in Scotland; Department of Health, Social Services, Northern Ireland.

Table 7.18 General practitioners, dentists and opticians:[1], by Strategic Health Authority, 30 September 2002

Numbers and percentages

	General medical services									General dental services[1,2]				
	Number of practices	Of which: practices with one GP (percentages)	Number of general medical practitioners (GPs)[1]	Percentage who were female GPs	Percentage aged Under 35	Percentage aged 65 or over	Part-time GPs (percentages)	Average list size per GP	Number of practice staff (WTE)[3]	Percentage who were direct care practice staff[3,4]	Number of dentists[5]	People registered with a dentist as a percentage of the population[6]	Average registrations per dentist	Number of opthalmic practitioners[7]
North East	403		1,487	34				1,745	3,700		889	55	1,554	
Country Durham and Tees Valley	168	21	645	29	11	1	18	1,808	1,778	3	379	56	1,684	222
Northumberland, Tyne and Wear	235	18	842	37	13	1	24	1,696	1,922	1	510	54	1,457	250
North West	1,362		3,808	34				1,851	9,325		2,397	52	1,470	
Cheshire and Merseyside	439	29	1,338	36	11	1	18	1,824	3,312	4	838	53	1,485	483
Cumbria and Lancashire	368	32	1,078	29	9	1	20	1,803	2,577	5	651	49	1,434	471
Greater Manchester	555	36	1,392	35	12	3	18	1,913	3,436	1	908	54	1,482	604
Yorkshire and the Humber	867		2,932	34				1,772	6,784		1,718	53	1,524	
North and East Yorkshire and Northern Lincolnshire	266	28	952	30	9	1	19	1,756	2,334	7	541	50	1,516	353
South Yorkshire	226	27	714	34	9	2	21	1,889	1,771	2	442	56	1,617	328
West Yorkshire	375	26	1,266	37	13	2	24	1,718	2,679	4	735	52	1,474	421
East Midlands	647		2,231	31				1,878	6,128		1,288	51	1,667	
Leicestershire, Northamptonshire and Rutland	223	22	816	30	11	1	21	1,922	1,992	2	458	50	1,728	493
Trent	424	22	1,415	31	12	1	20	1,853	4,136	4	830	51	1,633	576
West Midlands	1,027		2,902	31				1,897	6,966		1,698	46	1,449	
Birmingham and the Black Country	529	45	1,264	31	9	3	18	1,928	3,097	1	719	48	1,530	479
Coventry, Warwickshire, Herefordshire and Worcestershire	231	17	859	34	10	1	19	1,831	1,963	5	530	46	1,342	337
Shropshire and Staffordshire	267	37	779	26	7	2	16	1,919	1,906	3	449	43	1,444	367
East	804		2,955	32				1,866	7,326		2,023	49	1,317	
Bedfordshire and Hertfordshire	229	22	888	38	11	1	16	1,904	2,132	3	698	48	1,108	487
Essex	274	34	798	30	5	3	17	2,064	1,972	5	551	48	1,411	276
Norfolk, Suffolk and Cambridgeshire	301	12	1,269	29	8	0	23	1,716	3,222	13	774	51	1,439	329
London	1,675		3,994	42				2,034	9,506		3,142	40	926	
North Central London	310	46	700	44	9	4	15	1,992	1,628	2	614	40	801	476
North East London	378	51	790	34	7	7	14	2,086	2,020	0	499	38	1,161	536
North West London	448	43	977	44	10	4	16	2,089	2,157	1	865	41	856	454
South East London	297	37	827	41	9	3	20	1,971	2,115	3	554	39	1,078	504
South West London	242	28	700	45	13	3	20	2,014	1,586	1	610	38	822	651
South East	1,203		4,578	36				1,821	10,290		3,291	43	1,038	
Hampshire and Isle of Wight	240	10	1,031	38	10	0	22	1,737	2,373	2	647	45	1,238	478
Kent and Medway	299	37	845	29	7	1	17	1,903	2,038	2	583	43	1,166	330
Surrey and Sussex	367	16	1,436	35	10	1	22	1,846	3,135	3	1,185	45	971	660
Thames Valley	297	14	1,266	39	11	1	26	1,805	2,744	6	876	37	897	670
South West	760		3,144	33				1,597	7,082		1,954	47	1,202	
Avon, Gloucestershire and Wiltshire	323	12	1,329	38	10	0	31	1,676	2,706	5	868	44	1,104	496
Dorset and Somerset	185	12	780	32	8	0	33	1,515	1,799	9	468	53	1,356	262
South West Peninsula	252	11	1,035	28	9	0	27	1,556	2,577	5	618	48	1,224	240
England	8,748	28	28,031	34	10	2	21	1,838	67,107	4	18,400	47	1,276	
Wales	516	23	1,793	30	10	1	20	1,704	6,012	15	1,015	51	1,444	599
Scotland[5]	1,048	184	3,769	38	12	1	18	1,392	7,187		2,054	53	1,299	935
Northern Ireland[8]	367	18	1,076	34	10	0	..	1,651	..	..	701	51	1,245	476

1 Figures for GPs include unrestricted principals, PMS contracted GPs and PMS salaried GPs. Figures for General Dental Practitioners include principals, assistants and vocational dental practitioners. Salaried dentists, Hospital Dental Services and Community Dental Services are excluded.

2 Dentists are assigned to the region where they carry out their main work.

3 Other than GPs.

4 Figures relate to practice nurses, physiotherapists, chiropodists, counsellors, dispensers and complementary therapists.

5 Number of dentists in Scotland is at 30 March 2003.

6 Registrations with dentists practising in each region.

7 Optometrists and opthalmic medical practitioners contracted to perform NHS sight tests at 31 December 2002 (31 March 2002 for optometrists in Scotland). As some practitioners have contracts in more than one region, the sum of the regions does not equal country totals.

8 Average registrations per dentist for Northern Ireland is for 1 November 2002.

Source: Department of Health; National Assembly for Wales; Information and Statistics Division, NHS in Scotland; Central Services Agency, Northern Ireland

Table **7.19** **Council supported residents,[1] 31 March 2003**

Percentage and thousands

	Percentage cared for in type of registered care home				Total of all supported residents ('000s)	Percentage aged 18 to 64 in registered care homes				Percentage aged 65 and over	All ages in staffed care homes[5] ('000s)
	Council Staffed	Independent Residential[2]	Independent Nursing[3]	Unstaffed and other[4]		Physically/ sensorily disabled	People with learning disabilities	People with mental health problems	Others		
North East	11.3	57.2	28.9	2.6	19	3.2	7.4	3.3	0.7	85.4	18
North West	10.6	56.0	32.2	1.2	45	4.3	8.2	5.6	0.4	81.5	44
Yorkshire and the Humber	14.1	54.7	29.7	1.6	33	3.7	10.3	3.8	0.4	81.8	33
East Midlands	15.4	57.6	26.2	0.8	26	4.0	11.9	3.8	0.6	79.7	26
West Midlands	15.8	51.6	30.5	2.1	29	3.6	13.8	4.2	0.6	77.8	29
East	11.4	70.2	18.2	0.3	27	3.9	13.6	3.3	0.4	78.8	27
London	10.3	58.0	28.0	3.7	34	4.5	17.4	8.6	1.6	67.9	33
South East	10.9	61.9	25.1	2.1	41	4.5	16.1	4.0	0.5	74.8	40
South West	9.7	60.3	27.6	2.4	30	4.2	13.8	3.5	0.3	78.2	29
England	12.0	58.5	27.6	1.9	284	4.1	12.7	4.6	0.6	78.0	279

1 Aged 18 and over and includes clients formerly in receipt of preserved rights.
2 Voluntary and private residential care homes.
3 Includes general and mental nursing homes.
4 Includes supported residents in homes with less than four residential care places.
5 Council supported residents in CSSR and registered staffed care homes and other accommodation.

Source: Department of Health

Table **7.20** **Children looked after by local authorities[1], year ending 31 March 2002[2]**

	Total children looked after per ten thousand resident population[3]			Manner of accommodation (percentages)			Number of children looked after at 31 March (=100%)
	Started to be looked after	Ceased to be looked after	Looked after at 31 March	Foster homes	Children's homes & hostels[4]	Other[5]	
North East	28	31	60	65.4	11.2	23.4	3,400
North West	23	24	62	62.0	12.3	25.7	9,800
Yorkshire and the Humber	21	21	58	64.0	11.8	24.2	6,600
East Midlands	20	20	44	66.9	9.6	23.5	4,100
West Midlands	23	22	55	67.6	10.6	21.8	6,700
East	16	16	44	66.6	10.5	22.9	5,400
London	31	30	70	64.5	14.5	20.9	11,400
South East	16	18	41	66.2	9.8	24.1	7,400
South West	24	25	46	73.3	7.8	18.9	4,900
England	22	23	54	65.7	11.4	22.9	59,700
Wales[2]	24	22	55	73.8	6.4	19.7	3,640
Scotland[1]	43	38	102	28.0	14.0	58.0	11,240
Northern Ireland	27	25	54	61.7	12.2	26.1	2,450

1 English and Scottish figures do not include children who, at 31 March 2002, were being looked after in a planned series of short-term placements.
2 Data for Wales relate to 2000/01.
3 Rates are based on mid-2001 estimates of population aged under 18.
4 In England, includes homes and hostels both subject, and not subject, to Children's Homes Regulation and also includes Secure Units. Scottish figures relate to residential care homes for children.
5 Includes children looked after at home and children looked after through being under a supervision requirement made by the Scottish Children's Hearings System.

Source: Department of Health; National Assembly for Wales; Scottish Executive Education Department; Department of Health, Social Services and Public Safety, Northern Ireland.

Table **7.21** **Children and young people on child protection registers: by age and category, at 31 March 2002**

	Percentage aged					Number of children on registers[2] (=100%)	Rate per 10,000 children aged under 18[3]	Percentage of children in each category of abuse				
	Under 1	1 to 4	5 to 9[1]	10 to 15[1]	16 or over			Neglect	Physical injury	Sexual abuse	Emotional abuse	Multiple categories/ other[4]
North East	11	32	29	25	1	1,935	33	34	17	7	13	30
North West	10	29	31	28	2	3,390	21	40	20	9	18	13
Yorkshire and the Humber	11	30	29	28	2	2,850	25	35	18	15	12	20
East Midlands	9	30	29	28	3	2,370	25	31	15	16	19	18
West Midlands	11	30	28	28	2	2,995	24	42	16	11	19	11
East	9	28	31	29	2	2,490	20	40	15	11	23	11
London	9	28	29	30	3	4,500	27	46	13	7	18	15
South East	11	29	31	27	2	3,105	17	43	14	10	18	15
South West	11	31	28	28	2	2,095	20	35	20	13	19	14
England	10	29	30	28	2	25,700	23	39	16	11	18	16
Wales	11	32	29	26	2	1,970	30	40	21	10	21	..
Scotland	..	..	..	..	..	..	..	..	..	..	..	..
Northern Ireland[1]	7	25	41	23	4	1,530	34	41	23	10	14	..

1 Age bands for Northern Ireland are 5 to 11 and 12 to 15.
2 Includes a number of unborn children not included elsewhere in this table.
3 Figure for Northern Ireland calculated using the mid-2001 population estimate.
4 For England and Wales data relate to children or young people on the child protection registers who have not been allocated a specific single category.

Source: Department of Health; National Assembly for Wales; Department of Health, Social Services and Public Safety, Northern Ireland.

Chapter 8 Income and Lifestyles

Household income

Households in London had the highest average gross weekly income (AGHWI) of £676 from 1999 to 2002. Northern Ireland had the lowest AGHWI (under £400 per week). South East, London and the East of England all had an AGHWI higher than the UK average. (Table 8.1)

Wages and salaries made up the majority of household income in the United Kingdom between 1999 and 2002; Scotland and London had the highest proportion (70 per cent). Northern Ireland received the highest amount of income derived from social security benefits (21 per cent of all household income). (Table 8.1)

During the period 1999 to 2002, London and the South East had the highest percentage of households with a weekly income of £750 or over (33 and 29 per cent respectively). North East had the highest percentage of households with a weekly income of under £100. Wales had the lowest proportion of households with weekly income of £750 or over. (Table 8.2)

Income distribution and savings

London had the highest proportion of individual income after housing costs in both the top and the bottom quintiles of the UK as a whole. (Table 8.3)

Over a third of households in the South East, South West and East of England had at least one member with an ISA account in 2001/02. (Table 8.4)

Income tax

London had the highest percentage of individuals with an income liable to tax assessment in all income brackets over £20,000 in 2000/01. North East and Wales had the lowest percentage of individuals with an income liable to tax assessment of £50,000 and over in 2000/01. (Table 8.5)

Males in London had the highest average total income (over £33,000 in 2000/01). However, this was over £13,000 more, than the average for females in London. This compares to a difference between sexes of £9,000 at United Kingdom level. Women in Wales had the lowest average total income (just over £13,000). (Figure 8.6)

Receipt of benefit

Wales received the highest percentage of benefits of all regions in 2001/02 (75 per cent). Households receiving pension benefit were most numerous in the South West. (Table 8.8)

Expenditure

Total expenditure in London and the South East during the period 1999 and 2002 was over a sixth higher than the United Kingdom average whereas the North East was over a sixth lower. (Figure 8.9)

Children in Scotland spent just under £14 per head per week between 1999 and 2002, the highest amount in Great Britain. Children in South West spent a third less than those in Scotland with an average of just over £9 per head per week. (Figure 8.10)

Households in Scotland had the highest expenditure on alcoholic beverages and tobacco of just over £23 per week between 1999 and 2002, while those in East of England spent just over £17 per week. London had the highest expenditure per household on food. (Table 8.11)

The highest spenders on housing during the period 1999 to 2002 were households in London (£90.30 per week) compared to £34.50 per week in Northern Ireland. Households in London spent the most on leisure goods and services between 1999 and 2002 (£86.60 per week) compared to the North East which spent £53.50 per week. London had the highest average household expenditure of £463 per week. North East had an average household expenditure of £308.80 per week during the period 1999 to 2002. (Table 8.11)

London's residents spent the most on fruit in 2000/01 at £2 per person per week, whereas Northern Ireland's population spent the least at £1.16 per person per week. (Table 8.12)

Consumption

In 2001/02, London consumed the least amount of meat, Wales consumed the most vegetables and the South West consumed the most fruit. (Table 8.13)

Consumer goods

Over half of the households in United Kingdom had a mobile phone between 1999 and 2002. A quarter of households in the United Kingdom had dishwashers. London had the lowest percentage of households with microwave ovens. (Figure 8.14)

The proportion of households with access to the internet increased across all regions between 1999/2000 and 2001/02, over doubling for three quarters of the regions. (Figure 8.15)

Leisure

In 2000, in the UK, people spent nearly three hours a day watching TV, videos or DVD's (over 200 minutes a day in the North East). In the UK in general a similar amount of time was spent reading and listening to either music or the radio. (Table 8.16)

Tourism

Residents of the South East, London and East of England spent the most on holidays in 2001/02. (Figure 8.18)

In 2002, overseas visitors to the United Kingdom spent £11.6 billion and stayed almost 200 million nights. Just under half of the spending and nearly two-fifths of those nights were in London. (Table 8.19)

National Lottery

West Midlands and the North East spent the most on the National Lottery between 1999 and 2002 with an average weekly household expenditure of £4.50, while Northern Ireland spent the least (£3.90 per week). (Figure 8.20)

The region awarded the highest number of grants since the start of the National Lottery to the end of 2002 was Scotland (a seventh of the total for United Kingdom). The fewest grants were awarded to Northern Ireland. (Table 8.21)

Table 8.1   Household income: by source, 1999 to 2002[1]

Percentages and £

	Percentage of average gross weekly household income						Average gross weekly household income[3] (=100%) (£)
	Wages and salaries	Self-employ-ment	Invest-ments	Annuities and pensions[2]	Social security benefits[3]	Other income	
United Kingdom	67	9	4	7	12	1	510
North East	68	4	2	6	18	1	406
North West	66	6	3	8	16	1	444
Yorkshire and the Humber	67	7	3	7	14	2	436
East Midlands	68	8	4	6	12	1	480
West Midlands	68	8	4	6	13	1	476
East	68	9	4	8	10	1	538
London	70	14	4	4	7	1	676
South East	68	10	6	7	8	1	630
South West	61	11	6	9	13	1	483
England	67	9	4	7	11	1	526
Wales	64	6	2	9	18	1	407
Scotland	70	5	3	6	14	2	446
Northern Ireland	62	7	2	6	21	1	399

1 Combined data from the 1999/2000 and 2000/01 Family Expenditure Surveys and the 2001/02 Expenditure and Food Survey. See Notes and Definitions.
2 Other than social security benefits.
3 Excluding Housing Benefit and Council Tax Benefit (rates rebate in Northern Ireland).

Source: Expenditure and Food Survey, Office for National Statistics; Northern Ireland Statistics and Research Agency

Table 8.2   Distribution of household income, 1999 to 2002[1]

Percentages and £

	Percentage of households in each weekly income group								Average gross weekly income[2] (£)	
	Under £100	£100 but under £150	£150 but under £250	£250 but under £350	£350 but under £450	£450 but under £600	£600 but under £750	£750 or over	Per house-hold	Per person
United Kingdom	9	9	15	12	11	14	10	20	510	217
North East	16	11	16	11	11	15	8	12	406	171
North West	10	10	17	12	12	13	9	16	444	190
Yorkshire and the Humber	9	10	16	14	12	14	10	14	436	186
East Midlands	8	8	15	13	13	15	11	17	480	205
West Midlands	9	10	16	10	12	15	10	19	476	196
East	8	7	14	11	10	15	12	23	538	229
London	9	8	13	9	9	10	10	33	676	283
South East	7	8	11	11	10	14	11	29	630	276
South West	7	9	16	13	11	16	10	17	483	209
England	9	9	15	12	11	14	10	21	526	224
Wales	9	11	19	14	11	15	10	11	407	175
Scotland	11	10	17	11	11	14	9	16	446	194
Northern Ireland	10	13	20	13	11	13	9	12	399	152

1 Combined data from the 1999/2000 and 2000/01 Family Expenditure Surveys and the 2001/02 Expenditure and Food Survey. See Notes and Definitions.
2 Excluding Housing Benefit and Council Tax Benefit (rates rebate in Northern Ireland).

Source: Expenditure and Food Survey, Office for National Statistics; Northern Ireland Statistics and Research Agency

Table **8.3**   Income distribution of individuals, 2001/02[1,2]

Percentages

| | Quintile groups of individuals ranked by net equivalised household income | | | | | | | | | |
| | Before housing costs | | | | | After housing costs | | | | |
	Bottom fifth	Next fifth	Middle fifth	Next fifth	Top fifth	Bottom fifth	Next fifth	Middle fifth	Next fifth	Top fifth
Great Britain	20	20	20	20	20	20	20	20	20	20
North East	22	25	21	19	12	20	25	22	20	13
North West	23	22	21	20	14	21	23	21	21	15
Yorkshire and the Humber	23	23	23	17	14	22	24	23	18	14
East Midlands	22	22	21	22	14	20	22	22	20	16
West Midlands	22	21	23	20	15	21	21	23	20	15
East	15	18	20	23	24	16	17	19	23	24
London	19	16	15	18	32	24	14	15	18	29
South East	15	17	17	21	30	17	17	18	20	29
South West	19	21	22	20	18	19	21	22	20	18
England	20	20	20	20	21	20	20	20	20	21
Wales	24	23	21	20	12	22	23	22	20	13
Scotland	22	20	20	21	17	19	21	20	22	19

1 Total income of all members of the household after deductions of income tax and other contributions. See Notes and Definitions.
2 Figures for this year include the self employed.

Source: Households Below Average Income, Department for Work and Pensions

Table **8.4**   Households[1] with different types of saving, 2001/02

Percentages[2]

| | Accounts | | | | | Other savings | | | | | |
	Current[3]	Post Office	TESSA	ISA	Other bank/ building society[4]	Gilts or unit trusts	Stocks and shares[5]	National Savings	Save As You Earn	Premium Bonds	PEPs
Great Britain	88	7	11	29	57	6	25	4	1	24	10
North East	82	6	8	21	47	4	18	2	-	17	7
North West	88	7	9	28	53	5	23	4	1	20	9
Yorkshire and the Humber	84	6	11	29	56	5	22	3	1	23	9
East Midlands	86	6	9	27	53	4	20	3	1	20	7
West Midlands	84	6	11	28	56	5	20	4	-	22	8
East	93	9	13	35	67	7	32	5	1	32	13
London	89	7	11	28	55	7	28	4	1	23	10
South East	92	9	13	34	65	7	33	5	1	33	14
South West	92	9	11	34	63	8	27	6	1	31	13
England	88	7	11	30	58	6	26	4	1	25	10
Wales	87	7	9	25	48	4	18	3	1	21	8
Scotland	84	5	8	24	49	6	23	3	1	14	10

1 Households in which at least one member has an account. See Notes and Definitions.
2 As a percentage of all households.
3 A current account may be either a bank account or a building society account.
4 All bank/building society accounts excluding current accounts and TESSAs and ISAs plus other accounts yielding interest.
5 Includes membership of a Share Club.

Source: Family Resources Survey, Department for Work and Pensions

Table **8.5**   Distribution of income liable to assessment for tax, 2000/01[1]

Percentages and thousands

	Percentage of taxpayers in each income range								Individuals with incomes of £4,385 or more (=100%) (thousands)
	£4,385-£4,999	£5,000-£7,499	£7,500-£9,999	£10,000-£14,999	£15,000-£19,999	£20,000-£29,999	£30,000-£49,999	£50,000 and over	
United Kingdom[2]	2.7	13.1	12.8	22.4	16.8	18.4	9.6	4.3	29,300
North East	2.4	14.4	16.3	25.3	15.8	16.7	7.5	1.8	1,160
North West	2.9	13.9	13.8	23.8	17.0	17.6	8.1	2.9	3,220
Yorkshire and the Humber	3.2	14.7	14.1	24.4	16.1	17.2	7.6	2.6	2,390
East Midlands	3.1	13.7	14.7	23.1	16.9	16.5	8.6	3.3	2,080
West Midlands	3.1	13.4	12.7	23.7	17.3	18.1	8.6	3.0	2,530
East	2.4	12.2	11.5	20.8	16.9	19.4	11.4	5.5	2,750
London	2.2	11.5	10.0	17.8	16.5	21.2	12.9	7.9	3,610
South East	2.1	11.1	11.3	20.0	16.8	19.8	12.0	6.8	4,340
South West	2.9	14.1	13.0	23.5	17.2	17.5	8.4	3.5	2,590
England	2.7	12.9	12.6	21.9	16.8	18.5	9.9	4.6	24,700
Wales	2.7	15.0	15.9	24.7	16.1	16.4	7.3	1.8	1,330
Scotland	2.7	13.5	13.1	24.4	17.3	18.0	8.2	3.0	2,490
Northern Ireland	3.3	12.8	14.1	26.2	16.6	18.2	6.3	2.4	666

1 Includes taxpayers only and not those above the personal allowance threshold. See Notes and Definitions.
2 Figures for United Kingdom include members of HM Forces and others who are liable to some UK tax but reside overseas on a long-term basis. In addition, the United
   Kingdom total includes a very small number of individuals who could not be allocated to a region.

Source: Survey of Personal Incomes, Inland Revenue

Figure **8.6**   Average total income[1] and average income tax payable[2]: by sex, 2000/01

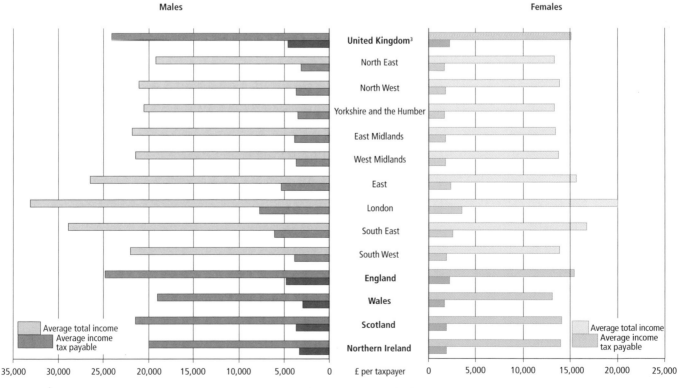

1 Figures are based on individuals with total income above the single person's allowance. See Notes and Definitions.
2 Figures relate to taxpayers only.
3 See Notes and Definitions.

Source: Survey of Personal Incomes, Inland Revenue

Map **8.7**

**Percentage of the population of working age claiming a key social security benefit:[1]
by local authority, May 2003[2]**

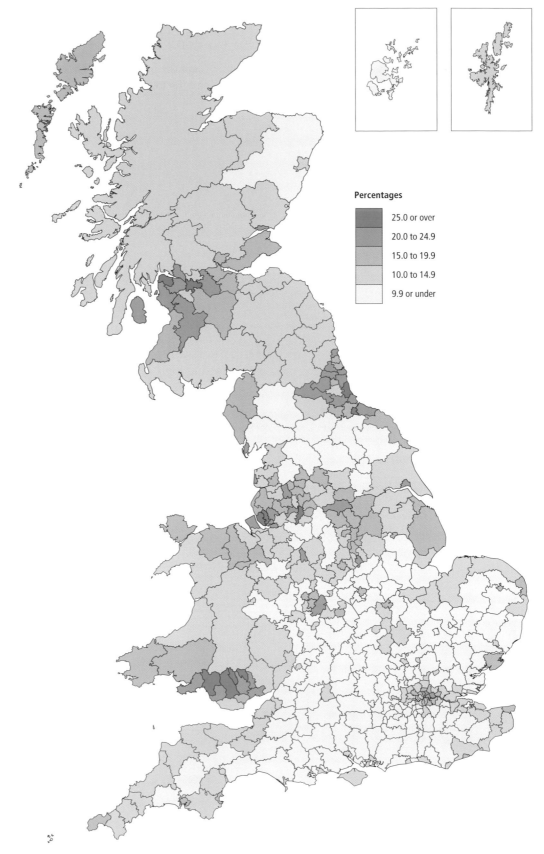

Percentages

25.0 or over

20.0 to 24.9

15.0 to 19.9

10.0 to 14.9

9.9 or under

1 *Key benefits are Jobseeker's Allowance (JSA), Incapacity Benefit (IB), Severe Disablement Allowance, Disability Living Allowance,
   Income Support and National Insurance credits only (through JSA or IB).*
2 *Based on 5 per cent statistical samples relating to May 2003.*

Source: IAD Information Centre, Department for Work and Pensions

Table **8.8**   **Households in receipt of benefit[1]: by type of benefit, 2001/02**

Percentages[2]

	Family Credit/ WFTC[3] or Income Support	Housing Benefit	Council Tax Benefit	Jobseeker's Allowance	Retirement Pension	Incapacity or Disablement Benefits[4]	Child Benefit	Any benefit
Great Britain	17	15	20	2	29	15	28	69
North East	22	22	29	3	30	24	27	74
North West	22	18	23	3	28	19	29	70
Yorkshire and the Humber	19	17	21	3	29	17	29	72
East Midlands	17	13	18	2	28	14	30	69
West Midlands	17	15	20	3	31	15	28	71
East	12	12	14	2	30	11	28	67
London	17	18	20	3	24	10	27	61
South East	10	10	13	2	28	10	28	66
South West	13	12	16	1	34	14	24	69
England	16	15	19	2	29	14	28	68
Wales	21	18	24	3	33	26	27	75
Scotland	19	19	24	2	29	20	26	70

1 Households in which at least one member is in receipt of benefit. See Notes and Definitions.
2 As a percentage of all households.
3 Working Families Tax Credit.
4 Incapacity Benefit, Disability Living Allowance (Care and Mobility components), Severe Disablement Allowance, Disability Working Allowance, Industrial Injuries Disablement Benefit, War Disablement Pension and Attendance Allowance. In October 1999 Disability Working Allowance was replaced by Disabled Person's Tax Credits.

Source: Family Resources Survey, Department for Work and Pensions

Figure **8.9**   **Total expenditure in relation to the UK average, 1999–2002[1]**

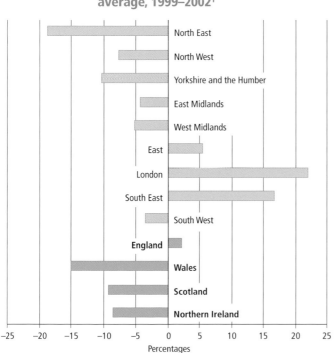

1 Combined data from the 1999/2000 and 2000/01 Family Expenditure Surveys and 2001/02 Expenditure and Food Survey. See Notes and Definitions.

Source: Expenditure and Food Survey, Office for National Statistics; Northern Ireland Statistics and Research Agency

Figure **8.10** **Children's spending[1], 1999–2002[2]**

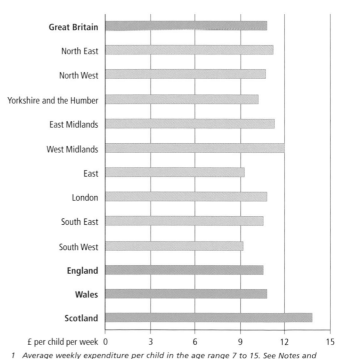

1 Average weekly expenditure per child in the age range 7 to 15. See Notes and Definitions.
2 Combined data from the 1999/2000 and 2000/01 Family Expenditure Surveys and 2001/02 Expenditure and Food Survey. See Notes and Definitions.

Source: Expenditure and Food Survey, Office for National Statistics

Table **8.11** Household expenditure[1]: by commodity and service, 1999-2002

£ per week and percentages

	Housing	Fuel, light and power	Food	Alcohol and tobacco	Clothing and footwear	House-hold goods and services	Motoring and fares	Leisure goods and services	Miscellan-eous and personal goods and services	Average house-hold expend-iture	Average expend-iture per person
£ per week											
United Kingdom	62.30	11.70	61.20	20.70	21.80	53.60	64.50	68.10	15.80	379.70	162.00
North East	47.70	11.40	53.70	22.60	19.60	41.00	48.20	53.50	11.00	308.80	130.90
North West	53.50	11.70	57.20	21.90	22.90	48.20	58.00	63.10	14.30	351.00	150.50
Yorkshire and the Humber	54.20	11.20	55.50	21.70	19.40	46.10	58.40	60.00	14.00	340.50	145.70
East Midlands	56.20	11.50	60.40	21.50	19.20	49.50	65.60	64.80	14.30	363.10	155.30
West Midlands	56.00	11.80	58.80	20.60	20.70	50.40	65.00	63.20	13.80	360.30	148.50
East	66.40	11.30	63.70	17.20	20.80	57.20	76.60	69.20	18.10	400.50	170.50
London	90.30	10.80	70.80	21.40	27.20	65.80	69.40	86.60	20.50	463.00	194.30
South East	76.40	11.60	65.30	19.30	22.50	65.60	77.50	84.90	19.90	443.00	194.40
South West	61.40	11.60	58.60	18.80	17.70	53.90	64.70	64.50	15.30	366.40	158.50
England	65.00	11.40	61.40	20.40	21.60	54.90	66.40	70.20	16.40	387.80	165.50
Wales	45.90	11.80	55.70	20.30	19.30	46.90	51.10	59.00	12.40	322.50	139.10
Scotland	53.60	12.30	59.80	23.10	22.60	46.50	56.40	57.10	13.30	344.70	150.20
Northern Ireland	34.50	16.80	68.20	22.90	28.40	49.90	56.00	56.80	13.80	347.30	132.70
As a percentage of average weekly household expenditure											
United Kingdom	16	3	16	5	6	14	17	18	4	100	
North East	15	4	17	7	6	13	16	17	4	100	
North West	15	3	16	6	7	14	17	18	4	100	
Yorkshire and the Humber	16	3	16	6	6	14	17	18	4	100	
East Midlands	15	3	17	6	5	14	18	18	4	100	
West Midlands	16	3	16	6	6	14	18	18	4	100	
East	17	3	16	4	5	14	19	17	5	100	
London	20	2	15	5	6	14	15	19	4	100	
South East	17	3	15	4	5	15	17	19	4	100	
South West	17	3	16	5	5	15	18	18	4	100	
England	17	3	16	5	6	14	17	18	4	100	
Wales	14	4	17	6	6	15	16	18	4	100	
Scotland	16	4	17	7	7	13	16	17	4	100	
Northern Ireland	10	5	20	7	8	14	16	16	4	100	

1 Combined data from the 1999/2000 and 2000/01 Family Expenditure Surveys and the 2001/02 Expenditure and Food Survey. See Notes and Definitions.

Source: Expenditure and Food Survey, Office for National Statistics; Northern Ireland Statistics and Research Agency

Table **8.12** Expenditure on selected foods bought for household consumption, 2000/01[1]

Pence per person per week

	Liquid and processed milk and cream	Cheese	Uncooked carcass meat and poultry	Other meat and meat products	Fish	Vegetables and vegetable products[2]	Fresh and other fruit	Bread	Cereals other than bread	Drinks and confec-tionery	Total house-hold food and drink
United Kingdom	143	54	197	224	90	257	148	79	269	413	2,109
North East	134	45	158	208	73	229	121	86	260	394	1,923
North West	142	43	203	214	77	228	126	81	243	394	1,976
Yorkshire and the Humber	138	40	176	204	90	217	118	79	260	381	1,908
East Midlands	145	55	196	201	84	251	133	77	261	381	2,009
West Midlands	135	52	188	212	87	247	125	78	257	393	1,976
East	137	55	207	231	91	280	167	72	300	420	2,208
London	140	59	206	221	121	309	200	76	293	411	2,284
South East	153	73	222	254	117	300	199	83	295	512	2,494
South West	152	56	188	227	98	267	162	72	263	423	2,153
England	143	54	197	222	95	262	154	78	271	418	2,132
Wales	142	52	174	211	67	245	121	80	248	350	1,924
Scotland	135	53	191	241	64	216	123	83	253	419	2,002
Northern Ireland	167	40	252	253	64	267	116	94	299	348	2,127

1 The National Food Survey (NFS) was replaced by the Expenditure and Food Survey on 1st April 2001. The 2000/01 data include adjusted estimates from the NFS. The adjustments are under review and may be revised. Classifications of various food categories have been revised. See Notes and Definitions.
2 Including tomatoes, fresh potatoes and potato products.

Source: Expenditure and Food Survey, Department for Environment, Food and Rural Affairs

Table **8.13** Household consumption of selected foods, 2001/02[1]

Kilogrammes per person per week[2]

	Liquid and processed milk and cream	Meat and meat products	Fish	Vegetables and vegetable products[3]	Fresh and other fruit	Cereals including bread
United Kingdom	2.0	1.0	0.2	2.0	1.2	1.7
North East	1.9	1.0	0.1	2.0	1.0	1.6
North West	2.1	1.1	0.2	1.9	1.1	1.7
Yorkshire and the Humber	2.1	1.0	0.2	1.9	0.9	1.6
East Midlands	2.1	1.1	0.2	2.1	1.1	1.7
West Midlands	2.0	1.1	0.1	2.1	1.0	1.6
East	2.1	1.1	0.2	2.0	1.3	1.7
London	1.8	0.9	0.2	1.8	1.3	1.6
South East	2.0	1.0	0.2	2.0	1.3	1.6
South West	2.2	1.0	0.2	2.1	1.4	1.7
England	2.0	1.0	0.2	2.0	1.2	1.6
Wales	2.0	1.2	0.2	2.3	1.0	1.7
Scotland	2.1	1.1	0.1	1.8	1.0	1.7
Northern Ireland	2.2	1.0	0.1	2.2	0.8	1.9

1 Data collected through the Expenditure and Food Survey in which 7500 households in the United Kingdom keep a record of the type, quantity and costs of foods entering the home during a two week period. Nutritional intakes are estimated from the survey data. See Notes and Definitions.
2 Except equivalent litres of milk and cream.
3 Including tomatoes, fresh potatoes and potato products.

Source: Expenditure and Food Survey, Department for Environment, Food and Rural Affairs

Table **8.14** Households with selected durable goods, 1999 to 2002[1]

Percentages

	Micro-wave oven	Washing machine	Dish-washer	Fridge-freezer or deep freezer	Tumble drier	Video recorder	Compact-disc player	Satellite receiver	Mobile phone
United Kingdom	83	92	25	93	53	88	76	37	52
North East	89	94	16	93	51	88	75	40	50
North West	86	91	20	94	52	89	76	38	51
Yorkshire and the Humber	86	94	21	93	53	89	75	34	54
East Midlands	85	95	25	94	57	88	78	37	55
West Midlands	85	91	23	94	57	89	75	38	54
East	82	94	30	95	54	87	78	36	51
London	75	89	27	92	44	85	77	39	52
South East	82	92	33	94	56	88	79	35	57
South West	83	92	28	94	53	87	77	32	51
England	83	92	26	94	53	88	77	37	53
Wales	87	92	18	93	55	89	72	47	51
Scotland	82	95	21	90	58	85	75	33	42
Northern Ireland	85	94	24	92	51	88	75	39	51

1 Combined data from the 1999/2000 and 2000/01 Family Expenditure Surveys and the 2001/02 Expenditure and Food Survey. See Notes and Definitions.

Source: Expenditure and Food Survey, Office for National Statistics; Northern Ireland Statistics and Research Agency

Figure **8.15** Households with Internet access, 1999/2000 and 2001/02[1]

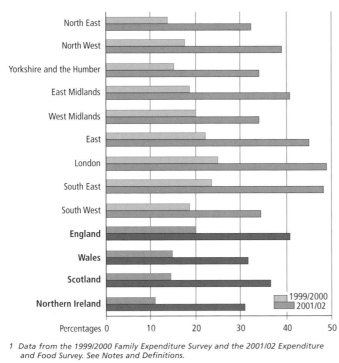

1 Data from the 1999/2000 Family Expenditure Survey and the 2001/02 Expenditure and Food Survey. See Notes and Definitions.

Source: Expenditure and Food Survey, Office for National Statistics; Northern Ireland Statistics and Research Agency

Table 8.16 Average time spent on various activities,[1] by region, 2000

Minutes per day

	TV & video/DVD	Radio & music	Reading	Gardening	DIY	Walking & running	Jogging & hiking	Biking	Fitness	Swimming	Other physical exercise
United Kingdom	171.8	46.3	40.0	9.5	6.4	3.8	0.2	0.5	1.7	0.8	6.6
North East	201.3	41.9	41.7	7.1	4.7	2.4	0.2	0.0	1.3	0.2	4.7
North West	180.3	44.0	37.0	7.3	8.1	4.4	0.3	0.7	2.0	0.5	7.2
Yorkshire and the Humber	183.5	39.9	37.5	8.0	3.1	3.1	0.3	0.3	1.7	0.8	6.5
East Midlands	174.3	47.8	38.5	11.1	6.6	4.1	0.2	0.8	1.7	0.8	4.4
West Midlands	175.1	44.2	33.0	10.7	6.9	3.3	0.5	0.2	2.0	0.8	6.9
East	164.1	45.9	42.5	14.3	7.5	4.4	0.1	1.1	2.1	0.8	8.5
London	155.8	47.6	40.4	5.2	3.9	2.5	0.2	0.2	1.3	1.0	6.3
South East	158.7	54.3	40.7	10.7	7.2	3.5	0.1	0.4	2.3	1.1	6.2
South West	165.4	49.0	42.7	13.5	9.1	5.1	0.0	0.5	1.2	0.7	7.5
Wales	182.5	47.5	47.8	14.1	9.3	4.6	0.0	0.6	1.1	0.7	5.1
Scotland	184.8	44.6	44.5	7.4	5.7	4.5	0.4	0.4	1.4	1.0	7.7
Northern Ireland	157.1	36.5	32.1	3.5	1.2	4.4	0.2	0.7	1.0	0.4	4.6

1 Combined main and secondary activity time. See Notes and Definitions.

Source: UK 2000 Time Use Survey, Office for National Statistics

Table 8.17 Library resources and use, 2001/02

	Library books issues per head of population to:		Number of visits to libraries per head of population	Expenditure (£ millions)	Expenditure per head of population (£)	Stock of books (thousands)	Stock of books per head of population	Resident population per library
	Adults	Children[1]						
United Kingdom	6.0	8.2	5.4	930.1	15.82	115,961	2.0	12,743
North East	6.8	7.0	5.5	42.0	16.68	5,049	2.0	10,985
North West	6.5	7.7	5.4	108.9	16.18	13,501	2.0	13,790
Yorkshire and the Humber	5.1	5.8	4.5	71.5	14.41	8,763	1.8	12,139
East Midlands	6.0	8.2	4.7	58.8	14.10	7,147	1.7	12,058
West Midlands	5.5	7.1	4.7	77.1	14.64	9,823	1.9	15,723
East	6.8	10.9	6.0	81.5	15.13	8,810	1.6	14,254
London	5.2	9.1	6.8	163.5	22.80	16,624	2.3	18,065
South East	6.1	9.6	5.7	112.5	14.06	13,992	1.7	14,926
South west	6.4	8.7	5.4	63.1	12.81	8,653	1.8	12,762
England	6.0	8.4	5.5	779.0	15.85	92,363	1.9	14,023
Wales	6.1	5.9	4.2	36.4	12.53	6,772	2.3	8,526
Scotland	6.2	7.6	5.7	93.8	18.52	13,124	2.6	8,289
Northern Ireland	4.2	7.3	3.9	20.8	12.36	3,703	2.2	10,674

1 Children are aged 14 and under.

Source: Library and Information Statistics Unit, Loughborough University

Figure **8.18** Expenditure on holidays in relation to the UK average, 2001/02[1]

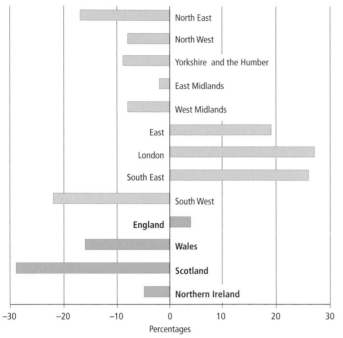

1 Data from the 2001/02 survey. See Notes and Definitions.

Source: Expenditure and Food Survey, Office for National Statistics; Northern Ireland Statistics and Research Agency

Table **8.19** Overseas visitors: by UK region of visit, 2002

Thousands and £ million

	Number of nights	Expenditure (£m)
Tourist Board Regions[1]		
United Kingdom[2]	199,285	11,618
Northumbria	3,871	169
Cumbria	971	41
North West	9,505	466
Yorkshire	7,481	303
East of England	13,600	616
Heart of England	21,129	881
London	75,402	5,788
Southern and South East England	31,373	1,504
South West	11,504	526
England[3]	175,257	10,313
Wales	6,622	252
Scotland	15,040	806
Northern Ireland	1,655	126

1 Tourist Board Regions – see map in Notes and Definitions.
2 Includes an amount which cannot be allocated to an individual country.
3 Includes the value of tourism in the Channel Islands, the Isle of Man, and a small amount where the region was unknown.

Source: International Passenger Survey, Office for National Statistics

Figure **8.20** Participation in the National Lottery[1], 1999-2002[2]

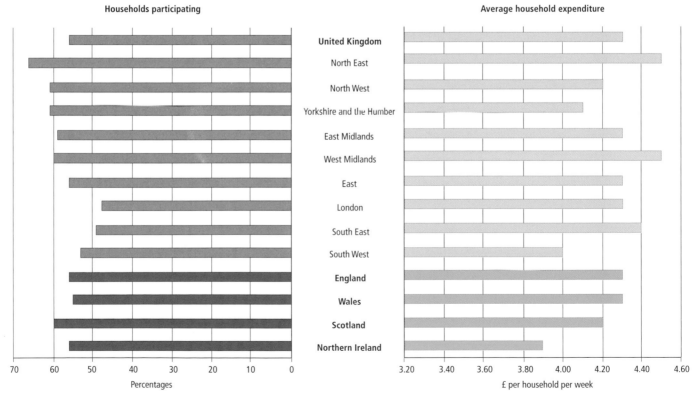

1 In the two-week diary-keeping period following interview; including scratchcards.
2 Combined data from the 1999/2000 and 2000/01 Family Expenditure Surveys and the 2001/02 Expenditure and Food Survey. See Notes and Definitions.
3 Average weekly expenditure of participating households.

Source: Expenditure and Food Survey, Office for National Statistics; Northern Ireland Statistics and Research Agency

Table **8.21** The National Lottery grants: cumulative totals from 1999 to 2002

Numbers and £ million

	Number of grants awarded from the start of Lottery to:				Total value of awards (£ million)			
	end 1999	end 2000	end 2001	end 2002	end 1999	end 2000	end 2001	end 2002
United Kingdom[1]	56,133	80,920	103,064	130,240	7,749.8	9,004.7	10,511.0	11,847.7
North East	2,889	4,248	5,175	6,475	358.0	403.9	458.9	517.2
North West	4,008	6,314	7,646	9,884	581.4	797.0	899.1	1,010.8
Yorkshire and the Humber	3,505	5,424	6,918	8,670	411.5	465.7	578.8	699.3
East Midlands	3,843	5,433	6,846	8,360	255.3	311.3	393.4	461.6
West Midlands	3,962	6,234	7,856	10,038	458.1	528.7	599.8	670.7
East	3,005	4,518	5,753	7,633	338.6	390.9	460.0	527.4
London	4,730	7,438	9,354	11,641	1,310.8	1,439.9	1,603.0	1,755.4
South East	4,360	6,617	8,238	9,889	473.4	582.3	677.0	765.0
South West	5,557	7,455	9,292	11,251	433.4	509.7	587.7	657.1
England[2]	37,553	56,194	71,027	90,139	5,476.7	6,457.4	7,549.7	8,526.5
Wales	4,932	6,487	7,921	9,725	380.1	444.3	511.8	593.8
Scotland	10,104	12,614	15,438	17,815	753.7	843.6	968.0	1,084.8
Northern Ireland	2,454	3,243	4,133	5,390	261.9	295.1	339.3	370.6

1 Includes grants made UK-wide or to institutions of national significance. Further grants have been made overseas. See Notes and Definitions.
2 Includes grants not allocated to a specific English region. See Notes and Definitions.

Source: **Department for Culture, Media and Sport**

Chapter 9 Crime and Justice

Recorded crimes

The total recorded crime rate (per 100,000 population) was around 1.8 times higher in London than in the South East in 2002/03. Recorded offences of burglary in Yorkshire and the Humber were almost 1.7 times higher than the average for England and Wales. (Table 9.1)

In 2002/03 the incidence of recorded thefts involving vehicles was higher in Yorkshire and the Humber than anywhere else in the United Kingdom. The recorded crime rate for robbery was significantly higher in London, around 2.9 times higher than the average for England and Wales. (Table 9.1)

Violent offences

The North East and Yorkshire and the Humber had the highest percentage of individuals wounded in a violent offence in 2002/03 (1.5 per cent). The total number of violent incidents was highest in Yorkshire and the Humber (4.6 per cent). The lowest rate was in Wales (2.8 per cent). (Table 9.2)

The percentage of individuals robbed at least once was highest in London in 2002/03 (1.3 per cent). The lowest proportions of individuals robbed were in the North East and South West (0.2 per cent). (Table 9.2)

Offences against households

The region in England with the lowest percentage of household offences in 2002/03 was the South West. Almost 25 per cent of all households were victimised at least once in 2002/03 in Yorkshire and the Humber. (Table 9.3)

In 2002/03 vandalism was highest in the South East: 8.9 per cent of households were victimised at least once. The percentage of households burgled at least once was highest in Yorkshire and the Humber: 5.5 per cent. The South West and East of England had the lowest rate of burglary of all regions in England and Wales. (Table 9.3)

Detection of crime

The region with the highest percentage of recorded crimes detected by the police in 2002/03 was Wales (36 per cent). The percentage of recorded crime detected by the police was lowest in London (15 per cent of total recorded crimes). (Table 9.4)

Firearms

In 2000/01, London had the highest number of offences recorded in which firearms were reported to have been used: 4,050. Wales had the lowest number: 614. The North West had the highest number of operations where firearms were issued to the police (1,999 incidents) and the lowest was in Scotland (74 incidents). (Table 9.5)

Seizure of controlled drugs

London had the highest number of all class A drugs (in excess of 6,900) and all class B drug seizures (just over 18,400) in 2001. Almost 35 per cent of seizures of class C drugs occurred in Scotland (788 in total). (Table 9.6)

Police manpower

In March 2002, the highest number of police officers on ordinary duty was in London: 26,987. The East had the lowest number of officers per head of population at 546. (Table 9.7)

One in five police officers in the West Midlands were women in March 2002. The proportion of women officers in London was lower: around 1 in 6. Almost 5 per cent of police officers in London were from minority ethnic group, the highest proportion of all UK regions. (Table 9.7)

People cautioned or found guilty

For people aged 10 to 17, the South West had the highest percentage of people cautioned for criminal damage at 70 per cent in 2001. The South West also held the highest percentage of total indictable offences at 65 per cent. (Table 9.8)

For people aged 18 and over the region with the highest proportion cautioned for a sexual offence was the South East (25 per cent of those found guilty or cautioned in 2001). (Table 9.8)

The proportion of minors (aged 10-17) found guilty or cautioned for burglary, robbery and theft was highest in the North East in 2001 (rate of 1941 people per 100,000 population in that age group). (Table 9.9)

The North East also had the largest proportion of males aged 18 or over found guilty or cautioned for a sexual offence in 2001. The lowest rates were in London and the East of England (16 people per 100,000 population aged 18 or over). (Table 9.9)

The highest proportion of persons found guilty who were fined in 2002 was in the East of England (76 per cent for males and 82 percent for females). (Table 9.10)

In Scotland in 2002, 14 per cent of all males and 6 per cent of all females sentenced were given an immediate custodial sentence (including sentence imposed following a sentence deferred for good behaviour). (Table 9.10)

Prisons and imprisonment

In 2002 London had the highest number of males (just over 14,800) and females (almost 1,600) aged 21 or over who were sentenced to immediate imprisonment for a principal offence. (Table 9.11)

The North East had the lowest number of males sentenced to immediate imprisonment at 3,905 and Wales had the lowest number of females (289 in 2002). (Table 9.11)

The regions with highest percentage of males sentenced to four years or longer in prison were London and South East (10 per cent of those sentenced). The South East also had the highest percentage of females sentenced to four years or more in prison (11 per cent of those sentenced in 2002). In 2002, females aged 21 or over who were sentenced to immediate imprisonment for four years or over were lowest in West Midlands and Wales at 2 per cent of all those imprisoned. (Table 9.11)

The region with the highest prison population in the UK was the North West: 11,100 inmates in April 2003. Wales had the lowest number of all regions; 2,400 inmates. (Table 9.12)

Feelings of insecurity

The highest proportion of females who felt 'very unsafe' at night when walking alone was approximately a quarter in the North West and West Midlands in 2002/03. (Table 9.13)

In 2002/03, a higher percentage of males in London felt insecure when walking alone at night (7 per cent), whereas in the South East, South West and Wales males felt least insecure. (Table 9.13)

Table **9.1**   Recorded crimes:[1] by offence group, 2002/03

Rates per 100,000 population

| | Violence against the person | Sexual offences | Burglary | Robbery | Theft and handling stolen goods | Of which: | | Fraud and forgery | Criminal damage | Drug offences | Other | Total |
						Theft of vehicles	Theft from vehicles					
England and Wales[2]	1,603	93	1,707	207	4,542	609	1,265	634	2,130	271	139	11,327
North East	1,556	89	1,797	126	4,229	551	1,118	410	2,816	358	162	11,543
North West	1,538	88	2,093	236	4,440	753	1,221	406	2,590	266	152	11,810
Yorkshire and the Humber	1,366	91	2,879	186	5,463	873	1,694	644	2,595	240	133	13,597
East Midlands	1,579	96	2,077	159	4,810	559	1,441	645	2,164	189	166	11,884
West Midlands	1,851	99	1,813	232	4,257	640	1,201	749	2,095	264	185	11,546
East	1,279	77	1,217	91	3,706	419	1,064	552	1,892	167	104	9,084
London	2,500	146	1,584	592	6,538	817	1,605	1,167	2,014	475	160	15,175
South East	1,155	75	1,162	82	3,640	395	1,001	491	1,707	208	111	8,631
South West	1,353	85	1,382	112	3,928	435	1,153	585	1,720	211	97	9,473
England	1,590	95	1,733	217	4,589	609	1,276	646	2,121	266	139	11,396
Wales	1,831	70	1,269	47	3,744	614	1,070	420	2,276	354	145	10,156
Scotland[3]	420	92	867	98	3,338	445	800	396	1,889	799	551	8,448
Northern Ireland[4]	1,684	87	1,105	148	2,481	498	423	521	2,165	114	131	8,435

1 Recorded crime statistics broadly cover the more serious offences. See Notes and Definitions.
2 In April 2002, all police forces in England and Wales adopted the National Crime Recording Standard (NCRS). See Notes and Definitions.
3 Scottish data refer to 2002.
4 Figures for Scotland and Northern Ireland are not comparable with those for England and Wales, nor with each other, because of the differences in the legal systems, recording practises and classifications.

Source: Home Office; Scottish Executive; The Police Service of Northern Ireland

Table **9.2**   Violent offences committed against the person, 2002/03[1]

Percentage of individuals victimised at least once

	Common assault[2]	Wounding	Robbery[3]	All violent incidents
England and Wales	2.4	1.1	0.6	4.1
North East	2.0	1.2	0.2	3.5
North West	2.3	1.5	0.8	4.5
Yorkshire and the Humber	2.6	1.5	0.7	4.6
East Midlands	2.5	0.9	0.4	3.7
West Midlands	2.1	1.0	0.4	3.4
East	2.8	1.0	0.4	4.3
London	2.3	0.6	1.3	4.3
South East	2.8	1.3	0.7	4.5
South West	2.1	1.3	0.2	3.5
England	2.4	1.1	0.6	4.1
Wales	1.6	1.0	0.3	2.8
Scotland	2.6	..	0.3	2.8
Northern Ireland	2.1	1.1	0.4	3.4

1 Data for Scotland relate to 1999. Data for Northern Ireland relate to the period 1 September 2000 to 31 August 2001.
2 'Assault' for Scotland includes both serious assaults and petty assaults.
3 Mugging (robbery and snatch theft from the person) in Northern Ireland.

Source: British Crime Survey, Home Office; Scottish Crime Survey, Scottish Executive; Northern Ireland Crime Survey, Northern Ireland Office

Table **9.3**   Offences committed against households,[1] 2002/03[2]

Rates per 10,000 households and percentages

	Offences per 10,000 households[3]				Percentage of households victimised at least once			
	Vandalism	Burglary[4]	Vehicle thefts[5]	All household offences[6]	Vandalism	Burglary[4]	Vehicle thefts[5]	All household offences[6]
England and Wales	1,145	439	1,399	3,428	7.3	3.4	10.8	21.0
North East	1,079	351	1,233	3,125	6.8	3.0	10.6	19.4
North West	1,199	570	1,495	3,685	7.8	4.1	11.6	22.4
Yorkshire and the Humber	950	704	1,878	4,163	6.8	5.5	13.5	24.9
East Midlands	1,293	339	1,338	3,528	7.6	2.7	10.0	21.4
West Midlands	1,114	455	1,310	3,291	7.2	3.4	10.2	20.2
East	1,227	339	1,201	3,298	7.0	2.6	9.3	19.6
London	982	514	1,776	3,304	6.8	4.1	13.6	21.2
South East	1,361	346	1,291	3,592	8.9	2.8	10.1	22.1
South West	1,129	364	1,174	3,125	6.9	2.6	9.3	19.0
England	1,157	450	1,417	3,480	7.4	3.5	10.9	21.3
Wales	940	258	1,099	2,563	5.6	1.9	8.1	15.4
Scotland	999	385	534	2,374	6.0	3.2	4.6	15.3
Northern Ireland	1,110	272	781	2,485	6.4	2.0	6.5	15.4

1 See Notes and Definitions for details of surveys.
2 Data for Scotland relate to 1999. Data for Northern Ireland relate to the period 1 September 2000 to 31 August 2001.
3 The vehicle theft risks are based on vehicle-owning households only.
4 The term used in Scotland is housebreaking. The figures include attempts at burglary/housebreaking.
5 Comprises theft of vehicles, thefts from vehicles and associated attempts.
6 Comprises the three individual categories plus thefts of bicycles and other household thefts.

Source: British Crime Survey, Home Office; Scottish Crime Survey, Scottish Executive; Northern Ireland Crime Survey, Northern Ireland Office

Table **9.4**   Recorded crimes detected by the police:[1] by offence group, 2002/03[2]

Percentages

	Violence against the person	Sexual offences	Burglary	Robbery	Theft and handling stolen goods	Fraud and forgery	Criminal damage[3]	Drug offences	Other[3]	All Offences[3]
England and Wales[4]	54	43	12	18	16	26	13	93	69	24
North East	66	53	14	24	23	47	15	98	83	30
North West	64	54	10	19	17	34	13	95	77	24
Yorkshire and the Humber	62	48	10	22	15	24	12	97	78	21
East Midlands	55	42	12	22	16	26	14	94	71	23
West Midlands	63	45	15	23	20	27	14	95	72	28
East	65	41	13	23	17	27	14	95	66	26
London	25	33	13	13	8	10	8	83	45	15
South East	63	44	13	26	17	30	15	97	70	26
South West	48	36	14	18	16	34	14	94	63	23
England	53	42	12	18	15	24	13	92	68	23
Wales	73	62	20	33	23	55	20	99	86	36
Scotland[5]	81	77	26	38	34	82	22	99	97	46
Northern Ireland[5,6]	51	47	10	13	14	28	13	68	40	23

1 See Notes and Definitions.
2 Some offences cleared up may have been initially recorded in an earlier year.
3 From 1st April 2002, most attempted thefts/ unauthorised taking of motor vehicles are recorded as vehicle interference due to a change in the Home Office counting rules. For England and Wales the 2002/03 figures are not comparable with those for earlier years.
4 Unadjusted, see Notes and Definitions.
5 Figures for Scotland and Northern Ireland are not comparable with those for England and Wales, nor with each other, because of the differences in the legal systems, recording practices and classifications.
6 The Northern Ireland figures exclude Offences against the State.

Source: Home Office; Scottish Executive; The Police Service of Northern Ireland

Table 9.5   Firearms 1994 to 2001

Numbers

	Offences recorded[1] by the police where firearms were reported[2] to have been used							Operations where firearms were issued to the police[3,4,5]						
	1994	1995	1996	1997	1998/99[6,7]	1999/2000[6,7]	2000/01[6,7]	1994/95	1995/96	1996/97	1997/98	1998/99[6]	1999/2000[6]	2000/01[6]
United Kingdom	15,985	15,730	16,177	14,424	15,778	18,716	19,457	5,960	8,671	12,649	12,134	11,184	11,056	11,183
North East	767	723	681	486	727	783	791	800	1,050	2,517	1,029	832	655	776
North West	2,044	2,308	2,426	1,751	2,308	2,619	3,012	420	922	1,578	1,462	1,611	1,390	1,999
Yorkshire and the Humber	2,264	2,270	2,175	1,968	2,079	2,206	2,541	427	1,026	1,128	1,506	1,183	1,304	1,179
East Midlands	970	1,014	1,187	1,140	1,407	1,619	1,440	283	346	470	671	736	867	1,011
West Midlands	1,394	1,510	1,570	1,251	1,092	1,375	1,638	237	420	730	751	935	840	957
East	808	771	730	607	761	996	1,052	620	871	1,172	1,327	1,327	1,239	1,288
London	2,376	2,248	2,605	2,930	3,005	4,123	4,050	2,129	2,453	2,747	2,885	2,889	2,987	1,865
South East	1,526	1,367	1,232	1,123	1,276	1,579	1,563	790	883	1,064	1,284	562	626	924
South West	569	588	608	560	628	934	888	284	511	575	403	294	305	504
England	12,718	12,799	13,214	11,816	13,283	16,234	16,975	5,673	8,232	11,981	11,318	10,292	10,213	10,503
Wales	449	635	662	594	591	712	614	151	244	398	524	636	702	606
Scotland	1,788	1,721	1,650	1,187	985	1,033	938	136	195	270	292	256	141	74
Northern Ireland	1,030	575	651	827	919	737	930	..	..	..	..	..	..	..

1 See Notes and Definitions for information on coverage of offences.
2 'Alleged' in Scotland.
3 In England and Wales, firearms were discharged in 6 incidents in 1994/95; 5 incidents in 1995/96; 4 incidents in both 1996/97 and 1997/98, 7 incidents in both 1998/99 and 1999/2000 and 9 incidents in 2000/01. In Scotland, police shots were fired in 4 operations in 1995/96, 9 in 1996/97, 1 in 1997/98, 8 in 1998/99, 3 in 1990/2000 and 4 in 2000/01.
4 In Northern Ireland, police officers are armed at all times.
5 Figures for the United Kingdom relate to Great Britain only.
6 The collection of recorded crime data in England and Wales changed to a financial year basis from 1 April 1998, which coincided with a change in the counting rules for recorded crime. Due to this, the data shown for 1998/99, 1999/00 and 2000/01 are not comparable with those shown for previous years. See Notes and Definitions.
7 In Scotland, data collection relating to offences involving firearms is based on calendar year data.
Source: Home Office; Her Majesty's Inspectorate of Constabulary; Scottish Executive Justice Department; Police Service of Northern Ireland

Table 9.6   Seizures of controlled drugs[1]: by type of drug, 2001

Number of seizures

	Class A drugs						Class B drugs			All class C drugs[2,3]
	Heroin	Cocaine	Crack	LSD	Ecstasy type	All class A drugs[2]	Cannabis	Ampheta-mines	All class B drugs[2]	
United Kingdom[4]	18,168	6,984	3,688	168	10,411	37,915	93,482	6,799	98,954	2,299
North East	1,029	239	39	7	963	2,223	4,476	602	4,977	246
North West	1,473	399	168	8	785	2,812	6,374	515	6,808	103
Yorkshire and the Humber	2,071	193	274	9	866	3,330	5,743	655	6,226	228
East Midlands	1,147	168	153	7	586	1,958	3,853	560	4,258	125
West Midlands	2,199	259	388	19	807	3,584	8,264	440	8,579	45
East	774	376	87	6	410	1,574	4,824	361	5,078	35
London	2,477	2,168	1,868	44	1,004	6,929	17,893	627	18,407	193
South East	1,212	598	227	25	991	2,914	8,985	736	9,489	115
South West	1,499	336	328	15	1,222	3,213	7,559	678	8,047	106
England	13,881	4,736	3,532	140	7,634	28,537	67,971	5,174	71,869	1,196
Wales	810	103	46	9	993	1,957	6,252	703	6,691	168
Scotland	3,123	523	51	10	1,337	4,860	14,062	735	14,639	788
Northern Ireland	79	19	1	7	285	390	1,226	66	1,259	24
National Crime Squad[4]	37	48	2	0	20	92	68	16	76	0
British Transport Police[4]	145	41	13	0	53	247	915	31	937	4
Customs and Excise[4]	93	1,514	43	2	89	1,832	2,988	74	3,483	119

1 See Notes and Definitions.
2 Since a seizure may involve drugs other than those listed and the seizure of more than one drug listed, figures for individual drugs cannot be added together to produce totals.
3 Class C drugs include benzodiazepines (including temazepam) and anabolic steroids.
4 Figures for the National Crime Squad, the British Transport Police and the Customs and Excise cannot be split by region or country, but are included in the UK totals.
Source: Home Office

Table **9.7**   Police manpower: by type, March 2002[1]

| | Police officers on ordinary duty[2] | | | | Special constables and civilian staff (rates per 1,000 officers on ordinary duty) | | |
| | | Percentage of which | | | | | |
	Number	Minority ethnic groups	Women officers	Population per officer[3]	Special constables[4]	Civilian staff	Traffic wardens (numbers)[5]
United Kingdom[6]	151,678	..	..	388	..	..	2,547
North East	7,004	1.0	17.6	359	68	384	102
North West	17,804	2.1	18.2	378	82	428	255
Yorkshire and the Humber	11,564	2.2	18.6	430	82	456	236
East Midlands	8,690	3.1	16.6	480	124	483	179
West Midlands	12,801	3.6	20.9	411	120	438	120
East	9,872	2.0	18.1	546	148	553	202
London	26,987	4.9	16.1	266	27	397	632
South East	15,482	1.7	19.0	517	105	527	164
South West	9,870	1.0	17.7	500	163	525	195
England	120,073	2.7	18.0	410	91	457	2,085
Wales	7,194	1.0	16.8	404	97	432	148
Scotland[7]	15,251	0.6	18.0	335	74	343	314
Northern Ireland[7,8]	9,160	..	..	185	109	359	..

1 Full-time equivalents as at 31 March 2002 for England and Wales. Actual numbers (whether full or part-time) as at 31 March 2002 for Northern Ireland and Scotland.
2 Includes full-time reserves in Northern Ireland.
3 Based on mid-2000 population estimates.
4 Part-time reserves in Northern Ireland.
5 Figures for Great Britain only.
6 Great Britain for minority ethnic groups.
7 For civilian staff and traffic wardens, part-time staff are counted as full-time equivalents.
8 The figure for civilian staff relates to those who work to the Chief Constable and not to those who work to the Police Authority for Northern Ireland.

Source: Home Office; Scottish Executive; The Police Service of Northern Ireland

Table **9.8**   **People given a police caution[1]: by type of offence and age, 2001**

Percentages and thousands

	Those cautioned as a percentage of people found guilty or cautioned for each offence category										All people found guilty or cautioned (thousands)	
	Violence against the person	Sexual offences	Burglary	Robbery	Theft and handling stolen goods	Fraud and forgery	Criminal damage	Other indict-able off-ences	Total indict-able off-ences	Sum-mary off-ences[2]	Indictable offences	Summary offences[2]
People aged 10 to 17												
England and Wales	56	52	46	15	65	55	42	23	56	55	113.1	63.0
North East	57	37	43	11	64	62	38	25	55	58	8.2	5.6
North West	44	34	40	5	58	50	34	14	47	48	15.7	9.7
Yorkshire and the Humber	63	40	43	16	64	52	29	22	54	59	11.1	6.7
East Midlands	59	63	47	20	66	56	55	29	59	60	9.1	5.4
West Midlands	60	46	50	4	61	52	28	24	54	58	13.2	7.6
East	63	68	57	18	70	54	54	29	64	56	9.9	4.8
London	49	53	43	20	66	58	27	23	54	47	15.6	6.9
South East	61	65	48	16	68	53	44	28	61	57	15.1	7.8
South West	62	57	50	22	70	58	70	35	65	56	7.9	4.5
England	56	52	46	15	65	55	42	23	56	55	105.9	58.9
Wales	45	38	42	5	64	60	57	26	55	54	7.3	4.2
People aged 18 or over												
England and Wales	28	17	6	2	21	21	13	7	23	11	346.0	463.2
North East	26	21	5	-	22	24	10	7	24	16	24.5	36.2
North West	19	9	4	-	18	15	7	3	18	11	51.3	76.2
Yorkshire and the Humber	23	11	3	-	14	13	4	4	14	11	33.9	41.8
East Midlands	19	17	4	-	17	16	14	5	17	7	24.8	42.3
West Midlands	36	19	7	2	22	21	4	8	25	15	41.2	44.1
East	36	21	9	2	22	20	17	10	26	10	25.5	36.0
London	30	16	8	4	28	28	6	6	29	6	57.8	65.3
South East	33	25	7	2	26	26	16	11	27	14	39.4	52.1
South West	29	24	7	3	20	22	26	12	26	11	25.1	36.4
England	28	18	6	2	21	21	11	7	23	11	323.4	430.4
Wales	19	14	5	-	23	16	26	6	25	11	22.6	32.8

1 People committing an offence who, on admission of guilt, were given a formal oral caution by the police as a proportion of those found guilty or cautioned. See notes and Definitions.
2 Excludes motoring offences for which written warnings were issued.

Source: Home Office

Table **9.9**   People found guilty or cautioned:[1] by type of offence and age, 2001

Rates per 100,000 population in the relevant age group

	People aged 10 to 17						People aged 18 or over					
	Violence against the person plus common assault[2]	Sexual off-ences	Burglary, robbery and theft[3]	Drugs off-ences	Other indict-able off-ences[4]	All indictable offences plus common assault[2]	Violence against the person plus common assault[2]	Sexual off-ences	Burglary, robbery and theft[3]	Drugs off-ences	Other indict-able off-ences[4]	All indictable offences plus common assault[2]
Males												
England and Wales	764	36	1,839	425	396	3,460	301	20	615	322	296	1,554
North East	946	37	2,673	628	483	4,766	352	25	903	467	363	2,110
North West	781	31	1,910	466	443	3,631	314	23	745	307	347	1,737
Yorkshire and the Humber	764	39	2,023	296	376	3,498	290	21	730	239	310	1,590
East Midlands	915	57	1,971	270	359	3,573	303	22	626	231	261	1,443
West Midlands	1,101	52	1,996	386	467	4,002	415	22	700	344	404	1,885
East	652	30	1,547	303	387	2,919	248	16	448	210	219	1,141
London	683	35	1,821	734	433	3,705	284	16	636	516	345	1,797
South East	635	27	1,661	344	324	2,991	257	18	448	253	218	1,194
South West	603	27	1,378	360	241	2,607	276	19	505	253	193	1,245
England	766	36	1,832	419	387	3,440	299	20	616	312	292	1,539
Wales	727	38	1,951	525	553	3,794	344	22	603	482	361	1,812
Females												
England and Wales	250	1	763	42	83	1,140	49	-	168	37	61	316
North East	329	0	1,169	61	110	1,669	70	1	326	71	98	565
North West	254	-	571	34	79	938	50	-	209	32	70	362
Yorkshire and the Humber	266	-	749	38	85	1,138	48	-	181	35	67	330
East Midlands	322	1	808	28	85	1,245	56	-	151	27	58	292
West Midlands	388	1	764	49	105	1,308	77	-	188	38	77	380
East	241	-	778	31	76	1,126	40	-	122	27	37	226
London	129	1	805	50	78	1,063	31	-	176	45	78	330
South East	203	1	773	35	71	1,084	39	-	126	30	41	237
South West	221	1	675	45	64	1,005	42	-	122	34	39	238
England	250	1	760	40	82	1,132	48	-	168	35	60	312
Wales	242	0	825	80	112	1,259	66	-	170	69	71	376
All people												
England and Wales	514	19	1,316	239	244	2,332	172	10	386	176	176	920
North East	646	19	1,941	352	301	3,258	210	13	613	268	230	1,333
North West	524	16	1,258	255	266	2,320	177	11	467	164	203	1,023
Yorkshire and the Humber	521	20	1,402	170	234	2,347	166	10	449	134	186	946
East Midlands	627	30	1,406	153	226	2,441	177	11	384	127	158	856
West Midlands	754	27	1,397	222	291	2,692	243	11	439	188	237	1,117
East	451	16	1,171	170	235	2,043	142	8	281	116	126	673
London	413	19	1,326	401	260	2,419	156	8	404	278	210	1,057
South East	426	15	1,230	194	202	2,066	145	9	283	138	127	702
South West	418	14	1,037	207	155	1,831	155	9	307	140	114	725
England	515	19	1,310	235	238	2,318	170	10	387	171	174	911
Wales	491	20	1,402	307	338	2,557	200	11	380	269	211	1,072

1 See Notes and Definitions for information on coverage of offences.
2 Following the introduction of a charging standard on 31 August 1994, some people who would have been charged with an indictable offence are now charged with common assault, a summary offence. Common assaults have therefore been included for comparability with figures in previous editions of Regional Trends.
3 Includes handling stolen goods.
4 Includes criminal damage and fraud and forgery.

Source: Home Office

Table **9.10** **People aged 21 or over found guilty of offences:[1] by sex and type of sentence, 2002**

	A percentage of number of people sentenced						All sentenced	
	Absolute or condit- ional discharge	Fine	All community penalties	Fully sus- pended sentence[2]	Immed- iate custodial sentence[3]	Otherwise dealt with	(=100%) (numbers)	Rates per 100,000 aged 21 or over
Males								
England and Wales	7	73	10	-	9	2	927,810	51
North East	12	66	10	-	8	5	50,570	57
North West	9	73	9	-	8	1	147,582	63
Yorkshire and the Humber	8	67	11	-	10	4	87,472	51
East Midlands	6	73	10	-	8	2	78,331	53
West Midlands	6	72	11	-	10	1	95,032	52
East	5	76	9	-	8	2	81,928	42
London	5	75	8	-	11	1	134,901	53
South East	6	74	9	-	8	2	112,362	40
South West	9	74	9	-	7	2	80,341	45
England	7	73	10	-	9	2	868,519	50
Wales	6	75	9	-	7	2	59,291	59
Scotland[5]	8	68	9	.	14	1	75,564	43
Northern Ireland[6]	4	71	5	7	9	4	17,537	31
Females								
England and Wales	9	79	8	-	3	1	228,763	11
North East	11	75	7	-	3	4	14,729	15
North West	9	79	8	-	3	1	40,535	16
Yorkshire and the Humber	9	76	9	-	3	2	23,936	13
East Midlands	8	80	8	-	2	2	19,496	12
West Midlands	9	77	9	-	4	1	20,457	10
East	7	82	7	-	3	1	19,456	9
London	7	80	7	-	5	1	31,032	11
South East	9	78	8	-	3	2	25,057	8
South West	12	77	8	-	2	1	18,029	9
England	9	79	8	-	3	1	212,727	11
Wales	8	82	7	-	2	1	16,036	14
Scotland[4]	18	63	11	.	6	1	12,653	6
Northern Ireland[5]	10	74	6	4	2	5	2,851	5

1 See Notes and Definitions. The coverage of the table is all offences, including motoring offences. A defendant is recorded only once for each set of court proceedings, against the principal offence.
2 Fully suspended sentences are not available to courts in Scotland. See Notes and Definitions for table 9.12.
3 Includes custodial sentences imposed following a sentence deferred for good behaviour in Scotland.
4 To improve comparability, this table excludes breaches of probation and community service orders normally included in Scottish figures.
5 Northern Ireland figures relate to 2000.

Source: Home Office; Scottish Executive; Northern Ireland Office

Table **9.11** People aged 21 or over sentenced to immediate imprisonment: by sex and length of sentence imposed for principal[1] offence, 2002

Percentages and numbers

	Males				Females			
	Length of sentence (percentages)			Total sentenced to immediate imprisonment (=100%) (numbers)	Length of sentence (percentages)			Total sentenced to immediate imprisonment (=100%) (numbers)
	One year or less	Over one year but less than four years	Four years or over		One year or less	Over one year but less than four years	Four years or over	
North East	71	21	8	3,905	78	18	3	395
North West	73	19	8	11,883	82	15	3	1,215
Yorkshire and the Humber	73	18	8	8,795	83	13	3	801
East Midlands	74	19	7	6,215	81	16	3	466
West Midlands	75	17	7	9,320	84	14	2	766
East	76	16	8	6,338	85	11	4	534
London	73	17	10	14,806	76	14	9	1,571
South East	72	18	10	8,679	75	14	11	785
South West	75	17	7	5,255	84	13	3	406
England	74	18	8	75,196	80	14	5	6,939
Wales	75	19	6	4,404	80	18	2	289
Scotland[1,2]	88	8	4	10,563	91	7	2	728
Northern Ireland[3]	80	16	4	1,525	83	13	4	48

1 Figures for Scotland are for the length of sentence in total and not just for the principal offence; they include sentence length not known. Figures on sentence lengths for principal offences only are not available for Scotland. Scottish data are for 2001.

2 To improve comparability, this table excludes breaches of probation and community service orders normally included in Scottish figures.

3 Data for Northern Ireland relate to 2000.

Source: Home Office; Scottish Executive; Northern Ireland Office

Table **9.12** Prison population in the United Kingdom: by prison service region[1], 30 April 2003

Thousands

	Prison population
United Kingdom	..
North East	4.3
North West	11.1
Yorkshire & Humberside	8.5
East Midlands North	4.0
East Midlands South	4.9
West Midlands	6.7
Eastern	6.3
London	7.0
Kent, Surrey & Sussex	6.2
Thames Valley & Hampshire	5.6
South West	6.4
Wales	2.4
Scotland	6.5
Northern Ireland	1.1

1 People in prison establishments in Prison Service region excluding female area and high security prisons. See Notes and Definitions.

Source: Home Office; Scottish Executive; Northern Ireland Office

Table **9.13** Feelings of insecurity:[1] by sex, 2002/03[2]

Percentages

	Percentage feeling 'very unsafe' at night when:			
	Alone at home		Walking alone[3]	
	Males	Females	Males	Females
England and Wales	-	2	5	21
North East	1	1	5	19
North West	-	2	6	25
Yorkshire and the Humber	1	2	5	21
East Midlands	-	2	4	19
West Midlands	1	2	6	24
East	-	2	4	19
London	1	2	7	22
South East	-	2	3	20
South West	-	3	3	19
England	-	2	5	21
Wales	1	2	3	17
Scotland	-	2	4	16
Northern Ireland	-	2	5	16

1 People aged 16 and over.

2 Data for Scotland relate to 2000. Data for Northern Ireland relate to 2001. See Notes and Definitions.

3 For Northern Ireland the question relates to fear of 'walking in the dark' (i.e. alone or with others); the figures also include those people who never go out.

Source: British Crime Survey, Home Office; Scottish Crime Survey, Scottish Executive; Northern Ireland Crime Survey, Northern Ireland Office

Chapter 10 Transport

Cars

New car registrations have risen in the United Kingdom since 1998 with the largest increase (43 per cent growth by 2002) in the South West. London was the only region to experience a decrease in new car registrations, of 9 per cent, and also had one of the smallest increases in the number of vehicles currently licensed. (Table 10.1)

Scotland, London and the North East had the highest proportions of households without regular use of a car or van (35 per cent in each area in 2001). The highest proportions with access to one or more cars were the South East (83 per cent) and South West (82 per cent) compared to the average for Great Britain which was 74 per cent. (Table 10.2)

The East of England had the highest proportion of males with full licenses in 1999-2001 (91 per cent) and the second highest proportion for females (69 per cent). However, in the South East the positions were reversed; the region had the highest proportion of females (71 per cent) and second highest for males (87 per cent). (Table 10.4)

Travel

With the exception of London, where the mean time taken to travel to work was 43 minutes in 2002, there was little variation in commuting times throughout the rest of Great Britain. The quickest average journey time was 19 minutes in the North East (excluding Tyne and Wear) whilst the slowest, 27 minutes, was in the Former Metropolitan County of West Midlands. (Table 10.5)

People in the East travelled the furthest distance 8,280 miles per person in 1999-2001, over 50 per cent further than Londoners, who travelled the least distance within Great Britain. (Table 10.6)

Londoners travelled further by public transport and by walking than residents of other areas. People living in Wales travelled the least distance by these modes (only one-third and two-thirds of Londoners' distance respectively). (Table 10.6)

The percentage of households within 13 minutes of a bus stop which had a service at least once an hour, increased during the 1990s throughout Great Britain; the overall average was 89 per cent of households in 1999–2001. London had greatest accessibility on this measure (99 per cent in 1999–2001) followed closely by the North East (98 per cent). (Figure 10.7)

Households in the South East had the greatest increase in accessibility of bus services between 1992-1994 and 1999-2001 (21 percentage points), although the proportion of households with access was still lower than most other areas. The East Midlands had the smallest increase (6 percentage points) in access to bus services over the same time period. (Figure 10.7)

Across Great Britain women made proportionally fewer commuting trips than men did during 1999–2001. The greatest differences were in the South West and Scotland, where nearly a fifth of men's trips were for commuting compared to an eighth of women's trips. (Table 10.8)

Travel by car, van, minibus or works van was the most frequent method of travel to work throughout the UK in autumn 2002. In Wales, 80 per cent of commuters used this method, almost twice the proportion in London. Walking was the second most common method of travelling to work in all regions except London and the North East where rail and bus/coach were the most usual mode respectively. (Table 10.9)

Walking was the most common method of travelling to and from school during 1999–2001. Nearly three-fifths of school trips in Yorkshire and the Humberside were made on foot, followed closely by Scotland and the West Midlands. (Table 10.10)

Pupils in the South West had the longest average journeys to school: 1.9 miles for those aged 5 to 10 years (over twice the distance travelled in the North East) and 3.8 miles for 11 to 16 year-olds (two-thirds more than in the West Midlands). (Table 10.10)

Expenditure on travel and roads

In 2002, the average weekly household expenditure on motoring was highest in the South East (£74.27 per car or van) over 60 per cent more than households in Yorkshire and the Humber (£46.25 per car or van). Average household expenditure on petrol, diesel and other motor oils varied considerably throughout the United Kingdom in 2002, from £17.69 per week in the South East to £11.53 per week in London. (Table 10.11)

Traffic

Average daily motor flows overall for Great Britain increased by 3 per cent between 2001 and 2002. London had the greatest increase, an 11 per cent rise for 'All roads' and generally had the highest traffic flows on major roads, whereas flows in Scotland showed a slight decline. (Table 10.13 and table 10.14 in Regional Trends 37)

The greatest increase in traffic on major roads (expressed as vehicle kilometres) was in the South East with a rise of over 24 per cent, between 1993 and 2002. London had the smallest traffic increase on major roads, (almost 3 per cent); overall the increase for Great Britain was 20 per cent. (Table 10.14)

Accidents

The total number of accidents on all roads in Great Britain decreased by just over 3 per cent between 2001 and 2002. The largest decrease was in London (7 per cent), while the number of accidents in North West increased by almost 19 per cent. (Table 10.15 and table 10.16 in Regional Trends 37)

The rate of fatal and serious accidents fell in all areas between 1991 and 2002; the largest reduction was in Scotland where the rate per 100,000 population fell by 43. Road casualties in general fell overall in Great Britain between 2001 and 2002, except in Wales and North East (four per cent and one per cent increases respectively). Over the same period, London had the largest reduction in overall road casualties at 7 per cent. (Tables 10.16 and 10.17)

Airports

In 2002, almost 80 per cent of all air passengers using UK airports travelled on international flights. The largest number of passengers, about one-third of the total, travelled through Heathrow Airport. The second busiest airport was Gatwick followed by Manchester. In the UK there was a four per cent average increase in the total number of air passengers between 2001 and 2002. Belfast City airport had the largest increase in passenger activity (59 per cent rise) whilst Cardiff had the largest fall (7 per cent decrease). (Table 10.18)

Seaports

East coast ports handled nearly half of all UK seaport freight tonnage in 2002 whilst over half of International sea passenger movements took place through Dover. (Table 10.19)

Table 10.1 Motor cars currently licensed and new registrations[1]

Thousands and percentages

	Currently licensed				Percentage company cars 2002[2]	New registrations		
	1994	1996	1998	2002[2]		1996	1998	2002[2]
United Kingdom[3]	21,708	22,784	23,878	25,782	9	2,077	2,366	2,682
North East	745	783	824	922	5	74	78	94
North West	2,375	2,501	2,647	2,876	11	235	265	322
Yorkshire and the Humber	1,633	1,707	1,808	2,000	8	138	157	203
East Midlands	1,532	1,609	1,698	1,927	9	140	173	223
West Midlands	2,070	2,183	2,290	2,562	17	275	288	333
East	2,168	2,295	2,429	2,694	8	200	232	276
London	2,310	2,362	2,369	2,473	7	277	270	246
South East	3,295	3,469	3,709	4,103	10	292	361	457
South West	1,976	2,109	2,230	2,495	9	130	138	198
England	18,104	19,018	20,006	22,052	10	1,762	1,961	2,352
Wales	1,012	1,067	1,129	1,269	4	73	83	100
Scotland	1,575	1,674	1,775	1,993	8	154	175	220
Northern Ireland	515	540	585	..	..	55	71	..

1 At 31 December 2002.
2 Figures for 2002 are for Great Britain.
3 Totals for the United Kingdom include motor vehicles where the country of the registered keeper is unknown, that are under disposal or from countries unknown within Great Britain (but not Northern Ireland).

Source: Annual Vehicle Census/Vehicle Information Database, Department for Transport; Department of the Environment, Northern Ireland

Table 10.2 Households with regular use of a car[1], 2001

Percentages

	Percentage of households with regular use of a car[1]			
	No car	One car	Two or more cars	Use of one car or more
Great Britain	26	46	28	74
North East	35	44	20	65
North West	29	46	25	71
Yorkshire and the Humber	31	46	23	69
East Midlands	21	49	30	79
West Midlands	25	47	28	75
East	21	46	33	79
London	35	46	19	65
South East	17	45	38	83
South West	18	47	35	82
England	25	46	28	75
Wales	25	47	28	75
Scotland	35	46	19	65
Northern Ireland[2]	27	45	28	73

1 Includes cars and light vans normally available to the household.
2 Northern Ireland data are for 2001/02.

Source: General Household Survey and Family Expenditure Survey, Office for National Statistics; National Travel Survey, Department for Transport; Continuous Household Survey, Northern Ireland Statistics and Research Agency

Table **10.3**   Age of household cars[1], 1992–1994 and 1999–2001

Percentages

	1992–1994			1999–2001		
	Less than 3 years old	3 to 6 years old	More than 6 years old	Less than 3 years old	3 to 6 years old	More than 6 years old
Great Britain	26	29	44	27	22	51
North East	32	29	39	32	22	46
North West	28	29	43	28	22	50
Yorkshire and the Humber	28	34	38	30	25	45
East Midlands	31	30	39	25	22	53
West Midlands	25	27	47	29	20	51
East	25	30	46	27	20	53
London	20	29	52	27	20	53
South East	29	30	41	26	23	51
South West	21	27	52	21	20	59
England	26	29	45	27	21	52
Wales	23	26	51	24	21	55
Scotland	31	33	36	33	27	40

1 Age of main or only car or light van normally available to the household. See Notes and Definitions.

Source: National Travel Survey, Department for Transport

Table **10.4**   Full car driving licence holders:[1] by sex, 1992–1994 and 1999–2001

Percentages

	Males		Females	
	1992–1994	1999–2001	1992–1994	1999–2001
Great Britain	81	82	54	60
North East	68	72	40	44
North West	77	82	49	61
Yorkshire and the Humber	77	79	51	54
East Midlands	84	83	55	60
West Midlands	80	83	51	57
East	88	91	62	69
London	78	76	51	57
South East	88	87	65	71
South West	88	85	61	65
England	82	83	55	61
Wales	83	83	48	57
Scotland	77	80	46	57

1 Aged 17 years and over. See Notes and Definitions.

Source: National Travel Survey, Department for Transport

Table **10.5**   **Time taken to travel to work by workplace, autumn 2002**

Percentages and minutes

	Cumulative percentage of journeys to workplace				Mean time (minutes)
	<20 minutes	<40 minutes	<60 minutes	<90 minutes	
Great Britain	46	79	90	97	25
North East	51	86	95	99	21
Tyne & Wear[1]	44	82	94	98	24
Rest	57	90	96	99	19
North West	47	84	93	99	23
Greater Manchester[1]	41	80	91	98	25
Merseyside[1]	43	86	96	100	22
Rest	54	86	94	98	21
Yorkshire and the Humber	47	84	94	99	23
South Yorkshire[1]	41	83	92	98	24
West Yorkshire[1]	44	82	93	99	24
Rest	55	89	96	99	20
East Midlands	54	87	94	99	21
West Midlands	47	83	93	98	23
West Midlands[1]	39	77	90	98	27
Rest	56	89	95	99	20
East	51	84	93	98	23
London	21	49	68	90	43
South East	49	82	91	97	24
South West	52	86	94	98	21
England	45	79	89	97	26
Wales	55	89	96	99	20
Scotland	48	82	92	98	24

1   Data relate to Former Metropolitain Counties.

Source: Labour Force Survey

Table **10.6**   Distance travelled per person[1] per year: by mode of transport, 1999–2001

Miles

| | Walk | Pedal cycle[2] | Cars and other private road vehicles | Public transport | | | | All modes of transport |
				Bus	Rail[2]	Taxi and other	All public transport	
Great Britain	189	39	5,714	245	425	204	873	6,815
North East	177	52	4,651	448	200	211	858	5,737
North West	173	36	5,407	265	249	204	717	6,333
Yorkshire and the Humber	190	42	5,490	279	282	199	761	6,483
East Midlands	165	51	6,156	237	..	134	648	7,020
West Midlands	175	31	5,694	269	..	222	613	6,513
East	176	51	7,056	138	699	161	998	8,280
London	237	32	3,647	333	996	206	1,536	5,452
South East	193	45	6,967	117	568	176	862	8,067
South West	178	41	6,015	157	..	179	592	6,826
England	188	41	5,719	234	449	188	871	6,819
Wales	165	15	5,438	179	..	187	494	6,111
Scotland	220	30	5,835	393	366	369	1,128	7,213

1 Within Great Britain only. Figures relate to region of residence of the traveller and include trips undertaken outside of this region. They include trips of less than one mile;
   these were excluded from the table in Regional Trends 32 and earlier editions. See Notes and Definitions.
2 For some regions, sample sizes are too small to provide reliable estimates.

Source: National Travel Survey, Department for Transport

Figure **10.7** Bus accessibility,[1] 1992–1994 and 1999–2001

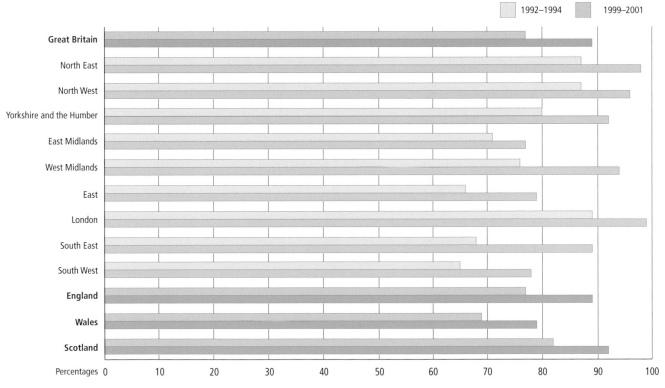

1 Households within 13 minutes of a bus stop with a service at least once an hour. See Notes and Definitions.
Source: National Travel Survey, Department for Transport

Table 10.8 Trips per person[1] per year: by purpose and sex, 1999–2001

Percentages and numbers

	Commuting	Business	Education	Shopping	Other personal business	Leisure	Average number of journeys (=100%)
Males							
Great Britain	18	5	7	19	21	31	1,031
North East	17	3	7	20	18	35	1,014
North West	17	4	7	19	21	32	1,056
Yorkshire and the Humber	18	5	7	19	19	31	1,023
East Midlands	20	5	6	19	19	30	981
West Midlands	19	4	7	18	21	30	1,043
East	19	6	6	18	22	29	1,062
London	18	5	7	18	22	30	1,005
South East	17	7	6	18	22	30	1,056
South West	19	5	5	19	21	31	1,021
England	18	5	7	19	21	31	1,033
Wales	18	5	6	19	20	32	955
Scotland	19	4	7	19	18	32	1,064
Females							
Great Britain	13	2	6	23	25	31	1,008
North East	14	2	6	25	22	32	951
North West	13	2	6	23	25	31	1,016
Yorkshire and the Humber	12	2	7	24	24	31	1,013
East Midlands	14	1	6	22	24	32	934
West Midlands	14	1	7	24	25	30	972
East	13	2	7	22	28	29	1,052
London	12	3	8	22	26	30	977
South East	13	2	6	23	27	29	1,061
South West	12	2	6	23	24	33	991
England	13	2	6	23	25	31	1,004
Wales	12	1	7	24	24	32	948
Scotland	12	1	7	24	23	33	1,083
All persons							
Great Britain	15	3	7	21	23	31	1,019
North East	15	2	6	23	20	33	980
North West	15	3	7	21	23	31	1,034
Yorkshire and the Humber	15	4	7	22	22	31	1,018
East Midlands	17	3	6	21	22	31	957
West Midlands	16	3	7	21	23	30	1,006
East	15	4	7	20	25	29	1,057
London	15	4	8	20	24	30	990
South East	15	4	6	21	24	30	1,059
South West	15	3	6	21	23	32	1,005
England	15	4	6	21	23	31	1,018
Wales	15	3	6	22	22	32	952
Scotland	15	3	7	22	21	33	1,074

1 Within Great Britain only. Figures relate to region of residence of the traveller and include trips undertaken outside of their region. They include trips of less than one mile; these were excluded from the table in Regional Trends 32 and earlier editions. See Notes and Definitions.

Source: National Travel Survey, Department for Transport

Table 10.9 Main method of travel to work, autumn 2002[1]

Percentages

	Car, van, minibus, works van	Motorbike, moped, scooter[2]	Bicycle[2]	Bus, coach, private bus	Rail[2]	Other rail[2,3]	Foot	Other[2,4]
United Kingdom	71.2	1.1	2.8	7.6	3.7	2.4	10.6	0.6
North East	72.4	..	1.4	11.5	..	1.4	11.1	..
North West	74.6	1.2	2.1	8.7	1.6	0.4	10.8	0.6
Yorkshire and the Humber	72.8	1.0	3.2	10.6	1.0	..	10.7	..
East Midlands	76.7	1.3	3.4	5.9	0.6	..	11.6	..
West Midlands	77.6	1.1	2.5	7.2	1.7	..	9.3	..
East	78.6	1.2	4.1	3.8	1.5	..	10.2	..
London	40.5	1.5	2.7	11.9	17.8	16.1	8.8	0.7
South East	77.8	1.1	3.7	4.1	2.7	..	9.8	0.7
South West	76.1	1.7	3.4	5.3	0.8	..	12.3	..
England	70.6	1.3	3.0	7.5	4.1	2.7	10.3	0.5
Wales	80.4	..	1.3	4.5	1.1	..	11.5	..
Scotland	69.6	..	1.7	11.4	2.9	..	12.5	1.1
Northern Ireland	79.9	..	..	5.0	..	..	11.4	1.6

1 Analyses excludes those on government schemes, those who work from home or in the same grounds or building as their home, and those who work in different places using their home as a base. See Notes and Definitions for Chapter 5 also.
2 For some regions, sample sizes are too small to provide a reliable estimate.
3 Underground, light railway and tram.
4 Includes taxi as main method.

Source: Labour Force Survey, Office for National Statistics; Department of Enterprise, Trade and Investment, Northern Ireland

Table 10.10 Trips to and from school: by main mode of transport, 1999–2001[1]

Percentages and miles

	Age 5 to 16				Average length (miles)	
	Walk	Car	Bus[2]	Other	Age 5 to 10	Age 11 to 16
Great Britain	48	29	18	4	1.4	2.9
North East	53	22	23	2	0.8	3.0
North West	43	31	22	3	1.4	2.5
Yorkshire and the Humber	58	25	15	2	1.0	2.4
East Midlands	45	27	25	3	1.4	3.0
West Midlands	56	27	17	-	1.7	2.3
East	44	36	12	8	1.7	3.4
London	50	22	20	8	1.1	3.2
South East	45	37	13	4	1.6	3.2
South West	41	34	18	7	1.9	3.8
England	48	30	18	5	1.4	3.0
Wales	45	25	28	2	1.1	3.0
Scotland	57	19	23	1	1.1	2.7

1 By region of residence. See Notes and Definitions.
2 Including school bus.

Source: National Travel Survey, Department for Transport

Table 10.11 Household expenditure on transport, 2002[1]

Average weekly household expenditure (£)

	Motoring costs per car/van						Fares and other travel costs			
	Cars, vans & motorcycles purchase and repairs	Spares & access-ories	Motor vehicle insurance & taxation	Petrol, diesel & other motor oils	Other motoring costs	Total Motoring expenditure per car/van	Rail & tube fares	Bus & coach fares	Other travel costs[2]	Total expenditure per household
United Kingdom	30.43	1.80	9.09	14.61	1.97	57.90	1.81	1.40	6.03	393.90
North East	28.74	2.13	7.25	12.31	1.70	52.09	1.23	1.63	6.38	344.01
North West	27.99	1.21	8.20	12.79	1.75	51.94	0.82	1.61	4.68	356.16
Yorkshire and the Humber	24.76	1.01	7.40	11.60	1.50	46.25	0.87	1.95	3.95	338.29
East Midlands	32.63	1.42	9.22	15.57	1.94	60.79	0.89	1.43	4.13	380.11
West Midlands	30.07	1.55	8.92	15.59	1.55	57.68	1.01	1.29	4.64	356.88
East	39.38	1.90	10.23	17.57	2.42	71.50	3.36	0.79	5.13	417.43
London	28.40	1.03	9.91	11.53	1.77	52.64	3.85	1.82	12.27	489.62
South East	39.60	3.25	11.18	17.69	2.55	74.27	3.17	0.94	7.81	474.55
South West	28.98	2.36	9.37	16.29	2.57	59.57	0.78	0.81	4.20	361.79
England	31.63	1.80	9.31	14.69	2.01	59.43	1.96	1.34	6.21	401.32
Wales	22.47	2.16	8.03	14.69	1.65	49.00	0.74	1.22	3.11	338.07
Scotland	24.78	1.54	7.00	13.21	1.92	48.44	1.48	2.10	5.84	357.42
Northern Ireland	26.06	1.95	11.29	16.71	1.47	57.48	0.23	1.13	6.32	384.98

1 Data from the 2001/2002 survey, based on FES categories.
2 Other travel costs include taxis, air and other travel, and bicycles and boats: purchase and repair.

Source: Expenditure and Food Survey, Office for National Statistics

Table 10.12 Public expenditure on roads, 2001/02

Millions (£)

	Motorways and trunk roads[1]				Local roads[2]				
	New construction/ improvement and structural maintenance	Public lighting and routine maintenance[3]	Total	Expenditure per 1,000 kilometres	New construction/ improvement and structural maintenance[4,5]	Public lighting and routine maintenance[3,6]	Revenue expenditure on road safety[7]	Total	Expenditure per 1,000 kilometres
North East	52.0	7.9	59.9	120.9	117.2	55.8	5.8	178.8	11.6
North West	157.1	23.9	181.0	123.4	267.2	137.9	17.3	422.4	12.4
Yorkshire and the Humber	121.4	18.5	139.9	131.0	195.2	107.7	12.5	315.4	10.2
East Midlands	107.1	16.3	123.4	87.2	178.9	61.2	10.1	250.2	8.7
West Midlands	94.9	14.4	109.3	89.2	207.6	85.4	11.4	304.4	9.8
East	141.8	21.6	163.4	116.5	243.5	97.3	17.7	358.5	9.9
London[8]	28.6	4.3	32.9	85.5	315.1	178.1	89.1	582.3	42.1
South East	205.1	31.2	236.3	156.5	254.8	161.7	19.7	436.2	9.7
South West	112.2	17.1	129.3	97.5	203.0	104.9	11.0	318.9	6.7
England	1,020.4	155.1	1,175.5	118.6	1,982.4	990.0	194.5	3,166.9	10.0
Wales[9]	78.3	28.9	107.2	..	135.8	84.5	22.5	242.9	..
Scotland[10]	..	..	..	..	122.2	292.0	61.1	427.8	..
Northern Ireland[11]	..	..	..	..	98.0	42.0	..	140.0	5.6

1 Expenditure on motorway and trunk roads excludes expenditure under Design, Build, Finance & Operate (DBFO) schemes.
2 Local Authority expenditure excludes car parks.
3 Includes expenditure on gritting and snow clearing.
4 In Northern Ireland, includes revenue expenditure on certain road safety items.
5 In Scotland, includes expenditure on the purchase and sale of vehicles, plant machinery and equipment.
6 In Northern Ireland, includes revenue expenditure on highway structures.
7 Scottish figures are for network and traffic management which include school's crossing patrols and other network and traffic management. The data for road safety was collected on a different basis from previous years and therefore cannot be compared.
8 Trunk roads were transferred to Transport for London in July 2000 and were reclassified as principal roads. Expenditure on these roads is now shown under the 'local roads' heading.
9 In Wales, the total figure for local roads includes construction and improvement capital figures and revenue figures which are on an accruals basis. The revenue expenditure for local roads are on a net current basis, which is the expenditure excluding that financed by sales fees and charges but including that financed by specific government grants.
10 In Scotland, the total figure for local roads includes construction and improvement capital figures which are on a cash basis and revenue figures which are on an accruals basis.
11 In Northern Ireland, figures for motorways and trunk roads are included in local roads totals.

Source: Department for Transport; Department for Regional Development, Northern Ireland; Scottish Executive; National Assembly for Wales

Table **10.13** Average daily motor vehicle flows:[1] by road class, 2002

Thousand vehicles per day

| | Major roads | | | Minor roads | | |
	Motorway	Rural	Urban	Rural	Urban	All roads
Great Britain	72.9	10.5	20.1	0.8	2.3	3.4
North East	50.7	12.9	20.8	0.7	2.7	3.3
North West	69.9	10.3	17.9	0.9	2.1	4.1
Yorkshire and the Humber	65.7	12.0	18.5	0.9	2.0	3.5
East Midlands	89.6	13.0	19.0	0.9	2.1	3.4
West Midlands	80.4	11.2	20.0	0.9	2.8	4.0
East	83.6	17.5	18.2	1.2	2.5	3.7
London	100.8	28.9	28.8	1.5	2.7	6.1
South East	91.8	17.7	19.4	1.4	2.5	4.9
South West	64.7	10.6	19.7	0.7	2.2	2.5
England	77.8	13.4	20.7	1.0	2.4	3.8
Wales	59.5	7.6	16.7	0.6	2.1	2.2
Scotland	39.8	4.7	15.9	0.5	1.8	1.9

1 Average daily flow is annual traffic divided by road length divided by the number of days in the year. See Notes and Definitions.

Source: National Road Traffic Survey, Department for Transport

Figure **10.14** Traffic[1] increase on major roads[2] between 1993 and 2002

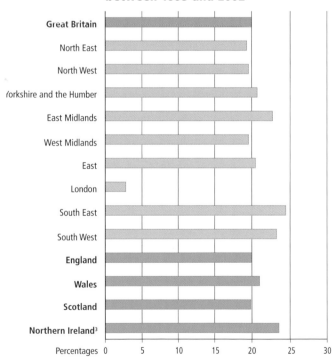

1 The volume of traffic is expressed as vehicle kilometres, which is calculated by multiplying the Annual Average Daily Flow by the corresponding length of road.
2 Motorways and A roads.
3 Traffic increase between 1991 and 1998.

Source: Department for Transport; Department of the Environment, Northern Ireland

Table 10.15 Road traffic and distribution of accidents on major[1] roads, 2002

Percentage and number

| | Motor vehicle traffic on major roads (percentages) | | | All major roads (=100%) (billion vehicle kilometres) | All roads (billion vehicle kilometres) | Distribution of accidents (percentages) | | | Total accidents | |
	Motorway	Urban 'A roads'	Rural 'A roads'			Motorway	Urban 'A roads'	Rural 'A roads'	On major[1] roads (=100%) (numbers)	On all roads (numbers)[2]
Great Britain	29.7	26.3	43.9	310.7	485.9	8.0	58.5	33.3	111,320	221,751
North East	10.2	35.2	54.6	10.8	19.4	3.1	50.4	46.5	3,626	8,280
North West	45.3	30.6	24.2	36.0	54.7	11.5	64.9	23.0	13,769	27,922
Yorkshire and the Humber	34.1	28.3	37.6	25.8	40.3	8.3	58.8	32.2	9,225	20,331
East Midlands	24.2	18.5	57.3	26.0	39.2	8.2	42.5	49.3	8,179	15,903
West Midlands	38.4	27.6	34.0	29.4	47.5	9.5	62.0	28.5	9,691	20,538
East	24.4	16.6	59.0	33.2	53.7	11.0	40.6	48.4	10,115	21,062
London	10.8	86.2	3.0	20.3	32.8	1.5	97.2	1.3	21,666	34,000
South East	38.8	18.3	42.9	56.4	85.2	14.0	43.9	42.1	15,541	31,248
South West	26.5	17.2	56.4	29.1	45.9	6.8	35.8	56.1	8,251	18,452
England	31.4	27.4	41.3	267.3	418.7	8.2	60.6	31.0	100,003	197,736
Wales	18.8	20.0	61.2	16.5	26.2	5.3	37.2	57.5	4,644	9,700
Scotland	20.8	19.3	59.9	26.9	41.0	7.0	41.7	51.2	6,673	14,315

1 Includes accidents on un allocated A roads. See Notes and Definitions for details of road classifications.
2 Includes B, C and unclassified roads. See Notes and Definitions.

Source: Department for Transport

Table 10.16 Fatal and serious road accidents[1]

Numbers and rates

| | Fatal and serious accidents on all roads | | | | | | Fatal and serious accidents on major roads[2] | | | |
| | Numbers | | | Rates per 100,000 population[4] | | | Numbers | | Rates per 100 million vehicle kms | |
	1991	1994–1998 average[3]	2002	1991	1994–1998 average[3]	2002	1991	2002	1991	2002
Great Britain	47,931	40,481	33,645	85	71	59	24,344	17,330	9.4	5.6
North East	1,769	1,295	1,064	68	50	42	734	462	5.9	4.3
North West	4,914	4,582	3,634	71	66	54	2,506	1,827	9.6	5.1
Yorkshire and the Humber	4,352	3,521	3,187	87	70	64	2,084	1,484	10.1	5.8
East Midlands	3,451	3,305	2,781	86	80	66	1,796	1,461	9.3	5.6
West Midlands	4,447	3,997	2,695	84	75	51	2,055	1,275	8.5	4.4
East	4,802	4,187	3,431	93	79	63	2,264	1,650	6.5	5.0
London	7,279	6,082	5,187	105	86	71	4,399	3,291	23.7	16.2
South East	5,843	5,170	4,773	76	65	59	2,882	2,408	6.9	4.3
South West	3,793	2,720	2,640	80	56	53	1,833	1,324	7.1	4.5
England	40,650	34,859	29,392	84	71	59	20,553	15,182	9.2	5.7
Wales	2,112	1,623	1,315	73	56	45	1,139	665	8.9	4.0
Scotland	5,169	3,999	2,938	101	78	58	2,652	1,483	12.1	5.5
Northern Ireland	1,381	1,280	1,241	86	77	73	643	..	9.5	..

1 An accident is defined as one involving personal injury on a public highway in which a road vehicle is involved. See Notes and Definitions.
2 Motorways, A(M) roads and A roads.
3 Used as a basis for the government targets for reducing road casualties in Great Britain by 40 per cent by the year 2010.
4 Latest population figures available at the time these figures were supplied.

Source: Department for Transport; The Police Service of Northern Ireland

Table 10.17 Road casualties:[1] by age and type of road user, 2002

Percentages and numbers

	Percentage of all road casualties								All road casualties (=100%) (numbers)	Per-centage change over 1994–1998 average[4]
	Who were aged[2]			Type of road user						
	0 to 15	16 to 59	60 or over	Pedes-trians	Pedal cyclists	Motor cyclists	Car occupants[3]	Other road users		
United Kingdom	12.8	77.2	10.0	12.2	3.8	6.5	69.7	8.0	314,519	–5.4
North East	13.8	76.3	10.0	14.0	4.9	5.5	67.2	8.4	11,706	–3.0
North West	13.6	79.8	9.6	13.5	5.3	6.4	67.9	6.9	39,995	–11.5
Yorkshire and the Humber	12.9	77.2	9.9	12.4	5.6	7.8	66.8	7.4	29,053	–0.9
East Midlands	11.8	78.9	9.4	10.5	5.3	9.5	67.8	6.9	22,515	–2.6
West Midlands	12.6	77.9	9.4	13.0	4.7	7.1	68.5	6.7	28,044	–1.9
East	10.1	79.9	9.9	9.9	6.2	9.3	69.8	5.7	29,158	–3.4
London	9.0	76.5	8.2	18.0	7.4	17.0	49.3	8.3	41,508	–9.4
South East	9.6	75.7	10.2	10.2	6.1	10.4	67.1	6.2	42,194	–6.1
South West	11.0	77.6	11.4	11.2	6.1	10.4	67.4	5.0	24,847	3.1
England	11.5	78.6	9.9	12.6	5.9	9.8	65.0	6.8	269,020	–4.9
Wales	12.9	76.5	10.6	11.5	3.5	5.9	72.7	6.5	14,336	–3.5
Scotland	14.3	74.2	11.6	17.2	4.3	6.0	63.3	9.2	19,249	–13.7
Northern Ireland	12.5	79.3	8.1	7.6	1.4	4.2	77.4	9.4	11,914	4.7

1 Casualties in accidents occurring on a public highway in which a road vehicle is involved. See Notes and Definitions.
2 Excludes age not reported.
3 Includes occupants of taxis and minibuses.
4 Used as a basis for the government targets for reducing road casualties in Great Britain by 40 per cent by the year 2010.

Source: Department for Transport; The Police Service of Northern Ireland

Table 10.18 Activity at major airports[1], 2002

Thousands and thousand tonnes

	Air passengers (thousands)[2]				Freight handled[3] (thousands tonnes)
		International			
	Domestic[3]	Scheduled	Non-scheduled	Total	
All UK Airports[4]	42,082	108,906	37,892	188,880	2,195
Newcastle	1,165	626	1,597	3,387	1
Manchester	2,743	6,463	9,412	18,618	113
Leeds/Bradford	477	486	563	1,526	-
Liverpool	736	1,685	414	2,835	14
East Midlands	548	1,097	1,588	3,233	219
Birmingham	1,222	3,762	2,928	7,911	13
Luton	1,745	3,665	1,064	6,474	20
Stansted	2,461	12,385	1,203	16,049	184
Heathrow	6,674	56,237	124	63,035	1,235
Gatwick	3,427	15,029	11,062	29,518	243
London City	417	1,184	1	1,602	
Bristol	925	1,194	1,296	3,415	-
Cardiff	108	344	964	1,416	1
Aberdeen	1,613	407	529	2,549	4
Edinburgh	5,079	1,418	415	6,911	21
Glasgow	4,297	1,157	2,315	7,769	5
Belfast City	1,886	1	3	1,890	1
Belfast International	2,683	182	686	3,551	29
Other UK airports	3,877	1,587	1,726	7,190	90

1 Airports handling one million passengers or more in 2002. Includes British Government/armed forces on official business and travel to/from oil rigs. Data are not comparable with years prior to 2001 because of the exclusion of air taxi operations before this date.
2 Arrivals and departures.
3 Domestic traffic is counted at airports on arrival and departure.
4 Including airports handling fewer than one million passengers.

Source: Civil Aviation Authority

Table 10.19 Activity at major seaports,[1] 2002

Millions and million tonnes

	International sea passenger movements[2] (millions)	Freight handled (million tonnes)
All UK ports	28.7	558.3
All East coast ports	3.3	272.6
Sullom Voe	-	29.4
Forth	0.1	42.2
Tees and Hartlepool	-	50.4
Hull	1.0	10.3
Grimsby and Immingham	0.0	55.7
Felixstowe	0.1	25.1
Harwich	1.3	3.5
All Thames and Kent ports	16.5	88.6
London	0.0	51.2
Ramsgate	0.1	1.8
Dover	16.3	20.2
All South coast ports	5.0	49.4
Portsmouth	3.4	4.4
Southampton	-	34.2
All West coast ports	3.9	126.3
Milford Haven	0.4	34.5
Holyhead	2.4	3.3
Liverpool	0.9	30.4
All Northern Ireland ports	-	21.4

1   Individual ports handling one million passengers or more in 2002 and/or 25 million tonnes of freight. See Notes and Definitions.
2   Excluding cruise and long sea passengers.

Source: Department for Transport

155

Chapter 11 Environment

Rainfall

In 2002, the UK had 15 per cent more rainfall than the 1961–1990 average. The level above this historic average in 2002 ranged from 8 per cent in Scotland to 28 per cent in the Thames region. (Table 11.1)

Atmospheric pollution

Estimated annual mean background sulphur and nitrogen dioxide concentrations were highest around London and other urban areas of England and Wales in 2002. Concentrations were lowest in Scotland, Wales the North East and the South West. (Maps 11.2 and 11.3)

Water consumption

Estimated water consumption in unmetered households was highest in the Thames water region with 164 litres per head per day consumed in 2002/03. Daily consumption per head decreased by almost 10 per cent in the Severn Trent water region between 2001/02 and 2002/03.

In 2002/03 metered households in England and Wales consumed on average 16 litres per head per day less than unmetered households; the difference was as high as 36 litres per head per day in the Anglian Region.

Almost half of billed households in the Anglian water region in 2002/03 were metered compared to just 8 per cent of households in the Northumbrian water region. (Table 11.4)

Water abstraction

In 2001, estimated abstractions from groundwater (for the purpose of public water supply) ranged from 118 megalitres per day in the North West to 1,378 megalitres per day in the Thames region. In England and Wales, 76 per cent of all estimated abstractions from groundwater in 2001, was used for public water supply. (Table 11.5)

Water quality

Chemical water quality in rivers and canals improved across all regions in England and Northern Ireland between 1990 and 2002. The most significant improvements in water quality were in the North West, London and the East Midlands. Since 1990, the North West has seen an extension of 660km in its surveyed rivers and canals.

Between 1990 and 2002, biological water quality improved across all regions of England, Wales and Scotland. In 1990, all rivers and canals in Northern Ireland were classified as either good or fair. However, in 2002, this fell to 97 per cent of all rivers and canals. (Table 11.6)

In 2003, Anglian, Southern, Thames and Northern Ireland coastal bathing waters complied with EC coliform standards. Northern Ireland reached 100 per cent compliance in 2003 (the first time since 2000). The percentage of coastal bathing water complying decreased in Wales and the North East between 2002 and 2003. (Table 11.7)

Prosecution for pollution

There were 757 prosecutions for pollution incidents in England and Wales in 2002, more than two-thirds of these were for waste pollution. In 2002, there was one prosecution for pollution caused by radioactive substances in England and Wales. This occurred in the North West Environment Agency Region. (Table 11.9)

Scheduled monuments

London was the only region, which had a decrease in the number of scheduled monuments (150 in 2002 to 149 in 2003). Although Ham House in Petersham, London is still a listed building it was descheduled in January 2003.

In 2003, the South West region had 6,929 scheduled monuments, an increase of 1.4 per cent since 2002. In comparison the number of monuments in Northern Ireland increased by 4.2 per cent. (Table 11.10)

Land

In 1998, arable and horticulture and grassland covered two-thirds of the land in England. Almost three-fifths of East Anglia was designated as arable land, but this region had the lowest proportion of woodland, 6.4 per cent. (Table 11.11)

National Park area made up around a fifth of the total areas of Wales and Yorkshire and the Humber in 2002. Almost a third of the area in each of the South East and South West is classified as an area of outstanding beauty. (Table 11.13)

Waste and recycling

During 2001/02, the North West produced on average 26.4 kilogrammes of waste per household per week, compared to London which produced the least amount of 21.1 kilogrammes. (Table 11.15)

The average English household recycled 151.7 kg of waste in 2001/02. The South East recycled the most waste per household, 222 kg; three and a half times the amount recycled by households in the North East. Paper, card and compost together made up about three fifths of all of England's recycled waste. (Table 11.16)

Over three-quarters of municipal waste disposed of in England was by landfill during 2001/2002. The West Midlands had the least proportion of waste disposed of using landfill methods (57 per cent) and the highest proportion by incineration with energy recovery, around a third of its municipal waste was disposed of in this way.

In 2001/02, the North East recycled or composted 7 per cent of its municipal waste compared to almost 20 per cent in the South East and South West. (Table 11.17)

Noise pollution

There were 683 noise offences (relating to motor vehicles) in the South East, almost a fifth of all noise offences in England in 2001.

Between 1996 and 2001, the North East was the only region which recorded an increase in the number of motor vehicle related noise offences. The largest decrease in noise offences was in London where there was a two-thirds reduction in the five year period to 2001. Overall, the number of noise offences fell by two-thirds between 1986 and 2001 in England and Wales. (Table 11.18)

Table **11.1** Average annual rainfall[1]

Percentages and millimetres

Water and sewerage companies	Annual rainfall as a percentage of the 1961-1990 rainfall average										1961-1990 rainfall average (=100%)
	1992	1993	1994	1995	1996	1997	1998	1999[2]	2000[2]	2001[2]	2002[2] (millimetres)
United Kingdom	113	107	113	98	87	98	121	117	123	95	115	1,080
North West	103	97	113	85	80	92	119	108	131	90	119	1,201
Northumbrian Water[3]	99	113	103	96	85	98	122	109	125	95	117	853
Severn Trent	112	111	114	90	82	98	117	120	130	102	116	754
Yorkshire	102	109	108	84	85	94	116	107	131	96	120	821
Anglian	118	122	108	91	79	97	120	112	128	123	121	596
Thames	116	112	108	100	78	91	118	110	136	113	128	688
Southern	103	117	122	98	83	101	112	104	143	111	126	778
Wessex	101	115	123	111	93	105	120	114	134	98	127	839
South West	96	118	126	100	96	102	122	104	119	86	116	1,173
England	106	111	113	93	83	96	117	111	131	103	120	823
Wales[4]	107	105	121	92	88	97	120	116	133	97	118	1,355
Scotland	121	104	112	104	88	99	121	116	111	88	108	1,436
Northern Ireland	109	109	110	101	102	99	120	115	114	83	127	1,059

1 The regions of England shown in this table correspond to the original nine English regions of the National Rivers Authority (NRA); the NRA became part of the Environment Agency upon its creation in April 1996. See Notes and Definitions.

2 Regional data are provisional.

3 Northumbrian Water is also known as Northumbrian-North and refers to the area served in the North East of England. Northumbrian-South was formerly Essex and Suffolk Water. The figures for Northumbrian-South are not included in this table.

4 The figures in this table relate to the country of Wales; not the Environment Agency Welsh Region.

Source: Met Office; Centre for Ecology and Hydrology, Wallingford

Map **11.2**

Sulphur dioxide concentration across the UK, 2002[1]

Map **11.3**

Nitrogen dioxide concentration across the UK, 2002[1]

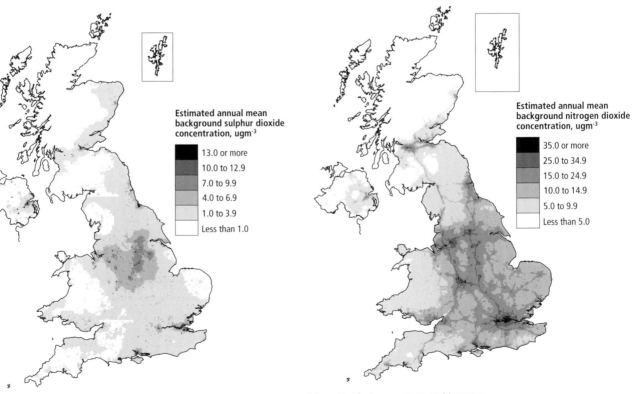

Estimated annual mean background sulphur dioxide concentration, ugm⁻³

- 13.0 or more
- 10.0 to 12.9
- 7.0 to 9.9
- 4.0 to 6.9
- 1.0 to 3.9
- Less than 1.0

Estimated annual mean background nitrogen dioxide concentration, ugm⁻³

- 35.0 or more
- 25.0 to 34.9
- 15.0 to 24.9
- 10.0 to 14.9
- 5.0 to 9.9
- Less than 5.0

1 In units of micrograms per cubic metre.

Source: Department for Environment, Food & Rural Affairs

1 In units of micrograms per cubic metre.

Source: Department for Environment, Food & Rural Affairs

Table **11.4**   Estimated household water consumption[1]

Litres per head per day and percentages

	Unmetered households			Metered households			Percentage of billed households metered		
	2000/01	2001/02	2002/03	2000/01	2001/02	2002/03	2000/01	2001/02	2002/03
Water and sewerage companies									
England and Wales[2]	152	153	153	134	136	137	*19*	*21*	*22*
United Utilities	141	142	149	135	136	128	*10*	*11*	*13*
Northumbrian Water[3]	148	148	146	130	128	128	*6*	*7*	*8*
Yorkshire[4]	140	149	146	131	138	137	*20*	*22*	*23*
Severn Trent	140	141	127	131	134	133	*19*	*20*	*22*
Anglian[5]	155	150	159	114	119	123	*45*	*48*	*49*
Thames	167	161	164	154	150	149	*17*	*18*	*19*
Southern	158	164	162	142	151	148	*20*	*21*	*23*
Wessex	143	147	147	130	129	129	*26*	*27*	*29*
South West	157	160	159	128	123	138	*28*	*31*	*37*
Dwr Cymru	147	151	151	138	132	140	*9*	*12*	*13*

1 *Excluding underground supply pipe leakage.*
2 *Figures for England and Wales are industry averages; these include both the 10 water and sewerage companies, and 12 water companies.*
3 *Northumbrian Water is also known as Northumbrian-North and refers to the area served in the North East of England. Northumbrian-South was formerly Essex and Suffolk Water. The figures for Northumbrian – South are not included in this table.*
4 *The entries for Yorkshire Water include the weighted averages for Yorkshire Water and York Waterworks that now operate under a single license.*
5 *The entries for Anglian Water include the weighted averages for Anglian Water and Hartlepool Water that now operate under a single license.*

Source: OFWAT

Table **11.5**   Estimated abstractions from groundwaters: by purpose, 2001[1]

Megalitres per day

	Public water supply	Spray irrigation	Agriculture (excluding spray irrigation)	Electricity supply	Other industry	Fish farming, etc	Private water supply[2]	Other[3]	Total
Environment Agency Regions[4]									
England and Wales	4,941	97	91	50	850	359	38	58	6,484
North East	332	13	12	9	95	10	4	-	475
North West	118	2	3	-	149	1	-	-	273
Midlands	856	23	9	33	136	3	7	-	1,068
Anglian	760	46	15	-	146	-	3	-	969
Thames	1,378	6	8	1	104	19	12	4	1,532
Southern	966	5	4	2	174	200	2	20	1,373
South West	485	2	35	2	26	125	9	34	718
England	4,895	97	86	47	830	358	37	58	6,406
Wales	47	1	5	2	21	-	1	-	77

1 *Some regions report licensed and actual abstractions for financial rather than calendar years. As figures represent an average for the whole year expressed in daily amounts, differences between amounts reported for financial and calendar years are small.*
2 *Private abstractions for domestic use by individual households.*
3 *'Other' includes some private domestic water supply wells and boreholes, public water supply transfer licenses and frost protection use.*
4 *The boundaries of the Environment Agency Regions are based on river catchment areas and not county borders. In particular, the figures shown for Wales are for the Environment Agency Region for Wales, the boundary of which does not coincide with the boundary of Wales. Figures for England are derived by adding up figures for the English regions. See Notes and Definitions.*

Source: Environment Agency

Table **11.6**   Rivers and canals: by biological[1] and chemical quality[2]

Percentages and kilometres

| | Chemical quality (percentages) | | | | Total length surveyed (=100%)[4] (kms) 1990[3] | Total length surveyed (=100%)[4] (kms) 2002[3] | Biological quality (percentages) | | | | Total length surveyed (=100%) (kms) 1990 | Total length surveyed (=100%) (kms) 2002 |
| | 1988-1990[3] | | 2000-2002[3] | | | | 1990 | | 2002 | | | |
	Good/ Fair	Poor/ Bad	Good/ Fair	Poor/ Bad			Good/ Fair	Poor/ Bad	Good/ Fair	Poor/ Bad		
North East	90	10	97	3	2,030	2,120	91	9	98	2	1,990	2,050
North West	70	30	91	9	4,770	5,430	69	31	86	14	3,790	4,710
Yorkshire and the Humber	76	24	90	10	3,530	4,070	81	19	90	10	2,330	3,560
East Midlands	79	21	97	3	3,410	3,550	93	7	96	4	2,830	3,260
West Midlands	82	18	94	6	3,590	3,940	91	9	92	8	2,200	3,350
East	82	18	92	8	3,530	3,580	96	4	99	1	3,050	3,430
London	71	29	87	13	390	420	65	35	82	18	290	360
South East	84	16	94	6	4,370	4,440	95	5	99	1	3,330	4,290
South West	93	7	97	3	6,460	6,570	97	3	99	1	5,800	6,320
England	84	16	94	6	30,740	36,190	89	11	95	5	26,770	33,500
Wales	98	2	98	2	3,520	4,570	98	2	99	1	3,330	4,380
Scotland[5]	..	..	98	2	..	25,440	97	3	99	1	10,870	25,440
Northern Ireland[6]	95	5	97	3	1,680	2,400	100	-	97	3	2,190	5,140

1 Classification based on the River Invertebrate Prediction and Classification System (RIVPACS). See Notes and Definitions.
2 England, Wales and Northern Ireland data are based on the chemical quality grade of the General Quality Assessment (GQA) scheme. Scottish data are based on a different combined classification scheme involving an assessment of chemical, biological, nutrient and aesthetic measures although predominantly chemical. See Notes and Definitions.
3 Based on three-year averages.
4 Figures for the English regions will not add to the national figure for England because a small amount of river lengths which are located along the border between England and Wales are counted in both the national figures for England and Wales.
5 Scottish data are based on data for the calendar year 2002. The methods used to measure river lengths have changed significantly between 1990 and 2002, so the figures are not directly comparable. Figures for biological and chemical quality include unmonitored stretches of rivers and canals.
6 1990 data for Northern Ireland relate to 1991.

Source: Department for Environment Food and Rural Affairs; Scottish Environment Protection Agency; Environment and Heritage Service, Northern Ireland

Table **11.7**   Bathing water – compliance with EC Bathing Water Directive[1] coliform standards[2]: by coastal region

Numbers and percentages

| | Identified coastal bathing waters (numbers) | | | | | | Percentage complying during the bathing season[3] | | | | | |
	1998	1999	2000	2001	2002	2003	1998	1999	2000	2001	2002	2003
Environment Agency Regions[4]												
United Kingdom	496	535	545	546	547	554	89	91	94	95	98	98
North East[5]	56	55	56	55	56	55	84	95	91	100	98	96
North West	34	34	34	34	34	34	62	68	82	88	97	97
Midlands[6]	..	..	..	..	..	..	..	..	..	..	..	..
Anglian[7]	36	36	37	37	38	38	100	94	100	97	100	100
Thames[8]	3	3	3	5	5	8	100	100	100	100	100	100
Southern	77	79	79	79	79	79	97	94	97	99	99	100
South West[9]	183	184	187	187	186	188	91	91	96	98	98	99
England	389	391	396	397	398	402	90	92	95	98	99	99
Wales	68	70	75	75	75	78	94	99	99	93	100	99
Scotland	23	58	58	58	58	58	52	88	84	84	91	95
Northern Ireland	16	16	16	16	16	16	94	100	100	81	94	100

1 Directive 76/160/EEC.
2 At least 95 per cent of samples must have counts not exceeding the mandatory limit values for total and faecal coliforms.
3 The bathing season is from mid-May to end-September in England and Wales, but is shorter in Scotland and Northern Ireland. Bathing waters which are closed for a season are excluded for that year.
4 In England and Wales. The boundaries of the Environment Agency Regions are based on river catchment areas and not county borders. In particular, the figures shown for Wales are for the Environment Agency Welsh Region, the boundary of which does not coincide with the boundary of Wales. See map at the start of Notes and Definitions.
5 Figures for 1998 include Alnmouth, which was undesignated in 1999. Earls Dyke was closed for the 2001 season but re-opened in 2002.
6 This table just covers coastal bathing waters and not inland bathing waters. As the Midlands is surrounded by other regions there are no beaches.
7 In 2002 a new beach was designated at Sea Palling.
8 In 2001 two new beaches were designated at Shoeburyness and Three Shells.
9 In 2001 and 2002 three beaches were closed for the bathing seasons at Redgate, Dartmouth Castle and Sugary Cove. In 2002 three further beaches were closed for the bathing season at Beacon Cove, Gunwalloe and West Bay West but two new beaches were designated at Trebarwith Strand and Crackington Haven.

Source: Environment Agency; Scottish Environment Protection Agency; Environment and Heritage Service, Northern Ireland

Table 11.8   Water pollution incidents: by source, 2002[1]

	Industrial		Sewage and water related		Agricultural		Other		Total Incidents			All Incidents (Category 1-4)	Number of prose-cutions[3,4]
	Category 1 "most serious" Incidents[2]	Category 2 incidents	Category 1 "most serious" Incidents[2]	Category 2 incidents	Category 1 "most serious" Incidents[2]	Category 2 incidents	Category 1 "most serious" Incidents[2]	Category 2 incidents	Category 1 "most serious"	Category 2 incidents	Category 1 and Category 2		
Environment Agency Regions[5]													
North East	2	17	1	26	2	12	7	49	12	104	116	3,849	16
North West	3	21	-	11	1	22	4	42	8	96	104	3,749	29
Midlands	1	14	1	18	3	22	5	67	10	121	131	5,611	39
Anglian	1	7	2	16	1	9	14	42	18	74	92	3,411	29
Thames	1	13	2	34	2	10	5	62	10	119	129	3,828	28
Southern	1	8	3	19	-	12	6	57	10	96	106	3,308	21
South West	-	5	1	18	4	29	3	31	8	83	91	3,772	34
Wales[5]	3	8	1	15	-	21	2	47	6	91	97	2,352	38
England and Wales[5]	12	93	11	157	13	137	46	397	82	784	866	29,880	234
Scotland[6]	55	..	46	..	38	..	48	..	82	..	..	..	..
Northern Ireland[7]	12	71	6	60	29	141	2	33	49	305	354	..	104

1 Data relate to substantiated reports of pollution only (Categories 1-4). See Notes and Definitions.

2 Formerly major incidents. For Scotland the term 'serious incidents' is used and compares broadly with all of Category 1 and most of Category 2 used by the Environment Agency. In Northern Ireland the term 'high severity' is used, this compares broadly with all of Category 1 used by the Environment Agency.

3 For England and Wales total prosecutions include cases concluded and prosecutions outstanding. Prosecutions concluded relate to cases which had been brought to court by 31 March 2000. In Scotland, this figure relates only to legal proceedings which resulted in a conviction during 2000/01. In Northern Ireland total prosecutions include cases concluded and prosecutions outstanding for incidents which took place in 2000.

4 The Environment Agency prosecute category 1 incidents where there is adequate evidence to support the case. A caution or warning is used for category 2 incidents where appropriate.

5 In England and Wales the boundaries of the Environment Agency Regions are based on river catchment areas and not county borders. In particular, the figures shown for Wales are for the Environment Agency Wales Region, the boundary of which does not coincide with the boundary of Wales. See Notes and Definitions.

6 Figures for Scotland relate to the financial year 2001/02.

7 Figures for Northern Ireland relate to 2001.

Source: Environment Agency; Scottish Environment Protection Agency; Department of the Environment, Northern Ireland

Table 11.9   Prosecutions[1] for pollution incidents, 2002

	Waste	Water pollution[2]	Integrated pollution control	Radioactive substances	Water abstraction	All
Environment Agency Regions[2]						
North East	58	16	-	-	-	74
North West	104	28	2	1	1	136
Midlands	76	36	1	-	2	115
Anglian	40	29	-	-	-	69
Thames	89	25	-	-	1	115
Southern	42	21	-	-	-	63
South West	41	34	-	-	1	76
England	450	189	3	1	5	648
Wales	67	35	-	-	7	109

1 Figures are for the total numbers of defendants (companies and individuals) prosecuted in 2002 by type of prosecution.

2 In England and Wales. The boundaries of the Environment Agency Regions are based on river catchment areas and not county borders. In particular, the figures shown for Wales are for the Environment Agency Region for Wales, the boundary of which does not coincide with the boundary of Wales. See Notes and Definitions.

Source: Environment Agency

Table 11.10 Scheduled monuments, 2003[1]

	Number
	Scheduled monuments
United Kingdom	32,356
North East	1,363
North West	1,290
Yorkshire and the Humber	2,606
East Midlands	1,509
West Midlands	1,402
East	1,683
London	149
South East	2,621
South West	6,929
England	19,552
Wales	3,558
Scotland[2]	7,631
Northern Ireland[3]	1,615

1 As at 30 June 2003 except for Scotland and Northern Ireland.
2 As at 31 March 2003.
3 As at July 2003.

Source: English Heritage; Cadw – Welsh Historic Monuments; Historic Scotland; Enviroment and Heritage Service (Northern Ireland)

Table 11.11 Land cover[1] by broad habitat[2] and Standard Statistical Regions, 1998

Percentage of land covered by

	Woodland[3]	Arable and horticulture	Grassland[4]	Dwarf shrub heath	Fen, marsh, swamp and bog	Standing open water and canals[5]	Inland rock[6]	Coastal (Littoral etc)	Unsurveyed urban and unclassified
England	9.9	33.3	35.2	2.7	1.9	0.9	10.8	1.2	4.1
North	10.0	16.6	47.9	9.8	5.7	0.8	6.3	1.4	1.6
North West	8.5	15.9	45.2	3.8	2.9	1.3	10.6	1.9	9.7
Yorkshire and the Humber	9.7	27.6	38.8	5.2	2.5	1.0	11.1	0.8	3.3
East Midlands	8.6	48.8	25.5	1.2	0.9	1.3	10.8	0.7	2.1
West Midlands	11.0	29.2	37.5	1.9	1.5	0.9	12.9	0.2	5.0
East Anglia	6.4	57.1	21.1	0.2	0.7	1.7	9.9	1.8	1.1
South East	9.7	41.8	27.5	0.3	0.6	0.7	10.8	1.4	7.3
South West	12.4	23.0	43.2	2.0	1.6	0.5	12.9	1.3	3.2

1 Estimates are based on extrapolation from a national sample and are associated with error terms which are not shown on this table.
2 See Notes and Definitions.
3 Woodland covers both coniferous and broadleaved/mixed.
4 Includes improved, neutral, acid and calcareous grasslands and bracken.
5 Includes rivers and streams.
6 Includes built up areas, boundary and linear features.

Source: Countryside Survey 2000, Department for Environment, Food and Rural Affairs; Centre for Ecology and Hydrology

Map **11.12**

Protected Areas,[1] as at 1 April 2000

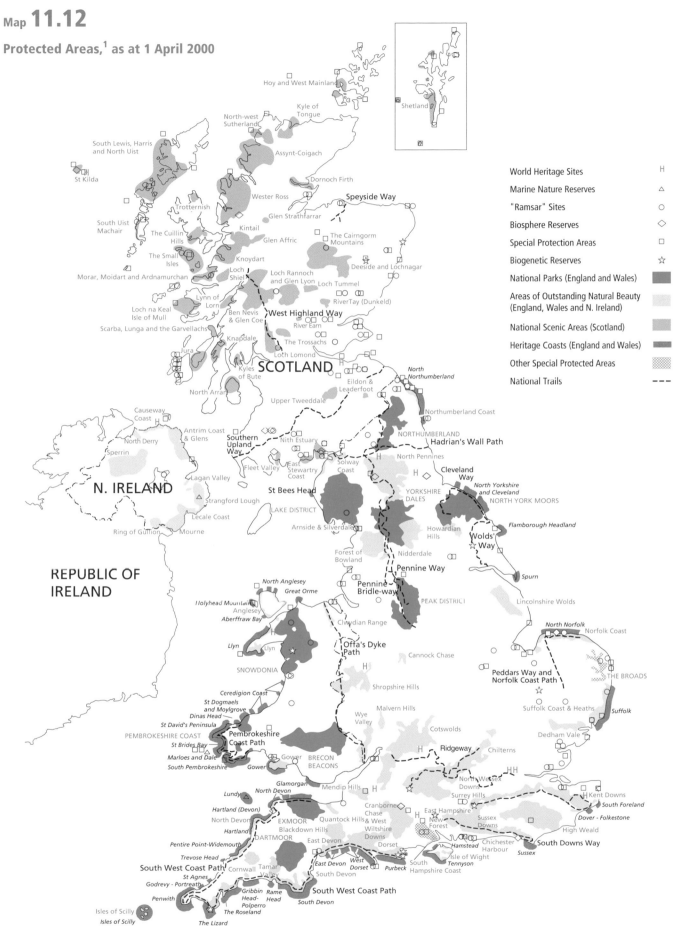

World Heritage Sites   H

Marine Nature Reserves   △

"Ramsar" Sites   ○

Biosphere Reserves   ◇

Special Protection Areas   □

Biogenetic Reserves   ☆

National Parks (England and Wales)

Areas of Outstanding Natural Beauty (England, Wales and N. Ireland)

National Scenic Areas (Scotland)

Heritage Coasts (England and Wales)

Other Special Protected Areas

National Trails   - - -

1 See Notes and Definitions.

Source: The Countryside Agency; Department of Culture, Media and Sport; Centre for Ecology and Hydrology; Office of the Deputy Prime Minister; Countryside Council for Wales; Scottish National Heritage; Department of the Environment, Northern Ireland

Table **11.13** Designated areas[1], March 2003

	National Parks		Areas of Outstanding Natural Beauty[2]		Defined Heritage Coasts length (km)
	Area (thousand hectares)	Percentage of total area in region	Area (thousand hectares)	Percentage of total area in region	
North East	111	13	147	17	138
North West	261	18	157	11	6
Yorkshire and the Humber	315	21	92	6	80
East Midlands	92	6	52	3	-
West Midlands	20	2	127	10	-
East	30	2	112	6	121
London[3]	..	..	..	..	..
South East	-	-	641	31	74
South West	165	7	712	30	638
England	994	7	2,040	16	1,057
Wales	413	20	83	4	496
Scotland	567	6	1,002	13	..
Northern Ireland	..	..	285	20	..

1 National Parks, Areas of Outstanding Natural Beauty, Defined Heritage Coasts, National Scenic Areas in Scotland are the major areas designated by legislation to protect their landscape importance. Other areas, such as National Nature Reserves, Special Protection Areas and Marine Nature Reserves are protected for their value as wildlife habitat. See Notes and Definitions. Some areas may be in more than one category.

2 National Scenic Areas in Scotland.

3 Data for London are included with the South East.

Source: Department for Environment, Food and Rural Affairs

Table **11.14** Land changing to residential use: by previous use, 1996-1999 [1,2]

Percentages and hectares

	Not previously-developed uses				Previously-developed uses					Annual average changes to residential use (=100%) (hectares)[5]
		Other not previously developed uses[3]	All not previously developed uses	Residential	Vacant		Other previously developed uses[4]	All previously developed uses		
	Agriculture				Previously developed	Not previously developed				
England	40	5	54	15	20	9	11	46		6,405
North East	45	5	61	9	25	11	5	39		285
North West	30	5	46	11	33	11	9	54		845
Yorkshire and the Humber	39	3	53	12	26	11	10	47		675
East Midlands	54	4	65	13	14	7	8	35		690
West Midlands	41	5	57	14	19	12	10	43		620
East	36	7	50	18	19	7	12	50		970
London	2	6	14	20	37	7	29	86		275
South East	35	8	52	20	16	10	12	48		1,210
South West	59	5	70	16	6	6	9	30		840

1 The data relate to map changes recorded by Ordnance Survey as at the end of 2002 for which the year of change has been estimated from available information. See Notes and Definitions.

2 Comparisons between regions should be treated with caution as changes from land which is vacant for a short period are more likely to be recorded in areas where surveying is more frequent.

3 Includes Forestry, Open Land & Water and Outdoor Recreation.

4 Includes Transport & Utilities, Industry & Commerce and Community Services.

5 Average hectares excludes data from 1999 and is thus 1996 to 1998 average.

Source: Office of the Deputy Prime Minister

Table 11.15 Household waste, 2001/02

Kilogrammes per household per week[1]

North East	23.4
North West	26.4
Yorkshire and the Humber	23.2
East Midlands	24.1
West Midlands	23.8
East	23.9
London	21.1
South East	24.3
South West	23.7
England	23.8

1 Table grossed-up from reported data with missing values estimated from household numbers.

Source: Department for Environment, Food and Rural Affairs

Table 11.16 Recycling of household waste[1], 2001/02

Kilogrammes per household per year

	Glass	Paper and card	Total cans	Plastics	Textiles	Scrap metal/ white goods	Compost	Other materials[2]	Total
North East	9.8	27.1	0.7	0.0	1.1	11.7	6.5	5.1	62.0
North West	13.1	39.1	0.4	0.3	1.6	12.2	42.5	11.6	120.7
Yorkshire and the Humber	13.9	26.2	0.5	0.3	1.2	12.6	32.9	18.3	105.9
East Midlands	18.5	43.8	1.0	0.7	2.0	19.8	64.5	20.7	171.1
West Midlands	17.4	37.9	0.6	0.1	1.8	18.2	32.5	14.9	123.2
East	26.9	56.0	3.1	0.4	2.8	20.2	79.5	24.3	213.3
London	17.0	50.2	0.9	0.2	1.9	10.3	12.8	7.6	100.9
South East	30.1	61.1	1.8	0.6	2.8	26.2	64.4	35.0	222.0
South West	32.1	56.8	2.2	1.0	2.3	27.1	60.6	12.8	195.0
England	20.7	46.3	1.3	0.4	2.0	17.8	45.4	17.8	151.7

1 Materials recycled by local authorities through civic amenity and bring/drop-off sites and kerbside collection schemes for household wastes.
2 Other materials includes oils, batteries, aluminium foil, books, shoes and co-mingled materials.

Source: Department for Environment, Food and Rural Affairs

Table 11.17 Municipal waste disposal: by method, 2001/02

Percentages

	Landfill	Incin-eration without energy recovery	Incin-eration with energy recovery	RDF[1] manu-facture	Recycled/ composted	Other	All methods
North East	78	-	16	-	7	-	100
North West	87	-	2	-	11	-	100
Yorkshire and the Humber	85	-	4	-	11	-	100
East Midlands	77	-	6	-	16	1	100
West Midlands	57	-	32	-	11	1	100
East	80	-	1	-	18	-	100
London	73	-	19	-	8	-	100
South East	79	-	-	2	19	-	100
South West	81	-	-	-	19	-	100
England	77	-	9	-	14	-	100
Wales	..	..	..	..	..	..	..

1 Refuse derived fuel.

Source: Department for Environment, Food and Rural Affairs; National Assembly for Wales

Table 11.18 Noise offences[1] relating to motor vehicles

Numbers

	1986[2]	1991	1996	2001
North East	683	319	232	373
North West	1,113	722	597	473
Yorkshire and the Humber	866	657	380	315
East Midlands	906	874	563	407
West Midlands	1,000	498	617	298
East	1,519	1,318	551	354
London	1,582	650	634	200
South East	1,597	1,276	1,069	683
South West	1,230	790	685	449
England	10,496	7,104	5,328	3,552
Wales	926	572	381	229

1 Includes written warnings issued for alleged offences, findings of guilt at Magistrates Courts and Fixed Penalty Notices.
2 Fixed Penalties not introduced until October 1986.

Source: Home Office

Chapter 12 **Regional Accounts**

Gross value added (GVA)

Gross value added (GVA) at current basic prices was highest in London and the South East in 2001, each area contributed approximately £140 billion. These two regions together accounted for almost one-third of United Kingdom total in 2001, Northern Ireland had the smallest share with two per cent (£19 billion). (Table 12.1)

GVA per head

London also had the highest GVA per head in 2001 at over £19,000. GVA per head was also above the national average in the East and South East of England. GVA per head was consistently above the United Kingdom average in the East of England, London and South East during the 1990s. (Table 12.1)

GVA per head was lowest in the North East at just over three-quarters (76 per cent) of the United Kingdom average in 2001, followed closely by Northern Ireland and Wales, at 78 and 79 per cent of the United Kingdom level respectively. The relative position of the North East has declined over the ten years to 2001 whereas that of Northern Ireland has increased slightly over the same period.
(Table 12.1 and Map 12.4)

GVA by component of income

The North East derived the highest proportion (68 per cent) of its GVA from compensation of employees (i.e. wages and salaries, insurance and pension contributions etc); this compared with 60 per cent for Northern Ireland in 2001.
(Table 12.3)

GVA by industry

The highest GVA at current prices from the agriculture, hunting, forestry and fishing industries was in the South West with just over £1,244 million in 2000, followed closely by Scotland with £1,235 million, this compared with the lowest amount of £17 million for London. Figures for the South West and Scotland fell from 1999.
(Table 12.5)

Hotels and restaurants in London contributed £5,364 million to GVA at current basic prices in 2000, this was around a fifth of the figure for United Kingdom as a whole. However, GVA generated by hotels and restaurants constituted four per cent of the total GVA for London. (Table 12.5)

In the same time period the South East produced the highest GVA from manufacturing of £19.7 billion (15 per cent of the region's total GVA). This was followed closely by the North West with £19.4 billion from manufacturing which was 23 per cent of total GVA in the North West. Each of these two regions accounted for an eighth of the UK total and showed an increase on the previous year. (Table 12.5)

Workplace-based GVA

Workplace-based estimates of GVA show little difference to residence based estimates for most regions except in London, South East and East of England. London had the highest workplace-based GVA of £163 billion; around 19 per cent of the UK total in 2001; whereas Northern Ireland had the lowest GVA at £19 billion.
(Tables 12.1 and 12.6)

In 2001 the lowest work-place based GVA per head was in the North East at £11,000, under half of the London figure: £22,200. The difference between the highest and lowest workplace-based estimates is £3,000 more than that of the residence-based estimates. There are only differences between work-place and residence-based estimates in the East of England, London and the South East. This is due to incomes of commuters being allocated to their place of work rather than their home for workplace estimates. GVA per head estimates can be inflated for regions like London where there are high levels of inward commuting. (Tables 12.6 and 12.1)

Total and gross disposable household income

Total household income has been steadily increasing over ten years from 1989 for all areas of the United Kingdom. The total UK figure increased from £475 billion to £931 billion with London and South East together making up nearly one-third. (Table 12.7)

London had the highest gross disposable household income per head of £12,207 in 1999 compared to £8,870 per head for Wales. (Table 12.7)

In 1999, the South West and Scotland were close to the United Kingdom average for disposable income per head - less than 1 and less than 3 percentage points below the average respectively. Only the East, South East and London had gross disposable incomes per head above the national average. (Table 12.7)

Between 1995 and 1999, the contribution that compensation of employees made to household income grew most strongly in London and South East, while the lowest growth was in Wales. (Table 12.10)

Apart from the North East, North West, West Midlands and Wales, there was a decline in the percentage of disposable income expressed as a proportion of total income between 1995 and 1999. This ranged from 62 per cent in London and the South East to 70 per cent in Northern Ireland in 1999. (Table 12.10)

Individual consumption expenditure (ICE)

During 1999, London and the South East together made up nearly one-third of individual consumption expenditure in the United Kingdom, which totalled nearly £587 billion. These regions had individual consumption expenditure of £12,250 and £11,392 per head respectively in 1999; the lowest ICE per head was in North East with just over £8,000. (Table 12.11)

London and the South East were the highest spenders for all the categories of individual expenditure in 1999. Over £34 billion was spent on housing and fuel by the combined households in London and South East in 1999, this constituted nearly one-third of the United Kingdom total. This equates to nearly £2,500 per person in London and nearly £2,100 per person in South East during the year. These same regions each spent over £13 billion on food, drink and tobacco during 1999, in excess of £1billion more than the next highest region, the North West. (Table 12.12 and population estimates published by ONS in September 2003)

During 1999 nearly £1.5 billion was spent by households in Northern Ireland on recreation compared to nearly £10 billion by the South East. This equates to almost £1,230 per person in the South East compared to nearly £860 per person in Northern Ireland; however the lowest expenditure per head on recreation was in the North East at just under £810. (Table 12.12)

Table **12.1** Gross value added[1] (GVA) at current basic prices

	1991	1992	1993	1994	1995	1996	1997[2]	1998[2]	1999[2]	2000[2]	2001[2,3]
£ million											
United Kingdom[4]	523,935	546,434	575,461	608,740	639,908	679,620	720,692	762,363	796,273	838,065	874,227
North East	19,560	20,511	21,399	22,402	23,229	23,963	24,762	25,497	25,910	26,740	27,729
North West	55,596	58,078	60,954	64,159	66,887	69,905	73,670	77,698	80,836	84,058	87,584
Yorkshire and the Humber	39,925	41,486	43,288	45,558	47,970	50,612	53,501	56,099	57,706	59,675	61,929
East Midlands	34,069	35,532	37,287	39,547	41,793	44,575	47,552	50,102	51,743	53,588	55,394
West Midlands	43,035	44,812	47,282	50,245	52,800	55,596	58,904	62,140	64,103	66,498	68,839
East	50,122	52,100	54,768	57,964	60,974	64,726	69,137	73,927	77,562	81,713	85,775
London	79,745	83,393	88,248	92,613	96,310	102,802	111,117	120,271	127,124	133,179	140,354
South East	75,209	78,480	82,914	88,204	93,376	99,855	108,091	117,440	124,875	132,147	138,877
South West	38,977	40,498	42,762	45,245	47,632	50,635	53,740	56,598	58,739	61,085	63,554
England	436,238	454,890	478,900	505,937	530,971	562,669	600,474	639,772	668,598	698,684	730,036
Wales	21,405	22,273	23,357	24,710	26,028	27,217	28,492	29,718	30,652	31,864	33,086
Scotland	45,276	47,597	49,949	52,943	55,431	58,079	60,828	63,285	64,932	67,150	69,179
Northern Ireland	10,990	11,715	12,574	13,412	14,273	15,182	16,057	16,913	17,665	18,414	19,108
United Kingdom less Extra-Regio[5] and statistical discrepancy	513,909	536,475	564,781	597,002	626,703	663,148	705,851	749,688	781,847	816,111	851,408
Extra-Regio	10,028	9,958	10,681	11,740	13,206	16,473	14,842	12,679	14,426	21,954	22,437
Statistical discrepancy	–	–	–	–	–	–	–	–	–	–	382
As a percentage of United Kingdom less Extra-Regio and statistical discrepancy											
United Kingdom	100.0	100.0	100.0	100.0	100.0	100.0	100.0	100.0	100.0	100.0	100.0
North East	3.8	3.8	3.8	3.8	3.7	3.6	3.5	3.4	3.3	3.3	3.3
North West	10.8	10.8	10.8	10.7	10.7	10.5	10.4	10.4	10.3	10.3	10.3
Yorkshire and the Humber	7.8	7.7	7.7	7.6	7.7	7.6	7.6	7.5	7.4	7.3	7.3
East Midlands	6.6	6.6	6.6	6.6	6.7	6.7	6.7	6.7	6.6	6.6	6.5
West Midlands	8.4	8.4	8.4	8.4	8.4	8.4	8.3	8.3	8.2	8.1	8.1
East	9.8	9.7	9.7	9.7	9.7	9.8	9.8	9.9	9.9	10.0	10.1
London	15.5	15.5	15.6	15.5	15.4	15.5	15.7	16.0	16.3	16.3	16.5
South East	14.6	14.6	14.7	14.8	14.9	15.1	15.3	15.7	16.0	16.2	16.3
South West	7.6	7.5	7.6	7.6	7.6	7.6	7.6	7.5	7.5	7.5	7.5
England	84.9	84.8	84.8	84.7	84.7	84.8	85.1	85.3	85.5	85.6	85.7
Wales	4.2	4.2	4.1	4.1	4.2	4.1	4.0	4.0	3.9	3.9	3.9
Scotland	8.8	8.9	8.8	8.9	8.8	8.8	8.6	8.4	8.3	8.2	8.1
Northern Ireland	2.1	2.2	2.2	2.2	2.3	2.3	2.3	2.3	2.3	2.3	2.2
GVA per head (£)											
United Kingdom	9,122	9,493	9,978	10,532	11,047	11,709	12,390	13,075	13,616	14,291	14,798
North East	7,561	7,922	8,267	8,676	9,027	9,344	9,696	10,021	10,235	10,600	11,009
North West	8,124	8,497	8,916	9,403	9,823	10,300	10,884	11,490	11,997	12,477	12,942
Yorkshire and the Humber	8,088	8,384	8,737	9,189	9,678	10,216	10,807	11,334	11,666	12,057	12,459
East Midlands	8,493	8,805	9,199	9,716	10,221	10,860	11,554	12,145	12,486	12,890	13,243
West Midlands	8,229	8,556	9,013	9,575	10,047	10,569	11,197	11,799	12,175	12,642	13,031
East	9,788	10,133	10,631	11,197	11,714	12,361	13,120	13,933	14,522	15,203	15,881
London	11,677	12,223	12,918	13,532	14,040	14,896	16,039	17,259	18,054	18,746	19,206
South East	9,858	10,251	10,808	11,439	12,026	12,794	13,757	14,882	15,698	16,555	17,313
South West	8,314	8,596	9,042	9,519	9,970	10,572	11,152	11,686	12,053	12,443	12,873
England	9,112	9,481	9,964	10,504	10,996	11,625	12,375	13,148	13,691	14,260	14,781
Wales	7,450	7,742	8,106	8,565	9,020	9,427	9,860	10,273	10,593	10,987	11,379
Scotland	8,907	9,359	9,809	10,376	10,861	11,406	11,966	12,465	12,802	13,263	13,660
Northern Ireland	6,837	7,217	7,688	8,160	8,655	9,136	9,608	10,081	10,521	10,941	11,311
United Kingdom less Extra-Regio[5]	8,947	9,320	9,793	10,329	10,819	11,425	12,135	12,858	13,369	13,917	14,418
GVA per head: indices (UK less Extra-Regio=100)											
United Kingdom	100.0	100.0	100.0	100.0	100.0	100.0	100.0	100.0	100.0	100.0	100.0
North East	84.5	85.0	84.4	84.0	83.4	81.8	79.9	77.9	76.6	76.2	76.4
North West	90.8	91.2	91.0	91.0	90.8	90.2	89.7	89.4	89.7	89.7	89.8
Yorkshire and the Humber	90.4	90.0	89.2	89.0	89.5	89.4	89.1	88.1	87.3	86.6	86.4
East Midlands	94.9	94.5	93.9	94.1	94.5	95.1	95.2	94.5	93.4	92.6	91.9
West Midlands	92.0	91.8	92.0	92.7	92.9	92.5	92.3	91.8	91.1	90.8	90.4
East	109.4	108.7	108.6	108.4	108.3	108.2	108.1	108.4	108.6	109.2	110.1
London	130.5	131.2	131.9	131.0	129.8	130.4	132.2	134.2	135.0	134.7	133.2
South East	110.2	110.0	110.4	110.7	111.2	112.0	113.4	115.7	117.4	119.0	120.1
South West	92.9	92.2	92.3	92.2	92.2	92.5	91.9	90.9	90.2	89.4	89.3
England	101.8	101.7	101.7	101.7	101.6	101.7	102.0	102.3	102.4	102.5	102.5
Wales	83.3	83.1	82.8	82.9	83.4	82.5	81.3	79.9	79.2	79.0	78.9
Scotland	99.5	100.4	100.2	100.5	100.4	99.8	98.6	96.9	95.8	95.3	94.7
Northern Ireland	76.4	77.4	78.5	79.0	80.0	80.0	79.2	78.4	78.7	78.6	78.4

1 Estimates of regional GVA in this table are on a residence basis, where income of commuters is allocated to where they live, rather than their place of work. The data are consistent with the headline series published on 20 August 2003. See Notes and Definitions.

2 Provisional.

3 The per head series in these data for 2001 are calculated using updated population estimates, that were not available in August 2003.

4 Components may not sum to totals as a result of rounding.

5 The GVA for Extra-Regio comprises compensation of employees and gross operating surplus which cannot be assigned to regions.

Source: Office for National Statistics

Figure **12.2** Gross value added[1] (GVA) at current basic prices

£ per head index, UK less Extra-Regio = 100

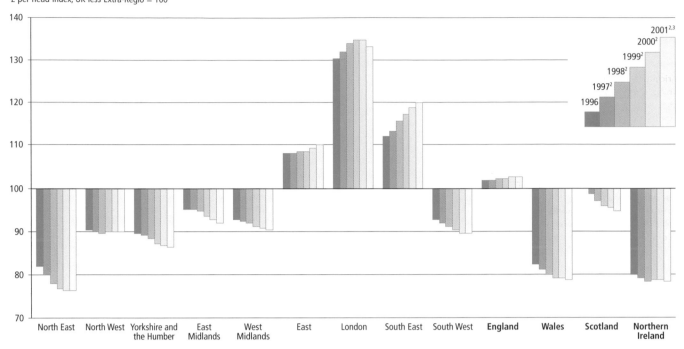

1 Estimates of regional GVA in this table are on a residence basis, where income of commuters is allocated to where they live, rather than their place of work. The data are consistent with the headline series published on 20 August 2003. See Notes and Definitions.

2 Provisional.

3 The per head series in these data for 2001 are calculated using updated population estimates, that were not available in August 2003.

Source: Office for National Statistics

Table **12.3** Gross value added[1] (GVA) by component of income at current basic prices, 2001[2]

Percentages and £ million

	Income components as a percentage of total GVA		Gross value added (=100%) (£ million)
	Compensation of employees	Operating surplus/ mixed income[3]	
United Kingdom[4]	65	35	851,408
North East	68	32	27,729
North West	66	34	87,584
Yorkshire and the Humber	66	34	61,929
East Midlands	65	35	55,394
West Midlands	65	35	68,839
East	66	34	85,775
London	66	34	140,354
South East	65	35	138,877
South West	61	39	63,554
England	65	35	730,036
Wales	65	35	33,086
Scotland	65	35	69,179
Northern Ireland	60	40	19,108
Extra-Regio[5]	7	93	22,437

1 Estimates of regional GVA in this table are on a residence basis, where the income of commuters is allocated to where they live, rather than their place of work. See Notes and Definitions.

2 Provisional.

3 Including taxes on production.

4 Excluding GVA for Extra-Regio and the allowance for statistical discrepancy.

5 The GVA for extra-Regio comprises compensation of employees and gross operating surplus which cannot be assigned to regions.

Source: Office for National Statistics

Map **12.4**

Gross value added per head at current basic[1] prices, 2001[2]

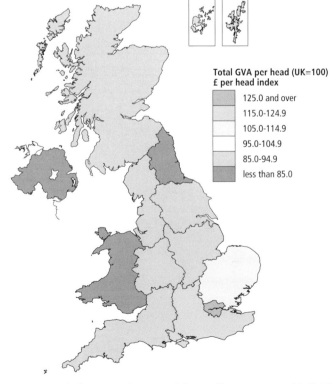

Total GVA per head (UK=100) £ per head index

- 125.0 and over
- 115.0-124.9
- 105.0-114.9
- 95.0-104.9
- 85.0-94.9
- less than 85.0

1 Consistent with the National Accounts (Blue Book). See Notes and Definitions.

2 Provisional.

Source: Office for National Statistics

Table 12.5 Gross value added[1] by industry groups, current basic prices by country and region

£ million

	1996	1997[2]	1998[2]	1999[2]	2000[2]	1996	1997[2]	1998[2]	1999[2]	2000[2]
	United Kingdom[3]					North East				
Agriculture, hunting, forestry and fishing	11,736	10,146	9,628	9,478	8,802	213	194	189	189	177
Mining, quarrying of energy producing materials	2,632	2,501	2,265	2,166	2,468	114	100	83	77	87
Other mining and quarrying	1,599	1,694	1,649	1,715	1,813	81	87	85	94	108
Manufacturing	146,078	152,299	153,412	152,402	153,671	6,772	6,799	6,660	6,433	6,427
Electricity, gas and water supply	16,280	16,141	15,960	15,968	15,731	608	609	651	718	756
Construction	34,587	36,879	39,097	41,516	44,047	1,320	1,399	1,430	1,455	1,509
Wholesale and retail trade (including motor trade)	79,667	86,747	93,503	99,144	102,332	2,464	2,617	2,755	2,850	2,876
Hotels and restaurants	20,138	22,383	24,331	26,099	28,297	631	691	746	796	855
Transport, storage and communication	53,474	57,412	62,230	65,096	68,842	1,820	1,895	1,939	1,876	1,893
Financial intermediation	40,913	40,584	45,313	43,189	45,785	754	751	852	811	867
Real estate, renting and business activities	128,776	143,286	163,277	178,318	193,963	3,568	3,842	4,188	4,383	4,638
Public administration and defence[4]	38,773	38,738	38,836	38,467	39,920	1,481	1,438	1,421	1,403	1,479
Education	36,540	38,802	41,355	45,418	49,163	1,587	1,605	1,656	1,805	1,966
Health and social work	44,566	46,892	49,570	52,783	56,495	1,963	2,045	2,154	2,310	2,489
Other services	29,969	33,743	37,261	40,209	42,731	947	1,042	1,126	1,176	1,199
Adjustment for financial services (FISIM[5])	−22,580	−22,396	−27,998	−30,121	−37,949	−358	−354	−439	−467	−588
Total	663,148	705,851	749,688	781,847	816,111	23,963	24,762	25,497	25,910	26,740

	1996	1997[2]	1998[2]	1999[2]	2000[2]	1996	1997[2]	1998[2]	1999[2]	2000[2]
	North West					Yorkshire and the Humber				
Agriculture, hunting, forestry and fishing	875	746	714	724	684	1,056	917	862	833	766
Mining, quarrying of energy producing materials	26	24	24	35	54	180	203	207	218	261
Other mining and quarrying	125	148	141	141	140	164	142	114	102	102
Manufacturing	19,151	19,471	19,388	19,323	19,423	13,621	14,125	13,948	13,438	13,322
Electricity, gas and water supply	1,678	1,695	1,691	1,707	1,700	1,176	1,215	1,227	1,224	1,188
Construction	3,532	3,758	3,940	4,166	4,406	2,826	2,968	3,128	3,338	3,566
Wholesale and retail trade (including motor trade)	8,834	9,653	10,406	10,956	11,234	6,303	6,787	7,256	7,661	7,917
Hotels and restaurants	1,986	2,191	2,365	2,509	2,700	1,464	1,618	1,759	1,893	2,053
Transport, storage and communication	5,241	5,526	5,987	6,324	6,702	3,978	4,306	4,612	4,701	4,850
Financial intermediation	2,898	2,882	3,319	3,229	3,462	2,233	2,258	2,597	2,495	2,604
Real estate, renting and business activities	11,789	12,956	14,501	15,470	16,549	7,602	8,316	9,255	9,864	10,512
Public administration and defence[4]	3,249	3,327	3,433	3,496	3,653	2,708	2,691	2,718	2,724	2,868
Education	4,117	4,366	4,708	5,262	5,764	3,020	3,190	3,423	3,770	4,052
Health and social work	5,245	5,461	5,718	6,057	6,477	3,668	3,946	4,253	4,573	4,891
Other services	2,690	2,979	3,289	3,530	3,739	1,798	2,018	2,262	2,484	2,676
Adjustment for financial services (FISIM[5])	1,529	1,513	−1,927	−2,094	−2,630	−1,183	−1,199	−1,521	−1,613	−1,955
Total	69,905	73,670	77,698	80,836	84,058	50,612	53,501	56,099	57,706	59,675

	1996	1997[2]	1998[2]	1999[2]	2000[2]	1996	1997[2]	1998[2]	1999[2]	2000[2]
	East Midlands					West Midlands				
Agriculture, hunting, forestry and fishing	1,134	969	925	916	851	1,070	927	881	864	799
Mining, quarrying of energy producing materials	184	182	163	156	178	64	63	55	49	53
Other mining and quarrying	206	201	194	205	235	103	111	118	134	144
Manufacturing	13,412	14,155	14,183	13,952	14,011	16,517	17,185	17,161	16,625	16,565
Electricity, gas and water supply	1,229	1,198	1,126	1,059	1,016	1,369	1,424	1,552	1,693	1,781
Construction	2,310	2,522	2,749	2,975	3,159	2,885	3,024	3,187	3,323	3,511
Wholesale and retail trade (including motor trade)	5,811	6,304	6,700	7,008	7,168	7,075	7,613	8,103	8,489	8,705
Hotels and restaurants	1,090	1,184	1,261	1,336	1,448	1,585	1,848	2,066	2,179	2,293
Transport, storage and communication	2,693	2,876	3,167	3,409	3,668	3,738	4,003	4,300	4,486	4,783
Financial intermediation	1,403	1,412	1,642	1,571	1,653	2,314	2,327	2,626	2,487	2,598
Real estate, renting and business activities	6,869	7,659	8,634	9,212	9,806	9,244	10,146	11,392	12,261	13,157
Public administration and defence[4]	1,968	1,993	2,027	2,033	2,135	2,435	2,441	2,463	2,438	2,518
Education	2,454	2,680	2,909	3,200	3,415	3,072	3,266	3,508	3,889	4,222
Health and social work	2,891	3,035	3,211	3,439	3,714	3,464	3,611	3,864	4,209	4,563
Other services	1,550	1,813	2,022	2,144	2,205	1,867	2,130	2,372	2,570	2,741
Adjustment for financial services (FISIM[5])	−632	−629	−813	−872	−1,073	−1,205	−1,216	−1,508	−1,592	−1,936
Total	44,575	47,552	50,102	51,743	53,588	55,596	58,904	62,140	64,103	66,498

Table 12.5 (Continued)

£ million

	1996	1997[2]	1998[2]	1999[2]	2000[2]	1996	1997[2]	1998[2]	1999[2]	2000[2]
	East					London				
Agriculture, hunting, forestry and fishing	1,587	1,355	1,283	1,253	1,155	49	25	13	6	17
Mining, quarrying of energy producing materials	226	184	153	154	188	217	203	188	180	199
Other mining and quarrying	96	103	98	104	110	60	58	52	49	48
Manufacturing	12,714	13,306	13,429	13,229	13,333	12,747	13,335	13,799	14,297	14,750
Electricity, gas and water supply	1,404	1,369	1,389	1,421	1,401	1,521	1,443	1,421	1,474	1,512
Construction	3,975	4,386	4,727	5,024	5,312	4,137	4,423	4,698	5,007	5,345
Wholesale and retail trade (including motor trade)	8,036	8,869	9,621	10,176	10,485	12,497	13,400	14,393	15,393	16,036
Hotels and restaurants	1,578	1,773	1,935	2,051	2,215	3,774	4,110	4,457	4,870	5,364
Transport, storage and communication	5,892	6,237	6,732	7,140	7,660	11,014	11,993	13,213	13,987	14,847
Financial intermediation	4,444	4,507	4,901	4,707	4,935	13,656	13,387	14,893	14,042	14,964
Real estate, renting and business activities	13,018	14,576	16,748	18,492	20,359	29,614	33,446	38,769	42,952	47,287
Public administration and defence[4]	3,442	3,511	3,576	3,583	3,732	4,961	4,641	4,417	4,178	4,309
Education	3,315	3,496	3,764	4,215	4,641	5,289	5,843	6,275	6,782	7,215
Health and social work	3,723	3,908	4,108	4,364	4,680	5,867	6,298	6,685	7,087	7,560
Other services	2,726	3,033	3,314	3,565	3,821	7,537	8,563	9,497	10,331	11,030
Adjustment for financial services (FISIM[5])	−1,449	−1,475	−1,851	−1,915	−2,316	−10,138	−10,051	−12,500	−13,512	−17,303
Total	64,726	69,137	73,927	77,562	81,713	102,802	111,117	120,271	127,124	133,179

	1996	1997[2]	1998[2]	1999[2]	2000[2]	1996	1997[2]	1998[2]	1999[2]	2000[2]
	South East					South West				
Agriculture, hunting, forestry and fishing	1,246	1,086	1,031	1,016	942	1,689	1,467	1,381	1,347	1,244
Mining, quarrying of energy producing materials	210	168	129	114	122	33	28	25	26	32
Other mining and quarrying	168	168	153	156	159	291	327	320	328	337
Manufacturing	17,143	18,243	18,947	19,335	19,738	10,461	11,179	11,497	11,642	11,872
Electricity, gas and water supply	2,340	2,226	2,138	2,142	2,088	1,722	1,704	1,619	1,529	1,436
Construction	5,275	5,661	6,042	6,496	6,946	2,689	2,863	3,052	3,260	3,451
Wholesale and retail trade (including motor trade)	12,374	13,884	15,410	16,687	17,367	5,888	6,382	6,801	7,178	7,393
Hotels and restaurants	2,639	2,839	3,057	3,347	3,714	1,669	1,814	1,938	2,073	2,256
Transport, storage and communication	9,382	10,268	11,312	11,926	12,661	3,199	3,452	3,694	3,772	3,935
Financial intermediation	6,023	6,090	6,758	6,553	6,981	2,801	2,667	2,909	2,743	2,895
Real estate, renting and business activities	23,741	26,895	31,322	35,054	38,769	9,087	10,006	11,270	12,221	13,184
Public administration and defence[4]	6,502	6,648	6,768	6,730	6,929	4,408	4,433	4,346	4,192	4,272
Education	4,642	4,888	5,159	5,617	6,059	2,610	2,829	3,052	3,408	3,751
Health and social work	6,099	6,376	6,702	7,081	7,557	3,486	3,664	3,882	4,118	4,393
Other services	4,525	5,101	5,636	6,063	6,484	2,135	2,372	2,569	2,771	2,966
Adjustment for financial services (FISIM[5])	−2,453	−2,448	−3,125	−3,441	−4,371	−1,534	−1,448	−1,757	−1,869	−2,332
Total	99,855	108,091	117,440	124,875	132,147	50,635	53,740	56,598	58,739	61,085

	1996	1997[2]	1998[2]	1999[2]	2000[2]	1996	1997[2]	1998[2]	1999[2]	2000[2]
	England					Wales				
Agriculture, hunting, forestry and fishing	8,919	7,685	7,279	7,147	6,635	538	486	498	514	491
Mining, quarrying of energy producing materials	1,254	1,156	1,028	1,009	1,174	104	84	65	57	60
Other mining and quarrying	1,295	1,346	1,275	1,312	1,383	99	113	123	128	133
Manufacturing	122,539	127,797	129,014	128,275	129,441	7,797	8,007	7,941	7,775	7,826
Electricity, gas and water supply	13,046	12,883	12,815	12,968	12,880	828	785	740	735	752
Construction	28,949	31,005	32,953	35,043	37,206	1,442	1,508	1,562	1,617	1,680
Wholesale and retail trade (including motor trade)	69,281	75,508	81,447	86,397	89,182	2,701	2,947	3,192	3,381	3,491
Hotels and restaurants	16,416	18,069	19,585	21,055	22,899	884	983	1,066	1,146	1,239
Transport, storage and communication	46,957	50,556	54,957	57,620	61,000	1,410	1,484	1,590	1,672	1,788
Financial intermediation	36,526	36,280	40,497	38,639	40,959	934	931	1,060	1,017	1,089
Real estate, renting and business activities	114,530	127,841	146,079	159,909	174,261	3,813	4,124	4,549	4,859	5,168
Public administration and defence[4]	31,154	31,124	31,169	30,777	31,895	1,815	1,772	1,729	1,686	1,750
Education	30,107	32,162	34,454	37,949	41,086	1,764	1,859	2,012	2,252	2,466
Health and social work	36,405	38,344	40,577	43,237	46,324	2,327	2,488	2,641	2,816	3,012
Other services	25,774	29,051	32,086	34,634	36,862	1,182	1,341	1,478	1,573	1,639
Adjustment for financial services (FISIM[5])	−20,482	−20,333	−25,440	−27,374	−34,502	−421	−419	−528	−574	−720
Total	562,669	600,474	639,772	668,598	698,684	27,217	28,492	29,718	30,652	31,864

Table **12.5** (Continued)

£ million

	1996	1997[2]	1998[2]	1999[2]	2000[2]	1996	1997[2]	1998[2]	1999[2]	2000[2]
	Scotland					Northern Ireland				
Agriculture, hunting, forestry and fishing	1,478	1,292	1,242	1,273	1,235	801	682	609	544	440
Mining, quarrying of energy producing materials	1,261	1,249	1,161	1,089	1,220	13	12	11	12	13
Other mining and quarrying	135	156	172	190	207	71	78	79	85	90
Manufacturing	12,638	13,182	13,034	12,787	12,673	3,104	3,313	3,423	3,565	3,731
Electricity, gas and water supply	1,972	2,044	1,990	1,860	1,710	434	430	416	405	389
Construction	3,346	3,437	3,563	3,715	3,898	850	929	1,020	1,141	1,264
Wholesale and retail trade (including motor trade)	6,003	6,404	6,800	7,146	7,354	1,682	1,888	2,064	2,220	2,305
Hotels and restaurants	2,447	2,901	3,217	3,402	3,622	392	430	464	495	537
Transport, storage and communication	4,329	4,520	4,748	4,818	5,011	778	851	936	987	1,043
Financial intermediation	2,930	2,868	3,201	3,011	3,181	524	505	556	521	556
Real estate, renting and business activities	8,781	9,449	10,481	11,148	11,907	1,651	1,872	2,168	2,402	2,628
Public administration and defence[4]	3,849	3,887	3,986	4,084	4,324	1,955	1,956	1,953	1,921	1,951
Education	3,516	3,551	3,603	3,872	4,212	1,154	1,231	1,286	1,345	1,399
Health and social work	4,379	4,573	4,818	5,129	5,473	1,455	1,488	1,535	1,602	1,687
Other services	2,443	2,718	3,008	3,270	3,459	569	633	688	732	771
Adjustment for financial services (FISIM[5])	–1,427	–1,402	–1,737	–1,861	–2,335	–250	–242	–293	–312	–392
Total	58,079	60,828	63,285	64,932	67,150	15,182	16,057	16,913	17,665	18,414

1 Estimates of regional GVA in this table are on a residence basis, where the income of commuters is allocated to where they live rather than their place of work. See Notes and Definitions.

2 Provisional.

3 Excludes GVA from Extra-Regio, which cannot be allocated to any particular region.

4 Public administration, national defence and compulsory social security.

5 Financial Intermediation Services Indirectly Measured.

Source: Office for National Statistics

Table 12.6 Workplace-based gross value added[1,2] (GVA) at current basic prices

	1991	1992	1993	1994	1995	1996	1997[3]	1998[3]	1999[3]	2000[3]	2001[3]
£ million											
United Kingdom	523,935	546,434	575,461	608,740	639,908	679,620	720,692	762,363	796,273	838,065	874,227
North East	19,560	20,511	21,399	22,402	23,229	23,963	24,762	25,497	25,910	26,740	27,729
North West	55,596	58,078	60,954	64,159	66,887	69,905	73,670	77,698	80,836	84,058	87,584
Yorkshire and the Humber	39,925	41,486	43,288	45,558	47,970	50,612	53,501	56,099	57,706	59,675	61,929
East Midlands	34,069	35,532	37,287	39,547	41,793	44,575	47,552	50,102	51,743	53,588	55,394
West Midlands	43,035	44,812	47,282	50,245	52,800	55,596	58,904	62,140	64,103	66,498	68,839
East	44,134	45,821	48,305	51,958	54,359	57,392	61,795	65,645	67,820	71,701	75,128
London	91,441	95,230	100,248	104,860	108,630	116,967	126,567	137,402	145,413	154,182	162,501
South East	69,501	72,922	77,376	81,963	87,672	93,024	99,983	108,591	116,329	121,156	127,377
South West	38,977	40,498	42,762	45,245	47,632	50,635	53,740	56,598	58,739	61,085	63,554
England	436,238	454,890	478,900	505,937	530,971	562,669	600,474	639,772	668,598	698,684	730,036
Wales	21,405	22,273	23,357	24,710	26,028	27,217	28,492	29,718	30,652	31,864	33,086
Scotland	45,276	47,597	49,949	52,943	55,431	58,079	60,828	63,285	64,932	67,150	69,179
Northern Ireland	10,990	11,715	12,574	13,412	14,273	15,182	16,057	16,913	17,665	18,414	19,108
United Kingdom less Extra-Regio[4] and statistical discrepancy	513,909	536,475	564,781	597,002	626,703	663,148	705,851	749,688	781,847	816,111	851,408
Extra-Regio	10,028	9,958	10,681	11,740	13,206	16,473	14,842	12,679	14,426	21,954	22,437
Statistical discrepancy	–	–	–	–	–	–	–	–	–	–	382
As a percentage of United Kingdom less Extra-Regio and statistical discrepancy											
United Kingdom	100.0	100.0	100.0	100.0	100.0	100.0	100.0	100.0	100.0	100.0	100.0
North East	3.8	3.8	3.8	3.8	3.7	3.6	3.5	3.4	3.3	3.3	3.3
North West	10.8	10.8	10.8	10.7	10.7	10.5	10.4	10.4	10.3	10.3	10.3
Yorkshire and the Humber	7.8	7.7	7.7	7.6	7.7	7.6	7.6	7.5	7.4	7.3	7.3
East Midlands	6.6	6.6	6.6	6.6	6.7	6.7	6.7	6.7	6.6	6.6	6.5
West Midlands	8.4	8.4	8.4	8.4	8.4	8.4	8.3	8.3	8.2	8.1	8.1
East	8.6	8.5	8.6	8.7	8.7	8.7	8.8	8.8	8.7	8.8	8.8
London	17.8	17.8	17.7	16.6	17.3	17.6	17.9	18.3	18.6	18.9	19.1
South East	13.5	13.6	13.7	13.7	14.0	14.0	14.2	14.5	14.9	14.8	15.0
South West	7.6	7.5	7.6	7.6	7.6	7.6	7.6	7.5	7.5	7.5	7.5
England	84.9	84.8	84.8	84.7	84.7	84.8	85.1	85.3	85.5	85.6	85.7
Wales	4.2	4.2	4.1	4.1	4.2	4.1	4.0	4.0	3.9	3.9	3.9
Scotland	8.8	8.9	8.8	8.9	8.8	8.8	8.6	8.4	8.3	8.2	8.1
Northern Ireland	2.1	2.2	2.2	2.2	2.3	2.3	2.3	2.3	2.3	2.3	2.2
GVA per head (£)											
United Kingdom	9,122	9,493	9,978	10,532	11,047	11,709	12,390	13,075	13,616	14,291	14,798
North East	7,561	7,922	8,267	8,676	9,027	9,344	9,696	10,021	10,235	10,600	11,009
North West	8,124	8,497	8,916	9,403	9,823	10,300	10,884	11,490	11,997	12,477	12,942
Yorkshire and the Humber	8,088	8,384	8,737	9,189	9,678	10,216	10,807	11,334	11,666	12,057	12,459
East Midlands	8,493	8,805	9,199	9,716	10,221	10,860	11,554	12,145	12,486	12,890	13,243
West Midlands	8,229	8,556	9,013	9,575	10,047	10,569	11,197	11,799	12,175	12,642	13,031
East	8,618	8,912	9,376	10,037	10,443	10,961	11,726	12,372	12,698	13,340	13,909
London	13,390	13,958	14,674	15,322	15,836	16,949	18,270	19,717	20,651	21,702	22,236
South East	9,110	9,525	10,086	10,629	11,292	11,918	12,725	13,761	14,623	15,178	15,880
South West	8,314	8,596	9,042	9,519	9,970	10,572	11,152	11,686	12,053	12,443	12,873
England	9,112	9,481	9,964	10,504	10,996	11,625	12,375	13,148	13,691	14,260	14,781
Wales	7,450	7,742	8,106	8,565	9,020	9,427	9,860	10,273	10,593	10,987	11,379
Scotland	8,907	9,359	9,809	10,376	10,861	11,406	11,966	12,465	12,802	13,263	13,660
Northern Ireland	6,837	7,217	7,688	8,160	8,655	9,136	9,608	10,081	10,521	10,941	11,311
United Kingdom less Extra-Regio[4]	8,947	9,320	9,793	10,329	10,819	11,425	12,135	12,858	13,369	13,917	14,418
GVA per head: indices (UK less Extra-Regio=100)											
United Kingdom	100.0	100.0	100.0	100.0	100.0	100.0	100.0	100.0	100.0	100.0	100.0
North East	84.5	85.0	84.4	84.0	83.4	81.8	79.9	77.9	76.6	76.2	76.4
North West	90.8	91.2	91.0	91.0	90.8	90.2	89.7	89.4	89.7	89.7	89.8
Yorkshire and the Humber	90.4	90.0	89.2	89.0	89.5	89.4	89.1	88.1	87.3	86.6	86.4
East Midlands	94.9	94.5	93.9	94.1	94.5	95.1	95.2	94.5	93.4	92.6	91.9
West Midlands	92.0	91.8	92.0	92.7	92.9	92.5	92.3	91.8	91.1	90.8	90.4
East	96.3	95.6	95.7	97.2	96.5	95.9	96.6	96.2	95.0	95.9	96.5
London	149.7	149.8	149.8	148.3	146.4	148.3	150.6	153.3	154.5	155.9	154.2
South East	101.8	102.2	103.0	102.9	104.4	104.3	104.9	107.0	109.4	109.1	110.1
South West	92.9	92.2	92.3	92.2	92.2	92.5	91.9	90.9	90.2	89.4	89.3
England	101.8	101.7	101.7	101.7	101.6	101.7	102.0	102.3	102.4	102.5	102.5
Wales	83.3	83.1	82.8	82.9	83.4	82.5	81.3	79.9	79.2	79.0	78.9
Scotland	99.5	100.4	100.2	100.5	100.4	99.8	98.6	96.9	95.8	95.3	94.7
Northern Ireland	76.4	77.4	78.5	79.0	80.0	80.0	79.2	78.4	78.7	78.6	78.4

1 Estimates of workplace based GVA allocate incomes to the region in which commuters work. The data are consistent with the headline workplace based series published in August 2003. See Notes and Definitions.

2 The per head series in these data for 2001 are calculated using updated population estimates that were not available in August 2003.

3 Provisional.

4 The GVA for Extra-Regio comprises compensation of employees and gross operating surplus which cannot be assigned to regions.

Source: Office for National Statistics

Table 12.7 Household income[1] and gross disposable household income[2]

	1989	1990	1991	1992	1993	1994	1995[3]	1996[3]	1997[3]	1998[3]	1999[3]
Total household income											
£ million											
United Kingdom[4]	475,104	529,272	574,225	614,110	640,471	667,658	754,140	796,674	843,244	893,466	930,887
North East	18,504	20,674	22,847	24,739	25,633	26,048	28,810	30,169	31,913	32,947	34,111
North West	52,842	58,866	64,261	67,957	70,450	73,328	80,562	84,957	89,563	93,569	97,705
Yorkshire and the Humber	37,742	41,777	45,489	48,024	50,938	52,652	57,964	61,943	64,684	68,748	70,011
East Midlands	31,512	34,554	37,368	39,979	41,771	44,400	49,436	52,692	55,061	57,759	60,480
West Midlands	39,113	44,015	47,684	51,481	53,417	55,989	63,732	66,702	69,466	73,738	77,569
East	46,734	51,963	55,708	59,870	61,057	63,949	72,767	77,164	81,804	87,008	90,712
London	67,727	76,647	83,339	88,594	92,888	96,515	109,563	116,859	126,154	136,966	143,088
South East	70,407	77,618	83,958	89,657	94,768	99,847	114,268	121,783	130,769	139,224	144,133
South West	38,261	42,545	45,817	49,085	50,774	52,403	61,585	64,561	68,719	72,928	75,627
England	402,843	448,658	486,471	519,385	541,697	565,129	638,687	676,831	718,134	762,887	793,435
Wales	20,755	22,895	25,059	26,901	27,787	29,051	32,551	33,981	35,209	36,592	37,926
Scotland	40,200	45,346	49,300	53,464	55,729	57,107	63,668	66,030	68,814	72,007	76,325
Northern Ireland	10,664	11,700	12,706	13,656	14,725	15,795	17,778	18,375	19,611	20,557	21,642
United Kingdom less Extra-Regio[5]	474,462	528,600	573,536	613,406	639,938	667,082	752,684	795,217	841,767	892,042	929,329
Extra-Regio[5]	642	672	689	704	533	576	1,456	1,457	1,477	1,424	1,558
Household Income											
£ per head											
North East	7,133	7,957	8,768	9,479	9,805	9,960	11,059	11,601	12,301	12,723	13,215
North West	7,705	8,572	9,326	9,850	10,200	10,606	11,676	12,328	13,009	13,579	14,200
Yorkshire and the Humber	7,626	8,418	9,129	9,603	10,155	10,472	11,525	12,301	12,842	13,633	13,872
East Midlands	7,888	8,608	9,265	9,858	10,242	10,831	11,988	12,723	13,247	13,853	14,430
West Midlands	7,462	8,383	9,050	9,750	10,095	10,562	12,010	12,546	13,056	13,828	14,538
East	9,177	10,162	10,834	11,578	11,760	12,258	13,841	14,579	15,336	16,181	16,740
London	9,960	11,184	12,103	12,824	13,405	13,863	15,636	16,519	17,713	19,057	19,641
South East	9,254	10,156	10,937	11,631	12,250	12,844	14,562	15,425	16,431	17,395	17,844
South West	8,182	9,063	9,716	10,356	10,657	10,937	12,759	13,335	14,093	14,879	15,323
England	8,425	9,348	10,093	10,737	11,162	11,604	13,060	13,788	14,571	15,414	15,948
Wales	7,232	7,955	8,669	9,277	9,559	9,967	11,160	11,633	12,029	12,474	12,913
Scotland	7,887	8,887	9,633	10,443	10,868	11,108	12,395	12,876	13,434	14,064	14,910
Northern Ireland	6,736	7,361	7,918	8,424	9,010	9,604	10,743	11,009	11,671	12,174	12,792
United Kingdom less Extra-Regio[5]	8,271	9,182	9,920	10,574	10,996	11,422	12,842	13,522	14,264	15,059	15,619
Gross disposable household income											
£ per head											
North East	4,908	5,506	6,111	6,690	7,053	7,095	7,522	7,972	8,554	8,585	9,018
North West	5,239	5,865	6,452	6,922	7,313	7,536	7,874	8,334	8,900	9,008	9,501
Yorkshire and the Humber	5,208	5,781	6,308	6,682	7,232	7,417	7,780	8,323	8,776	9,106	9,325
East Midlands	5,280	5,801	6,284	6,810	7,214	7,569	7,869	8,401	8,835	8,935	9,409
West Midlands	4,934	5,605	6,127	6,716	7,112	7,391	7,939	8,313	8,748	8,981	9,541
East	6,097	6,803	7,312	7,962	8,248	8,540	9,011	9,484	10,025	10,147	10,638
London	6,549	7,302	8,001	8,640	9,311	9,612	10,102	10,650	11,485	11,811	12,207
South East	6,110	6,680	7,292	7,880	8,519	8,873	9,282	9,814	10,579	10,698	11,055
South West	5,638	6,222	6,718	7,255	7,608	7,767	8,606	8,915	9,511	9,725	10,073
England	5,643	6,273	6,842	7,395	7,867	8,127	8,592	9,070	9,674	9,862	10,284
Wales	4,994	5,534	6,169	6,672	6,986	7,235	7,742	8,056	8,389	8,529	8,870
Scotland	5,355	6,124	6,643	7,301	7,704	7,773	8,287	8,541	8,977	9,154	9,870
Northern Ireland	4,729	5,240	5,610	5,993	6,540	6,959	7,678	7,834	8,365	8,500	8,998
United Kingdom less Extra-Regio[5]	5,560	6,194	6,757	7,311	7,771	8,019	8,497	8,938	9,513	9,696	10,142
Gross disposable household income per head, indices											
UK less Extra-Regio=100											
United Kingdom	100.0	100.0	100.0	100.0	100.0	100.0	100.0	100.0	100.0	100.0	100.0
North East	88.3	88.9	90.4	91.5	90.8	88.5	88.5	89.2	89.9	88.5	88.9
North West	94.2	94.7	95.5	94.7	94.1	94.0	92.7	93.2	93.6	92.9	93.7
Yorkshire and the Humber	93.7	93.3	93.4	91.4	93.1	92.5	91.6	93.1	92.3	93.9	91.9
East Midlands	95.0	93.7	93.0	93.2	92.8	94.4	92.6	94.0	92.9	92.2	92.8
West Midlands	88.7	90.5	90.7	91.9	91.5	92.2	93.4	93.0	92.0	92.6	94.1
East	109.7	109.8	108.2	108.9	106.1	106.5	106.0	106.1	105.4	104.6	104.9
London	117.8	117.9	118.4	118.2	119.8	119.9	118.9	119.1	120.7	121.8	120.4
South East	109.9	107.8	107.9	107.8	109.6	110.6	109.2	109.8	111.2	110.3	109.0
South West	101.4	100.4	99.4	99.2	97.9	96.9	101.3	99.7	100.0	100.3	99.3
England	101.5	101.3	101.3	101.1	101.2	101.4	101.1	101.5	101.7	101.7	101.4
Wales	89.8	89.3	91.3	91.3	89.9	90.2	91.1	90.1	88.2	88.0	87.5
Scotland	96.3	98.9	98.3	99.9	99.1	96.9	97.5	95.6	94.4	94.4	97.3
Northern Ireland	85.1	84.6	83.0	82.0	84.2	86.8	90.4	87.6	87.9	87.7	88.7

1 Household income covers the income received by households and non-profit institutions serving households.
2. Data for 1989 to 1994 are based on Blue Book 2000, whilst data for 1995 to 1999 are revised (based on Blue Book 2001). Therefore the time series are not consistent with current National Accounts.
3. Data for 1995 to 1999 are consistent with those published on 26 March 2002.
4 Components may not sum to totals as a result of rounding.
5 Parts of the UK economic territory that cannot be attached to a particular region.

Source: Office for National Statistics

Figure **12.8** Gross disposable household income[1] per head

£ per head index, UK[2] less Extra-Regio[3] = 100

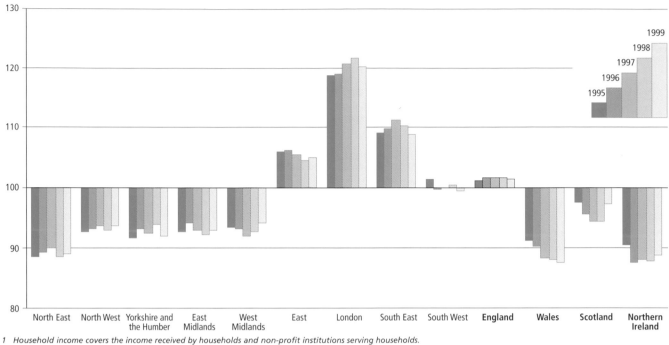

1 Household income covers the income received by households and non-profit institutions serving households.

2 Components may not sum to totals as a result of rounding.

3 Parts of the UK economic territory that cannot be attached to a particular region.

Source: Office for National Statistics

Figure **12.9** Gross disposable household income,[1] 1999

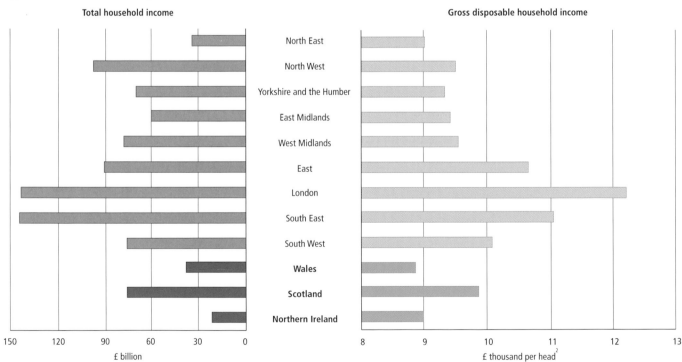

1 Household income covers the income received by households and non-profit institutions serving households.

2 Disposable household income adjusted for taxes and certain other outgoings.

Source: Office for National Statistics

Table **12.10** Sources of household income[1]

£ million and percentage

	Gross operating surplus	Gross mixed income	Compen-sation of employees	Net property income[2]	All pensions[3]	Other social benefits[4]	Net other income[5]	Total income	Disposable income	Disposable income as % of total income
1991										
United Kingdom	29,162	31,635	333,787	47,446	63,401	46,276	22,518	574,225	391,316	68
North East	796	779	13,597	1,647	2,494	2,480	1,054	22,847	15,923	70
North West	2,828	2,851	36,798	6,125	6,857	6,001	2,802	64,261	44,460	69
Yorkshire and the Humber	2,060	2,210	26,246	4,233	4,606	4,006	2,128	45,489	31,434	69
East Midlands	1,870	2,090	22,151	3,011	3,855	2,814	1,579	37,368	25,342	68
West Midlands	2,419	2,486	28,540	3,384	4,714	4,121	2,020	47,684	32,282	68
East	2,924	3,791	32,686	4,816	6,312	3,317	1,862	55,708	37,602	67
London	4,801	5,511	50,477	6,044	7,416	6,098	2,992	83,339	55,093	66
South East	5,220	5,030	47,836	6,397	11,469	5,185	2,822	83,958	55,978	67
South West	2,795	2,868	24,310	4,075	6,780	3,247	1,743	45,817	31,681	69
England	25,713	27,616	282,640	39,732	54,502	37,267	19,001	486,471	329,794	68
Wales	1,265	1,285	13,625	2,143	3,027	2,703	1,011	25,059	17,834	71
Scotland	1,795	1,988	29,616	4,329	4,996	4,575	2,001	49,300	33,997	69
Northern Ireland	388	747	7,216	1,243	877	1,731	504	12,706	9,002	71
Extra-Regio[6]	-	-	689	-	-	-	-	689	689	-
1995[7]										
United Kingdom	38,165	46,647	386,422	101,455	82,686	66,920	31,845	754,140	499,059	66
North East	1,149	1,085	14,979	3,334	3,526	3,435	1,301	28,810	19,597	68
North West	3,874	4,493	40,768	10,059	8,991	8,748	3,628	80,562	54,329	67
Yorkshire and the Humber	2,645	3,054	30,040	7,422	6,533	5,663	2,608	57,964	39,131	68
East Midlands	2,345	2,974	25,517	6,786	5,384	4,207	2,224	49,436	32,450	66
West Midlands	3,103	3,631	32,953	8,601	6,627	5,907	2,909	63,732	42,127	66
East	3,791	5,106	38,067	10,103	7,732	4,962	3,006	72,767	47,373	65
London	5,880	7,953	57,570	15,316	9,166	9,794	3,884	109,563	70,785	65
South East	6,940	7,388	57,447	16,790	13,807	7,348	4,548	114,268	72,840	64
South West	3,449	4,399	28,994	8,789	8,442	4,793	2,719	61,585	41,542	67
England	33,176	40,083	326,336	87,201	70,208	54,858	26,825	638,687	420,175	66
Wales	1,605	1,753	15,781	4,298	3,882	3,727	1,505	32,551	22,582	69
Scotland	2,758	3,493	33,987	7,826	6,926	5,999	2,678	63,668	42,568	67
Northern Ireland	626	1,318	8,862	2,131	1,669	2,336	837	17,778	12,707	71
Extra-Regio[6]	-	-	1,456	-	-	-	-	1,456	1,456	-
1999[7]										
United Kingdom	51,197	52,464	494,387	118,539	109,967	68,533	35,800	930,887	604,543	65
North East	1,422	1,170	18,635	3,355	4,665	3,422	1,442	34,111	23,278	68
North West	4,695	5,003	51,561	11,838	11,719	8,851	4,038	97,705	65,372	67
Yorkshire and the Humber	3,157	3,567	37,199	8,821	8,558	5,791	2,917	70,011	47,061	67
East Midlands	2,893	3,157	32,578	7,755	7,240	4,345	2,512	60,480	39,436	65
West Midlands	3,901	3,920	42,163	9,502	8,831	6,016	3,236	77,569	50,909	66
East	5,136	5,824	48,506	12,133	10,587	5,123	3,403	90,712	57,647	64
London	9,556	9,424	79,011	19,163	11,814	9,725	4,395	143,088	88,930	62
South East	9,578	8,806	74,139	20,162	18,824	7,466	5,158	144,133	89,299	62
South West	4,770	4,771	36,250	10,445	11,367	4,952	3,071	75,627	49,718	66
England	45,108	45,641	420,044	103,173	93,606	55,691	30,172	793,435	511,651	64
Wales	1,990	2,045	19,191	4,193	5,084	3,723	1,699	37,926	26,051	69
Scotland	3,125	3,105	42,766	8,916	9,108	6,336	2,969	76,325	50,529	66
Northern Ireland	974	1,673	10,826	2,257	2,169	2,783	960	21,642	15,223	70
Extra-Regio[6]	-	-	1,558	-	-	-	-	1,558	1,558	-

1 Household income covers the income received by households and non-profit institutions serving households.
2 Net Property Income is the difference between Property Income (Uses) & Property Income (Resources).
3 Includes Retirement & Widows' Pensions, Unfunded Social Benefits and Privately Funded Social Benefits.
4 Social Benefits excluding pensions.
5 Includes Imputed Social Contributions, Non Life Insurance Claims and Miscellaneous Current Transfers.
6 Parts of UK economic territory that cannot be attached to any particular region.
7 Data for 1991 are based on Blue Book 2000, whilst data for 1995 to 1999 are based on Blue Book 2001. The time series are therefore not consistent with the current National Accounts.

Source: Office for National Statistics

Table 12.11 Individual consumption expenditure

	Individual consumption expenditure (£ million)			Regional shares of the UK (percentages)			£ Per head			Per head, indices UK = 100		
	1997	1998	1999[1]	1997	1998	1999[1]	1997	1998	1999[1]	1997	1998	1999[1]
United Kingdom	517,910	551,823	586,906	100.0	100.0	100.0	8,776	9,316	9,864	100.0	100.0	100.0
North East	20,150	20,998	20,659	3.9	3.8	3.5	7,744	8,086	8,003	88.2	86.8	81.1
North West	57,489	59,774	64,133	11.1	10.8	10.9	8,331	8,662	9,321	94.9	93.0	94.5
Yorkshire and the Humber	41,255	44,248	44,956	8.0	8.0	7.7	8,177	8,763	8,907	93.2	94.1	90.3
East Midlands	34,787	36,261	37,961	6.7	6.6	6.5	8,370	8,695	9,057	95.4	93.3	91.8
West Midlands	43,309	46,107	49,416	8.4	8.4	8.4	8,128	8,640	9,262	92.6	92.7	93.9
East	47,712	52,258	54,607	9.2	9.5	9.3	8,963	9,740	10,077	102.1	104.6	102.2
London	72,873	80,737	89,241	14.1	14.6	15.2	10,248	11,264	12,250	116.8	120.9	124.2
South East	78,921	85,207	92,024	15.2	15.4	15.7	9,938	10,656	11,392	113.2	114.4	115.5
South West	41,784	43,887	47,384	8.1	8.0	8.1	8,584	8,961	9,600	97.8	96.2	97.3
England	438,280	469,478	500,380	84.6	85.1	85.3	8,895	9,488	10,057	101.4	101.9	102.0
Wales	23,553	23,716	24,103	4.5	4.3	4.1	8,041	8,079	8,206	91.6	86.7	83.2
Scotland	43,556	45,520	48,421	8.4	8.2	8.3	8,488	8,874	9,459	96.7	95.3	95.9
Northern Ireland	12,521	13,109	14,009	2.4	2.4	2.4	7,463	7,749	8,281	85.0	83.2	83.9

1 Provisional.

Source: Office for National Statistics

Table 12.12 Individual consumption expenditure: by broad function, 1999[1]

£ million

	Food, drink and tobacco	Clothing and footwear	Housing and fuel	Household goods and services	Vehicles, transport and comm-unications	Recreation	Other goods and services	Consump-tion expenditure in the UK[2]	Total consump-tion expenditure[3]
United Kingdom	99,473	34,601	103,887	34,781	93,181	65,467	128,878	560,268	586,906
North East	3,970	1,317	3,454	1,289	3,189	2,085	3,825	19,128	20,659
North West	11,973	4,063	10,740	3,505	10,036	7,566	13,036	60,919	64,133
Yorkshire and the Humber	8,110	2,459	7,341	2,514	6,734	5,470	9,512	42,140	44,956
East Midlands	6,908	1,896	6,638	2,401	5,805	4,347	7,859	35,853	37,961
West Midlands	8,409	2,688	8,106	3,182	7,903	5,795	10,448	46,531	49,416
East	8,662	2,919	9,830	3,489	8,839	6,136	12,067	51,943	54,607
London	13,263	6,451	17,467	4,928	14,811	8,941	22,591	88,453	89,241
South East	13,847	4,782	16,585	5,706	15,845	9,914	21,097	87,776	92,024
South West	7,745	2,297	9,049	2,859	6,988	5,412	11,132	45,482	47,384
England	82,888	28,872	89,211	29,874	80,148	55,666	111,566	478,225	500,380
Wales	4,479	1,486	4,327	1,370	3,464	2,618	4,884	22,627	24,103
Scotland	9,358	3,129	8,236	2,693	7,468	5,739	9,738	46,361	48,421
Northern Ireland	2,747	1,114	2,113	844	2,101	1,451	2,690	13,061	14,009

1 Provisional.
2 Expenditure by UK households and foreign residents in the United Kingdom.
3 Expenditure by UK consumers, including non-profit institutions serving households but excluding expenditure in the United Kingdom by foreign residents.

Source: Office for National Statistics

Chapter 13 Industry and Agriculture

Gross value added – Industry

In 2000 gross value added (GVA) derived from industry was 27 per cent of total GVA for the United Kingdom. The highest proportion of Industry derived GVA (35 per cent in 2000) was in the East Midlands. (Map 13.1)

Industry and services

The area with the highest percentage of business sites in the service sector (as a proportion of all businesses) was Inner London with 91 per cent. Omagh in Northern Ireland had the lowest proportion of businesses in the service sector (38 per cent) while Magherafelt in Northern Ireland had the highest level in the industry sector (26 per cent). (Map 13.2)

In the UK there were over 2.5 million business sites registered for VAT and /or PAYE in March 2002. London and the South East had the highest number of business sites, each with 385 thousand. The North East had less than a fifth of this number at just under 75 thousand. (Table 13.3)

Agriculture accounted for almost a quarter of all business sites in Northern Ireland. The highest proportions of businesses in construction were in the East of England and Northern Ireland (10.9 per cent in each area), and lowest in London (5.6 per cent). (Table 13.3)

In manufacturing industries the North East had the highest net capital expenditure per employee at £7,291 in 2001, this was more that twice the amount spent per employee in London (£3,262). Net capital expenditure in total for manufacturing was highest in the North West at over £2 billion in 2001. (Table 13.5)

Exports and imports

The North East had the smallest number of companies exporting to the European Union (EU) and also had one of the lowest regional shares of export trade to the EU. Most exports from the North East in 2002 were traded within European Union countries (73 per cent), whilst many regions exported more than 40 per cent outside the EU; London and the West Midlands exported the most outside the EU. Scotland received the highest proportion of its imports, 66 per cent, from countries outside the EU. (Table 13.7)

Investment

The number of project successes as result of direct inward investment in manufacturing decreased by almost 30 per cent between 1998/99 and 2002/03 in the UK. However, over the same period, project investment successes relating to non-manufacturing industries increased by almost 39 per cent. (Table 13.8)

Research and development

Businesses in the South East spent the highest amount on research and development. This expenditure accounted for 2.4 per cent of its total regional GVA. The North East business sector spent the lowest amount on research and development at £119 million in 2001, equivalent to 0.4 per cent of the region's GVA, the same proportion as Wales. (Table 13.9)

Preferential assistance

Of the English regions the North East received the highest annual regional preferential assistance to industry, £36.2m in 2001/02. Other areas of the United Kingdom received more assistance than the total for all the English regions. (Table 13.10)

Assisted Areas

Objective 1 funding (allocated from EU Structural Funds) was reduced by a fifth between 2001 and 2003 in the UK overall. The North West had a £46 million decrease over the same period. Wales obtained £178 million in 2003, accounting for 94 per cent of all structural funding the region received from the EU. (Table 13.11)

Businesses

In 2001 the South East had the largest net change, an increase of 3,100 in registrations minus de-registrations with an end of year stock of 277,500 businesses. The change in 2002 was considerably less, with London having the largest net change of all UK regions with a reduction of 2100 businesses. (Table 13.12)

Between 1999 and 2000, businesses surviving over 12 months in the UK increased by 1.8 percentage points to 91.4 per cent. All regions showed an increase, but Northern Ireland had a higher increase in proportion than most other areas, 2.7 percentage points. Business survival rate of 24 months also increased in the UK, from 75.5 per cent in 1998 to 77.2 per cent in 1999. Around two-thirds of businesses across the UK survived for 36 months after registration in 1998.(Table 13.13)

Construction

The value of contractors' output in construction increased across the UK by 47 per cent between 1997 and 2002. London had the largest increase (70 per cent) over the same time period, whereas the increase in Wales was only 15 per cent. Of the construction work in London in 2002, over three-fifths was new work, the largest proportion in the UK. (Table 13.14)

Tourism

Expenditure from overseas visitors was highest in London, accounting for nearly half of the UK total in 2002. However, the number of overseas visitors in London decreased from 12.3 million in 1996 to 11.6 million in 2002. Overall expenditure by overseas residents in the UK also decreased between 1996 and 2002. (Table 13.15)

The number of trips taken by UK residents within the UK increased by over 13 million between 1996 and 2002. Expenditure by UK residents increased, in line with visits, by 17 per cent. However, although the UK showed an overall increase in number of visits by UK residents, the East of England, Scotland, Wales and Northern Ireland showed decreases in the number of visits and expenditure between 1996 and 2002. In the South East the number of visits decreased over the same period of time but expenditure increased from £1.2 billion to £1.4 billion. (Table 13.15)

Agriculture

The percentage of gross value added (GVA) derived from agriculture in 2000, varied across the UK from 0 per cent in London to 2.4 per cent in Northern Ireland. Since 1998 the overall percentage of GVA derived from agriculture decreased across the UK apart from the North East. Northern Ireland showed the largest reduction from 4 per cent in 1998 to 2.4 per cent in 2000. (See 13.16 RT37) (Map 13.16)

In Northern Ireland just under a third of total business units were in agriculture, the highest proportion of all UK regions in 2002. (Map 13.17)

Scotland had the highest number of agricultural holdings in the UK in 2002. The proportion of arable land in Wales, Scotland and Northern Ireland was significantly lower than in the English regions. Grasslands were the predominant type of agricultural land accounting for over three-quarters in each of these three countries. In line with this Wales, Scotland and Northern Ireland have high proportions of farms grazing cattle and sheep on less favoured areas (35, 30 and 55 per cent respectively). (Table13.18 and 3.19)

Throughout the UK, the area devoted to wheat and the crop yield increased between 2001 and 2002. Although the area of barley and rape (for oilseed) decreased, the yield of these crops increased between 2001 and 2002. (Table 13.20)

Wales and Scotland together accounted for more than half of all sheep and lambs in the UK in 2002. In the East of England pigs outnumbered sheep and lambs by almost four to one. (Table 13.21)

Map **13.1**

Percentage of gross value added[1] derived from industry and services, 2000

Industry

Industry[2] as a percentage of total GVA

- 37.0 or over
- 32.0 to 36.9
- 27.0 to 31.9
- 22.0 to 26.9
- 21.9 or under

Services

Services[3] as a percentage of total GVA

- 75.0 or over
- 70.0 to 74.9
- 65.0 to 69.9
- 60.0 to 64.9
- 59.9 or under

1 Current basic prices. See Notes and Definitions.
2 Standard Industrial Classification sections C, D, E, F. See Notes and Definitions.
3 Standard Industrial Classification sections G, H, I, J, K, L, M, N, O. See Notes and Definitions.

Source: Office for National Statistics

Map **13.2**

Industry and services[1] local units as a percentage of total business sites,[2] 2002[3]

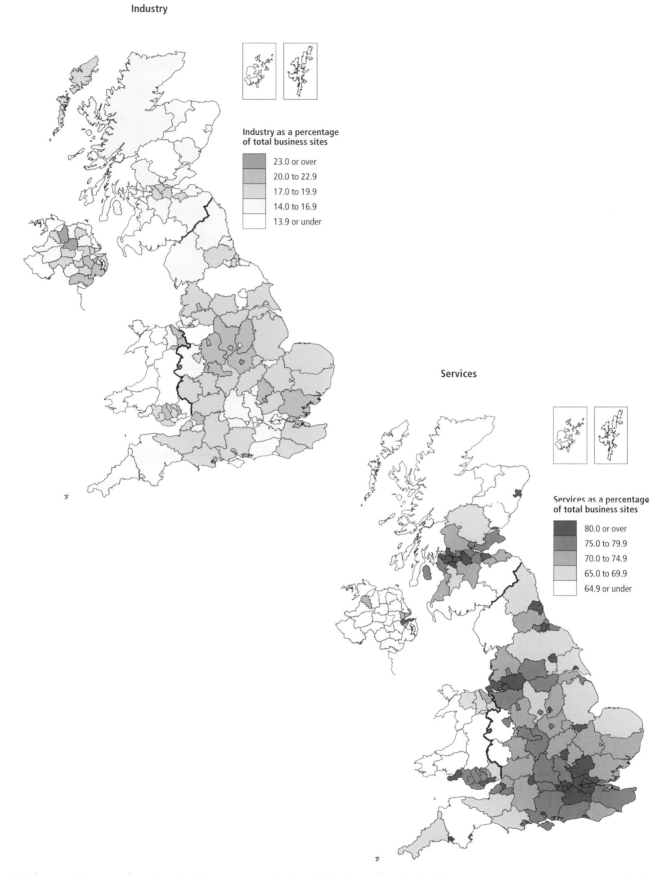

Industry

Industry as a percentage
of total business sites

- 23.0 or over
- 20.0 to 22.9
- 17.0 to 19.9
- 14.0 to 16.9
- 13.9 or under

Services

Services as a percentage
of total business sites

- 80.0 or over
- 75.0 to 79.9
- 70.0 to 74.9
- 65.0 to 69.9
- 64.9 or under

1 Industry: mining, manufacturing, electricity, gas, water. Sevices: wholesale, retail, repair, hotels, restaurants, transport, storage, communications, finance, real estate, public administration, education, health, other community. See Notes and Definitions.
2 Registered for VAT and/or PAYE, sites are allocated to countries or regions on local unit basis, e.g. an individual factory or shop
3 The maps relate to the subregions (counties/UAs) in existence at 1 April 1998.

Source: Inter-Departmental Business Register, Office for National Statistics

Table **13.3**   Classification[1] of business sites[2], March 2002

Percentages and thousands

	Agriculture, hunting, forestry & fishing	Mining & quarrying, energy, water supply & manu-facturing	Con-struction	Distrib-ution, hotels & catering; repairs	Transport & com-munication	Financial intermed-iation, real estate renting & business activities	Education & health	Public admini-stration & other services	Total business sites (=100%) (thousands)
United Kingdom	6.9	7.8	8.7	28.2	4.3	26.8	7.1	10.1	2,538.1
North East	6.1	8.0	7.9	32.8	4.5	20.3	9.3	11.3	74.6
North West	5.3	8.2	8.2	32.0	4.5	24.7	7.8	9.2	253.9
Yorkshire and the Humber	7.0	9.1	8.7	31.7	4.9	21.4	7.6	9.6	187.0
East Midlands	7.6	10.7	9.4	29.0	4.8	21.7	7.3	9.5	171.4
West Midlands	6.6	10.8	9.0	29.6	4.5	23.7	7.1	8.8	209.4
East	6.0	8.3	10.9	26.2	4.9	28.3	6.4	9.0	248.0
London	0.3	6.0	5.6	25.5	3.9	40.6	5.7	12.5	384.9
South East	3.7	7.3	9.8	25.4	4.0	32.8	6.7	10.4	384.6
South West	11.0	7.4	9.8	28.2	3.9	23.5	7.2	8.9	235.1
England	5.3	8.1	8.7	28.1	4.3	28.5	6.9	10.1	2,148.8
Wales	16.2	6.8	9.1	29.8	4.3	16.9	7.7	9.3	114.4
Scotland	11.7	6.3	7.7	30.0	4.3	20.4	8.1	11.4	195.9
Northern Ireland	24.3	6.3	10.9	25.3	3.9	11.8	9.7	8.0	79.0

1 Based on Standard Industrial Classification 1992. See Notes and Definitions.
2 Registered for VAT and/or PAYE, sites are allocated to counties or regions on local unit basis, eg an individual factory or shop. See Notes and Definitions.

Source: Inter-Departmental Business Register, Office for National Statistics

Table **13.4**   Manufacturing[1] industry business sites:[2] by employment sizeband[3], March 2002

Percentages and thousands

	Percentage of manufacturing local units with an employment sizeband[3] of								Total manu-facturing local units (=100%) (thousands)
	1 to 9	10 to 19	20 to 49	50 to 99	100 to 199	200 to 499	500 to 999	1,000 or over	
United Kingdom	72.9	11.2	8.4	3.7	2.1	1.3	0.3	0.1	192.2
North East	66.3	12.2	10.2	4.6	3.4	2.4	0.7	0.1	5.7
North West	69.1	12.3	9.4	4.4	2.7	1.5	0.4	0.1	20.4
Yorkshire and the Humber	68.8	12.3	9.7	4.5	2.6	1.7	0.4	0.1	16.5
East Midlands	70.1	12.0	9.5	4.2	2.4	1.3	0.4	0.1	17.3
West Midlands	69.0	12.5	10.2	4.1	2.3	1.5	0.3	0.1	22.1
East	75.6	10.1	7.8	3.3	1.7	1.1	0.3	0.1	20.1
London	81.6	9.4	5.4	1.9	1.0	0.6	0.1	0.1	22.9
South East	76.6	10.3	7.1	3.1	1.7	0.9	0.3	0.1	27.1
South West	75.5	10.4	7.7	3.1	1.7	1.2	0.3	0.1	16.7
England	73.4	11.1	8.3	3.6	2.0	1.2	0.3	0.1	168.9
Wales	70.0	11.0	9.0	4.3	2.9	2.1	0.5	0.3	7.3
Scotland	68.3	11.8	9.9	4.6	2.9	1.8	0.5	0.2	11.3
Northern Ireland	70.6	12.3	9.4	3.7	2.1	1.5	0.3	0.1	4.7

1 Based on Standard Industrial Classification 1992 Section D. See Notes and Definitions.
2 Registered for VAT and/or PAYE, sites are allocated to counties or regions on local unit basis, eg an individual factory or shop. See Notes and Definitions.
3 Includes paid full and part-time employees and working proprietors.

Source: Inter-Departmental Business Register, Office for National Statistics

Table **13.5**   Turnover, expenditure and gross value added in manufacturing[1], 2001

£ million and £ per person employed

	Total turnover (£ million)	Purchases of goods and services (£ million)	Total employment costs		Net capital expenditure		Gross value added at basic prices	
			£ million	£ per person employed	£ million	£ per person employed	£ million	£ per person employed
United Kingdom	450,196	287,614	85,056	22,161	16,157	4,210	143,530	37,396
North East	20,765	14,024	3,523	21,695	1,184	7,291	5,734	35,310
North West	59,414	36,513	10,799	22,342	2,045	4,231	19,539	40,424
Yorkshire and the Humber	39,061	26,051	7,903	20,359	1,412	3,638	12,876	33,171
East Midlands	35,597	21,015	7,315	19,735	1,286	3,469	12,631	34,077
West Midlands	48,825	32,203	10,016	21,207	1,789	3,788	16,038	33,958
East	38,374	25,945	7,784	22,842	1,438	4,220	12,295	36,079
London	38,105	24,440	7,416	26,442	915	3,262	13,606	48,512
South East	57,015	35,369	10,882	25,328	1,825	4,248	18,301	42,596
South West	32,466	20,450	6,780	21,797	1,493	4,800	10,783	34,666
England	369,622	236,011	72,416	22,359	13,386	4,133	121,804	37,608
Wales	27,655	17,155	4,085	20,953	863	4,427	6,866	35,217
Scotland	39,425	27,992	6,707	22,205	1,459	4,830	10,930	36,186
Northern Ireland	13,493	6,456	1,849	18,077	449	4,390	3,930	38,423

1   Based on Standard Industrial Classification 1992 Section D. See Notes and Definitions.
Source: Annual Business Inquiry, Office for National Statistics

Table **13.6**   Gross value added in manufacturing[1]: by size of local unit, 2001

Percentages and £ million

	Percentage of gross value added by number employed[2]							Total (=100%) (£ million)
	1 to 19	20 to 49	50 to 99	100 to 199	200 to 499	500 to 999	1,000 or over	
United Kingdom	15.1	11.9	11.7	14.3	20.0	13.1	14.0	143,530
North East	10.2	9.4	10.4	16.6	23.2	19.5	10.8	5,734
North West	11.7	10.0	11.3	14.4	17.4	13.9	21.4	19,539
Yorkshire and the Humber	13.7	12.4	12.6	15.0	20.3	16.7	9.2	12,876
East Midlands	13.8	12.6	12.5	15.3	18.3	11.8	15.7	12,631
West Midlands	14.8	13.2	12.2	14.1	20.6	10.0	15.1	16,038
East	17.8	13.6	13.5	13.4	22.7	9.8	9.2	12,295
London	22.4	12.9	9.9	14.5	16.0	13.6	10.8	13,606
South East	17.3	12.1	12.5	13.5	19.2	13.4	11.9	18,301
South West	15.6	11.7	10.5	14.3	20.0	14.0	14.0	10,783
England	15.5	12.1	11.8	14.4	19.4	13.2	13.7	121,804
Wales	9.2	9.5	10.8	14.7	33.7	10.5	11.6	6,866
Scotland	15.0	12.1	12.1	15.2	19.5	13.6	12.6	10,930
Northern Ireland	13.0	8.7	8.4	10.0	17.3	12.3	30.1	3,930

1   Based on Standard Industrial Classification 1992 Section D. See Notes and Definitions.
2   Number employed at time of selection of inquiry, including full and part-time employees and working proprietors.
Source: Annual Business Inquiry, Office for National Statistics

Table **13.7**   Export and import trade with EU and non-EU countries[1], 2002

£ million, percentages and numbers

	Exports									
	£ million			Percentages		As a percentage of UK regional share of export trade			Average number of companies exporting[2]	
	All export trade	To the EU	Outside the EU	To the EU	Outside the EU	All export trade	To the EU	Outside the EU	To the EU[3]	Outside the EU[3]
United Kingdom	186,978	108,933	78,045	58.3	41.7	100.0	100.0	100.0	19,420	65,562
North East	6,938	5,042	1,896	72.7	27.3	3.7	4.6	2.4	496	1,315
North West	16,871	9,814	7,057	58.2	41.8	9.0	9.0	9.0	2,063	6,164
Yorkshire and the Humber	9,077	5,732	3,346	63.1	36.9	4.9	5.3	4.3	1,497	4,717
East Midlands	12,864	7,341	5,523	57.1	42.9	6.9	6.7	7.1	1,600	5,168
West Midlands	13,800	7,821	5,979	56.7	43.3	7.4	7.2	7.7	1,944	6,414
East	16,228	10,065	6,163	62.0	38.0	8.7	9.2	7.9	2,026	7,321
London	25,981	14,783	11,197	56.9	43.1	13.9	13.6	14.3	2,614	13,038
South East	25,745	15,097	10,648	58.6	41.4	13.8	13.9	13.6	3,311	11,524
South West	7,535	5,162	2,373	68.5	31.5	4.0	4.7	3.0	1,250	4,548
England	135,039	80,858	54,181	59.9	40.1	72.2	74.2	69.4	16,801	60,209
Wales	6,619	4,691	1,928	70.9	29.1	3.5	4.3	2.5	633	1,596
Scotland	15,616	9,291	6,324	59.5	40.5	8.4	8.5	8.1	1,008	3,182
Northern Ireland	3,343	2,171	1,172	64.9	35.1	1.8	2.0	1.5	978	575
Unallocatable Trade	26,362	11,922	14,440	45.2	54.8	14.1	10.9	18.5	..	..

	Imports									
	£ million			Percentages		As a percentage of UK regional share of import trade			Average number of companies importing[2]	
	All import trade	From the EU	From outside the EU	From the EU	From outside the EU	All import trade	From the EU	From outside the EU	From the EU[3]	From outside the EU[3]
United Kingdom	227,445	120,084	107,361	52.8	47.2	100.0	100.0	100.0	24,925	95,869
North East	5,039	2,614	2,425	51.9	48.1	2.2	2.2	2.3	566	1,818
North West	15,779	7,409	8,370	47.0	53.1	6.9	6.2	7.8	2,612	8,770
Yorkshire and the Humber	10,662	5,590	5,072	52.4	47.6	4.7	4.7	4.7	1,920	6,128
East Midlands	12,275	6,232	6,043	50.8	49.2	5.4	5.2	5.6	2,179	6,745
West Midlands	16,091	9,634	6,457	59.9	40.1	7.1	8.0	6.0	2,601	8,215
East	29,947	19,013	10,934	63.5	36.5	13.2	15.8	10.2	2,585	9,835
London	38,799	15,534	23,265	40.0	60.0	17.1	12.9	21.7	3,743	22,041
South East	51,097	31,379	19,719	61.4	38.6	22.5	26.1	18.4	4,311	17,041
South West	10,560	4,359	6,201	41.3	58.7	4.6	3.6	5.8	1,509	6,630
England	190,249	101,763	88,486	53.5	46.5	83.6	84.7	82.4	22,026	87,223
Wales	5,851	2,376	3,475	40.6	59.4	2.6	2.0	3.2	657	2,346
Scotland	8,911	3,004	5,907	33.7	66.3	3.9	2.5	5.5	1,106	4,571
Northern Ireland	3,741	2,084	1,657	55.7	44.3	1.6	1.7	1.5	1,136	1,729
Unallocatable Trade	18,693	10,857	7,836	58.1	41.9	8.2	9.0	7.3	..	..

1   EU data are from Intraset declarations and do not cover all EU trade, see Notes and Definitions.
2   Companies who trade with both EU countries and countries outside the EU will appear more than once in the company count.
3   Over four quarters of 2002.

Source: HM Customs and Excise

Table **13.8** Direct inward investment:[1] project successes[2]

Numbers

	Manufacturing					Non- Manufacturing				
	1998/99	1999/2000	2000/01	2001/02	2002/03	1998/99	1999/2000	2000/01	2001/02	2002/03
United Kingdom[3]	311	328	232	253	220	353	472	637	511	489
North East	28	28	16	33	28	7	21	18	23	33
North West	42	41	11	8	20	24	39	28	25	40
Yorkshire and the Humber	63	31	19	31	20	23	13	14	9	15
East Midlands	8	17	9	7	19	11	14	8	10	13
West Midlands	41	56	47	38	17	30	43	56	60	35
East	8	9	6	13	14	33	28	50	41	28
London	1	9	14	16	9	104	150	206	160	146
South East	23	30	24	18	21	51	80	167	108	97
South West	16	16	16	10	7	18	31	22	20	26
England	230	237	162	174	155	301	419	569	456	433
Wales	35	36	26	46	39	13	11	13	15	21
Scotland	26	40	32	25	20	28	36	40	34	29
Northern Ireland	20	14	11	8	5	11	6	11	6	6

1 Data on projects which have attracted inward investment appear in this table. They are based on information provided to Invest UK, part of British Trade International, by companies at the time of the decision to invest. See Notes and Definitions.
2 A project success is defined as a case where an overseas company specifies an interest and successfully completes an investment in the UK.
3 The UK figures for 1999/2000, 2000/01 and 2002/03 do not total the sum of individual countries as they include UK-wide projects.

Source: Invest-UK, Department of Trade and Industry

Table **13.9** Expenditure on research and development, 2001

£ million and percentages

	Expenditure within (£ million)			Expenditure as a percentage of total regional GVA[1]		
	Businesses[1]	Government[1,2]	Higher education institutions	Businesses[1]	Government[1,2]	Higher education institutions
United Kingdom	12,336	1,829	4,035	1.4	0.2	0.5
North East	119	4	142	0.4	0.0	0.5
North West	1,512	66	322	1.7	0.1	0.4
Yorkshire and the Humber	298	50	317	0.5	0.1	0.5
East Midlands	951	68	224	1.7	0.1	0.4
West Midlands	662	65	207	1.0	0.1	0.3
East	2,916	277	366	3.4	0.3	0.4
London	738	238	980	0.5	0.2	0.7
South East	3,317	515	562	2.4	0.4	0.4
South West	1,025	254	178	1.6	0.4	0.3
England	11,538	1,537	3,297	1.6	0.2	0.5
Wales	136	49	155	0.4	0.1	0.5
Scotland	512	226	510	0.7	0.3	0.7
Northern Ireland	150	16	73	0.8	0.1	0.4

1 See Notes and Definitions.
2 Figures include estimates of NHS and local authorities' research and development and estimates for those areas in Central Government not available from the Government Survey and local authorities.

Source: Office for National Statistics

Table 13.10 Government expenditure on regional preferential assistance to industry

£ million

	1992/93	1993/94	1994/95	1995/96	1996/97	1997/98	1998/99	1999/2000	2000/01	2001/02
Great Britain[1]	364.0	394.4	368.9	343.0	371.1	430.4	393.8	335.0	383.3	357.4
North East	48.3	52.7	38.4	46.4	24.3	38.1	22.3	18.1	25.8	36.2
North West	36.8	40.3	32.4	24.3	23.2	19.4	25.9	25.0	29.5	32.1
Yorkshire and the Humber	13.7	35.6	23.0	19.7	11.1	12.7	11.9	9.8	9.1	7.7
East Midlands	1.2	1.9	5.2	7.3	10.5	10.5	7.1	4.0	5.8	7.3
West Midlands	10.8	14.4	14.7	14.2	25.5	29.8	30.6	20.5	35.8	12.0
East	..	..	0.7	2.1	1.5	2.2	0.7	0.5	0.9	0.9
London	..	..	0.6	1.7	2.9	2.7	3.2	2.3	1.3	1.2
South East	..	..	0.9	4.2	4.1	5.4	3.3	5.0	4.1	4.3
South West	8.2	9.5	9.4	7.7	7.4	4.5	9.4	4.1	4.0	6.5
England[2]	119.0	154.4	125.3	127.6	110.5	125.3	114.4	89.3	116.3	108.2
Wales	104.4	121.2	134.4	117.4	128.2	172.6	153.9	107.8	108.3	122.5
Scotland	140.6	118.8	109.2	98.0	132.4	132.5	125.5	137.9	158.7	126.7
Northern Ireland	105.6	117.6	132.9	131.2	137.1	156.1	153.3	133.0	132.5	130.8

1 The system of assistance available in Northern Ireland is not comparable with that operating in Great Britain, and thus UK figures are not produced. See Notes and Definitions.
2 Payments for European Regional Incentives, General Consultancy Contracts and Regional Selective Assistance Payments to the European Commission are not included.

Source: Department of Trade and Industry; Department of Economic Development, Northern Ireland

Table 13.11 Allocation of EU Structural Funds[1]

£ million at 1999 prices

	Objective 1[2]			Objective 2[2]			Objectives 1 and 2		
	2001	2002	2003	2001	2002	2003	2001	2002	2003
United Kingdom	621	587	498	505	460	480	1,126	1,047	978
North East	..	..	..	70	66	71	70	66	71
North West	132	120	86	87	78	80	219	198	166
Yorkshire and the Humber	116	106	75	53	49	51	169	155	126
East Midlands	..	..	..	38	36	37	38	36	37
West Midlands	..	..	..	89	81	85	89	81	85
East	..	..	..	16	15	15	16	15	15
London	..	..	..	25	23	26	25	23	26
South East	..	..	..	4	4	4	4	4	4
South West	49	45	29	19	17	19	68	62	48
England	297	271	190	401	369	388	698	640	578
Wales	184	167	178	14	12	12	198	179	190
Scotland	36	39	33	90	79	80	126	118	113
Northern Ireland	104	110	97	..	..	..	104	110	97

1 Only allocations resulting from the Commission's Single Programming Documents are shown. Allocations resulting from Community Initiatives, the value of which is about 8 per cent of the total Objective 1 and 2 allocations, are not included because not all of these can be allocated to the Government Office Regions in the table.
2 See Notes and Definitions for further information.

Source: Department of Trade and Industry

Table **13.12** Business registrations and deregistrations[1]

Thousands and rates

	2001						2002					
	Regist-rations	Deregist-rations	Net change	End-year stock	Regist-ration rates[2]	Deregist-ration rates[2]	Regist-rations	Deregist-rations	Net change	End-year stock	Regist-ration rates[2]	Deregist-ration rates[2]
United Kingdom	174.6	167.2	7.4	1,762.4	37	35	175.8	176.0	−0.2	1,762.1	37	37
North East	4.1	4.4	-0.3	43.7	20	22	4.2	4.1	0.1	43.8	21	20
North West	17.4	16.6	0.9	169.9	33	31	17.6	17.8	−0.2	169.7	33	33
Yorkshire and the Humber	11.7	12.0	-0.4	124.6	30	30	12.1	12.3	−0.2	124.4	31	31
East Midlands	11.4	10.8	0.6	119.5	34	32	12.1	11.1	1.0	120.5	36	33
West Midlands	14.1	13.4	0.6	146.2	34	32	14.3	14.2	0.1	146.3	34	34
East	17.3	16.9	0.4	177.4	40	39	17.7	17.2	0.5	177.9	41	40
London	34.4	32.6	1.8	282.9	59	56	33.5	35.6	−2.1	280.8	57	60
South East	28.5	25.5	3.1	277.5	44	40	28.5	27.4	1.1	278.7	44	42
South West	14.6	14.2	0.4	163.8	36	35	15.0	15.3	−0.3	163.5	37	38
England	153.5	146.4	7.2	1,505.6	39	37	154.9	154.9	−0.1	1,505.5	39	39
Wales	6.0	6.0	0.0	77.0	26	26	6.1	6.8	−0.7	76.3	26	29
Scotland	11.5	11.3	0.2	124.0	28	28	11.4	11.1	0.2	124.2	28	27
Northern Ireland	3.6	3.5	0.1	55.8	28	27	3.5	3.2	0.3	56.1	27	24

1 Enterprises registered for VAT. See Notes and Definitions.
2 Registrations and deregistrations during the year per 10,000 of the resident adult population. Each year's rate is based on the same year's mid-year population figure.

Source: Small Business Service

Table **13.13** Business survival rates[1]

Percentages

	The percentage of businesses surviving the stated number of months after year of registration								
	12 months				24 months			36 months	
	1997	1998	1999	2000	1997	1998	1999	1997	1998
United Kingdom	88.7	88.9	89.6	91.4	75.9	75.5	77.2	64.4	64.0
North East	88.8	88.6	89.1	91.2	74.5	75.2	75.6	63.5	64.0
North West	86.3	87.1	88.4	90.6	72.3	73.8	75.7	61.0	62.8
Yorkshire and the Humber	88.1	89.1	88.9	90.9	75.0	74.5	76.1	63.7	62.4
East Midlands	88.4	88.4	89.4	90.1	75.5	74.8	76.7	63.8	63.7
West Midlands	87.2	88.0	88.8	91.1	73.9	74.5	75.9	62.9	63.7
East	90.7	90.7	90.9	91.3	78.6	77.9	78.3	66.8	66.6
London	88.1	88.2	89.2	91.6	74.2	73.3	76.1	61.3	60.3
South East	90.6	90.7	91.3	92.7	78.9	78.5	79.9	68.0	67.5
South West	90.3	89.4	90.3	91.9	78.1	77.1	78.2	67.4	66.5
England	88.8	89.0	89.7	91.4	75.9	75.5	77.2	64.3	64.0
Wales	87.9	87.3	88.5	90.4	75.2	74.2	76.8	64.3	63.9
Scotland	87.3	88.0	87.9	91.1	74.2	74.2	75.8	63.6	62.6
Northern Ireland	90.3	89.4	91.1	93.8	81.2	79.1	82.4	72.4	70.8

1 Provisional.

Source: Small Business Service

Table 13.14 Construction: value at current prices of contractors' output[1]

£ million and percentages

	Total work (£ million)						Of which new work (percentages)[2]					
	1997	1998	1999	2000	2001	2002[3]	1997	1998	1999	2000	2001	2002[3]
Great Britain	55,220	59,027	62,858	66,624	71,992	81,074	53.9	54.8	56.4	56.3	55.3	56.0
North East	2,132	2,336	2,374	2,309	2,310	2,811	59.2	59.7	63.3	58.8	58.1	58.0
North West	6,061	6,336	6,614	6,833	7,035	8,189	53.4	53.6	56.1	56.9	54.9	58.0
Yorkshire and the Humber	4,555	4,833	5,295	5,276	5,386	6,380	51.1	52.8	54.3	56.9	55.2	54.0
East Midlands	4,213	4,382	4,513	4,263	4,300	5,382	58.0	58.2	59.3	58.1	55.7	55.0
West Midlands	4,773	5,248	5,459	6,377	7,051	7,633	51.6	54.2	57.0	58.4	54.7	53.0
East	5,222	5,422	5,825	6,427	7,378	8,245	48.6	47.8	47.9	52.4	52.9	54.0
London	7,957	8,954	9,675	10,260	12,115	13,524	59.3	60.4	61.9	57.6	61.0	62.0
South East	8,178	8,833	9,846	10,728	11,517	12,032	49.0	50.4	51.5	50.4	49.9	49.0
South West	4,398	4,719	4,975	5,195	5,875	7,280	48.9	50.2	51.9	54.0	51.8	54.0
England	47,490	51,063	54,576	57,667	62,967	71,477	53.0	54.0	55.5	55.2	54.8	55.0
Wales	2,539	2,641	2,631	2,541	2,488	2,915	58.7	59.0	61.7	59.8	57.9	59.0
Scotland	5,191	5,323	5,651	6,416	6,537	6,682	60.4	60.3	62.5	63.9	59.2	61.0

1 Output of contractors, including estimates of unrecorded output by small firms and self-employed workers, classified to construction in Standard Industrial Classification 1992.
2 For new work, figures relate to the region in which the site is located; for repair and maintenance, figures are for the region in which the reporting unit is based.
3 Data for 2002 are provisional.

Source: Construction Market intelligence, Department of Trade and Industry

Table 13.15 Tourism, 1996 and 2002

Millions and £ million

	1996				2002			
	UK residents[1]		Overseas residents[2]		UK residents[1]		Overseas residents[2]	
	Number of trips (millions)	Expenditure (£ million)	Number of visits (millions)	Expenditure (£ million)	Number of trips (millions)	Expenditure (£ million)	Number of visits (millions)	Expenditure (£ million)
Tourist Board Regions[3]								
United Kingdom	154.2	22,041	25.2	12,290	167.3	26,699	24.2	11,618
Northumbria	3.7	402	0.4	158	4.8	868	0.5	169
Cumbria	3.7	503	0.3	58	4.3	728	0.2	41
North West	11.9	1,632	1.2	381	14.5	2,316	1.4	466
Yorkshire	11.9	1,713	1.0	280	12.2	1,595	0.9	303
East of England	15.8	1,860	1.4	473	14.5	1,704	1.7	616
Heart of England	18.9	2,164	1.9	632	24.6	3,166	2.6	881
London	12.9	1,633	12.3	6,007	16.1	2,818	11.6	5,788
Southern	11.5	1,586	1.9	739	14.6	2,065	2.0	841
South East England	11.9	1,240	2.3	699	10.9	1,355	2.0	663
South West	17.5	3,029	1.7	570	21.0	3,901	1.8	740
England	117.3	15,763	19.5	10,016	134.9	20,787	20.5	10,313
Wales	13.6	1,781	0.8	198	11.9	1,543	0.9	252
Scotland	19.6	3,276	1.8	839	18.5	3,683	1.6	806
Northern Ireland	3.8	698	0.1	46	2.8	525	0.3	126

1 The United Kingdom figures include the value of tourism in the Channel Islands, the Isle of Man, and a small amount where the region was unknown.
2 The expenditure in this table excludes spending of overseas visitors departing directly from the Channel Islands and that of nil nights transit visitors.
3 For information on Tourist Board boundaries see map at start of Notes and Definitions.

Source: United Kingdom Tourism Survey, sponsored by the National Tourist Boards; International Passenger Survey, Office for National Statistics

Map **13.16**

Percentage of gross value added[1] derived from agriculture[2], 2000

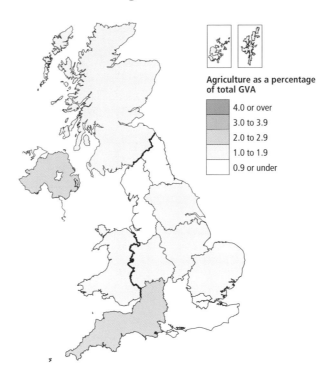

Agriculture as a percentage
of total GVA

- 4.0 or over
- 3.0 to 3.9
- 2.0 to 2.9
- 1.0 to 1.9
- 0.9 or under

1 Current basic prices. See Notes and Definitions.
2 "Agriculture" is defined as Agriculture, hunting, forestry and fishing.

Source: Office for National Statistics

Map **13.17**

Agricultural enterprises as a percentage of total enterprises,[1,2] 2002

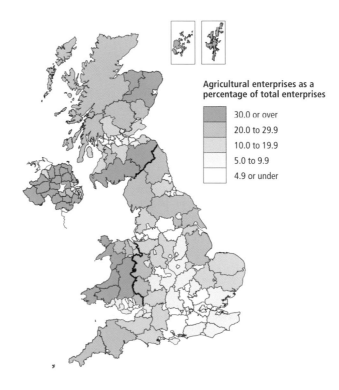

Agricultural enterprises as a
percentage of total enterprises

- 30.0 or over
- 20.0 to 29.9
- 10.0 to 19.9
- 5.0 to 9.9
- 4.9 or under

1 The figures include only those enterprises that are registered for VAT. Some smaller holdings will therefore not be included.
  See Notes and Definitions.
2 Geographic boundaries relate to the sub-regions (Counties/Unitary Authorities) in existence on 1 April 1998.

Source: Inter-Departmental Business Register, Office for National Statistics

Table **13.18** Agricultural holdings[1]: by area of crops and grass, and by land use, June 2002

Percentages and numbers

	None[2]	Under 10 hectares	10-49.9 hectares	50 hectares or over	Total holdings (=100%) (numbers)	Arable land[3]	Grass five years old and over (including sole right rough grazing)	Set-aside land	Other land on agri-cultural holdings including Woodland[4]	Total area on agri-cultural holdings (=100%) (thousand hectares)
United Kingdom	16.7	34.6	25.6	23.1	303,046	34.0	57.7	3.6	4.7	17,154
North East	17.3	27.4	19.6	35.7	6,321	30.9	61.2	4.1	3.8	582
North West	20.5	33.5	24.3	21.7	22,133	22.2	73.6	1.3	2.9	884
Yorkshire and the Humber	18.3	34.1	21.9	25.7	20,870	51.4	39.6	5.6	3.3	1,093
East Midlands	17.7	32.2	22.2	27.9	20,023	64.7	24.1	7.7	3.5	1,220
West Midlands	18.9	36.4	23.2	21.4	24,725	49.7	41.0	4.9	4.4	928
East	17.4	35.4	18.7	28.4	21,882	73.2	11.9	8.6	6.4	1,471
London	21.6	45.1	19.9	13.3	472	43.6	40.8	7.6	8.0	12
South East	19.5	38.9	21.5	20.2	23,972	52.6	31.0	7.6	8.8	1,143
South West	20.7	35.9	23.2	20.2	47,473	39.4	51.6	3.8	5.3	1,766
England	19.2	35.1	22.2	23.4	187,871	50.2	39.1	5.7	5.0	9,099
Wales	15.5	34.0	26.3	24.2	36,473	13.4	82.5	0.3	3.8	1,452
Scotland	17.1	39.4	20.1	23.4	50,189	16.0	77.5	1.5	5.0	5,536
Northern Ireland	1.3	23.7	56.5	18.5	28,513	17.7	80.5	0.3	1.5	1,067

1 Includes estimates for minor holdings and set-aside land. See Notes and Definitions.
2 These holdings have either a zero farmed area at present or consist only of rough grazing, woodland or other land.
3 Crops, bare fallow and all grass under five years old.
4 In Great Britain this includes farm roads, yards, buildings (except glasshouses), ponds and derelict land. In Northern Ireland it includes land under bog, water, roads, buildings etc and wasteland not used for agriculture.

Source: Department for Environment, Food and Rural Affairs; The Scottish Executive Rural Affairs Department; Department of Agriculture and Rural Development in Northern Ireland

Table **13.19** Agricultural holdings by farm type, June 2002

Percentages and numbers

	Cereals	General cropping	Horti-culture	Pigs and poultry	Dairy	Cattle and sheep (LFA[1])	Cattle and sheep (low-ground)	Mixed	Other	Total holdings (=100%) (numbers)
United Kingdom	8.5	4.1	3.7	3.0	7.8	18.3	14.4	4.7	35.6	303,046
North East	14.7	1.9	1.8	2.7	3.6	24.1	11.5	7.9	31.8	6,321
North West	2.6	2.5	3.9	3.2	15.2	14.9	15.4	3.2	39.3	22,133
Yorkshire and the Humber	14.1	7.0	3.0	5.2	6.2	12.2	12.3	6.3	33.6	20,870
East Midlands	19.5	8.4	4.3	3.6	5.5	4.5	15.0	5.8	33.2	20,023
West Midlands	7.4	4.5	4.9	3.1	8.8	5.6	22.1	6.6	37.0	24,725
East	24.8	14.6	7.2	5.4	1.0	0.0	9.4	4.6	33.1	21,882
London	9.3	3.6	15.7	4.0	1.5	0.0	11.2	4.0	50.6	472
South East	12.4	2.1	8.2	3.6	3.0	0.0	21.7	5.8	43.3	23,972
South West	5.6	1.1	4.7	3.2	11.0	4.4	23.8	5.4	40.8	47,473
England	11.3	4.9	5.1	3.7	7.6	6.3	18.0	5.5	37.7	187,871
Wales	0.8	0.3	1.4	1.7	8.7	35.1	10.0	1.9	40.0	36,473
Scotland	7.3	5.3	1.4	2.1	3.3	30.2	3.0	4.5	42.8	50,189
Northern Ireland	1.7	1.1	1.2	1.8	16.1	54.8	16.4	3.5	3.4	28,513

1 Less favoured areas. See Notes and Definitions.

Source: Department for Environment, Food and Rural Affairs; National Assembly for Wales; The Scottish Executive Rural Affairs Department; Department of Agriculture and Rural Development for Northern Ireland

Table 13.20 Areas and estimated yields of selected crops[1], 2001 and 2002

Thousand hectares and tonnes per hectare

| | Area (thousand hectares) | | | | | | Estimated yields (tonnes per hectare) | | | | | |
| | Wheat | | Barley | | Rape (for oilseed)[2] | | Wheat | | Barley | | Rape (for oilseed)[2] | |
	2001	2002	2001	2002	2001	2002	2001	2002	2001	2002	2001	2002
United Kingdom	1,635	1,996	1,245	1,101	404	357	7.1	8.0	5.4	5.6	2.6	3.5
North East	58	70	47	43	20	18	6.8	8.1	4.9	6.3	..	..
North West	21	27	50	38	4	3	5.1	6.8	4.6	4.9	..	..
Yorkshire and the Humber	201	247	135	120	46	41	7.6	8.5	5.8	6.4	..	..
East Midlands	317	387	104	94	86	81	7.0	8.3	5.5	6.0	..	..
West Midlands	129	163	77	66	28	23	6.4	7.5	4.7	6.0	..	..
East	440	528	185	166	78	75	7.3	8.2	5.4	6.0	..	..
London	2	2	1	1	1	0	..	..	..	..	..	..
South East	211	257	104	82	69	56	6.9	8.0	5.2	5.8	..	..
South West	163	194	145	114	36	27	6.8	7.5	5.2	5.3	..	..
England	1,540	1,876	848	722	367	325	7.1	8.1	5.3	5.9	2.5	3.5
Wales	11	15	27	25	14	1	6.3	7.3	4.7	4.9	..	..
Scotland	80	97	337	325	35	31	7.7	7.6	5.7	5.2	3.0	3.4
Northern Ireland	4	7	33	28	-	-	6.2	6.5	5.1	3.9	..	..

1 Regional Figures do not include minor holdings. Therefore they may not add up to the country and UK totals.
2 Excludes crops grown on set-aside scheme land. See Notes and Definitions.

Source: Department for Environment, Food and Rural Affairs; National Assembly for Wales; The Scottish Executive Rural Affairs Department; Department of Agriculture and Rural Development for Northern Ireland

Table 13.21 Livestock on agricultural holdings[1], June 2002

Thousands

| | Cattle and calves | | | Sheep and lambs | Pigs | Poultry | | Total poultry |
	Total herd[2]	Dairy cows	Beef cows			Total fowls[3]	Total laying flock[4]	
United Kingdom	10,345	2,227	1,657	35,834	5,588	155,005	28,778	169,449
North East	285	23	74	1,931	78	1,727	264	1,818
North West	934	316	79	2,733	191	8,985	1,924	9,805
Yorkshire and the Humber	558	116	78	2,086	1,441	12,894	1,649	15,531
East Midlands	523	115	68	1,312	461	22,372	4,756	23,736
West Midlands	759	215	81	2,306	266	16,716	3,257	18,167
East	231	37	42	362	1,280	23,144	2,513	28,782
London	4	1	1	3	3	266	31	274
South East	481	112	69	1,429	384	12,864	3,734	13,455
South West	1,755	527	174	3,235	526	18,349	4,973	19,404
England	5,531	1,462	665	15,397	4,630	117,318	23,100	130,971
Wales	1,195	268	196	10,050	44	5,828	930	6,072
Scotland	1,935	199	489	8,063	526	15,446	2,648	15,544
Northern Ireland	1,684	298	307	2,324	388	16,413	2,099	16,862

1 Regional figures include minor holdings. See Notes and Definitions.
2 Includes bulls, in-calf heifers and fattening cattle and calves.
3 Excludes ducks, geese and turkeys.
4 Excludes growing pullets (from day-old to point of lay).

Source: Department for Environment, Food and Rural Affairs, National Assembly for Wales; The Scottish Executive Rural Affairs Department; Department of Agriculture and Rural Development for Northern Ireland

Chapter 14 Sub-regions of England

Government Office Regions, Counties and Unitary Authorities in England[1]

1 Hartlepool
2 Middlesbrough
3 Redcar and Cleveland
4 Stockton-on-Tees
5 Darlington
6 Halton
7 Warrington
8 Blackburn with Darwen
9 Blackpool
10 East Riding of Yorkshire
11 City of Kingston upon Hull
12 North East Lincolnshire
13 North Lincolnshire
14 York
15 Derby
16 Leicester
17 Rutland
18 Nottingham
19 County of Herefordshire
20 Telford and Wrekin
21 Stoke-on-Trent
22 Luton
23 Peterborough
24 Southend-on-Sea
25 Thurrock
26 Bracknell Forest
27 Reading
28 Slough
29 West Berkshire (Newbury)
30 Windsor and Maidenhead
31 Wokingham
32 Milton Keynes
33 Brighton and Hove
34 Portsmouth
35 Southampton
36 Isle of Wight
37 Medway
38 Bath and North
   East Somerset
39 City of Bristol
40 North Somerset
41 South Gloucestershire
42 Plymouth
43 Torbay
44 Bournemouth
45 Poole
46 Swindon

Table **14.1**   Area and population: by local authority[1], 2002[2]

	Area (sq km)	People per sq km	Population (thousands) Males	Females	Total	Total population percentage change 1982-2002	Total fertility rate (TFR)[3]	Standardised mortality ratio (UK=100) (SMR)[4]	Percentage of population aged: Under 5	5 to 15	16 up to pension age[5]	Pension age[5] or over
United Kingdom	242,514	244	28,911	30,318	59,229	5.2	1.63	100	5.8	14.1	61.7	18.4
England	130,281	380	24,240	25,319	49,559	5.9	1.64	98	5.8	14.1	61.8	18.4
North East	8,573	293	1,219	1,294	2,513	-4.2	1.58	111	5.3	14.1	61.3	19.3
Darlington UA	197	496	47	51	98	-0.8	1.76	114	5.8	14.3	60.3	19.6
Hartlepool UA	94	940	42	46	88	-6.2	1.87	119	5.8	15.6	59.5	19.1
Middlesbrough UA	54	2,485	65	69	134	-10.6	1.78	119	6.0	15.6	61.0	17.5
Redcar and Cleveland UA	245	569	67	72	139	-7.3	1.70	105	5.3	14.8	60.0	19.9
Stockton-on-Tees UA	204	881	88	92	180	4.0	1.66	112	5.6	15.0	61.8	17.5
Durham	2,226	221	239	253	492	-3.2	1.50	110	5.1	13.7	61.7	19.5
Chester-le-Street	68	788	26	27	53	2.8	1.54	103	5.3	13.7	62.3	18.7
Derwentside	271	314	41	44	85	-2.7	1.67	115	5.2	13.8	60.6	20.3
Durham	187	470	43	45	88	-0.4	1.17	104	4.5	11.4	66.9	17.3
Easington	145	648	45	48	94	-6.7	1.60	113	5.4	14.8	59.6	20.1
Sedgefield	217	399	42	45	87	-6.1	1.71	115	5.4	14.4	60.9	19.3
Teesdale	836	29	12	12	25	0.1	1.47	97	4.3	13.0	60.2	22.5
Wear Valley	503	122	29	32	61	-4.2	1.74	109	5.3	14.1	59.9	20.7
Northumberland	5,013	62	150	158	308	3.0	1.65	102	5.0	13.6	60.7	20.7
Alnwick	1,080	29	15	16	31	8.9	1.75	83	5.0	12.8	59.1	23.1
Berwick-upon-Tweed	972	27	13	14	26	-0.6	1.39	92	4.4	12.6	57.5	25.6
Blyth Valley	70	1,160	40	42	82	4.9	1.67	111	5.5	14.2	62.9	17.3
Castle Morpeth	618	79	24	25	49	-2.2	1.57	95	4.6	13.1	59.6	22.7
Tynedale	2,206	27	29	30	59	9.4	1.70	98	4.9	14.0	60.0	21.1
Wansbeck	67	914	30	31	61	-2.2	1.66	119	5.2	13.4	61.3	20.1
Tyne and Wear (Met County)	540	1,988	521	553	1,074	-6.7	1.51	113	5.3	13.8	61.6	19.3
Gateshead	142	1,340	92	98	191	-9.8	1.62	116	5.5	13.6	60.6	20.3
Newcastle upon Tyne	113	2,294	127	133	260	-7.4	1.45	112	5.3	13.0	63.7	18.0
North Tyneside	82	2,321	92	99	191	-3.1	1.59	106	5.3	13.7	60.5	20.5
South Tyneside	64	2,365	74	79	152	-5.1	1.57	108	5.3	14.6	59.6	20.6
Sunderland	137	2,030	136	143	279	-7.1	1.51	121	5.3	14.3	62.1	18.4
North West	14,106	480	3,287	3,484	6,771	-2.0	1.66	109	5.7	14.6	61.0	18.6
Blackburn with Darwen UA	137	1,018	69	71	139	-2.3	2.21	113	7.5	17.5	59.8	15.2
Blackpool UA	35	4,065	69	73	142	-4.1	1.66	118	5.2	13.5	58.7	22.6
Halton UA	79	1,494	57	61	118	-4.3	1.81	122	6.0	15.3	62.7	16.0
Warrington UA	181	1,064	94	98	192	11.8	1.67	107	5.9	14.7	62.4	16.9
Cheshire	2,083	324	329	347	676	6.1	1.59	97	5.4	14.0	60.9	19.7
Chester	448	265	57	62	119	1.6	1.47	94	5.2	12.9	61.7	20.2
Congleton	211	432	45	46	91	13.4	1.46	95	5.3	13.7	62.1	19.0
Crewe and Nantwich	430	259	55	57	112	13.3	1.71	106	5.7	14.7	60.6	19.1
Ellesmere Port and Neston	88	920	40	42	81	-1.2	1.59	92	5.6	15.0	59.9	19.5
Macclesfield	525	285	72	77	150	1.3	1.54	94	5.2	13.5	60.0	21.3
Vale Royal	380	324	60	63	123	10.8	1.78	100	5.7	14.8	61.1	18.4
Cumbria	6,768	72	238	250	489	1.3	1.61	100	5.0	13.6	59.9	21.5
Allerdale	1,242	75	46	48	94	-1.9	1.66	106	5.0	13.8	59.8	21.4
Barrow-in-Furness	78	919	35	37	72	-3.3	1.78	105	5.5	15.0	59.7	19.8
Carlisle	1,040	97	49	52	101	0.4	1.44	107	5.0	13.5	60.8	20.7
Copeland	732	95	34	35	69	-5.0	1.62	102	5.1	14.2	61.0	19.7
Eden	2,142	23	25	25	50	16.0	1.67	85	5.0	13.0	60.0	22.1
South Lakeland	1,534	67	50	53	103	7.4	1.56	91	4.6	12.6	58.4	24.4
Greater Manchester (Met County)	1,276	1,970	1,229	1,285	2,513	-3.3	1.69	113	6.0	14.8	61.9	17.3
Bolton	140	1,871	127	134	262	0.1	1.86	107	6.2	15.2	61.2	17.4
Bury	99	1,823	88	93	181	3.1	1.75	108	6.0	15.3	61.2	17.4
Manchester	116	3,652	208	214	422	-7.0	1.52	125	6.0	14.0	65.1	14.9
Oldham	142	1,535	107	112	219	-0.7	2.11	110	6.8	15.9	60.6	16.7
Rochdale	158	1,305	101	106	206	-0.1	1.89	116	6.4	16.0	61.0	16.6
Salford	97	2,224	107	109	216	-12.6	1.67	120	5.6	14.2	61.7	18.5
Stockport	126	2,246	137	146	283	-2.7	1.56	99	5.6	14.5	60.6	19.3
Tameside	103	2,063	103	110	213	-1.7	1.75	116	5.9	15.3	61.4	17.5
Trafford	106	1,978	102	108	210	-5.0	1.64	99	5.7	14.3	61.3	18.7
Wigan	188	1,603	148	154	302	-1.2	1.63	123	5.6	14.6	62.5	17.2

Table **14.1** (continued)

	Area (sq km)	People per sq km	Population (thousands) Males	Females	Total	Total population percentage change 1982-2002	Total fertility rate (TFR)[3]	Standardised mortality ratio (UK=100) (SMR)[4]	Percentage of population aged: Under 5	5 to 15	16 up to pension age[5]	Pension age[5] or over
Lancashire	2,903	393	554	587	1,141	4.3	1.67	105	5.5	14.6	60.5	19.4
Burnley	111	804	43	46	89	−3.3	1.83	109	6.2	16.3	59.9	17.7
Chorley	203	500	50	51	101	9.5	1.60	107	5.4	14.1	63.6	17.0
Fylde	166	447	36	38	74	8.5	1.67	97	4.7	12.6	57.0	25.8
Hyndburn	73	1,121	40	42	82	3.2	1.96	113	6.4	16.1	59.8	17.7
Lancaster	576	232	64	70	134	6.0	1.40	101	5.1	13.3	61.1	20.5
Pendle	169	533	44	46	90	4.8	1.94	104	6.4	15.8	60.1	17.7
Preston	142	914	64	66	130	2.6	1.67	116	5.8	14.4	62.9	16.8
Ribble Valley	583	94	27	28	55	1.7	1.57	97	5.2	14.4	60.3	20.1
Rossendale	138	477	32	34	66	1.2	1.83	115	6.0	16.1	61.3	16.6
South Ribble	113	926	51	53	105	8.1	1.71	101	5.4	14.6	61.6	18.4
West Lancashire	347	313	52	56	109	0.0	1.65	110	5.5	14.5	61.2	18.9
Wyre	283	378	51	56	107	8.4	1.60	94	4.8	13.5	56.0	25.7
Merseyside (Met County)	645	2,110	649	712	1,361	−9.9	1.57	115	5.4	14.8	60.4	19.4
Knowsley	86	1,745	72	79	151	−12.4	1.73	122	6.0	16.2	60.3	17.5
Liverpool	112	3,947	213	229	441	−13.7	1.47	127	5.4	14.0	63.1	17.5
St. Helens	136	1,296	86	91	177	−6.6	1.60	116	5.5	15.0	60.8	18.6
Sefton	153	1,840	133	149	282	−5.4	1.58	108	5.0	14.9	58.0	22.1
Wirral	157	1,975	146	164	310	−8.5	1.74	106	5.5	14.9	58.5	21.0
Yorkshire and the Humber	15,408	323	2,424	2,559	4,983	1.5	1.67	101	5.7	14.5	61.1	18.7
East Riding of Yorkshire UA	2,408	132	155	163	318	16.6	1.60	93	5.0	13.6	59.7	21.7
Kingston upon Hull, City of UA	71	3,379	118	123	241	−11.4	1.62	111	5.9	15.3	61.3	17.6
North East Lincolnshire UA	192	824	77	81	158	−2.0	1.71	101	5.8	15.9	58.9	19.4
North Lincolnshire UA	846	182	75	79	154	2.1	1.79	101	5.5	14.5	60.2	19.8
York UA	272	670	88	95	182	9.7	1.36	94	5.0	12.1	63.4	19.5
North Yorkshire	8,038	71	280	293	573	12.2	1.64	90	5.1	14.0	59.7	21.3
Craven	1,177	46	26	28	54	12.5	1.59	88	4.8	13.9	57.8	23.5
Hambleton	1,311	65	42	43	85	12.8	1.70	87	5.0	13.9	60.3	20.8
Harrogate	1,308	115	73	77	151	10.5	1.58	89	5.2	13.9	60.3	20.6
Richmondshire	1,319	36	25	23	48	10.4	1.87	95	6.1	13.5	62.6	17.8
Ryedale	1,507	34	25	26	51	17.5	1.51	79	4.7	13.9	57.7	23.8
Scarborough	817	131	51	56	107	4.8	1.60	93	4.6	13.4	57.3	24.7
Selby	599	130	38	40	78	24.5	1.67	99	5.4	15.3	62.1	17.2
South Yorkshire (Met County)	1,552	817	618	649	1,267	−3.4	1.63	105	5.6	14.2	61.3	18.8
Barnsley	329	662	106	112	218	−3.5	1.64	112	5.6	14.5	61.0	18.9
Doncaster	568	506	141	147	288	−0.2	1.85	105	5.8	14.8	60.3	19.2
Rotherham	287	871	121	128	249	−1.5	1.74	104	5.8	14.9	60.8	18.4
Sheffield	368	1,392	250	262	512	−6.0	1.53	101	5.5	13.4	62.3	18.9
West Yorkshire (Met County)	2,029	1,030	1,013	1,076	2,089	1.4	1.73	104	6.1	14.9	61.6	17.4
Bradford	366	1,292	230	243	473	2.1	2.18	109	7.1	15.9	60.5	16.5
Calderdale	364	531	94	100	193	1.1	1.85	102	6.1	15.0	60.8	18.1
Kirklees	409	953	189	200	389	3.2	1.87	107	6.5	15.1	61.5	17.0
Leeds	552	1,299	346	370	717	0.2	1.44	99	5.5	14.1	62.7	17.7
Wakefield	339	934	154	163	316	0.9	1.59	110	5.5	14.6	61.7	18.1
East Midlands	15,607	270	2,074	2,141	4,215	9.5	1.61	99	5.6	14.2	61.6	18.6
Derby UA	78	2,861	110	113	223	3.4	1.75	101	6.0	14.6	61.0	18.4
Leicester UA	73	3,868	138	145	284	0.3	1.72	110	6.7	14.9	63.3	15.2
Nottingham UA	75	3,619	136	134	270	−2.9	1.48	115	5.6	13.4	65.0	16.0
Rutland UA	382	91	18	17	35	5.1	1.67	78	5.3	14.9	59.8	20.0
Derbyshire	2,547	290	363	376	739	6.4	1.61	101	5.4	14.1	61.1	19.5
Amber Valley	265	441	57	60	117	7.8	1.64	97	5.4	14.0	61.2	19.3
Bolsover	160	452	36	37	72	2.4	1.70	106	5.3	14.3	60.5	19.8
Chesterfield	66	1,500	48	51	99	1.3	1.49	107	5.3	13.8	60.6	20.3
Derbyshire Dales	792	88	34	35	69	2.6	1.68	97	4.9	13.1	59.7	22.3
Erewash	110	1,009	54	56	111	6.8	1.61	102	5.5	14.6	61.5	18.4
High Peak	539	166	44	46	90	9.4	1.60	94	5.7	14.6	61.4	18.2
North East Derbyshire	276	352	48	49	97	0.9	1.52	100	4.7	13.5	60.7	21.1
South Derbyshire	338	248	42	42	84	22.5	1.66	104	5.9	14.7	62.6	16.8

Table **14.1** (continued)

	Area (sq km)	People per sq km	Population (thousands)			Total population percentage change 1982-2002	Total fertility rate (TFR)[3]	Standardised mortality ratio (UK=100) (SMR)[4]	Percentage of population aged:			
			Males	Females	Total				Under 5	5 to 15	16 up to pension age[5]	Pension age[5] or over
Leicestershire	2,083	295	304	311	615	13.2	1.56	90	5.5	13.9	62.2	18.4
Blaby	130	702	45	46	92	18.9	1.55	76	5.6	14.2	61.9	18.2
Charnwood	279	550	76	77	153	9.5	1.48	96	5.2	13.6	63.8	17.3
Harborough	592	132	39	39	78	27.1	1.70	92	5.9	14.2	61.6	18.3
Hinckley and Bosworth	297	339	49	51	101	13.2	1.57	90	5.4	13.5	62.2	18.9
Melton	481	100	24	25	48	10.1	1.53	91	5.5	14.1	61.6	18.7
North West Leicestershire	279	310	43	44	87	9.4	1.72	93	5.8	13.8	61.8	18.6
Oadby and Wigston	24	2,411	28	29	57	6.8	1.46	85	5.0	14.5	60.6	19.9
Lincolnshire	5,921	111	322	336	658	19.2	1.61	96	5.1	13.8	59.2	21.9
Boston	362	157	28	29	57	7.7	1.75	99	5.2	13.4	58.8	22.7
East Lindsey	1,760	75	65	67	133	25.7	1.63	96	4.5	12.8	56.8	26.0
Lincoln	36	2,408	42	44	86	11.9	1.46	98	5.7	13.9	62.9	17.5
North Kesteven	922	105	47	49	97	22.4	1.64	96	5.2	14.1	59.3	21.4
South Holland	742	107	39	41	79	27.1	1.67	99	4.9	13.0	57.4	24.8
South Kesteven	943	133	61	64	126	26.9	1.68	89	5.4	14.8	60.5	19.3
West Lindsey	1,156	70	40	41	81	5.7	1.57	97	4.9	14.7	59.0	21.4
Northamptonshire	2,364	270	315	323	638	18.9	1.74	94	6.0	14.9	62.5	16.6
Corby	80	669	26	27	54	2.8	1.88	109	5.9	16.2	61.3	16.6
Daventry	663	111	37	37	74	25.9	1.75	94	5.9	15.6	62.6	16.0
East Northamptonshire	510	154	39	40	78	25.5	1.71	93	6.1	15.1	61.6	17.3
Kettering	233	355	41	42	83	15.8	1.79	90	6.0	14.5	61.7	17.9
Northampton	81	2,404	95	99	194	20.0	1.68	96	6.2	14.4	63.6	15.9
South Northamptonshire	634	129	41	41	82	25.0	1.75	84	6.1	15.2	62.7	16.1
Wellingborough	163	453	37	37	74	14.2	1.78	93	6.0	14.9	61.8	17.3
Nottinghamshire	2,085	361	368	385	753	5.7	1.54	101	5.3	14.2	61.3	19.2
Ashfield	110	1,043	56	59	114	8.0	1.56	112	5.6	14.3	62.0	18.1
Bassetlaw	638	170	54	55	108	5.6	1.64	108	5.3	14.4	61.2	19.1
Broxtowe	80	1,345	53	55	108	3.8	1.39	98	5.0	13.6	62.3	19.2
Gedling	120	933	54	58	112	3.7	1.47	88	5.1	13.7	61.4	19.8
Mansfield	77	1,278	48	50	98	−1.3	1.58	107	5.2	15.2	60.5	19.1
Newark and Sherwood	651	164	52	55	107	6.2	1.73	103	5.4	14.5	59.8	20.3
Rushcliffe	409	259	52	54	106	14.9	1.44	95	5.5	13.9	61.8	18.8
West Midlands	12,998	408	2,602	2,702	5,304	2.4	1.74	101	5.9	14.6	60.9	18.6
Herefordshire, County of UA	2,180	81	86	90	176	17.6	1.63	88	5.2	13.9	58.5	22.4
Stoke-on-Trent UA	93	2,553	116	122	239	−5.1	1.63	110	5.6	14.0	61.6	18.8
Telford and Wrekin UA	290	553	79	82	161	27.1	1.71	105	6.4	15.6	63.0	15.0
Shropshire	3,197	89	141	144	285	12.2	1.62	93	5.2	13.8	59.8	21.3
Bridgnorth	633	83	27	26	52	5.2	1.45	97	4.6	12.8	62.1	20.5
North Shropshire	679	86	29	29	58	14.6	1.75	91	5.5	13.9	59.9	20.7
Oswestry	256	149	18	20	38	20.7	1.35	103	5.2	14.8	59.4	20.6
Shrewsbury and Atcham	602	159	47	49	95	8.6	1.70	88	5.4	14.3	59.9	20.4
South Shropshire	1,027	40	20	21	41	20.4	1.75	92	5.0	12.8	56.7	25.5
Staffordshire	2,620	309	396	412	809	5.7	1.59	102	5.4	14.1	61.8	18.7
Cannock Chase	79	1,182	46	47	93	9.0	1.66	103	6.1	14.9	62.6	16.4
East Staffordshire	387	270	51	54	104	9.0	1.87	113	6.1	15.2	60.4	18.4
Lichfield	331	281	46	48	93	4.7	1.54	104	5.2	14.1	61.6	19.1
Newcastle-under-Lyme	211	579	59	63	122	1.7	1.41	98	5.0	13.3	61.9	19.7
South Staffordshire	407	261	52	54	106	9.7	1.44	94	4.9	14.1	61.6	19.4
Stafford	598	201	59	61	120	3.2	1.53	97	5.0	13.2	61.8	20.0
Staffordshire Moorlands	576	165	47	48	95	−0.6	1.54	101	4.9	13.2	61.2	20.7
Tamworth	31	2,418	37	38	75	12.9	1.79	114	6.4	15.8	64.1	13.7
Warwickshire	1,975	260	252	261	513	7.4	1.60	97	5.5	13.8	61.8	18.9
North Warwickshire	284	221	31	32	63	5.0	1.65	106	5.2	14.0	63.0	17.7
Nuneaton and Bedworth	79	1,518	59	61	120	5.3	1.77	107	5.8	15.1	61.5	17.6
Rugby	351	253	44	45	89	2.1	1.74	96	5.9	14.2	61.3	18.6
Stratford-on-Avon	978	116	55	58	113	12.0	1.61	92	5.3	13.2	60.1	21.4
Warwick	283	453	63	65	128	10.7	1.35	90	5.3	12.7	63.3	18.8
West Midlands (Met County)	902	2,857	1,264	1,312	2,576	−3.7	1.85	104	6.3	15.2	60.5	18.0
Birmingham	268	3,697	485	505	990	−3.4	1.95	107	7.0	15.9	60.7	16.4
Coventry	99	3,089	153	152	305	−3.9	1.68	99	6.0	14.6	62.0	17.5
Dudley	98	3,112	150	155	305	1.2	1.70	101	5.6	14.2	60.5	19.7
Sandwell	86	3,329	139	146	285	−7.8	1.92	116	6.3	15.1	59.8	18.8
Solihull	178	1,119	97	103	200	0.2	1.63	89	5.4	15.3	59.6	19.6
Walsall	104	2,428	123	130	252	−5.2	1.98	102	6.4	15.2	59.2	19.2
Wolverhampton	69	3,447	118	121	239	−6.6	1.78	100	5.8	14.6	60.4	19.3

Table **14.1** (continued)

	Area (sq km)	People per sq km	Population (thousands)			Total population percentage change 1982-2002	Total fertility rate (TFR)[3]	Standardised mortality ratio (UK=100) (SMR)[4]	Percentage of population aged:			
			Males	Females	Total				Under 5	5 to 15	16 up to pension age[5]	Pension age[5] or over
Worcestershire	1,741	314	268	278	546	13.8	1.62	96	5.4	13.9	61.4	19.3
Bromsgrove	217	412	44	45	89	11.9	1.53	98	5.1	14.3	60.6	20.0
Malvern Hills	577	126	35	37	73	7.3	1.65	91	4.6	13.5	57.6	24.2
Redditch	54	1,459	39	40	79	14.9	1.74	98	6.2	15.0	64.4	14.5
Worcester	33	2,801	45	48	93	21.0	1.59	100	6.3	13.7	63.3	16.7
Wychavon	664	172	56	58	114	20.9	1.59	89	5.2	13.4	60.7	20.6
Wyre Forest	195	498	48	49	97	6.0	1.59	103	5.1	13.5	61.6	19.8
East	19,110	284	2,657	2,763	5,420	11.2	1.67	92	5.8	14.1	61.0	19.1
Luton UA	43	4,295	94	92	186	12.7	2.02	110	7.1	15.9	62.9	14.1
Peterborough UA	343	460	78	80	158	15.4	1.84	105	6.4	15.2	62.2	16.3
Southend-on-Sea UA	42	3,802	76	83	159	1.1	1.84	105	6.0	14.0	58.4	21.6
Thurrock UA	163	889	71	75	145	15.2	1.66	98	6.8	14.9	63.0	15.3
Bedfordshire	1,192	323	191	194	385	11.8	1.70	94	6.2	14.8	62.4	16.5
Bedford	476	313	74	75	149	12.7	1.61	92	6.1	14.5	62.1	17.3
Mid Bedfordshire	503	243	61	61	122	17.5	1.69	89	6.4	14.7	63.3	15.6
South Bedfordshire	213	533	56	57	113	5.2	1.82	102	6.2	15.3	61.9	16.6
Cambridgeshire	3,046	183	278	281	558	21.5	1.48	89	5.7	13.5	63.6	17.3
Cambridge	41	2,719	56	54	111	8.8	1.19	89	4.6	9.7	71.1	14.6
East Cambridgeshire	651	114	37	38	74	38.6	1.57	80	5.9	13.8	61.1	19.2
Fenland	546	154	41	43	84	26.2	1.73	108	5.6	13.9	58.4	22.1
Huntingdonshire	906	174	79	79	158	24.2	1.73	89	6.3	15.1	63.0	15.6
South Cambridgeshire	902	145	65	66	131	18.9	1.60	81	5.9	14.3	62.6	17.3
Essex	3,465	381	643	675	1,318	9.9	1.65	92	5.7	14.1	60.6	19.5
Basildon	110	1,512	80	86	166	7.7	1.77	93	6.4	14.8	61.4	17.3
Braintree	612	220	66	68	134	18.8	1.71	101	6.1	14.6	61.9	17.3
Brentwood	153	448	33	35	69	−5.2	1.55	85	5.3	13.9	59.3	21.4
Castle Point	45	1,935	43	45	87	0.3	1.64	90	5.1	13.9	60.2	20.8
Chelmsford	339	465	78	80	158	11.7	1.47	85	5.5	14.3	62.9	17.3
Colchester	329	472	77	79	155	12.2	1.50	92	5.9	13.8	62.9	17.3
Epping Forest	339	358	59	63	121	5.8	1.64	90	6.0	13.8	60.8	19.5
Harlow	31	2,572	38	40	79	−0.8	1.84	94	6.6	14.7	61.7	17.1
Maldon	359	168	30	30	60	24.2	1.70	94	5.7	14.4	61.6	18.3
Rochford	169	468	38	41	79	6.3	1.67	84	5.5	14.2	59.7	20.6
Tendring	338	415	67	73	140	23.3	1.72	94	4.8	12.6	53.0	29.6
Uttlesford	641	108	35	35	69	10.7	1.68	95	5.7	14.8	61.5	18.0
Hertfordshire	1,643	631	506	530	1,036	6.7	1.70	93	6.2	14.5	61.8	17.5
Broxbourne	51	1,701	42	45	87	9.6	1.74	92	6.0	14.7	61.8	17.4
Dacorum	212	650	68	70	138	5.1	1.80	91	6.2	14.7	61.7	17.5
East Hertfordshire	476	273	64	66	130	17.3	1.63	90	6.2	14.7	63.0	16.1
Hertsmere	101	924	45	49	93	3.7	1.63	95	6.0	14.5	60.8	18.7
North Hertfordshire	375	315	58	61	118	8.4	1.75	105	6.1	14.2	61.2	18.4
St. Albans	161	800	63	66	129	2.9	1.72	84	6.7	14.1	62.0	17.2
Stevenage	26	3,068	39	40	80	6.2	1.72	97	6.3	15.7	61.8	16.2
Three Rivers	89	929	40	43	83	2.8	1.70	86	6.1	14.7	60.4	18.9
Watford	21	3,751	40	40	80	7.4	1.68	108	6.3	13.8	64.7	15.2
Welwyn Hatfield	130	751	47	50	97	3.5	1.61	86	5.8	13.9	60.7	19.6
Norfolk	5,371	149	391	411	803	13.7	1.56	89	5.0	12.9	59.0	23.1
Breckland	1,305	94	60	62	122	24.9	1.62	91	5.4	13.8	58.5	22.4
Broadland	552	216	58	61	119	21.3	1.54	88	5.1	12.9	59.5	22.5
Great Yarmouth	174	526	44	47	92	12.1	1.80	99	5.0	13.7	58.6	22.7
King's Lynn and West Norfolk	1,429	96	67	71	137	12.5	1.77	92	5.0	12.8	57.5	24.6
North Norfolk	964	103	48	51	99	18.7	1.49	85	4.1	11.7	55.0	29.3
Norwich	39	3,117	60	62	122	−4.2	1.27	85	4.9	11.8	64.6	18.7
South Norfolk	908	124	55	58	112	16.7	1.62	81	5.1	13.5	58.8	22.5
Suffolk	3,801	177	330	342	672	10.6	1.72	90	5.6	14.0	59.1	21.3
Babergh	594	143	41	43	85	12.8	1.52	86	5.3	14.2	59.1	21.3
Forest Heath	378	147	28	27	56	5.0	1.92	95	6.7	13.0	62.9	17.3
Ipswich	39	2,976	57	60	117	−2.6	1.69	95	5.9	14.8	60.3	19.0
Mid Suffolk	871	101	44	44	88	22.7	1.76	87	5.6	14.1	59.9	20.4
St. Edmundsbury	657	150	49	50	98	11.4	1.76	91	5.6	13.6	61.3	19.5
Suffolk Coastal	892	129	56	59	115	17.2	1.60	86	5.0	14.0	56.7	24.3
Waveney	370	306	55	59	113	12.3	1.77	90	5.2	14.0	56.1	24.7

Table **14.1** (continued)

	Area (sq km)	People per sq km	Population (thousands)			Total population percentage change 1982-2002	Total fertility rate (TFR)[3]	Standardised mortality ratio (UK=100) (SMR)[4]	Percentage of population aged:			
			Males	Females	Total				Under 5	5 to 15	16 up to pension age[5]	Pension age[5] or over
London[6]	1,572	4,679	3,632	3,724	7,355	8.7	1.62	98	6.4	13.1	66.4	14.0
Inner London	319	8,980	1,431	1,437	2,867	13.7	1.62	104	6.6	12.1	69.8	11.5
Inner London – West	109	9,297	501	512	1,013	10.5	..	..	5.8	9.4	72.3	12.4
Camden	22	9,498	102	105	207	17.9	1.35	105	5.8	10.4	71.9	11.9
City of London	3	2,694	4	4	8	17.3	0.80	50	3.3	5.6	76.8	14.2
Hammersmith and Fulham	16	10,566	86	87	173	16.4	1.38	91	6.0	9.9	72.2	11.9
Kensington and Chelsea	12	13,609	81	84	165	18.5	1.34	73	6.1	9.2	70.4	14.3
Wandsworth	34	7,859	132	137	269	3.7	1.47	110	6.1	9.7	72.8	11.4
Westminster	21	8,875	96	95	191	2.2	1.39	90	5.2	7.8	73.6	13.4
Inner London – East	210	8,816	930	924	1,854	15.6	..	..	7.0	13.5	68.5	11.0
Hackney	19	11,027	103	107	210	14.9	2.07	101	8.0	14.7	66.8	10.5
Haringey	30	7,609	112	113	225	9.7	1.80	104	6.6	13.2	69.2	11.1
Islington	15	12,181	89	92	181	11.9	1.38	115	6.0	11.5	71.1	11.4
Lambeth	27	10,136	139	133	272	9.6	1.65	110	6.5	11.7	71.3	10.4
Lewisham	35	7,220	125	129	254	7.6	1.60	113	6.8	13.5	67.3	12.4
Newham	36	7,013	129	125	254	20.1	2.19	115	8.0	16.6	65.3	10.0
Southwark	29	8,710	126	125	251	16.7	1.67	107	6.8	12.8	68.8	11.7
Tower Hamlets	20	10,462	107	100	207	44.1	1.81	119	7.4	14.2	68.2	10.2
Outer London	1,253	3,582	2,201	2,287	4,488	5.7	1.64	94	6.3	13.8	64.2	15.7
Outer London – East and North East	432	3,656	771	810	1,581	3.3	..	..	6.4	14.4	62.9	16.2
Barking and Dagenham	36	4,636	80	87	167	4.1	1.86	109	7.4	15.6	61.0	16.0
Bexley	61	3,612	105	114	219	0.5	1.73	93	6.0	14.8	60.8	18.4
Enfield	81	3,486	138	144	282	7.9	1.70	93	6.4	14.1	63.8	15.6
Greenwich	47	4,677	108	113	221	3.3	1.74	106	7.0	13.9	64.6	14.4
Havering	112	1,997	108	116	224	−7.4	1.64	95	5.5	14.3	59.9	20.4
Redbridge	56	4,326	121	124	244	11.1	1.69	93	6.3	14.6	63.3	15.7
Waltham Forest	39	5,751	111	112	223	3.6	1.81	110	6.8	13.9	66.2	13.2
Outer London – South	355	3,255	565	592	1,157	6.1	..	..	6.3	13.8	63.7	16.2
Bromley	150	1,977	142	154	297	−0.5	1.58	90	6.1	13.7	60.8	19.3
Croydon	87	3,890	164	172	337	4.8	1.67	93	6.5	14.9	63.8	14.8
Kingston upon Thames	37	4,031	74	76	150	12.6	1.44	95	6.1	12.5	66.7	14.8
Merton	38	5,112	96	97	192	15.0	1.59	92	6.4	12.5	66.6	14.5
Sutton	44	4,126	88	93	181	6.1	1.50	100	6.2	14.4	62.8	16.6
Outer London – West and North West	465	3,764	866	885	1,751	7.9	..	..	6.2	13.3	65.7	14.8
Barnet	87	3,694	155	165	320	9.3	1.53	89	6.3	13.6	63.9	16.3
Brent	43	6,302	136	136	272	10.2	1.61	92	6.0	12.9	67.7	13.4
Ealing	56	5,554	155	153	308	8.7	1.62	95	6.1	12.9	67.8	13.2
Harrow	50	4,193	104	107	212	5.6	1.59	79	5.7	14.0	63.8	16.6
Hillingdon	116	2,131	121	126	247	5.7	1.66	94	6.3	14.4	63.3	15.9
Hounslow	56	3,870	109	108	217	7.1	1.67	103	6.4	13.4	67.1	13.0
Richmond upon Thames	57	3,038	86	89	174	7.2	1.54	86	6.7	11.9	66.1	15.3
South East	19,069	421	3,931	4,106	8,037	10.5	1.62	91	5.7	14.0	61.4	18.9
Bracknell Forest UA	109	1,002	55	55	110	28.4	1.59	95	6.7	15.3	65.1	12.9
Brighton and Hove UA	83	3,023	122	128	250	4.8	1.34	98	5.2	11.3	65.6	17.9
Isle of Wight UA	380	355	65	70	135	13.7	1.64	89	4.6	13.4	56.7	25.3
Medway UA	192	1,307	124	127	251	4.5	1.74	106	6.3	15.9	62.8	15.0
Milton Keynes UA	309	682	105	105	210	58.3	1.83	100	6.7	15.7	65.4	12.2
Portsmouth UA	40	4,671	93	95	188	−1.6	1.46	101	5.7	13.2	63.9	17.2
Reading UA	40	3,574	74	71	144	4.5	1.59	95	6.0	12.5	67.3	14.2
Slough UA	33	3,725	62	60	121	19.4	1.83	108	6.7	15.1	65.1	13.2
Southampton UA	50	4,438	112	109	221	6.3	1.39	90	5.3	12.4	66.1	16.2
West Berkshire UA	704	204	72	72	144	16.2	1.58	89	5.9	14.9	63.4	15.7
Windsor and Maidenhead UA	197	678	66	68	133	−2.2	1.73	96	6.1	13.9	62.2	17.8
Wokingham UA	179	845	76	76	151	27.5	1.52	85	5.9	14.7	64.9	14.5
Buckinghamshire	1,565	306	234	244	478	7.6	1.67	90	6.3	14.6	61.8	17.3
Aylesbury Vale	903	185	83	84	167	23.6	1.61	94	6.5	14.8	63.4	15.3
Chiltern	196	451	43	46	88	−2.4	1.74	86	6.0	14.6	59.4	20.0
South Bucks	141	437	30	32	62	1.6	1.62	89	5.5	14.5	59.4	20.6
Wycombe	325	497	79	82	161	2.1	1.71	88	6.5	14.5	62.5	16.5
East Sussex	1,709	289	234	260	494	14.7	1.71	90	5.2	13.6	55.5	25.8
Eastbourne	44	2,055	42	49	91	15.5	1.64	92	5.1	12.7	55.1	27.1
Hastings	30	2,886	41	45	86	12.0	1.77	110	6.0	14.9	58.9	20.2
Lewes	292	319	45	48	93	17.6	1.75	83	5.1	13.5	55.8	25.6
Rother	509	168	40	45	85	11.0	1.62	90	4.4	12.5	51.0	32.1
Wealden	833	167	66	73	139	16.5	1.72	82	5.3	14.1	56.1	24.5

Table **14.1** (continued)

	Area (sq km)	People per sq km	Population (thousands)			Total population percentage change	Total fertility rate	Standardised mortality ratio (UK=100)	Percentage of population aged:			
			Males	Females	Total	1982-2002	(TFR)[3]	(SMR)[4]	Under 5	5 to 15	16 up to pension age[5]	Pension age[5] or over
Hampshire	3,679	338	610	634	1,244	14.3	1.63	87	5.7	14.3	61.1	19.0
Basingstoke and Deane	634	241	76	77	153	15.1	1.65	88	6.4	14.6	64.0	14.9
East Hampshire	514	213	54	56	110	19.1	1.78	91	5.7	14.7	60.8	18.8
Eastleigh	80	1,454	57	59	116	23.2	1.54	88	5.6	15.0	61.9	17.5
Fareham	74	1,466	53	56	109	24.0	1.68	87	5.4	13.9	60.3	20.4
Gosport	25	3,043	38	39	77	−0.4	1.61	101	5.9	14.1	61.2	18.8
Hart	215	391	42	42	84	19.2	1.60	77	6.1	14.5	63.9	15.5
Havant	55	2,103	56	60	116	0.1	1.78	94	5.3	14.3	58.4	22.1
New Forest	753	226	81	89	170	16.7	1.62	75	4.9	13.2	56.0	25.9
Rushmoor	39	2,320	46	45	91	4.1	1.64	99	6.6	14.3	65.4	13.6
Test Valley	628	176	54	56	111	20.1	1.59	92	5.7	15.2	61.4	17.7
Winchester	661	163	53	55	108	16.4	1.55	84	5.2	13.3	61.8	19.7
Kent	3,544	378	648	690	1,338	7.4	1.74	94	5.7	14.6	59.8	19.8
Ashford	581	180	51	54	105	20.4	1.90	85	6.3	14.8	60.3	18.6
Canterbury	309	440	64	71	136	10.4	1.45	93	5.1	13.3	59.9	21.8
Dartford	73	1,188	42	44	86	6.5	1.68	105	6.2	14.9	62.0	16.9
Dover	315	333	50	54	105	2.0	1.81	99	5.4	14.6	58.4	21.6
Gravesham	99	971	47	49	96	0.7	1.77	92	5.9	15.2	60.8	18.1
Maidstone	393	355	69	71	139	6.8	1.67	93	5.7	13.9	62.0	18.4
Sevenoaks	369	294	52	56	109	−1.4	1.81	81	5.7	14.6	59.3	20.4
Shepway	357	271	47	50	97	11.5	1.79	99	5.4	14.0	57.6	23.1
Swale	373	336	62	64	126	14.0	1.85	102	6.1	15.3	61.2	17.4
Thanet	103	1,236	61	67	128	4.4	1.80	100	5.4	14.6	55.6	24.4
Tonbridge and Malling	240	453	53	56	109	10.1	1.86	89	6.2	15.3	60.6	17.9
Tunbridge Wells	331	313	50	54	104	5.2	1.70	87	5.9	15.0	60.4	18.8
Oxfordshire	2,605	233	301	306	607	11.4	1.54	87	5.8	13.5	63.8	17.0
Cherwell	589	222	65	66	131	17.7	1.73	94	6.5	14.3	63.1	16.1
Oxford	46	2,952	67	67	135	3.3	1.32	85	4.8	10.7	69.9	14.6
South Oxfordshire	679	189	63	65	128	9.4	1.73	86	6.1	13.9	61.9	18.1
Vale of White Horse	578	202	58	59	117	12.1	1.64	80	5.7	14.6	61.7	18.0
West Oxfordshire	714	135	48	49	97	17.4	1.68	89	5.8	14.3	61.2	18.7
Surrey	1,663	638	517	543	1,060	5.0	1.57	87	5.8	13.5	61.8	18.9
Elmbridge	95	1,307	61	64	124	10.9	1.65	85	6.4	13.9	61.2	18.5
Epsom and Ewell	34	1,960	32	35	67	−3.5	1.56	85	5.9	13.4	61.2	19.5
Guildford	271	476	64	65	129	3.7	1.43	78	5.4	12.5	64.4	17.7
Mole Valley	258	311	39	41	80	3.5	1.63	84	5.4	13.5	58.9	22.1
Reigate and Banstead	129	978	62	65	126	8.1	1.61	100	6.0	13.6	61.7	18.8
Runnymede	78	1,011	38	41	79	8.8	1.48	92	5.2	12.0	64.5	18.4
Spelthorne	45	1,998	44	46	90	−0.9	1.60	86	5.6	13.3	61.4	19.6
Surrey Heath	95	838	39	40	80	6.1	1.52	93	6.1	14.4	63.0	16.5
Tandridge	248	321	38	41	80	4.8	1.70	88	5.9	14.4	60.2	19.5
Waverley	345	336	56	60	116	3.0	1.63	84	5.6	13.8	60.2	20.4
Woking	64	1,406	43	46	89	7.9	1.64	87	6.2	14.3	62.5	17.0
West Sussex	1,991	380	362	394	756	12.1	1.67	91	5.5	13.6	58.0	23.0
Adur	42	1,448	29	32	61	3.7	1.71	85	5.3	13.5	56.9	24.3
Arun	221	643	67	75	142	17.9	1.74	94	4.9	12.3	53.8	29.1
Chichester	786	136	51	56	107	8.0	1.62	89	4.8	12.7	56.4	26.1
Crawley	45	2,219	49	50	100	20.9	1.62	88	6.4	14.6	62.3	16.7
Horsham	530	231	59	63	122	19.9	1.64	84	5.8	14.8	60.0	19.5
Mid Sussex	334	381	62	66	127	6.2	1.67	93	5.8	14.4	60.6	19.3
Worthing	32	3,000	46	52	97	5.1	1.74	99	5.4	13.0	56.1	25.6
South West	23,837	208	2,413	2,546	4,960	12.7	1.58	90	5.3	13.5	59.7	21.5
Bath and North East Somerset UA	346	491	82	87	170	5.2	1.45	82	5.2	12.9	61.5	20.4
Bournemouth UA	46	3,547	79	85	164	13.2	1.32	95	4.9	11.6	60.5	23.0
Bristol, City of UA	110	3,482	188	193	382	−4.8	1.51	102	6.0	12.6	64.9	16.6
North Somerset UA	374	507	92	98	189	16.0	1.74	92	5.4	13.5	58.8	22.3
Plymouth UA	80	3,000	117	123	239	−6.2	1.54	99	5.3	13.9	62.1	18.6
Poole UA	65	2,130	66	72	138	13.4	1.55	82	5.0	13.2	58.4	23.3
South Gloucestershire UA	497	496	122	125	246	20.4	1.56	83	6.0	14.7	62.1	17.2
Swindon UA	230	785	90	91	181	18.3	1.73	101	6.1	14.6	63.3	16.0
Torbay UA	63	2,081	62	68	131	16.0	1.53	94	4.6	13.2	56.4	25.8

Table **14.1**   (continued)

	Area (sq km)	People per sq km	Population (thousands)			Total population percentage change 1982-2002	Total fertility rate (TFR)[3]	Standardised mortality ratio (UK=100) (SMR)[4]	Percentage of population aged:			
			Males	Females	Total				Under 5	5 to 15	16 up to pension age[5]	Pension age[5] or over
Cornwall and the Isles of Scilly	3,563	143	246	262	508	18.2	1.64	90	5.1	13.3	58.4	23.3
Caradon	664	120	39	41	80	15.4	1.73	90	4.7	13.4	59.3	22.6
Carrick	458	194	42	46	89	16.1	1.52	85	4.8	12.9	58.1	24.2
Kerrier	474	198	46	48	94	11.5	1.71	93	5.4	13.3	59.1	22.2
North Cornwall	1,195	69	40	42	82	25.4	1.74	88	5.1	13.6	57.3	24.0
Penwith	304	210	31	33	64	19.0	1.49	93	4.9	12.8	57.7	24.6
Restormel	452	216	48	50	98	23.6	1.70	93	5.3	13.5	58.8	22.5
Isles of Scilly	16	132	1	1	2	7.7	0.95	76	5.3	11.7	61.1	21.8
Devon	6,564	108	343	368	710	18.6	1.57	88	4.8	13.1	58.1	24.1
East Devon	814	155	59	67	126	17.1	1.54	86	4.3	12.1	53.3	30.4
Exeter	47	2,363	54	57	111	9.7	1.30	90	4.9	11.9	64.7	18.5
Mid Devon	913	77	35	36	71	20.4	1.83	85	5.5	14.1	58.8	21.7
North Devon	1,086	81	43	46	88	12.7	1.76	94	5.0	13.8	57.6	23.5
South Hams	886	92	40	42	82	22.9	1.61	80	4.6	13.5	57.8	24.1
Teignbridge	674	181	58	64	122	27.9	1.67	87	4.9	13.5	56.6	25.1
Torridge	984	61	29	31	60	24.0	1.63	94	4.6	13.6	57.8	24.0
West Devon	1,160	44	25	25	51	18.0	1.79	94	4.6	13.4	59.6	22.4
Dorset	2,542	155	191	204	395	16.7	1.67	82	4.6	13.2	55.4	26.8
Christchurch	50	900	21	24	45	13.2	1.74	80	4.2	11.6	51.3	32.9
East Dorset	354	239	40	44	85	20.5	1.61	75	4.4	12.7	53.8	29.2
North Dorset	609	102	31	31	62	27.2	1.56	80	4.6	15.1	57.1	23.2
Purbeck	404	109	21	23	44	9.7	1.74	77	4.5	13.4	56.6	25.4
West Dorset	1,081	87	45	49	94	16.8	1.74	84	4.6	13.1	54.5	27.7
Weymouth and Portland	42	1,539	32	33	64	10.5	1.63	94	5.0	13.3	59.5	22.3
Gloucestershire	2,653	214	277	290	567	12.1	1.61	90	5.6	14.0	60.4	20.1
Cheltenham	47	2,360	53	57	110	6.9	1.39	89	5.2	13.0	62.2	19.7
Cotswold	1,165	69	39	41	80	14.1	1.59	86	5.3	13.3	58.5	23.0
Forest of Dean	527	153	39	41	81	10.4	1.56	94	5.4	13.9	60.3	20.3
Gloucester	41	2,727	54	56	111	10.2	1.75	95	6.3	15.2	61.1	17.4
Stroud	461	235	53	55	108	12.6	1.77	92	5.5	14.5	59.5	20.4
Tewkesbury	414	187	38	40	77	22.4	1.71	86	5.5	13.8	59.9	20.8
Somerset	3,451	146	244	259	503	16.5	1.68	88	5.3	14.1	58.3	22.3
Mendip	739	142	51	54	105	16.2	1.63	89	5.5	15.0	59.4	20.1
Sedgemoor	564	191	52	55	108	19.0	1.69	91	5.3	14.3	58.4	22.0
South Somerset	959	158	74	77	151	13.1	1.78	87	5.5	14.0	57.9	22.7
Taunton Deane	462	224	50	54	104	17.4	1.60	86	5.2	13.9	59.1	21.8
West Somerset	725	50	17	19	36	22.3	1.65	84	4.1	11.8	54.5	29.6
Wiltshire	3,255	134	215	222	436	15.7	1.70	90	6.0	14.4	60.4	19.2
Kennet	967	77	37	37	74	9.1	1.98	83	6.2	14.4	60.9	18.6
North Wiltshire	768	164	62	64	126	20.0	1.65	94	6.1	15.1	61.4	17.3
Salisbury	1,004	115	56	59	115	11.4	1.56	89	5.6	13.7	59.7	20.9
West Wiltshire	517	234	59	62	121	20.0	1.73	92	6.0	14.4	59.7	20.0

1 *Local government structure as at 1 April 1998. See Notes and Definitions.*

2 *Mid-2002 Population Estimates for the UK, England and Manchester include provisional results from the Manchester Matching Exercise, published in November 2003.*

3 *The total fertility rate (TFR) is the number of children that would be born to a woman if current patterns of fertility persisted throughout her child-bearing life. The TFRs in this table relate to 2001. The population estimates used to calculate those for Manchester, Greater Manchester and the North West take account of the provisional results from the Manchester matching exercise published in November 2003. The national TFR's are unaffected by these results.*

4 *The standardised mortality ratio (SMR) takes account of the age structure of the population. The SMRs in this table relate to 2001. They are based on the UK population estimates published in September 2003, except those for Manchester, Greater Manchester and the North West, which take into account the provisional results from the Manchester matching exercise published in November 2003.*

5 *Pension age is 65 for men and 60 for women.*

6 *London is presented by NUTS levels 1, 2, 3 and 4. See Notes and Definitions.*

Source: Office for National Statistics

Table **14.2** Vital[1,2] and social statistics[3]

	Live births[2,4] per 1,000 population		Deaths[2,4] per 1,000 population		Perinatal mortality rate[5]	Infant mortality rate[6]	Percentage of live births under 2.5 kg	Percentage of live births outside marriage
	1991	2001	1991	2001	2000-2002	2000-2002	2001	2001
United Kingdom	13.8	11.3	11.2	10.2	8.1	5.5	..	40.1
England	13.7	11.4	11.1	10.1	8.2	5.4	7.6	39.6
North East	13.4	10.3	12.2	11.3	8.2	5.7	7.4	50.9
Darlington UA	14.3	11.0	13.9	12.4	9.1	4.9	7.2	50.1
Hartlepool UA	14.9	11.6	11.5	11.4	8.3	5.8	9.0	59.5
Middlesbrough UA	15.1	12.3	11.1	10.6	9.9	7.2	9.7	53.7
Redcar and Cleveland UA	14.0	10.3	10.9	10.8	7.7	4.8	8.1	56.8
Stockton-on-Tees UA	14.9	10.9	10.4	10.1	7.6	6.4	7.4	47.7
Durham County	12.8	9.7	12.1	11.2	8.1	6.3	7.2	51.4
Northumberland	11.8	9.4	12.6	11.3	8.0	4.9	6.1	42.3
Tyne and Wear (Met County)	13.4	10.3	12.7	11.5	8.0	5.5	7.4	51.7
Tees Valley	14.7	11.2	11.1	11.0	..	..	8.3	53.0
Tees Valley less Darlington	14.7	11.2	10.9	10.8	..	..	8.5	53.5
Former county of Durham	13.0	9.9	12.4	11.4	..	..	7.2	51.1
North West	14.2	11.1	12.0	11.1	8.6	5.8	7.9	46.3
Blackburn with Darwen UA	17.2	15.0	12.2	9.7	10.7	7.8	10.7	37.7
Blackpool UA	13.0	9.8	16.0	14.9	9.0	5.3	7.6	61.0
Halton UA	15.5	12.2	10.1	10.3	9.4	6.6	7.2	57.3
Warrington UA	14.7	11.2	10.6	9.7	8.0	4.5	5.6	41.2
Cheshire County	12.7	10.3	10.8	10.4	7.7	4.6	6.6	35.5
Cumbria	12.7	9.5	12.7	11.6	6.8	3.7	6.8	42.5
Greater Manchester (Met County)	14.9	11.9	11.8	10.7	9.1	6.3	8.3	46.3
Lancashire County	13.7	10.7	12.3	11.1	8.3	6.2	8.4	42.2
Merseyside (Met County)	14.0	10.6	12.4	11.8	8.4	5.6	7.8	55.7
Former county of Cheshire	13.5	10.7	10.7	10.2	..	..	6.5	39.7
Former county of Lancashire	13.9	11.0	12.7	11.4	..	..	8.6	43.3
Yorkshire and the Humber	13.8	11.2	11.5	10.5	8.8	6.4	8.1	43.3
East Riding of Yorkshire UA	11.8	8.9	12.0	10.8	5.7	4.8	6.9	39.7
Kingston upon Hull, City of UA	15.6	11.7	10.9	10.6	7.1	5.3	8.7	63.0
North East Lincolnshire UA	14.5	10.4	10.9	10.6	10.0	7.7	7.7	58.5
North Lincolnshire UA	13.0	10.5	11.2	10.7	10.6	7.2	8.0	48.2
York UA	12.3	10.1	11.6	10.2	8.2	5.4	6.5	42.0
North Yorkshire County	11.8	9.5	12.4	10.7	6.1	3.5	5.7	31.8
South Yorkshire (Met County)	13.7	10.9	11.7	10.7	8.6	6.3	8.0	48.5
West Yorkshire (Met County)	14.5	12.3	11.2	10.1	9.7	7.4	8.8	40.0
The Humber	13.7	10.2	11.3	10.7	..	..	7.8	52.2
Former county of North Yorkshire	11.8	9.7	12.2	10.6	..	..	5.9	34.4
East Midlands	13.4	10.7	10.9	10.2	8.1	5.3	7.5	42.6
Derby UA	15.4	12.5	11.8	10.3	9.3	6.4	8.2	44.4
Leicester UA	16.5	14.1	11.3	9.8	12.3	6.6	9.6	41.9
Nottingham UA	15.8	12.2	11.1	10.5	9.5	8.9	9.7	58.1
Rutland UA	9.8	8.6	8.7	8.5	7.4	5.3	7.4	29.8
Derbyshire County	12.8	9.9	11.6	10.9	7.5	4.8	6.9	43.1
Leicestershire County	12.5	10.2	9.4	9.1	7.9	3.7	6.9	33.8
Lincolnshire	11.7	9.3	11.8	11.3	7.2	5.0	6.9	43.2
Northamptonshire	14.0	11.7	10.3	8.8	7.3	4.5	7.2	41.5
Nottinghamshire County	12.9	9.9	10.6	10.6	6.9	5.7	7.2	43.6
Former county of Derbyshire	13.4	10.5	11.6	10.7	..	..	7.3	43.4
Former county of Leicestershire	13.7	11.3	10.0	9.3	..	..	8.0	36.8
Former county of Nottinghamshire	13.7	10.5	10.8	10.6	..	..	8.0	48.0
West Midlands	14.1	11.5	10.8	10.2	9.6	6.6	8.6	40.3
Herefordshire, County of UA	..	9.1	..	10.7	7.1	2.3	6.7	38.2
Stoke-on-Trent UA	14.3	11.4	12.1	11.2	11.0	9.6	8.9	51.7
Telford and Wrekin UA	15.5	11.8	8.8	8.5	10.8	6.7	8.5	49.5
Shropshire County	12.1	9.3	11.3	10.8	8.6	5.2	6.2	35.8
Staffordshire County	12.9	10.0	10.3	10.1	7.8	5.6	7.9	38.6
Warwickshire	12.5	10.4	10.5	10.2	5.5	4.0	7.3	36.2
West Midlands (Met County)	15.2	12.9	11.0	10.2	10.9	7.7	9.5	40.8
Worcestershire County	..	10.3	..	10.3	8.4	4.9	7.6	37.6
Herefordshire and Worcestershire	12.6	10.0	10.7	10.4	..	..	7.4	37.7
Former county of Shropshire	13.3	10.2	10.4	10.0	..	..	7.2	41.5
Former county of Staffordshire	13.2	10.3	10.7	10.4	..	..	8.2	41.9

Table **14.2** (continued)

	Live births[2,4] per 1,000 population		Deaths[2,4] per 1,000 population		Perinatal mortality rate[5]	Infant mortality rate[6]	Percent- age of live births under 2.5 kg	Percent- age of live births outside marriage
	1991	2001	1991	2001	2000-2002	2000-2002	2001	2001
East	13.3	11.1	10.3	9.9	7.2	4.4	6.7	35.9
Luton UA	18.5	15.3	8.8	8.4	12.4	7.8	9.7	30.6
Peterborough UA	15.8	13.1	8.8	9.4	9.2	5.9	7.8	41.3
Southend-on-Sea UA	13.8	11.9	14.2	13.8	7.5	3.5	6.2	48.1
Thurrock UA	15.7	12.5	9.4	8.1	9.3	4.8	5.8	46.7
Bedfordshire County	13.6	11.7	9.1	8.6	7.5	4.3	7.4	32.2
Cambridgeshire County	13.0	10.6	9.3	8.8	5.8	4.2	6.9	32.1
Essex County	13.0	10.7	10.3	9.9	6.9	4.4	6.2	36.5
Hertfordshire	13.6	12.3	9.5	9.1	6.7	4.3	6.3	31.4
Norfolk	11.6	9.3	12.1	11.4	6.6	4.1	6.8	42.4
Suffolk	12.8	10.4	11.2	10.7	6.9	3.7	6.5	35.7
Former county of Bedfordshire	15.2	12.9	9.0	8.5	..	..	8.3	31.6
Former county of Cambridgeshire	13.6	11.1	9.2	8.9	..	..	7.1	34.5
Former county of Essex	13.3	11.0	10.6	10.1	..	..	6.2	38.8
London	15.5	14.3	10.1	8.0	9.1	5.7	8.1	34.6
Inner London	16.4	15.9	9.8	7.1	9.6	6.3	8.7	36.6
Outer London	14.7	13.2	10.1	8.6	8.7	5.3	7.7	33.1
South East	13.0	11.0	10.8	9.9	6.8	4.4	6.9	34.8
Bracknell Forest UA	15.2	12.4	8.6	6.9	6.5	4.1	7.6	30.6
Brighton and Hove UA	12.1	11.3	13.9	11.1	7.3	5.4	7.1	46.2
Isle of Wight UA	10.6	8.3	15.5	13.2	8.3	3.0	6.2	46.8
Medway UA	15.6	12.1	8.7	8.7	6.1	5.4	7.1	45.3
Milton Keynes UA	17.1	13.5	7.2	7.1	8.9	6.4	8.6	41.8
Portsmouth UA	14.2	11.4	12.0	10.4	10.3	7.5	9.1	45.1
Reading UA	14.2	13.6	12.0	8.0	10.5	6.3	8.3	38.3
Slough UA	18.2	15.4	7.8	8.0	8.8	4.9	9.5	31.9
Southampton UA	13.8	11.1	11.1	8.6	6.7	6.0	7.8	48.0
West Berkshire UA	13.8	10.9	11.1	7.9	7.4	4.2	6.8	31.6
Windsor and Maidenhead UA	12.4	12.0	9.8	9.7	8.5	5.4	7.5	26.2
Wokingham UA	12.7	11.0	6.8	6.8	5.8	2.8	5.3	20.8
Buckinghamshire County	13.3	11.4	8.8	8.7	7.9	4.9	6.7	25.5
East Sussex County	11.2	9.3	15.5	13.9	6.5	4.9	6.2	39.5
Hampshire County	12.7	10.4	9.5	9.3	5.9	3.9	6.5	32.7
Kent County	13.0	11.0	11.7	10.6	6.7	4.0	6.9	40.9
Oxfordshire	13.7	11.6	8.8	8.4	6.1	3.6	6.8	29.8
Surrey	12.3	11.1	10.4	9.5	5.7	3.8	6.2	26.3
West Sussex	11.7	10.3	13.5	12.4	6.4	3.5	6.9	33.9
Former county of Berkshire	14.3	12.5	8.5	7.9	..	..	7.5	30.2
Former county of Buckinghamshire	14.3	12.0	8.4	8.2	..	..	7.3	31.1
Former county of East Sussex	11.5	9.9	15.0	12.9	..	..	6.5	42.1
Former county of Hampshire	13.1	10.6	10.0	9.3	..	..	7.0	36.4
Former county of Kent	13.4	11.2	11.2	10.3	..	..	6.9	41.7
South West	12.2	9.9	11.9	11.0	6.9	4.8	6.7	39.3
Bath and North East Somerset UA	11.1	9.8	11.4	9.7	5.3	3.4	5.6	35.3
Bournemouth UA	11.1	9.4	16.0	13.9	7.5	6.3	7.2	40.6
Bristol, City of UA	13.9	12.2	11.2	10.0	7.2	6.0	7.3	45.7
North Somerset UA	11.0	9.9	12.2	11.9	6.1	5.4	6.9	38.2
Plymouth UA	13.8	10.6	10.6	10.3	7.9	5.2	6.6	48.7
Poole UA	12.2	9.7	12.7	11.0	6.3	3.7	6.5	37.6
South Gloucestershire UA	13.9	10.9	8.4	7.6	6.8	4.7	6.0	32.0
Swindon UA	15.1	12.4	9.5	8.8	8.4	5.9	9.0	42.5
Torbay UA	10.6	8.2	15.6	14.7	7.9	5.3	7.8	47.2
Cornwall and the Isles of Scilly	11.5	8.9	12.9	11.8	6.3	4.8	6.5	44.1
Devon County	11.2	8.8	13.2	12.2	6.0	4.2	5.9	39.2
Dorset County	10.6	8.4	13.0	12.4	7.3	4.7	6.6	35.6
Gloucestershire	12.6	10.2	10.8	10.3	7.1	4.0	6.8	38.4
Somerset	12.1	9.5	11.9	11.1	5.9	4.9	6.5	37.9
Wiltshire County	12.9	10.6	10.5	9.7	8.1	4.9	6.3	31.5
Bristol/Bath area	12.9	11.0	10.8	9.7	..	..	6.7	39.5
Former county of Devon	11.8	9.1	12.9	12.1	..	..	6.3	42.5
Former county of Dorset	11.1	8.9	13.7	12.4	..	..	6.7	37.3
Former county of Wiltshire	13.5	11.1	10.2	9.5	..	..	7.2	35.1

1 Births and deaths are based on the usual area of residence of the mother/deceased. See Notes and Definitions to the Population chapter for details of the inclusion/exclusion of births to non-resident mothers and deaths of non-resident persons.

2 Births data are on the basis of year of occurrence in England and Wales and year of registration in Scotland and Northern Ireland. All deaths data relate to year of registration.

3 Counties and unitary authorities in existence from 1 April 1998. See Notes and Definitions.

4 The population estimates used to calculate rates for Greater Manchester and the North West take account of the provisional results of the Census matching exercise for Manchester published on 4 November 2003. The national rates are unaffected by these results.

5 Still births and deaths of infants under 1 week of age per 1,000 live and still births.

6 Deaths of infants under 1 year of age per 1,000 live births.

Source: Office for National Statistics; Department of Health

Table 14.3   Health and care of people[1], 2001

Percentages and thousands

	Percentage of individuals:					Households with one or more person with a limiting long-term illness (percentages)	All house-holds (thousands)
	With limiting long-term illness[2]	Of working age[3] with limiting long-term illness	Claiming good health[4]	Individuals providing 50 hours or more unpaid care[5] per week	All people (thousands)		
England	17.9	8.2	68.8	2.0	49,139	33.6	20,451
North East	22.7	10.9	64.3	2.7	2,515	41.1	1,066
Darlington UA	20.4	9.3	66.4	2.4	98	36.0	42
Hartlepool UA	24.4	12.1	64.2	3.0	89	44.2	37
Middlesbrough UA	22.3	10.9	65.2	3.0	135	41.8	55
Redcar and Cleveland UA	23.3	11.0	63.4	3.0	139	43.0	57
Stockton-on-Tees UA	19.9	9.4	66.9	2.6	178	37.2	73
Durham	24.5	12.2	62.6	2.9	493	44.1	207
Chester-le-Street	21.5	10.6	65.1	2.6	54	38.5	23
Derwentside	25.0	12.1	61.4	3.0	85	44.0	36
Durham	20.1	10.2	67.0	2.2	88	38.3	35
Easington	30.8	16.3	57.8	3.9	94	54.9	39
Sedgefield	24.8	12.2	62.5	3.0	87	44.2	38
Teesdale	19.9	8.5	67.1	2.4	24	36.0	10
Wear Valley	24.7	11.6	61.7	2.9	61	43.6	26
Northumberland	20.9	9.7	65.6	2.4	307	37.5	131
Alnwick	19.2	8.0	67.4	1.9	31	34.3	14
Berwick-upon-Tweed	20.7	8.2	65.1	2.3	26	35.8	12
Blyth Valley	21.3	10.8	64.9	2.7	81	38.7	35
Castle Morpeth	20.0	8.9	67.8	2.1	49	35.2	20
Tynedale	18.2	7.8	69.0	1.7	59	33.2	25
Wansbeck	24.6	12.1	60.8	3.1	61	43.8	26
Tyne and Wear (Met County)	23.0	11.0	64.1	2.7	1,076	41.3	463
Gateshead	23.9	11.6	62.6	2.9	191	42.3	84
Newcastle upon Tyne	21.6	10.4	65.1	2.5	260	39.1	111
North Tyneside	21.8	9.9	64.9	2.6	192	38.5	85
South Tyneside	23.6	11.0	63.9	2.7	153	42.3	66
Sunderland	24.0	12.0	63.9	3.0	281	44.0	116
North West	20.7	10.0	66.9	2.4	6,730	38.4	2,813
Blackburn with Darwen UA	20.3	10.5	66.6	2.4	137	39.8	53
Blackpool UA	25.4	12.0	61.1	3.1	142	42.9	64
Halton UA	21.5	11.4	66.5	3.1	118	40.9	48
Warrington UA	17.9	8.5	70.6	2.2	191	34.0	78
Cheshire	17.4	7.5	70.6	2.0	674	32.5	280
Chester	17.5	7.6	71.4	2.0	118	32.3	50
Congleton	16.1	6.9	71.6	1.7	91	30.6	37
Crewe and Nantwich	17.9	7.9	68.9	1.9	111	33.8	46
Ellesmere Port and Neston	18.9	8.6	69.0	2.5	82	36.5	33
Macclesfield	16.4	6.5	72.0	1.6	150	29.5	64
Vale Royal	18.1	8.2	69.7	2.2	122	34.4	50
Cumbria	20.0	9.0	67.1	2.2	488	36.5	209
Allerdale	20.2	8.9	66.6	2.2	93	37.1	40
Barrow-in-Furness	24.8	12.7	63.1	3.0	72	45.1	31
Carlisle	19.3	8.7	67.4	2.0	101	34.8	44
Copeland	20.4	9.8	66.7	2.4	69	37.5	29
Eden	17.1	7.3	69.7	1.7	50	31.9	21
South Lakeland	18.5	7.1	69.2	1.8	102	33.3	44
Greater Manchester (Met County)	20.4	10.1	66.4	2.3	2,482	38.1	1,040
Bolton	20.3	9.8	67.0	2.4	261	38.5	108
Bury	19.0	9.1	67.8	2.2	181	35.7	74
Manchester	21.5	11.5	64.6	2.3	393	39.5	167
Oldham	20.3	10.1	65.7	2.4	217	39.1	88
Rochdale	20.6	10.5	66.1	2.3	205	39.3	83
Salford	22.8	11.1	64.7	2.6	216	41.0	94
Stockport	17.7	7.8	69.2	2.0	285	33.3	120
Tameside	20.9	10.3	65.2	2.5	213	38.6	90
Trafford	17.7	7.9	69.8	1.9	210	33.1	89
Wigan	22.3	11.5	65.5	2.6	301	41.5	125

Table 14.3 (continued)

Percentages and thousands

	Percentage of individuals:				Households with one or more person with a limiting long-term illness (percentages)	All house-holds (thousands)
	With limiting long-term illness[2]	Of working age[3] with limiting long-term illness	Claiming good health[4]	Individuals providing 50 hours or more unpaid care[5] per week	All people (thousands)	
Lancashire	20.2	9.3	67.2	2.3	1,135	37.3	469
Burnley	22.1	11.0	64.8	2.5	90	41.1	37
Chorley	18.5	9.1	69.1	2.0	100	34.2	41
Fylde	21.3	8.2	66.7	2.2	73	36.0	32
Hyndburn	22.0	10.9	64.4	2.5	81	41.4	33
Lancaster	19.9	8.8	67.4	2.2	134	36.4	56
Pendle	20.9	10.2	65.3	2.2	89	40.1	36
Preston	19.2	9.4	67.3	2.2	130	36.3	53
Ribble Valley	17.2	7.4	71.6	1.7	54	31.6	22
Rossendale	20.3	10.3	66.9	2.3	66	37.9	27
South Ribble	18.1	8.3	69.2	2.1	104	34.5	43
West Lancashire	19.8	9.4	69.1	2.6	108	37.7	44
Wyre	22.6	8.8	65.3	2.9	106	40.1	45
Merseyside (Met County)	23.5	11.6	65.7	3.0	1,362	42.9	571
Knowsley	24.7	12.8	65.0	3.5	150	46.7	61
Liverpool	24.6	12.9	64.5	3.2	439	44.4	188
St. Helens	23.6	11.9	64.8	3.0	177	43.8	73
Sefton	22.2	10.0	67.0	2.7	283	40.6	117
Wirral	22.5	10.4	66.9	2.8	312	40.7	133
Yorkshire and the Humber	19.5	8.9	67.0	2.3	4,965	36.2	2,065
East Riding of Yorkshire UA	18.1	7.5	68.8	2.1	314	33.2	131
Kingston upon Hull, City of UA	20.7	9.9	65.2	2.6	244	37.5	104
North East Lincolnshire UA	19.0	8.3	67.6	2.4	158	35.1	66
North Lincolnshire UA	19.2	8.5	66.5	2.4	153	35.2	64
York UA	16.6	6.9	70.3	1.7	181	30.6	77
North Yorkshire	17.1	6.9	70.3	1.8	570	31.6	238
Craven	17.2	6.3	70.1	1.8	54	31.6	23
Hambleton	16.0	6.5	71.8	1.7	84	30.4	35
Harrogate	15.6	6.1	72.1	1.5	151	28.5	63
Richmondshire	15.3	6.6	73.0	1.5	47	30.5	18
Ryedale	16.9	6.4	69.4	1.8	51	31.2	21
Scarborough	21.6	8.7	65.4	2.5	106	37.2	47
Selby	16.1	7.2	70.5	1.8	76	31.3	31
South Yorkshire (Met County)	22.3	10.5	64.3	2.8	1,266	40.7	531
Barnsley	25.2	12.8	61.3	3.1	218	45.2	92
Doncaster	22.9	11.0	64.5	2.8	287	42.1	119
Rotherham	22.4	10.5	64.5	3.0	248	41.4	102
Sheffield	20.6	9.2	65.2	2.5	513	37.6	218
West Yorkshire (Met County)	18.8	8.7	67.3	2.2	2,079	35.6	854
Bradford	18.5	8.7	67.3	2.2	468	36.4	180
Calderdale	18.4	8.3	67.6	2.0	192	34.7	81
Kirklees	18.0	8.3	67.7	2.1	389	34.4	159
Leeds	18.0	8.1	68.3	2.0	715	33.6	302
Wakefield	22.4	11.0	64.6	2.7	315	40.7	132
East Midlands	18.4	8.4	67.6	2.1	4,172	34.2	1,732
Derby UA	19.3	8.8	66.5	2.2	222	35.9	92
Leicester UA	18.8	9.3	65.5	2.3	280	35.9	111
Nottingham UA	20.1	10.2	65.0	2.3	267	36.3	116
Rutland UA	14.3	5.9	72.9	1.5	35	28.0	13
Derbyshire	20.1	9.1	65.8	2.4	735	37.0	309
Amber Valley	19.7	8.7	66.0	2.3	116	36.1	49
Bolsover	25.8	12.5	59.8	3.5	72	45.6	30
Chesterfield	23.1	10.7	62.4	2.7	99	40.7	43
Derbyshire Dales	17.9	7.3	69.1	1.8	69	33.3	29
Erewash	18.3	8.2	66.7	2.1	110	34.2	46
High Peak	17.5	7.9	69.2	1.9	89	33.5	37
North East Derbyshire	21.7	9.6	64.4	2.6	97	39.7	41
South Derbyshire	17.6	8.2	69.0	2.1	82	33.4	33

Table 14.3 (continued)

Percentages and thousands

	With limiting long-term illness[2]	Of working age[3] with limiting long-term illness	Claiming good health[4]	Individuals providing 50 hours or more unpaid care[5] per week	All people (thousands)	Households with one or more person with a limiting long-term illness (percentages)	All house-holds (thousands)
	Percentage of individuals:						
Leicestershire	15.4	6.6	70.4	1.7	610	30.1	245
Blaby	14.7	6.3	71.3	1.6	90	28.9	36
Charnwood	15.0	6.6	70.5	1.5	153	29.6	60
Harborough	13.7	5.8	73.2	1.4	77	26.8	31
Hinckley and Bosworth	16.3	6.9	69.4	1.9	100	31.5	41
Melton	14.5	6.0	72.3	1.7	48	28.5	20
North West Leicestershire	17.8	7.8	67.4	2.1	86	33.7	35
Oadby and Wigston	15.7	6.4	70.0	1.8	56	30.9	22
Lincolnshire	19.3	8.5	66.9	2.3	647	35.0	272
Boston	20.3	9.4	64.6	2.4	56	36.0	24
East Lindsey	23.7	10.4	62.5	3.3	130	41.2	56
Lincoln	19.2	9.3	67.2	2.1	86	34.6	37
North Kesteven	17.8	7.5	69.6	2.1	94	32.8	39
South Holland	19.6	8.0	64.9	2.4	77	35.0	33
South Kesteven	15.9	6.8	70.6	1.7	125	30.0	51
West Lindsey	18.7	8.1	68.3	2.1	80	34.3	33
Northamptonshire	15.5	7.1	70.6	1.7	630	29.6	259
Corby	18.4	9.3	68.1	2.3	53	35.3	22
Daventry	13.6	6.2	73.4	1.4	72	26.8	29
East Northamptonshire	15.2	6.5	70.6	1.6	77	28.9	31
Kettering	16.2	7.0	69.9	1.7	82	30.2	34
Northampton	15.9	7.4	70.0	1.8	194	29.6	81
South Northamptonshire	12.9	5.5	74.5	1.3	79	26.2	32
Wellingborough	16.7	7.7	67.8	1.7	73	31.8	30
Nottinghamshire	20.0	9.4	66.8	2.3	749	36.4	314
Ashfield	22.1	10.9	63.1	2.7	111	40.0	47
Bassetlaw	21.9	10.8	65.3	2.6	108	39.4	45
Broxtowe	18.1	8.2	68.1	2.0	108	33.5	45
Gedling	18.3	8.1	68.1	2.0	112	33.6	48
Mansfield	24.2	12.1	62.7	3.0	98	43.3	42
Newark and Sherwood	19.7	9.0	67.3	2.4	106	36.0	44
Rushcliffe	15.6	6.5	72.8	1.5	106	29.3	44
West Midlands	18.9	8.6	67.2	2.3	5,267	35.7	2,154
Herefordshire, County of UA	18.0	7.5	68.7	1.9	175	33.0	74
Stoke-on-Trent UA	23.9	11.9	63.1	2.9	241	42.5	103
Telford and Wrekin UA	18.0	9.3	68.6	2.4	158	34.7	64
Shropshire	17.9	7.5	69.4	1.9	283	33.3	117
Bridgnorth	16.7	6.9	70.3	1.8	52	32.4	21
North Shropshire	18.3	7.8	68.7	2.1	57	34.8	23
Oswestry	18.7	8.2	69.9	2.1	37	33.8	16
Shrewsbury and Atcham	17.5	7.5	69.8	1.8	96	32.0	40
South Shropshire	19.4	7.4	67.4	2.1	40	35.0	17
Staffordshire	18.3	8.3	68.6	2.2	807	34.6	328
Cannock Chase	19.9	9.5	66.9	2.5	92	38.0	37
East Staffordshire	17.1	7.6	69.4	2.0	104	32.1	43
Lichfield	17.2	7.5	70.0	2.0	93	32.2	38
Newcastle-under-Lyme	20.8	9.6	66.1	2.4	122	38.6	51
South Staffordshire	17.0	7.2	70.4	2.1	106	32.6	42
Stafford	17.6	7.6	69.6	1.9	121	32.4	50
Staffordshire Moorlands	19.9	9.0	67.5	2.2	94	36.8	39
Tamworth	16.8	8.6	69.1	2.4	75	33.8	29
Warwickshire	16.8	7.2	69.9	1.9	506	31.6	211
North Warwickshire	18.3	8.6	67.9	2.3	62	35.1	25
Nuneaton and Bedworth	19.1	9.0	67.4	2.4	119	36.4	49
Rugby	16.1	6.8	70.3	1.8	87	30.4	36
Stratford-on-Avon	15.4	6.0	71.5	1.5	111	28.8	47
Warwick	15.4	6.3	71.6	1.5	126	28.8	53
West Midlands (Met County)	19.6	9.1	65.7	2.4	2,556	37.7	1,033
Birmingham	19.7	9.4	65.7	2.5	977	37.9	391
Coventry	18.6	8.6	67.4	2.1	301	35.8	122
Dudley	19.1	8.4	65.8	2.4	305	36.3	125
Sandwell	21.7	10.0	62.6	2.8	283	41.1	115
Solihull	16.3	7.0	70.9	1.9	200	31.9	81
Walsall	20.4	9.4	64.7	2.7	253	39.4	101
Wolverhampton	21.2	9.6	63.6	2.6	237	39.6	97

Table **14.3**   (continued)

	Percentage of individuals:					Households with one or more person with a limiting long-term illness (percentages)	All house-holds (thousands)
	With limiting long-term illness[2]	Of working age[3] with limiting long-term illness	Claiming good health[4]	Individuals providing 50 hours or more unpaid care[5] per week	All people (thousands)		
Worcestershire	16.7	7.2	69.7	1.9	542	31.5	223
Bromsgrove	16.7	6.7	71.1	1.8	88	31.6	35
Malvern Hills	18.1	6.9	69.1	1.9	72	32.6	30
Redditch	15.8	7.7	70.2	2.0	79	31.2	32
Worcester	15.9	7.3	69.9	1.8	93	30.0	39
Wychavon	16.1	6.6	70.4	1.9	113	30.5	47
Wyre Forest	17.9	8.1	67.5	2.0	97	33.3	40
East	16.2	7.0	70.4	1.8	5,388	30.8	2,232
Luton UA	15.3	7.7	69.6	1.8	184	31.5	71
Peterborough UA	16.8	8.1	68.6	2.0	156	31.9	65
Southend-on-Sea UA	19.1	7.8	66.9	2.0	160	33.7	71
Thurrock UA	16.1	7.7	70.1	2.0	143	31.9	58
Bedfordshire	14.3	6.4	72.5	1.6	382	28.1	154
Bedford	15.6	7.0	71.3	1.6	148	30.1	60
Mid Bedfordshire	12.9	5.7	74.2	1.4	121	25.9	49
South Bedfordshire	14.1	6.3	72.3	1.6	113	27.7	46
Cambridgeshire	14.6	6.4	72.5	1.6	553	28.5	223
Cambridge	13.7	6.4	74.1	1.1	109	27.5	43
East Cambridgeshire	15.2	6.3	71.4	1.6	73	29.2	30
Fenland	19.4	8.4	65.6	2.4	84	35.3	35
Huntingdonshire	13.5	6.2	73.4	1.6	157	26.9	63
South Cambridgeshire	13.3	5.5	75.1	1.3	130	26.3	52
Essex	16.4	7.0	70.5	1.8	1,311	31.2	545
Basildon	16.9	7.7	69.5	2.1	166	32.5	69
Braintree	15.5	6.8	71.6	1.7	132	29.4	54
Brentwood	15.4	6.1	72.9	1.5	68	28.4	29
Castle Point	17.1	7.2	69.3	2.2	87	33.3	35
Chelmsford	13.6	5.9	73.9	1.4	157	26.8	65
Colchester	15.9	7.4	71.3	1.7	156	30.6	64
Epping Forest	15.5	6.5	71.7	1.7	121	29.9	51
Harlow	16.2	7.5	68.6	1.8	79	31.2	33
Maldon	15.5	6.8	71.7	1.7	59	30.4	24
Rochford	15.8	6.3	71.1	1.9	78	31.2	32
Tendring	24.0	9.0	62.5	2.8	139	40.6	61
Uttlesford	13.2	5.4	74.8	1.3	69	26.5	28
Hertfordshire	14.1	5.9	73.1	1.5	1,034	27.5	421
Broxbourne	14.3	6.2	71.5	1.7	87	29.3	35
Dacorum	13.8	5.9	73.3	1.5	138	27.3	56
East Hertfordshire	12.4	5.3	75.2	1.2	129	24.6	52
Hertsmere	14.7	5.9	73.2	1.5	94	28.2	38
North Hertfordshire	14.7	5.9	72.1	1.5	117	27.7	49
St. Albans	13.1	5.3	75.5	1.3	129	25.4	53
Stevenage	15.1	6.8	70.9	1.9	80	29.5	33
Three Rivers	14.3	5.5	73.6	1.4	83	28.0	33
Watford	14.2	6.3	72.6	1.6	80	27.4	32
Welwyn Hatfield	15.3	6.2	71.2	1.6	98	30.0	40
Norfolk	19.4	8.1	66.1	2.1	797	34.7	343
Breckland	18.6	7.7	67.0	2.1	121	34.1	51
Broadland	17.5	7.1	68.7	1.7	119	31.3	50
Great Yarmouth	21.8	9.6	63.3	2.7	91	38.7	39
King's Lynn and West Norfolk	20.4	8.4	65.1	2.5	135	36.5	58
North Norfolk	21.5	8.2	63.9	2.3	98	36.8	44
Norwich	19.4	9.2	64.9	1.9	122	34.3	55
South Norfolk	17.0	7.0	68.9	1.7	111	31.5	47
Suffolk	17.1	7.0	69.4	1.9	669	31.8	281
Babergh	16.1	6.3	70.4	1.7	83	30.2	35
Forest Heath	14.4	6.1	72.6	1.6	56	28.1	23
Ipswich	18.0	8.0	68.1	2.1	117	33.1	50
Mid Suffolk	15.5	6.2	71.5	1.6	87	29.9	35
St. Edmundsbury	15.5	6.6	70.9	1.6	98	29.2	41
Suffolk Coastal	17.2	6.5	69.8	1.9	115	31.8	49
Waveney	20.7	8.4	65.1	2.4	112	37.2	48

Table **14.3** (continued)

Percentages and thousands

	Percentage of individuals:					Households with one or more person with a limiting long-term illness (percentages)	All house-holds (thousands)
	With limiting long-term illness[2]	Of working age[3] with limiting long-term illness	Claiming good health[4]	Individuals providing 50 hours or more unpaid care[5] per week	All people (thousands)		
London	15.5	7.8	70.8	1.7	7,172	29.7	3,016
Inner London	15.6	8.7	70.7	1.6	2,766	29.0	1,220
Camden	15.8	9.3	71.3	1.3	198	28.3	92
City of London	13.3	7.3	73.8	1.1	7	19.3	4
Hackney	18.1	10.5	68.4	1.7	203	34.7	86
Hammersmith and Fulham	14.7	8.0	73.0	1.2	165	27.0	75
Haringey	15.5	8.7	70.2	1.5	217	29.5	92
Islington	17.9	10.6	68.0	1.6	176	32.0	82
Kensington and Chelsea	13.6	7.1	75.2	1.0	159	23.5	79
Lambeth	14.4	8.1	71.6	1.3	266	26.4	118
Lewisham	15.6	8.2	69.2	1.7	249	29.4	107
Newham	17.3	9.8	68.0	2.2	244	36.5	92
Southwark	15.6	8.5	70.3	1.7	245	29.7	106
Tower Hamlets	17.2	9.9	67.9	2.4	196	33.8	79
Wandsworth	13.4	6.8	74.6	1.2	260	24.1	116
Westminster	14.8	8.0	72.4	1.2	181	25.0	91
Outer London	15.4	7.2	70.9	1.7	4,406	30.1	1,796
Barking and Dagenham	19.9	9.6	65.5	2.7	164	38.6	67
Barnet	14.6	6.4	72.5	1.5	315	28.4	127
Bexley	15.6	6.4	70.3	1.9	218	30.7	89
Brent	15.6	8.2	70.0	1.7	263	32.4	100
Bromley	15.0	6.2	72.4	1.6	296	28.2	126
Croydon	14.7	7.1	70.7	1.6	331	27.9	139
Ealing	15.1	7.7	71.1	1.7	301	30.4	118
Enfield	16.2	7.7	69.5	1.8	274	31.5	110
Greenwich	17.4	8.7	68.4	2.0	214	32.5	93
Harrow	14.9	6.5	72.1	1.7	207	30.6	79
Havering	17.2	7.0	69.7	2.1	224	33.2	92
Hillingdon	14.9	6.9	71.3	1.8	243	30.0	97
Hounslow	14.9	7.8	70.9	1.7	212	30.2	84
Kingston upon Thames	12.9	5.7	73.9	1.2	147	24.9	61
Merton	13.8	6.3	72.7	1.4	188	26.6	79
Redbridge	16.3	7.6	69.8	2.0	239	33.0	92
Richmond upon Thames	12.4	5.2	76.3	1.1	172	23.0	76
Sutton	14.8	6.5	71.5	1.6	180	27.7	76
Waltham Forest	16.5	8.5	68.6	1.9	218	32.0	90
South East	15.5	6.5	71.5	1.6	8,001	29.4	3,287
Bracknell Forest UA	11.7	5.6	75.3	1.3	110	23.4	43
Brighton and Hove UA	18.1	8.5	68.1	1.7	248	31.1	114
Isle of Wight UA	22.0	9.0	65.1	2.5	133	38.1	58
Medway UA	15.6	7.5	69.8	1.9	249	31.0	100
Milton Keynes UA	14.1	7.3	72.5	1.7	207	27.9	83
Portsmouth UA	17.4	7.9	67.9	1.8	187	32.3	79
Reading UA	13.5	6.3	72.5	1.4	143	26.6	58
Slough UA	14.3	6.9	70.5	1.7	119	30.3	45
Southampton UA	17.4	8.4	68.3	1.8	217	33.1	91
West Berkshire UA	12.4	5.5	74.9	1.2	144	24.8	57
Windsor and Maidenhead UA	12.6	4.9	75.4	1.3	134	24.5	54
Wokingham UA	10.9	4.9	77.6	1.1	150	22.6	57
Buckinghamshire	12.8	5.3	74.9	1.3	479	25.8	188
Aylesbury Vale	12.7	5.8	74.6	1.3	166	25.6	65
Chiltern	13.0	5.0	75.8	1.2	89	25.7	35
South Bucks	13.1	4.8	75.3	1.3	62	26.1	25
Wycombe	12.6	5.3	74.5	1.4	162	26.1	64
East Sussex	19.8	7.4	66.8	2.0	492	34.4	215
Eastbourne	21.6	7.8	64.2	2.0	90	35.8	41
Hastings	21.7	10.2	63.3	2.3	85	36.8	38
Lewes	18.8	6.9	68.2	1.8	92	33.8	40
Rother	22.0	7.2	65.2	2.2	85	36.4	38
Wealden	16.8	6.1	70.6	1.7	140	31.0	58

Table **14.3** (continued)

Percentages and thousands

	Percentage of individuals:					Households with one or more person with a limiting long-term illness (percentages)	All house-holds (thousands)
	With limiting long-term illness[2]	Of working age[3] with limiting long-term illness	Claiming good health[4]	Individuals providing 50 hours or more unpaid care[5] per week	All people (thousands)		
Hampshire	14.9	6.2	72.5	1.6	1,240	28.8	503
Basingstoke and Deane	13.1	6.1	74.3	1.4	153	25.9	62
East Hampshire	14.2	5.9	74.1	1.4	109	26.9	44
Eastleigh	14.4	6.2	73.3	1.6	116	28.3	47
Fareham	15.3	6.0	72.2	1.6	108	29.4	44
Gosport	16.8	7.2	68.9	2.0	76	31.9	31
Hart	11.2	4.8	77.2	1.1	84	23.1	32
Havant	18.3	7.6	67.9	2.3	117	34.5	48
New Forest	17.8	6.6	69.4	1.9	169	32.2	72
Rushmoor	13.2	6.3	73.5	1.4	91	26.9	35
Test Valley	14.1	6.0	73.7	1.5	110	27.5	44
Winchester	14.2	5.7	74.6	1.3	107	27.3	43
Kent	17.3	7.4	69.2	1.9	1,330	32.4	547
Ashford	16.1	7.1	70.2	1.8	103	31.4	41
Canterbury	18.9	7.5	67.6	2.0	135	34.6	56
Dartford	15.1	6.8	70.4	1.7	86	28.3	35
Dover	20.5	8.8	66.4	2.3	105	36.7	44
Gravesham	16.3	7.6	69.4	1.9	96	32.7	38
Maidstone	15.2	6.7	71.2	1.6	139	29.3	56
Sevenoaks	14.5	5.8	72.9	1.5	109	28.1	44
Shepway	20.5	8.6	66.1	2.2	96	36.3	41
Swale	17.6	8.2	68.3	2.3	123	33.7	49
Thanet	22.9	9.4	63.2	2.7	127	39.4	55
Tonbridge and Malling	14.0	6.0	72.5	1.5	108	28.1	43
Tunbridge Wells	14.5	6.0	72.9	1.3	104	27.3	43
Oxfordshire	13.4	5.6	73.9	1.4	605	26.6	241
Cherwell	13.3	5.9	73.0	1.5	132	26.3	53
Oxford	13.8	6.4	73.1	1.3	134	28.1	52
South Oxfordshire	13.1	5.2	74.7	1.3	128	25.6	52
Vale of White Horse	13.1	5.2	74.9	1.5	116	26.4	46
West Oxfordshire	13.7	5.4	73.8	1.3	96	26.8	38
Surrey	13.5	5.4	74.5	1.3	1,059	25.9	433
Elmbridge	12.4	4.6	76.2	1.2	122	23.9	51
Epsom and Ewell	14.3	5.8	73.8	1.4	67	27.0	27
Guildford	12.9	5.3	75.2	1.3	130	25.6	52
Mole Valley	14.5	5.4	74.2	1.3	80	27.3	34
Reigate and Banstead	14.2	5.9	73.8	1.3	127	26.4	52
Runnymede	13.5	5.3	73.7	1.4	78	26.2	32
Spelthorne	14.1	5.8	72.5	1.5	90	27.2	38
Surrey Heath	11.7	4.9	76.7	1.3	80	23.4	32
Tandridge	14.4	5.8	73.6	1.4	79	26.9	32
Waverley	14.1	5.4	74.5	1.3	116	26.6	47
Woking	13.0	5.4	74.4	1.3	90	25.4	37
West Sussex	16.8	6.2	70.1	1.7	754	30.4	321
Adur	19.2	7.3	66.7	2.0	60	35.0	26
Arun	20.8	7.1	65.6	2.2	141	35.0	63
Chichester	17.0	5.9	70.4	1.6	106	30.6	46
Crawley	14.6	6.4	71.2	1.7	100	29.1	40
Horsham	13.5	5.1	74.2	1.3	122	25.7	50
Mid Sussex	13.5	5.2	74.4	1.3	127	25.6	52
Worthing	20.1	7.2	66.3	1.9	98	33.4	44
South West	18.1	7.6	68.9	2.0	4,928	33.1	2,086
Bath and North East Somerset UA	15.8	6.3	71.5	1.5	169	30.0	71
Bournemouth UA	20.0	8.2	66.7	1.9	163	34.1	72
Bristol, City of UA	17.8	8.1	68.6	2.1	381	32.8	162
North Somerset UA	18.5	7.5	69.0	1.9	189	33.0	80
Plymouth UA	20.6	10.0	66.8	2.5	241	37.4	103
Poole UA	18.5	7.3	68.3	2.0	138	33.6	59
South Gloucestershire UA	14.5	6.3	72.4	1.7	246	28.2	99
Swindon UA	15.3	7.0	70.7	1.8	180	29.1	75
Torbay UA	23.0	9.4	63.7	2.8	130	39.0	57

Table **14.3** (continued)

	Percentage of individuals:					Households with one or more person with a limiting long-term illness (percentages)	All house-holds (thousands)
	With limiting long-term illness[2]	Of working age[3] with limiting long-term illness	Claiming good health[4]	Individuals providing 50 hours or more unpaid care[5] per week	All people (thousands)		
Cornwall and the Isles of Scilly	21.2	9.2	65.8	2.6	501	37.9	216
Caradon	20.1	8.6	67.2	2.5	80	36.6	34
Carrick	20.8	8.3	66.6	2.4	88	36.6	39
Kerrier	21.9	10.1	65.4	2.8	93	39.9	39
North Cornwall	20.6	8.8	65.9	2.5	81	36.7	34
Penwith	23.6	10.4	63.6	2.7	63	40.7	28
Restormel	20.9	9.2	65.7	2.8	96	37.9	40
Isles of Scilly	12.9	4.9	74.2	1.0	2	25.2	1
Devon	19.0	7.7	68.3	2.1	704	34.1	299
East Devon	20.3	6.8	67.1	2.0	126	35.2	55
Exeter	17.6	8.2	70.1	1.8	111	32.0	47
Mid Devon	17.0	7.2	69.5	1.9	70	32.3	29
North Devon	18.7	7.8	67.9	2.1	88	34.1	37
South Hams	18.7	7.6	69.7	2.0	82	33.8	35
Teignbridge	20.0	7.8	67.6	2.2	121	35.1	51
Torridge	19.9	8.5	65.7	2.4	59	36.2	25
West Devon	19.0	8.1	68.4	2.1	49	34.1	20
Dorset	19.2	7.1	68.1	2.0	391	34.5	168
Christchurch	22.1	6.9	64.3	2.5	45	37.5	21
East Dorset	18.4	6.0	68.9	2.0	84	33.6	36
North Dorset	16.6	6.4	71.1	1.7	62	32.1	25
Purbeck	18.6	7.0	68.3	1.9	44	34.3	19
West Dorset	19.3	7.0	68.2	1.9	92	34.1	41
Weymouth and Portland	20.9	9.5	66.5	2.3	64	36.5	27
Gloucestershire	16.1	6.7	70.5	1.7	565	30.0	238
Cheltenham	15.6	6.4	71.2	1.5	110	27.7	48
Cotswold	15.1	5.5	72.1	1.4	80	28.0	34
Forest of Dean	18.0	8.0	68.0	2.0	80	34.6	33
Gloucester	16.9	7.7	69.2	1.8	110	31.4	46
Stroud	15.8	6.5	71.0	1.6	108	29.7	45
Tewkesbury	15.5	6.1	71.8	1.7	76	29.1	32
Somerset	18.1	7.4	68.3	1.9	498	33.1	211
Mendip	16.8	7.1	70.1	1.7	104	31.4	43
Sedgemoor	18.9	8.0	66.8	2.2	106	34.7	44
South Somerset	17.4	6.9	68.6	1.8	151	32.3	64
Taunton Deane	18.2	7.4	68.9	1.8	102	32.7	44
West Somerset	22.3	8.3	64.7	2.2	35	38.3	16
Wiltshire	15.1	6.3	72.5	1.6	433	28.9	177
Kennet	14.1	6.0	73.7	1.5	75	27.8	30
North Wiltshire	13.9	5.9	73.9	1.5	125	27.3	50
Salisbury	16.0	6.5	72.3	1.6	115	30.2	47
West Wiltshire	16.1	6.7	70.5	1.7	118	30.2	49

1   Cells in this table have been adjusted to avoid the release of confidential data.
2   Limiting long-term illness covers any long-term illness, health problems or disability which limits daily activities or work.
3   Working age population is 16 to 64 inclusive for men and 16 to 59 inclusive for women.
4   Good general health refers to health over the 12 months prior to Census day (29 April 2001).
5   Provision of unpaid care: looking after, giving help or support to family members, friends, neighbours or others because of long-term physical or mental ill-health or disability or problems relating to old age.

Source: Office for National Statistics

Table **14.4**   Education and training: by local education authority[1]

| | Three- and four-year-olds in early years education[2] | | | | | Pupils and students participating in post-compulsory education[7] (percentages) 2000/01 | Percentage of pupils in last year of compulsory schooling[8,9] 2001/02 with: | | Average GCE/VCE A/AS level points score[9,10] 2001/02 |
| | Participation rates[3] (percentages) | | | Pupil/teacher ratio[6] 2002/03 (numbers) | | | | 5 or more GCSE Grades A*-C/ Standard Grades 1-3 (or equivalent) | |
	All schools Jan. 2002[4]	Private and voluntary providers[5] Jan. 2002[4]	All providers Jan. 2002[4]	Primary schools	Secondary schools		No graded results		
United Kingdom	64	29	93	22.0	16.4	79	5.1	50.8	..
England	64	32	96	22.6	17.0	77	5.1	49.5	240.5
North East	87	12	99	21.9	16.7	74	6.4	44.3	224.4
Darlington	91	22	113	23.5	17.8	70	4.4	48.7	280.3
Durham	83	12	94	21.1	16.9	68	6.6	41.1	217.4
Gateshead	79	18	98	21.0	15.5	76	6.9	51.9	228.8
Hartlepool	95	8	102	23.3	17.1	75	6.0	42.0	256.1
Middlesbrough	101	7	108	21.3	15.8	75	9.7	35.8	190.6
Newcastle upon Tyne	83	18	101	22.6	16.6	77	11.8	38.0	194.7
North Tyneside	92	12	104	22.7	16.8	79	5.5	48.0	217.9
Northumberland	82	15	97	22.3	18.0	77	4.7	51.4	231.2
Redcar and Cleveland	100	5	105	22.3	16.0	69	5.9	48.6	246.5
South Tyneside	86	10	96	21.0	15.8	63	4.7	42.2	198.7
Stockton-on-Tees	90	9	99	22.6	16.8	87	4.8	46.1	229.8
Sunderland	89	7	96	21.7	15.8	69	5.4	41.6	235.6
North West	70	27	97	22.3	16.4	74	5.3	48.0	246.7
Blackburn with Darwen	66	24	90	21.5	16.4	81	6.4	42.0	236.7
Blackpool	51	52	103	22.3	17.4	69	4.9	36.4	241.3
Bolton	73	24	97	21.9	16.4	73	3.4	46.7	245.7
Bury	65	26	91	24.0	17.6	73	1.9	56.3	230.3
Cheshire	57	42	99	22.3	16.9	81	3.5	58.2	264.5
Cumbria	69	22	91	21.5	16.3	78	4.6	52.7	259.3
Halton	62	32	94	21.4	15.9	70	5.0	42.7	209.6
Knowsley	99	6	105	22.1	16.0	63	10.9	30.1	175.0
Lancashire	58	34	91	22.5	16.8	74	4.0	51.7	272.6
Liverpool	84	20	103	21.5	15.4	73	8.1	39.2	212.6
Manchester	93	11	104	22.1	15.2	68	12.6	33.3	213.5
Oldham	72	21	93	23.9	15.7	77	5.4	42.9	251.5
Rochdale	67	25	92	22.9	17.0	64	7.0	40.0	173.5
St. Helens	73	22	95	22.9	15.8	81	5.8	45.5	258.1
Salford	96	12	109	22.5	16.1	57	6.0	35.9	206.1
Sefton	80	20	100	21.6	16.1	87	4.4	52.6	244.5
Stockport	75	21	96	23.0	16.5	75	5.7	52.4	216.0
Tameside	78	16	94	22.7	16.9	70	5.8	43.1	244.1
Trafford	83	26	109	23.7	17.2	74	2.9	60.1	287.5
Warrington	59	45	105	22.6	16.7	79	4.5	51.9	250.6
Wigan	62	32	94	22.2	16.3	70	3.7	49.3	256.7
Wirral	69	34	103	21.7	16.0	76	5.5	53.1	262.8
Yorkshire and the Humber	73	24	97	22.7	16.9	76	6.1	44.2	245.6
Barnsley	75	13	88	23.7	17.9	60	7.0	35.4	197.9
Bradford	82	15	97	21.8	16.0	88	7.2	37.3	212.0
Calderdale	70	25	95	22.4	16.6	77	4.5	50.5	227.4
Doncaster	84	8	92	23.1	16.2	77	7.0	39.6	244.0
East Riding of Yorkshire	60	43	103	23.4	17.7	80	5.3	49.7	252.1
Kingston upon Hull, City of	77	18	94	23.1	20.0	62	9.9	28.9	218.3
Kirklees	66	24	90	22.4	17.5	75	3.7	47.5	282.6
Leeds	80	16	95	22.4	16.6	76	7.9	42.4	225.4
North East Lincolnshire	69	26	95	22.9	19.2	71	5.5	37.8	239.9
North Lincolnshire	65	38	103	24.2	18.2	80	2.9	42.6	272.4
North Yorkshire	60	42	102	21.6	16.2	87	3.7	60.2	283.1
Rotherham	79	18	97	22.9	15.9	76	6.3	41.6	237.9
Sheffield	71	28	99	23.5	17.0	67	8.7	41.4	233.3
Wakefield	88	14	102	23.3	17.5	72	4.1	45.6	242.2
York	62	49	111	22.0	16.0	78	4.1	56.4	283.1

Table **14.4** (continued)

| | Three- and four-year-olds in early years education[2] | | | Pupil/teacher ratio[6] 2002/03 (numbers) | | Pupils and students participating in post-compulsory education[7] (percentages) 2000/01 | Percentage of pupils in last year of compulsory schooling[8,9] 2001/02 with: | | Average GCE/VCE A/AS level points score[9,10] 2001/02 |
| | Participation rates[3] (percentages) | | | | | | 5 or more GCSE Grades A*-C/ | | |
	All schools Jan. 2002[4]	Private and voluntary providers[5] Jan. 2002[4]	All providers Jan. 2002[4]	Primary schools	Secondary schools		No graded results	Standard Grades 1-3 (or equivalent)	
East Midlands	64	34	98	23.1	17.2	75	5.0	49.2	245.5
Derby	82	29	112	23.0	16.7	72	5.6	45.2	237.0
Derbyshire	69	33	102	23.8	17.0	73	4.2	53.0	265.2
Leicester	78	15	93	22.6	16.7	74	5.4	40.5	211.7
Leicestershire	38	56	94	23.4	17.5	84	4.1	52.5	247.8
Lincolnshire	58	32	90	23.4	17.2	79	3.8	54.4	275.3
Northamptonshire	57	42	99	22.6	17.6	75	5.8	50.6	236.4
Nottingham	92	20	112	21.2	15.8	65	11.2	31.4	222.6
Nottinghamshire	68	28	96	23.6	17.3	73	5.0	46.9	234.4
Rutland	56	59	114	20.4	17.3	82	0.7	61.1	..
West Midlands	69	25	95	22.5	17.0	76	5.3	48.1	237.5
Birmingham	73	18	91	21.6	16.0	75	5.3	45.3	241.2
Coventry	71	22	94	21.5	17.1	75	7.0	43.2	232.1
Dudley	77	26	103	22.5	16.9	72	4.2	51.7	218.9
Herefordshire	50	47	97	22.0	17.0	73	4.0	56.0	278.8
Sandwell	91	4	94	23.7	17.3	70	7.9	34.2	163.5
Shropshire	43	58	101	23.0	17.1	81	3.0	58.4	273.3
Solihull	87	17	104	22.2	17.5	79	4.3	58.2	226.2
Staffordshire	62	27	90	23.3	17.3	79	4.3	50.1	241.0
Stoke-on-Trent	80	11	91	23.6	17.1	66	5.6	38.6	201.9
Telford and Wrekin	53	43	97	24.1	16.7	75	4.6	49.7	247.6
Walsall	93	4	97	23.2	16.2	77	5.2	42.4	242.6
Warwickshire	56	37	93	22.4	17.1	78	4.9	51.7	251.8
Wolverhampton	96	8	104	23.3	17.2	74	7.0	43.3	192.9
Worcestershire	56	40	96	22.1	18.1	84	6.4	52.1	248.6
East	56	40	95	22.8	17.5	80	4.7	53.0	242.3
Bedfordshire	60	37	97	22.6	18.7	83	4.8	51.2	253.3
Cambridgeshire	48	47	95	23.7	18.2	78	4.5	54.3	281.6
Essex	43	51	94	23.0	17.6	75	4.4	53.5	245.2
Hertfordshire	78	24	102	23.0	17.0	93	4.4	56.7	241.9
Luton	62	24	87	23.5	17.9	75	4.1	39.5	207.0
Norfolk	53	45	98	21.7	17.1	74	5.1	50.4	229.5
Peterborough	46	49	95	23.1	17.4	78	7.7	42.8	212.2
Southend-on-Sea	57	32	90	23.3	17.3	75	7.3	56.0	272.6
Suffolk	51	37	88	21.7	16.9	77	3.8	56.5	236.3
Thurrock	50	37	86	23.6	19.8	71	4.6	46.8	170.1
London	72	20	92	23.3	16.9	81	4.5	48.5	216.8
Inner London	79	16	95	22.6	16.2	77	4.7	41.0	188.5
Camden	..	..	..	21.4	14.8	..	6.1	48.4	251.3
City of London	..	..	..	..	.	..	.	.	.
Hackney	..	..	..	23.5	16.3	..	8.7	31.1	143.4
Hammersmith and Fulham	..	..	..	23.2	18.0	..	2.8	50.5	202.0
Haringey	..	..	..	23.8	15.3	..	8.0	35.6	163.8
Islington	..	..	..	22.7	16.2	..	11.6	32.9	150.9
Kensington and Chelsea	..	..	..	20.8	16.9	..	4.7	55.7	231.4
Lambeth	..	..	..	21.4	16.2	..	3.7	40.1	162.1
Lewisham	..	..	..	20.6	15.4	..	4.3	38.7	199.7
Newham	..	..	..	24.9	16.7	..	0.6	42.4	175.8
Southwark	..	..	..	22.8	17.1	..	4.4	35.8	166.7
Tower Hamlets	..	..	..	22.9	16.2	..	1.9	43.7	160.9
Wandsworth	..	..	..	21.4	16.4	..	4.2	48.6	182.7
Westminster	..	..	..	22.1	15.6	..	6.0	41.5	183.2
Outer London	68	22	90	23.7	17.2	83	4.3	51.9	227.1
Barking and Dagenham	..	..	..	24.1	17.4	..	7.2	42.4	192.8
Barnet	..	..	..	22.7	15.4	..	5.1	59.2	246.9
Bexley	..	..	..	25.1	18.7	..	3.4	52.6	259.0
Brent	..	..	..	23.6	16.3	..	3.8	49.7	224.1
Bromley	..	..	..	23.7	17.6	..	3.7	59.9	233.6
Croydon	..	..	..	22.8	17.3	..	3.9	48.9	172.5
Ealing	..	..	..	24.8	17.6	..	0.9	49.9	227.4
Enfield	..	..	..	23.6	17.2	..	4.2	46.3	209.4
Greenwich	..	..	..	22.8	16.4	..	6.9	33.5	170.2

Table 14.4 (continued)

	Three- and four-year-olds in early years education[2] — Participation rates[3] (percentages)			Pupil/teacher ratio[6] 2002/03 (numbers)		Pupils and students participating in post-compulsory education[7] (percentages) 2000/01	Percentage of pupils in last year of compulsory schooling[8,9] 2001/02 with:		Average GCE/VCE A/AS level points score[9,10] 2001/02
	All schools Jan. 2002[4]	Private and voluntary providers[5] Jan. 2002[4]	All providers Jan. 2002[4]	Primary schools	Secondary schools		No graded results	5 or more GCSE Grades A*-C/ Standard Grades 1-3 (or equivalent)	
Harrow	..	..	..	23.8	17.3	..	2.6	59.1	207.3
Havering	..	..	..	24.2	17.5	..	3.7	57.3	259.7
Hillingdon	..	..	..	25.5	18.5	..	5.3	46.0	215.9
Hounslow	..	..	..	23.7	17.4	..	4.5	49.5	196.7
Kingston upon Thames	..	..	..	23.2	17.1	..	8.3	60.1	240.4
Merton	..	..	..	22.7	18.1	..	8.7	40.9	229.6
Redbridge	..	..	..	23.2	16.9	..	1.4	63.7	249.1
Richmond upon Thames	..	..	..	21.9	17.6	..	6.6	51.4	231.6
Sutton	..	..	..	24.7	17.7	..	3.3	64.8	300.6
Waltham Forest	..	..	..	24.5	16.8	..	4.8	44.3	188.8
South East	48	45	93	22.4	17.3	78	4.5	53.6	251.5
Bracknell Forest	38	55	93	23.6	17.6	73	3.7	45.5	217.9
Brighton and Hove	62	39	101	21.6	16.2	80	5.9	45.6	261.4
Buckinghamshire	49	48	97	22.5	18.4	81	3.9	64.4	281.2
East Sussex	46	49	95	21.3	16.5	78	4.8	51.2	233.8
Hampshire	41	60	102	22.5	17.3	74	3.2	56.2	262.4
Isle of Wight	43	57	100	21.2	17.6	83	7.5	44.1	221.4
Kent	45	44	88	23.1	17.5	79	4.5	53.9	258.0
Medway	45	50	95	23.6	17.7	81	3.6	49.1	248.8
Milton Keynes	48	29	77	23.0	17.6	61	5.0	46.0	231.9
Oxfordshire	43	47	90	21.6	17.3	76	5.2	51.5	240.5
Portsmouth	51	46	97	21.4	18.3	76	8.0	36.5	214.6
Reading	59	45	104	22.7	16.3	76	9.6	44.3	237.4
Slough	86	11	97	23.9	17.6	79	3.1	50.5	230.1
Southampton	47	49	96	22.1	16.5	73	5.7	43.3	207.9
Surrey	59	24	84	22.7	18.1	82	4.5	58.4	250.1
West Berkshire	50	42	92	21.3	16.0	84	3.9	57.1	256.1
West Sussex	44	53	97	22.0	16.6	82	4.7	53.7	237.1
Windsor and Maidenhead	54	43	98	22.5	17.3	76	4.2	56.4	251.7
Wokingham	40	57	97	22.5	17.0	82	4.0	62.6	266.5
South West	49	51	100	22.4	17.2	79	4.4	53.5	245.2
Bath and North East Somerset	51	62	113	22.5	16.8	96	5.5	58.4	228.0
Bournemouth	45	62	107	23.3	17.5	80	5.5	53.5	318.9
Bristol, City of	74	25	99	22.8	15.9	69	11.2	31.0	211.0
Cornwall	52	40	92	22.4	17.6	80	3.2	54.1	239.9
Devon	53	50	103	22.4	17.4	77	4.3	50.4	234.3
Dorset	42	63	105	21.9	17.8	76	4.1	59.0	238.5
Gloucestershire	39	64	103	21.2	16.8	79	2.9	60.9	258.2
Isles of Scilly[11]	31	43	73	10.6	.	..	..	63.0	..
North Somerset	41	47	88	23.9	17.2	76	4.5	53.3	268.4
Plymouth	55	49	105	22.7	16.9	81	4.7	51.4	252.8
Poole	39	50	89	22.7	16.5	83	2.7	60.9	241.2
Somerset	44	53	97	22.1	18.2	79	2.7	54.8	264.7
South Gloucestershire	46	59	104	23.2	16.5	85	3.3	52.4	248.3
Swindon	49	53	101	23.7	18.0	73	6.5	46.9	202.0
Torbay	66	28	95	23.0	17.0	84	5.5	54.3	250.6
Wiltshire	43	54	97	22.4	17.2	78	4.5	57.0	245.1

1　Local Education Authorities as at 1 April 1998. See Notes and Definitions.

2　Headcounts of children aged three and four at 31 December in the previous calendar year. Numbers of three- and four-year-olds in schools may include some two-year-olds. These figures must be interpreted carefully in the light of differing types of education providers between the countries. In the UK figures, any child attending more than one provider in England, or in Scotland, may have been counted twice.

3　Figures relate to all pupils as a percentage of the three- and four-year-old population. As some pupils are aged two, this can lead to participation rates greater than 100 per cent.

4　Provisional data for 2002/03 for England are shown in Department for Education and Skills (DfES) Statistical First Release (SFR) 15/2003.

5　Includes some local authority providers (other than schools) registered to receive nursery education grants.

6　Public sector schools only. Data for 2002/03 are provisional.

7　Pupils and students aged 16 in education as a percentage of the 16 year old population (ages measured at the beginning of the academic year). Provisional data for England up to 2002/03 [i.e. end 2002] are shown in Department for Education and Skills (DfES) Statistical First Release (SFR) 31/2003. The figure in the United Kingdom row refers to Great Britain.

8　Pupils in their last year of compulsory schooling as a percentage of the school population of the same age.

9　Figures relate to maintained schools only; hence they are not directly comparable with those in Tables 4.5, 16.3 and 17.3, which are for all schools.

10　The points scores for 2001/02 throughout England reflect the Universities and Colleges Admissions Service (UCAS) Tariff, and data are not directly comparable with earlier years, or with Wales. See Notes and Definitions for derivation of points scores.

11　Figures for pupils and students participating in post-compulsory education are included with those for Cornwall.

Source: Department for Education and Skills

Table 14.5 Housing and households[1]

| | Housing completions[2] 2001-02 (numbers) | | Stock of dwellings 1991[3] (thousands) | Households 2001[4] | | | | Local authority average weekly rent per dwelling (£) April 2003[6,7] | Average Council Tax (£)[8] April 2003 |
	Private enterprise	Registered Social Landlords, Local Authorities, etc		All household mid year estimates (thousands)	Average household size (number of people)	Lone parents[5] as a percentage of all households	One-person households as a percentage of all households		
England	115,749	14,550	19,671	20,715	2.34	6.2	30.0	51.26	1,102
North East	5,897	493	1,074	1,079	2.30	7.0	31.3	42.46	1,161
Darlington UA	335	15	..	41	2.31	6.3	31.9	43.01	1,003
Hartlepool UA	311	0	..	37	2.39	7.6	30.0	44.82	1,212
Middlesbrough UA	94	11	..	56	2.38	10.8	30.1	48.59	1,086
Redcar and Cleveland UA	299	59	..	59	2.33	6.8	29.5	.	1,132
Stockton-on-Tees UA	1,141	0	..	75	2.36	7.0	30.1	44.68	1,089
Durham County	1,607	94	..	209	2.33	6.2	29.4	42.72	1,211
Chester-le-Street	159	0	22	23	2.28	5.0	28.0	41.15	1,138
Derwentside	363	31	36	37	2.30	7.1	30.4	43.40	1,221
Durham	156	0	33	36	2.40	5.8	29.0	42.85	1,157
Easington	215	0	41	40	2.33	6.3	30.7	43.02	1,272
Sedgefield	220	13	37	37	2.32	7.1	27.8	42.49	1,294
Teesdale	37	16	11	10	2.33	3.1	30.6	42.88	1,159
Wear Valley	110	15	27	26	2.30	6.4	29.7	42.74	1,167
Northumberland	914	61	129	130	2.32	4.6	29.5	38.94	1,204
Alnwick	86	22	14	13	2.28	5.0	27.9	41.06	1,201
Berwick-upon-Tweed	20	0	13	12	2.20	3.6	34.6	42.96	1,197
Blyth Valley	71	0	33	35	2.32	5.2	29.7	37.40	1,183
Castle Morpeth	136	6	20	20	2.34	3.2	28.4	43.90	1,234
Tynedale	184	18	24	24	2.34	4.6	29.5	.	1,213
Wansbeck	162	6	26	26	2.35	5.2	28.7	36.52	1,193
Tyne and Wear (Met County)	1,531	268	474	471	2.26	7.7	33.3	41.73	1,162
Gateshead	421	60	86	84	2.25	6.7	33.5	43.19	1,238
Newcastle upon Tyne	434	17	120	116	2.21	8.5	36.9	42.64	1,241
North Tyneside	220	73	84	86	2.21	6.5	33.1	40.74	1,171
South Tyneside	50	0	66	67	2.26	8.6	33.9	39.52	1,128
Sunderland	369	91	118	118	2.35	7.9	29.5	.	1,049
Tees Valley	..	..	..	..	..	..	..	..	1,100
Tees Valley less Darlington	..	..	222	..	..	..	..	..	1,119
Former county of Durham	..	..	249	..	..	..	..	..	1,174
North West	14,219	1,673	2,222	2,823	2.35	7.4	30.3	46.29	1,135
Blackburn with Darwen UA	338	62	..	53	2.55	8.1	29.1	.	1,161
Blackpool UA	521	0	..	61	2.23	5.5	33.9	46.22	1,078
Halton UA	152	0	..	49	2.41	10.7	26.9	44.80	1,010
Warrington UA	472	0	..	81	2.34	7.3	29.9	50.75	995
Cheshire County	2,500	92	..	283	2.35	4.3	27.6	42.73	1,134
Chester	316	2	49	51	2.27	5.8	31.1	.	1,138
Congleton	158	19	34	37	2.42	2.9	26.2	.	1,143
Crewe and Nantwich	505	11	43	46	2.37	4.0	27.9	.	1,124
Ellesmere Port and Neston	49	0	32	34	2.38	5.5	26.5	38.00	1,138
Macclesfield	361	0	63	65	2.28	3.9	27.9	48.36	1,126
Vale Royal	402	0	45	50	2.43	3.9	25.3	.	1,139
Cumbria	1,368	105	210	210	2.28	4.2	31.2	46.80	1,175
Allerdale	224	34	41	40	2.30	3.9	32.3	.	1,158
Barrow-in-Furness	173	0	31	31	2.30	5.3	31.0	48.03	1,194
Carlisle	396	6	43	44	2.28	4.6	31.0	.	1,185
Copeland	142	3	29	29	2.33	5.6	30.0	44.71	1,176
Eden	161	54	20	21	2.30	3.0	28.5	.	1,165
South Lakeland	272	8	46	45	2.21	2.9	32.7	48.15	1,174
Greater Manchester (Met County)	4,062	913	1,051	1,046	2.35	8.2	31.2	46.18	1,111
Bolton	516	118	106	108	2.39	6.6	30.1	41.08	1,118
Bury	141	64	72	75	2.39	6.0	29.7	46.48	1,084
Manchester	1,025	221	184	171	2.26	14.6	36.1	51.29	1,106
Oldham	246	121	89	90	2.40	7.7	30.3	43.21	1,222
Rochdale	231	133	84	85	2.39	8.0	30.3	40.74	1,100
Salford	331	27	98	93	2.30	9.2	34.4	47.68	1,237
Stockport	234	93	117	121	2.33	6.1	30.1	42.39	1,150
Tameside	399	131	90	89	2.38	6.5	29.0	.	1,090
Trafford	364	18	87	89	2.33	6.9	30.7	48.25	922
Wigan	574	0	123	125	2.40	5.7	27.9	44.06	1,098

Table 14.5 (continued)

	Housing completions[2] 2001-02 (numbers)			Households 2001[4]				Local authority average weekly rent per dwelling (£) April 2003[6,7]	Average Council Tax (£)[8] April 2003
	Private enterprise	Registered Social Landlords, Local Authorities, etc	Stock of dwellings 1991[3] (thousands)	All household mid year estimates (thousands)	Average household size (number of people)	Lone parents[5] as a percentage of all households	One-person households as a percentage of all households		
Lancashire County	3,840	205	..	473	2.36	6.4	29.5	43.98	1,190
Burnley	96	0	38	37	2.37	9.2	29.6	.	1,228
Chorley	404	0	38	41	2.39	5.6	25.8	41.50	1,180
Fylde	151	33	31	32	2.21	4.0	32.3	.	1,154
Hyndburn	143	0	33	34	2.39	7.6	29.8	44.34	1,200
Lancaster	164	8	53	56	2.32	7.0	31.3	45.17	1,167
Pendle	272	0	36	37	2.38	6.6	31.7	43.38	1,226
Preston	309	92	52	54	2.33	7.9	33.1	46.84	1,234
Ribble Valley	172	0	21	21	2.43	4.1	27.9	40.56	1,149
Rossendale	148	0	27	27	2.40	6.5	27.8	43.45	1,234
South Ribble	313	17	40	43	2.42	4.8	25.5	.	1,186
West Lancashire	256	18	42	45	2.40	7.4	26.5	42.77	1,190
Wyre	381	17	43	45	2.29	4.6	30.7	.	1,159
Merseyside (Met County)	2,449	358	575	567	2.36	9.4	30.7	48.52	1,151
Knowsley	142	35	57	61	2.45	15.3	26.0	.	1,114
Liverpool	598	109	194	183	2.36	10.4	33.3	46.28	1,181
St. Helens	597	8	71	72	2.43	6.0	25.4	.	1,142
Sefton	376	88	116	117	2.35	7.7	30.9	48.42	1,130
Wirral	442	19	136	133	2.30	8.8	31.8	51.50	1,151
Former county of Cheshire	..	..	386	..	..	..	..	..	1,096
Former county of Lancashire	..	..	574	..	..	..	..	..	1,177
Yorkshire and the Humber	12,354	885	2,025	2,092	2.34	6.2	29.9	42.55	1,071
East Riding of Yorkshire UA	964	0	..	133	2.34	3.9	27.5	45.60	1,109
Kingston upon Hull, City of UA	401	54	..	104	2.30	8.4	33.3	46.10	1,036
North East Lincolnshire UA	259	0	..	66	2.37	7.6	28.1	42.90	1,174
North Lincolnshire UA	738	0	..	63	2.38	5.6	26.3	41.20	1,157
York UA	535	4	..	77	2.31	4.9	30.3	48.63	988
North Yorkshire County	1,734	79	..	238	2.33	4.2	29.0	48.83	1,127
Craven	108	0	22	23	2.29	4.6	30.8	49.75	1,127
Hambleton	278	11	32	34	2.39	3.0	26.5	.	1,055
Harrogate	279	8	60	63	2.32	4.3	30.1	52.08	1,145
Richmondshire	70	0	19	18	2.43	3.7	28.1	47.86	1,145
Ryedale	61	0	39	21	2.37	2.9	27.5	.	1,142
Scarborough	158	32	49	47	2.20	5.4	32.5	48.98	1,141
Selby	181	16	36	31	2.41	4.3	24.6	44.94	1,136
South Yorkshire (Met County)	2,969	170	528	536	2.34	6.2	29.6	40.40	1,095
Barnsley	783	0	91	90	2.40	6.0	26.6	39.68	1,045
Doncaster	577	15	116	120	2.36	6.0	27.6	40.68	1,040
Rotherham	942	64	101	104	2.38	6.4	27.5	38.10	1,085
Sheffield	667	50	221	222	2.29	6.2	32.8	41.56	1,155
West Yorkshire (Met County)	5,286	542	840	874	2.35	6.9	30.7	42.54	1,028
Bradford	1,112	147	183	188	2.46	7.8	29.9	.	1,016
Calderdale	422	10	81	82	2.31	6.1	30.6	.	1,131
Kirklees	874	25	155	163	2.36	6.5	30.6	45.11	1,089
Leeds	1,639	289	293	308	2.29	7.5	32.1	41.70	985
Wakefield	1,239	44	127	133	2.35	5.0	29.2	42.17	1,006
The Humber	..	..	356	..	..	..	..	..	1,111
Former county of North Yorkshire	..	..	301	..	..	..	..	..	1,095
East Midlands	13,413	649	1,638	1,740	2.37	5.3	27.9	44.44	1,125
Derby UA	303	4	..	92	2.36	7.0	30.3	45.06	1,016
Leicester UA	177	55	..	112	2.46	9.6	30.8	44.64	1,042
Nottingham UA	520	89	..	113	2.32	10.3	32.1	42.40	1,144
Rutland UA	85	3	..	14	2.45	3.7	25.6	48.77	1,236
Derbyshire County	2,179	110	..	310	2.34	4.2	27.9	42.18	1,178
Amber Valley	206	0	47	49	2.35	3.9	27.1	.	1,174
Bolsover	356	0	29	30	2.42	4.0	25.7	39.20	1,212
Chesterfield	241	81	43	43	2.26	4.3	32.3	40.79	1,142
Derbyshire Dales	144	0	29	29	2.34	3.2	27.4	.	1,196
Erewash	60	16	44	47	2.33	5.3	28.4	.	1,158
High Peak	188	9	35	38	2.35	4.8	28.6	48.23	1,179
North East Derbyshire	159	0	39	42	2.31	4.2	27.1	40.89	1,218
South Derbyshire	497	0	29	33	2.44	3.7	25.6	47.20	1,155

Table 14.5 (continued)

| | Housing completions[2] 2001-02 (numbers) | | Stock of dwellings 1991[3] (thousands) | Households 2001[4] | | | | Local authority average weekly rent per dwelling (£) April 2003[6,7] | Average Council Tax (£)[8] April 2003 |
	Private enterprise	Registered Social Landlords, Local Authorities, etc		All household mid year estimates (thousands)	Average household size (number of people)	Lone parents[5] as a percentage of all households	One-person households as a percentage of all households		
Leicestershire County	2,531	132	..	250	2.41	3.8	26.0	43.59	1,099
Blaby	277	43	32	36	2.48	3.5	23.6	42.52	1,109
Charnwood	459	0	57	62	2.44	4.4	27.4	41.79	1,090
Harborough	602	6	27	32	2.40	2.9	26.6	49.88	1,111
Hinckley and Bosworth	344	25	39	42	2.36	3.6	26.5	42.96	1,061
Melton	105	0	18	20	2.37	3.6	26.4	43.43	1,099
North West Leicestershire	209	0	32	36	2.38	4.0	26.3	44.25	1,128
Oadby and Wigston	28	0	20	22	2.48	4.3	23.5	42.81	1,112
Lincolnshire	3,313	224	250	273	2.33	4.3	27.4	43.40	1,053
Boston	229	0	23	24	2.34	3.8	28.6	.	1,055
East Lindsey	402	146	52	56	2.29	3.6	27.6	.	1,026
Lincoln	196	0	36	37	2.25	6.6	34.6	42.38	1,085
North Kesteven	941	23	33	39	2.37	4.2	23.3	44.06	1,064
South Holland	572	0	29	33	2.33	2.9	25.6	41.30	1,054
South Kesteven	475	0	45	52	2.37	4.6	26.5	45.53	1,033
West Lindsey	498	55	31	33	2.38	3.9	26.4	.	1,082
Northamptonshire	3,102	63	236	259	2.40	5.3	26.3	49.78	1,071
Corby	77	0	21	21	2.52	9.6	22.3	45.97	1,063
Daventry	406	0	25	29	2.47	3.3	23.7	45.40	1,053
East Northamptonshire	593	29	28	31	2.43	3.8	25.3	.	1,064
Kettering	591	0	32	34	2.38	4.4	27.6	45.29	1,069
Northampton	562	0	75	82	2.34	6.1	28.9	54.76	1,091
South Northamptonshire	688	8	28	32	2.44	3.7	24.0	52.96	1,083
Wellingborough	175	23	28	30	2.37	6.6	26.8	45.98	1,037
Nottinghamshire County	2,288	120	..	315	2.35	4.7	27.7	44.16	1,249
Ashfield	413	24	44	46	2.39	5.3	27.2	44.17	1,248
Bassetlaw	314	0	42	45	2.37	4.2	26.7	48.71	1,246
Broxtowe	77	0	45	47	2.29	5.0	28.4	38.65	1,247
Gedling	66	0	45	48	2.32	3.7	28.6	41.50	1,223
Mansfield	145	0	42	41	2.35	6.3	27.3	44.98	1,265
Newark and Sherwood	498	7	42	44	2.37	4.7	27.5	43.11	1,294
Rushcliffe	255	0	39	44	2.35	4.1	28.3	.	1,226
Former county of Derbyshire	..	..	387	..	..	..	..	..	1,143
Former county of Leicestershire	..	..	351	..	..	..	..	..	1,091
Former county of Nottinghamshire	..	..	414	..	..	..	..	..	1,225
West Midlands	12,261	1,198	2,083	2,155	2.41	6.2	28.5	46.74	1,093
Herefordshire, County of UA	557	46	..	72	2.39	4.1	27.1	.	1,071
Stoke-on-Trent UA	451	0	..	100	2.39	6.1	29.1	44.22	1,029
Telford and Wrekin UA	563	12	..	63	2.48	6.7	24.9	.	1,047
Shropshire County	1,363	139	..	118	2.36	3.8	28.6	45.91	1,148
Bridgnorth	49	15	20	21	2.41	4.1	26.2	49.02	1,130
North Shropshire	218	15	21	23	2.44	2.5	26.7	43.66	1,155
Oswestry	130	0	14	16	2.34	4.1	31.4	44.85	1,190
Shrewsbury and Atcham	193	22	38	40	2.33	4.8	30.7	.	1,123
South Shropshire	210	10	16	17	2.31	2.9	26.3	.	1,185
Staffordshire County	3,208	167	..	328	2.43	4.3	25.4	46.17	1,084
Cannock Chase	440	47	34	37	2.48	5.1	24.5	49.52	1,108
East Staffordshire	329	0	40	42	2.45	4.1	25.8	.	1,111
Lichfield	514	26	35	37	2.44	3.3	23.3	.	1,077
Newcastle-under-Lyme	96	20	49	51	2.38	4.8	29.2	.	1,088
South Staffordshire	252	16	40	43	2.43	3.9	23.7	.	1,058
Stafford	582	28	47	49	2.39	3.9	26.2	43.86	1,079
Staffordshire Moorlands	301	0	38	39	2.41	3.6	25.5	.	1,095
Tamworth	210	30	26	30	2.48	6.6	23.3	48.89	1,051
Warwickshire	1,962	152	197	211	2.37	4.7	27.7	47.77	1,133
North Warwickshire	127	0	24	25	2.42	4.5	26.6	47.24	1,189
Nuneaton and Bedworth	432	59	46	49	2.44	5.6	25.9	45.63	1,157
Rugby	313	0	34	37	2.36	5.2	27.5	47.19	1,139
Stratford-on-Avon	279	38	44	47	2.33	2.7	28.8	.	1,119
Warwick	796	48	49	53	2.33	5.3	29.1	50.90	1,102

Table **14.5**   (continued)

	Housing completions[2] 2001-02 (numbers)			Households 2001[4]				Local authority average weekly rent per dwelling (£) April 2003[6,7]	Average Council Tax (£)[8] April 2003
	Private enterprise	Registered Social Landlords, Local Authorities, etc	Stock of dwellings 1991[3] (thousands)	All household mid year estimates (thousands)	Average household size (number of people)	Lone parents[5] as a percentage of all households	One-person households as a percentage of all households		
West Midlands (Met County)	3,610	617	1,036	1,037	2.44	7.8	30.4	48.98	1,091
Birmingham	1,445	400	392	391	2.47	10.0	32.5	46.81	1,079
Coventry	468	34	122	126	2.36	8.6	31.7	.	1,172
Dudley	317	0	123	125	2.41	4.6	27.6	48.18	1,008
Sandwell	465	0	119	116	2.43	6.3	30.5	50.71	1,095
Solihull	458	14	78	82	2.43	5.3	27.0	48.98	1,008
Walsall	243	52	101	101	2.49	5.8	26.8	.	1,190
Wolverhampton	178	34	99	97	2.40	8.3	29.9	44.73	1,132
Worcestershire County	2,118	123	..	226	2.37	4.7	26.7	48.13	1,090
Bromsgrove	411	5	35	36	2.42	3.1	23.5	51.17	1,095
Malvern Hills	86	0	36	30	2.35	3.4	27.8	.	1,101
Redditch	198	33	30	32	2.45	6.9	24.6	48.85	1,112
Worcester	199	0	34	40	2.32	6.3	28.6	45.08	1,075
Wychavon	387	16	41	48	2.35	4.1	26.6	.	1,063
Wyre Forest	259	23	38	41	2.33	4.3	28.5	.	1,111
Herefordshire and Worcestershire	..	..	274	..	..	..	..	..	1,086
Former county of Shropshire	..	..	165	..	..	..	..	..	1,116
Former county of Staffordshire	..	..	411	..	..	..	..	..	1,073
East	14,105	1,512	2,098	2,264	2.35	4.8	28.3	52.76	1,115
Luton UA	183	11	..	74	2.47	7.1	28.1	53.94	990
Peterborough UA	334	66	..	67	2.33	7.3	29.7	53.42	1,047
Southend-on-Sea UA	45	37	..	70	2.23	5.7	32.5	50.08	944
Thurrock UA	810	14	..	58	2.46	6.5	24.8	55.15	1,010
Bedfordshire County	1,383	111	..	159	2.38	4.6	27.6	58.27	1,194
Bedford	392	16	54	62	2.35	5.4	29.7	.	1,170
Mid Bedfordshire	452	0	44	49	2.41	3.1	26.7	.	1,181
South Bedfordshire	329	4	43	47	2.39	5.2	25.7	58.27	1,237
Cambridgeshire County	2,211	376	..	230	2.37	4.3	27.8	54.58	1,045
Cambridge	31	99	41	47	2.26	6.6	36.2	55.40	1,037
East Cambridgeshire	368	43	25	30	2.40	2.4	25.9	.	1,053
Fenland	269	56	32	36	2.33	3.5	27.8	50.05	1,106
Huntingdonshire	463	27	57	64	2.40	5.0	24.9	.	1,041
South Cambridgeshire	620	44	47	53	2.44	3.0	25.1	56.52	1,020
Essex County	4,020	380	..	550	2.36	4.6	28.3	53.92	1,150
Basildon	392	12	64	70	2.37	6.0	27.8	54.69	1,189
Braintree	382	14	49	55	2.37	4.9	28.0	51.86	1,135
Brentwood	48	5	29	29	2.35	3.5	29.3	57.17	1,135
Castle Point	75	0	34	36	2.42	3.4	24.7	59.63	1,174
Chelmsford	409	110	61	66	2.37	4.1	27.5	.	1,136
Colchester	532	1	59	65	2.35	6.0	28.4	52.45	1,135
Epping Forest	337	27	47	51	2.37	4.2	28.5	55.83	1,152
Harlow	77	117	30	33	2.39	7.0	30.1	53.87	1,198
Maldon	143	0	21	25	2.40	3.7	25.9	.	1,141
Rochford	151	0	29	32	2.42	3.8	26.2	51.64	1,157
Tendring	429	8	59	62	2.20	3.6	33.2	47.61	1,118
Uttlesford	179	30	26	28	2.44	3.5	25.8	58.59	1,139
Hertfordshire	2,146	120	394	428	2.38	4.8	28.5	57.78	1,104
Broxbourne	175	47	32	35	2.48	3.7	24.4	62.89	1,034
Dacorum	213	0	53	59	2.33	5.4	29.8	55.44	1,077
East Hertfordshire	376	57	47	52	2.44	3.2	26.1	.	1,104
Hertsmere	147	9	35	38	2.41	5.0	26.9	.	1,087
North Hertfordshire	263	0	45	49	2.34	4.3	29.7	.	1,111
St. Albans	201	0	50	53	2.37	4.2	28.5	59.25	1,117
Stevenage	210	6	30	33	2.39	7.2	27.1	58.24	1,100
Three Rivers	388	0	31	34	2.41	4.1	28.6	60.48	1,117
Watford	49	0	30	34	2.30	6.4	32.0	58.63	1,174
Welwyn Hatfield	55	0	39	41	2.38	4.9	30.8	55.65	1,131

Table 14.5 (continued)

	Housing completions[2] 2001-02 (numbers)			Households 2001[4]				Local authority average weekly rent per dwelling (£) April 2003[6,7]	Average Council Tax (£)[8] April 2003
	Private enterprise	Registered Social Landlords, Local Authorities, etc	Stock of dwellings 1991[3] (thousands)	All household mid year estimates (thousands)	Average household size (number of people)	Lone parents[5] as a percentage of all households	One-person households as a percentage of all households		
Norfolk	2,325	302	328	345	2.27	4.7	28.8	45.25	1,131
Breckland	623	21	45	51	2.34	4.1	27.0	.	1,090
Broadland	323	99	43	50	2.36	3.2	24.4	.	1,129
Great Yarmouth	146	22	38	39	2.27	5.4	30.3	41.91	1,117
King's Lynn and West Norfolk	362	0	57	58	2.29	4.1	28.2	47.58	1,129
North Norfolk	202	0	45	43	2.20	3.7	30.1	44.83	1,131
Norwich	275	150	55	56	2.12	8.3	35.2	45.16	1,179
South Norfolk	394	0	43	47	2.34	3.8	25.8	47.18	1,143
Suffolk	2,020	223	269	283	2.33	4.2	28.1	48.88	1,164
Babergh	186	0	33	35	2.34	3.7	26.3	53.23	1,158
Forest Heath	118	32	22	23	2.35	5.4	27.3	48.70	1,155
Ipswich	320	59	49	50	2.32	6.5	31.1	48.54	1,256
Mid Suffolk	257	46	32	36	2.40	3.0	24.9	49.64	1,151
St. Edmundsbury	379	45	37	41	2.33	3.5	26.1	.	1,158
Suffolk Coastal	379	10	47	49	2.30	2.9	29.3	.	1,141
Waveney	381	30	47	49	2.27	4.5	29.6	45.82	1,122
Former county of Bedfordshire	..	..	209	..	..	..	..	..	1,138
Former county of Cambridgeshire	..	..	267	..	..	..	..	..	1,045
Former county of Essex	..	..	632	..	..	..	..	..	1,119
London	10,324	3,846	2,916	3,121	2.27	8.6	34.0	66.53	1,058
Inner London	..	..	..	1,270	2.14	11.3	38.3	67.28	995
Inner London – West	..	..	..	..	..	..	..	73.14	963
Camden	240	17	85	93	2.05	9.3	42.9	70.06	1,158
City of London	105	0	3	4	1.69	4.7	54.2	65.61	742
Hammersmith and Fulham	26	0	74	81	2.01	8.9	41.3	64.80	1,073
Kensington and Chelsea	119	11	79	83	1.86	7.1	49.4	76.45	905
Wandsworth	336	0	114	120	2.14	9.2	34.9	77.48	584
Westminster	309	243	101	90	1.89	6.4	48.2	81.53	570
Inner London – East	..	..	..	..	..	..	..	65.23	1,054
Hackney	528	84	80	90	2.25	14.1	36.7	65.82	1,158
Haringey	38	140	88	96	2.23	11.9	35.6	67.06	1,174
Islington	209	5	77	82	2.10	12.6	38.0	69.43	1,049
Lambeth	226	58	114	128	2.05	14.5	36.8	66.08	995
Lewisham	25	264	103	112	2.21	12.0	33.1	60.74	1,082
Newham	562	160	85	94	2.59	12.9	30.4	60.19	1,005
Southwark	341	22	104	114	2.14	13.5	37.7	63.49	1,034
Tower Hamlets	1,014	415	70	84	2.30	13.2	36.6	70.19	957
Outer London	..	..	..	1,851	2.36	6.7	31.0	65.32	1,126
Outer London – East and North East	..	..	..	..	..	..	..	62.34	1,122
Barking and Dagenham	107	57	60	66	2.46	8.2	30.9	58.46	1,048
Bexley	196	27	88	91	2.39	5.3	27.4	.	1,102
Enfield	1,548	312	106	114	2.40	7.2	29.1	64.72	1,123
Greenwich	1,027	72	89	93	2.30	11.0	32.3	62.75	1,088
Havering	174	133	92	93	2.40	4.9	27.6	53.98	1,216
Redbridge	289	12	92	96	2.47	4.7	30.2	71.32	1,078
Waltham Forest	46	83	91	94	2.30	8.7	33.4	70.76	1,171
Outer London – South	..	..	..	..	..	..	..	66.47	1,083
Bromley	350	9	124	128	2.30	4.8	31.2	.	973
Croydon	158	114	131	139	2.36	7.9	30.1	67.92	1,086
Kingston upon Thames	196	4	57	63	2.32	4.5	32.9	71.99	1,222
Merton	427	81	73	82	2.30	6.2	30.6	67.60	1,144
Sutton	108	83	72	77	2.31	5.5	31.2	59.61	1,099
Outer London – West and North West	..	..	..	..	..	..	..	68.67	1,159
Barnet	399	72	121	130	2.39	6.0	32.3	64.15	1,135
Brent	182	294	99	111	2.36	11.0	32.1	70.67	1,075
Ealing	167	157	113	127	2.35	7.9	32.9	68.21	1,114
Harrow	85	8	79	84	2.46	5.1	27.8	75.26	1,226
Hillingdon	154	134	94	100	2.40	5.7	29.8	77.13	1,154
Hounslow	205	87	83	88	2.40	6.9	30.7	62.22	1,180
Richmond upon Thames	119	28	73	78	2.18	4.4	37.4	.	1,268

Table 14.5 (continued)

	Housing completions[2] 2001-02 (numbers)		Stock of dwellings 1991[3] (thousands)	Households 2001[4]				Local authority average weekly rent per dwelling (£) April 2003[6,7]	Average Council Tax (£)[8] April 2003
	Private enterprise	Registered Social Landlords, Local Authorities, etc		All household mid year estimates (thousands)	Average household size (number of people)	Lone parents[5] as a percentage of all households	One-person households as a percentage of all households		
South East	19,045	2,850	3,106	3,346	2.35	4.7	28.9	51.26	1,098
Bracknell Forest UA	313	18	..	44	2.45	5.5	25.5	57.63	963
Brighton and Hove UA	425	147	..	116	2.09	6.0	38.0	.	1,074
Isle of Wight UA	344	32	..	57	2.25	4.4	30.9	63.60	1,134
Medway UA	519	43	..	99	2.49	5.6	25.3	52.27	921
Milton Keynes UA	1,198	48	..	87	2.37	7.0	27.2	.	1,023
Portsmouth UA	151	76	..	78	2.33	8.0	31.7	52.39	998
Reading UA	429	168	..	62	2.27	6.7	32.2	63.51	1,156
Slough UA	442	89	..	49	2.43	7.5	29.5	53.68	988
Southampton UA	416	23	..	90	2.37	7.1	32.7	68.69	1,085
West Berkshire UA	77	22	..	59	2.43	3.7	25.2	61.39	1,134
Windsor and Maidenhead UA	197	45	..	55	2.39	3.4	29.1	48.18	971
Wokingham UA	243	8	..	59	2.49	3.1	23.6	.	1,139
Buckinghamshire County	2,323	216	..	194	2.43	3.9	26.4	58.16	1,098
Aylesbury Vale	516	18	57	67	2.42	3.4	26.1	.	1,095
Chiltern	112	63	35	37	2.40	4.1	26.7	61.71	1,115
South Bucks	109	11	25	25	2.41	4.5	25.9	58.49	1,089
Wycombe	437	27	61	66	2.45	4.1	26.8	.	1,093
East Sussex County	1,524	444	..	217	2.21	4.6	32.8	65.45	1,207
Eastbourne	451	47	39	41	2.11	5.7	36.5	.	1,209
Hastings	187	31	37	38	2.20	6.8	36.2	52.07	1,216
Lewes	143	9	38	41	2.22	4.3	32.0	51.46	1,217
Rother	134	201	39	38	2.20	3.4	32.5	.	1,178
Wealden	187	4	55	60	2.30	3.4	28.9	55.09	1,214
Hampshire County	3,601	692	..	514	2.37	4.4	26.4	49.67	1,083
Basingstoke and Deane	568	143	56	63	2.41	4.7	25.0		1,042
East Hampshire	164	76	40	45	2.38	4.1	26.2	57.41	1,097
Eastleigh	97	25	43	48	2.42	4.5	24.7	.	1,100
Fareham	238	55	40	45	2.38	3.7	24.6	.	1,062
Gosport	218	42	31	32	2.32	6.5	28.3	.	1,098
Hart	344	10	30	33	2.45	4.0	23.6	55.55	1,105
Havant	128	39	48	49	2.35	5.4	27.1	50.56	1,085
New Forest	508	51	69	74	2.25	3.8	29.0	.	1,111
Rushmoor	115	57	31	37	2.39	5.0	26.2	.	1,090
Test Valley	442	11	40	45	2.41	4.1	26.1	62.21	1,052
Winchester	212	74	39	44	2.39	3.1	28.6	.	1,083
Kent County	3,986	353	..	554	2.36	4.9	28.9	58.41	1,095
Ashford	640	38	38	43	2.38	4.8	28.3	.	1,060
Canterbury	567	25	53	56	2.36	5.2	30.7	54.91	1,083
Dartford	185	5	32	35	2.43	4.2	28.2	57.37	1,088
Dover	103	62	44	44	2.31	5.3	31.3	54.10	1,091
Gravesham	32	11	37	39	2.44	6.2	26.6	56.82	1,073
Maidstone	359	15	54	57	2.39	4.0	26.5	57.26	1,131
Sevenoaks	171	59	43	45	2.38	3.7	27.2	51.19	1,125
Shepway	330	6	42	42	2.23	5.8	32.3	56.59	1,121
Swale	456	32	47	50	2.45	5.3	25.4	.	1,073
Thanet	222	0	56	55	2.24	6.2	32.9	52.50	1,107
Tonbridge and Malling	273	19	40	43	2.46	4.0	25.4	.	1,101
Tunbridge Wells	106	0	41	44	2.33	3.4	31.0	52.38	1,074
Oxfordshire	1,555	264	219	246	2.41	4.7	27.6	.	1,128
Cherwell	406	17	47	54	2.41	4.9	26.2	.	1,139
Oxford	379	69	46	54	2.42	7.3	33.1	59.09	1,184
South Oxfordshire	173	70	47	52	2.41	3.8	26.2	58.64	1,137
Vale of White Horse	311	30	43	47	2.45	3.2	25.3	59.30	1,097
West Oxfordshire	235	69	36	40	2.38	4.1	26.4	.	1,077

Table **14.5** (continued)

	Housing completions[2] 2001-02 (numbers)			Households 2001[4]				Local authority average weekly rent per dwelling (£) April 2003[6,7]	Average Council Tax (£)[8] April 2003
	Private enterprise	Registered Social Landlords, Local Authorities, etc	Stock of dwellings 1991[3] (thousands)	All household mid year estimates (thousands)	Average household size (number of people)	Lone parents[5] as a percentage of all households	One-person households as a percentage of all households		
Surrey	2,283	353	412	439	2.36	3.8	28.5	.	1,128
Elmbridge	461	14	48	51	2.37	4.4	28.9	.	1,150
Epsom and Ewell	183	66	26	27	2.39	3.8	29.9	63.36	1,108
Guildford	156	6	50	54	2.37	4.3	28.4	.	1,125
Mole Valley	179	5	32	34	2.32	3.0	29.4	.	1,109
Reigate and Banstead	340	13	48	53	2.35	3.5	29.2	66.57	1,140
Runnymede	68	56	29	32	2.36	3.3	29.7	55.34	1,072
Spelthorne	170	77	38	38	2.34	3.5	28.4	.	1,105
Surrey Heath	214	37	30	32	2.44	4.0	23.9	67.73	1,139
Tandridge	173	49	30	32	2.42	3.1	28.1	.	1,141
Waverley	92	5	46	48	2.36	4.1	28.7	.	1,143
Woking	236	16	35	38	2.33	4.7	28.0	57.68	1,147
West Sussex	1,290	146	304	326	2.27	4.1	31.0	63.63	1,112
Adur	30	0	25	26	2.30	4.4	30.5	66.29	1,172
Arun	484	0	60	64	2.14	3.6	33.0	60.76	1,121
Chichester	243	94	45	46	2.26	3.8	31.1	59.30	1,097
Crawley	39	0	35	41	2.40	6.0	26.8	57.94	1,111
Horsham	326	30	45	52	2.34	2.9	28.6	.	1,094
Mid Sussex	128	0	49	53	2.36	4.0	28.7	62.40	1,112
Worthing	40	22	44	45	2.13	4.5	37.5	.	1,112
Former county of Berkshire	..	..	290	..	..	..	..	.	1,065
Former county of Buckinghamshire	..	..	250	..	..	..	..	.	1,078
Former county of East Sussex	..	..	321	..	..	..	..	..	1,166
Former county of Hampshire	..	..	629	..	..	..	..	..	1,075
Former county of Kent	..	..	924	..	..	..	..	..	1,071
South West	14,131	1,444	1,973	2,097	2.30	4.8	29.3	49.39	1,113
Bath and North East Somerset UA	218	12	..	72	2.33	4.7	29.5	.	1,075
Bournemouth UA	455	0	..	72	2.17	5.6	34.8	49.06	1,109
Bristol, City of UA	309	48	..	165	2.27	7.4	32.9	46.74	1,171
North Somerset UA	769	85	..	80	2.31	4.1	28.0	57.64	1,076
Plymouth UA	249	24	..	101	2.32	6.9	29.7	45.20	1,046
Poole UA	203	8	..	60	2.28	4.1	30.3	51.30	1,072
South Gloucestershire UA	853	97	..	100	2.42	4.5	25.8	51.34	1,105
Swindon UA	516	111	..	76	2.36	5.5	26.2	47.60	1,048
Torbay UA	285	31	..	56	2.22	6.1	31.3	.	1,061
Cornwall and the Isles of Scilly	2,014	124	207	214	2.30	4.9	28.5	48.30	1,050
Caradon	120	10	34	34	2.32	4.5	26.1	46.18	1,058
Carrick	312	4	37	38	2.26	4.3	30.0	51.47	1,055
Kerrier	343	10	37	39	2.34	5.5	27.2	.	1,065
North Cornwall	439	51	34	34	2.30	4.3	28.6	46.91	1,068
Penwith	271	22	28	27	2.24	5.6	29.9	.	1,030
Restormel	401	0	36	40	2.31	5.0	29.2	.	1,028
Isles of Scilly	0	0	1	1	2.48	7.2	23.5	51.67	828
Devon County	2,841	190	..	303	2.27	4.1	30.4	48.40	1,142
East Devon	380	0	53	56	2.17	4.0	31.9	45.38	1,120
Exeter	210	13	41	48	2.27	5.7	34.1	44.11	1,105
Mid Devon	376	22	27	29	2.36	3.4	28.5	48.29	1,174
North Devon	231	26	36	38	2.26	4.5	30.1	.	1,164
South Hams	148	50	37	35	2.28	3.5	29.3	.	1,139
Teignbridge	418	4	47	52	2.27	3.6	29.4	57.01	1,156
Torridge	402	4	23	25	2.35	3.2	27.9	51.31	1,133
West Devon	142	16	19	21	2.31	3.8	28.9	.	1,177
Dorset County	2,039	61	..	171	2.24	3.8	30.0	55.32	1,186
Christchurch	49	0	20	21	2.14	4.4	32.3	.	1,157
East Dorset	197	0	33	37	2.26	2.9	26.0	.	1,194
North Dorset	386	40	23	26	2.36	3.7	28.9	.	1,151
Purbeck	64	2	19	19	2.27	2.7	29.4	55.32	1,191
West Dorset	423	0	39	41	2.20	3.0	32.1	.	1,183
Weymouth and Portland	209	6	26	28	2.18	6.4	31.6	.	1,240

Table 14.5 (continued)

	Housing completions[2] 2001-02 (numbers)			Households 2001[4]				Local authority average weekly rent per dwelling (£) April 2003[6,7]	Average Council Tax (£)[8] April 2003
	Private enterprise	Registered Social Landlords, Local Authorities, etc	Stock of dwellings 1991[3] (thousands)	All household mid year estimates (thousands)	Average household size (number of people)	Lone parents[5] as a percentage of all households	One-person households as a percentage of all households		
Gloucestershire	1,478	284	222	239	2.32	4.7	29.1	53.09	1,142
Cheltenham	412	60	45	49	2.20	6.0	34.8	58.64	1,138
Cotswold	175	60	33	35	2.30	3.3	28.8	.	1,141
Forest of Dean	88	8	30	32	2.44	3.3	25.7	48.96	1,164
Gloucester	319	142	41	46	2.34	6.7	28.8	50.62	1,128
Stroud	269	1	42	45	2.37	4.1	27.5	52.87	1,183
Tewkesbury	208	0	29	32	2.33	3.4	27.0	.	1,089
Somerset	1,670	141	195	211	2.33	4.1	29.0	47.20	1,110
Mendip	285	47	39	43	2.39	4.2	29.5	.	1,125
Sedgemoor	373	0	41	45	2.34	4.2	27.4	47.17	1,093
South Somerset	519	59	60	64	2.33	3.5	28.6	.	1,127
Taunton Deane	427	34	39	44	2.29	5.3	30.6	47.21	1,088
West Somerset	66	0	15	15	2.22	2.9	30.2	.	1,113
Wiltshire County	1,940	402	..	177	2.39	4.2	25.8	61.78	1,108
Kennet	226	48	28	29	2.46	4.0	24.0	.	1,098
North Wiltshire	448	26	45	51	2.43	4.8	23.7	.	1,126
Salisbury	235	64	43	47	2.36	3.9	26.9	61.78	1,083
West Wiltshire	515	153	44	50	2.35	4.0	27.9	.	1,118
Bristol/Bath area	..	..	391	..	..	..	..	..	1,116
Former county of Devon	..	..	440	..	..	..	..	..	1,115
Former county of Dorset	..	..	287	..	..	..	..	..	1,147
Former county of Wiltshire	..	..	231	..	..	..	..	..	1,091

1 The table reflects the local government structure at 1 April 1998. For some new areas data are not available. See Notes and Definitions.

2 District figures do not always add to county totals. See Notes and Definitions.

3 The figures for housing stock at local authority level shown in this table are derived using different methods from the regional stock figures shown in Table 6.1. This has led to small discrepancies between the two sets of figures. The figures in Table 6.1 provide the definitive regional estimates.

4 These figures are based on the provisional 2001 mid year estimates. In comparison figures in table 3.19 use the revised estimates from ODPM.
Lone parents with dependent children only.

6 Some local authorities have no housing stock following large scale voluntary transfers to Registered Social Landlords.

7 Unrebated rent and provisional.

8 See Notes and Definitions.

Source: Office of the Deputy Prime Minister

Table **14.6** Labour market statistics[1]

	Total in employment[2,3] 2001-2002[4] (thousands)	Employment rate[3] 2001-2002[4] (percentages)	Unemploy-ment rate[3] 2001-2002[4] (percentages)[5]	Average gross weekly full-time earnings[6], April 2002 (£)						All people total
				Males			Females			
					10 per cent earned			10 per cent earned		
				Total	Less than	More than	Total	Less than	More than	
United Kingdom	28,274	74.4	5.0	511.3	237.0	832.6	382.1	194.5	612.6	462.6
England	23,921	75.0	4.8	521.3	240.0	852.6	388.0	196.2	623.8	471.7
North East	1,101	68.7	7.4	439.1	218.1	668.0	332.1	182.0	543.4	399.3
Darlington UA	45	74.2	6.4	405.8	196.5	665.1	..	..	..	374.8
Hartlepool UA	38	66.5	8.7	..	..	..	..	..	..	..
Middlesbrough UA	55	62.4	10.0	..	..	..	322.6	168.8	509.5	391.8
Redcar and Cleveland UA	53	64.8	8.7	470.9	225.2	693.8	..	..	..	419.7
Stockton-on-Tees UA	81	68.4	7.2	454.5	233.6	691.2	..	..	..	412.6
Durham	224	70.7	6.1	419.1	220.9	629.9	330.1	182.9	554.5	384.8
Northumberland	142	72.9	5.9	..	..	..	320.7	166.6	536.6	..
Tyne and Wear (Met County)	462	67.6	7.9	437.3	218.7	675.8	341.9	186.9	549.2	400.8
North West	3,094	71.5	5.2	471.1	228.8	747.0	354.3	188.0	571.5	426.8
Blackburn with Darwen UA	54	65.7	7.0	..	..	..	330.1	185.6	494.1	370.2
Blackpool UA	70	74.7	3.4	..	..	..	314.1	176.1	494.1	368.4
Halton UA	50	65.5	7.2	463.9	250.6	738.5	360.5	188.5	609.4	427.2
Warrington UA	91	75.9	3.9	475.4	222.7	773.2	..	..	..	444.0
Cheshire	320	76.7	2.9	520.9	240.2	863.7	379.2	190.4	608.3	469.5
Cumbria	218	72.1	6.6	441.9	232.9	690.5	307.8	177.9	507.1	396.2
Greater Manchester (Met County)	1,186	72.1	5.0	471.8	230.3	763.5	359.0	195.6	570.4	427.9
Lancashire	528	73.7	3.8	456.0	224.6	698.4	341.7	180.0	551.1	416.8
Merseyside (Met County)	577	66.1	7.7	475.9	224.9	751.5	355.5	191.7	586.9	425.6
Yorkshire and the Humber	2,347	73.8	5.1	447.1	229.7	706.4	345.0	186.2	565.3	409.9
East Riding of Yorkshire UA	158	77.9	4.2	449.5	240.5	762.3	323.2	165.8	536.8	412.8
Kingston upon Hull, City of UA	99	65.2	9.2	419.2	230.0	673.2	329.2	172.4	545.5	385.8
North East Lincolnshire UA	65	70.6	9.2	437.3	216.4	654.5	..	..	..	377.0
North Lincolnshire UA	70	74.0	5.1	..	..	..	317.0	179.1	534.8	438.2
York UA	91	79.8	3.9	465.2	240.7	727.4	356.7	196.7	553.7	432.2
North Yorkshire	286	80.3	2.7	446.6	229.7	681.2	331.0	179.6	565.3	403.4
South Yorkshire (Met County)	582	71.0	5.5	426.9	225.3	656.6	347.6	191.2	579.3	398.2
West Yorkshire (Met County)	995	73.9	5.0	456.3	228.6	735.7	354.0	192.4	565.3	417.3
East Midlands	2,025	75.9	4.6	454.2	232.6	709.4	334.8	182.3	553.3	413.0
Derby UA	107	72.7	6.1	493.1	245.4	739.4	364.8	188.2	577.6	454.7
Leicester UA	119	66.7	6.3	419.8	216.3	661.2	323.5	194.5	480.3	385.0
Nottingham UA	115	64.7	7.7	460.2	226.8	748.1	346.0	193.0	598.1	418.7
Rutland UA	20	78.6	..	..	..	..	..	..	..	..
Derbyshire	360	76.6	4.3	456.8	223.0	647.1	317.5	174.4	534.8	411.9
Leicestershire	324	81.9	4.3	466.7	249.6	741.4	337.1	175.7	562.9	422.7
Lincolnshire	299	75.9	4.9	426.8	228.0	650.5	323.8	174.4	565.3	392.7
Northamptonshire	327	81.0	3.5	464.0	249.3	738.9	350.6	200.7	565.4	423.5
Nottinghamshire	354	74.3	4.1	452.7	226.9	736.5	324.9	175.1	542.0	406.1
West Midlands	2,480	74.3	5.3	469.6	235.6	732.6	353.0	187.9	568.1	427.3
Herefordshire, County of UA	81	79.0	3.5	404.3	241.1	658.4	324.2	179.5	537.1	375.7
Stoke-on-Trent UA	108	69.5	7.5	403.7	210.4	607.6	325.1	183.8	549.5	370.8
Telford and Wrekin UA	73	75.6	4.6	441.1	230.6	695.2	329.4	176.6	542.6	401.3
Shropshire	142	78.6	3.3	434.8	223.2	751.8	324.1	159.8	541.3	392.0
Staffordshire	409	79.6	3.0	443.2	226.6	663.3	351.2	175.7	580.4	411.2
Warwickshire	256	79.0	3.8	521.2	251.5	785.8	346.3	203.1	525.7	457.4
West Midlands (Met County)	1,133	69.9	7.2	483.9	239.9	744.7	367.6	191.9	591.6	442.1
Worcestershire	277	80.5	2.4	442.6	233.0	738.5	326.6	183.2	565.3	400.5

Table **14.6** (continued)

	Total in employment[2,3] 2001-2002[4] (thousands)	Employment rate[3] 2001-2002[4] (percentages)	Unemploy- ment rate[3] 2001-2002[4] (percentages)[5]	Average gross weekly full-time earnings[6], April 2002 (£)						All people total
				Males			Females			
				Total	10 per cent earned		Total	10 per cent earned		
					Less than	More than		Less than	More than	
East	2,749	79.0	3.7	506.3	241.0	826.4	375.1	197.5	596.6	459.6
Luton UA	84	74.1	5.5	551.8	238.5	1,012.3	379.8	190.8	631.1	480.2
Peterborough UA	76	76.9	5.2	475.5	250.5	766.2	..	..	..	..
Southend-on-Sea UA	83	74.4	5.6	466.5	207.2	833.6	389.8	212.9	629.8	431.4
Thurrock UA	67	78.1	3.6	518.3	303.0	811.5	..	..	..	472.8
Bedfordshire	205	80.5	3.7	508.3	243.5	853.8	374.1	189.9	613.5	458.2
Cambridgeshire	302	80.0	3.8	526.3	239.9	875.7	382.2	203.1	605.5	479.4
Essex	667	79.2	3.2	506.5	246.6	835.5	363.0	198.0	578.5	454.8
Hertfordshire	548	80.4	3.2	579.7	259.1	924.5	415.5	219.3	661.4	519.9
Norfolk	382	77.6	4.1	436.5	232.4	694.4	342.5	187.9	534.8	403.1
Suffolk	334	79.8	3.6	453.0	230.3	715.4	339.3	182.6	568.1	414.0
London	3,513	70.4	6.6	704.8	278.2	1,247.6	503.6	243.0	797.4	624.1
South East	4,154	80.0	3.3	555.3	259.1	937.4	398.6	207.9	631.3	496.7
Bracknell Forest UA	60	82.5	2.6	703.3	300.2	1,318.4	..	..	..	613.5
Brighton and Hove UA	131	75.3	5.2	484.0	230.9	821.7	363.6	226.8	573.2	432.1
Isle of Wight UA	56	72.7	6.4	394.7	208.5	588.5	..	..	..	370.3
Medway UA	123	77.0	5.0	509.6	275.1	825.8	333.7	189.1	534.8	441.9
Milton Keynes UA	117	82.1	3.5	554.3	257.1	911.7	395.0	216.0	665.5	491.0
Portsmouth UA	92	75.5	5.3	519.8	249.5	931.4	379.0	202.1	603.8	467.3
Reading UA	76	78.6	4.1	593.6	264.3	963.5	441.8	264.0	676.1	534.3
Slough UA	54	76.8	4.2	..	..	..	426.2	216.8	671.7	605.2
Southampton UA	105	76.0	3.9	..	..	..	347.9	204.3	516.7	487.3
West Berkshire UA	81	85.6	2.1	586.5	261.5	947.5	436.8	219.0	830.9	535.9
Windsor and Maidenhead UA	72	76.1	3.6	..	..	..	..	..	..	567.4
Wokingham UA	77	81.2	3.0	..	..	..	..	..	..	..
Buckinghamshire	255	81.4	3.5	570.7	270.1	998.1	444.0	230.2	760.6	521.2
East Sussex	225	77.1	4.7	425.8	228.3	677.6	344.7	182.2	565.3	393.9
Hampshire	663	82.6	2.6	551.3	264.5	914.7	388.0	206.6	613.1	494.8
Kent	661	77.6	3.7	476.1	243.4	758.8	366.4	188.5	591.1	433.2
Oxfordshire	347	82.0	2.1	539.9	271.6	882.7	389.4	209.9	617.2	485.8
Surrey	582	82.6	2.5	655.2	278.8	1,124.2	459.5	230.3	742.7	582.0
West Sussex	376	81.1	2.3	506.2	240.9	841.5	378.4	207.5	603.5	457.3
South West	2,457	79.3	3.7	463.3	231.2	750.2	350.0	191.6	565.3	421.7
Bath and North East Somerset UA	87	79.3	3.4	493.4	239.6	862.3	372.7	203.3	609.6	440.5
Bournemouth UA	75	74.9	5.4	..	..	..	..	..	..	393.6
Bristol, City of UA	210	78.3	3.2	502.4	249.9	815.8	377.6	207.7	568.4	453.9
North Somerset UA	97	80.4	3.3	..	..	..	322.9	183.9	554.3	..
Plymouth UA	120	74.1	6.3	454.3	221.8	746.3	349.5	196.0	558.5	415.7
Poole UA	68	80.1	3.2	529.4	231.0	964.7	..	..	..	473.1
South Gloucestershire UA	136	83.6	..	521.5	270.3	842.7	359.9	188.1	595.0	474.3
Swindon UA	99	84.2	..	530.3	252.4	920.4	385.3	212.0	589.8	474.5
Torbay UA	56	73.2	5.4	..	..	..	301.5	172.2	479.4	340.2
Cornwall and the Isles of Scilly	222	73.2	6.0	362.9	194.0	561.1	322.9	180.1	523.9	348.0
Devon	339	78.5	4.0	404.6	215.6	613.8	323.3	182.1	526.1	376.7
Dorset	188	79.6	..	431.6	230.9	668.8	330.8	196.2	532.6	397.4
Gloucestershire	287	81.0	3.8	497.8	254.4	768.5	358.4	203.6	599.4	447.5
Somerset	242	81.5	3.0	441.3	236.9	711.1	347.5	186.5	605.5	407.5
Wiltshire	231	84.2	2.6	459.7	235.7	726.2	343.4	192.8	565.6	418.0

1 Local government structure as at 1 April 1998. See Notes and Definitions to the Labour Market chapter. In some cases sample sizes are too small to provide reliable estimates.
2 Includes those on government-supported employment and training schemes and unpaid family workers.
3 Employment totals and unemployment rates are for people aged 16 and over, while employment rates are for those of working age only. Working age is 16 to 64 for males and 16 to 59 for females.
4 Data are from the Annual Local Area Labour Force Survey and relate to the period March 2001 to February 2002. These data have not been adjusted to take account of the 2001 Census population estimates.
5 As a percentage of the economically active.
6 Earnings estimates have been derived from the New Earnings Survey 2002 and relate to full-time employees whose pay for the survey pay-period was not affected by absence.
Source: Office for National Statistics

Table **14.7** Labour market,[1] benefit and economic statistics

| | Economically active[2] 2001-2002[3] (percentages) | Benefit statistics | | | | Economic statistics | | |
| | | Claimant count[4], March 2003 | | | Income Support bene-ficiaries[6,7] May 2003 (percentages) | Businesses registered for VAT 2002 | | Stock of businesses end 2001 (thousands) |
		Level (thousands)	Females (percentage of claimants)	Percentage claiming over 12 months, computerised claims only[5]		Registration rates[8] (percentages)	De-registration rates[8] (percentages)	
United Kingdom	78.4	992.3	24.6	14.6	..	10	10	1,762.4
England	78.9	801.5	25.0	14.5	10	10	10	1,505.6
North East	74.2	57.9	21.7	15.1	13	10	9	43.7
Darlington UA	79.1	2.1	21.4	12.7	12	9	10	2.1
Hartlepool UA	73.0	2.7	19.4	15.5	17	9	9	1.2
Middlesbrough UA	69.5	4.9	19.4	16.1	17	9	11	1.9
Redcar and Cleveland UA	71.0	3.5	19.4	18.1	13	8	9	1.8
Stockton-on-Tees UA	73.6	4.5	21.1	14.7	11	9	10	3.0
Durham County	75.3	7.8	24.2	9.8	13	9	8	9.0
Chester-le-Street	81.8	0.7	21.7	8.8	10	8	8	0.8
Derwentside	74.8	1.3	25.4	9.0	15	9	8	1.5
Durham	80.4	1.2	23.9	10.4	8	10	9	1.5
Easington	64.3	1.4	22.7	10.2	17	9	8	1.1
Sedgefield	80.6	1.6	25.9	8.1	13	10	8	1.5
Teesdale	86.4	0.2	27.0	10.8	8	6	7	1.2
Wear Valley	65.0	1.3	23.9	12.1	16	10	8	1.4
Northumberland	77.6	5.7	28.0	12.1	9	8	8	7.8
Alnwick	75.6	0.5	30.5	12.3	8	5	7	1.1
Berwick-upon-Tweed	82.4	0.5	31.6	8.5	9	6	5	1.1
Blyth Valley	75.7	1.8	26.6	12.6	13	13	9	1.1
Castle Morpeth	78.1	0.6	26.0	14.8	6	8	9	1.4
Tynedale	83.1	0.7	30.3	11.3	6	8	7	2.4
Wansbeck	73.9	1.6	27.4	11.8	10	8	8	0.7
Tyne and Wear (Met County)	73.5	26.6	20.6	16.9	15	11	10	16.7
Gateshead	75.9	3.9	21.6	16.2	14	12	10	3.3
Newcastle upon Tyne	71.5	6.8	18.0	20.4	15	10	10	5.0
North Tyneside	76.3	4.3	21.6	15.8	12	11	8	2.8
South Tyneside	73.4	5.0	20.4	18.3	16	11	11	1.8
Sunderland	71.9	6.7	22.2	13.4	16	11	11	3.8
Tees Valley	..	..	..	..	..	9	10	10.0
Tees Valley less Darlington	..	15.7	19.9	16.0	..	9	10	7.9
Former county of Durham	..	9.8	23.6	10.4	..	9	8	11.1
North West	75.5	121.1	22.3	14.6	12	10	10	169.9
Blackburn with Darwen UA	70.8	2.3	22.7	7.7	16	11	11	3.1
Blackpool UA	77.3	3.3	22.0	8.5	16	9	11	3.0
Halton UA	70.7	3.0	23.0	12.5	15	11	9	2.0
Warrington UA	79.1	2.5	25.2	10.7	8	12	11	4.8
Cheshire County	78.9	6.4	24.3	8.8	7	10	9	21.9
Chester	79.4	1.1	23.8	11.7	8	10	10	3.9
Congleton	80.0	0.8	24.9	6.1	6	9	9	3.0
Crewe and Nantwich	78.1	1.1	27.4	8.4	7	9	10	3.2
Ellesmere Port and Neston	81.6	0.9	22.3	7.8	9	11	10	1.4
Macclesfield	81.4	1.0	23.1	7.1	6	10	9	6.8
Vale Royal	73.4	1.4	23.9	10.0	7	10	10	3.6
Cumbria	77.3	7.0	23.9	12.2	8	7	7	16.3
Allerdale	78.6	1.6	23.3	13.0	10	7	7	3.1
Barrow-in-Furness	73.7	1.3	19.8	8.9	12	7	10	1.0
Carlisle	79.4	1.6	26.3	13.5	8	8	8	3.0
Copeland	72.7	1.5	22.5	16.0	10	7	7	1.5
Eden	85.2	0.3	30.2	11.5	5	7	6	3.1
South Lakeland	75.7	0.7	28.7	5.0	5	8	7	4.6

Table **14.7** (continued)

| | Economically active[2] 2001-2002[3] (percentages) | Benefit statistics | | | Income Support bene-ficiaries[6,7] May 2003 (percentages) | Economic statistics | | Stock of businesses end 2001 (thousands) |
| | | Claimant count[4], March 2003 | | | | Businesses registered for VAT 2002 | | |
		Level (thousands)	Females (percentage of claimants)	Percentage claiming over 12 months, computerised claims only[5]		Registration rates[8] (percentages)	De-registration rates[8] (percentages)	
Greater Manchester (Met County)	75.9	46.5	21.8	13.3	13	11	11	60.8
Bolton	77.5	4.3	22.6	10.2	13	10	11	6.1
Bury	76.7	2.2	22.1	7.4	11	12	12	4.3
Manchester	66.6	13.9	20.5	18.9	20	11	15	11.3
Oldham	76.3	4.0	22.7	10.0	13	11	9	4.5
Rochdale	75.9	4.1	21.5	11.5	15	11	10	4.2
Salford	73.0	4.0	20.9	12.3	16	13	11	4.9
Stockport	81.6	3.1	22.6	12.3	8	10	10	8.1
Tameside	80.7	3.4	23.8	10.0	13	10	10	4.5
Trafford	79.7	2.6	21.1	12.4	9	12	13	7.1
Wigan	78.6	4.9	23.2	11.7	11	11	9	5.9
Lancashire County	76.8	14.1	23.6	10.8	10	9	9	30.6
Burnley	69.0	1.1	24.3	7.5	13	12	11	1.7
Chorley	80.3	1.0	24.5	7.8	7	10	10	2.8
Fylde	76.7	0.5	23.3	10.5	7	9	11	2.2
Hyndburn	74.8	1.0	26.1	7.0	13	10	9	1.7
Lancaster	76.5	2.3	23.3	12.0	10	9	8	3.2
Pendle	75.5	1.2	25.3	5.7	12	9	8	2.2
Preston	71.5	2.3	20.8	14.6	13	9	12	3.6
Ribble Valley	80.1	0.2	24.9	4.7	5	10	8	2.3
Rossendale	84.1	0.7	25.2	8 7	13	9	9	1.9
South Ribble	81.8	0.8	23.4	7.8	6	9	10	2.7
West Lancashire	77.7	1.9	23.6	18.1	10	8	10	3.2
Wyre	76.6	1.0	23.7	6.8	9	9	8	3.1
Merseyside (Met County)	71.7	36.1	21.5	20.5	16	10	11	23.0
Knowsley	67.8	4.4	22.6	19.3	21	11	10	1.7
Liverpool	67.5	15.6	21.0	25.1	21	11	12	7.7
St. Helens	75.9	3.8	22.7	14.4	13	10	9	2.9
Sefton	73.2	5.5	21.0	21.2	12	10	11	5.4
Wirral	75.8	6.8	21.3	13.9	14	10	10	5.3
Former county of Cheshire	..	11.9	24.2	10.1	..	10	10	28.7
Former county of Lancashire	..	19.7	23.2	10.0	..	9	10	36.6
Yorkshire and the Humber	77.8	90.9	23.5	13.0	11	10	10	124.6
East Riding of Yorkshire UA	81.4	4.3	27.2	14.4	8	9	9	9.6
Kingston upon Hull, City of UA	71.9	8.9	22.6	14.8	17	11	9	4.2
North East Lincolnshire UA	77.9	3.9	23.4	12.5	12	9	11	3.3
North Lincolnshire UA	78.0	2.6	27.2	9.6	9	9	8	4.0
York UA	83.1	1.9	24.1	8.6	6	10	9	4.4
North Yorkshire County	82.5	5.5	27.6	11.4	6	8	7	23.8
Craven	80.0	0.3	30.1	10.5	5	7	6	2.7
Hambleton	84.1	0.6	27.6	11.7	5	7	7	4.0
Harrogate	85.8	1.0	26.9	9.4	5	10	8	6.4
Richmondshire	84.4	0.4	37.3	9.2	4	6	7	2.1
Ryedale	73.6	0.4	30.6	12.1	6	6	6	3.0
Scarborough	78.2	2.0	25.1	14.7	12	8	8	3.1
Selby	85.3	0.7	27.7	6.4	5	10	8	2.5
South Yorkshire (Met County)	75.2	24.9	22.6	13.8	12	10	10	24.7
Barnsley	72.2	3.6	26.3	7.8	13	10	11	4.2
Doncaster	75.4	5.4	23.4	13.8	12	10	8	5.3
Rotherham	77.8	4.6	21.6	12.1	12	11	9	4.4
Sheffield	75.2	11.3	21.4	16.6	12	10	11	10.8
West Yorkshire (Met County)	77.8	39.0	23.0	12.7	11	11	11	49.9
Bradford	74.1	10.9	21.8	14.9	13	10	11	10.5
Calderdale	81.6	3.5	23.6	14.4	11	10	10	5.7
Kirklees	76.3	6.1	23.6	11.6	11	10	10	10.0
Leeds	80.7	13.2	22.6	12.4	10	11	12	17.6
Wakefield	76.4	5.2	25.7	8.9	11	11	9	6.2
The Humber	..	19.7	24.4	13.6	..	9	9	21.2
Former county of North Yorkshire	..	7.4	26.7	10.7	..	8	8	28.2

Table **14.7** (continued)

| | | Benefit statistics | | | | Economic statistics | | |
| | | Claimant count[4], March 2003 | | | | Businesses registered for VAT 2002 | | |
	Economically active[2] 2001-2002[3] (percentages)	Level (thousands)	Females (percentage of claimants)	Percentage claiming over 12 months, computerised claims only[5]	Income Support beneficiaries[6,7] May 2003 (percentages)	Registration rates[8] (percentages)	De-registration rates[8] (percentages)	Stock of businesses end 2001 (thousands)
East Midlands	79.6	62.6	25.9	13.1	9	10	9	119.5
Derby UA	77.5	5.0	23.0	16.3	11	11	11	4.3
Leicester UA	71.2	9.0	25.3	17.4	15	12	12	7.6
Nottingham UA	70.3	7.7	20.7	18.5	16	10	11	6.1
Rutland UA	80.7	0.1	29.0	1.5	3	9	7	1.5
Derbyshire County	80.1	9.8	28.2	12.3	9	10	8	20.3
Amber Valley	76.8	1.4	32.1	10.7	8	11	9	3.1
Bolsover	74.5	1.1	24.8	11.5	12	10	9	1.4
Chesterfield	76.1	2.0	27.2	14.4	12	11	9	2.3
Derbyshire Dales	85.2	0.5	29.6	12.3	5	8	7	3.5
Erewash	83.9	1.7	31.1	11.6	9	10	8	2.6
High Peak	82.6	0.9	24.1	8.0	7	10	8	2.7
North East Derbyshire	77.8	1.4	26.2	14.8	10	10	8	2.5
South Derbyshire	84.6	0.7	29.5	12.8	7	12	8	2.2
Leicestershire County	85.6	6.0	29.4	12.4	5	10	9	19.6
Blaby	87.9	0.8	29.8	13.8	4	10	7	2.4
Charnwood	81.9	1.8	27.6	14.3	6	9	9	4.3
Harborough	85.3	0.5	28.9	9.4	4	9	10	3.6
Hinckley and Bosworth	86.2	1.1	31.8	8.7	6	10	8	3.3
Melton	88.2	0.3	31.4	7.4	5	10	7	1.9
North West Leicestershire	85.3	0.8	30.3	12.9	7	11	8	2.8
Oadby and Wigston	90.1	0.7	28.0	16.1	6	10	10	1.3
Lincolnshire	80.0	7.4	26.3	7.7	9	9	8	20.5
Boston	78.8	0.5	25.0	2.2	10	10	8	1.8
East Lindsey	75.6	1.8	27.3	5.6	11	8	8	4.6
Lincoln	74.5	1.6	19.8	8.9	12	13	9	1.7
North Kesteven	82.0	0.7	31.0	7.0	7	9	8	2.7
South Holland	78.1	0.6	27.8	6.4	8	6	7	2.9
South Kesteven	87.4	1.0	30.5	5.9	5	10	8	4.1
West Lindsey	81.1	1.1	27.5	15.0	8	8	8	2.7
Northamptonshire	84.0	7.9	27.6	9.2	7	11	9	21.2
Corby	75.0	1.1	25.3	6.2	10	9	8	1.1
Daventry	84.3	0.7	32.3	6.6	4	10	7	3.2
East Northamptonshire	86.1	0.7	32.0	5.8	6	9	8	2.6
Kettering	86.3	0.9	29.8	9.0	8	10	8	2.3
Northampton	82.3	3.1	25.3	12.9	8	10	10	5.3
South Northamptonshire	89.4	0.4	28.6	6.5	4	9	8	3.6
Wellingborough	83.4	1.0	28.7	6.0	8	16	12	3.1
Nottinghamshire County	77.5	9.6	26.0	11.8	8	11	9	17.7
Ashfield	74.9	1.9	28.4	12.7	10	12	9	2.1
Bassetlaw	75.0	1.5	25.9	14.6	10	9	9	2.8
Broxtowe	81.4	1.3	25.7	13.5	6	12	9	2.2
Gedling	84.5	1.4	23.4	14.6	7	11	10	2.4
Mansfield	75.0	1.6	25.3	7.4	11	10	9	1.8
Newark and Sherwood	76.4	1.2	26.6	7.0	8	11	7	3.3
Rushcliffe	75.0	0.8	26.0	13.3	5	10	10	3.2
Former county of Derbyshire	..	14.7	26.4	13.6	..	10	9	24.6
Former county of Leicestershire	..	15.2	27.0	15.2	..	10	9	28.7
Former county of Nottinghamshire	..	17.4	23.6	14.8	..	11	10	23.8
West Midlands	78.5	99.4	23.7	15.6	11	10	10	146.2
Herefordshire, County of UA	81.8	1.8	26.9	7.2	7	8	7	8.0
Stoke-on-Trent UA	75.2	4.9	23.1	8.8	14	10	10	4.6
Telford and Wrekin UA	79.3	2.2	27.4	9.7	11	13	9	3.4
Shropshire County	81.5	2.6	25.9	10.9	7	7	7	11.7
Bridgnorth	84.6	0.4	31.7	9.8	6	7	6	2.3
North Shropshire	81.6	0.5	26.0	10.8	8	7	8	2.6
Oswestry	76.7	0.4	31.1	15.1	7	8	6	1.3
Shrewsbury and Atcham	83.1	0.9	22.2	9.1	7	9	8	3.1
South Shropshire	77.3	0.3	21.4	12.1	7	6	6	2.3

Table **14.7**   (continued)

		Benefit statistics				Economic statistics		
		Claimant count[4], March 2003			Income Support bene-ficiaries[6,7] May 2003 (percentages)	Businesses registered for VAT 2002		Stock of businesses end 2001 (thousands)
	Economically active[2] 2001-2002[3] (percentages)	Level (thousands)	Females (percentage of claimants)	Percentage claiming over 12 months, computerised claims only[5]		Registration rates[8] (percentages)	De-registration rates[8] (percentages)	
Staffordshire County	82.1	9.6	27.6	9.4	7	10	9	23.6
Cannock Chase	84.3	1.3	30.0	8.7	9	11	8	2.4
East Staffordshire	86.7	1.2	27.5	4.8	8	10	8	3.3
Lichfield	73.9	1.0	26.9	9.7	7	10	9	3.4
Newcastle-under-Lyme	81.0	1.5	25.6	9.0	8	9	10	2.7
South Staffordshire	86.3	1.3	25.8	12.2	7	9	8	3.1
Stafford	79.4	1.4	25.1	12.2	6	9	9	3.8
Staffordshire Moorlands	80.4	1.0	31.6	7.3	7	8	7	3.2
Tamworth	86.3	1.1	30.0	10.6	9	13	9	1.7
Warwickshire	82.3	5.3	26.4	11.5	7	10	9	18.0
North Warwickshire	76.2	0.6	29.5	11.3	7	10	7	2.1
Nuneaton and Bedworth	80.8	1.6	26.1	9.0	9	10	9	2.4
Rugby	85.3	1.1	26.2	14.4	6	9	7	2.7
Stratford-on-Avon	84.5	0.7	28.4	11.2	6	9	8	5.9
Warwick	82.5	1.3	24.4	12.2	6	11	10	4.9
West Midlands (Met County)	75.4	67.2	22.4	18.6	14	11	11	57.6
Birmingham	71.1	31.8	21.6	23.2	16	11	12	22.2
Coventry	78.1	6.7	20.8	14.2	12	11	9	5.6
Dudley	82.2	6.1	24.7	17.0	11	10	9	7.7
Sandwell	75.3	7.8	23.0	17.1	16	11	9	6.1
Solihull	82.4	2.5	26.0	10.3	7	10	10	4.9
Walsall	76.8	5.6	24.1	11.8	15	11	11	5.7
Wolverhampton	74.4	6.7	22.8	13.7	14	11	16	5.5
Worcestershire County	82.6	5.9	26.0	8.5	7	9	9	18.7
Bromsgrove	85.1	1.1	25.8	10.7	5	10	10	3.1
Malvern Hills	83.2	0.5	25.8	6.4	6	8	8	3.3
Redditch	77.9	1.1	26.2	8.0	9	11	9	2.1
Worcester	82.7	1.2	24.5	9.7	8	10	12	2.3
Wychavon	84.0	0.8	27.8	5.3	7	9	8	5.1
Wyre Forest	82.3	1.2	26.4	8.7	8	10	9	2.8
Herefordshire and Worcestershire	..	7.7	26.2	8.2	..	9	8	26.6
Former county of Shropshire	..	4.7	26.6	10.3	..	9	7	15.1
Former county of Staffordshire	..	14.5	26.1	9.2	..	10	9	28.2
East	82.1	62.5	27.1	11.1	7	10	10	177.4
Luton UA	78.4	3.9	25.4	12.8	10	12	10	3.8
Peterborough UA	81.2	2.4	23.1	6.7	11	12	11	4.0
Southend-on-Sea UA	78.9	2.9	23.3	15.0	11	11	15	4.8
Thurrock UA	81.2	2.0	31.1	11.4	9	14	10	3.0
Bedfordshire County	83.8	4.6	26.8	11.8	6	10	9	12.7
Bedford	82.2	2.3	24.3	14.6	8	10	8	4.3
Mid Bedfordshire	84.5	1.0	31.5	10.9	5	10	9	4.7
South Bedfordshire	84.8	1.4	27.9	7.7	5	11	9	3.7
Cambridgeshire County	83.0	4.8	27.7	9.0	6	9	8	20.0
Cambridge	79.4	1.4	26.0	10.9	6	10	9	3.5
East Cambridgeshire	88.6	0.6	28.5	9.8	5	9	7	3.0
Fenland	81.9	0.8	29.1	8.9	10	9	9	2.7
Huntingdonshire	82.5	1.2	30.1	6.1	5	9	8	5.5
South Cambridgeshire	85.0	0.8	25.2	9.4	4	8	7	5.4
Essex County	81.9	13.4	28.7	10.1	7	10	10	42.2
Basildon	78.8	2.3	28.4	7.9	11	11	10	4.5
Braintree	85.7	1.3	30.0	9.8	7	10	9	4.7
Brentwood	82.2	0.5	28.9	7.3	5	11	10	2.7
Castle Point	80.6	0.7	31.2	6.0	7	11	10	2.3
Chelmsford	84.9	1.3	28.8	13.4	6	11	10	4.9
Colchester	82.2	1.4	29.8	6.6	6	11	9	4.7
Epping Forest	82.4	1.3	33.4	11.5	7	11	11	4.8
Harlow	83.5	1.1	27.5	12.3	10	13	10	1.6
Maldon	79.4	0.5	27.8	15.5	6	11	9	2.6
Rochford	82.6	0.7	29.1	10.0	6	10	10	2.4
Tendring	76.6	2.0	24.4	11.5	10	9	9	3.3
Uttlesford	82.6	0.4	27.8	9.7	4	9	8	3.7

Table 14.7 (continued)

	Economically active[2] 2001-2002[3] (percentages)	Benefit statistics			Income Support bene-ficiaries[6,7] May 2003 (percentages)	Economic statistics		Stock of businesses end 2001 (thousands)
		Claimant count[4], March 2003				Businesses registered for VAT 2002		
		Level (thousands)	Females (percentage of claimants)	Percentage claiming over 12 months, computerised claims only[5]		Registration rates[8] (percentages)	De-registration rates[8] (percentages)	
Hertfordshire	83.0	9.4	28.8	9.5	6	10	10	38.6
Broxbourne	82.2	0.8	34.8	12.4	7	12	10	2.6
Dacorum	82.9	1.4	29.5	8.2	6	9	10	5.3
East Hertfordshire	86.5	0.8	29.8	7.3	5	10	9	5.5
Hertsmere	78.4	0.9	26.8	9.4	7	11	10	3.7
North Hertfordshire	83.8	1.1	34.4	6.9	6	9	8	5.1
St. Albans	79.2	0.9	24.7	8.0	5	10	10	5.5
Stevenage	82.5	1.0	26.0	9.4	8	11	10	1.8
Three Rivers	82.2	0.7	27.4	12.7	5	10	11	3.2
Watford	81.4	0.9	26.0	12.3	6	11	12	2.9
Welwyn Hatfield	91.5	0.9	27.2	10.0	6	9	9	3.2
Norfolk	80.9	10.7	26.0	11.7	9	8	8	24.6
Breckland	85.8	1.0	27.8	6.8	7	9	8	3.9
Broadland	85.6	0.8	26.8	13.3	6	8	9	3.4
Great Yarmouth	73.7	2.7	26.1	12.4	12	7	8	2.3
King's Lynn and West Norfolk	80.8	1.6	25.9	11.2	10	8	7	4.2
North Norfolk	79.0	1.1	26.7	11.0	8	7	8	3.4
Norwich	76.3	2.6	23.2	13.1	13	9	10	3.2
South Norfolk	82.8	0.8	30.4	10.7	6	7	8	4.1
Suffolk	82.9	8.5	26.1	13.8	7	9	9	21.9
Babergh	81.8	0.7	29.4	11.9	6	8	9	3.3
Forest Heath	89.4	0.4	37.8	4.5	6	10	10	2.0
Ipswich	79.1	2.8	23.1	16.8	10	12	11	2.6
Mid Suffolk	82.2	0.6	29.5	10.9	5	8	7	3.8
St. Edmundsbury	85.3	0.8	28.6	7.8	6	10	8	3.3
Suffolk Coastal	84.0	1.1	26.1	11.5	6	9	9	4.1
Waveney	80.3	2.0	24.9	16.8	10	9	8	2.8
Former county of Bedfordshire	..	8.5	26.2	12.3	..	11	9	16.6
Former county of Cambridgeshire	..	7.2	26.2	8.2	..	10	8	24.0
Former county of Essex	..	18.2	28.1	11.0	..	11	10	49.9
London	75.5	174.0	27.9	18.9	11	12	13	282.9
Inner London	..	92.8	27.6	21.6	14	12	12	150.8
Inner London – West	..	24.5	29.6	21.2	10	..	..	..
Camden	71.3	6.0	28.4	23.0	13	10	11	18.6
City of London	..	0.1	31.6	29.8	4	8	11	12.1
Hammersmith and Fulham	77.4	4.9	27.8	20.5	11	13	12	8.4
Kensington and Chelsea	69.9	3.2	32.8	21.7	9	11	10	9.8
Wandsworth	83.0	5.8	29.8	19.4	9	12	11	9.5
Westminster	69.3	4.6	30.4	21.2	10	12	13	38.5
Inner London – East	..	68.3	26.9	21.7	16	..	..	..
Hackney	65.5	8.6	27.5	17.0	19	14	13	7.1
Haringey	66.9	7.9	27.0	23.5	15	13	13	6.4
Islington	71.6	6.5	29.9	21.0	17	12	13	10.3
Lambeth	75.1	10.8	26.9	21.9	13	14	10	6.7
Lewisham	73.8	8.5	27.9	21.1	12	13	12	4.5
Newham	61.1	7.9	25.5	18.0	17	15	13	3.8
Southwark	72.1	9.7	27.6	27.1	14	12	11	7.9
Tower Hamlets	62.0	8.4	23.6	23.0	19	14	11	7.3
Outer London	..	81.2	28.2	15.9	9	12	13	130.2
Outer London – East and North East	..	31.2	28.7	15.1	11	..	..	..
Barking and Dagenham	72.7	3.3	28.2	14.5	15	13	10	2.5
Bexley	79.3	3.0	30.5	12.6	7	11	10	5.0
Enfield	74.7	5.8	28.8	15.1	12	13	13	6.7
Greenwich	75.6	6.1	29.3	17.3	13	13	12	4.0
Havering	81.0	2.6	31.5	11.8	8	11	12	5.7
Redbridge	77.1	4.3	28.8	11.7	9	13	15	5.8
Waltham Forest	74.0	6.1	26.2	18.5	12	14	14	4.7
Outer London – South	..	17.7	28.4	16.1	7	..	..	..
Bromley	81.0	4.0	28.2	14.1	7	11	11	9.1
Croydon	80.8	6.8	28.9	17.1	9	12	12	8.6
Kingston upon Thames	81.6	1.8	28.3	15.6	5	11	12	5.3
Merton	81.5	3.1	27.5	15.3	6	11	12	5.7
Sutton	86.7	2.0	28.4	18.3	6	10	11	5.2

Table **14.7** (continued)

	Economically active[2] 2001-2002[3] (percentages)	Benefit statistics			Income Support bene-ficiaries[6,7] May 2003 (percentages)	Economic statistics		Stock of businesses end 2001 (thousands)
		Claimant count[4], March 2003				Businesses registered for VAT 2002		
		Level (thousands)	Females (percentage of claimants)	Percentage claiming over 12 months, computerised claims only[5]		Registration rates[8] (percentages)	De-registration rates[8] (percentages)	
Outer London – West and North West	..	32.3	27.7	16.6	9	..	..	..
Barnet	79.6	5.9	29.3	16.9	9	11	18	13.6
Brent	74.7	8.3	26.7	24.6	12	12	13	8.5
Ealing	73.9	6.3	25.9	16.1	10	12	12	9.7
Harrow	76.7	3.0	28.8	15.7	8	13	13	7.3
Hillingdon	80.3	3.5	27.6	10.3	9	11	11	7.4
Hounslow	78.9	3.4	28.6	7.4	11	12	12	6.9
Richmond upon Thames	83.1	2.1	29.9	12.7	5	12	11	8.7
South East	**82.8**	**79.8**	**25.5**	**11.0**	**6**	**10**	**10**	**277.5**
Bracknell Forest UA	84.7	1.0	28.3	9.5	5	12	11	3.4
Brighton and Hove UA	79.5	5.2	26.2	20.0	11	11	10	7.9
Isle of Wight UA	77.9	2.4	24.4	12.3	9	8	9	3.5
Medway UA	81.1	3.7	26.5	13.1	8	11	10	5.2
Milton Keynes UA	85.0	2.8	27.0	9.7	7	12	11	6.8
Portsmouth UA	79.8	2.8	22.3	11.7	9	13	10	3.8
Reading UA	82.0	2.2	25.0	9.3	7	11	11	4.3
Slough UA	80.0	2.4	26.5	15.3	9	13	12	3.2
Southampton UA	79.1	3.5	19.5	8.0	10	11	13	4.7
West Berkshire UA	87.4	1.0	26.7	8.4	4	10	9	6.5
Windsor and Maidenhead UA	79.1	1.4	28.4	13.4	5	10	10	6.8
Wokingham UA	83.8	1.0	27.9	8.2	3	10	9	5.8
Buckinghamshire County	84.6	4.1	25.0	12.2	5	10	9	22.5
Aylesbury Vale	85.6	1.1	24.3	9.0	5	10	9	6.8
Chiltern	82.4	0.7	24.4	9.4	5	9	9	4.5
South Bucks	83.4	0.5	29.7	12.6	3	9	10	3.7
Wycombe	85.1	1.8	24.3	15.2	5	9	9	7.6
East Sussex County	80.8	5.6	24.2	13.4	8	10	9	16.2
Eastbourne	79.6	1.3	24.1	15.1	9	11	12	2.0
Hastings	75.8	1.9	22.2	12.3	13	11	11	1.8
Lewes	83.7	0.9	26.8	12.9	7	9	8	3.0
Rother	79.7	0.8	25.1	15.7	7	9	10	3.1
Wealden	83.6	0.8	25.4	11.4	5	9	8	6.2
Hampshire County	84.9	8.6	26.3	6.3	5	10	9	41.4
Basingstoke and Deane	85.9	1.0	27.2	8.6	5	10	10	5.2
East Hampshire	82.4	0.7	24.3	11.1	5	10	9	4.8
Eastleigh	89.3	0.7	27.8	6.5	4	10	10	3.6
Fareham	88.0	0.6	24.5	6.2	4	10	9	3.1
Gosport	80.8	0.6	22.9	2.3	7	10	10	1.1
Hart	87.0	0.4	29.5	5.3	3	10	10	3.6
Havant	80.4	1.5	25.7	6.5	9	11	10	2.8
New Forest	81.2	1.0	26.3	5.5	6	9	9	5.9
Rushmoor	83.7	0.8	30.6	6.3	4	11	11	2.3
Test Valley	87.1	0.6	26.7	3.0	5	10	9	4.3
Winchester	87.8	0.6	23.3	6.7	4	9	9	4.7
Kent County	80.7	15.8	25.8	11.3	8	11	10	40.3
Ashford	83.2	1.1	22.5	8.3	6	10	10	3.9
Canterbury	83.1	1.5	25.4	10.2	8	11	10	3.4
Dartford	85.3	1.0	30.6	8.8	6	11	9	2.2
Dover	81.7	1.5	25.2	11.5	9	10	10	2.4
Gravesham	78.2	1.6	28.5	11.9	8	11	9	2.2
Maidstone	80.7	1.2	24.7	6.3	7	11	9	5.0
Sevenoaks	80.9	0.7	27.5	10.3	6	9	10	4.7
Shepway	83.8	1.4	23.5	14.1	10	10	9	2.6
Swale	77.2	1.8	27.2	13.1	10	10	10	3.4
Thanet	76.0	2.7	24.6	15.0	13	12	10	2.3
Tonbridge and Malling	80.3	0.8	25.6	9.1	6	10	10	3.7
Tunbridge Wells	79.1	0.7	25.2	8.1	7	12	10	4.7
Oxfordshire	83.9	4.4	26.4	10.4	5	10	9	22.3
Cherwell	87.2	0.8	26.2	5.6	6	9	9	4.7
Oxford	78.8	1.7	22.2	13.8	7	11	9	3.1
South Oxfordshire	83.1	0.8	30.5	10.7	4	9	9	6.1
Vale of White Horse	87.1	0.7	29.2	11.1	4	10	9	4.3
West Oxfordshire	84.7	0.5	30.0	5.8	4	9	8	4.2

Table **14.7** (continued)

	Economically active[2] 2001-2002[3] (percentages)	Benefit statistics				Economic statistics		
		Claimant count[4], March 2003			Income Support bene-ficiaries[6,7] May 2003 (percentages)	Businesses registered for VAT 2002		Stock of businesses end 2001 (thousands)
		Level (thousands)	Females (percentage of claimants)	Percentage claiming over 12 months, computerised claims only[5]		Registration rates[8] (percentages)	De-registration rates[8] (percentages)	
Surrey	84.7	6.5	27.2	7.2	5	10	10	45.1
Elmbridge	80.2	0.8	26.5	5.7	4	9	11	5.9
Epsom and Ewell	79.9	0.4	28.6	9.0	4	11	10	2.2
Guildford	84.2	0.8	26.8	8.8	4	10	10	5.5
Mole Valley	81.9	0.4	24.9	9.0	5	8	9	4.1
Reigate and Banstead	89.2	0.7	27.3	3.4	5	9	11	5.0
Runnymede	84.4	0.5	26.0	7.7	4	10	10	3.1
Spelthorne	88.2	0.7	31.8	10.6	6	9	11	3.1
Surrey Heath	78.4	0.5	29.0	3.9	4	10	10	3.5
Tandridge	87.7	0.4	27.5	5.8	5	10	10	3.6
Waverley	87.7	0.6	26.2	8.3	4	9	9	5.7
Woking	89.0	0.6	24.0	6.7	5	10	10	3.4
West Sussex	83.1	5.4	24.7	10.6	6	10	10	26.0
Adur	80.9	0.5	24.8	13.1	7	12	8	1.5
Arun	80.1	1.0	27.1	11.6	8	10	11	4.0
Chichester	82.7	0.7	28.6	9.1	5	8	9	5.1
Crawley	87.6	1.0	25.5	8.9	7	13	14	2.2
Horsham	85.6	0.8	23.4	13.2	4	8	9	5.4
Mid Sussex	83.6	0.6	24.5	6.9	4	10	9	5.1
Worthing	80.4	0.8	18.4	11.6	9	9	13	2.6
Former county of Berkshire	..	8.9	26.7	11.3	..	11	10	30.0
Former county of Buckinghamshire	..	7.0	25.9	11.2	..	10	10	29.2
Former county of East Sussex	..	10.8	25.2	16.6	..	10	10	24.1
Former county of Hampshire	..	14.8	23.9	7.7	..	10	10	49.8
Former county of Kent	..	19.6	25.9	11.7	..	11	10	45.4
South West	82.4	53.2	26.6	10.8	8	9	9	163.8
Bath and North East Somerset UA	82.2	1.3	29.0	7.0	6	9	8	5.8
Bournemouth UA	79.4	1.8	23.4	8.8	10	10	12	4.7
Bristol, City of UA	81.0	6.2	23.0	11.4	12	12	11	11.1
North Somerset UA	83.2	1.5	24.1	4.7	8	10	8	5.5
Plymouth UA	79.1	4.4	25.0	13.2	11	11	10	3.7
Poole UA	82.8	1.0	24.7	4.0	7	11	9	4.0
South Gloucestershire UA	85.7	1.7	27.2	9.2	6	11	11	6.5
Swindon UA	86.6	2.6	26.6	13.2	8	11	12	4.3
Torbay UA	77.5	2.6	25.1	11.4	13	10	13	3.2
Cornwall and the Isles of Scilly	77.9	7.1	29.6	11.4	9	8	8	17.6
Caradon	80.4	0.9	28.8	8.1	8	8	7	2.8
Carrick	73.1	1.1	26.8	10.1	8	8	8	3.2
Kerrier	79.1	1.5	27.9	14.3	10	7	8	2.7
North Cornwall	80.7	1.1	30.8	13.4	9	7	7	3.9
Penwith	71.9	1.2	30.3	12.1	12	9	8	2.1
Restormel	80.4	1.4	32.3	9.2	9	9	9	2.9
Isles of Scilly	..	0.0	41.2	5.9	3	6	6	0.2
Devon County	81.7	7.1	28.0	11.6	8	8	8	28.0
East Devon	81.4	0.8	27.4	7.7	6	8	9	4.6
Exeter	81.2	1.4	22.8	13.8	8	10	10	2.8
Mid Devon	80.5	0.6	28.0	11.0	7	6	7	3.5
North Devon	79.8	1.2	32.1	13.2	9	8	8	3.8
South Hams	82.5	0.7	30.6	5.6	7	8	7	3.8
Teignbridge	81.4	1.2	26.9	10.4	8	9	10	4.3
Torridge	87.5	0.8	29.5	18.2	8	7	7	2.8
West Devon	81.1	0.4	30.7	9.3	6	6	7	2.5
Dorset County	81.9	2.4	27.2	5.6	6	8	8	13.9
Christchurch	79.4	0.3	25.4	5.2	6	10	9	1.4
East Dorset	83.0	0.4	27.2	7.2	5	8	8	3.2
North Dorset	86.9	0.2	32.6	5.8	5	7	8	2.6
Purbeck	82.1	0.2	21.1	5.2	7	10	8	1.5
West Dorset	81.1	0.5	30.4	4.5	7	7	8	4.0
Weymouth and Portland	78.1	0.7	25.5	5.5	9	11	10	1.2

Table **14.7** (continued)

| | Economically active[2] 2001-2002[3] (percentages) | Benefit statistics | | | | Economic statistics | | |
| | | Claimant count[4], March 2003 | | | Income Support bene-ficiaries[6,7] May 2003 (percentages) | Businesses registered for VAT 2002 | | Stock of businesses end 2001 (thousands) |
		Level (thousands)	Females (percentage of claimants)	Percentage claiming over 12 months, computerised claims only[5]		Registration rates[8] (percentages)	De-registration rates[8] (percentages)	
Gloucestershire	84.3	6.2	26.2	13.8	7	9	10	20.6
Cheltenham	80.1	1.2	21.7	15.6	6	10	12	3.5
Cotswold	87.2	0.5	28.4	7.6	5	8	9	4.5
Forest of Dean	83.5	1.0	32.4	11.0	7	9	9	3.0
Gloucester	83.4	1.9	24.4	18.2	9	10	14	2.5
Stroud	84.7	1.0	28.7	10.0	6	9	8	4.3
Tewkesbury	88.6	0.6	25.0	12.7	6	8	9	2.8
Somerset	84.2	4.3	27.9	11.5	8	8	8	18.1
Mendip	85.9	1.1	30.0	13.9	7	9	8	4.1
Sedgemoor	81.4	1.1	29.3	12.9	9	7	8	3.7
South Somerset	84.9	1.0	28.1	10.9	7	8	8	5.4
Taunton Deane	85.5	0.8	24.2	8.2	8	9	10	3.4
West Somerset	78.9	0.4	26.0	9.1	8	8	7	1.5
Wiltshire County	86.6	3.1	28.8	6.7	5	9	8	15.4
Kennet	85.3	0.5	30.9	5.3	5	9	8	3.0
North Wiltshire	83.8	1.0	30.8	7.1	4	10	8	4.8
Salisbury	89.4	0.5	26.8	4.5	5	9	10	4.0
West Wiltshire	87.7	1.0	26.7	8.0	5	10	8	3.6
Bristol/Bath area	..	10.7	24.6	9.6	..	11	10	28.9
Former county of Devon	..	14.0	26.6	12.1	..	8	9	34.9
Former county of Dorset	..	5.2	25.4	6.4	..	9	9	22.6
Former county of Wiltshire	..	5.6	27.8	9.6	..	10	9	19.7

1 See Notes and Definitions to the Labour Market chapter for labour market definitions.

2 For those of working age.

3 Data are from the Annual Local Area Labour Force Survey and relate to the period March 2001 to February 2002. These data have not been adjusted to reflect the 2001 Census population estimates.

4 Count of claimants of unemployment-related benefit, i.e. Jobseeker's Allowance.

5 People who have been claiming for more than 12 months (computerised claims only), as a percentage of total computerised claimants.

6 Claimants and their partners aged 16 or over, as a percentage of the population aged 16 or over. Data are from the Income Support Quarterly Statistical Enquiry. United Kingdom figure not supplied as latest data available for Northern Ireland is February 2002.

7 Mid 2002 population estimates for England and Manchester include provisional results from the Manchester Matching Exercise, published in November 2003.

8 Registrations/de-registrations during 2002, as a percentage of the stock at the end of 2001.

Source: Office for National Statistics; Department of Trade and Industry; Small Business Service; IAD Information Centre, Department for Work and Pensions

NUTS levels 1, 2 and 3 in England,[1] 1998

NUTS level 3 areas

1 South Teeside
2 Hartlepool & Stockton
3 Darlington
4 Sunderland
5 Tyneside
6 Halton & Warrington
7 Gt Manchester North
8 Gt Manchester South
9 Blackburn with Darwen
10 Blackpool
11 Sefton
12 Wirral
13 East Merseyside
14 Liverpool
15 East Riding of Yorkshire
16 City of Kingston upon Hull
17 North & North East Lincolnshire
18 York
19 Leeds
20 Bradford
21 Calderdale, Kirklees & Wakefield
22 Sheffield
23 Barnsley, Doncaster & Rotherham
24 Derby
25 South & West Derbyshire
26 East Derbyshire
27 Leicester City
28 Leicestershire CC & Rutland
29 Northamptonshire
30 Nottingham
31 North Nottinghamshire
32 South Nottinghamshire
33 The Wrekin
34 Stoke-on-Trent
35 Staffordshire CC
36 Walsall & Wolverhampton
37 Birmingham
38 Coventry
39 Solihull
40 Dudley & Sandwell
41 Luton
42 Bedfordshire CC
43 Peterborough
44 Southend-on-Sea
45 Thurrock
46 Hertfordshire
47 Inner London - East
48 Inner London - West
49 Outer London - E & NE
50 Outer London - South
51 Outer London - W & NW
52 Milton Keynes
53 Buckinghamshire CC
54 Brighton & Hove

55 Portsmouth
56 Southampton
57 Medway
58 Kent CC
59 N & NE Somerset, South Gloucestershire
60 City of Bristol
61 Plymouth
62 Torbay
63 Bournemouth & Poole
64 Swindon

1 NUTS (Nomenclature of Units for Territorial Statistics) is a hierarchical classification of areas that provides a breakdown of the EU's economic territory.
See Notes and Definitions.

Table **14.8**   Gross value added (GVA) and gross disposable household income by NUTS 1, 2 and 3 area at current basic prices[1, 2]

Country NUTS 1 NUTS 2 NUTS 3	GVA £ million				GVA £ per head				GVA £ per head (UK=100)				Gross disposable household income £ per Head (UK=100)[3] 3 year average
	1998	1999	2000	2001	1998	1999	2000	2001	1998	1999	2000	2001	1997-1999
United Kingdom[4]	749,688	781,847	816,111	851,408	12,858	13,369	13,917	14,418	100	100	100	100	100
England	639,772	668,598	698,684	730,036	13,148	13,691	14,260	14,781	102	102	103	103	102
North East	25,497	25,910	26,740	27,729	10,021	10,235	10,600	11,009	78	77	76	76	89
Tees Valley and Durham	11,053	11,156	11,494	11,905	9,685	9,809	10,124	10,502	75	73	73	73	89
Hartlepool and Stockton-on-Tees	2,988	3,043	3,161	3,287	11,243	11,441	11,849	12,295	87	86	85	85	89
South Teesside	2,628	2,627	2,685	2,778	9,420	9,485	9,751	10,114	73	71	70	70	86
Darlington	1,178	1,190	1,211	1,256	11,934	12,119	12,349	12,831	93	91	89	89	89
Durham CC	4,259	4,296	4,437	4,584	8,555	8,658	8,961	9,285	67	65	64	64	90
Northumberland and Tyne and Wear	14,444	14,754	15,245	15,824	10,294	10,583	10,989	11,423	80	79	79	79	89
Northumberland	2,623	2,603	2,633	2,681	8,539	8,465	8,567	8,722	66	63	62	60	96
Tyneside	8,923	9,200	9,568	9,995	11,027	11,466	11,997	12,539	86	86	86	87	90
Sunderland	2,898	2,952	3,044	3,149	10,108	10,382	10,781	11,215	79	78	77	78	82
North West	77,698	80,836	84,058	87,584	11,490	11,997	12,477	12,942	89	90	90	90	93
Cumbria	5,273	5,283	5,321	5,410	10,763	10,807	10,901	11,092	84	81	78	77	94
West Cumbria	2,483	2,480	2,494	2,530	10,469	10,484	10,599	10,776	81	78	76	75	85
East Cumbria	2,790	2,803	2,827	2,881	11,038	11,109	11,182	11,385	86	83	80	79	101
Cheshire	14,059	14,520	14,968	15,545	14,330	14,822	15,248	15,797	111	111	110	110	103
Halton and Warrington	4,448	4,593	4,759	4,963	14,328	14,818	15,368	16,022	111	111	110	111	96
Cheshire CC	9,611	9,927	10,209	10,582	14,330	14,825	15,192	15,694	111	111	109	109	106
Greater Manchester	30,313	31,863	33,377	34,971	12,131	12,804	13,421	13,920	94	96	96	97	92
Greater Manchester South	19,135	20,474	21,670	22,861	14,369	15,485	16,408	17,015	112	116	118	118	93
Greater Manchester North	11,177	11,389	11,707	12,110	9,578	9,764	10,040	10,361	74	73	72	72	91
Lancashire	15,319	15,954	16,700	17,436	10,849	11,316	11,820	12,301	84	85	85	85	91
Blackburn With Darwen	1,548	1,577	1,622	1,677	11,182	11,431	11,784	12,103	87	86	85	84	83
Blackpool	1,357	1,402	1,454	1,512	9,380	9,789	10,160	10,626	73	73	73	74	89
Lancashire CC	12,415	12,976	13,624	14,247	10,996	11,496	12,034	12,534	86	86	86	87	92
Merseyside	12,733	13,215	13,692	14,221	9,227	9,637	10,012	10,414	72	72	72	72	92
East Merseyside	2,672	2,764	2,884	3,008	8,121	8,432	8,804	9,165	63	63	63	64	79
Liverpool	5,210	5,462	5,667	5,890	11,581	12,268	12,790	13,317	90	92	92	92	83
Sefton	2,344	2,425	2,523	2,635	8,232	8,546	8,909	9,315	64	64	64	65	110
Wirral	2,508	2,564	2,618	2,689	7,924	8,154	8,343	8,611	62	61	60	60	101
Yorkshire and the Humber	56,099	57,706	59,675	61,929	11,334	11,666	12,057	12,459	88	87	87	86	93
East Riding and North Lincolnshire	9,966	9,972	10,131	10,375	11,437	11,476	11,678	11,938	89	86	84	83	91
Kingston upon Hull, City of	2,913	2,960	3,074	3,198	11,475	11,828	12,483	13,143	89	88	90	91	81
East Riding of Yorkshire	2,956	2,919	2,945	3,007	9,624	9,450	9,459	9,549	75	71	68	66	99
North and North East Lincolnshire	4,097	4,093	4,113	4,170	13,201	13,212	13,266	13,413	103	99	95	93	93
North Yorkshire	8,610	8,960	9,376	9,791	11,719	12,119	12,585	13,031	91	91	90	90	107
York	2,639	2,774	2,919	3,052	14,964	15,595	16,258	16,833	116	117	117	117	105
North Yorkshire CC	5,971	6,186	6,457	6,740	10,694	11,018	11,419	11,822	83	82	82	82	107
South Yorkshire	12,278	12,576	12,997	13,466	9,633	9,899	10,259	10,633·	75	74	74	74	87
Barnsley, Doncaster and Rotherham	6,440	6,563	6,767	6,983	8,498	8,694	8,988	9,270	66	65	65	64	85
Sheffield	5,838	6,013	6,230	6,483	11,298	11,664	12,119	12,634	88	87	87	88	91
West Yorkshire	25,245	26,198	27,171	28,297	12,201	12,668	13,125	13,581	95	95	94	94	92
Bradford	5,146	5,295	5,430	5,605	11,053	11,408	11,695	11,895	86	85	84	82	86
Leeds	10,493	11,019	11,539	12,097	14,687	15,442	16,193	16,904	114	116	116	117	97
Calderdale, Kirklees and Wakefield	9,606	9,884	10,202	10,595	10,803	11,102	11,421	11,815	84	83	82	82	90

Table **14.8** (continued)

Country													Gross disposable household income £ per Head (UK=100)[3]
NUTS 1 NUTS 2	GVA £ million				GVA £ per head				GVA £ per head (UK=100)				3 year average
NUTS 3	1998	1999	2000	2001	1998	1999	2000	2001	1998	1999	2000	2001	1997-1999
East Midlands	50,102	51,743	53,588	55,394	12,145	12,486	12,890	13,243	95	93	93	92	93
Derbyshire and Nottinghamshire	23,279	24,072	24,970	25,819	11,819	12,209	12,672	13,066	92	91	91	91	90
Derby	3,601	3,874	4,046	4,146	15,992	17,255	18,146	18,584	124	129	130	129	90
East Derbyshire	2,324	2,412	2,490	2,570	8,701	9,031	9,319	9,602	68	68	67	67	81
South and West Derbyshire	5,239	5,230	5,227	5,290	11,407	11,316	11,230	11,322	89	85	81	79	92
Nottingham	5,023	5,121	5,343	5,595	18,307	18,829	19,863	20,782	142	141	143	144	81
North Nottinghamshire	4,270	4,418	4,624	4,800	10,163	10,476	10,955	11,327	79	78	79	79	88
South Nottinghamshire	2,822	3,018	3,240	3,418	8,724	9,309	10,004	10,516	68	70	72	73	102
Leicestershire, Rutland and Northamptonshire	20,348	21,060	21,820	22,544	13,313	13,689	14,116	14,460	104	102	101	100	95
Leicester	4,219	4,338	4,487	4,639	14,873	15,344	15,987	16,381	116	115	115	114	81
Leicestershire CC and Rutland	7,777	7,772	7,859	8,016	12,346	12,232	12,281	12,431	96	91	88	86	99
Northamptonshire	8,352	8,950	9,474	9,889	13,584	14,427	15,155	15,671	106	108	109	109	97
Lincolnshire[5]	6,475	6,612	6,798	7,031	10,321	10,429	10,607	10,857	80	78	76	75	97
West Midlands	62,140	64,103	66,498	68,839	11,799	12,175	12,642	13,031	92	91	91	90	93
Herefordshire, Worcestershire and Warwickshire	13,955	14,587	15,341	15,983	11,558	12,047	12,618	13,065	90	90	91	91	100
Herefordshire, County of	1,734	1,768	1,829	1,901	10,182	10,282	10,535	10,872	79	77	76	75	94
Worcestershire	5,637	5,957	6,348	6,636	10,490	11,059	11,744	12,239	82	83	84	85	101
Warwickshire	6,584	6,862	7,164	7,445	13,176	13,719	14,279	14,708	102	103	103	102	102
Shropshire and Staffordshire	15,664	15,951	16,288	16,631	10,582	10,766	10,974	11,166	82	81	79	77	95
Telford and Wrekin	2,072	2,096	2,110	2,137	13,608	13,613	13,530	13,476	106	102	97	93	96
Shropshire CC	2,716	2,804	2,880	2,943	9,733	10,019	10,218	10,392	76	75	73	72	97
Stoke-on-Trent	2,830	2,773	2,774	2,809	11,506	11,356	11,463	11,684	89	85	82	81	83
Staffordshire CC	8,047	8,278	8,524	8,741	10,019	10,301	10,596	10,829	78	77	76	75	97
West Midlands	32,520	33,565	34,869	36,226	12,610	13,046	13,621	14,095	98	98	98	98	88
Birmingham	13,257	13,840	14,463	15,127	13,437	14,067	14,785	15,344	105	105	106	106	87
Solihull	2,545	2,681	2,832	2,984	12,659	13,375	14,213	14,951	98	100	102	104	106
Coventry	4,359	4,539	4,696	4,843	14,378	14,982	15,601	15,979	112	112	112	111	88
Dudley and Sandwell	6,655	6,695	6,868	7,072	11,234	11,334	11,668	11,988	87	85	84	83	86
Walsall and Wolverhampton	5,705	5,810	6,010	6,199	11,506	11,742	12,195	12,611	89	88	88	87	89
East	65,645	67,820	71,701	75,128	12,372	12,698	13,340	13,909	96	95	96	96	105
East Anglia	25,413	25,975	27,242	28,455	11,834	12,031	12,534	13,046	92	90	90	90	97
Peterborough	2,299	2,349	2,425	2,497	14,702	15,052	15,549	15,847	114	113	112	110	101
Cambridgeshire CC	7,252	7,555	8,034	8,465	13,312	13,786	14,576	15,256	104	103	105	106	103
Norfolk	8,324	8,472	8,786	9,095	10,653	10,767	11,072	11,387	83	81	80	79	94
Suffolk	7,538	7,599	7,998	8,398	11,337	11,373	11,886	12,534	88	85	85	87	95
Bedfordshire and Hertfordshire	22,974	24,054	25,688	27,024	14,632	15,192	16,127	16,849	114	114	116	117	113
Luton	2,494	2,565	2,698	2,824	13,586	13,879	14,605	15,173	106	104	105	105	88
Bedfordshire CC	4,494	4,555	4,769	4,960	12,130	12,155	12,603	12,980	94	91	91	90	111
Hertfordshire	15,986	16,934	18,221	19,240	15,732	16,540	17,696	18,578	122	124	127	129	118
Essex	17,258	17,791	18,771	19,650	10,867	11,128	11,669	12,158	85	83	84	84	108
Southend-on-Sea	1,676	1,716	1,781	1,853	10,212	10,524	11,014	11,553	79	79	79	80	99
Thurrock	1,797	1,868	1,980	2,056	13,042	13,354	13,970	14,349	101	100	100	100	99
Essex CC	13,785	14,206	15,009	15,741	10,717	10,964	11,501	11,992	83	82	83	83	110
London	137,402	145,413	154,182	162,501	19,717	20,651	21,702	22,236	153	155	156	154	121
Inner London	82,347	87,564	93,144	99,014	31,208	32,654	34,214	34,888	243	244	246	242	127
Inner London – West	54,903	58,319	61,681	65,426	60,818	63,322	65,342	65,641	473	474	470	455	164
Inner London – East	27,444	29,245	31,463	33,588	15,810	16,611	17,692	18,241	123	124	127	127	106
Outer London	55,055	57,849	61,038	63,487	12,714	13,269	13,929	14,203	99	99	100	99	117
Outer London – East and North East	14,534	15,054	15,859	16,423	9,479	9,780	10,257	10,463	74	73	74	73	112
Outer London – South	13,342	13,694	14,196	14,623	11,910	12,140	12,506	12,669	93	91	90	88	120
Outer London – West and North West	27,180	29,102	30,983	32,441	16,210	17,194	18,219	18,580	126	129	131	129	119

Table **14.8** (continued)

Country NUTS 1 NUTS 2 NUTS 3	GVA £ million				GVA £ per head				GVA £ per head (UK=100)				Gross disposable household income £ per Head (UK=100)[3] 3 year average 1997-1999
	1998	1999	2000	2001	1998	1999	2000	2001	1998	1999	2000	2001	
South East	108,591	116,329	121,156	127,377	13,761	14,623	15,178	15,880	107	109	109	110	110
Berkshire, Buckinghamshire and Oxfordshire	35,607	38,959	41,147	43,430	17,238	18,730	19,701	20,686	134	140	142	143	115
Berkshire	15,525	17,236	18,332	19,381	19,492	21,625	22,931	24,115	152	162	165	167	116
Milton Keynes	3,702	3,997	4,179	4,428	18,507	19,696	20,348	21,172	144	147	146	147	98
Buckinghamshire CC	7,258	7,777	8,175	8,608	15,320	16,279	17,099	17,967	119	122	123	125	120
Oxfordshire	9,123	9,950	10,461	11,012	15,323	16,517	17,273	18,128	119	124	124	126	114
Surrey, East and West Sussex	34,499	36,642	37,891	39,841	13,723	14,410	14,870	15,571	107	108	107	108	118
Brighton and Hove	2,814	2,924	3,042	3,236	11,499	11,864	12,307	12,934	89	89	88	90	105
East Sussex CC	4,499	4,610	4,707	4,923	9,257	9,412	9,571	9,983	72	70	69	69	103
Surrey	17,093	18,578	19,421	20,483	16,421	17,589	18,382	19,318	128	132	132	134	131
West Sussex	10,093	10,530	10,721	11,199	13,597	14,034	14,245	14,831	106	105	102	103	114
Hampshire and Isle of Wight	22,090	23,241	23,924	25,019	12,575	13,158	13,511	14,037	98	98	97	97	101
Portsmouth	2,639	2,752	2,817	2,955	14,083	14,783	15,114	15,698	110	111	109	109	87
Southampton	3,232	3,332	3,333	3,415	15,003	15,390	15,386	15,542	117	115	111	108	88
Hampshire CC	15,243	16,099	16,644	17,433	12,438	13,049	13,461	14,043	97	98	97	97	107
Isle of Wight	977	1,058	1,131	1,216	7,607	8,141	8,606	9,147	59	61	62	63	89
Kent	16,394	17,487	18,194	19,088	10,543	11,168	11,554	12,074	82	84	83	84	101
Medway	2,121	2,294	2,392	2,500	8,692	9,309	9,626	10,013	68	70	69	69	99
Kent CC	14,273	15,194	15,802	16,587	10,887	11,515	11,915	12,461	85	86	86	86	101
South West	56,598	58,739	61,085	63,554	11,686	12,053	12,443	12,873	91	90	89	89	100
Gloucestershire, Wiltshire and North Somerset	29,949	31,026	32,147	33,396	14,067	14,467	14,913	15,416	109	108	107	107	103
Bristol, City of	6,849	7,057	7,230	7,463	17,917	18,432	18,949	19,450	139	138	136	135	94
North and North East Somerset, South Gloucestershire	7,602	7,940	8,318	8,687	12,895	13,345	13,844	14,382	100	100	99	100	108
Gloucestershire	7,018	7,334	7,639	7,945	12,611	13,060	13,521	14,062	98	98	97	98	104
Swindon	3,607	3,733	3,842	3,967	20,282	20,784	21,371	22,025	158	155	154	153	103
Wiltshire CC	4,872	4,963	5,118	5,334	11,521	11,660	11,944	12,305	90	87	86	85	104
Dorset and Somerset	12,077	12,645	13,214	13,749	10,308	10,748	11,149	11,533	80	80	80	80	102
Bournemouth and Poole	3,529	3,749	3,952	4,134	11,753	12,483	13,121	13,693	91	93	94	95	102
Dorset CC	3,553	3,703	3,869	4,017	9,249	9,617	9,931	10,259	72	72	71	71	105
Somerset	4,995	5,193	5,393	5,598	10,252	10,574	10,907	11,225	80	79	78	78	99
Cornwall and Isles of Scilly[5]	3,681	3,801	3,965	4,123	7,543	7,718	7,971	8,212	59	58	57	57	90
Devon	10,891	11,267	11,759	12,286	10,328	10,630	10,981	11,413	80	80	79	79	95
Plymouth	2,780	2,872	3,011	3,174	11,416	11,892	12,475	13,174	89	89	90	91	87
Torbay	1,249	1,292	1,360	1,423	9,996	10,253	10,597	10,949	78	77	76	76	90
Devon CC	6,862	7,103	7,388	7,688	10,002	10,258	10,537	10,897	78	77	76	76	99

1 Estimates for GVA data are provisional.
2 Components may not sum to totals due to rounding.
3 Household Income estimates are consistent with those published on 26 March 2002.
4 Excluding GVA for Extra-regio, which comprises compensation of employees and gross operating surplus which cannot be assigned to regions.
5 This area is represented at more than one NUTS level.

Source: Office for National Statistics

Chapter 15 **Sub-regions of Wales**

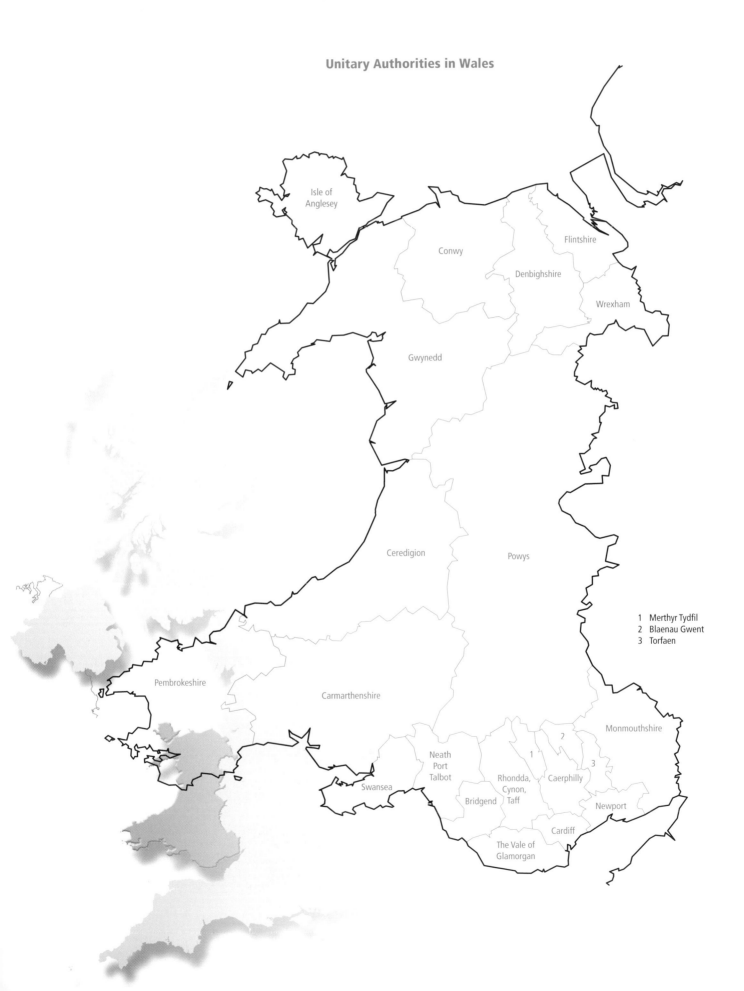

Unitary Authorities in Wales

Isle of Anglesey

Conwy

Flintshire

Denbighshire

Wrexham

Gwynedd

Ceredigion

Powys

1 Merthyr Tydfil
2 Blaenau Gwent
3 Torfaen

Pembrokeshire

Carmarthenshire

Monmouthshire

Neath Port Talbot

2

1

Caerphilly

3

Rhondda, Cynon, Taff

Swansea

Bridgend

Newport

Cardiff

The Vale of Glamorgan

Table 15.1   Area and population by unitary authority, 2002[1]

| | Area (sq km) | People per sq km | Population (thousands) | | | Total population percentage change 1982-2002 | Total fertility rate (TFR)[2] | Standardised mortality ratio (UK=100) (SMR)[3] | Percentage of population aged: | | |
			Males	Females	Total				0 to 15	16 up to pension age[4]	Pension age[4] or over
United Kingdom	242,514	244	28,911	30,318	59,229	5.2	1.63	100	19.9	61.7	18.4
Wales	20,732	141	1,411	1,508	2,919	4.1	1.66	103	19.9	59.9	20.2
Blaenau Gwent	109	638	33	36	69	-7.2	1.73	119	20.9	59.4	19.7
Bridgend	251	514	63	66	129	2.0	1.84	105	20.1	60.5	19.4
Caerphilly	278	613	83	87	170	-0.6	1.81	115	21.4	60.7	18.0
Cardiff	139	2,222	148	161	309	7.9	1.46	102	20.1	63.6	16.3
Carmarthenshire	2,394	73	84	91	176	7.2	1.69	109	19.3	58.2	22.4
Ceredigion	1,792	43	37	40	77	25.6	1.34	83	16.6	61.8	21.6
Conwy	1,126	98	53	58	110	11.8	1.86	100	18.3	55.3	26.5
Denbighshire	837	113	45	49	94	11.1	1.75	100	19.5	57.4	23.1
Flintshire	438	341	73	76	149	7.7	1.70	100	20.3	61.8	17.9
Gwynedd	2,535	46	56	61	117	4.6	1.66	95	19.3	58.6	22.1
Isle of Anglesey	711	95	33	35	68	-0.8	1.72	98	19.2	58.5	22.2
Merthyr Tydfil	111	504	27	29	56	-7.4	1.74	118	20.9	60.3	18.8
Monmouthshire	849	100	41	44	85	11.5	1.68	96	20.0	58.8	21.2
Neath Port Talbot	441	305	65	70	135	-4.6	1.70	111	19.3	59.5	21.1
Newport	190	729	67	72	139	4.7	1.81	106	22.0	59.5	18.5
Pembrokeshire	1,589	72	55	59	114	6.0	1.92	103	20.4	57.1	22.5
Powys	5,181	25	63	65	127	13.8	1.81	94	19.2	57.7	23.1
Rhondda, Cynon, Taff	424	545	112	119	231	-2.7	1.64	110	20.6	60.4	19.0
Swansea	378	591	108	115	224	-1.7	1.66	99	18.6	60.3	21.1
Torfaen	126	723	44	47	91	0.9	1.77	105	21.0	59.4	19.7
The Vale of Glamorgan	331	363	57	63	120	6.5	1.67	99	21.2	59.2	19.5
Wrexham	504	257	63	66	129	6.8	1.67	109	19.5	62.0	18.6

1 Mid-2002 Population Estimates for the UK include provisional results from the Manchester Matching Exercise, published in November 2003.

2 The total fertility rate (TFR) is the number of children that would be born to a woman if current patterns of fertility persisted throughout her child-bearing life. The TFRs in this table relate to 2001.

3 The standardised mortality ratio (SMR) takes account of the age structure of the population. The SMRs in this table relate to 2001 and are based on the UK population estimates published in September 2003.

4 Pension age is 65 for men and 60 for women.

Source: Office for National Statistics

Table **15.2** Vital[1,2] and social statistics

	Live births per 1,000 population		Deaths per 1,000 population		Perinatal mortality rate[3]	Infant mortality rate[4]	Percentage of live births under 2.5 kg	Percentage of live births outside marriage
	1991	2001	1991	2001	2000-2002	2000-2002	2001	2001
United Kingdom	13.8	11.3	11.2	10.2	8.1	5.5	..	40.1
Wales	13.2	10.5	11.8	11.4	7.5	5.1	7.5	48.3
Blaenau Gwent	14.8	10.3	12.5	12.8	9.0	4.3	9.4	63.5
Bridgend	13.3	11.2	11.6	10.9	6.2	3.5	6.4	48.4
Caerphilly	14.2	11.6	10.0	10.9	7.5	4.7	8.6	52.9
Cardiff	14.8	11.7	10.8	9.6	8.0	7.1	7.7	45.0
Carmarthenshire	11.3	9.6	13.0	13.5	4.7	4.3	7.4	48.4
Ceredigion	10.8	7.5	12.6	9.9	9.0	5.1	5.0	42.4
Conwy	11.8	9.7	15.6	15.1	7.9	4.5	7.5	50.2
Denbighshire	12.6	10.0	13.9	13.3	8.7	4.7	6.3	48.9
Flintshire	13.4	11.1	10.5	9.7	7.7	4.9	6.6	39.6
Gwynedd	12.2	10.3	13.0	11.5	4.4	3.6	7.5	48.5
Isle of Anglesey	12.2	9.7	11.6	11.8	8.6	4.1	8.4	47.3
Merthyr Tydfil	14.7	10.7	11.7	11.6	8.2	2.2	9.1	63.0
Monmouthshire	11.8	9.3	11.1	11.1	4.1	3.7	6.5	35.2
Neath Port Talbot	12.4	10.0	13.2	12.9	7.4	6.4	8.0	51.3
Newport	15.3	11.5	10.6	10.7	8.9	7.3	7.9	47.7
Pembrokeshire	13.0	10.3	11.2	12.2	7.6	6.7	8.0	47.6
Powys	12.0	9.4	12.4	12.0	7.0	4.2	6.8	39.9
Rhondda, Cynon, Taff	13.4	10.8	11.6	11.2	7.0	4.5	8.4	56.4
Swansea	12.5	10.7	11.8	11.6	8.9	6.4	7.6	48.9
Torfaen	14.3	10.6	11.4	10.7	7.1	4.4	7.3	51.5
The Vale of Glamorgan	13.4	10.0	11.5	10.9	8.4	5.5	6.3	43.3
Wrexham	13.1	11.1	11.2	11.4	9.0	4.1	6.3	45.9

1 Births and deaths data are based on the usual area of residence of the mother/deceased. See Notes and Definitions to the Population chapter for details of the inclusion/exclusion of births to non-resident mothers and deaths of non-resident persons.
2 Births data are on the basis of year of occurrence in England and Wales and year of registration in Scotland and Northern Ireland. All deaths data relate to year of registration.
3 Still births and deaths of infants under 1 week of age per 1,000 live and still births.
4 Deaths of infants under 1 year of age per 1,000 live births.

Source: Office for National Statistics; National Assembly for Wales

Table **15.3** Health and care of people, April 2001[1]

Percentages and thousands

	Percentage of individuals:						
	With limiting long-term illness[2] (percentage)	Of working age[3] with limiting long-term illness (percentage)	Claiming good health[4] (percentages)	Individuals providing 50 hours or more unpaid care[5] per week (percentage)	All people (thousands)	Households with one or more person with a limiting long-term illness (percentages)	All house-holds (thousands)
Wales	23.3	11.0	65.1	3.1	2,903	42.4	1,209
Blaenau Gwent	28.3	14.5	59.3	3.8	70	50.3	30
Bridgend	25.0	12.0	63.5	3.4	129	45.2	53
Caerphilly	26.3	13.6	61.6	3.6	170	48.0	69
Cardiff	18.8	8.9	69.0	2.4	305	35.8	124
Carmarthenshire	26.3	12.3	62.4	3.6	173	46.6	73
Ceredigion	20.7	9.9	67.0	2.6	75	38.8	31
Conwy	23.5	9.6	65.2	3.0	110	40.4	48
Denbighshire	23.4	10.1	66.0	3.0	93	40.9	40
Flintshire	19.2	9.1	69.6	2.6	149	37.0	61
Gwynedd	20.6	9.1	69.2	2.7	117	38.2	49
Isle of Anglesey	22.4	10.4	67.4	3.0	67	40.6	28
Merthyr Tydfil	30.0	15.9	58.6	3.9	56	53.6	23
Monmouthshire	19.1	8.1	68.6	2.4	85	35.3	35
Neath Port Talbot	29.4	14.3	59.7	4.2	134	51.1	58
Newport	21.6	10.1	65.4	2.9	137	40.1	57
Pembrokeshire	22.3	10.1	65.6	3.1	114	40.6	48
Powys	20.4	8.7	66.8	2.5	126	37.4	54
Rhondda, Cynon, Taff	27.2	13.7	61.0	3.8	232	49.8	95
Swansea	24.7	11.4	64.6	3.4	223	44.4	94
Torfaen	24.8	12.0	62.2	3.2	91	45.2	38
The Vale of Glamorgan	19.9	8.7	68.3	2.6	119	36.9	49
Wrexham	21.5	10.1	67.0	2.6	128	39.8	53

1 Data relate to Census day 29 April 2001. Cells in this table have been adjusted to avoid the release of confidential data.

2 Limiting long-term illness covers any long-term illness, health problems or disability which limits daily activities or work.

3 Working age population is 16 to 64 inclusive for men and 16 to 59 inclusive for women.

4 General health refers to health over the 12 months prior to Census day.

5 Provision of unpaid care. looking after, giving help or support to family members, friends, neighbours or others because of long-term physical or mental ill-health or disability or problems relating to old age.

Source: Office for National Statistics

Table **15.4**   Education and training

	Three- and four-year-olds in early years education[1]			Pupil/teacher ratio 2002/03[3](numbers)		Pupils and students participating in post-compulsory education[4] (percentages) 2000/01	Percentage of pupils in last year of compulsory schooling[5,6] 2001/02 with:		Average A/AS level points score 2001/02
	Participation rates[2] (percentages)						5 or more GCSE Grades A*-C/ Standard		
	All schools Jan. 2002	Private and voluntary providers Jan. 2002	All providers Jan. 2002	Primary schools	Secondary schools		No graded results	Grades 1-3 (or equivalent)	
United Kingdom	64	29	93	22.0	16.4	79	5.1	50.8	..
Wales	79	..	79	20.7	16.5	79	7.6	49.7	19.8
Blaenau Gwent	75	..	75	21.7	16.5	..	7.6	35.5	14.9
Bridgend	73	..	73	22.2	16.5	..	7.1	46.7	19.6
Caerphilly	84	..	84	21.9	17.2	..	10.2	42.7	18.2
Cardiff	78	..	78	20.0	16.1	..	11.0	46.4	20.6
Carmarthenshire	74	..	74	18.8	16.5	..	5.0	56.9	19.7
Ceredigion	61	..	61	16.5	15.4	..	4.7	61.8	22.5
Conwy	82	..	82	20.7	17.0	..	7.0	53.6	19.4
Denbighshire	83	..	83	22.1	17.1	..	7.1	51.6	19.6
Flintshire	82	..	82	22.4	16.9	..	8.2	50.9	18.1
Gwynedd	71	..	71	18.6	14.4	..	4.2	57.5	19.9
Isle of Anglesey	66	..	66	20.0	15.4	..	4.5	54.0	21.8
Merthyr Tydfil	92	..	92	20.6	16.1	..	10.9	35.3	17.2
Monmouthshire	55	..	55	21.8	16.5	..	9.3	53.3	22.1
Neath Port Talbot	94	..	94	19.4	15.7	..	5.2	50.9	20.4
Newport	73	..	73	22.8	16.9	..	8.1	44.6	18.9
Pembrokeshire	80	..	80	20.1	16.8	..	5.4	52.3	20.6
Powys	59	..	59	18.7	15.4	..	5.7	59.9	21.3
Rhondda, Cynon, Taff	91	..	91	22.1	17.0	..	9.1	45.8	17.4
Swansea	94	..	94	20.3	17.3	..	8.8	48.8	20.5
Torfaen	77	..	77	22.4	17.5	..	4.4	51.8	19.6
The Vale of Glamorgan	80	..	80	20.6	16.9	..	5.1	59.7	21.8
Wrexham	78	..	78	21.8	16.5	..	9.6	45.2	21.1

1 Headcounts of children aged three and four at 31 December in the previous calendar year. These figures must be interpreted carefully in the light of differing types of education providers between the countries. In the UK figures, any child attending more than one provider in England, or in Scotland, may have been counted twice.
2 Number of three- and four-year-olds attending provider expressed as a percentage of the three- and four-year-old population.
3 Provisional. Public sector schools only.
4 Pupils and students aged 16 in education as a percentage of the 16-year-old population (ages measured at the beginning of the academic year).
5 Pupils in their last year of compulsory schooling as a percentage of the school population of the same age.
6 Figures relate to maintained schools only; hence they are not directly comparable with those in Tables 4.5, 16.3 and 17.3, which are for all schools.

Source: National Assembly for Wales; Department for Education and Skills

Table 15.5 Housing and households

	Housing completions 2002[1] (numbers)		Stock of dwellings 1 April 2002[3] (thousands)	All households[4] April 2001 (thousands)	Local authority tenants: average weekly unrebated rent per dwelling (£) April 2001	Council Tax (£)[5] April 2001-02
	Private enterprise	Registered social landlords[2], local authorities etc				
Wales	7,403	756	1,282	1,209	43.96	710
Blaenau Gwent	88	27	32	30	42.94	796
Bridgend	553	38	58	53	42.84	768
Caerphilly	285	28	72	69	45.94	697
Cardiff	1,231	81	129	124	49.24	691
Carmarthenshire	292	-	76	73	41.76	747
Ceredigion	165	-	31	31	..	761
Conwy	221	11	52	48	41.02	600
Denbighshire	226	28	39	40	40.26	774
Flintshire	136	26	62	61	43.03	702
Gwynedd	152	-	57	49	41.79	695
Isle of Anglesey	131	-	32	28	40.78	647
Merthyr Tydfil	43	-	25	23	39.06	870
Monmouthshire	304	7	36	35	47.64	674
Neath Port Talbot	303	78	67	58	42.14	884
Newport	571	135	59	57	46.41	576
Pembrokeshire	188	25	54	48	..	609
Powys	369	8	57	54	45.45	673
Rhondda, Cynon, Taff	586	86	104	95	43.47	810
Swansea	536	144	96	94	43.71	710
Torfaen	122	23	39	38	48.30	654
The Vale of Glamorgan	555	11	51	49	49.56	655
Wrexham	346	-	55	53	39.05	729

1 Figures include all dwellings inspected by the National House Building Council.
2 Excludes acquisitions, rehabilitation's and hostel bedspaces.
3 Estimates based on information collected in the Census of Population for 2001 adjusted to take account of new housebuilding and demolitions. The breakdown of dwelling stock tenure is estimated from the Census information, local authority returns and Registered Social Landlord returns.
4 Estimate on Census day 29 April 2001.
5 Amounts shown for Council Tax are average Council Tax for the area of each billing authority for Band D, 2 adults, before Council Tax benefit. See Notes and Definitions.

Source: National Assembly for Wales

Table **15.6** Labour market and benefit statistics[1]

| | Economically active[2] 2001-2002[3] (percentages) | Total in employment[2,4] 2001-2002[3] (thousands) | Employment rate[2] 2001-2002[3] (percentages) | Unemploy- ment rate[2] 2001-2002[3] (percentages)[5] | Claimant count[6], March 2003 | | | Average gross weekly full-time earnings, all people[8] April 2002 (£) | Income Support bene- ficiaries[9] May 2003 (percentages) |
					Level (thousands)	Females (percentage of claimants)	Percentage claiming over 12 months, computerised claims only[7]		
United Kingdom	78.4	28,274	74.4	5.0	992.3	24.6	14.6	462.6	..
Wales	73.4	1,265	69.3	5.5	49.0	23.2	13.5	399.7	12
Blaenau Gwent	68.5	27	63.1	7.8	1.7	19.7	19.4	..	17
Bridgend	74.7	58	71.2	4.6	2.1	24.3	8.3	394.4	12
Caerphilly	71.1	68	65.2	8.3	3.0	23.7	11.8	378.4	14
Cardiff	73.3	148	69.3	5.4	5.7	19.4	11.9	442.1	12
Carmarthenshire	70.1	67	65.3	6.7	2.7	24.3	12.6	374.7	12
Ceredigion	69.4	31	65.1	5.9	0.9	27.4	10.9	..	8
Conwy	74.9	48	72.4	3.4	1.7	23.8	18.0	353.1	11
Denbighshire	77.8	41	74.4	4.3	1.3	24.7	15.8	..	12
Flintshire	77.7	70	73.6	5.0	1.7	25.6	15.9	435.7	8
Gwynedd	72.5	48	68.4	5.5	2.3	22.2	25.9	393.4	11
Isle of Anglesey	72.6	27	69.0	4.8	1.6	27.1	31.8	..	11
Merthyr Tydfil	65.2	20	60.8	6.7	1.2	20.8	16.4	..	16
Monmouthshire	79.7	42	75.8	4.7	0.9	27.0	8.9	377.1	7
Neath Port Talbot	67.4	52	63.3	6.0	2.5	23.1	8.3	417.3	15
Newport	75.8	61	72.4	4.7	2.9	21.1	15.5	400.1	12
Pembrokeshire	72.5	48	67.6	6.4	2.5	27.3	11.9	..	12
Powys	80.2	61	77.1	3.7	1.3	29.7	11.6	371.2	8
Rhondda, Cynon, Taff	68.3	96	64.2	6.1	3.8	22.6	8.8	385.3	15
Swansea	74.4	100	69.5	6.4	4.1	21.4	11.4	383.9	14
Torfaen	75.0	38	70.4	6.0	1.5	24.3	13.5	387.5	13
The Vale of Glamorgan	78.3	58	75.2	3.9	2.0	21.7	11.0	425.4	8
Wrexham	75.4	58	72.6	3.5	1.7	24.9	10.4	378.7	11

1 See Notes and Definitions to the Labour Market chapter. In some cases sample sizes are too small to provide reliable estimates. Due to the sample size in Wales, the National Assembly for Wales has adopted the use of a four quarter average for Wales as the standard methodology for analysing and publishing LFS data. Thus, the data in this table may not correspond to other analyses released by the National Assembly for Wales.

2 Employment totals and unemployment rates are for people aged 16 and over, while employment rates and economic activity rates are for those of working age only. Working age is defined as 16 to 64 for males and 16 to 59 for females.

3 Data are from the Annual Local Area Labour Force Survey and relate to the period March 2001 to February 2002. These data have not been adjusted to reflect the 2001 Census population estimates.

4 Includes those on government-supported employment and training schemes and unpaid family workers.

5 As a percentage of the economically active.

6 Count of claimants of unemployment-related benefit, i.e. Jobseeker's Allowance.

7 People who have been claiming for more than 12 months (computerised claims only), as a percentage of total computerised claimants.

8 Earnings estimates have been derived from the New Earnings Survey and relate to full-time employees whose pay for the survey pay-period was not affected by absence.

9 Claimants and their partners aged 16 or over as a percentage of the population aged 16 or over. Data are from the Income Support Quarterly Statistical Enquiry. United Kingdom figure not supplied as latest data available for Northern Ireland is February 2002.

Source: Office for National Statistics; IAD Information Centre, Department for Work and Pensions

NUTS levels 1, 2 and 3 in Wales,[1] 1998

NUTS level 2
NUTS level 3

Isle of Anglesey

Conwy & Denbighshire

Flintshire & Wrexham

Gwynedd

Powys

East Wales

West Wales & The Valleys

South West Wales

Monmouthshire and Newport

Central Valleys

Gwent Valleys

Swansea

Bridgend & Neath Port Talbot

Cardiff and The Vale of Glamorgan

1 NUTS (Nomenclature of Units for Territorial Statistics) is a hierarchical classification of areas that provides a breakdown of the EU's economic territory. The NUTS level 1 area is the whole country. See Notes and Definitions.

Table **15.7** **Gross value added (GVA) and gross disposable household income by NUTS 1, 2 and 3 area at current basic prices**[1, 2]

| | GVA £ million | | | | GVA £ per head | | | | GVA £ per head (UK=100) | | | | Gross disposable household income £ per head (UK=100)[3] 3 year average |
	1998	1999	2000	2001	1998	1999	2000	2001	1998	1999	2000	2001	1997-99
Wales[4]	29,718	30,652	31,864	33,086	10,273	10,593	10,987	11,379	80	79	79	79	88
West Wales and the Valleys	16,407	16,757	17,337	17,934	8,857	9,056	9,364	9,669	69	68	67	67	87
Isle of Anglesey	441	461	489	517	6,545	6,868	7,299	7,636	51	51	52	53	95
Gwynedd	1,050	1,047	1,055	1,085	9,010	9,024	9,058	9,290	70	67	65	64	84
Conwy and Denbighshire	1,688	1,719	1,780	1,847	8,439	8,581	8,832	9,106	66	64	63	63	94
South West Wales	2,914	3,018	3,163	3,303	8,190	8,438	8,783	9,122	64	63	63	63	86
Central Valleys	2,489	2,526	2,603	2,681	8,525	8,713	9,029	9,306	66	65	65	65	76
Gwent Valleys	2,752	2,816	2,899	2,975	8,305	8,506	8,758	9,002	65	64	63	62	86
Bridgend and Neath Port Talbot	2,764	2,755	2,797	2,856	10,427	10,421	10,622	10,855	81	78	76	75	92
Swansea	2,309	2,415	2,550	2,669	10,297	10,790	11,402	11,943	80	81	82	83	90
East Wales	13,312	13,895	14,527	15,152	12,793	13,317	13,854	14,391	99	100	100	100	90
Monmouthshire and Newport	2,693	2,897	3,077	3,227	12,217	13,144	13,920	14,491	95	98	100	101	92
Cardiff and Vale of Glamorgan	5,761	6,110	6,480	6,857	13,657	14,441	15,229	16,074	106	108	109	111	90
Flintshire and Wrexham	3,596	3,617	3,691	3,776	13,171	13,183	13,376	13,623	102	99	96	94	92
Powys	1,262	1,272	1,279	1,291	10,072	10,130	10,143	10,216	78	76	73	71	82

1 Estimates for GVA data are provisional.
2 Components may not sum to totals due to rounding.
3 Household income estimates are consistent with those published on 26 March 2002.
4 Excluding GVA for Extra-regio, which comprises compensation of employees and gross operating surplus which cannot be assigned to regions.

Source: Office for National Statistics

Chapter 16 Sub-regions of Scotland

New Councils in Scotland

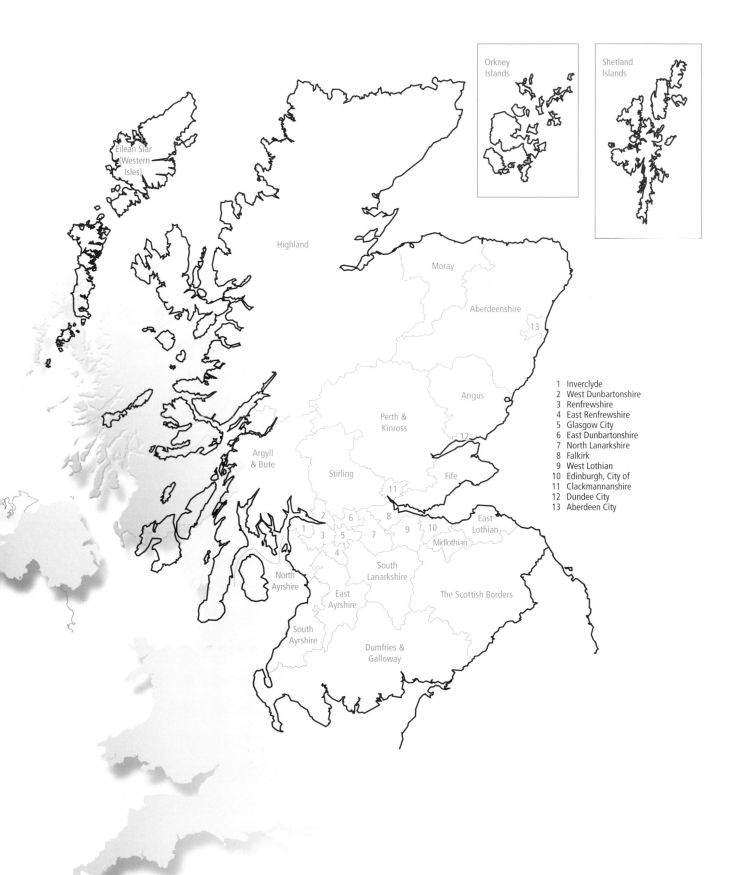

Orkney Islands

Shetland Islands

Eilean Siar (Western Isles)

Highland

Moray

Aberdeenshire

Angus

Perth & Kinross

Argyll & Bute

Stirling

Fife

East Lothian

Midlothian

North Ayrshire

South Lanarkshire

East Ayrshire

The Scottish Borders

South Ayrshire

Dumfries & Galloway

1 Inverclyde
2 West Dunbartonshire
3 Renfrewshire
4 East Renfrewshire
5 Glasgow City
6 East Dunbartonshire
7 North Lanarkshire
8 Falkirk
9 West Lothian
10 Edinburgh, City of
11 Clackmannanshire
12 Dundee City
13 Aberdeen City

Table **16.1**   Area and population by council area, 2002[1]

| | Area (sq km) | People per sq km | Population (thousands) | | | Total population percentage change 1982-2002 | Total fertility rate (TFR)[2] | Standardised mortality ratio (UK=100) (SMR)[3] | Percentage of population aged | | |
			Males	Females	Total				0 to 15	16 up to pension age[4]	Pension age[4] or over
United Kingdom	242,514	244	28,911	30,318	59,229	5.2	1.63	100	19.9	61.7	18.4
Scotland	77,925	65	2,432	2,623	5,055	-2.1	1.49	114	18.9	62.3	18.8
Aberdeen City	186	1,127	103	107	209	-1.9	1.25	107	16.2	66.0	17.8
Aberdeenshire	6,313	36	113	115	227	18.0	1.62	97	20.7	62.2	17.1
Angus	2,182	50	52	56	108	2.7	1.76	107	18.7	60.1	21.2
Argyll & Bute	6,909	13	45	46	91	0.1	1.54	105	18.4	59.6	22.0
Clackmannanshire	159	302	23	25	48	-0.1	1.74	119	20.5	62.1	17.4
Dumfries & Galloway	6,426	23	71	76	147	1.3	1.59	103	18.5	58.6	22.9
Dundee City	60	2,410	68	76	144	-14.3	1.39	120	17.5	61.9	20.6
East Ayrshire	1,262	95	58	62	120	-5.4	1.55	126	19.6	61.3	19.1
East Dunbartonshire	175	615	52	56	107	-2.6	1.46	93	19.9	61.0	19.1
East Lothian	679	134	43	47	91	12.1	1.70	100	20.6	59.3	20.1
East Renfrewshire	174	516	43	47	90	11.4	1.72	93	21.2	60.1	18.7
Edinburgh, City of	264	1,699	215	233	448	0.8	1.19	106	16.1	66.2	17.7
Eilean Siar[5]	3,071	9	13	13	26	-16.8	1.60	105	18.6	58.3	23.2
Falkirk	297	490	70	75	146	0.7	1.46	114	19.3	62.4	18.4
Fife	1,325	265	168	183	351	2.5	1.59	110	19.3	61.6	19.1
Glasgow City	175	3,290	274	304	577	-17.8	1.38	139	17.9	64.1	17.9
Highland	25,659	8	102	106	208	6.8	1.76	111	19.3	60.8	19.9
Inverclyde	160	521	40	44	84	-16.8	1.54	129	19.0	61.5	19.5
Midlothian	354	228	38	42	81	-3.1	1.77	112	20.6	61.5	17.9
Moray	2,238	39	44	43	87	2.7	1.67	107	19.7	61.0	19.3
North Ayrshire	885	153	64	72	136	-1.1	1.63	121	19.7	60.9	19.4
North Lanarkshire	470	684	154	167	321	-5.5	1.59	130	20.2	63.1	16.7
Orkney Islands	990	19	9	10	19	0.6	1.56	108	19.7	60.1	20.2
Perth & Kinross	5,286	26	65	70	135	10.6	1.70	97	18.7	59.5	21.8
Renfrewshire	261	659	82	90	172	-6.6	1.50	124	19.2	62.4	18.4
Scottish Borders	4,732	23	52	56	107	6.3	1.71	100	18.8	59.2	22.0
Shetland Islands	1,466	15	11	11	22	-9.0	1.85	108	21.5	61.6	16.8
South Ayrshire	1,222	91	53	58	112	-1.3	1.59	110	17.8	59.7	22.5
South Lanarkshire	1,772	171	144	158	302	-2.1	1.54	118	19.5	62.3	18.2
Stirling	2,187	39	41	45	86	6.8	1.40	110	19.2	62.1	18.7
West Dunbartonshire	159	584	44	49	93	-11.3	1.51	131	19.5	62.0	18.5
West Lothian	427	374	77	83	160	14.4	1.72	126	21.7	64.1	14.2

1 Population figures for 2002 are based on the 2002 mid-year population estimates. Mid-2002 Population Estimates for the UK include provisional results from the Manchester Matching Exercise, published in November 2003.
2 The total fertility rate (TFR) is the number of live births per 1,000 women aged 15 to 44. Rates are for 2001.
3 Data are for 2001. Adjusted for the age structure of the population. See Notes and Definitions to the Population chapter.
4 Pension age is 65 for men and 60 for women.
5 Formerly known as the Western Isles.

Source: Office for National Statistics; General Register Office for Scotland

Table 16.2 Vital[1,2] and social statistics

	Live births per 1,000 population		Deaths per 1,000 population		Perinatal mortality rate[3]	Infant mortality rate[4]	Percentage of live births outside marriage
	1991	2001	1991	2001	2000-2002	2000-2002	2001
United Kingdom	13.8	11.3	11.2	10.2	8.1	5.5	40.1
Scotland	13.1	10.4	12.0	11.3	8.2	5.5	43.3
Aberdeen City	12.5	9.9	10.8	10.3	8.8	3.3	42.5
Aberdeenshire	13.5	9.9	9.6	9.1	7.1	4.5	30.7
Angus	12.3	10.2	12.9	12.3	5.0	4.4	41.7
Argyll & Bute	13.0	8.5	12.7	12.4	9.8	6.4	36.5
Clackmannanshire	13.7	11.0	10.1	10.8	6.6	6.0	48.2
Dumfries & Galloway	12.1	8.7	13.1	12.0	8.5	5.5	42.6
Dundee City	12.9	10.1	12.4	12.9	8.4	8.2	58.2
East Ayrshire	13.9	10.0	11.9	12.5	7.8	6.7	47.5
East Dunbartonshire	12.4	9.1	8.7	8.7	8.9	4.5	26.7
East Lothian	13.1	10.4	12.6	10.9	7.6	3.8	35.5
East Renfrewshire	13.0	10.7	9.5	9.1	7.8	5.7	23.9
Edinburgh, City of	12.9	10.0	12.5	10.5	7.5	5.9	39.8
Eilean Siar[5]	11.2	8.5	14.9	13.5	10.0	4.3	26.1
Falkirk	13.5	10.0	11.5	10.8	8.4	6.2	43.2
Fife	12.6	10.4	11.9	11.2	8.4	5.0	44.9
Glasgow City	14.3	11.5	14.4	13.3	10.9	7.1	53.1
Highland	13.0	10.2	11.5	11.5	8.3	4.5	42.2
Inverclyde	12.9	10.1	13.6	13.2	7.2	6.4	48.2
Midlothian	13.5	11.4	10.6	10.4	4.0	4.1	41.8
Moray	13.8	10.0	11.2	10.8	6.4	5.6	34.8
North Ayrshire	13.9	10.5	11.7	12.1	8.3	6.4	52.4
North Lanarkshire	13.6	11.4	11.1	10.7	7.9	5.6	47.7
Orkney Islands	12.1	9.1	11.8	11.9	8.1	2.0	32.8
Perth & Kinross	12.2	9.9	13.0	11.4	4.6	3.8	35.5
Renfrewshire	12.6	10.4	11.5	11.7	7.8	6.3	45.3
Scottish Borders	12.1	10.0	13.8	12.0	7.6	3.5	36.1
Shetland Islands	14.4	11.2	10.4	10.2	1.5	0.0	38.1
South Ayrshire	10.8	9.4	13.3	13.1	12.6	9.1	45.1
South Lanarkshire	13.3	10.5	10.5	10.9	7.6	4.8	41.4
Stirling	11.9	9.7	11.8	10.9	7.0	4.7	34.0
West Dunbartonshire	13.1	10.4	12.5	12.5	11.6	7.2	50.4
West Lothian	14.3	12.5	9.2	9.2	6.1	3.8	43.8

1 Births and deaths data are based on the usual area of residence of the mother/deceased. See Notes and Definitions to the Population chapter for details of the inclusion/exclusion of births to non-resident mothers and deaths of non-resident persons.
2 Births data are on the basis of year of occurrence in England and Wales and year of registration in Scotland and Northern Ireland. All deaths data relate to year of registration.
3 Still births and deaths of infants under 1 week of age per 1,000 live and still births.
4 Deaths of infants under 1 year of age per 1,000 live births.
5 Formerly known as the Western Isles.

Source: Office for National Statistics; General Register Office for Scotland

Table **16.3** Education and training

| | Three- and four-year-olds in early years education[1] | | | Pupil/teacher ratio 2002/03 (numbers) | | Pupils and students participating in post-compulsory education[5] (percentages) 2000/01 | Percentage of pupils in last year of compulsory schooling[6,7] 2001/02 with: | |
| | Participation rates[2] (percentages) | | | | | | | |
	All schools[3] Jan. 2002	Private and voluntary providers[4] Jan. 2002	All providers Jan. 2002	Primary schools	Secondary schools		No graded results	5 or more Grades 1-3 SCE Standard Grade (or equivalent)
United Kingdom	64	29	93	22.0	16.4	79	5.4	52.5
Scotland	60	22	82	18.0	12.7	79	4.6	60.4
Aberdeen City	55	29	84	16.4	12.0	..	3.4	59.4
Aberdeenshire	48	35	83	17.2	12.4	..	1.9	72.4
Angus	65	18	83	18.4	12.0	..	4.8	61.9
Argyll & Bute	43	52	95	17.8	12.4	..	1.6	67.4
Clackmannanshire	59	10	68	19.4	12.6	..	9.1	56.1
Dumfries & Galloway	56	32	88	17.6	12.0	..	3.7	63.3
Dundee City	68	12	80	16.9	11.3	..	7.9	48.0
East Ayrshire	68	11	80	20.1	13.4	..	4.8	59.9
East Dunbartonshire	46	47	93	20.7	13.8	..	1.4	74.3
East Lothian	80	8	87	18.1	12.3	..	8.9	59.3
East Renfrewshire	65	25	91	20.1	13.9	..	1.0	83.3
Edinburgh, City of	59	23	82	17.3	12.6	..	6.9	61.6
Eilean Siar[8]	6	71	77	11.4	9.6	..	2.8	73.1
Falkirk	51	7	58	18.8	13.1	..	4.8	50.7
Fife	74	14	88	16.6	12.9	..	5.4	57.8
Glasgow City	67	18	85	18.7	13.3	..	7.7	51.3
Highland	48	41	89	16.6	11.3	..	3.4	66.7
Inverclyde	37	22	59	19.8	12.7	..	2.8	63.0
Midlothian	70	12	83	17.6	13.2	..	3.2	57.7
Moray	45	48	92	17.2	11.9	..	9.3	62.8
North Ayrshire	57	25	82	21.0	13.5	..	2.8	56.6
North Lanarkshire	64	14	78	19.5	12.9	..	3.2	54.9
Orkney Islands	71	9	80	13.1	11.2	..	2.1	74.2
Perth & Kinross	55	30	85	16.2	11.9	..	8.1	58.5
Renfrewshire	46	19	65	20.0	13.7	..	0.7	62.4
Scottish Borders	66	25	91	15.7	11.9	..	2.4	69.6
Shetland Islands	50	23	73	10.3	7.7	..	2.5	76.7
South Ayrshire	63	21	84	19.3	13.3	..	3.2	61.5
South Lanarkshire	61	20	82	19.5	13.3	..	4.3	60.0
Stirling	67	26	93	17.8	12.8	..	2.2	67.5
West Dunbartonshire	55	12	67	19.3	13.5	..	4.8	54.4
West Lothian	64	8	72	18.0	12.7	..	5.5	54.6

1 Headcounts of children aged three and four at 31 December in the previous calendar year. These figures must be interpreted carefully in the light of differing types of education providers between the countries. Any child attending more than one provider in Scotland (and also in England, in the UK figures) may have been counted twice.
2 Number of three- and four-year-olds attending provider expressed as a percentage of the three- and four-year-old population.
3 Local Authority (LA) figures relate to nursery schools and nursery classes in primary schools.
4 Centres not run by LAs which provide pre-school education in partnership with LAs.
5 In Scotland, pupils and students in schools and further education aged 16 and 17 but excluding 16-year-olds who leave school in the winter term at the minimum statutory age. Figures are not directly comparable with those shown in previous editions of Regional Trends.
6 Pupils in their last year of compulsory schooling as a percentage of the school population of the same age. See Notes and Definitions for Table 4.6.
7 Figures relate to all schools; hence they are not directly comparable with those in Tables 14.3 and 15.3 which are for maintained schools only.
8 Formerly known as the Western Isles.

Source: Scottish Executive; Department for Education and Skills

Table **16.4** Housing and households

	Housing completions 2002 (numbers)		Stock of dwellings[3,4] 2002 (thousands)	Household estimates mid-2001 (thousands)	Local authority tenants: average weekly unrebated rent per dwelling (£) 2002-03	Council Tax (£)[5] 2002-03
	Private enterprise[1]	Housing associations local authorities etc[2]				
Scotland	18,749	4,578	2,340	2,192	41.0	971
Aberdeen City	451	79	106	97	38.3	981
Aberdeenshire	1,161	184	98	91	36.4	919
Angus	377	157	51	47	35.1	881
Argyll & Bute	169	4	45	39	41.0	1,009
Clackmannanshire	206	72	22	21	37.4	978
Dumfries & Galloway	310	37	68	64	38.9	899
Dundee City	397	302	72	67	42.2	1,079
East Ayrshire	321	4	53	50	36.9	967
East Dunbartonshire	79	10	43	42	40.0	915
East Lothian	443	18	40	38	35.2	955
East Renfrewshire	270	0	36	35	38.7	910
Edinburgh, City of	1,164	510	218	205	47.1	1,001
Eilean Siar[6]	97	21	14	11	43.0	815
Falkirk	724	68	65	63	39.7	863
Fife	1,618	303	159	150	37.1	935
Glasgow City	2,137	1,250	289	272	48.5	1,141
Highland	635	142	101	90	44.4	939
Inverclyde	319	84	39	37	46.8	1,062
Midlothian	115	12	33	33	31.4	1,036
Moray	452	8	39	36	32.0	865
North Ayrshire	379	42	63	59	35.0	927
North Lanarkshire	1,354	196	138	133	40.5	939
Orkney Islands	77	43	10	8	37.0	824
Perth & Kinross	779	208	63	58	33.6	936
Renfrewshire	422	92	81	75	42.1	941
Scottish Borders	728	85	52	47	..	864
Shetland Islands	71	12	10	9	48.3	810
South Ayrshire	206	131	51	49	37.5	918
South Lanarkshire	1,370	269	132	127	41.0	947
Stirling	513	96	37	36	38.3	1,011
West Dunbartonshire	198	119	44	41	38.5	1,050
West Lothian	1,207	20	67	65	43.5	951

1 Includes estimates for outstanding returns.
2 Excludes completions built for private use originally, but acquired by Housing Association; these are included under private sector.
3 Number of residential dwellings taken from the Council Tax Register
4 All figures are individually rounded to the nearest thousand. As a result the Scotland figure may not be the same as the sum of all Local Authorities.
5 Band D Council Tax, figures exclude water and sewerage charges. All figures are rounded to the nearest pound. See Notes and Definitions.
6 Formerly known as the Western Isles.

Source: Scottish Executive; General Register for Scotland

Table **16.5** Labour market and benefit statistics[1]

	Economically active[2] 2001-2002[3] (percentages)	Total in employment[2,4] 2001-2002[3] (thousands)	Employment rate[2] 2001-2002[3] (percentages)	Unemploy-ment rate[2] 2001-2002[3] (percentages)[5]	Claimant count[6], March 2003 Level (thousands)	Females (percentage of claimants)	Percentage claiming over 12 months, computerised claims only[7]	Average gross weekly full-time earnings, all people[8] April 2002 (£)	Income Support bene-ficiaries[9] May 2003 (percentages)
United Kingdom	78.4	28,274	74.4	5.0	992.3	24.6	14.6	462.6	..
Scotland	78.5	2,374	73.2	6.7	107.2	23.0	13.0	427.0	12
Aberdeen City	81.2	108	76.2	6.0	2.7	22.1	6.9	504.5	9
Aberdeenshire	84.3	122	81.6	..	2.0	26.9	7.9	414.1	7
Angus	85.9	55	81.6	..	2.0	27.8	12.9	380.6	9
Argyll & Bute	81.8	40	76.6	..	1.7	26.9	17.7	390.3	10
Clackmannanshire	66.4	19	64.9	..	1.1	22.5	13.1	..	10
Dumfries & Galloway	78.9	65	74.7	..	2.8	28.6	15.3	386.7	10
Dundee City	75.9	60	68.8	9.3	4.7	21.7	18.3	411.4	15
East Ayrshire	75.1	51	69.1	..	3.6	24.9	15.7	..	14
East Dunbartonshire	80.6	56	76.5	..	1.3	21.7	10.0	..	7
East Lothian	78.5	43	76.1	..	1.0	19.7	5.4	399.6	10
East Renfrewshire	82.8	42	75.9	..	1.0	22.2	11.5	..	7
Edinburgh, City of	80.6	235	77.5	3.8	7.6	22.3	11.2	480.6	9
Eilean Siar[10]	84.7	11	78.5	..	0.6	15.4	19.5	..	13
Falkirk	76.5	68	69.3	9.2	3.2	22.3	11.6	391.7	10
Fife	79.2	165	72.3	8.4	8.9	23.2	14.9	390.1	9
Glasgow City	68.2	238	60.6	11.1	17.8	20.3	16.6	421.4	22
Highland	83.4	99	78.8	5.5	4.5	24.2	10.6	411.8	10
Inverclyde	74.6	32	67.5	..	2.6	19.0	9.3	354.7	16
Midlothian	86.9	40	84.5	..	1.0	19.6	8.0	397.5	8
Moray	83.3	43	79.3	..	1.3	31.8	5.8	346.1	7
North Ayrshire	75.1	58	67.8	9.5	4.4	26.2	11.4	372.8	13
North Lanarkshire	74.6	144	68.0	8.8	7.8	22.5	11.9	413.2	15
Orkney Islands	78.6	8	75.9	..	0.2	30.6	15.3	..	7
Perth & Kinross	85.3	68	81.2	..	1.7	26.3	8.2	369.4	8
Renfrewshire	81.1	85	75.8	6.4	4.0	20.0	11.5	447.7	14
Scottish Borders	82.9	52	81.6	..	1.3	28.5	8.2	346.2	9
Shetland Islands	87.1	10	84.8	..	0.3	21.8	10.2	..	8
South Ayrshire	79.3	51	71.4	..	2.6	24.7	12.5	421.1	11
South Lanarkshire	79.9	144	75.0	6.0	5.8	23.1	11.9	434.2	13
Stirling	78.3	35	72.8	..	1.4	25.6	14.0	..	8
West Dunbartonshire	77.6	44	70.3	..	2.9	22.2	16.8	376.5	16
West Lothian	83.6	83	78.7	..	3.1	24.0	8.7	430.1	11

1 See Notes and Definitions for the Labour Market chapter. In some cases sample sizes are too small to provide reliable estimates.

2 Employment totals and unemployment rates are for people aged 16 and over, while employment rates and economic activity rates are for those of working age only. Working age is defined as 16 to 64 for males and 16 to 59 for females.

3 Data are from the Annual Local Area Labour Force Survey and relate to the period March 2001 to February 2002. These data have not been adjusted to reflect the 2001 Census population estimates.

4 Includes those on government-supported employment and training schemes and unpaid family workers.

5 As a percentage of the economically active.

6 Count of claimants of unemployment-related benefit, i.e. Jobseeker's Allowance.

7 People who have been claiming for more than 12 months (computerised claims only), as a percentage of total computerised claimants.

8 Earnings estimates have been derived from the New Earnings Survey and relate to full-time employees whose pay for the survey pay-period was not affected by absence.

9 Claimants and their partners aged 16 or over as a percentage of the population aged 16 or over. Data are from the Income Support Quarterly Statistical Enquiry. United Kingdom figure not supplied as latest data available for Northern Ireland is February 2002.

10 Formerly known as the Western Isles.

Source: Office for National Statistics; IAD Information Centre, Department for Work and Pensions

Table **16.6** Gross value added (GVA) and gross disposable household income by NUTS 1, 2 and 3 area at current basic prices[1, 2]

NUTS 1 NUTS 2 NUTS 3	GVA £ million				GVA £ per head				GVA £ per head (UK=100)				Gross disposable household income £ per head (UK=100)[3] 3 year average
	1998	1999	2000	2001	1998	1999	2000	2001	1998	1999	2000	2001	1997-99
United Kingdom[4]	749,688	781,847	816,111	851,408	12,858	13,369	13,917	14,418	100	100	100	100	100
Scotland	63,285	64,932	67,150	69,179	12,465	12,802	13,263	13,660	97	96	95	95	95
North Eastern Scotland (Aberdeen City, Aberdeenshire and North East Moray)	8,838	9,056	9,489	9,711	17,462	17,893	18,809	19,300	136	134	135	134	102
Eastern Scotland	24,295	24,865	25,625	26,441	12,844	13,118	13,483	13,886	100	98	97	96	99
Angus and Dundee City	2,999	3,019	3,061	3,119	11,560	11,722	11,984	12,289	90	88	86	85	98
Clackmannanshire and Fife	3,661	3,727	3,859	4,003	9,269	9,429	9,732	10,061	72	71	70	70	91
East Lothian and Midlothian	1,395	1,438	1,487	1,528	8,279	8,470	8,692	8,931	64	63	62	62	96
Scottish Borders	996	990	986	994	9,390	9,359	9,285	9,298	73	70	67	64	93
Edinburgh, City of	8,699	9,066	9,510	9,954	19,495	20,273	21,207	22,168	152	152	152	154	113
Falkirk	1,769	1,752	1,748	1,760	12,295	12,121	12,087	12,114	96	91	87	84	87
Perth and Kinross and Stirling	2,530	2,568	2,609	2,673	11,539	11,638	11,798	12,085	90	87	85	84	108
West Lothian	2,245	2,305	2,364	2,410	14,657	14,897	15,055	15,154	114	111	108	105	84
South Western Scotland	26,803	27,564	28,459	29,350	11,615	11,990	12,439	12,831	90	90	89	89	92
East and West Dunbartonshire, Helensburgh and Lomond	1,841	1,863	1,911	1,948	7,957	8,080	8,306	8,498	62	60	60	59	96
Dumfries and Galloway	1,390	1,427	1,474	1,521	9,342	9,630	9,989	10,293	73	72	72	71	94
East Ayrshire and North Ayrshire Mainland	2,418	2,435	2,454	2,480	9,590	9,689	9,816	9,934	75	72	71	69	84
Glasgow City	9,681	10,135	10,595	11,059	16,490	17,385	18,361	19,110	128	130	132	133	87
Inverclyde, East Renfrewshire and Renfrewshire	4,154	4,094	4,100	4,148	11,887	11,758	11,804	11,974	92	88	85	83	101
North Lanarkshire	2,880	2,968	3,094	3,215	8,939	9,214	9,628	10,010	70	69	69	69	89
South Ayrshire	1,312	1,355	1,396	1,434	11,578	12,004	12,430	12,783	90	90	89	89	93
South Lanarkshire	3,127	3,286	3,435	3,546	10,310	10,859	11,365	11,729	80	81	82	81	98
Highlands and Islands	3,348	3,448	3,577	3,677	9,006	9,283	9,668	9,954	70	69	69	69	90
Caithness and Sutherland and Ross and Cromarty[5]	674	717	770	806	7,517	8,028	8,648	9,090	58	60	62	63	⎫ 90
Inverness and Nairn and Moray, Badenoch and Strathspey[5]	1,046	1,081	1,130	1,170	9,506	9,765	10,162	10,440	74	73	73	72	⎬
Lochaber, Skye and Lochalsh and Argyll and the Islands[5]	896	909	931	952	8,759	8,894	9,173	9,428	68	67	66	65	⎭
Eilean Siar (Western Isles)[6]	245	254	261	264	8,885	9,318	9,742	9,969	69	70	70	69	⎫ 88
Orkney Islands[6]	205	201	199	198	10,446	10,329	10,327	10,321	81	77	74	72	⎬
Shetland Islands[6]	283	286	286	286	12,485	12,719	12,887	13,034	97	95	93	90	⎭

1 Estimates for GVA data are provisional.
2 Components may not sum to totals due to rounding.
3 Household income estimates are consistent with those published on 26 March 2002.
4 Excluding GVA for Extra-regio, which comprises compensation of employees and gross operating surplus which cannot be assigned to regions.
5 Figure for Gross Disposable Household Income – Caithness and Sutherland and Ross and Cromarty; Inverness and Nairn and Moray, Badenoch and Strathspey; Lochaber, Skye and Lochalsh and Argyll and the Islands combined.
6 Figure for Gross Disposable Household Income – Eilean Siar (Western Isles), Orkney Isles and Shetland Isles combined.

Source: Office for National Statistics

NUTS levels 1, 2 and 3 in Scotland,[1] 1998

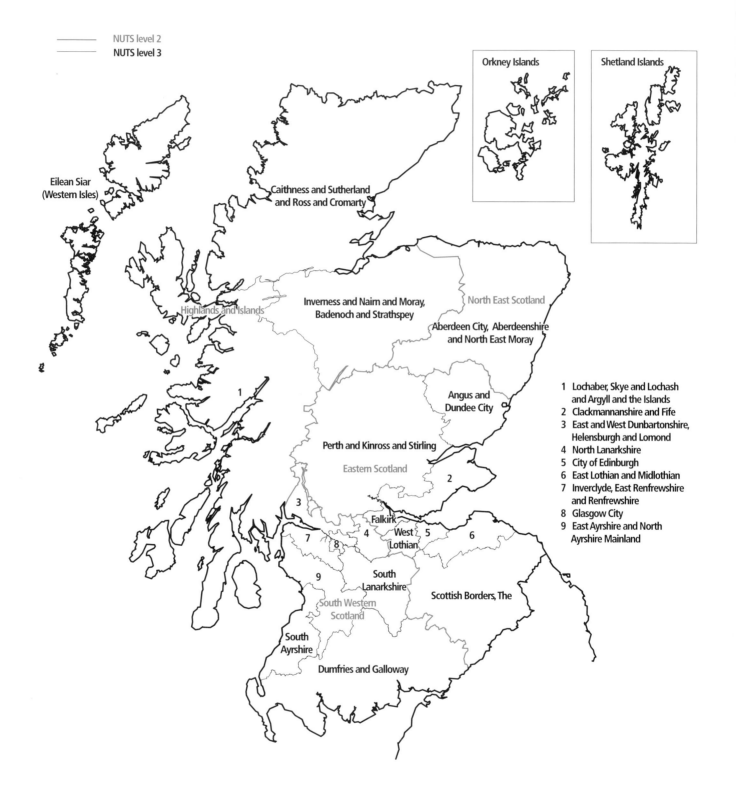

NUTS level 2
NUTS level 3

Orkney Islands

Shetland Islands

Eilean Siar
(Western Isles)

Caithness and Sutherland
and Ross and Cromarty

Highlands and Islands

Inverness and Nairn and Moray,
Badenoch and Strathspey

North East Scotland

Aberdeen City, Aberdeenshire
and North East Moray

Angus and
Dundee City

1

Perth and Kinross and Stirling

Eastern Scotland

2

3

Falkirk

4   West
    Lothian

5

6

7

8

9

South
Lanarkshire

Scottish Borders, The

South Western
Scotland

South
Ayrshire

Dumfries and Galloway

1 Lochaber, Skye and Lochash
   and Argyll and the Islands
2 Clackmannanshire and Fife
3 East and West Dunbartonshire,
   Helensburgh and Lomond
4 North Lanarkshire
5 City of Edinburgh
6 East Lothian and Midlothian
7 Inverclyde, East Renfrewshire
   and Renfrewshire
8 Glasgow City
9 East Ayrshire and North
   Ayrshire Mainland

1 NUTS (Nomenclature of Units for Territorial Statistics) is a hierarchical classification of areas that provides a breakdown of the EU's economic territory.
   The NUTS level 1 area is the whole country. See Notes and Definitions.

Chapter 17 Sub-regions of Northern Ireland

Boards and Travel-to-work areas in Northern Ireland

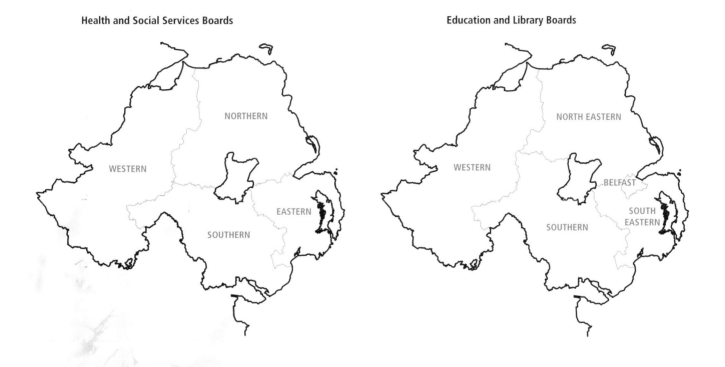

Health and Social Services Boards

NORTHERN

WESTERN

EASTERN

SOUTHERN

Education and Library Boards

NORTH EASTERN

WESTERN

BELFAST

SOUTHERN

SOUTH EASTERN

Travel-to-work areas

COLERAINE

DERRY

BALLYMENA

STRABANE

MID ULSTER

OMAGH

DUNGANNON

BELFAST

ENNISKILLEN

CRAIGAVON

NEWRY

Table **17.1** Area and population: by board[1] and district, 2002[2]

	Area (sq km)	People per sq km	Population (thousands)			Total population percentage change 1982-2002	Total fertility rate (TFR)[3]	Standardised mortality ratio (UK=100) (SMR)[4]	Percentage of population aged		
			Males	Females	Total				0 to 15	16 up to pension age[5]	Pension age[5] or over
United Kingdom	242,514	244	28,911	30,318	59,229	5.2	1.63	100	19.9	61.7	18.4
Northern Ireland	13,576	125	829	868	1,697	9.8	1.81	99	23.2	61.1	15.7
Eastern	1,751	380	319	347	666	3.9	..	99	21.8	61.2	17.1
Ards	380	195	36	38	74	25.8	1.66	95	20.9	62.3	16.8
Belfast	110	2,501	128	146	274	-12.2	1.63	110	21.2	61.1	17.6
Castlereagh	85	780	32	35	66	9.5	1.79	98	21.4	59.4	19.3
Down	649	100	32	33	65	19.1	1.96	100	24.3	60.6	15.1
Lisburn	447	245	53	56	109	25.7	1.78	99	24.2	61.6	14.2
North Down	81	952	37	40	77	13.8	1.68	91	19.4	61.6	19.0
Northern	4,093	105	211	219	430	13.7	..	99	22.7	61.3	16.0
Antrim	421	116	25	24	49	6.1	1.99	103	23.7	63.1	13.2
Ballymena	630	94	29	30	59	6.9	1.76	98	21.8	61.0	17.2
Ballymoney	416	66	14	14	27	18.7	1.88	92	23.3	60.6	16.1
Carrickfergus	81	472	19	20	38	32.4	1.66	108	22.1	62.1	15.9
Coleraine	486	116	27	29	56	18.3	1.58	92	22.1	60.6	17.3
Cookstown	514	64	16	17	33	15.6	1.72	98	25.3	60.9	13.8
Larne	336	92	15	16	31	7.2	1.60	96	21.1	61.2	17.7
Magherafelt	564	72	20	20	40	22.1	2.16	92	25.5	61.0	13.6
Moyle	494	33	8	8	16	11.4	1.74	110	23.1	59.6	14.7
Newtownabbey	151	531	39	41	80	10.1	1.56	97	21.4	61.6	17.0
Southern	3,075	103	157	159	316	15.0	..	105	24.8	60.6	14.6
Armagh	671	82	27	28	55	11.0	1.89	111	24.5	60.8	14.7
Banbridge	451	94	21	21	42	40.0	1.70	100	23.1	62.0	14.9
Craigavon	282	290	40	41	82	12.1	1.94	100	24.2	60.7	15.1
Dungannon	772	62	24	24	48	9.6	1.99	106	25.4	59.8	14.8
Newry and Mourne	898	99	44	45	89	13.7	2.18	108	26.2	60.1	13.7
Western	4,658	61	142	143	285	13.5	..	110	25.2	61.5	13.3
Derry	381	279	52	54	106	16.4	1.95	110	26.3	61.8	11.9
Fermanagh	1,699	34	29	29	58	11.0	1.91	112	23.3	60.6	16.1
Limavady	586	57	17	16	33	21.4	1.87	103	25.2	63.0	11.8
Omagh	1,130	43	25	24	49	10.1	1.94	110	25.1	61.4	13.5
Strabane	862	45	19	19	38	7.8	1.89	116	25.2	60.7	14.1

1 Health and Social Services Board areas.

2 Population figures for 2002 are the first in a new series that are based on the 2001 Census.

3 The total fertility rate (TFR) is the number of live births per 1,000 women aged 15 to 44. Figures for Northern Ireland are based on births and population data for the previous three years.

4 Averaged for the years 2000, 2001 and 2002 and adjusted for the age structure of the population.

5 Pension age is 65 for males and 60 for females.

Source: Office for National Statistics; Northern Ireland Statistics and Research Agency

Table **17.2**   Vital[1,2] and social statistics: by board[3]

	Live births per 1,000 population		Deaths per 1,000 population		Perinatal mortality rate[4]	Infant mortality rate[5]	Percentage of live births outside marriage
	1991	2001	1991	2001	2001	2001	2001
United Kingdom	13.8	11.3	11.2	10.2	8.0	5.5	*40.1*
Northern Ireland	16.2	13.0	9.4	8.6	8.4	6.0	*32.5*
Eastern	15.7	12.1	10.3	9.4	8.8	5.8	*38.9*
Northern	15.1	12.6	8.7	8.1	8.8	6.1	*29.7*
Southern	17.5	14.6	8.9	8.0	8.1	7.0	*24.5*
Western	17.6	13.9	8.7	7.9	7.2	5.2	*32.6*

1 *Births and deaths data are based on the usual area of residence of the mother/deceased. See Notes and Definitions to the Population chapter for details of the inclusion/exclusion of births to non-resident mothers and deaths of non-resident persons.*

2 *Births data are on the basis of year of occurrence in England and Wales and year of registration in Scotland and Northern Ireland. All deaths data relate to year of registration.*

3 *Health and Social Service Board Areas.*

4 *Still births and deaths of infants under 1 week of age per 1,000 live and still births.*

5 *Deaths of infants under 1 year of age per 1,000 live births.*

Source: Northern Ireland Statistics and Research Agency; Department of Health, Social Services and Public Safety, Northern Ireland

Table 17.3 Education and training: by board[1]

| | Three- and four-year-olds in early years education[2] | | | Pupil/teacher ratio 2002/03[4](numbers) | | Pupils and students participating in post-compulsory education[6] (percentages) 2001/02 | Percentage of pupils in last year of compulsory schooling[7,8] 2001/02 with: | |
| | Participation rates[3] (percentages) | | | | | | | |
	All schools Jan. 2002	Private and voluntary providers Jan. 2002	All providers Jan. 2002	Primary schools[5]	Secondary schools		No graded results	5 or more GCSE Grades A*-C/ Standard Grades 1-3 (or equivalent)
United Kingdom	64	29	93	22.0	16.4	..	5.4	52.5
Northern Ireland	56	11	67	19.6	14.4	76	4.4	58.7
Belfast	..	..	..	18.5	14.2	..	5.5	60.1
South Eastern	..	..	..	19.7	14.4	..	3.8	56.3
Southern	..	..	..	19.3	14.5	..	3.9	60.0
North Eastern	..	..	..	21.1	14.5	..	3.8	58.8
Western	..	..	..	19.5	14.3	..	5.0	57.7

1 Education and Library Boards.

2 Headcounts of children aged three and four at 31 December in the previous calendar year. These figures must be interpreted carefully in the light of differing types of education providers between the countries. In the UK figures, any child attending more than one provider in England, or in Scotland, may have been counted twice.

3 Number of three- and four-year-olds attending provider expressed as a percentage of the three- and four-year-old population.

4 Provisional.

5 In Northern Ireland the primary pupil-teacher ratio includes preparatory departments of Grammar schools.

6 Pupils and students aged 16 at 1 July. Figures for Northern Ireland exclude those in part-time further education.

7 Pupils in their last year of compulsory schooling as a percentage of the school population of the same age. See Notes and Definitions for table 4.6.

8 Figures relate to all schools; hence they are not directly comparable with those in Tables 14.3 and 15.3, which are for maintained schools only.

Source: Department for Education and Skills; Northern Ireland Department of Education

Table 17.4 Labour market[1] and benefit statistics: by district

Thousands and percentages

| | Economically active 2001-2002[2] (percentages) | Employment rate 2001-2002[2] (percentages) | Claimant count[3], March 2003 | | | Income Support bene-ficiaries[5] Feb 2002 (percentages) |
			Level (thousands)	Females (percentage of claimants)	Percentage claiming over 12 months, computerised claims only[4]	
United Kingdom	78.4	74.4	992.3	24.6	14.6	..
Northern Ireland	71.2	66.7	34.6	22.2	22.0	16
Eastern	..	..	14.1	19.9	20.8	15
Ards	75.5	73.5	1.2	23.0	17.8	10
Belfast	69.8	64.4	8.2	18.4	23.1	22
Castlereagh	79.0	77.9	0.8	18.2	14.5	8
Down	70.1	67.4	1.2	21.5	19.9	12
Lisburn	70.1	67.0	1.6	21.4	20.2	13
North Down	77.3	74.7	1.2	24.9	16.0	9
Northern	..	..	7.1	25.0	20.6	13
Antrim	72.6	69.3	0.7	23.9	19.4	13
Ballymena	79.1	76.6	0.9	29.5	21.8	11
Ballymoney	74.1	64.4	0.4	24.2	13.7	13
Carrickfergus	77.7	73.6	0.8	23.8	17.6	9
Coleraine	71.9	64.5	1.3	24.2	23.9	14
Cookstown	68.6	66.2	0.4	29.7	18.6	22
Larne	77.2	71.2	0.7	26.2	18.0	12
Magherafelt	66.3	65.5	0.4	31.4	16.8	16
Moyle	66.7	..	0.4	21.7	23.1	18
Newtownabbey	80.4	77.4	1.4	21.3	23.6	11
Southern	..	..	5.3	24.6	22.1	17
Armagh	77.4	73.2	0.9	25.0	22.2	13
Banbridge	77.5	72.5	0.5	25.9	17.9	10
Craigavon	67.9	62.9	1.3	22.6	19.5	16
Dungannon	66.6	62.9	0.6	29.3	25.2	21
Newry and Mourne	63.8	58.8	2.0	24.0	24.7	20
Western	..	..	8.1	22.1	24.6	20
Derry	65.2	58.2	3.5	20.3	19.5	23
Fermanagh	72.3	66.4	1.6	23.6	31.5	18
Limavady	68.8	62.2	0.7	22.1	21.0	16
Omagh	58.3	54.0	1.1	27.0	28.5	18
Strabane	58.1	49.7	1.2	21.1	30.1	22

1 See Notes and Definitions to the Labour Market chapter.

2 Based on the population of working age. Data are from the Annual Local Area Labour Force Survey and relate to the period March 2001 to February 2002. These data have not been adjusted to reflect the 2001 Census population estimates.

3 Count of claimants of unemployment-related benefits, i.e. Jobseeker's Allowance.

4 People who have been claiming for more than 12 months (computerised claims only), as a percentage of total computerised claimants.

5 Claimants and their partners aged 16 or over as a percentage of the population aged 16 or over (using the mid-2002 population estimates). The figure for Northern Ireland includes those who could not be assigned to a council.

Source: Office for National Statistics; Department of Enterprise, Trade and Investment; Department of Health, Social Services and Public Safety, Northern Ireland; Department for Social Development, Northern Ireland

Table **17.5** **Gross value added (GVA) and gross disposable household income by NUTS 1, 2 and 3 area at current basic prices[1, 2, 3]**

NUTS 1 and 2 NUTS 3	GVA £ million				GVA £ per head				GVA £ per head (UK=100)				Gross disposable household income £ per head (UK=100)[3] 3 year average 1997-99
	1998	1999	2000	2001	1998	1999	2000	2001	1998	1999	2000	2001	
United Kingdom[4]	749,688	781,847	816,111	851,408	12,858	13,369	13,917	14,418	100	100	100	100	100
Northern Ireland	16,913	17,665	18,414	19,108	10,081	10,521	10,941	11,311	78	79	79	78	88
Belfast	4,855	5,121	5,397	5,688	16,932	18,082	19,216	20,521	132	135	138	142	104
Outer Belfast	2,945	3,074	3,199	3,317	8,001	8,357	8,667	8,965	62	63	62	62	95
East of Northern Ireland	3,833	4,018	4,209	4,354	9,852	10,246	10,651	10,927	77	77	77	76	90
North of Northern Ireland	2,297	2,397	2,486	2,556	8,439	8,764	9,050	9,274	66	66	65	64	72
West and South of Northern Ireland	2,983	3,054	3,123	3,193	8,248	8,431	8,599	8,675	64	63	62	60	79

1 Estimates for GVA data are provisional.
2 Components may not sum to totals due to rounding.
3 Household income estimates are consistent with those published on 26 March 2002.
4 Excluding GDP for Extra-regio, which comprises compensation of employees and gross operating surplus which cannot be assigned to regions.

Source: Office for National Statistics

NUTS levels 1, 2 and 3 in Northern Ireland,[1] 1998

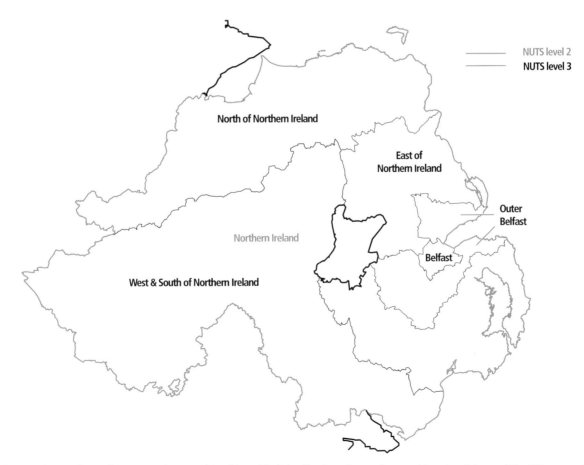

1 NUTS (Nomenclature of Units for Territorial Statistics) is a hierarchical classification of areas that provides a breakdown of the EU's economic territory. The NUTS levels 1 and 2 are represented by the whole country. See Notes and Definitions.

Notes and Definitions

Government Office Regions within England

Most of the statistics in *Regional Trends* are on the based on the Government Office Regions (GORs) of England, together with Wales, Scotland and Northern Ireland. Government Offices for the Regions were established across England in 1994. Changes were implemented in order that government departments could work effectively in partnership with local people and organisations to improve the quality of life and prosperity within their area. In 1996, GORs became the primary classification for the presentation of regional statistics. The Government Office for the North West merged with the Government Office for Merseyside in August 1998, so figures for Merseyside are no longer shown separately. In tables, the Government Office for the East of England (formerly the Eastern Region) is referred to as East.

Sub-regions of England

The implementation of local government re-organisation in England, (which took place in four phases on 1 April in each year from 1995 to 1998) is summarised below. The reorganisation involved only the non-metropolitan counties. Unitary Authorities (UA) have replaced the two tier system of County Councils and Local Authority District Councils in parts of some shire counties and, in some instances, across the whole county. For statistical purposes grouping UAs by geography can be helpful. In Chapter 14 the following areas are included, where data are available:

Tees Valley less Darlington relates to the abolished administrative county of Cleveland (*Tees Valley* relates to the area covered by five UAs; Darlington, Hartlepool, Middlesborough, Redcar and Cleveland, and Stockton-on-Tees.); *The Humber* relates to the abolished administrative county of Humberside. *Herefordshire and Worcestershire* relate to the former administrative county of Hereford and Worcestershire. *Bristol/Bath* relates to the abolished administrative county of Avon.

By legal definition all unitary authorities in England are counties. However, for many purposes the UAs are treated as districts. For the majority of UAs their establishment has been achieved without geographical change. However, for a few unitary authorities, there are some boundary changes at District and Ward levels, most notably, the County of Herefordshire UA in the West Midlands and Peterborough UA in the East of England.

The local government structure at 1 April 1998 is used in Chapter 14 and throughout the rest of the book unless otherwise specified.

Unitary Authorities of Wales

On 1 April 1996, the 8 counties and 37 districts of Wales were replaced by 22 Unitary Authorities. In Chapter 15, the Unitary Authorities are presented in the tables in alphabetical order.

New Councils of Scotland

On 1 April 1996, the 10 Local Authority regions and 56 districts of Scotland were replaced by 32 Unitary Councils. In Chapter 16, the New Councils are presented in the tables in alphabetical order.

Northern Ireland

The 26 districts of Northern Ireland are listed in Chapter 17. For some topics, they have been grouped into either the five Education and Library Boards or the four Health and Social Services Boards. The districts comprising the Education and Library Boards are as follows:

Board	Districts
Belfast	Belfast
South	Eastern Ards, Castlereagh, Down, Lisburn, North Down.
Southern	Armagh, Banbridge, Cookstown, Craigavon, Dungannon, Newry and Mourne.
North Eastern	Antrim, Ballymena, Ballymoney, Carrickfergus, Coleraine, Larne, Magherafelt, Moyle, Newtownabbey
Western	Derry, Fermanagh, Limavady, Omagh, Strabane.

Health and Social Services Boards are as follows:

Northern	as North Eastern Education and Library Board but including Cookstown.
Eastern	as South Eastern Education and Library Board but including Belfast.
Southern	as Southern Education and Library Board but excluding Cookstown.
Western	as Western Education and Library Board.

NUTS (Nomenclature of Territorial Statistics) area classification

NUTS is a hierarchical classification of areas that provide a breakdown of the European Union's economic territory for producing regional statistics that are comparable across the Union. It has been used since 1988 in EU legislation for determining the distribution of the Structural Funds. The NUTS five-tier structure for the UK was reviewed during 1998 as a consequence of the move to using Government Office Regions as the principal classification for English Regions and the local government re-organisation, which took place in the same year. The NUTS structure comprises current national administrative areas, except in Scotland where some NUTS areas comprise whole and /or part local enterprise company areas. As a result of a European Union wide NUTS regulation enacted in June 2003 it is now obligatory to use the NUTS geographies in the regulation (including the new codes) and not those in the current gentleman's agreement. There are only minimal changes for the UK although NUTS levels 4 and 5 no longer have any official status and should now be referred to as LAU (Local Administrative Unit) 1 and 2 respectively.

Other regional classifications

The UK Continental Shelf, now referred to as Extra-Regio, is treated as a separate region in Tables in Chapter 12 (see the Notes and Definitions to Chapter 12 Regional accounts).

Maps

Since the Tourist Board map was produced the West Country has been renamed South West, with some small boundary changes, and Lincolnshire has moved from the East of England to the Heart of England region. For further information contact VisitBritain.

Chapter 2: European Union

The data appearing in this chapter are based on information in the statistical database produced by the Statistical Office of the European Communities (EUROSTAT) which uses the Nomenclature of Territorial Units for Statistics (NUTS) classification, described earlier. Data relate to the NUTS level 1 areas for countries in the European Union.

Table 2.3 Economic statistics

Employment statistics are derived from the annual Community Labour Force Survey (CLFS), which uses national Labour Force Survey (LFS) data although there may be

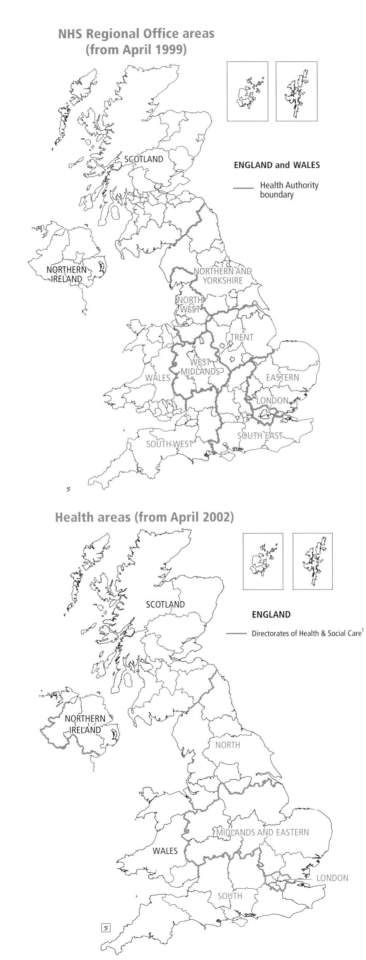

NHS Regional Office areas (from April 1999)

SCOTLAND

NORTHERN IRELAND

NORTHERN AND YORKSHIRE

NORTH WEST

TRENT

WEST MIDLANDS

WALES

EASTERN

LONDON

SOUTH EAST

SOUTH-WEST

ENGLAND and WALES

——— Health Authority boundary

Health areas (from April 2002)

SCOTLAND

NORTHERN IRELAND

NORTH

MIDLANDS AND EASTERN

WALES

LONDON

SOUTH

ENGLAND

——— Directorates of Health & Social Care[1]

1 DHSCs apply only to England, Boards in Scotland report to the Scottish Executive, the 3 Welsh Regional Offices are administered by the NHS Wales Department, HSSBs report to the Northern Ireland Executive.

Police Force areas

Northern   Northern

GREAT BRITAIN

—— Police Force area
boundary

Northern

Grampian

Tayside

Central   Fife

Strathclyde

Lothian &
Borders

Dumfries
& Galloway   Northumbria

Northern
Ireland

Cumbria   Durham   Cleveland

North Yorkshire

Lancashire   Humberside
W. Yorks

Merseyside   G.M.P.   S. Yorks

Cheshire   Derbys   Lincolnshire

North Wales   Notts

Staffs   Leicester   Norfolk

West   W. Mids   Suffolk
Mercia   Warks   Northants

Dyfed-Powys   Cambs
Beds

Gwent   Gloucs   Herts   Essex
Thames   City
South Wales   Valley   Met.

Avon and   Wiltshire   Surrey   Kent
Somerset

Devon and   Hampshire   Sussex
Cornwall   Dorset

Prison Service regions

ENGLAND and WALES

—— Prison Service region
boundary

North East

Lancashire
and Cumbria
(North West)

Yorkshire
and Humberside

Manchester,
Mersey and
Cheshire
(North West)

East Midlands
North

West Midlands   East
Midlands
South

Wales   Eastern

Thames
Valley and
Hampshire
(South East)   London

Kent, Surrey and
Sussex (South East)

South West

Tourist Board areas

UNITED KINGDOM

—— Tourist Board boundary

SCOTLAND

NORTHUMBRIA

NORTHERN
IRELAND   CUMBRIA

YORKSHIRE

NORTH
WEST

HEART OF
ENGLAND   EAST OF
ENGLAND

WALES   LONDON

SOUTH WEST   SOUTHERN   SOUTH EAST
ENGLAND

minor differences in interpretation compared with the national LFS. Since the survey is conducted on a sample basis, results relating to small regions should be treated with caution. One of the main statistical objectives of the CLFS is to divide the population of working age into three groups: people in employment, unemployed people and inactive people (those not classified as employed or unemployed). The groups are used to derive the following measures:

a) Activity rates: the labour force as a percentage of the population of working-age;

b) Employment/population ratios: people in employment as a percentage of the population of working-age; and

c) Unemployment rates: unemployed people as a percentage of the labour force.

The definitions of employment and unemployment used in the CLFS closely follow those adopted by the 13th International Conference of Labour Statisticians and promulgated by the International Labour Organisation (ILO). They are:

Employment: the employed comprise all people above a specified age who during a specified brief period either one week or one day were in the following categories:

a) Paid employment: at work or with a job but not at work i.e. temporarily absent but in receipt of a wage or salary;

b) Self-employment: at work i.e. people who during the reference period performed some work for profit or family gain, in cash or kind, or with an enterprise but not at work i.e. temporarily absent. (An 'enterprise' may be a business enterprise, a farm or a service undertaking.)

Unemployment: people above a specified age who, during the reference period, were:

a) Without work: i.e. were not in paid employment or self-employment;

b) Currently available for work: i.e. were available for paid employment or self-employment during the reference period;

c) Seeking work: i.e. had taken specific steps in a specified recent period to seek paid employment or self-employment.

Long-term unemployment: people who had been unemployed for 12 or more consecutive months.

Table 2.3 Purchasing Power Standard
The Purchasing Power Standard (PPS) is a unit of measurement calculated by scaling Purchasing Power Parities (PPPs) so that the aggregate for the EU-15 as a whole is the same whether expressed in EUROs (ECUs) or in PPS. Purchasing Power Parities are

conversion factors, which make it possible to eliminate the combined effect of price level differences and other factors from a comparison of economic aggregates and thereby obtain a real volume comparison between countries.

Table 2.4 Agricultural statistics
The 'gross margin' of an agricultural enterprise is defined as the monetary value of gross production from which corresponding specific costs (other than building, machinery and labour force) are deducted. The 'Standard Gross Margin' (SGM) is the value of gross margin corresponding to the average situation in a given region for each agricultural characteristic, eg crop production, livestock production. 'Gross production' is the sum of the value of the principal product(s) and of any secondary product(s). The values are calculated by multiplying production per unit (less any losses) by the farm-gate price, excluding VAT. Gross production also includes subsidies linked to products, to area and/or to livestock.

Basic data are collected in Member States from farm accounts, specific surveys or compiled from appropriate calculations for a reference period which covers three successive years or agricultural production years. The reference period is the same for all Member States. SGMs are first calculated in Member States national currencies and then converted into European currency units (ECUs) using the average exchange rates for the reference period.

Chapter 3: Population and Migration

Tables 3.1, 3.2, 3.3, 3.4, 3.5 and 3.13 Resident population
The estimated population of an area includes all those usually resident in the area, whatever their nationality. HM Forces stationed outside the United Kingdom are excluded but foreign forces stationed here are included. Students are taken to be resident at their term-time address. The population estimates for mid-2002 shown in tables in chapter 1, part of table 3.1 and tables 3.2, 14.1, 15.1, 16.1 and 17.1, are based upon information from the 2001 Census. With appropriate adjustments for undercounting and definitional differences between the Census and the population estimates, the mid-2002 estimates make allowances for births, deaths, migration, and other changes and ageing of the population since the Census. Table 3.1 includes the revised mid-2001 population estimates released in November 2003. The figures for years earlier than 1991, shown in the rest of *Regional Trends 38* are unrevised and are inconsistent with the mid-2002 estimates. The mid-1991 population estimates were revised in February 2003.

Table 3.6 Social class
Based on the Labour Force Survey (see Notes and Definitions to the Labour Market chapter), the table gives percentages of working age people in each socio-economic class based on the National Statistics Socio-economic Classification (NS-SEC). The NS-SEC is an occupationally based classification but has rules to provide coverage of the whole adult population. The information required to create the NS-SEC is occupation coded to the unit groups (OUG) of the Standard Occupational Classification 2000 (SOC2000) and details of employment status (whether an employer, self-employed or employee; whether a supervisor; and number of employees at the workplace). Similar information was previously required for earlier social classifications: Social Class and Socio-economic Group. The version of the classification which will be used for most analyses (the analytic version), has eight classes, the first of which can be subdivided.

The National Statistics Socio-economic Classification Analytic Classes:

1. Higher managerial and professional occupations

1.1. Large employers and higher managerial occupations

1.2. Higher professional occupations

2. Lower managerial and professional occupations

3. Intermediate occupations

4. Small employers and own account workers

5. Lower supervisory and technical occupations

6. Semi-routine occupations

7. Routine occupations

8. Never worked and long-term unemployed

For complete coverage, the three categories Students, Occupations not stated or inadequately described, and Not classifiable for other reasons are added as 'Not elsewhere classified (n.e.c.) included under 8 above'.

For those in employment in the reference week of the survey, their occupation was their main job, and for those not in employment, their last occupation if they had done any paid work in the previous eight years.

Table 3.7 Ethnic group
The information for the ethnic group of each respondent is based on the data and categorisation generated from the 2001 Census from ONS, the General Register Office for Scotland and the Northern Ireland Statistics and Research Agency.

In both 1991 and 2001 respondents were asked to which ethnic group they considered themselves to belong. The question asked in 2001 was more extensive than that asked in 1991, so that people could tick 'Mixed' for the first time. This change in answer categories may account for a small part of the observed increase in the minority ethnic population over the period. Different versions of the ethnic group question were asked in England and Wales, in Scotland and in Northern Ireland, to reflect local differences in the requirement for information. However, results are comparable across the UK as a whole.

White includes British, Scottish, Irish and Other British and Other White sub-categories as defined in the 2001 census. Mixed includes the sub-categories White and Black Caribbean, White and Black African, White and Asian and Other mixed.

Table 3.9 Projected population

As with population estimates, the projected population of an area includes all those usually resident in the area, whatever their nationality. HM Forces stationed outside the United Kingdom are excluded but foreign forces stationed here are included. Students are taken to be resident at their term-time address.

The projected population change figures for Wales and for England, Scotland and Northern Ireland are not directly comparable with previous editions of Regional Trends as later projections are used. There are changes to the assumptions for fertility, mortality and migration in the preparation of each set of projections.

This table uses 1996-based subnational projections for England, 2000-based projections for Wales, Scotland and Northern Ireland. The Northern Ireland data are the 2000 based population projections for 2000-2015.

Tables 3.10, 3.13 and 3.14
Births and deaths

Within England and Wales, births are assigned to areas according to the usual residence of the mother at the date of birth, as stated at registration. If the address of usual residence is outside England and Wales, the birth is included in any aggregate for England and Wales as a whole (and hence in the UK total), but excluded from the figures for any individual region or area.

Birth figures for Scotland include births to both resident and non-resident mothers. Where subnational data are given (Table 16.2), births have been allocated to the usual residence of the mother if this was in Scotland and to the area of occurrence if the mother's usual residence was outside Scotland.

All figures given for Northern Ireland (including the subregional figures in Table 17.2) exclude births to mothers not usually resident in Northern Ireland. However, the UK total includes such births.

As with births, within England and Wales, a death is normally assigned to the area of usual residence of the deceased. If this is outside England and Wales, the death is included in any aggregate for England and Wales as a whole (and hence in the UK total), but excluded from the figures for any individual region or area.

Death figures for Scotland and Northern Ireland include deaths of both residents and non-residents. Where subnational data are given (Tables 16.2 and 17.2), deaths of Scottish or Northern Irish residents have been allocated to the usual area of residence, while deaths of non-residents have been allocated to the area of occurrence.

Table 3.10 Birth and death rates and rate of natural change.

Unlike Table 3.11, which relates to population change from mid-year to mid-year, the numbers shown in this table relate to calendar years. Crude birth/death rates and natural change are affected by the age and sex structure of the population. For example, for any given levels of fertility and mortality, a population with a relatively high proportion of persons in the younger age groups will have a higher crude birth rate and consequently a higher rate of natural change than a population with a higher proportion of elderly people.

Table 3.12 Conceptions

The date of conception is estimated using recorded gestation for abortion and stillbirths, and assuming 38 weeks gestation for live births. A woman's age at conception is calculated as the interval in complete years between her date of birth and the estimated age of conception. The postcode of the woman's address is used to determine the area she was living in at the time of the conception.

Table 3.13 Total Fertility Rate

The total fertility rate (TFR) is the average number of children that would be born to a woman if she experiences the current age-specific fertility rates throughout her childbearing years. It is sometimes called the total period fertility rate (TPFR).

Table 3.14 Standardised mortality ratio

The standardised mortality ratio (SMR) compares overall mortality in a region with that for the UK. The ratio expresses the number of deaths in a region as a percentage of the hypothetical number that would have occurred if the region's population had

experienced the sex/age-specific rates of the UK that year.

Tables 3.15 and 3.16
Interregional movements

Estimates for internal population movements are based on the movement of NHS doctors' patients between Health Authorities (HAs) in England and Wales and Area Health Boards (AHBs) in Scotland and Northern Ireland. These transfers are recorded at the NHS Central Registers (NHSCRs), Southport and Edinburgh, and at the Central Services Agency, Belfast. The figures have been adjusted to take account of differences in recorded cross-border flows between England and Wales, Scotland, and Northern Ireland and provide a detailed indicator of population movement within the UK. However, they should not be regarded as a perfect measure of migration as there is variation in the delay between a person moving and registering with a new doctor. Additionally, some moves may not result in a re-registration i.e. individuals may migrate again before registering with a doctor. Conversely, there may be others who move and re-register several times in a year.

The NHSCR at Southport was computerised in 1991. Before 1991, the time lag was assumed to be three months between a person moving and the re-registration with an NHS doctor being processed onto the NHSCR. (It was estimated that processing at NHSCR took two months.) Since computerisation, estimates of internal migration derived from the NHSCR are based on the date of acceptance of the new patient by the HA/HSA (not previously available), and a one-month time lag assumed

Research is ongoing into whether there is a need to revise internal migration estimates in light of the results of the 2001 Census. ONS will report on the necessity and feasibility of producing revised internal migration estimates in late 2003.

Table 3.15 Migration

An international migrant is defined as someone who changes his or her country of usual residence for a period of at least a year, so that the country of destination effectively becomes the country of usual residence. The estimates of international migration shown in Table 3.15 have recently been revised in line with the results of the 2001 Census.

The main source of international migration data is the International Passenger Survey (IPS). This is a continuous voluntary sample survey that provides information on passengers entering and leaving the UK by the principal air, sea and tunnel routes. The IPS has been running since 1961 and is used to collect information on tourism and the Balance of Payments, as well as on migration. In 2001, 256,000 travellers were interviewed, representing 0.2 per cent of all passengers.

Being a sample survey, the IPS results are subject to some uncertainty; therefore it should be noted that international migration estimates, in particular the differences between inflow and outflow, may be subject to large sampling errors. Given the structure of the sample, the standard error for an estimate of 1,000 migrants is around 40 per cent, while that for an estimate of 40,000 migrants reduces to about 10 per cent. For the UK in 2001, the overall standard error for estimated inflow of 372,000 migrants is 4.1 per cent and for outflow of 251,000 migrants is 5.2 per cent. The IPS excludes routes between the Channel Islands, the Isle of Man and the rest of the world.

The IPS data are supplemented with three types of additional information in order to provide a full picture of total international migration:

1. The IPS is based on intentions to migrate and intentions are liable to change. Adjustments are made for visitor switchers (those who intend to stay in the UK or abroad for less than one year but subsequently stay for longer and become migrants) and migrant switchers (those who intend to stay in the UK or abroad for one year or more but then return earlier so are no longer migrants). These adjustments are primarily based on IPS data but for years prior to 2001, Home Office data on short-term visitors who were subsequently granted an extension of stay for a year or longer for other reasons have been incorporated.

2. Home Office data on applications for asylum and dependants of asylum seekers entering the UK are used to estimate inflows of asylum seekers and dependants not already captured by the IPS. In addition, Home Office data on removals and refusals are used to estimate outflows of failed asylum seekers not identified by the IPS.

3. Migration flows between the UK and Ireland are added to IPS data, as the IPS did not cover this route until recently and the quality of these data are still being assessed. Migration flows are obtained primarily from the Irish Quarterly National Household Survey and are agreed between the Irish Central Statistics Office and ONS.

A consistent methodology (based primarily on the IPS) has been used to derive international migration estimates for the constituent countries of the UK and Government Office Regions within England. This methodology is currently under review as part of the National Statistics Quality Review of International Migration. Given the small sample size of the IPS for Scotland and Northern Ireland residents, adjustment of these estimates using data from administrative records is currently

made for the purposes of population estimation in Scotland and Northern Ireland.

Table 3.19 Household projections
The household projections are trend-based; they illustrate what would happen if past trends in household formation were to continue into the future. They are therefore not policy-based forecasts of what is expected to happen, but provide a starting point for policy decisions. The projections are heavily dependent on the assumptions involved, particularly international and internal migration, the marital status projections (in England and Wales only) and the continuation of past trends in household formation.

Chapter 4: Education and Training

Table 4.1 Pupils and teachers by type of school
Qualified teachers only are included for all schools (i.e. all other teaching staff at these schools are excluded).

The pupil/teacher ratio in a school is the ratio of all pupils on the register to all qualified teachers employed within the schools during the census week. Part-time teachers and part-time pupils are included on a full-time equivalent basis. The difference in the age at which pupils transfer from primary to secondary school affects the comparison of pupil/teacher ratios between Scotland and the rest of the United Kingdom.

Table 4.2 Three- and-four-year-olds by type of early years education provider
Figures in this table must be interpreted carefully in light of the differing types of early years education provision within the four home countries.

Table 4.3 Class sizes for all classes
Figures for England, Wales and Scotland include classes where more than one teacher may be present. In Northern Ireland a class is defined as a group of pupils normally under the control of one teacher. Figures previously shown in this publication for England, prior to 1999/2000, related to classes taught by one teacher only. In England, in 2002/03, the average Key Stage 1 class, taught by one teacher, had 25.5 pupils, with 1.1 per cent of classes having 31 or more pupils. Further information, including one-teacher class size data for Key Stage 2, primary and secondary school class sizes can be found in DfES Statistical First Release 09/2003.

Table 4.4 School meal arrangements
Information is collected for the numbers of full- and part-time pupils (up to and including and above minimum school leaving age) on each school's register known to be eligible for

a free school meal and those who took a free school meal. Prior to 2001, the numbers eligible for a free school meal were those pupils who had, or whose parents had, satisfied the relevant authority that they were receiving Income Support or income based Jobseeker's Allowance or support provided under Part 6 of the Immigration and Asylum Act 1999. For the 2001 census, this definition was modified to include only pupils where parents had indicated that they wished their child to have a free meal and had confirmed benefit receipt with the LEA or school.

Table 4.5 Pupil absence from maintained primary and secondary schools in England
In law, parents of children of compulsory school age (5 to 16) are required to ensure that they receive a suitable education by regular attendance at school or otherwise. Failure to comply with this statutory duty can lead to prosecution. Local Education Authorities (LEAs) are responsible in law for making sure that pupils attend school.

Schools are required to take attendance registers twice a day: once at the beginning of the morning session and once during the afternoon session. In their register, schools are required to distinguish whether pupils are present, engaged in an approved educational activity, or are absent. Where a day pupil of compulsory school age is absent, schools have to indicate in their register whether the absence is authorised by the school or unauthorised.

Authorised absence is absence with permission from a teacher or other authorised representative of the school. This includes instances of absences for which a satisfactory explanation has been provided (for example, illness). Unauthorised absence is absence without permission from a teacher or other authorised representative of the school. This includes all unexplained or unjustified absences.

Tables 4.6 and 4.8, and Map 4.7 Examination achievements
The main examination for pupils at the minimum school-leaving age in England, Wales and Northern Ireland is the General Certificate of Secondary Education (GCSE); in Scotland it is the Standard Grade. From 1999/2000 National Qualifications (NQ) were introduced in Scotland. NQs include Standard Grades, Intermediate 1 & 2 and Higher. The GCSE is awarded in eight grades, A*-G, while in Scotland the Standard Grade is awarded in seven levels, 1-7. Standard Grade courses begin in the third year and continue to the end of the fourth year. Each subject has a number of elements, some of which are internally assessed in school. The award for the subject as a whole is given on a 7-point scale at three levels: Credit (1 and 2), General

(3 and 4) and Foundation (5 and 6). An award of 7 means that the course has been completed. Pupils who do not complete the course or do not sit all parts of the examination get 'no award'.

GCSE figures relate to achievements by 16-year-olds at the end of the academic year and are shown as percentages of 16-year-olds in school. Standard Grades (in Scotland) relate to achievements by pupils in year S4 at the end of the academic year. That is, the achievements of pupils by the end of their last year of compulsory schooling: some may have been passed a year earlier.

GCE A levels are usually taken after a further two years of post-compulsory education, passes being graded from A-E. The SCE/NQ Higher Grade requires only one year of post-compulsory study, and for the more able candidates the range of subjects taken may be as wide as at Standard Grade. The Highers figures in Table 4.6 combine the new NQ Higher and the old SCE Higher. GCE A level and equivalent figures for pupils aged between 18 and 19 at the end of the academic year in England, aged 18 in Wales and aged 17 to 19 in Northern Ireland, are shown as a percentage of the 18-year-old population. This age spread in the examination result figures takes account of those pupils sitting examinations a year early or resitting them. Scottish Higher figures are based on the 17-year-old population as Highers are normally taken one year earlier (in year S5) than A levels, although they can resit them or take additional subjects in year S6.

Average GCE/VCE (Vocational Certificate of Education) A/AS points scores are shown in Table 4.6. Points scores are determined by totalling pupils' individual GCE/VCE A/AS results: an A level pass and an AS examination pass are classified at grade E or above. Each grade at AS examination is counted as half that grade at A level. VCE A level double awards count as 2 A levels. From 2001/02, the number of points assigned to grades within GCE/VCE qualifications, in England, has changed to reflect the Universities and Colleges Admissions Service (UCAS) Tariff. Scores are calculated as shown below:

GCE/VCE AS level:

Grade	UCCA points	UCAS points
A	5	60
B	4	50
C	3	40
D	2	30
E	1	20

GCE/VCE A level:

Grade	UCCA points	UCAS points
A	10	120
B	8	100
C	6	80
D	4	60
E	2	40

VCE A level double award:

Grade	UCAS points
AA	240
AB	220
BB	200
BC	180
CC	160
CD	140
DD	120
DE	100
EE	80

Advanced GNVQ:

Grade	Comparable GCE grade	Previous point allocation (12 units)	Previous point allocation (18 units)	UCAS points
Distinction	A/B	18	27	100
Merit	C	12	18	80
Pass	D/E	6	9	60

In Wales, at below GCSE standard, the Certificate of Education examination is also available and is widely used by schools. Many pupils take Welsh as a first language at GCSE. In all countries pupils may sit non-GCE/GCSE examinations such as BTEC (SCOTVEC in Scotland), City and Guilds, RSA and Pitman. A proportion of pupils who are recorded as achieving no GCSE, AS or A level qualification will have passes in one or more of these other examinations.

In Table 4.8, Mathematics figures exclude computing science (England) and computer studies and statistics (Wales) while 'any science' in England and Wales includes double award, single award and individual science subjects. Double award science was introduced with the GCSEs in 1988. Success in double award science means that the pupil has achieved two GCSEs rather than just one pass with single science or the individual sciences of biology, physics and chemistry. The majority of 15-year-olds now attempt GCSE double award science in preference to the single science subjects, although the individual sciences are still popular in the independent sector. There is no equivalent to double award science in Standard Grade.

Comparisons of examination results for England, Wales and Northern Ireland with those for Scotland are not straightforward because of the different education and examination systems. However, the following should be used as a rough guideline:

5 or more GCSEs at grades A*-C = 5 or more Standard Grades at levels 1-3/Intermediate 2 A-C/Intermediate 1 A-B;

1-4 GCSEs at grades A*-C = 1-4 awards of Standard Grades at levels 1-3/ Intermediate 2 A-C/ Intermediate 1 A-B;

GCSEs at grades D-G only = Standard Grades at levels 4-7 only/Intermediate 1 (C)/Access 3 (pass);

2 or more GCE A levels passes at A-E = either 3 or more Higher Grade passes, 2 or more Advanced Highers, or 1 Advanced Higher with 2 or more Higher Passes.

Also see the National Curriculum notes for Table 4.9

Table 4.9 The National Curriculum: Assessments and Tests

Under the *Education Reform Act (1988)* a National Curriculum has been progressively introduced into primary and secondary schools in England and Wales. This consists of mathematics, English (or the option of Welsh as a first language in Wales) and science as core subjects, with a modern language, history, geography, information technology, design and technology, music, art and physical education (and Welsh as a second language in Wales) as foundation subjects. The *Education Act 2002* extended the National Curriculum for England to include the foundation (i.e. early years education) stage, for suitable areas of learning. Measurable local targets have been defined for four key stages, corresponding to ages 7, 11, 14 and 16.

Pupils are assessed formally at the ages of 7, 11 and 14 by a mixture of teacher assessments and by national tests in the core subjects of English, mathematics and science (and in Welsh in Welsh speaking schools in Wales), though the method varies between subjects and countries. Sixteen-year-olds are assessed by means of the GCSE examination. Statutory authorities have been set up for England and Wales to advise government on the National Curriculum and promote curriculum development generally. Northern Ireland has its own common curriculum, which is similar, but not identical to, the National Curriculum in England and Wales. Assessment arrangements in Northern Ireland became statutory from September 1996, and Key Stage 1 pupils are assessed at the age of 8. Pupils in Northern Ireland are not assessed in science at Key Stages 1 and 2. The National Curriculum does not apply in Scotland, where school curricula are the responsibility of education authorities and individual head teachers, and in practice almost all 14- to-16-year-olds study mathematics, English, science, a modern foreign language, a social subject, physical education, technology and a creative and aesthetic subject. The Key Stage 1, 2 and 3 figures for England cover all types of school (eg maintained and independent). The Government Office Region figures cover LEA maintained schools only.

Tables 4.10 and 4.11 Post-compulsory and further (including adult) education

Further education (FE) includes home students on courses of further education (FE) in further education institutions. The FE sector includes all provision outside schools that is below higher education (HE) level. This ranges from courses in independent living skills for students with severe learning difficulties up to GCE A level, and level 3 NVQ/SVQ and other vocational courses. The FE sector also includes many students pursuing recreational courses not leading to a formal qualification. Students in England and Wales are counted once only, irrespective of the number of courses for which a student has enrolled. In Scotland and Northern Ireland, students enrolled on more than one course in unrelated subjects are counted for each of these courses with the exception of those on Standard Grade/GCSE and/or Highers/GCE courses, who are counted once only irrespective of the number of levels/grades. Most FE students are in FE colleges and (in England) sixth form colleges that were formerly maintained by Local Education Authorities (LEAs) but in April 1993 became independent self-governing institutions receiving funding through the Further Education Funding Council (FEFC). However, from April 2001, the Learning and Skills Council (LSC) took over the responsibility for funding the FE sector in England, and the National Council for Education and Training for Wales (part of Education and Learning Wales - ELWa) did so for Wales. The Scottish FEFC (SFEFC) funds FE colleges in Scotland, while the Department for Employment and Learning funds FE colleges in Northern Ireland. There are also a small number of FE students in higher education (HE) institutions, and conversely some HE students in FE institutions.

Students may be of any age from 16 upwards (no minimum age in Scotland), and full- or part-time. Full-time students aged under 19 are exempt from tuition fees and fully funded by the respective further education funding bodies in England, Wales, Scotland and Northern Ireland. Students aged 16 to 18 on FE courses in the Scottish FEIs are exempt from tuition fees, at the discretion of the individual colleges. Students are eligible to apply for support (bursary); the policy for eligibility is at the discretion of the colleges. For other students, tuition fees are payable

but may be remitted for students in receipt of certain social security benefits. In some cases discretionary grants may be available from LEAs or the colleges themselves. LEAs continue to make some FE provision (often referred to as 'adult education') exclusively part-time and predominantly recreational. The majority of LEAs make part or all of this provision directly themselves, but some pay other organisations (usually FE colleges) to do so on their behalf, i.e. 'contracted out' provision.

Part-time day courses are mainly those organised for students released by their employers either for one or two days a week (or any part of a week in Scotland), or for a period (or periods) of block release.

Sandwich courses are those where periods of full-time study are broken by a period (or periods) of associated industrial training or experience, and where the total period (or periods) of full-time study over the whole course averages more than 19 weeks per academic year (18 weeks in Scotland). Sandwich course students are classed as full-time students.

National Vocational Qualifications (NVQs) and Scottish Vocational Qualifications (SVQs) are occupational qualifications, available at five levels, and are based on up-to-date standards set by employers.

General National Vocational Qualifications (GNVQs) and General Scottish Vocational Qualifications (GSVQs) combine general and vocational education and are available at three levels:

Foundation – broadly equivalent to four GCSEs at grades D-G or four SCE Standard Grades at levels 4-7.

Intermediate – broadly equivalent to five GCSEs at grades A*-C or five SCE Standard Grades at levels 1-3.

Advanced – broadly equivalent to two GCE A levels, or three SCE Higher Grade passes. Advanced GNVQs were redesigned and re-launched as vocational 'A' levels (or, more formally, Advanced Vocational Certificates of Education (VCEs)). They are available as 'AS' levels (three units), 'A' levels (six units) and double awards (twelve units).

The figures for FE students in England for 2001/02 are extracted from the Individualised Student Record (ISR). They include all students studying in FE institutions (i.e. including external institutions and specialist designated colleges, which were previously excluded) who were undergoing learning at 1 November 2001. The figures are not directly comparable with pre 2001/02 figures published previously in Regional Trends. Until 1995/96 figures were taken from the Further Education Statistical Record (FESR). Due to differences in data collection and methodology between the two sources, the

ISR figures are not directly comparable with figures derived from the FESR. Since April 2001, the publication of data on further education in England has been the responsibility of the Learning and Skills Council (LSC), which has taken over the funding of further education from the FEFC.

The participation rates for regions in England in Table 4.10 have been calculated in the following way:

the numbers of pupils in maintained, special and independent schools attending schools in the area; the number of full-time and part-time further education students resident in the area regardless of where they study; trainees on government-supported training, according to the Training and Enterprise Council (TEC) area with which their training is contracted; divided by the estimated population of the area in January 2001 who were 16 or 17 respectively at 31 August 2000.

Table 4.12 Higher education

Higher education (HE) students are those on courses that are of a standard that is higher than GCE A level, Scottish SCE/NQ Higher Grade, GNVQ/NVQ level 3 or the BTEC or SCOTVEC National Certificate or Diploma. Higher education in publicly funded institutions is funded by block grants from the three Higher Education Funding Councils (HEFCs) in Great Britain and the Department for Employment and Learning in Northern Ireland (DELNI). Some HE activity takes place in FE sector institutions, some of which is funded by the HEFCs and some by the FE funding bodies.

The figures for HE students in FE colleges in England and Wales for 2001/02 are extracted from the Individualised Student Record (ISR). Figures for England include all students studying in FE institutions (i.e. including external institutions and specialist designated colleges, which were previously excluded) who were undergoing learning at 1 November 2001. They are not directly comparable with figures published in Regional Trends prior to 2001/02. Figures for Wales refer to students at 1 December 2001.

Table 4.14 Population of working age by highest qualification

Table 4.14 covers all people of working age (16 to 64 for males, 16 to 59 for females). Please also see notes to Tables 4.6 and 4.8.

Degree or equivalent includes higher and first degrees, NVQ level 5 and other degree level qualifications such as graduate membership of a professional institute.

Higher education qualification below degree level includes NVQ level 4, higher level BTEC/SCOTVEC, HNC/HND, RSA Higher diploma and nursing and teaching qualifications.

GCE A level or equivalent includes NVQ level 3, GNVQ advanced, BTEC/SCOTVEC National Certificate, RSA Advanced diploma, City and Guilds advanced craft, A/AS levels or equivalent, Scottish Highers, Scottish Certificate of Sixth Year Studies and trade apprenticeships.

GCSE grades A*-C or equivalent includes NVQ level 2, GNVQ intermediate, RSA diploma, City and Guilds craft, BTEC/SCOTVEC First or general diploma, GCSE grades A*-C or equivalent, O level and CSE Grade 1.

Other qualifications at NVQ level 1 or below include GNVQ, GSVO foundation level, GCSE grade D-G, CSE below grade 1, BTEC/SCOTVEC First or general certificate, other RSA and City and Guilds qualifications, Youth Training certificate and any other professional, vocational or foreign qualifications for which the level is unknown.

Table 4.15 Public Service Agreement Targets

Various Public Service Agreement (PSA) Targets have now superseded the 2002 National Learning Targets. Table 4.15 shows the proportions of people meeting the required qualification levels for some of these PSA Targets. The Targets shown are split into two groups - those for young people and those for adults - and they have been set using the competence-based National Vocational Qualifications (NVQs) and their vocational and academic equivalents. It should be noted that the data in Table 4.15 relate to the regions in which people were resident, and not where they obtained their qualifications. This can lead to some distortion of the regional picture of educational standards.

PSA Objective 4 is to raise attainment between the ages of 14 and 19. As part of this Objective, Target 5 includes an aim of ensuring that the proportion of 19-year-olds who achieve qualifications equivalent to 5 GCSEs at grades A*-C rises by 3 percentage points between 2002 and 2004, with a further increase of 3 percentage points by 2006. PSA Objective 6 is to tackle the adult skills deficit, and Target 11 of this Objective is to reduce by at least 40 per cent the number of adults in the UK workforce who lack NVQ level 2 or equivalent qualifications by 2010. Working towards this, the aim is that 1 million adults already in the workforce should achieve level 2 between 2003 and 2006.

Alongside the PSA targets, the DfES has a "Delivering Results" strategy with three main objectives, which aim to assist children, young people and adults respectively in their education and development. Objective 2 includes a target to increase the proportion of 19-year-olds achieving a level 3 qualification from 51 per cent in 2000 to 55 per cent in 2004. Objective 3 includes a target to

increase the percentage of adults attaining a level 3 qualification from 47 per cent, with the aim of reaching 52 per cent in 2004.

Table 4.17 Work-based learning

Work-based Learning for Adults (previously known as Work-based Training for Adults) replaced the former Training for Work (TfW) initiative in April 1998 and is aimed at getting unemployed adults back into work.

Work-based Learning for Young People (formerly Work-based Training for Young People) consists of Advanced Modern Apprenticeships (AMA), Foundation Modern Apprenticeships (FMA), Life Skills/Life Build (not recorded in Table 4.17) and Other Training (OT) for young people (formerly known as Youth Training). These programmes aim to provide the participants with learning towards a recognised National Vocational Qualification at levels 2 and 3 or above.

Up to 25 March 2001, these programmes were delivered through the network of Training and Enterprise Councils in England and Wales and Local Enterprise Companies (LECs) in Scotland (although data for Scotland are not available for Table 4.17). After that date the Learning and Skills Council (LSC) assumed responsibility for these programmes in England along with Education and Learning Wales (ELWa) in Wales. In England and Wales, leavers are followed up six months after they leave the programme, whereas in Scotland they are followed up three months after completing training.

For Northern Ireland, figures relate to people on the Jobskills Programme. The Programme focuses on the delivery and attainment of NVQs and in line with national policy guarantees all 16- and 17-year-olds the opportunity of a learning place. For statistical purposes, young people on Jobskills are classified as those who were under 18 years of age on joining the programme. As trainees can stay on Jobskills for up to three years, outcomes for leavers during 2000/01 may not necessarily be fully representative of outcomes in the longer term.

Chapter 5: Labour Market

Interpretation of the labour market requires a number of different sources of data to be used. There are five main sources in this chapter: the Labour Force Survey (LFS), the Annual Business Inquiry (ABI), the Northern Ireland Quarterly Employment Survey (QES), the New Earnings Survey (NES) and the claimant count. Problems can arise in drawing together data on the same subject from different sources. For example, the question in the LFS as to whether the respondent is employed produces a measure of employment based on the number of people, whereas a question addressed to employers asking the number of people they employ, as in the ABI, produces a measure of the

number of jobs. Thus if someone has a second job they will be included twice.

Labour Force Survey (LFS)

LFS estimates are prone to sampling variability. For example, in the March to May 2003 period, unemployment in the United Kingdom according to the ILO definition (seasonally adjusted) stood at 1,474,000. If another sample for the same period were drawn, a different result might be achieved. In theory, many samples could be drawn, each giving a different result. This is because each sample would be made up of different people giving different answers to the questions. The spread of these results is the sampling variability. Sampling variability is determined by a number of factors including the sample size, the variability of the population from which the sample is drawn and the sample design. Once the sampling variability is known, it is possible to calculate a range of values about the sample estimate that represents the expected variation with a given level of assurance. This is called a confidence interval. For a 95 per cent confidence interval, widely used within ONS and elsewhere, we expect that in 95 per cent of the samples (19 times out of 20) the confidence interval will contain the true value that would be obtained by surveying the entire population. For the example given above, we can be 95 per cent confident that the true value was in the range 1,422,000 to 1,526,000.

In general, the larger the number of people in the sample the smaller the variation between estimates. For this reason estimates based on the LFS for the whole of the UK are more accurate than those for smaller geographical areas or subsets of the population. Generally, the sampling variability around regional estimates is, proportionately, around three times that for national estimates.

Estimates of small numbers have relatively wide confidence intervals, making them less reliable. For this reason, the ONS does not publish figures based on LFS estimates which fall below 10,000 when grossed-up from the sample. Data from the LFS Annual Local Area Database are more precise than those from the quarterly survey because the database is derived from four quarters of the LFS and hence represents an increase of 60 per cent over the quarterly sample size. Estimates can therefore be published for a larger number of areas. The 2001/02 Local Area Database included a boosted sample for some local areas in England and Wales. This means that the publication threshold varies for each local area, depending on the size of the boost in each area. Thresholds in England are 2,000, 4,000 or 6,000 in each area, while in Wales the figures are 1,000, 2,000, 3,000 or 4,000. Full details can be found in the LFS User Guide, Volume 6.

Sampling variability also affects changes over time. For example, LFS employment in the United Kingdom rose by 101,000 (seasonally adjusted) between winter 2002/03 (December 2002 to February 2003) and spring 2003 (March to May), and the 95 per cent confidence interval for this change is the range -20,000 to +222,000. Quarterly changes may be lower than the level that is explainable by sampling variability.

Changes over time are best viewed using changes in rates rather than levels in order to view them in a wider context of changes in the overall population. Rates are also subject to sampling variability. The best estimate of the quarterly change in economic activity rate between winter 2002/03 and spring 2003 was that it rose by 0.1 per cent (seasonally adjusted). We can be 95 per cent confident that the true change in economic activity lay within the range -0.1 per cent to +0.3 per cent.

The LFS began in 1973. Since 1998 the results have been published 12 times a year, showing on each occasion the average for a three-month period. In this publication, the three-month period used is usually the spring quarter (March to May). Other three-month periods commonly used here and in other publications are the summer (June to August), autumn (September to November) and winter (December to February) quarters.

Interim Labour Force Survey estimates consistent with 2001 Census UK LFS estimates

On 27 February 2003, ONS published final population estimates for 1991-2000, by local authority, sex and age, consistent with the 2001 Census. These replaced the interim UK population estimates published in October 2002. Revised interim UK LFS estimates from March to May 1992, based on these population estimates were produced and were included in the Labour Market release published on 16 April 2003. The methods used to produce these estimates were consistent with those used for the interim series since November 2002, details of which are available on the website. Interim UK LFS estimates from mid-2001 were not revised. These data were based on population estimates for 2001, and interim population projections for 2002-03, produced by the Government Actuaries Department (GAD). Revised UK population estimates for 1984-1991 were made available on the website on 30 April 2003.

Revised national and regional mid-year population estimates for 2001 and 2002 were published on 26 September 2003, and revised mid-year population estimates for 1992 to 2000 were published on 23 October 2003. These revisions were the result of a number of studies that ONS has carried out since September 2002 to improve the

understanding of population estimates. These revised population estimates have now been incorporated in the LFS estimates together with consistent best estimates of population projections for 2003 and 2004 which were compiled by ONS in advance of the Government Actuary's Department 2002-based projections published in December 2003. On 4 November 2003, ONS published new provisional population estimates for Manchester for the years 2001 and 2002 as a result of additional research carried out over the last year. No back series are currently available for these estimates and the overall effect is small, so these revisions have not been included in the latest LFS revisions. These revisions will be incorporated into the LFS during 2004.

Regional LFS estimates

The publication in February 2003 of Census-2001-consistent population estimates at local authority level allowed the production of interim regional LFS estimates, consistent with the 2001 Census, for the first time. Interim regional estimates have been produced for all periods back to the three-month period ending February 1997. Regional level LFS time series for earlier periods will be compiled and released as part of ONS's full LFS reweighting exercise in spring 2004. Estimates for geographies below regions have not been reweighted using the interim method, but these also will be released in spring 2004. The methodology used to produce these estimates is broadly consistent with that used to produce the UK interim LFS estimates.

Users of the interim regional LFS estimates should note that the interim methodology used does not achieve full additivity between the regional estimates and the national LFS estimates (though the differences are small). Full additivity in the series will be restored by the full reweighting exercise in spring 2004.

Glossary of Terms

Claimant count
A count, derived from administrative sources, of those people who are claiming

unemployment-related benefits at Jobcentre Plus local offices.

Claimant count rate
At a national and regional level, the claimant count rate is normally calculated by expressing the number of people claiming unemployment-related benefits (the numerator) as a percentage of the estimated total workforce (the denominator), which is the sum of claimants, employee jobs, self-employment jobs, HM armed forces and government-supported trainees. At a subregional level, a different denominator is used: the resident working-age population of the area. Where national and regional claimant count rates are presented in the

same table as subregional rates, then the denominator for all the rates is also the resident working-age population of the area.

Economically active/labour force
The labour force (otherwise known as the economically active population) consists of those in employment *plus* the unemployed.

Economic activity rate
The percentage of the population which is in the labour force.

Economically inactive
People who are neither part of the labour force in employment nor unemployed (according to the ILO definition). For example, all people under 16, those retired or looking after a home, or those permanently unable to work.

Employees (Labour Force Survey)
A household-based measure of people aged 16 or over who regard themselves as paid employees. In this publication, people are counted only once in their main job.

Employee jobs (Employer Survey)
A measure, obtained from surveys of employers, of jobs held by civilians. People with two or more jobs are counted in each job.

Unemployed
An International Labour Organisation (ILO) recommended measure, used in household surveys such as the LFS, which counts as unemployed those aged 16 or over who are without a job, are available to start work in the next two weeks and who have been seeking a job in the last four weeks, or were waiting to start a job already obtained in the next two weeks.

Unemployment rate
The percentage of the economically active who are unemployed.

Labour force in employment (Labour Force Survey)
A household-based measure of employees, self-employed people, participants in government-supported training and employment programmes, and people doing unpaid work for a family business.

Population of working age
Men aged 16 to 64 years and women aged 16 to 59 years.

Self-employed
A household-based measure (from the Labour Force Survey) of people aged 16 or over who regard themselves as self-employed in their main job.

Workforce jobs
A measure of employee jobs (obtained from employer surveys), self-employment jobs (obtained from the Labour Force Survey), all

HM Forces, and government-supported trainees (obtained from the Department for Work and Pensions and its Scottish and Welsh counterparts).

Tables 5.1 and 5.2 Labour force
The labour force includes people aged 16 and over who are either in employment (whether employed, self-employed, on a work-related government-supported employment and training programme or an unpaid family worker) or unemployed. The ILO definition of unemployment counts as unemployed people without a job who were available to start work within two weeks and had either looked for work in the past four weeks or were waiting to start a job they had already obtained in the next two weeks.

Tables 5.4 and 5.5 Annual Business Inquiry, Short-term Employment Survey and Quarterly Employment Survey
The Annual Business Inquiry (ABI) is a sample survey which ran for the first time in 1998 and replaced the Annual Employment Survey. The ABI is the only source of employment statistics for Great Britain analysed by local area and by detailed industrial classification. The sample is drawn from the Inter-Departmental Business Register (IDBR), and the ABI 1999 sample comprised 78,000 enterprises. An enterprise is roughly defined as a combination of local units (i.e. individual workplaces with PAYE schemes or registered for VAT) under common ownership. These enterprises covered 0.5 million local units and 15 million employees (out of a total population of roughly 25 million employees in employment). The ABI results are used to benchmark the monthly/quarterly employment surveys (STES) which measure 'movements', by region and industrial group, between the annual survey dates.

The Quarterly Employment Survey (QES) for Northern Ireland is a voluntary survey which covers all employers with at least 25 employees, all public sector employers and a representative sample of smaller firms. Data are collected for both male and female, full-time and part-time employees. Estimates for Northern Ireland are produced on a quarterly basis with unadjusted figures available at the two-digit or division level of the 1992 Standard Industrial Classification and seasonally adjusted figures available at a broad sector level.

Table 5.7 Economic activity rates
The economic activity rate is the percentage of the population in a given age group which is in the labour force.

Table 5.12 Elementary occupational group
This group covers occupations which require the knowledge and experience necessary to perform mostly routine tasks, often involving the use of simple hand-held tools and, in some cases, requiring a degree of physical effort.

Most occupations in this group do not require formal educational qualifications but will usually have an associated short period of formal experience-related training. All non-managerial agricultural occupations are also included in this group, primarily because of the difficulty of distinguishing between those occupations which require only a limited knowledge of agricultural techniques, animal husbandry, etc., from those which require specific training and experience in these areas.

Table 5.13 Labour disputes
The table shows rates per 1,000 employees of working days lost for all industries and services. The statistics relate only to disputes connected with terms and conditions of employment. Stoppages involving fewer than ten workers or lasting less than one day are excluded except where the aggregate of working days lost is 100 or more. When interpreting the figures the following points should be borne in mind:

a)   geographical variations in industrial structure affect overall regional comparisons;

b)   a few large stoppages affecting a small number of firms may have a significant effect;

c)   the number of working days lost and workers involved relate to people both directly and indirectly involved at the establishments where the disputes occurred;

d)   the regional figures involve a greater degree of estimation than the national figures as some large national stoppages cannot be disaggregated to a regional level and are only shown in the figure for the United Kingdom.

Tables 5.16 and 5.17 New Earnings Survey
These tables contain some of the regional results of the New Earnings Survey 2002, fuller details of which are given for the Government Office Regions in the 'Great Britain: streamlined and summary analyses' and the 'Analyses by region, county and small areas' volumes of the report New Earnings Survey 2002 (National Statistics Direct). Results for Northern Ireland are published separately by the Department of Enterprise, Trade and Investment, Northern Ireland. The survey measured gross earnings of a 1 per cent sample of employees, most of whom were members of Pay-As-You-Earn (PAYE) schemes for a pay-period which included 10 April 2002. The earnings information collected was converted to a weekly basis where necessary, and to an hourly basis where normal basic hours were reported.

Figures are given where the number of employees reporting in the survey was 30 or more and the standard error of average weekly earnings was 5 per cent or less. Figures for the Northern Ireland New Earnings Survey are given where the number of employees reporting in the survey was 10 or more. Gross earnings are measured before tax, National Insurance or other deductions. They include overtime pay, bonuses and other additions to basic pay but exclude any payments for earlier periods (for example, back pay), income in kind, tips and gratuities. All the results in this volume relate to full-time male and female employees on adult rates whose pay for the survey pay-period was not affected by absence. Employees were classified to the region in which they worked (or were based if mobile) using postcode information, and to manual or non-manual occupations on the basis of the Standard Occupational Classification 1990 (SOC 90). The 'Great Britain: streamlined and summary analyses' and 'United Kingdom: streamlined and summary analyses' volumes of the report for Great Britain give full details of definitions used in the survey. Full-time employees are defined as those normally expected to work more than 30 hours per week, excluding overtime and main meal breaks (but 25 hours or more in the case of teachers) or, if their normal hours were not specified, as those regarded as full-time by the employer.

Tables 5.18, 5.20, 5.23 and 5.24 Unemployment
The International Labour Organisation (ILO) definition of unemployment is measured through the Labour Force Survey and covers those people who are looking for work and are available for work (see Glossary of terms). The unemployment rate is the percentage of economically active people who are unemployed.

Counts of claimants of unemployment-related benefits are also published. There are advantages and disadvantages with both, but the two series are complementary. The unemployment rate is the number of people who are unemployed as a proportion of the resident economically active population of the area concerned. The claimant count rate at the national and regional level is the number of people claiming unemployment–related benefits as a proportion of claimants and jobs in each area. This explains why the unemployment rate for London, where inward commuting is an important feature of the local labour market, tends to be significantly higher than the equivalent claimant count rate. The differential is much smaller for a region such as the South East where people commute out of the region into London. At a subregional level, the claimant count rate is the number of claimants in an area as a proportion of the resident working-age population of the area. A fuller description of unemployment and claimant count, and the way they relate to one another is in the booklet 'How exactly is unemployment measured?', available from the Office for National Statistics.

Tables 5.19 and 5.21, and Map 5.22 Claimant Count Statistics

From 7 October 1996, a new single benefit, the Jobseeker's Allowance (JSA), replaced Unemployment Benefit and Income Support for unemployed people. People who qualify for JSA through their National Insurance contributions are eligible for a personal allowance (known as contribution-based JSA) for a maximum of six months. People who do not qualify for contribution-based JSA, or whose needs are not met by it, are able to claim a means-tested allowance (known as income-based JSA) for themselves and their dependants for as long as they need it. All those eligible for and claiming JSA, as well as those claiming National Insurance credits, continue to be included in the monthly claimant count.

National and regional claimant count rates are calculated by expressing the number of claimants as a percentage of the estimated total workforce (the sum of claimants, employee jobs, self-employment jobs, HM Armed Forces and government-supported trainees). At a subregional level, the claimant count rate is the number of claimants in an area as a proportion of the resident working-age population of the area.

Table 5.24 Qualifications

Degree or equivalent includes higher and first degrees, NVQ level 5 and other degree level qualifications such as graduate membership of a professional institute.

Higher education qualification below degree level includes NVQ level 4, higher level BTEC/SCOTVEC, HNC/HND, RSA Higher diploma and nursing and teaching qualifications.

GCE A level or equivalent includes NVQ level 3, GNVQ advanced, BTEC/SCOTVEC National Certificate, RSA Advanced diploma, City and Guilds advanced craft, A/AS levels or equivalent, Scottish Highers, Scottish Certificate of Sixth Year Studies and trade apprenticeships.

GCSE grades A*-C or equivalent includes NVQ level 2, GNVQ intermediate, RSA diploma, City and Guilds craft, BTEC/SCOTVEC First or general diploma, GCSE grades A*-C or equivalent, O level and CSE Grade 1.

Other qualifications at NVQ level 1 or below include GNVQ, GSVQ foundation level, GCSE grade D-G, CSE below grade 1, BTEC/SCOTVEC First or general certificate,

other RSA and City and Guilds qualifications, Youth Training certificate and any other professional, vocational or foreign qualifications for which the level is unknown.

Chart 5.25 Redundancies

Estimates cover:

a) the number of people who were not in employment during the reference week and who reported that they had been made redundant in the month of the reference week or in the two calendar months prior to this; plus

b) the number of people who were in employment during the reference week who started their job in the same calendar month as, or the two calendar months prior to, the reference week, and who reported that they had been made redundant in the month of the reference week or in the two calendar months prior to this.

Table 5.26 Vacancies at Jobcentres

Statistics of vacancies notified to Jobcentres are not comprehensive. Only a proportion of all vacancies in the economy is notified and the proportion may tend to vary by region, by occupation, by industry as well as over time.

2000 is the latest year for which the Jobcentre vacancy stock data are available. Publication of the Jobcentre vacancy series since May 2001 has been deferred due to distortions to the data caused by the introduction of Employer Direct, which is a major change involving the transfer of the vacancy-taking process from local Jobcentres to regional customer service centres. Employer Direct has been gradually introduced across Great Britain, as part of the modernisation of the former Employment Service (now part of Jobcentre Plus) and has had the following effects:

1. a temporary reduction in the recorded level of outflows and placings owing to some delays in following up vacancies with employers associated with the introduction of the new arrangements;

2. an increase in the recorded level of newly notified vacancies.

Both the above effects have led to an increase in the recorded stock of unfilled vacancies

Tables 5.27 The New Deal

The New Deal for the young unemployed is available to young people aged 18 to 24 who have been unemployed for more than six months, through four options:

1. a job attracting a wage subsidy of £60 a week, payable to employees for up to six months;

2. a work placement with a voluntary organisation;

3. a six-month work placement with an Environment Task Force;

4. for those without basic qualifications, a place on a full-time education and training course, which might last for up to one year.

All the options include an element of training. For each young person the programme begins with a 'gateway' period of careers advice and intensive help with work, and with training in the skills needed for the world of work.

People in New Deal jobs are those who are recorded by the Employment Service as having been placed into subsidised employment, plus those who are recorded as having terminated their Jobseeker's Allowance (JSA) claim in order to go into a job. This will undercount the total number going into a job: some who go into a job will not, for whatever reason, record this as the reason for termination of their JSA claim. These will be counted as 'not known'. Past research indicates that the destinations of those who do not give a reason for termination follow a similar pattern to those who do give a reason. Where a young person returns to JSA within 13 weeks of starting an unsubsidised job, the job is discounted.

Chapter 6: Housing

Tables 6.1 and 6.4

In the 2001 Census, a dwelling was defined as a self-contained unit of accommodation: with all the rooms behind a door, which only that household can use. The figures in Table 6.1 include vacant dwellings and temporary dwellings occupied as a normal place of residence. Estimates of the stock in England, Wales and Scotland are based on data from the 2001 Census and projected forward yearly. In addition, local authority and other public sector landlords' figures supplement the data for Wales and Scotland. Estimates of the dwelling stock by tenure in Table 6.4 are also based on the latest Census for owner-occupied and privately rented dwellings. However Registered Social Landlord's stock is more accurately taken from the Housing Corporation's own data.

Table 6.2 New Dwellings completed

The figures in table 6.2 relate to new permanent dwellings only, i.e. dwellings with a life expectancy of 60 years or more. A dwelling is counted as completed when it becomes ready for occupation, whether actually occupied or not. The figures for private sector completions in Northern Ireland have been statistically adjusted to correct, as far as possible, the proven under-recording of private sector completions in Northern Ireland. The figures for private sector completions in Scotland include estimates for some local authorities in latter years.

Table 6.7 Householders' satisfaction with their area

In the Survey of English Housing, householders were asked to rate their satisfaction with the area in which they lived, while in the Scottish Household Survey, adults were asked to rate their neighbourhood as a place to live. In table 6.7, the categories shown are the responses for the Survey of English Housing and the table below shows how the Scottish responses compare.

Categories in table 6.7

Survey of English Housing 2001/02	Scottish Household Survey 2001/02
Very Satisfied	Very good
Fairly Satisfied	Fairly good
Neither satisfied nor dissatisfied	No opinion
Slightly dissatisfied	Fairly poor
Very dissatisfied	Very poor

Table 6.8 Selected housing costs of owner occupied

Prior to Regional Trends 36 each category included owner-occupiers who did not make any payments. This group of people has now been excluded from this table.

Mortgage payments: mortgage interest plus any premiums on mortgage protection policies for loans used to purchase the property. For repayment mortgages, interest is calculated using the amount of loan outstanding and the standard interest rate at time of interview.

Endowment policies: premium on endowment policies covering the repayment of mortgages and loans used to purchase the property.

Structural insurance: includes cases where insurance also covers furniture and contents and the structural element cannot be separately identified.

Services: includes payments of ground rent, feu duties (applies in Scotland), chief rent, service charges, compulsory or regular maintenance charges, site rent (caravans), factoring (payments to a land steward) and any other regular payments in connection with the accommodation.

Table 6.9 Average dwelling prices

Average prices in this table are calculated from data collected by the Land Registry. Because of the time lag between the completion of a house purchase and its subsequent lodgement with the Land Registry, data for the final quarter of 2001 are not as complete as those for the final quarter of 2000. The table includes all sales registered up to 31 March 2002.

Table 6.10 Mortgage advances, income for mortgage purchases

Figures in this table are taken from the Office of the Deputy Prime Minister's (ODPM) Survey of Mortgage Lenders. This is conducted in partnership with the Council of Mortgage Lenders and has, for most of its thirty-five year history, involved a variety of mortgage lenders supplying a five per cent sample of their completions on a monthly basis. Over the past few years, the number of completions received each month from mortgage lenders has increased significantly with some lenders now supplying all their completions. However, figures in Table 6.10 are taken from the five per cent sample.

First-time buyers include sitting tenant purchases.

Table 6.11 Average weekly rents: by tenure

Figures in this table are the average amounts of rent eligible for Housing Benefit paid by a household, calculated before the deduction of any Housing Benefit but after taking off certain expenses such as service charges and council tax. Individual households where the amount is £nil or less than £nil are all treated as £nil, and included in the calculation of the average.

Table 6.12 Dwellings in Council Tax bands

Council Tax bands in Scotland differ from those in England and Wales. The bands are as follows:

Bands in table 6.12	Scotland	England and Wales
Band A	Under £27,000	Under £40,000
Band B	£27,001-£35,000	£40,001-£52,000
Band C	£35,001-£45,000	£52,001-£68,000
Band D	£45,001-£58,000	£68,001-£88,000
Band E	£58,001-£80,000	£88,00 -£120,000
Band F	£80,001-£106,000	£120,001-£160,000
Band G	£106,001-£212,000	£160,001-£320,000
Band H	Over £212,000	Over £320,000.

Table 6.13 County Court actions for mortgage possessions

The figures do not indicate how many houses have been repossessed through the courts; not all the orders will have resulted in the issue and execution of warrants of possession. The regional breakdown relates to the location of the court rather than the address of the property.

Actions entered: a claimant begins an action for an order of possession of residential property by way of a summons in a county court.

Orders made: the court, following a judicial hearing, may grant an order for possession immediately. This entitles the claimant to apply for a warrant to have the defendant evicted. However, even where a warrant for possession is issued, the parties can still negotiate a compromise to prevent eviction.

Suspended orders: frequently, the court grants the mortgage lender possession but suspends the operation of the order. Provided the defendant complies with the terms of the suspension, which usually require them to pay the current mortgage instalments plus some of the accrued arrears, the possession order cannot be enforced.

Chapter 7: Health and Care

On 1 April 2002 a new organisation was introduced for the National Health Service (NHS) in England, whereby Primary Care Trusts (PCTs) and care groups were created to become the lead NHS organisations in assessing need, planning and securing all health services, and improving health. These care trusts will forge new partnerships with local communities and lead the NHS contribution to joint work with local government and other partners.

In Wales the 5 Health Authorities were replaced by 22 Local Health Boards on 1 April 2003. These are responsible for commissioning, securing and delivering health care in partnership with local authorities and the voluntary sector. Their boundaries are coterminus with Unitary Authorities.

NHS Trusts will continue to provide services, working within delivery agreements with PCTs. Trusts will be expected to devolve greater responsibility to clinical teams and to foster and encourage the growth of clinical networks across NHS organisations. High performing Trusts will earn greater freedoms and autonomy in recognition of their achievements. Primary Care Trusts will be able to secure treatment for their patients from a range of providers who are best suited to deliver.

Twenty-eight Strategic Health Authorities (StHA) have replaced the old ninety-five Health Authorities. These will step back from service planning and commissioning to lead the strategic development of the local health service and performance manage PCTs and NHS Trusts on the basis of local accountability agreements.

The Department of Health will change the way it relates to the NHS, focusing on supporting the delivery of the NHS Plan. Four new Regional Directors of Health and Social Care who will oversee the development of the NHS and provide the link between NHS organisations and the central department have replaced Regional Offices of the Department of Health.

Tables 7.3, 7.11 and 7.12 General Household Survey and Continuous Household Survey

The General Household Survey (GHS) and Continuous Household Survey (CHS) are continuous surveys that have been running since 1971 for the GHS and 1983 for the CHS. They are based each year on samples of the general population resident in private (non-institutional) households in Great Britain and Northern Ireland. As multi-purpose surveys, they provide information on aspects of housing, employment, education, health and social services, health-related behaviour, transport, population and social security. Since 1988, GHS fieldwork has been based on a financial rather than calendar year and as a result data were not collected for the first quarter of 1988.

Tables 7.5 and 7.7 Age-standardised mortality rates

Mortality rates vary with age so the rates for different areas can be affected by the age-structure of their populations. The figures in Tables 7.5 and 7.7 have been adjusted to take into account these differences. The rates have been standardised to the mid-1991 United Kingdom population for males and females

separately. This means it is valid to compare rates across areas for each sex, but not to compare males with females.

The causes of death included in Table 7.5 correspond to International Classification of Diseases (10th Revision) codes (ICD10) as follows:

all circulatory diseases	I00-I99;
ischaemic heart disease	I20-I25;
cerebrovascular disease	I60-I69;
all respiratory diseases	J00-J99;
bronchitis *et al*	J40-J44;
cancer (malignant neoplasms)	C00-C97;
all injuries and poisoning	V01-Y89;
Land Transport	V01-V89;
suicides and open verdicts	X60-X84 and Y10-Y34.

The data in these tables relate to registrations in the reference year.

Table 7.7 Cervical and breast cancer screening

Figures for the two cancer screening programmes are snapshots of the coverage of the target population for each programme at 31 March 2002.

Figures for the Scottish Breast Screening Programme are an estimate of the coverage of the target population in the three-year period: 1 April 1999 to 31 March 2002. These figures are derived from the number of women aged 50 to 54, 55 to 59 and 60 to 64 who have attended a routine screening appointment, or a self/GP referral appointment, during this period and a mid-year estimate of the female population in Scotland aged 50 to 64 in 2000. Medically ineligible women are not excluded from the target population.

Northern Ireland figures for breast screening may include a small number of women who have been counted more than once because of an early recall for screening during the relevant three-year period. The maximum extent of any such double count can be calculated as less than 0.4 per cent. All

population data for Scotland were obtained from the General Register Office for Scotland.

Figure 7.8 Standardised cancer registration rates

Figure 7.8 shows the Standardised Registration Ratios (SRRs) for various cancers in each of the Government Office areas in England. Registrations are to usual region of residence of the patient and relate to 2000, but include registrations notified up to July 2003.

For each cancer, the registration rates in England are taken as standards (with the sexes considered separately). For example, the SSR for cancer of the stomach for the East Midlands was calculated as:

SRR = 100 x No. of registrations of cancer of the stomach in East Midlands

 $\sum_{\text{Age group}}$ [Population in each age group. East Midlands GOR x registration rate for cancer of the stomach for that age, England]

Incidence of cancer registrations are for malignant neoplasms, classified according to the tenth revision of the International Classification of Diseases (ICD10):

Type of cancer:

Stomach	C16	Malignant neoplasm of stomach
Lung	C33-C34	Malignant neoplasm of trachea, bronchus and lung
Breast	C50	Malignant neoplasm of breast
Prostate	C61	Malignant neoplasm of prostate
Skin	C43	Malignant melanoma of skin
Leukaemia	C91-C95	All leukaemias

Three-year average age-standardised registration rates of newly diagnosed cancers per 100,000 population for the United Kingdom and England for 1998-2000 were:

Registration rates 1998-2000 Figure 7.8	United Kingdom		England	
Selected sites	Male	Female	Male	Female
Stomach	18.7	7.3	18.2	6.9
Lung	71.9	36.0	70.1	34.5
Breast	..	113.9	..	114.0
Prostate	73.3	..	73.7	..
Skin	8.9	10.3	8.8	10.3
Leukaemias	11.9	7.2	11.7	7.2

Data obtained from 'Cancer Statistics Registrations 2000'.

Table 7.10 National Food Survey

The National Food Survey (NFS) is a continuous sample survey of about 6,000 households per year in Great Britain keeping a record of the type, quantity and costs of foods entering their homes during a one-week period. From April 2001 these data have been collected as part of the new Expenditure and Food Survey (EFS), see notes to Chapter 8. For further details. A separate annual report on food will continue to be published by the Department for Environment, Food and Rural Affairs (DEFRA).

Nutritional intakes are estimated from the survey data. Recent developments include, from 1996, the participation in the survey of about 700 households in Northern Ireland. From 1994, data are also available on food eaten out in Great Britain (but not Northern Ireland).

Detailed survey results and definitions are published by The Stationery Office in an annual report *National Food Survey*. The edition published in November 2001 (for the data year 2000) was the last one based on data from the National Food Survey (NFS).

Table 7.12 Alcohol consumption

A unit of alcohol is 8 grams of pure alcohol, approximately equivalent to half a pint of ordinary strength beer, a glass of wine, or a pub measure of spirits. *Sensible Drinking*, the 1995 inter-departmental review of scientific and medical evidence on the effects of drinking alcohol, concluded that daily benchmarks were more appropriate than the previously recommended weekly levels. The daily recommendations could help individuals decide how much to drink on single occasions and how to avoid episodes of intoxication with their attendant health and social risks. The report concluded that regular consumption of between three and four units a day for men, and two to three units for women, does not carry a significant health risk. However, consistently drinking more than four units a day for men, or more than three for women, is not advised as a sensible drinking level because of the progressive health risk it carries. The government's advice on sensible drinking is now based on these daily benchmarks.

Figure 7.13 Drug use

Results for England and Wales can be found in Aust, R., Sharp, C. and Goulden, C. (2002) *Prevalence of drug use: key findings from the 2001/2002 British Crime Survey.* London: Home Office.

Table 7.15 NHS hospital waiting lists

The waiting list figures for England are based on the population of the Strategic Health Authority (StHA). That is, they are based on figures received from health authority-based returns and include all patients resident within the StHA boundary plus all patients registered with GPs who are members of a primary care group or trust (PCG/PCT) for which the StHA is responsible, but are resident in another authority. They exclude patients resident in the StHA, but registered with a GP who is a member of a PCG/PCT responsible to a different StHA. Other exclusions are patients living outside England and privately funded patients waiting for treatment in NHS hospitals. However, they do include NHS-funded patients living in England who are waiting for treatment in Scotland, Wales, Northern Ireland, abroad, and at private hospitals who are not included in the corresponding provider-based return.

In Scotland data are collected by trusts for each individual patient waiting for NHS in-patient or day care treatment. Information on Scottish residents waiting outside Scotland is not collected centrally. Average waiting times are calculated from the waiting time associated with each individual patient record.

Figures from Northern Ireland are provider-based. They include all patients waiting for treatment at Northern Ireland Trusts including private patients and patients from outside Northern Ireland.

Mean waiting time. This is an approximate calculation for the total waiting times of patients still on the list divided by the corresponding number of people waiting.

Median waiting time. The waiting time of 50 per cent of those patients admitted from waiting lists will be less than the median length. This is a better indicator of the 'average' case since it is generally unaffected by abnormally long or short waiting times at the end of the distribution.

Table 7.16 NHS hospital activity

Data for England are based on finished consultant episodes (FCEs). FCE is a completed period of care of a patient using a NHS hospital bed, under one consultant within one healthcare provider. If a patient is transferred from one consultant to another, even if this is within the same provider unit, the episode ends and another one begins. The transfer of a patient from one hospital to another with the same consultant and within the same NHS Trust does not end the episode. Data for Wales are based on discharges and deaths. Data for Scotland and Northern Ireland are based on a system where transfers between consultants do not count as a discharge. Although in Scotland figures include patients transferred from one consultant to another within the same hospital – provided there is a change of speciality (or significant facilities eg a change of ward) – but transfers from one hospital to another with the same consultant count as a discharge. New-born babies are included for Northern Ireland but excluded from England, Wales and Scotland. Deaths in hospitals are included in all four.

For Scotland, figures include NHS beds/activity in joint-user and contractual hospitals; these hospitals account for a relatively small proportion of total NHS activity.

A day case is a patient who comes for investigation, treatment or operation under clinical supervision on a planned non-resident basis, who occupies a bed for part or all of that day, and returns home the same day. Scottish figures also include day cases that have been transferred to or from in-patient care.

An outpatient is a non-resident of a hospital seen by a consultant for treatment or advice at a clinical outpatient department. A new outpatient is one whose first attendance (or only attendance) is part of a continuous series for the same course of treatment falling within the period in question. Each outpatient attendance of a series is included in the year the attendance occurred. People attending more than one department are counted in each department.

In Northern Ireland, the outpatient figures are separated into referrals and consultant-initiated attendances. It is possible for a first attendance to be initiated by a consultant. The number of attendances in 'new attendances' refers to referrals only, and therefore may not include all new attendances. (referrals can include self-referrals and requests from other consultants or from staff in Accident and Emergency Departments).

Mean duration of stay is calculated as the total bed-days divided by the number of ordinary admissions (finished consultant episodes in England and Wales, in-patient discharges (including transfers) in Scotland, and deaths and discharges in Northern Ireland). An ordinary admission is one where the patient is expected to remain in hospital for at least one night. Scottish figures exclude patients with learning disabilities and those requiring non-psychiatric specialities. Population figures are based on estimates for 1999 Health Authorities for people of all ages.

For Northern Ireland, mid-year population estimates for 2000 have been used. It should be noted that where figures are presented to the nearest whole number, this is to facilitate the calculation of rates and the aggregation of age bands. Cases treated per available bed are for ordinary admissions (in-patient discharges including transfers in Scotland) and do not include day case admissions.

Table 7.17 NHS hospital and community health service directly employed staff

General medical practitioners (i.e. family GPs), general dental practitioners, the staff employed by the practitioners, pharmacists in general pharmaceutical services and staff working in other contracted out services are not included in the figures. Medical and dental staff that are included are those holding permanent, paid (whole-time, part-time, sessional) and/or honorary appointments in NHS hospitals and Community Health services. Figures include clinical assistants and hospital practitioners. Bank staff maintain service delivery by covering staffing shortfalls and fluctuating workloads and, as a consequence their input to the service is difficult to measure.

Previously there has been much confusion over non-medical staff groups. To address this issue the health service have now classified the staff into three key areas:

1. Clinical staff – professionally qualified staff treating patients

2. Support to Clinical Staff – staff providing direct support to clinical staff, often with direct patient care, who free up the time of clinical staff allowing them more time to treat patients

3. Staff supporting NHS infrastructure - staff essential to the day-to-day running of the organisations

Unqualified and trainee nurses, health professionals and scientific staff are included under 'Support to clinical staff' as are ambulance staff. Formerly all ambulance, paramedics and support workers, were included in figures for other management and support staff.

Occasional sessional staff in Community Health medical and dental services for whom no whole-time equivalent is collected are not included. Nursing, midwifery and health visiting staff included healthcare assistants, and excluded nurse teachers and students on '1992' courses. Scientific, therapeutic and technical staff comprises scientific and professional and technical staff incorporating PAMs. Administration and estates comprise administration and clerical, senior managers and works staff. Other staff are ancillary, ambulance staff and support staff. All direct care staff are in medical and dental; nursing, midwifery and health visiting; and scientific, therapeutic and technical groups.

Table 7.18 General practitioners and dentists
The figures for general medical practitioners (GPs) include unrestricted principals and equivalents (UPEs), personal medical service (PMS) contracted GPs and PMS salaried GPs. An unrestricted principal is a practitioner who provides the full range of general medical services and whose list is not limited to any particular group of people. In a few cases, they may be relieved of the liability for emergency out-of-hours calls from patients that are not their own. Most people have an unrestricted principal as their GP. Doctors may

also practice in the general medical services as restricted principals, assistants, associated or GP registrars.

A PMS contracted doctor is a practitioner who provides the full range of services through the PMS pilot contract and like unrestricted principals they have a patient list. A PMS salaried doctor is employed to work in a PMS pilot, provides the full range of services and has a list of registered patients.

Other types of general medical practitioners include GP retainers, restricted principals, assistants, associates (Scotland only), GP registrars, salaried doctors (para 52 SFA) and PMS other.

The figures for general dental practitioners include principals, assistants and vocational dental practitioners in the general dental service. Salaried dentists are excluded. Some dentists have contracts in more than one health authority. These dentists have been counted only once in the authority in which they hold their main contract. Neither the hospital dental service nor the community dental services are included. All Scottish data are provisional.

Table 7.19 Council supported residents.
The figures for England relate to the number of residents who are supported (funded) by Councils with Social Services Responsibilities (CSSR) in residential, independent nursing and other unstaffed homes. They include residential places.

Chapter 8: Income and Lifestyles

Tables 8.1, 8.2, 8.11, 8.12, 8.13, 8.14 and figures 8.9, 8.10, 8.15, 8.18 and 8.20 Expenditure and Food Survey
In April 2001 the Expenditure and Food Survey (EFS) replaced the Family Expenditure Survey (FES) and the National Food Survey (NFS). The EFS is being coded to a new set of expenditure codes based on the United Nations and European classification of consumer goods and services, Classification by Individual Consumption by Purpose (COICOP). The EFS is a continuous survey conducted by the Office for National Statistics. Three year averages have been used wherever possible due to volatility of the data. However, because of changes in coding with the EFS, a number of tables present only one year's data.

The Family Expenditure Survey (FES) was a continuous, random sample survey of private households in the United Kingdom and collected information about incomes as well as detailed information on expenditure. All members of the household aged 16 or over kept individual diaries of all spending for two weeks. Over the three surveys, held between 1998/99 and 2000/01, a combined total of 20,364 households took part. See the FES

annual report, *Family Spending*, for a description of the concepts used and details of the definitions of expenditure and income.

The National Food Survey (NFS) was a continuous sample survey in which about 6,000 households per year in Great Britain kept a record of the type, quantity and costs of foods entering the home during a one-week period. Nutrient intakes were estimated from the information collected. Data from the NFS have been presented using calendar years. Recent developments included, from 1996, the participation in the survey of about 700 households in Northern Ireland (though figures quoted in this report and elsewhere still generally cover GB for the sake of continuity). From 1994 data were also available on food eaten out in Great Britain (but not Northern Ireland), although these are not included in this report to maintain continuity. The last NFS data available are for 2000. The 2000/01 figures use NFS data that has been adjusted to match the EFS.

Table 8.3 Measure of income
The measure of income used in compiling Table 8.3 is that used in the Department for Work and Pensions, *Households Below Average Income* series which is derived from the Family Resources Survey. The income of a household, before housing costs, is defined as the total income of all members of the household after the deduction of income tax, National Insurance contributions, contributions to occupational pension schemes, additional voluntary contributions to personal pensions, maintenance/child support payments, parental contributions to students living away from home and Council Tax.

Income includes earnings from employment and self-employment, social security benefits including housing benefit and tax credits, occupational and private pensions, investment income, maintenance payments, educational grants, scholarships and top-up loans and some in-kind benefits such as luncheon vouchers. Income after housing costs is derived by deducting a measure of housing costs from the above income. This includes rent, water rates, mortgage interest payments (net of tax relief) structural insurance premiums, ground rent and service charges.

No adjustment has been made in Table 8.3 for any differences between regions in cost of living, as the necessary data for adjustment are not available. In the analysis of regions it is therefore assumed that there is no difference in the cost of living between regions, although the 'after housing costs' measure will partly take into account differences in housing costs. As this assumption is unlikely to be true, statements have been sensitivity tested where possible against alternative cost of living regimes. Results suggest that estimates of income before housing costs are not sensitive to regional price differentials, but results after housing costs are. In particular, for London and to a lesser extent the South West, living standards may be overstated, and in Wales, the North East, and in Yorkshire and the Humber living standards may be understated.

Income is adjusted for household size and composition by means of the McClements equivalence scale (see below). This reflects the common sense notion that a household of five will need a higher income than a single person living alone in order to enjoy a comparable standard of living. The total equivalised income of a household is used to represent the income level of every individual in that household; all individuals are then ranked according to this level.

McClement's equivalence scale

	Before housing costs	After housing costs
Household member:		
First adult (head)	0.61	0.55
Spouse of head	0.39	0.45
Other second adult	0.46	0.45
Third adult	0.42	0.45
Subsequent adults	0.36	0.40
Each dependent aged:		
0 to 1	0.09	0.07
2 to 4	0.18	0.18
5 to 7	0.21	0.21
8 to 10	0.23	0.23
11 to 12	0.25	0.26
13 to 15	0.27	0.28
16 or over	0.36	0.38

Tables 8.4 and 8.8 Family Resources Survey

The Family Resources Survey (FRS) is a continuous survey of approximately 25,000 private households in Great Britain and is sponsored by the Department for Work and Pensions. The estimates are based on sample counts that have been adjusted for non-response using multi-purpose grossing factors that control for tenure type, council tax band and a number of demographic variables. Estimates are subject to sampling error and to variability in non-response.

The overall response rate was 66 per cent for 2001/02 but varied regionally. Benefit receipt is based on self-assessment and therefore may be subject to mis-reporting.

Table 8.5 and figure 8.6 Survey of Personal Incomes

The Survey of Personal Incomes uses a sample of around 200,000 cases drawn from all individuals for whom income tax records are

held by the Inland Revenue. Not all cases in the sample are taxpayers - about 15 per cent do not pay tax because the operation of personal allowances and reliefs removes them from liability. The data in Table 8.5 relate to individuals who have a liability to tax by having income greater than the single person's allowance (£4,385 in 2000/01). Below this threshold, coverage of incomes is incomplete in tax records. A more complete description of the survey appears on the Inland Revenue's website (http://www.inlandrevenue.gov.uk/).

Table 8.5 Distribution of income liable to assessment for tax

The income shown is that which is liable to assessment in the tax year. In most cases, this is the amount earned or receivable in that year, but for business profits and professional earnings the assessments are normally based on the amount of income arising in the trading account ending in the previous year. Those types of income that were specifically exempt from tax, eg certain social security benefits are excluded.

Income is allocated throughout the UK according to the place of residence of the recipient, except for the self-employed, where allocation is according to the business address. For many self-employed people their home is their business address.

The table classifies incomes by range of total income. This is defined as gross income, whether earned or unearned and includes estimates of employees' superannuation contributions after deducting employment expenses, losses, capital allowances, and any expenses allowable as a deduction from gross income from lettings or overseas investment income.

Superannuation contributions have been estimated and distributed among earners in the Survey of Personal Incomes consistently with information about numbers contracted in or out of the State Earnings Related Pension Scheme and the proportion of their earnings contribution. The coverage of unearned income also includes estimates of that part of the investment income (whose liability to tax at basic rate has been satisfied at source) not known to tax offices. Sampling errors should be allowed for when interpreting small differences in income distributions between regions.

Figure 8.6 Average total income and average income tax payable

Income tax is calculated as the liability for the income tax year, regardless of when the tax may have been paid or how it was collected. The income tax liability shown here is calculated from the individual's total income, including tax credits on dividends, and interest received after the deduction of tax grossed up at the appropriate rate. Allowable

reliefs etc, and personal allowances are deducted from total income in order to calculate the tax liability. However, relief given at source on mortgage interest is not deducted, as it cannot be estimated with sufficient reliability below a national level. The average of total incomes for males and females by Government Office Region are based on all individuals with total income in excess of the single person's allowance, which was £4,385 in 2000/01. The average income tax payable for males and females by Government Office Region are based on those individuals who are liable to tax.

Figures for United Kingdom include members of HM Forces and others who are liable to some UK tax but reside overseas on a long-term basis. In addition, the United Kingdom total includes a very small number of individuals who could not be allocated to a region.

Table 8.8 Households in receipt of benefit

Income support is a non-contributory benefit payable to people working less than 16 hours a week, whose incomes are below the levels (called 'applicable amounts') laid down by Parliament. The applicable amounts generally consist of personal allowances for members of the family and premiums for families, lone parents, pensioners, the disabled and carers. Amounts for certain housing costs (mainly mortgage interest) are also included. Local authorities administer housing benefit; people are eligible only if they are liable to pay rent in respect of the dwelling they occupy as their home. Couples are treated as a single benefit unit. The amount of benefit depends on eligible rent, income, deductions in respect of non-dependants and the applicable amount. 'Eligible rent' is the amount of a tenant's rental liability, which can be met by housing benefit. Payments made by owner-occupiers do not count. Deductions are made for service charged on rent that relates to personal needs.

Local authorities also administer council tax benefit. Generally, it mirrors the housing benefit scheme in the calculation of the claimant's applicable amount, resources and deductions in respect of any non-dependants.

Jobseeker's allowance (JSA) replaced unemployment benefit and income support for unemployed people on 7 October 1996. It is payable to people under pensionable age who are available for, and actively seeking, work of at least 40 hours per week. Certain groups of people, including carers, are able to restrict their availability to less than 40 hours depending on their circumstances. There are contribution-based and income-based routes of entry to JSA. Both types of JSA are included under the 'jobseeker's allowance' column of the table.

Retirement pensions are paid to men aged 65 or over and women aged 60 or over who have paid sufficient National Insurance contributions over their working life. A wife who cannot claim a pension in her own right may qualify on the basis of her husband's contributions. Incapacity benefit replaced sickness and invalidity benefits from 13 April 1995. It is paid to people who are assessed as being incapable of work and who meet the contribution conditions. The figures do not include expenditure for Statutory Sick Pay (SSP).

Industrial injuries include pensions, gratuities and sundry allowances for disablement and specified deaths arising from industrial causes.

Child benefit is normally paid in respect of children up to the age of 16. Benefit may continue up to age 19 for children in full-time education up to 'A' level standard; 16-and-17-year-olds are also eligible for a short period after leaving school.

A brief description of the main features of the various benefits paid in Great Britain is set out in *Social Security Statistics* (published annually by Department for Work and Pensions). Detailed information on benefits paid in Northern Ireland is contained in *Northern Ireland Annual Abstract of Statistics* and *Northern Ireland* Social *Security Statistics*.

Figure 8.10 Children's spending
The data for 1999-2002 are not directly comparable to the previous three year averages. The previous spending figures included money spent on school dinners, and on fares to and from school but money spent directly by the parent on these items is excluded. The current data are £ per child per week solely attributable to children aged 7 to 15 years living in households.

Figures 8.9 and 8.18 and table 8.11 Household expenditure
Expenditure excludes savings or investments (eg life assurance premiums), income tax payments, National Insurance contributions and the part of rent paid by housing benefit. Housing expenditure of households living in owner-occupied dwellings consists of the payments by these households for Council Tax (rates in Northern Ireland), water, ground rent, etc, insurance of the structure and mortgage interest payments. Mortgage capital repayments and amounts paid for the outright purchase of the dwelling or for major structural alterations are not included as housing expenditure.

Estimates of household expenditure on a few items are below those which might be expected by comparison with other sources eg. alcoholic drink, tobacco and, to a lesser extent, confectionery and ice cream.

Table 8.16 UK 2000 Time Use Survey
The survey had new weights, based on the 2001 Census information, applied in June

2003 and this together with improved guidelines on the diary quality to be used in analysis has resulted in minor changes to previously released data.

The results shown in table 8.16 are for combined primary and secondary (i.e. where respondents were doing two things at the same time) activities. This has been done because TV viewing, radio and music listening and reading often happen at the same time as another activity (for example reading on the train) and to get a true measure of the time spent in these activities it is sensible to look at the total time. The other activities in this table have almost no secondary time (i.e. they are usually done as a single activity).

Table 8.21 The National Lottery Grants
Up to the end of 2002, National Lottery grants included 5,211 grants worth £1,215 million made throughout the UK or to institutions of national significance. They include 1,946 grants worth £22 million allocated to specific areas within Great Britain. A further 644 grants worth £134 million were made overseas.

Chapter 9: Crime and Justice

Tables 9.1, 9.4, 9.5, 9.8, 9.9, and 9.10 Offences
Figures are compiled from police returns to the Home Office or directly from court computer systems; from police returns to the Scottish Executive Justice Department and from statistics supplied by the Police Service of Northern Ireland.

Recorded crime statistics broadly cover the more serious offences. Up to March 1998 most indictable and triable-either-way offences were included, as well as some summary ones; from April 1998, all indictable and triable-either-way offences were included, plus a few closely related summary ones. Recorded offences are the most readily available measures of the incidence of crime, but do not necessarily indicate the true level of crime. Many less serious offences are not reported to the police and cannot therefore be recorded while some offences are not recorded due to lack of evidence. Moreover, the propensity of the public to report offences to the police is influenced by a number of factors and may change over time.

In England, Wales and Northern Ireland, indictable offences cover those offences which must or may be tried by jury in the Crown Court and include the more serious offences. Summary offences are those for which a defendant would normally be tried at a magistrates' court and are generally less serious; the majority of motoring offences fall into this category. In general in Northern Ireland non-indictable offences are dealt with at a magistrates' court. Some indictable offences can also be dealt with there.

England and Wales
In England and Wales, Home Office counting rules for recorded crime were revised with effect from 1 April 2002, principally to take account of the National Crime Recording Standard (NCRS) which was produced by the Association of Chief Police Officers (ACPO) in consultation with the Home Office. The Standard aims to promote greater consistency between police forces in recording crime and to take a more victim orientated approach to crime recording. The national picture for total crime in England and Wales demonstrates an overall NCRS impact of 10 per cent on the recorded crime statistics for 2002/03. Crimes counted in 2002/03 were 10 per cent higher than they would have been under the pre-NCRS recording reflecting the change in recording practice, rather than a real increase in crime. Estimates of the percentage impact of the NCRS on recorded crime vary considerably between offence types: violence against the person (23 per cent), robbery (3 per cent), all theft (9 per cent), criminal damage (9 per cent).

The revisions will significantly increase the numbers of crimes in the recorded crime count and were introduced across all police forces from April 2002. Some police forces implemented the principles of the standard in advance of this date, and this will have had some effect on the recorded crime statistics reported here. There has also been a more general impetus over recent years both from the Association of Chief Police Officers (ACPO) and from the Home Office to increase the recording of crimes reported to the police, and this will also have impacted on the recorded crime figures. As with the 1998 counting rule changes, it may take several years for the changes to bed down.

In Scotland the term 'crimes' is generally used for the more serious criminal acts (roughly equivalent to indictable offences); less serious are termed 'offences'. In general, the procurator fiscal makes the decision as to which court a case should be tried in or, for lesser offences, whether alternatives to prosecution such as a fixed penalty might be considered. Certain crimes, such as rape and murder, must be tried by a jury in the High Court; cases can also be tried by jury in the Sheriff Court. The majority of cases (97 per cent) are tried summarily (without a jury), either in the Sheriff Court or in the lay District Court.

Cautions
If a person admits to committing an offence he may be given a formal police caution by, or on the instruction of, a senior police officer as an alternative to court proceedings. The figures exclude informal warnings given by the police, written warnings issued for motoring offences and warnings given by non-police bodies, eg a department store in the case of shoplifting. Cautions by the police

are not available in Scotland, but warnings may be issued on behalf of the Procurator Fiscal.

Tables 9.3 and 9.13 Crime Surveys

The British Crime Survey (BCS) was conducted by the Home Office in 1982, 1984, 1988, 1992, 1994, 1996, 1998 and 2000, and annually on a continuous basis from 2001. From 2001/02 the survey has measured crimes experienced by respondents in the 12 months prior to their interview including those not reported to the police. The survey also covers other matters of Home Office interest including fear of crime, contacts with the police, and drug misuse. The 2002/03 survey had a nationally representative sample of 36,479 respondents in England and Wales with an additional 2,827 ethnic boost sample. The sample was drawn from the Small User Postcode Address File - a listing of all postal delivery points. The response rate in the core sample was 74 per cent. The first results from the 2002/03 sweep of the BCS were published in July 2003.

Scotland participated in sweeps of the BCS in 1982 and 1988 and ran its own Scottish Crime Surveys in 1993, 1996 and 2000 based on nationally representative samples of around 5,000 respondents aged 16 and over interviewed in their homes. In addition around 400 young people aged between 12 and 15 completed questionnaires in each of the surveys. The sample was drawn from addresses randomly generated from the Postcode Address file. Both the 1993 and 1996 surveys had response rates of 77 per cent and the 2000 survey had a response rate of 72 per cent. The results of the 2000 Scottish Crime Survey were published in spring 2002.

The Northern Ireland Crime Survey (NICS) was conducted on behalf of the Northern Ireland Office (NIO) in 1994/95, 1998 and 2001. Closely mirroring the format and questions of the BCS, the fieldwork for NICS 2001 was conducted between August 2001 and January 2002, with a recall period of 1 September 2000 to 31 August 2001. 3,010 people aged 16 years and above participated in the survey. Their addresses were randomly sampled from the Valuation and Lands Agency domestic property database. The response rate was approximately 70 per cent.

In each of the surveys, respondents answered questions about offences against their household (such as theft or damage of household property) and about offences against them personally (such as assault or robbery). However, none of the surveys provides a complete count of crime. Many offence types cannot be covered in a household victim oriented survey (for example shop lifting, fraud or drug offences). Crime surveys are also prone to various forms of error, mainly to do with the difficulty of ensuring that samples are representative, the

frailty of respondents' memories, their reticence to talk about their experiences as victims, and their failure to realise an incident is relevant to the survey.

Table 9.4 Detection rates

In England, Wales and Northern Ireland detected offences recorded by the police include offences for which individuals have been charged, summonsed or cautioned; those admitted and taken into consideration when individuals are tried for other offences, and others where the police can take no action for various reasons. In Scotland a revised definition of 'cleared up' came into effect from 1 April 1996. Under the revised definition a crime or offence is regarded as cleared up where there is sufficient evidence under Scots Law to justify consideration of criminal proceedings not withstanding that a report is not submitted to the procurator fiscal because either:

a) by standing agreement with the procurator fiscal, the police warn the accused due to the minor nature of the offence, or

b) reporting is inappropriate due to the age of the accused, death of the accused or other similar circumstances.

The detection rate is the ratio of offences cleared up in the year to offences recorded in the year. Some offences detected may relate to offences recorded in previous years. There is some variation between police forces in the emphasis placed on certain of the methods listed above and, as some methods are more resource intensive than others, this can have a significant effect on a force's overall detection rate.

In April 1999, there was a change in the way detections are counted, with some circumstances no longer qualifying as detections. The new instructions provide more precise and rigorous criteria for recording a detection, with the underlying emphasis on the successful result of a police investigation. The most significant of these criteria is that there must be significant evidence to charge the suspect with a crime (whether or not a charge is actually imposed) so that, if given in court, it would be likely to result in a conviction. Detections obtained by the interview of a convicted prisoner are no longer included, and any detections where no further police action is taken generally have to be approved by a senior police officer or the Crown Prosecution Service. An offence is said to be cleared up in the following circumstances:

- a person has been charged or summonsed for the offence.

- a person has been cautioned.

- the offence has been taken into consideration (TIC) by the court.

or where no further action is taken and the case is not proceeded with because, for example, the offender is under the age of criminal responsibility, the offender has died, because the victim or an essential witness is permanently unable to give evidence, or no useful purpose would be served by proceeding with the charge.

With the effect of the National Crime Recording Standard (NCRS), the detection rate in 2002/03 was 23.5 per cent, slightly higher than the rate in 2001/02 (23.4 per cent). However, the full introduction of the NCRS in April 2002 may have depressed the current detection rate. Precise quantification is not possible, but on a comparable basis to the pre-NCRS crime count, the detection rate in 2002/03 is estimated to have been between 24 and 26 per cent.

Table 9.6 Seizures of controlled drugs

The figures in this table, which are compiled from returns to the Home Office, relate to seizures made by the police and officials of HM Customs and Excise, and to drugs controlled under the *Misuse of Drugs Act 1971*. The Act divides drugs into three main categories according to their harmfulness. A full list of drugs in each category is given in Schedule 2 to the *Misuse of Drugs Act 1971*, as amended by Orders in Council.

Table 9.10 People found guilty of offences

In England, Wales and Northern Ireland the term 'suspended sentence' is known as 'fully suspended sentence' and 'immediate custody' includes unsuspended sentences of imprisonment and sentence to detention in a young offender institution. Fully suspended sentences are not available to Scottish courts.

Tables 9.11 and 9.12 Sentencing and prison population

Imprisonment: is the custodial sentence for adult offenders. The *Criminal Justice Act 1991* abolished remission and substantially changed the parole scheme in England and Wales.

Those serving sentences of under four years, imposed on or after 1 October 1992, are subject to automatic conditional release and are released, subject to certain criteria, halfway through their sentence.

Home detention curfews result in selected prisoners in England and Wales being released up to two months early with a tag that monitors their presence during curfew hours. Those serving sentences of four years or longer are considered for discretionary conditional release after having served half their sentence, but are automatically released at the two-thirds point of sentence.

The *Crime (Sentences) Act 1997* implemented on 1 October 1997 included for people aged 18 and over sentenced in England and Wales automatic life sentences for second serious violent or sexual offences unless circumstances are exceptional. All offenders sentenced in England and Wales to a sentence of 12 months or more are supervised in the community until the three-quarter point of sentence.

In Scotland, the release of prisoners sentenced after 1 October 1993 is governed by the *Prisoners and Criminal Proceedings (Scotland) Act 1993*. Under the 1993 Act prisoners serving determinate sentences of less than four years are released unconditionally after having served half of their sentence. Those serving sentences of four years or more (i.e. long-term sentences) are eligible for parole at half sentence. If parole is not granted then they will automatically be released on licence at the two-thirds point of sentence, subject to any additional days for breaches of prison rules. The licence remains in force until the entire period specified in the sentence expires.

In addition, there is provision under the *Crime and Disorder Act 1998* for courts to impose additional post-release supervision (known as an extended sentence) of up to 10 years for sex offenders, and 5 years for violent offenders who have received a long-term sentence. During the period of extended sentence, the offender must comply with licence conditions. Extended sentences can also be imposed for sex offenders who received a short-term custodial sentence. Similarly, the court has a power to impose a supervised release order for those who received a short-term sentence for a violent offence, which ensures social work supervision for a period following release. Where a prisoner, released from a long-term sentence, fails to comply with the terms of his licence there are options available to the Courts and to Scottish Ministers for dealing with reports of a breach of licence. One of these is to revoke the licence and order the prisoners' return or recall to custody. This may mean the prisoner being detained until the sentence expiry date. A life sentence prisoner sentenced in Scotland may be released on licence subject to supervision and is always liable to recall.

Disposals for mentally disordered offenders: various hospital, community and custodial disposals are available to the courts. In some cases a hospital order, which sends the offender to hospital until such time as treatment is no longer required, may be appropriate.

A hospital order may be combined with a restriction order for offenders who pose a risk to the public, in which case Home Office or Scottish Ministers' consent is needed for release or transfer. A new disposal, the 'hospital direction', was introduced in 1997. The court, when imposing a period of imprisonment, can direct that the offender be sent initially to hospital for treatment. Upon

recovery from the mental disorder, the offender is sent to prison to serve the balance of his or her sentence.

Fully suspended sentences: may only be passed in exceptional circumstances. In England, Wales and Northern Ireland, sentences of imprisonment of two years or less may be fully suspended. A court should not pass a suspended sentence unless a sentence of imprisonment would be appropriate in the absence of a power to suspend. The result of suspending a sentence is that it will not take effect, unless during the period specified the offender is convicted of another offence punishable with imprisonment. Suspended sentences are not available in Scotland.

Fines: The *Criminal Justice Act 1993* introduced new arrangements on 20 September 1993 whereby courts are now required to fit an amount for the fine which reflects the seriousness of the offence, but which also takes account of an offender's means. This system replaced the more formal unit fines scheme included in the *Criminal Justice Act 1991*. The Act also introduced the power for courts to arrange deduction of fines from income benefit for those offenders receiving such benefits. The *Law Reform (Miscellaneous Provision) (Scotland) Act 1990* as amended by the *Criminal Procedure (Scotland) Act 1995* provides for the use of supervised attendance orders by selected courts in Scotland. The *Criminal Procedure (Scotland) Act 1995* also makes it easier for courts to impose a supervised attendance order in the event of a default and enables the court to impose a supervised attendance order in the first instance for 16-and-17-year-olds.

Custody Probation Order: an order introduced uniquely to Northern Ireland by the *Criminal Justice (Northern Ireland) Order 1996*. It reflects the different regime which applies in respect of remission and the general absence of release on licence. The custodial sentence is followed by a period of supervision for a period of between twelve months and three years.

Chapter 10: Transport

Table 10.3 Age of household cars
The main or only car available to the household applies to the vehicle with the greatest annual mileage. In the majority of cases this will be the newest car.

Tables 10.3, 10.6 and 10.10 and figures 10.4, 10.7 and 10.8 National Travel Survey
The National Travel Survey (NTS) is the only comprehensive national source of travel information for Great Britain that links different kinds of travel with the characteristics of travellers and their families.

The 1985/86 survey ran from July 1985 to June 1986 and collected data successfully from 10,266 households.

Since July 1988, the NTS has been conducted on a small-scale continuous basis with an annual sample about one-third the size of the 1985/86 survey. Data from the continuous survey are normally aggregated into three-year blocks for publication. From about 3,400 households in Great Britain each year, every member provides personal information (for example, age, sex, working status, driving licence, season ticket) and details of journeys carried out in a sample week, including purpose of journey, method of travel, time of day, length, duration and cost of any tickets bought.

Travel included in the NTS covers all journeys by British residents (living in private households) within Great Britain for personal reasons, including travel in the course of work, (for example, a doctor on their rounds or a businessman travelling to a meeting). It does not include journeys made by people whose work is to travel (such as bus drivers, postmen and deliverymen).

Most personal travel over 50 yards is included, including walking. However, to reduce the burden on respondents, short walks of less than a mile are only recorded on the last day of the diary. These walks are grossed up by a factor of 7 when publishing data.

In the NTS a trip is defined as a one-way course of travel having a single main purpose. It is the basic unit of personal travel in the survey. A round journey is split into two trips, with the first ending at a convenient point about halfway round as a notional stopping point for the outward destination. A stage is that portion of a journey defined by the use of a specific method of transport or of a specific ticket (a new stage being defined if either the mode or ticket changes).

The purpose of a trip is normally taken to be the activity at the destination, unless that destination is 'home' in which case the purpose is defined by the origin of the trip. The classification of 'trips to work' is also dependent on the origin of the trip. A trip cannot have two separate purposes, but trivial subsidiary purposes (such as a stop to buy a newspaper) are disregarded.

The main mode used for trips is that which is used for the longest stage of the trip (by length), the mode is that used for a stage within a trip. The definition of a 'trip' is not the same as a 'journey'

The following purposes are distinguished:

Commuting:
Trips to a usual place of work from home, or from work to home.

Business:
Trips in the course of work, including a trip in the course of work which is returning to work. This includes all work trips by people with no usual place of work (eg site workers) and those who work at or from home.

Education:
Trips to school or college, etc. by full-time students, students on day release and part-time students following vocational courses.

Shopping:
All trips to shops or from shops to home, even when there is no intention to buy.

Personal Business:
Visits to services, for example hairdressers, launderettes, dry-cleaners, betting shops, solicitors, banks, estate agents, libraries, churches; or for medical consultations or treatment, or for eating and drinking unless the main purpose is entertainment or social.

Leisure:
Travel for leisure purposes is normally included. However, journeys which are themselves a form of recreation are not. Travel by foot away from the public highway is excluded unless both the surface is paved or tarred and there is unrestricted access. Thus walks across open countryside on unsurfaced paths are excluded; and so are walks in pedestrian precincts or parks that are closed at night.

Tables 10.13, 10.14 and 10.15 Roads
Major roads: motorways and A roads.

Principal roads: important regional or local roads for which local authorities are the Highway Authorities (non-trunk A roads).

A Roads: trunk and principal roads (excluding motorways).

Minor roads: comprise of B, C and unclassified roads.

Department for Transport have introduced an Urban/Rural classification for roads, which replaces the previously used 'Built-up' and 'Non-built up' categories. This change in definition means that data for 2002 can not be compared with earlier years.

Definitions used in Regional Trends 38

Urban Roads: major and minor roads within an urban area with a population of 10,000 or more.

Rural Roads: major roads and minor roads outside urban areas having a population of less than 10,000.

Previous categories:

Built-up roads: all those having a speed limit of 40 mph or less (irrespective of whether there are buildings or not).

Non built-up roads: all those with a speed limit in excess of 40 mph.

The previous categorisation created difficulties in producing meaningful disaggregated traffic estimates because an increasing number of clearly rural roads were subject to a 40mph speed limit for safety reasons. The urban/rural split of roads is largely determined by whether roads lie within the boundaries of urban areas with a population of 10,000 or more with adjustments in some cases for major roads at the boundary.

Tables 10.13 and figure 10.14 Traffic flow
The figures for 1993 to 2002 have been calculated on a different basis from years prior to 1993. Therefore, figures prior to 1993 are not directly comparable with estimates for later years. Estimates on the new basis for 1993 and subsequent years were first published by the Department for Transport in May 2003 in *Traffic in Great Britain Q1 2003 SB(03)6*.

In summary the main methodological changes that have taken place over the last couple of years are:

Traffic estimates are now disaggregated for roads in urban and rural areas rather than between built-up and non built-up roads. See definitions above. Allocation of data to specific categories of roads in this publication is provisional as definitions of urban and rural had not been finalised at time of compilation.

Traffic estimates are based on the results of many 12-hour manual counts in every year which are grossed-up to estimates of annual average daily flows using expansion factors based on data from automatic traffic counters on similar roads. These averages are needed so that traffic in off-peak times, at weekends and in the summer and winter months (when only special counts are undertaken) can be taken into account when assessing the traffic at each site. For this purpose roads are now sorted into 22 groupings (previously there were only 7) and this allows a better match of manual count sites with automatic count sites. These groupings are based on a detailed analyses of the results from all the individual automatic count sites and take into account groupings below a national level, road category (i.e. both the urban/rural classification of the road and the road class) and traffic flow levels. The groupings range from lightly trafficked, rural minor roads in holiday areas such as Cornwall and Devon to major roads in Central London.

Tables 10.5, 10.7 and 10.9 The Labour Force Survey
The Labour Force Survey (LFS) is a quarterly sample survey of households living at private addresses in Great Britain. The LFS is a large sample survey in which around 10,000 people aged 16 and over are interviewed each week.

Its purpose is to provide information on the UK labour market that can then be used to develop, manage, evaluate and report on labour market policies.

The survey seeks information on respondents' personal circumstances and their labour market status during a specific reference period, normally a period of one week or four weeks (depending on the topic) immediately prior to the interview. For further details of the Labour Force Survey consult notes to Chapter 5.

Tables 10.15 to 10.17 Road accidents
An accident is one involving personal injury occurring on the public highway (including footways) in which a road vehicle is involved and which becomes known to the police within 30 days. The vehicle need not be moving and it need not be in collision with anything. Individuals killed are those who sustained injuries which caused death less than 30 days after the incident.

A serious injury is one for which a person is detained in hospital as an in-patient, or sustains any of the following injuries whether or not they are detained in hospital: fractures, concussion, internal injuries, crushing, severe cuts and lacerations, severe general shock requiring medical treatment, or injuries causing death 30 or more days after the accident. There are many reasons why accident rates per head of population (for all roads) and per 100 million vehicle kilometres (for major roads) vary from one area to another including the mix of pedestrian and vehicle traffic, and the considerable differences in vehicle ownership. In addition, an area that 'imports' large numbers of visitors or commuters will have a relatively high proportion of accidents related to vehicles or drivers from outside the area. A rural area of low population density but high road mileage can be expected, other things being equal, to have lower than average accident rates.

Table 10.19 Seaports
The Coastal regions are defined as:

East Coast – Orkneys to Harwich inclusive;

Thames and Kent – Colchester to Folkstone inclusive;

South Coast – Newhaven to Lands End;

West Coast – Lands End to Stornoway.

Chapter 11: Environment

Tables 11.1, 11.5 to 11.9 The Environment Agency
The Environment Agency for England and Wales was formally created on 8 August 1995 by the *Environment Act 1995*. It took up its statutory duties on 1 April 1996. The Agency brings together the functions

previously carried out by the National Rivers Authority, Her Majesty's Inspectorate of Pollution, the waste regulatory functions of 83 local authorities and a small number of units from the then Department of the Environment dealing with the aspects of waste regulation and contaminated land. One of the key reasons for setting up the Agency was to promote a more coherent and integrated approach to environmental management.

Table 11.6 Rivers and canals: by chemical quality

The chemical quality of rivers and canal waters in the United Kingdom is monitored in a series of separate national surveys in England and Wales, Scotland and Northern Ireland. In England and Wales the National Rivers Authority (now superseded by the Environment Agency) developed and introduced the General Quality Assessment (GQA) scheme to provide a rigorous and objective method for assessing the basic chemical quality of rivers and canals based on three determinands: dissolved oxygen, biochemical oxygen demand (BOD) and ammoniacal nitrogen. The GQA grades stretches of river into six categories (A-F) of chemical quality and these in turn have been grouped into two broader groups - good/fair (classes A, B, C and D) and poor/bad (classes E and F).

In Northern Ireland, the grading of the 1991 and 1995 surveys is also based on the GQA scheme. In Scotland, the classification system for chemical quality is not directly comparable with the GQA; the system was changed in 1996. In the table the 'good/fair' column for Scotland includes classes A1, A2 and B, plus 'unclassified' river stretches – which are river stretches that are not routinely monitored because they are generally expected to be of good quality.

Table 11.8 Water pollution incidents

The Environment Agency for England and Wales defines four categories of pollution incidents:

Category 1

A major incident involving one or more of the following:

a) potential or actual persistent effect on water quality or aquatic life;

b) closure of potable water, industrial or agriculture abstraction necessary;

c) major damage to aquatic ecosystem;

d) major damage to agriculture and/or commerce;

e) serious impact on man;

f) major effect on amenity value.

Category 2

A significant pollution which involves one or more of the following:

a) notification to abstractors;

b) significant damage to aquatic ecosystem;

c) significant effect on water quality;

d) damage to agriculture and/or commerce;

e) impact on man;

f) effect on amenity value to the public, owners or users.

Category 3

Minor incident involving one or more of the following:

a) a minimal effect on water quality;

b) minor damage to ecosystem;

c) amenity value only marginally affected;

d) minimal impact on agriculture and/or commerce.

Category 4

An incident where no impact on the environment occurred.

Department of the Environment (Northern Ireland) defines four categories of pollution incidents: High Severity; Medium Severity; Low Severity and Unsubstantiated. Apart from the last, these are broadly equivalent to the categories used by the Environment Agency.

The Scottish Environment Protection Agency (SEPA) presently reports on two categories of pollution incidents:

Category 1

Serious incidents are those which cause a breach of any appropriate environmental quality standard in the receiving water. These incidents are reported as 'significant' in SEPA's annual report and compare broadly with all of Category 1 and a, b, c and d of Category 2 used by the Environment Agency.

Category 2

Minor incidents are those which do not cause a breach of any appropriate environmental quality standard in the receiving water. These incidents are reported as 'minor' in SEPA's annual report and compare broadly with e and f of Category 2, and all of Category 3 used by the Environment Agency.

Table 11.11 Land cover by broad habitat

Land cover specifically refers to the make-up of the land surface, for example, woods, grasslands and buildings. The estimates used for this table are taken from the Countryside Survey 2000 database and have been derived using translation software that more or less matches the broad habitats (BHs) developed within the UK Biodiversity Action Plan.

Tables 11.13 Designated areas

National parks, areas of outstanding natural beauty in England and Wales and Northern Ireland, defined heritage coasts in England and Wales and national scenic areas in

Scotland are the major areas designated by legislation to protect their landscape importance.

Table 11.14 Land use change statistics

Details of changes in land use are recorded for the Office of the Deputy Prime Minister by Ordnance Survey (OS) as part of its map revision work in England. The data recorded by OS, in any one year, depend on OS resources and how these are deployed on different types of map revision survey. The main consequence of this is that physical development (eg new houses) tends to be recorded relatively sooner than changes between other uses (eg between agriculture and forestry), some of which may not be recorded for some years. The statistics are best suited to analyses of changes to urban uses and of the recycling of land already in urban uses.

Chapter 12: Regional Accounts

Tables 12.1, 12.3, 12.5, 12.6, figure 12.2, and map 12.4 Gross value added (GVA)

Regional GVA is measured as the sum of incomes earned from the production of goods and services in the region. Regional estimates are calculated for individual income components: compensation of employees (formerly known as income from employment); gross operating surplus; mixed income; and taxes (less subsidies) on production. The GVA estimates presented here are based on the European System of Accounts 1995 (ESA95). The figures for all United Kingdom NUTS1 areas are consistent with the UK National Accounts (Blue Book) 2002.

The industry definitions used are in accordance with the Standard Industrial Classification Revised 1992 (SIC92).

Under the European System of Accounts 1995 (ESA95), the term gross value added (GVA) is used to denote estimates that were previously known as gross domestic product (GDP) at basic prices. Under ESA95, the term GDP denotes GVA plus taxes (less subsidies) on products, i.e. at market prices. UK Regional Accounts are currently only published at basic prices so should be referred to as GVA rather than GDP.

Regional GVA is currently calculated both on a workplace and a residence basis. Residence-based GVA allocates the incomes of commuters to where they live, whereas workplace GVA allocates their incomes to where they work. The main GVA estimates are on a residence basis. However, workplace-based estimates are also provided. These differ from the residence-based estimates only in London, the South East and the East of England.

The methodology and data sources used in compiling regional gross value added were described in a booklet in the *Studies in Official Statistics series, No 31, Regional Accounts*, (HMSO) and more recently in a methodological article included in the December 2000 edition of *Economic Trends* (TSO).

GVA data for NUTS levels 2 and 3 areas, and by industry at NUTS-1, are currently only available up to 2001. The NUTS levels 2 and 3 GVA estimates are only produced on a workplace basis.

Tables 12.7, 12.10 and figures 12.8 and 12.9 Household income and gross disposable household income

The household sector covers people living in traditional households as well as those living in institutions. The latter (about 1.5 per cent of the UK population) includes people living in retirement homes, hostels, boarding houses, hotels and prisons. The household sector also includes sole trader enterprises and non-profit institutions serving households (NPISHs) which do not have separate legal status, examples of the latter being charities and most universities.

Total household income is the sum of incomes for the sector, i.e. wages and salaries, pensions and social security benefits. Gross disposable household income is the total income less certain cost items such as tax payments and social security contributions. In essence, this is the value of the resources that the household sector actually has available to spend.

The consumption of fixed capital (i e the depreciation in value of property) is not deducted from either form of income at the regional level and both are expressed at current prices.

In addition to these areas an estimate for a pseudo-geography called Extra-regio is also included in the regional household sector accounts. Included in this area are the earnings of UK residents employed in UK enclaves in other countries, mainly civil servants, diplomats and armed forces.

Household sector Extra-regio income differs from that included in regional gross value added (GVA). The biggest difference between the two is that the earnings of offshore (North Sea) oil workers are not classified as extra-regio in household income, but are allocated to mainland UK regions. Regional household income is derived using a variety of data sources. The methodology reflects the aims and definitions of the ESA95.

The estimates published here are consistent with the national accounts published in the *UK National Accounts (Blue Book) 2000*. Like the GVA estimates, they are based on ESA95. The methodologies and data sources used in compiling Regional Household Income were described in the

August 2001 and May 2002 editions of *Economic Trends*.

Tables 12.11 and 12.12 Individual consumption expenditure (ICE)

ICE measures spending by households and NPISHs in a region. The estimates are consistent with *UK National Accounts (Blue Book) 2000*, and are also based on ESA95.

Regional estimates of ICE complement household income (discussed above); together they complete the current account of that sector. The margins of error on both sets of figures make it unwise to compare the two in practice.

Estimates of ICE are published by category of expenditure using the Classification of Individual Consumption by Purpose (COICOP). This classification structure is defined by the ESA95 and estimates of ICE are therefore available on a consistent basis across all EU Member States.

The methodologies and data sources used in compiling ICE estimates were also described in the 2000 edition of *Economic Trends*.

Chapter 13: Industry and Agriculture

Maps 13.1, 13.16, 13.17 figure 13.2, and tables 13.3, 13.4, 13.5 and 13.6 Current basic prices

The regional gross value added (GVA) estimates are consistent with the national accounts published in the *United Kingdom National Accounts 2002*. Under the European system of accounts 1995 (ESA 95) the term GVA is used to denote estimates that were previously known as gross domestic product (GDP) at basic prices.

GVA percentages for industry and services do not sum to exactly 100 per cent due to the adjustment of data for Financial Intermediation Services Indirectly Measured (FISIM). FISIM is an indirect measure of the value of the services for which financial intermediaries do not charge explicitly. The total value of FISIM is measured as the total property income receivable by financial intermediaries other than insurance corporations and pension funds *less* their total interest payable.

Excluding Extra-regio

The GVA for Extra-regio comprises compensation of employees and gross operating surplus, which cannot be assigned to the regions.

The industrial breakdown used is in accordance with the Standard Industrial Classification (SIC) Revised 1992. Agriculture, industry and services are broken down as follows:

AGRICULTURE:

Section A	Agriculture, hunting and forestry
Section B	Fishing

INDUSTRY:

Section C	Mining and quarrying
Section D	Manufacturing
Section E	Electricity, gas and water supply
Section F	Construction

SERVICES:

Section G	Wholesale and retail trade; repair of motor vehicles, motorcycles and personal and household goods
Section H	Hotels and restaurants
Section I	Transport, storage and communications
Section J	Financial intermediation
Section K	Real estate, renting and business activities
Section L	Public administration and defence; compulsory social security
Section M	Education
Section N	Health and social work
Section O	Other community, social and personal service activities

Tables 13.3 and 13.4 Inter-Departmental Business Register

The Inter-Departmental Business Register (IDBR) is a structured list of business units used for the selection, mailing and grossing of statistical inquiries as well as for analysis. Information is provided at both the enterprise and local unit level. The enterprise is the level at which the business has some control or independence; the local units are the individual sites (or factories, shops etc.) operated by the enterprise. The IDBR covers more than 99 per cent of UK output, and covers around two-thirds of the total stock of enterprises. The register comprises information on companies, partnerships, sole-proprietors, public authorities, central government departments, local authorities and non-profit bodies. The main administrative sources for the IDBR are HM Customs and Excise for VAT information (passed to the ONS under the *Value Added Tax Act 1994*), and Inland Revenue for PAYE information (transferred under the *Finance Act 1969*). Other information is added to the register for ONS statistical purposes.

Tables 13.5 and 13.6 Annual Business Inquiry

The Annual Business Inquiry is a sample survey, which covers UK businesses including those engaged in the production and construction industries (formerly the Annual Inquiry into production). Production and construction industries are Divisions 1-5 of the Standard Industrial Classification (SIC) Revised 1980 and Section C to F of the SIC Revised 1992.

Businesses often conduct their activities at more than one address (local unit) but it is not usually possible for them to provide the full range of data for each. For this reason, data are usually collected at the enterprise level. Gross value added (GVA) is estimated for each local unit by apportioning the total GVA for the business in proportion to the total employment at each local unit using employment from the IDBR.

GVA at basic prices is defined as:

The value of total sales and work done, adjusted by any changes during the year in work in progress and goods on hand for sale

less: the value of purchases, adjusted by any changes in the stocks of material, stores and fuel etc.

less: payments for industrial services received

less: net duties and levies etc.

less: the cost of non-industrial services, rates and motor vehicle licences.

It includes taxes on production (like business rates) net subsidies but excludes taxes less subsidies on production (for example, VAT and excise duty). GVA per head is derived by dividing the estimated GVA by the total number of people employed. The data include estimates for businesses not responding, or not required to respond, to the inquiry.

Table 13.7 Export and import trade with EU and non-EU countries
Data are sourced from customs declarations submitted in respect of trade with countries outside the European Union and 'Supplementary Declarations' submitted under the Intrastat EU statistical reporting system. While all imports and exports outside the EU are recorded, the Intrastat system is based on returns from registered companies that exceed a set annual threshold in their trading with the EU (set at £233,000 for 2003). Trade is regionalised according to the postcode of declarants and adjustments are made to address the distortion caused by head offices reporting on behalf of their group.

Improvements to the regional trade statistics methodology have been carried out during 2003 to ensure that the total trade reported for *Regional Trade Statistics* mirror the trade published for the UK as a whole (the '*UK Overseas Trade Statistics*'). Certain goods, such as North Sea crude oil, ships and aircraft stores, and transactions involving overseas companies with no place of business in the

UK, cannot be allocated to a specific area within the UK and this trade is shown as 'Unknown Region'. Due to these improvements, figures in Table 13.7 are not comparable with those published in previous editions of *Regional Trends*.

Table 13.8 Direct inward investment: project successes
Data on projects which have attracted inward investment appear in this table. They are based on information provided to Invest UK, part of the Department of Trade and Industry, by the beneficiary companies at the time of the decision to invest. There is no obligation to notify the department, so the figures relate only to those projects where Invest UK or its regional partners were involved or have come to their notice. They also take no account of subsequent developments. For example, if a company goes bankrupt several years later.

Table 13.9 Expenditure on research and development
On 1 July 2001, the Government research agency, the Defence Evaluation and Research Agency (DERA) was disestablished and two new organisations were created. Around a quarter of DERA remained with the Ministry of Defence (MOD) as a government agency whilst the remaining three-quarters became a private limited company (PLC). As a PLC its Research and Development (R&D) activities are now classified and included within the Business sector.

Table 13.10 Government expenditure on regional preferential assistance to industry
The Department of Trade and Industry is the lead sponsor for the eight Regional Development Agencies in the UK and the London Development Agency. Their activities cover economic development and re-generation, promoting business efficiency, investment and competitiveness, promoting employment and skills development and contributing to the achievement of sustainable development in the UK.

The types of assistance included in this table for Great Britain are: Regional Development Grants prior to 1996/97; Regional Selective Assistance; Regional Enterprise Grants; expenditure on Land and Factories by the English Industrial Estates Corporation (until 1993/94 after which this falls under the province of the Single Regeneration Budget), Scottish Enterprise, the Welsh Development Agency; and expenditure on Land and Factories and Grants by the Development Board for Rural Wales (until 1998/99) and Highlands and Islands Enterprise.

Northern Ireland has a different range of financial incentives available and so the figures have not been aggregated into a UK total. The items included are Industrial Development Board grants and loans;

expenditure on land and factories; Standard Capital Grants; and Local Enterprise Development Unit grants and loans.

All figures are gross and include payments to nationalised industries. GB payments relate only to projects situated in the Assisted Areas of Great Britain.

Table 13.11 EU Structural Funds
Regions may be eligible for funding in one of two categories. 'Objective 1' funds promote the development of regions, which are lagging behind the rest of the European Union. To be eligible, regions need to have a per capita GDP of 75 per cent or less of the EU average. In these areas, emphasis is placed on creating a sound infrastructure, modernising transport and communication links, improving energy and water supplies, encouraging research and development, providing training and helping small businesses.

Areas suffering from industrial decline may be designated 'Objective 2'. These areas need help adjusting their economies to new industrial activities; they have high unemployment rates, and a high but declining share of industrial activity. EU grants may be provided to help create jobs, encourage new businesses, renovate land and buildings, promote research and development, and foster links between universities and industry.

In addition, rural areas where economic development needs to be encouraged may be designated 'Objective 2'. In these areas the focus is on developing jobs outside agriculture in small businesses and tourism, and improvements to transport and basic services are promoted to prevent rural depopulation.

Grants under Objectives 1 and 2 are disbursed under the terms of Single Programming Documents or their equivalents, which provide a strategic framework relevant to the region concerned.

The other objective under which grants are allocated, Objective 3, which covers long-term unemployment, jobs for young people and modernisation of farms, is not defined geographically. In addition the Structural Funds provide support for Community-wide Initiatives. These Initiatives account for 8 per cent of the Structural Funds budget.

Table 13.12 Business registration and de-registrations
Annual estimates of registrations and de-registrations are compiled by the Small Business Service an agency of the Department of Trade and Industry. They are based on VAT information held by the Office for National Statistics (ONS). The estimates are a good indicator of the pattern of business start-ups and closures, although they exclude firms not

registered for VAT, either because their main activity is exempt from VAT; or because they have a turnover below the VAT threshold (£51,000 with effect from 1 April 1999, £52,000 from 1 April 2000, £54,000 from 1 April 2001 and £55,000 from April 2002) and have not registered voluntarily. Large rises in the VAT threshold in 1991 and 1993 affected the extent to which the VAT system covers the small business population. This means that the estimates are not entirely comparable before and after these years.

Tables 13.17 to 13.21 Agriculture census
The annual census encompasses the 239 thousand main agricultural holdings in the United Kingdom in 2002. Estimates for minor holdings are included in the national totals for England, Wales, Scotland and Northern Ireland; these estimates are not included for the English regions. Generally, minor holdings are characterised by a small agricultural area, low economic activity and a small labour input.

Table 13.19 Less favoured areas
Land in the Less favoured areas is commonly infertile, unsuitable for cultivation and with limited potential which cannot be increased except at excessive cost. Such land is mainly suitable for extensive livestock farming.

Table 13.20 Areas and yields
The figures for specific crops relate to those in the ground on the date of the June census or for which the land is being prepared for sowing at that date. In England and Wales cereal production is estimated from sample surveys held in September, November and April; oilseed rape production is estimated from a sample survey held in August. In Scotland, cereals and oilseed rape yields are estimated mid-September, followed by sample surveys later in the year. The Department of Agriculture for Northern Ireland estimates cereal and oilseed rape yields from a stratified sample survey of 200 farms carried out in the autumn of each year.

Chapters 14 to 17: Subregional statistics

Subregional data complement the data shown regionally in Chapters 3 to 13. A wide range of data are presented, covering population, vital statistics, education, housing and households, labour market, deprivation and economic statistics. The statistics cover countries, regions, counties/unitary authorities and, where available, local authority districts in England; Unitary Authorities in Wales; the Council areas in Scotland; Health and Social Service Boards/Education and Library Boards/districts as available in Northern Ireland. English education statistics are presented by Local Education Authority. Tables 14.8, 15.7, 16.6 and 17.5 present data

on the NUTS area classification (see Regional Classifications at the beginning of Notes and Definitions).

In the local authority tables for England, where data are often collected at district and unitary authority level and can be easily combined, county, regional and national totals are given to make comparison easier. However, for national surveys, local estimates have to be derived by disaggregating and sometimes different sources are used to derive estimates for lower geographical levels. It is not therefore necessarily the case that data in this chapter are strictly comparable with data in other chapters. These data identify local as well as regional trends and because of the level of disaggregation more caution in interpretation is necessary.

There are specific and known problems in comparing population, employment and unemployment data for small areas. Allowing for the difficulties in interpreting such geographically de-segregated data, the figures in the relevant subregional tables can be used to give a broad picture of a particular local authority and how it compares with others. The tables are intended to take a reasonably broad sweep across a range of subjects. More detailed statistics on specific topics may be readily available. For example:

Key population and vital statistics (local and health authority areas of England and Wales)

Local Housing statistics (annual statistics by local authority area)

Projections of Households in England to 2001 (statistics for counties, metropolitan districts and London boroughs)

Labour Market Trends (unemployment by local authority districts and parliamentary constituencies).

Tables 14.1, 15.1, 16.1 and 17.1 Area and population
New population estimates for 2001 based on the 2001 Census of Population, were published in October 2002.

The standardised mortality ratio (SMR) compares an overall mortality in a region with that for the United Kingdom. The ratio expresses the number of deaths in a region as a percentage of the hypothetical number that would have occurred if the region's population had experienced the sex/age specific rates of the United Kingdom in that year.

Tables 14.4, 15.4, 16.3 and 17.3 Education
Pupils in last year of compulsory schooling with no graded results are those who either did not attempt any GCSE, GCE, CSE or SCE examinations or did not achieve a sufficient standard to be awarded a grade.

In Table 14.4, the column showing the average points score is based on students

aged 16 to 18 at the start of the academic year who entered for a GCE or VCE A level or VCE Double Award in Summer 2002. Coverage is maintained schools and FE sector colleges, and the points scores are based on the cumulative results of these students, obtained in academic years 2000/01 and 2001/02.

The points scores for England for 2001/02 (Table 14.4) reflect the Universities and Colleges Admissions Service (UCAS) Tariff. In Table 15.4, GCSE and AS/A level data for Wales include vocational equivalents. In addition, points scores for Wales for 2001/02 in Table 15.4 reflect the previous points system and cannot be compared directly with points scores for England. The Notes and Definitions for Chapter 4 contain more details. See also Statistical First Release SFR07/2003 on the DfES website.

Tables 14.5, 15.5 and 16.4 Council Tax
Amounts shown for Council Tax are headline Council Tax for the area of each billing authority for Band D, 2 adults, before Council Tax benefit. The ratios of other bands are: A 6/9, B 7/9, C 8/9, E 11/9, F 13/9, G 15/9 and F 18/9.

Averages are calculated by dividing the sum of the tax requirement for each area by the tax base for the area. The tax base is calculated by weighting each dwelling on the valuation list to take account of exemptions, discounts and disabled relief and the valuation band it falls into. It therefore represents the number of B and D equivalent (fully chargeable) dwellings.

Tables 14.6, 15.6 and 16.5 Labour market statistics
These tables include some of the regional results of the New Earnings Survey 2002. Full details are given for the countries and regions in *'Great Britain: streamlined and summary analyses'* and the *'Analyses by region, county and small areas'* volumes of the report New Earnings Survey 2002, (National Statistics Direct). Results for Northern Ireland are published separately by the Department of Enterprise, Trade and Investment, Northern Ireland. The survey measured gross earnings of a 1 per cent sample of employees, most of whom were members of Pay-As-You-Earn (PAYE) schemes for a pay-period which included 10 April 2002. The earnings information collected was converted to a weekly basis where necessary, and to an hourly basis where normal basic hours were reported.

Figures are given where the number of employees reporting in the survey was 30 or more and the standard error of average weekly earnings was 5 per cent or less. Gross earnings are measured before tax, National Insurance or other deductions. They include overtime pay, bonuses and other additions to basic pay but exclude any payments for earlier periods (for example, back pay), most income in kind, tips and gratuities. All the results in this volume relate to full-time male and female employees on adult rates whose pay for the survey pay-period was not affected by absence. Employees were classified to the region in which they worked (or were based if mobile) using postcode information, and to manual or non-manual occupations on the basis of the Standard Occupational Classification 1990 (SOC 90). The *'Great Britain: streamlined and summary analyses'* and *'United Kingdom: streamlined and summary analyses'* volumes of the report give full details of definitions used in the survey. Full-time employees are defined as those normally expected to work more than 30 hours per week, excluding overtime and main meal breaks (but 25 hours or more in the case of teachers) or, if their normal hours were not specified, as those regarded as full-time by the employer.

Labour Force Survey (LFS) Annual Local Area Database

Annual Local Area LFS data for 2001/02 are more accurate than those from the quarterly survey because the sample is larger. It was derived from four quarters of the LFS boosted by an additional sample in England funded by the Department for Work and Pensions and the Department for Education and Skills. This represents an increase of one and a quarter times the quarterly sample. Estimates can therefore be published down to 6,000 for unboosted areas in England, meaning that reliable data are available for more areas. Annual data for 2001/02 also included a boost for Wales, allowing estimates to be published down to between 1,000 and 4,000. Full details can be found in the *LFS User Guide, Volume 6*.

Table 14.7 Business registrations and de-registrations

Annual estimates of registrations and de-registrations are compiled by the Department of Trade and Industry. They are based on VAT information held by the Office for National Statistics (ONS). The estimates are a good indicator of the pattern of business start-ups and closures, although they exclude firms not registered for VAT, either because their main activity is exempt from VAT; or because they have a turnover below the VAT threshold (£51,000 with effect from 1 April 1999, £52,000 from 1 April 2000 and £54,000 from 1 April 2001) and have not registered voluntarily. Large rises in the VAT threshold in 1991 and 1993 affected the extent to which the VAT system covers the small business population. This means that the estimates are not entirely comparable before and after these years.

Symbols and conventions

Reference years. Where a choice of years has to be made, the most recent year or a run of recent years is shows, together with the past population census years (1991, 1998, 2001 etc.) and sometimes the mid-points between census years (1996 etc.) Other years may be added if they represent a peak or trough in the series or relate to a specific benchmark or target.

Rounding of figures. In tables where the figures have been rounded to the nearest final digit, there may be an apparent discrepancy between the sum of the constituent items and the total as shown.

Billion. This term is used to represent a thousand million.

Provisional and estimated data. Some data for the latest year (and occasionally for earlier years) are provisional or estimated. To keep footnotes to a minimum, these have not been indicated; source departments will be able to advise if revised data are available.

Survey data. Many of the tables and figures in Regional Trends present the results of household surveys that can be subject to large sampling errors. Care should therefore be taken in drawing conclusions about regional differences, and especially with subnational changes over time.

Non-calendar years. Data covering more than one year, eg. 1998, 1999 and 2000 would be shown as 1998-2000.

Financial years. For example April 2000 to March 2001 and academic years, for example September 2000 to August 2001, would be shown as 2000/01.

Units. Figures are shown in italics when they represent percentages.

Symbols. The following symbols have been used throughout Regional Trends:

    .. not available

    . not applicable

    - negligible (less than half the first digit shown)

    - 0 nil

Index

285